Urban Planet

Global urbanization promises better services, stronger economies, and more connections; it also carries risks and unforeseeable consequences. To deepen our understanding of this complex process and its importance for global sustainability, we need to build interdisciplinary knowledge around a systems approach.

Urban Planet takes an integrative look at our urban environment, bringing together scholars from a diverse range of disciplines: from sociology and political science to evolutionary biology, geography, economics, and engineering. It includes the perspectives of often neglected voices: architects, journalists, artists, and activists. The book provides a much needed cross-scale perspective, connecting challenges and solutions on a local scale with drivers and policy frameworks on a regional and global scale. The authors argue that to overcome the major challenges we are facing, we must embark on a large-scale reinvention of how we live together, grounded in inclusiveness and sustainability. This title is also available Open Access from www.cambridge.org/core.

Thomas Elmqvist is a Professor in Natural Resource Management at Stockholm Resilience Centre, Stockholm University, Sweden.

Xuemei Bai is a Professor of Urban Environment and Human Ecology at Fenner School of Environment and Society, Australian National University, Australia.

Niki Frantzeskaki is Associate Professor on Sustainability Transitions Governance at the Dutch Research Institute for Transitions (DRIFT) at Erasmus University Rotterdam, the Netherlands.

Corrie Griffith is Program Manager of the Global Consortium for Sustainability Outcomes at Arizona State University, AZ, USA.

David Maddox is the founder and Executive Director of The Nature of Cities, a transdisciplinary essay site with more than 600 writers from around the world, from scientists to civil society, designers to artists.

Timon McPhearson is Associate Professor of Urban Ecology and Director of the Urban Systems Lab at The New School, New York, NY, USA, and a Research Fellow at the Cary Institute of Ecosystem Studies and Stockholm Resilience Centre, Sweden.

Susan Parnell is Professor of Human Geography , University of Bristol and Emeritus Professor at the African Centre for Cities at the University of Cape Town.

Patricia Romero-Lankao is Senior Research Scientist at the US National Center for Atmospheric Research based in Colorado, where she is currently leading the "Urban Futures" initiative.

David Simon is Director of Mistra Urban Futures at Chalmers University of Technology, Gothenburg, Sweden, and Professor of Development Geography at Royal Holloway, University of London, United Kingdom.

Mark Watkins is Program Manager for the Central Arizona-Phoenix Long-Term Ecological Research Program (CAP LTER), part of the US LTER network.

The Urban Planet

Knowledge Towards Sustainable Cities

Edited by

Thomas Elmqvist
Stockholm Resilience Centre

Xuemei Bai
Australian National University

Niki Frantzeskaki
Erasmus University Rotterdam

Corrie Griffith
Arizona State University

David Maddox
The Nature of Cities

Timon McPhearson
The New School

Susan Parnell
University of Bristol & University of Cape Town

Patricia Romero-Lankao
National Center for Atmospheric Research

David Simon
Chalmers University of Technology

Mark Watkins
Arizona State University

CAMBRIDGE
UNIVERSITY PRESS

University Printing House, Cambridge CB2 8BS, United Kingdom

One Liberty Plaza, 20th Floor, New York, NY 10006, USA

477 Williamstown Road, Port Melbourne, VIC 3207, Australia

314–321, 3rd Floor, Plot 3, Splendor Forum, Jasola District Centre, New Delhi – 110025, India

79 Anson Road, #06–04/06, Singapore 079906

Cambridge University Press is part of the University of Cambridge.

It furthers the University's mission by disseminating knowledge in the pursuit of education, learning, and research at the highest international levels of excellence.

www.cambridge.org
Information on this title: www.cambridge.org/9781107196933
DOI: 10.1017/9781316647554

© Cambridge University Press 2018

First published in 2018

A catalogue record for this publication is available from the British Library.

ISBN 978-1-107-19693-3 Hardback

Cambridge University Press has no responsibility for the persistence or accuracy of URLs for external or third-party internet websites referred to in this publication and does not guarantee that any content on such websites is, or will remain, accurate or appropriate.

Contents

Figures

Tables

Contributors

Marina Alberti, Department of Urban Design and Planning, University of Washington, USA

Lorraine Amollo Ambole, University of Nairobi, Kenya

Emma Arnold, University of Oslo, Norway

Flor Avelino, The Dutch Research Institute for Transitions, Erasmus University Rotterdam, The Netherlands

Thomas Baar, Centre for Innovation, Leiden University, The Netherlands

Xuemei Bai, Fenner School of the Environment, Australian National University, Australia

Tim Baynes, Commonwealth Scientific and Industrial Research Organisation (CSIRO), Australia

Victoria Beard, World Resources Institute, USA

Elena Bennett, Department of Natural Resource Sciences and the McGill School of Environment, McGill University, Canada

Reinette (Oonsie) Biggs, Centre for Complex Systems in Transition, Stellenbosch University, South Africa, and Stockholm Resilience Centre, Stockholm University, Sweden

Edgardo Bilsky, United Cities and Local Governments, Spain

Eugénie L. Birch, Department of City and Regional Planning, School of Design, University of Pennsylvania and the Penn Institute for Urban Research, USA

Karina Blanco Ochoa, London School of Economics and Political Science (LSE), UK, and the United Nations Joint Environmental Unit (JEU)

Jo Ivey Boufford, New York University School of Medicine, USA

Sarah Burch, Sustainability Governance and Innovation, University of Waterloo, Canada

Kareem Buyana, Trans-Urban Knowledge Network, Uganda

Maruxa Cardama, Urban Adviser, Cities Alliance

Abel Chávez, Sustainable and Resilient Communities, Western State Colorado University, USA

Bin Chen School of Environment, Beijing Normal University, China

Shaoqing Chen, School of Environment, Beijing Normal University, China

Marian Chertow, Industrial Environmental Management Program, Yale School of Forestry and Environmental Studies, Yale University, USA

Mikhail Chester, Civil, Environmental, and Sustainable Engineering, Arizona State University, USA

Michael Cohen, Milano School for International Affairs, Management and Urban Policy, The New School, USA

Bharat Dahiya, Chulalongkorn University, Thailand

McKenna Davis, Ecologic Institute, Germany

PK Das, PK Das and Associates, India

Anna Dietzsch, Davis, Brody, and Bond Architects, Brazil

Paul Downton, Ecopolis, Australia

Adina Dumitru, University of A Coruña, Spain

Thomas Elmqvist, Stockholm Resilience Center, Stockholm University, Sweden

Niki Frantzeskaki, The Dutch Research Institute for Transitions, Erasmus University Rotterdam, The Netherlands

Richard Friend, University of York, UK

Franz W. Gatzweiler, Institute of Urban Environment, Chinese Academy of Sciences, China

Manuela Gervasi, ICLEI Cities Biodiversity Center, South Africa

Sarah Giest, Institute of Public Administration, Leiden University, The Netherlands

David Gómez-Álvarez, Public Policy Institute, Guadalajara University, Mexico

Andrew Gonzalez Department of Biology, McGill University, Canada

Andrew Grant, Grant Associates, UK

Corrie Griffith, UGEC Project and GCSO, Arizona State University, USA

Burak Güneralp, Texas A&M University, USA

Dagmar Haase, Humboldt University of Berlin, Germany

Cecilia Herzog, Inverde Institute, Brazil

Oliver Hillel, Secretariat of the Convention of Biological Diversity, Canada

Sara Hughes, University of Toronto, Canada

Keitaro Ito, Kyushu Institute of Technology, Japan

Chris Kennedy, Civil Engineering, University of Victoria, Canada

Radhika Khosla, Oxford India Centre for Sustainable Development, University of Oxford, UK

Todd Lester, Lanchonete, Brazil

Lesley Lokko, University of Johannesburg, South Africa

Eduardo López-Moreno, United Nations Human Settlements Programme, Kenya

Karen MacClune, Institute for Social and Environmental Transition-International, USA

David Maddox, The Nature Of Cities, USA

Anjali Mahendra, World Resources Institute, USA

Mahim Maher, *The Friday Times*, Pakistan

Nivedita Mani, Gorakhpur Environmental Action Group, India

Ulrich Mans, Centre for Innovation, Leiden University, The Netherlands

Umamah Masum, Global Kids, Inc., USA

Gora Mboup, Global Observatory Linking Research to Action (GORA), USA

Kes McCormick, International Institute for Industrial Environmental Economics, Lund University, Sweden

Robert McDonald, The Nature Conservancy, USA

Timon McPhearson Urban Systems Lab, Environmental Studies, The New School, USA

Mary Miss, Artist, USA

Michele-Lee Moore, Dept of Geography, University of Victoria, Canada, and Stockholm Resilience Centre, Stockholm University, Sweden

Harini Nagendra, Azim Premji University, India

Sandra Naumann, Ecologic Institute, Germany

Albert Norström Stockholm Resilience Centre, Stockholm University, Sweden

Per Olsson, Stockholm Resilience Centre, Stockholm University, Sweden

Efrén Osorio Lara, Sister Cities and International Affairs of the Municipal Government of Zapopan, México

Susan Parnell, School of Geographical Sciences, University of Bristol, UK, and University of Cape Town, South Africa

Laura M. Pereira, Centre for Complex Systems in Transition, Stellenbosch University, South Africa

Sascha Petersen, Adaptation International, USA

Garry Peterson, Stockholm Resilience Centre, Stockholm University, Sweden

Troy Pickard, City of Joondalup, Australia

Rika Preiser, Centre for Complex Systems in Transition, Stellenbosch University, South Africa

Guillermina Ramirez, Marcha de Mujeres Originarias por el Buen Vivir, Patagonia

Ciara Raudsepp-Hearne, Sustainability Science Lab, McGill University, Canada

Aromar Revi, Indian Institute for Human Settlements (IIHS), India

Andrew Revkin, ProPublica, USA

Debra Roberts, Environmental Planning and Climate Protection Department, EThekwini Municipality, South Africa

Patricia Romero-Lankao Urban Futures, National Center for Atmospheric Research, USA

Mary Rowe, Independent Urbanist, USA

Andrew Rudd, UN-Habitat's Urban Planning & Design Branch, USA

Cristina Rumbaitis del Rio, Action on Climate Today, India

Rebecca Salminen Witt, Detroit Historical Society, USA

David Satterthwaite, International Institute for Environment and Development, UK

Kate Scherer, Global Kids, Inc., USA

Heike Schroeder, School of International Development, University of East Anglia, UK

Huda Shaka, Arup, United Arab Emirates

Lena Simet, Milano School for International Affairs, Management and Urban Policy, The New School, USA

David Simon, Mistra Urban Futures, Chalmers University of Technology, Sweden, and Department of Geography, Royal Holloway University of London, UK

Ajay Kumar Singh, Gorakhpur Environmental Action Group, India

Bijay Kumar Singh, Gorakhpur Environmental Action Group, India

Gurbir Singh, Nivara Hakk Housing Rights Organization, India

Sverker Sörlin, KTH Royal Institute of Technology, Sweden

Takeshi Takama, Sustainability & Resilience (su-re.co), Indonesia

Thomas Tang, Partnerships for Eco-Business, Singapore

Reyhaneh Vahidian, Tehran Municipality, Iran

Kanmani Venkateswaran, Institute for Social and Environmental Transition-International, USA

Joost Vervoort, Climate Change, Agriculture and Food Security (CCAFS), CGIAR

Bolanle Wahab, Department of Urban and Regional Planning, University of Ibadan, Nigeria

Mark Watkins Central Arizona-Phoenix Long-Term Ecological Research Program, Arizona State University, USA

Diana Wiesner, Fundación Cerros de Bogotá, Colombia

Olga Wilhelmi, National Center for Atmospheric Research, USA

Julia Wittmayer, The Dutch Research Institute for Transitions, Erasmus University Rotterdam, The Netherlands

Pengfei Xie, C40 Climate Leadership Group, China

Lorena Zárate, Habitat International Coalition, Mexico

Preface

The Urban Planet is the result of a collaborative project within Future Earth (www.futureearth.org). It emphasizes the need for a new knowledge generation agenda, given the urgency of understanding the sustainability challenges and options for a rapidly urbanizing planet. Our urban future will determine the viability and vitality of the human endeavor towards global sustainability. This centrality of cities to the sustainability of people, planet, and prosperity points to the need for continuous investments in an expanded and flexible urban science and practical knowledge generation that is forged out of innovative interdisciplinary and multisectoral understandings of the complex systems that both drive and derive from the prevalence of urban ways of being. Greater understanding of urbanization processes and the multiscale interactions and feedbacks with the earth system is required for addressing the complex issues related to urbanization and sustainability, and for aiding in the solutions. This book aims, therefore, not only to provide a synthesis of existing knowledge across the different disciplines, but also to showcase new ways of producing and integrating knowledge, extending the frontier of urban research, and providing new directions in research and practice that will help us achieve the cities we want now and in the future.

In addition to academic scholars, this book gathers important urban stakeholders from a diverse range of disciplines to jointly show ways of coproducing knowledge. These urban stakeholders are critical, because ours is a book that aspires to make a difference in the real world of city building, city renovation, and city invention. To do so, the ideas of academics and thought leaders are paralleled by voices on the front lines of urban development and change – by stakeholders such as journalists, artists, designers, architects, landscape architects, activists, youth, and urban practitioners from city governments to civil society – whose perspectives are typically left out of academic books. The fourth part of *The Urban Planet* comprises contributions by 39 such diverse stakeholders, from the perspective of where the urban "rubber hits the road."

The *Urban Planet* thus draws from diverse authors and intellectual traditions to engage the emerging science and practice of cities, and evolving ideas about global urbanism. This large-scale undertaking (with over 100 contributors) represents a diverse range of disciplines as well as important urban stakeholders. This new generation of scholars will be responsible for producing the evolving analysis, knowledge, and methods necessary to spark the innovation that will be required to make cities the most efficient, equitable, and sustainable places to live. Much of what happens, both in cities and across the global urban system, will result from the actions of citizens and political decision-makers. But knowledge gaps and poorly understood urban design – its patterns, processes, and risks – in our urban planet will inevitably lead to poor decisions. Solid knowledge and knowledge-driven practice will be key to the future of life on Earth.

As editors and authors, we put considerable effort into addressing the scale issues and heterogeneity in urban issues (for example, differences in geography, biophysical conditions, size, growth rate, socioeconomic conditions, and demography). This is to avoid the usual generalizations that flow from the typically small selection of northern hemisphere and Global North cities included in similar volumes. Furthermore, we have tried to apply a knowledge coproduction mode of operation. The selection and assembly of the chapter-author teams intentionally include disciplinary, regional, and gender diversity for more holistic perspectives on the respective chapter topics. This is likewise true of the authors of the provocations, who represent many communities of practice from around the world in both the Global North and South.

We believe that integrating knowledge from science and practice – or, more abstract research ideas with lived experience – will be critical to building better cities. Decision-makers at various levels of government require knowledge that is both grounded in science and data, and also consistent with proven practice on the ground, at street and neighborhood levels. This belief led us to include both perspectives – academic, practitioner, and the many gradations between – in this volume as a single book, perspectives that are typically sequestered into separate forums.

But, as in real life, integrating diverse, even radically different, perspectives and points of view is challenging. Much of this process has evolved organically during the production of the book, allowing us to follow needs and address emerging issues in novel collaborations of authors. Indeed, we examined various approaches to integrating academic and practitioner perspectives: having practitioner responses interrogate academic chapters; interspersing academic and practitioner contributions; and gathering each point of view in their own section. In the end, we chose the latter path, and pursued three academic sections around major themes (Parts I, II, and III), and a section called "Provocations from Practice" (Part IV). We found that this arrangement best honored the unique contributions of each.

We can also see how different the perspective often are. There is still much work to be done to integrate research and practice into integrated urban knowledge. This book continues a march in that direction. While there are many profound differences among the chapters and sections, all share a common interest: discovering and sharing ideas that can help produce future cities that are better for both people and nature.

The Urban Planet

Structured in four major sections comprising 18 diverse academic chapters and 36 provocations written by nonacademic knowledge holders and practitioners, the book tracks the surge of urbanization globally. We pose this question: What new thinking is required to radically shift the urban trajectory onto a more sustainable path, a mandate for urbanism that international policy-makers provided when they endorsed the 2030 Agenda in 2015 (UN 2015) and the New Urban Agenda in 2016 (UN-Habitat 2016)? Taken together, the book's contents speak to the new multilateral demand that cities be given greater prominence in development. They also reflect the complexity and range of city realities and highlight the multiple, even competing, concerns of what we may frame as existing or contemporary urban science.

The book's four parts are I) Dynamic Urban Planet; II) Global Urban Sustainable Development; III) Urban Transformations to Sustainability – corresponding to the three crosscutting themes that underpin the research framework of Future Earth; and IV) Provocations from Practice.

Part I: Dynamic Urban Planet

In the first part, we seek to define the continuum of urbanity since there is a surprising lack of common understanding among scientific disciplines on what characterizes or defines an urban area or urbanization, making comparative and composite assessments of urban change difficult. This part of the book presents leading views, models, and new data from a diverse set of disciplines to advance our understanding of the urban, including the fundamental complexity of urban systems and how these intersect and interact with politics, justice, health, climate risks, and economics. The current framework of cities as social-technological systems is too narrow and should be complemented with the view of cities as complex social-ecological-technological systems that has recently advanced within urban ecology and social-ecological systems perspectives. This advance is critical given that the continuum of urbanity includes many characteristics and processes other than the particular density of people or land area covered by human-made structures. Furthermore, the conventional view of the urban-rural dichotomy is vastly outdated and needs to be challenged and replaced.

The first three chapters of the book deal with the different pathways of global urbanization; how they relate to different social, economic, historical, and geographical contexts, as well as different drivers and impacts; and the multifaceted dynamics of growing and shrinking urban areas. Different types of urban-rural interactions and urban teleconnections are introduced and discussed. An important dimension is the shift from cities as social-technological systems to complex social-ecological-technological systems.

Chapter 3 focuses on urban metabolism and challenges in the Anthropocene. Chapter 4, on dynamics of risk and vulnerability, examines existing and forward-looking approaches to risk, vulnerability, and resilience – for example, in coastal, mountain, and desert cities as well as in rapidly growing, affluent, and shrinking cities. It discusses vulnerability and resilience at multiple scales (for example, from the city to the neighborhood), and it examines infrastructural resilience and its relationship to vulnerability as well as the significance of governance and politics in shaping urban risk.

Chapter 5, on urbanization and health, outlines the current major threats to urban health and well-being worldwide, for example, an aging population, the epidemiological shift from infectious to noncommunicable diseases, and climate change, which is changing both disease patterns and quality of life in cities. For coping with urban health challenges, a transdisciplinary systems approach is taken, which conceptualizes urban health disorders as emergent properties of urban systems. Among the lessons learned are that changing urban environments can have a broader and more cost-effective impact than changing individual behavior. As a result of health determinants being highly interconnected, a health-in-all-policies approach promises sustainable and equitable urban development outcomes.

Finally, Chapter 6 covers urbanization and macroeconomy and demonstrates that aggregate economic growth and productivity are closely correlated with urbanization levels. Yet, while urbanization and productivity regularly rise in tandem, not all cities are equally productive. The chapter explores explanations of why urban poverty and intra-urban inequalities continue to persist and even intensify despite increased per capita productivity. The chapter concludes with an outlook on future challenges and opportunities. Rising inequalities and pressures from global market economies are expected to increasingly affect cities, threatening economic and social opportunity. However, moving towards a green economy could have tangible and considerable positive effects on the environment, productivity, and economic growth. International collaboration also represents an opportunity to hold local and national governments accountable for their actions. Ultimately, proactive local governments are needed to reduce local constraints to productivity, as well as strong social programs and distributive mechanisms to create opportunities for all citizens.

Part II: Global Urban Sustainable Development

Although widely sloganized and even abused by greenwashing, sustainability as an aspirational and perhaps normative concept remains remarkably durable.

Ironically, perhaps, it is even experiencing something of a resurgence rather than being eclipsed by "resilience" as many had anticipated. This is explicable in at least three ways, namely that sustainability is broader and has resilience as one of its characteristics; that similar analytical ambiguities and operational weaknesses identified with respect to sustainability also apply to resilience; and that any such concept is open to contestation, discipline- or context-specific interpretation, and weakening through popularization.

The urban represents one crucial arena in which such debates are manifested, and the catalytic and often contradictory roles of towns and cities as fulcra of population concentration, resource-intensive production, mobility, consumption, and both waste and opportunity generation – albeit in different combinations in different contexts – are now almost universally recognized. A key stimulus in this regard has been the explosion of research, political debate, and commitment to climate change mitigation, adaptation, and resilience. This has been further sharpened by increasing evidence of the devastating impact of increasingly severe and frequent extreme events on urban areas, both the highly vulnerable and the supposedly well protected and resilient.

All too often, however, debates over how to promote urban sustainability and resilience in progressive terms remain trapped in narratives that assume or imply that this is possible within cities in isolation from their hinterlands. Yet precisely because urban areas are not islands but integral parts of their natural, economic, and political regions, urban sustainability must be conceived and pursued as part of national and broader societal sustainability efforts.

The six chapters in this part examine ongoing conceptual (re)formulations and more practical initiatives to achieve urban sustainability by harnessing new information sources, technologies, and tools; creating and exploiting opportunities in international initiatives like the Sustainable Development Goals (SDG) and New Urban Agenda; and by applying new approaches to engage key stakeholder groups, especially those normally marginalized by and from conventional urban planning, design, and management procedures in order to achieve greater traction, acceptability, and local appropriateness. Several connective threads weave throughout these chapters that are important to highlight, particularly as they offer key messages for urban sustainability research, policy, and practice.

The first major thread concerns equity and justice principles, and thus links to where Part I ended. For example, Chapter 7 begins by pointing out that the "social" sphere of the traditional three-pronged approach of sustainability discourse has been, to date, heavily underemphasized within both research and practice, while resilience efforts are often critiqued for lacking critical examination of underlying power structures or conditions that maintain the status quo. That is, inequality and corruption may be highly resilient systems, but they are clearly undesirable if the goal is to foster greater livability in the era of global urbanization. Inequality is further examined in light of the increasing trend of utilizing big data in the urban context. This brings to the forefront questions of what and how data are being collected or accessed, distributed, and used, by whom, and who is benefiting from these applications. As the use of crowd-sourced and remote sensing data and other technologies increase to support "smart" cities around the world, it is imperative that data-driven, or rather "data-informed," solutions support equitable and just urban areas.

Closely related to equity is the second thread – the importance of finding new and more appropriate (and democratic) methodologies and instruments for "the urban." Acknowledging that traditional or conventional (mainly Northern-derived and -centric) urban planning, development, and management approaches are often inadequate, the chapters emphasize the importance of nonexpert knowledge and participatory opportunities; citizen science or coproduction; and capitalizing on the innovation space that urban areas offer, such as the use of "living laboratories" that might help catalyze social innovations and lead to the transformation of more inclusive and effective urban governance structures. These approaches, which are in many ways complementary to one another and to novel and more democratic forms of generating and using big data, represent promising ways forward for the next generation of urban research and action.

The third collective message from the chapters is the continuing challenge of scale, that is, the inherent difficulty of reconciling the distinctiveness of specifically urban contexts with the need for integrated urban sustainability planning at the scale of functional/ecological urban regions, and also advancing sustainability through urbanization at the global scale (that is, ensuring that sustainability efforts in one location do not erode efforts or conditions in another). This tension is central to the book's premise of the need to situate urban sustainability within an understanding of "planetary urbanization." This is particularly evident in the two chapters that connect to the most recent UN-led sustainability developments, such as the new urban SDG, the New Urban Agenda, and Agenda 2030. What is clear is the need for holistic, localized indices and indicator sets for planning and management purposes, but this will also be crucial for the implementation of such global sustainability agendas.

The six chapters in Part II have been arranged to provide a logical flow of arguments and illustrative cases from the broad and contextual to the more specific. The first three are also global in scope, respectively addressing the evolution and use of the core concepts in different settings; the ongoing process via which urban sustainability and resilience indicators within the UN system have developed increasing sophistication and universal relevance over successive generations; and the unprecedented process of formulating and gaining international political approval for the most ambitious global urban sustainability agenda within a broader sustainable development approach. The latter three chapters survey and illustrate three innovative and potentially complementary urban research approaches that emphasize substantive participation and coproduction.

Altogether this part seeks to showcase a diversity of perspectives, an evolution and "state of the art" in sustainability and resilience interpretations, and the actions that seek to improve urban areas worldwide. These new and, in some cases, unconventional approaches help to move agendas forward and open new potentials for our urbanizing planet, many of which are presented in Part III.

Part III: Urban Transformations to Sustainability

Governance shapes transformations towards urban sustainability and resilience. In Part III, we identify opportunities and challenges facing city officials and private and civil society actors in their efforts to develop governance solutions that support sustainable and resilient urban development. We introduce key urban governance terms and describe the governance factors shaping social and environmental change in urban areas. Chapter 13 describes policy actions seeking to mitigate or prevent environmental risks and impacts, and to adapt to environmental threats and disruptions. It analyzes the sectoral and jurisdictional actor-networks involved in designing and implementing actions, and the opportunities, barriers, and limits that multilevel governance poses to local climate and environmental policy. The remaining chapters throughout this part take a close look at the governance of environmental change and transformations through different forms of experimentation.

This part also examines the diversifying role of civil society organizations in fostering Europe's sustainability pathways in cities. First, civil society initiatives can pioneer new practices, eventually leading to radical changes in the ways of organizing urban life. Therefore, these initiatives can be an integral component of urban transformations and can fill the void left by a retreating welfare state, thereby safeguarding and servicing social needs but also backing up such a rollback of the welfare state. Finally, civil society organizations can function as a hidden innovator – contributing to sustainability but remaining disconnected from the wider society. While civil society organizations currently play a noteworthy role in decision-making around sustainability, some dangers also exist. Civil society initiatives can be used by neoliberal agendas to legitimize existing power structures and deepen social inequalities between and within communities, given their uneven capacities to self-sustain and self-organize.

Good Anthropocene futures are envisaged through the collection and use of "seeds," defined as initiatives that exist at least in prototype form but are not currently dominant in our world. These seeds are used to explore the potential for fostering radically different futures. The authors highlight the synergies and tensions between the underlying values reflected in the seeds, and also how these seeds can be used to think about an urban planet. They conclude by presenting new research directions suggested by this project.

The part ends by describing conceptual and theoretical tools that have emerged in the attempt to understand the role of collaboration in transitioning towards sustainable futures. The chapter explores experiments in collaboration that have shaped local politics and models of governance. It underscores the capacity of local governance actors to respond to identified sustainability challenges, the networks of interaction they form, and the scale of transformation that takes place over time. It questions whether collaborations among public and private actors can deliver on multiple priorities simultaneously, and seeks to analyze how experiments in collaboration may be reshaping urban politics more broadly, or just revealing new governance questions.

Part IV: Provocations from Practice

"Provocations from Practice" is a novel inclusion for an academic book, but it is key for addressing the breadth of knowledge that is actually required to build better cities. What do we mean by provocations? One of our core themes of the book is knowledge: What knowledge do we need for cities of the future that are more sustainable, livable, resilient, and just? Where will it come from? How can it be produced (or coproduced)? How will it be used (or misused)? These questions are starting points for provocations. The contributors inspire us to think about these issues in new or different ways from their point of view and/or practice. Further, they speak of urbanism and its knowledge as a lived reality, from practitioners of all sorts who build cities from the ground up: architects (Paul Downton, P.K. Das, Anna Dietszch), landscape architects (Andrew Grant, Diana Wiesner), artists (Lesley Lokko, Mary Miss), activists (Cecilia Herzog, Guillermina Ramirez, Gurbir Singh), civil society actors (Cristina Rumbaitis del Rio, Mary Rowe), government and elected officials (Troy Pickard, Debra Roberts), journalists (Mahim Maher, Andrew Revkin), specialists from NGOs (Robert McDonald, Kareem Buyana, Pengfei Xie, Lorena Zarate), young students (Kate Scherer, Umamah Masum), and others. They may comment specifically about the ideas included in the academic chapters or take us in new and/or otherwise missing directions. A key question of these provocations is this: What knowledge is needed to build cities at the street and neighborhood level?

And: What is missing from standard academic discussions of sustainability and livability? In these important senses, we have intended not to privilege the academic contributions as being more important, or more central, to the concept of sustainability. At 36 in total – from 39 authors in 31 cities on 6 continents – these provocations from practice offer key voices and ideas that are central to the struggle for urban sustainability.

Many pieces illustrate the fact that it is not only urban academic research that is flourishing. Cities around the world increasingly benefit from greater participation and activism by civil society, practitioners, and regular citizens. This activism has three key benefits. First, it facilitates the grounded practice of making better cities not just through knowledge, but *action:* the design of neighborhoods, infrastructure, and open spaces – that is, *places* – that are better for both people and nature (see Keitaro Ito, Cecilia Herzog, Anna Dietzsch, Rebecca Salminen Witt, Lorraine Amollo Ambole). Second, it demonstrates that justice, livability, and participation by urban citizens in decision-making and urban creation should be key drivers in any connection between academic knowledge and policy (see Robert McDonald, Diana Wiesner, Lorena Zarate, Anjali Mahendra and Victoria Beard, and P.K. Das). Indeed, what knowledge do cities themselves feel they need? What kind of cities to they want? Third, it unveils that there is a clear role for imagination to the creation of cities, not only in the forms of art but also in innovation (see Mary Miss, Paul Downton, Debra Roberts, Andrew Grant, Emma Arnold, and Todd Lester).

The overarching message of the provocations is the growing vibrancy of civil society and communities of practice around the world, which put people and nature at the center of movements to make cities that are better for both people and nature.

Final Words

The editors would like to thank Future Earth for generously sponsoring this project, support which has made it possible to organize several editorial meetings. The book project is part of a larger effort by Future Earth to build mechanisms for cogeneration of knowledge for urban sustainability. We want to thank Mistra Urban Futures for generously sponsoring the open-access publication of the book and, in particular, Helen Arfvidsson for support and hard work with planning meetings and keeping track of the project. We thank Stockholm Resilience Centre for continuous support and the Urbanization and Global Environmental Change (UGEC) community for providing an inspiring intellectual environment for discussing these things. The Integrated Research Systems for Sustainability Science (IR3S) at the University of Tokyo (Prof. K.

Takeuchi and Prof. K. Fukushi) kindly hosted one of the editors (Thomas Elmqvist) in early 2017, which greatly facilitated the editorial process. We also want to thank Jerker Lokrantz, Azote, for producing the illustrations.

The Future Earth Urban Knowledge and Action Network was launched at the Habitat III conference in Quito, Ecuador, in October 2016. This network represents an integrative and transdisciplinary approach to engage researchers, policy-makers, and other stakeholders on urban issues at various levels, thus facilitating the knowledge coproduction needed to address urban challenges. We hope that this book may be the source of initiating lively debates, innovative partnerships, and a wealth of codesign, coproduction, and co-implementation initiatives within the new Future Earth Urban Knowledge and Action Network and other urban knowledge generation networks.

Thomas Elmqvist
Xuemei Bai
Niki Frantzeskaki
Corrie Griffith
David Maddox
Timon McPhearson
Susan Parnell
Patricia Romero-Lankao
David Simon
Mark Watkins

References

UN 2015. Sustainable Development Goals. https://sustainabledevelopment.un.org/post2015/transformingourworld

UN 2016. The New Urban Agenda. United Nations Conference on Housing and Sustainable Urban Development (Habitat III) Quito, 17–20 October 2016 http://habitat3.org/the-new-urban-agenda

Introduction: Situating Knowledge and Action for an Urban Planet

Susan Parnell, Thomas Elmqvist, Timon McPhearson, Harini Nagendra, and Sverker Sörlin

The shared acceptance that we now live in a majority urban world and that cities will surely determine our future does not mean we agree on why or how the urban age is important. The *Urban Planet* thus draws from diverse intellectual traditions to grapple with the conceptual and operational challenges of sustainable urban development. The purpose of this book is to foster a community of global urban leaders through engaging the emerging science of cities and some of its critiques. The aspiration is that by generating ideas about global urbanism that situate the city at the core of the planet's future, we will provide pathways for evidence-based interventions to ensure ambitious changes. This is a significant undertaking (with over 100 contributors from urbanists drawn from both outside and inside the academy). The project on which this book is based is important because, over the next 30 years, based on population growth, the urbanization process will both accelerate and consolidate to make cities and towns, particularly settlements of the global south, an ever more dominant form of twenty-first-century human settlement. Moreover, this generation of scholars now finds itself responsible for producing the new information and analysis necessary to feed the innovation that will be required to make cities the most safe, resilient, equitable, and sustainable way of living.

Much of what happens across the global urban system will be down to citizens, political decision-makers, and the appropriateness of the institutions (including but not limited to states) on which we depend to manage ourselves and our environment. To meet the challenges that lie ahead, we argue that revisionist modes of urban knowledge and practice are imperative: Producing this requires an excitement and curiosity about cities to fuel a massive scaling up of our collective wisdom about the urban world we inhabit.

In setting the course for this volume, this chapter thus departs from the conventional format of an introduction that provides a summary or roadmap of the book. Note that such an overview of chapters is provided in the Preface, and the concluding chapter ("Synthesis") provides a review of the main points and details recurring, highlighting significant points that emerge from the book as a whole. Here we highlight four overarching points of departure in an effort to bring disparate readers into a common frame of reference from which they can engage with *The Urban Planet*. *First*, we reflect on what exactly is meant by "the urban," as this is the common but not universally understood object with which the chapters all grapple. *Second*, we locate the recent call among urban scholars (Acuto and Parnell 2016; Bai et al. 2017; McPhearson et al. 2016a; Batty 2013) for greater attention to be given to building a *science of cities* in historical context by exploring the importance of urbanism in the evolution of science and critical urban theory, here using the example of urban natures. *Third*, we underscore twin imperatives for the future science of cities: the increasing impacts of cities in global change and the *southern concentration of urbanization* – noting how attention to speed and geography must prioritize the focus of global urban inquiry (McPhearson et al. 2016b). *Fourth* and finally, we foreground the tensions of working across disciplinary boundaries and methods, and concede the tensions inherent in *coproducing urban knowledge*. However, these preparatory points, about defining the urban, the imperative of being mindful of history and geography and the possibly insurmountable dilemmas of coproduction, and inter-/trans-disciplinarity should stimulate and not detract in any way from the urgency of galvanizing research capacity to advance the understanding of the urban planet.

0.1 What Is Urban?

Given the consensus that this is an urban age and that cities present both critical opportunities and threats for a common future, it is perhaps surprising that there is so little agreement on what constitutes or defines "the urban." This is an immensely challenging question with no simple answer, and the approaches taken in social and natural sciences to global urbanism have only limited concerns (Parnell and Robinson 2017). There is a surprising lack of common understanding even among scientific disciplines on what characterizes or defines an urban area or urbanization, making comparative and composite assessments of urban change difficult. To underscore the obvious – while it is accepted that there is a common urban future which will in large part determine the state of the urban planet – there is neither a shared definition of "the urban" nor an agreement on city experiences or forms from which to engage or predict the outcomes of our urban futures (Robinson 2016; Simon 2016; Mitlin and Sattherthwaite 2013). This diversity of perspective and definition is understandably also reflected in the chapters of *The Urban Planet*.

As discussed in many of the following chapters, there are multiple dimensions to urbanity. Different perspectives or big ideas that are brought to bear on our core research issue include not just meta-theoretical differences but overlapping, competing, and even disparate research entry points. In positive terms, these varied conceptual and methodological points of departure highlight different ideologies and interests. They also encompass research on multiple elements of the urban – reflecting the diverse specialties of scholars from natural systems science, the design profession and economics (McPhearson et al. 2016a; Bai et al. 2017). But, not least because of this diversity of entry points, incommensurability remains a problem for urban science and comparative urbanism, and a central objective of the book is to address the need to accommodate the range of scholarly perspectives and to suggest how we may proceed to somehow make these speak to each other, thereby crafting a new and deeper holistic understanding of global urban processes. The common themes provide a starting point for presenting global urbanization as a story of great diversity, but perhaps we should count on diversity in solutions and modes of progress too. Variation in specific city experience should, however, not detract from the impact of the amalgamation of urban development on global change; and there is no doubt that, while the evolving science of cities will always need to grapple with the wicked problem of specificity, it must simultaneously generate if not a universal narrative but at least a comprehensive understanding of the complexities of urban change.

The current impetus to give greater weight to cities in general derives in large part from the massive expansion of the urban population over the last century and in part from the argument that an urban or industrial way of life has profoundly ruptured the geological and climate change in the earth system. It is, however, naive to regard the process of global urbanization as a unified or unidirectional phenomenon. Rather, in making the case that the urban is an important determinant of environmental, political, or social change, it helps to look back as well as forward. It is also helpful to interrogate more than demographic and biophysical evidence and to consider the impacts of the rise of the city and urbanism over the last 200 years as a plural, albeit of course very massive, historical phenomenon.

The Anthropocene narrative in this is both useful and obfuscating. It has unifying, sometimes also (suggestive) simplifying, storylines that tend to draw attention away from the diversity of human conditions (Biermann et al. 2016). Still, it suggests many key issues, and it lays out the land nicely with tons of "technofossil" data. Just consider the fact (Zalasiewicz et al. 2017) that, out of the 30 trillion tons of human materiality produced, cities account for (weigh, literally) 11 trillion tons, or 36 percent. Imagining the sheer scale of the urban is hard. In the late part of this century, one city, Dhaka, is projected to have

80 million people. That is one Germany. Our conventional language breaks down in the face of such massive numbers, perhaps our politics, too. The challenges are obvious, but there is also a potential in the growth of cities. Cities are increasingly becoming regional and even global actors in their own right, either alone or in shaping alliances with other cities. Knowing the number of people in Dhaka is of course a limited frame of understanding. We need to compare, for instance, the consumption footprint of Dhaka versus Germany to understand this better. The Anthropocene is a compelling heuristic, but we need more and sharper analytical instruments in approaching the urban. In this, we would do well to consider the urban analytics of the past, as well as to develop new analytics of the future that engage more deeply with normative concerns *and* science.

0.2 The Global Frame of Urbanism and a Science of Cities

In the current notion of "planetary urbanism," Brenner and Schmid (2014) argue that urbanism is now the celebrated form of development (Florida 2002) that is recognized as a triumphal force for economic growth (Glaeser 2011). However, there is a long history of planetary urbanism, where cities have been centers of innovation and economic growth and have been driving formation of global trade networks and spread of ideas, technology, and capital for more than 4,000 years (Clark 2016). As the importance of cities is once again on the rise, there is a sense we may return to the power dynamics of the Middle Ages. Now, as then, how cities are run in this century may determine much of the world's future. Now, as then, the shifting role of cities in global change cannot be uncoupled from the way nature and ecologies are present in those urban developments and the connections between urban places (Clark 2016).

While there are many threads through which the history of cities and civilization are intertwined – political, economic, and social – the urban experience is also an experience of nature and environment. Cities belong in nature, having grown to be the largest environmental actor, indeed the sole creature of humanity that is most comprehensively entangled with the natural world – paradoxically since the city was also meant to be the exception from nature, a *civitas* where the rules of nature did not apply or at least were tempered. The city was, it was once thought, what nature was not (Elmqvist et al. 2013). Nature for a long time had mostly an emblematic role in the description of the urban. In the historiography of cities, gardens and other forms of nature play their distinct role. Nature also appears in the history of urban infrastructures, such as waterways and sewage systems, and it is visible in utopian design ideals such as garden cities and suburbia, and dystopian narratives of diseases and disaster associated with urban infrastructure failure.

Research across a wide set of disciplines in recent years is now questioning the old dichotomy of a well or poorly managed split or interface between the city and nature (e.g. Melosi 1993 2010; Rosen and Tarr 1994; Sedrez 2005; Sharan 2014; Braun 2005; Heynen, Kaika, and Swyngedouw 2006; Gandy 2013). The growth of cities and their contribution to climate change (Rosenzweig et al. 2010) or health (Hodson 2016) is a good reason to stop keeping urban nature and culture apart. While the well-documented role of cities in driving climate change is widely acknowledged, less is known of other relationships between cities and other earth systems. Botanists and ecologists in European cities from the 1930s carried out early work on urban ecological interactions, but the roots of the study of urban botany go back to early modern times (Sukopp 2002). The most comprehensive work was carried out by a group led by Herbert Sukopp in West Berlin in the 1950s. They studied the return of vegetation to the war-torn urban landscape and found a fascinating array of new vegetation combinations (Lachmund 2011). Since the 1970s there has been a steadily growing interest in urban ecology that matured in the 1990s and now has its own established field with textbooks and journals (Elmqvist et al. 2013). Some of the major hubs in this line of work are in Europe (Helsinki, Stockholm) but there are concentrations in Australia (Melbourne), South Africa (Cape Town), China (Beijing), and India (Bangalore). In the United States, the movement was largely led by Baltimore and Phoenix, where long-term ecological research sites were established with funding from the National Science Foundation that saw a global scaling of traditionally anti-urban scientists in tracking cities.

Scholars' deep roots in the natural sciences marked the rise of urban sites in observational ecology. There was little interest in societal conflicts and how power relations shape urban ecologies, an interest that has been growing only recently (Ernstson and Sörlin 2018). It seems obvious that future research on the urban must better learn how to combine systems approaches with analysis of social and political dimensions, or at least work across those boundaries. There is already a rich, and indeed older, literature on social conflicts, class, race, and gender that could be of use for more synthetic approaches, but that literature on the other hand took marginal interest in nature until the appearance of works such as William Cronon's *Nature's Metropolis: Chicago and the Great West* (1991) or Erik Swyngedouw's (1996, 2004) on water, power, and the city.

Borrowing from human ecology and metabolic understandings of urban processes, much recent work has analyzed water, waste, sewage, electricity, and other substances/energies as "sociomaterial flows" with their own biophysical properties and "social relations," playing a role in the circulation of capital, upholding social structures, and producing often unequal urban environments (Warren-Rhodes and Koening 2001; Heynen et al. 2006; Bai et al. 2017. As has been argued in the most recent work on comparative global, and especially southern urbanism (Ernstson et al. 2014; Erixon Aalto and Ernstson 2017; Ernstson and Sörlin 2018), the concept of urban nature has become a much more complex phenomenon. Urban natures are now linking research to achieve ecological sustainability with critical studies and strategies for justice and equality in cities, as inseparable processes. In this regard, the situation for a building a complex knowledge of the urban experience, politics, and its future sustainability has greatly improved: for example, a new project called "cosmopolitics," about *learning with nonhumans*, focuses on how to live in cohabitation (Hinchliffe 2008; Hinchliffe and Whatmore 2006; Biehler 2011).

As Ernstson and Sörlin (2018) suggest in their review of the literature, it was in earnest only after 2000, after a slow and winding build-up period in the late twentieth century, that an "accidental discovery" of urban nature took place. To this discovery, all these and many other strands of academic work and practice contributed with their various pieces of the whole. However, they were almost invariably working in exclusive separation from each other and with quite little interest in bridging across scientific specialties. What remains is therefore, to a large extent, to bring the various research communities on the urban in closer and long-term relations with each other to spare no effort in carving roads forward for the major global challenge, and opportunity, that is urban growth.

One lasting finding found the new critical urban natures approaches and in the parallel body of critical urban studies is that diversity is an overarching theme that cannot be ignored in the global generalization or universalizing (Parnell and Robinson, 2017). While there is endless diversity, the urban planet is also unified by a set of mega-challenges, some of which are truly global, such as climate. Others are omnipresent without being global, such as justice, wealth, welfare, and sustainability. These mega-challenges may have local expressions, but they require national, regional, and international collaboration to be adequately addressed. No city is an island; they are all parts of the main. Our knowledge of the whole is patchy, and, crucially, we know least about those parts of the urban planet where change is occurring most rapidly and where the urban crisis is most acute, reinforcing the need for knowledge holders to reorient their view on global urbanism and to self-consciously try to "see cities from the south" (Watson 2009).

0.3 Cities of the Global South Are a Priority

The global urban condition is not a composite of equivalent types or parts – all cities are not the same – in size, in function in wealth or in exposure to risk. In the remaining decades of the twenty-first century, projections indicate that most of the growth (>90 percent) will come from the global south. The two continents that will experience the greatest share of twenty-first-century urbanization are Asia and Africa – with India, China, and Nigeria accounting for over a third of all urban growth (UN 2014). Thus, the everyday reality of the twenty-first-century urban is, out of necessity, *the focus on the cities of the global south*. What does this mean for urban research, planning, and envisioning? We need a "southern sensibility" towards urbanization that takes in the reality that cities will increasingly become locations of contrasts. These "southern leanings" will include a focus on contrasts between informal and planned urban expansion; between local place-making and global teleconnections; between shanties and high-rise buildings; between urban sprawl and congested inner cities; between waste dumps and pristine restored parks; and of course, to the spaces of urban power that lie between states, business, criminals, and traditional powers. Urban reality now and in the immediate future will include deep social, ecological, economic, and technological rifts between cities as loci of upward mobility and as a wicked nexus of poverty, pollution, and powerlessness. The gradual realignment of the divisions between rich and poor within and between cities will spill beyond the life struggles for upward mobility and survival, drawing from the vitality of the urban planet. Urbanism in the global south will share certain generic features with their nineteenth-and twentieth-century northern counterparts, but they will not copy or emulate them. What an 80 million inhabitant version of Dhaka will become, nobody really knows. What is the word for it? Is it a community, a region, a global subject? Or a concept yet to come? It is equally important to recognize that there is not a universal notion of *cities of global south*, as they exhibit as much disparity among themselves as when compared to those in the global north.

The challenge for mediating extremes absences and excesses in southern cities along the lines already claimed by northern urbanites is exacerbated by our absolute lack of knowledge and thus inability to put together dynamic analyses of urban change across most of the urbanizing world. In comparison to the vast amount of literature on cities in Europe, the Americas, and even China, we know relatively little about the southern cities, or their interactions with natural systems, in Congo, Pakistan, or Indonesia. This is further complicated by the extreme heterogeneity that characterizes the trajectories that different cities, large to small, have taken across different locations, as well as across different points in time. What is clear is that the growth of cities that lack planning capacity and local ecological expertise face problems. For instance, the semi-arid Indian city of Bangalore, built to deal with droughts via an engineered system of rainwater harvesting via topographically interconnected tanks, now faces a perverse challenge of flooding in the monsoon season due to construction over water channels coupled with the ever-present challenge of drought in summer (Nagendra 2016). Kampala in Uganda faces iatropic challenges (events that necessitate medical care that are common to many southern cities) with technical interventions such as the establishment of sewage treatment plants (to deal with the city's burgeoning sewage problem), leading to perverse outcomes of biodiversity loss in rich wetlands, further reducing the city's capacity to naturally treat its sewage, and making it increasingly dependent on technical solutions (Lwasa 2010).

These experiences that reflect the interplay of urban systems are not unique to Bangalore and Kampala. They represent a wider problem: that formal approaches to city planning tend to prioritize technology and infrastructure provisioning and solutions, with the idea that social and ecological problems can be tackled later, by fitting piecemeal "solutions" onto an already engineered system. Yet experience tells us that this is impossible. Cities are also social-ecological *systems*, and the social, ecological, and indeed, cultural elements need to be designed with an explicit focus on multilevel, adaptive *system* design, integrated with technological aspects, from the start. For instance, recent research on food waste, a growing challenge in most southern cities, indicates that urban planning, transportation, and street design play a major role in shaping diets, food packaging, and energy usage in cities (Seto and Ramankutty 2016). The fact that the growth in most southern cities is yet to take place thus creates a formidable opportunity, one that helps us to take cognizance of the mistakes made in urban planning of the past, and move towards a new approach that is data based but which also takes into account the local cultural and ecological requirements of diverse locations and governance regimes to connect formal and informal planning, ideally achieving equitable city improvements by leapfrogging technology innovation and with planned, macroeconomic investment-heavy urban growth.

The global concentration of people suggests that challenges of the urban planet will be won or lost in cities of the global south, but only if action is swift (Figure 0.1). A comparison of the waves of globalization in the last two centuries with the earlier waves (Clark 2016) shows clearly that the duration of each wave is becoming shorter, in what we might think of as a great urban acceleration (McPhearson et al. 2016c). Where waves of change once lasted a century or more, they now appear to run their course in as little as 15 to 20 years, and in the future this duration may be even shorter. If the global economy becomes

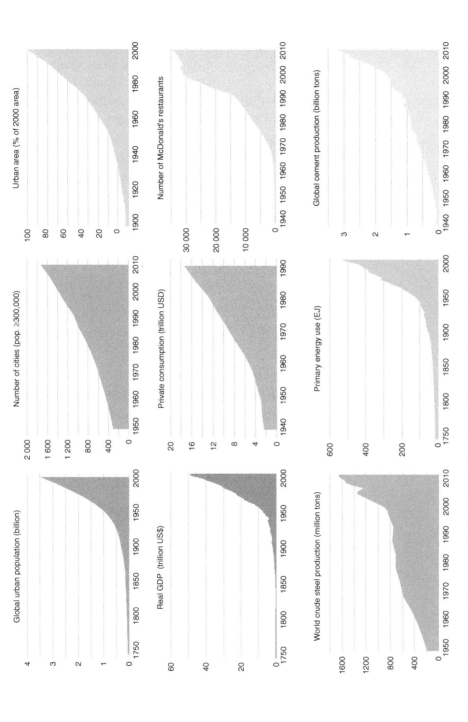

Figure 0.1 Cities and urban areas will house nearly all of the world's net population growth over the next two decades with 1.4 million people added to urban areas each week (UN 2014), equal to roughly the population of Stockholm. Cities are engines of national and global growth, accounting for 80 percent of global economic output. In China, four city clusters account for nearly half of China's GDP (Shao et al. 2006). Cities are also key drivers of global energy demand and greenhouse gas emissions, accounting for around 70 percent of both (IEA 2008). Meanwhile, urban land area could triple globally from 2000 to 2030 (Seto et al. 2012). This is equivalent to adding an area larger than Manhattan every day. Accelerating urban development boosts private consumption (Dobbs et al. 2008) and requires significant infrastructure, including carbon-intensive manufacturing and construction consuming massive quantities of concrete and steel consumption, particularly in the early phases of urbanization (Wang 2007).

ever more integrated, globalizing city waves will increasingly come to resemble global economic cycles, and the windows of opportunity for cities to participate will close quickly.

Although there are vast differences between the networks of cities along the ancient silk roads and the twenty-first-century system of global value chains and competitive advantage, there are also striking parallels (Clark 2016). Today's cities can learn much from how those in previous waves built and sustained their competitive attributes, and how to avoid becoming locked into unsustainable or unproductive cycles of development. History shows this is a risk if cities lose competitiveness in traded sectors, fail to embrace innovation or to project influence, are closed to immigration and entrepreneurship, or are unable to adapt to a changing geopolitical or geo-economic center of gravity. The ingredients of today's most successful cities are sometimes hard for other cities to emulate directly, and so alternative strategies and pathways to global engagement have arisen. Over time, these alternative pathways result in very different kinds of global, or local and regional, cities.

0.4 Knowledge for an Urban Planet

The Urban Planet is full of provocations from artists, practitioners, and activists who remind us repeatedly that a bookish science of cities is not enough to change the hearts, minds, and actions of the millions of urban residents; they point out that generalization without authentication will never generate useful or legitimate knowledge. It is not easy to reconcile this unambiguous message with the equally stark assertion that scientists must be at the forefront of generating the evidence that underpins global urban reform; or that for science and scholarship to have the impact required at the necessary scale and pace, a massive expansion in research capacity and coverage is required. These are the competing, even contrasting imperatives of the knowledge spectrum that must inform the urban planet going forward. Clearly unlocking a more sustainable urban future will require more than a singular effort.

Locating cities in a global frame is by its nature a multiscalar exercise and necessitates an interdisciplinary and systems perspective – alongside approaches from nonsystemic and nomothetic fields such as the social sciences and the humanities. A global view on urbanism demands learning from past waves of globalization, understanding the reach and impact of technology (telecoms, renewables, etc.) on the individual and household as well as in the formation of worldwide city networks. The demand for new knowledge for this global urbanism does not negate old disciplinary contributions, but it demands the investigation of new places, greater urgency, and an understanding of complexity. A global view of the urban transition hopes to bring all cities into the picture through establishing major causal dynamics, fostering comparability, and acknowledging difference – these are demands that are the imperatives for new urban knowledge innovation.

The centrality of cities to the sustainability of people, the planet, and prosperity points to the need for continuous investments in an expanded and flexible urban science that is forged out of innovative interdisciplinary understandings of the complex systems that both drive and derive from the prevalence of urban ways of being (Parnell et al. 2017). This volume draws together nascent interdisciplinary and cross-stakeholder urban dialogues, with some contributors actively self-defining as part of a new urban science community and others presenting themselves as concerned thinkers or contributors to a more open-ended debate on the significance of the urban planet. While there are clearly incommensurate ideas evident across the chapters that follow, not least in the schism between scholar- and practitioner-produced texts, but all contributors to *The Urban Planet* share a commitment of generating new knowledge as an integral part of building a better urban future. Together we argue for greater understanding of specialist concerns, like water or air quality, and system-based analyses of the cities where we each live. Local understanding of general processes lies at the core of doing things better in cities, but case-based research is not enough. Large-scale interactions between urban life and the cultural, social, political, economic, and the ecological processes that we highlight in this book are all increasingly dominated by cities and require perspectives based on local knowledge alongside summative and trend assessments.

The contributions in this volume all, even when dealing with micro details, intersperse local reality and global exploration of the complex system relationships between nature and the city. Simultaneously tracking global trajectories and highlighting place- and issue-specific problems reveals the shortage of sophisticated analysis of the interactions across sectors and cities, and the absence of clear messaging from science to practice. Tracking the surges of urbanization globally, we pose two overarching questions. First, what new thinking and evidence is required to radically shift the urban trajectory onto a more sustainable path. Second how, using evidence drawn in different ways and from cities across the world, can we reimagine and motivate for the changes that are required to implement the alternative global urban agenda. There has already been some success in the new urban endeavor – the call for a city-centric change to how we understand and regulate the world, which was endorsed by the 2030 Agenda in 2015 (UN 2015), was underpinned by the work of scientists. The approval of an urban Sustainable Development Goal and a number of other multilateral agreements to put cities at the core of global development has since confirmed the collective acceptance of the importance of the city to global environmental change. The immediate aftermath of the radical pro-city realignment of global policy scientists welcomed the role that evidence had played in securing global policy realignment (Barnett and Parnell 2016), but note, too, the imperative of ensuring ongoing evidence-led multilateral action in amending policy direction and monitoring implementation of urban sustainable development objectives. In addition, both individual scholars and organized science have endorsed very different modes of knowledge production: The new urban science has aspirations to inter- and transdisciplinarity and to coproduction.

As we highlight in the concluding chapter, substantive methodological and philosophical challenges remain in placing the study of cities in the crosshairs of sometimes-conflicting disciplinary rationalities. Similarly, the demands of integrating the ideas of non academic voices into the scientific text should not be underestimated. Notwithstanding these challenges, the imperative for a new science of cities and cogenerating knowledge across scholars, artists, residents, and practitioners remains an aspiration we endorse and have sought to pursue in *The Urban Planet*, even while we are aware of the different registers and even dissonant voices that this approach creates. Taken together, the book's contents, from right across the multidisciplinary and artist-practitioner-activist-scholar spectrum, all affirm the multilateral demand that cities be given greater prominence in global development in ways that reflect the geographical complexity and range of city realities. The *Urban Planet* highlights the multiple, even competing, concerns of what we may frame as existing or contemporary urban theory, but we are unambiguous of the need to put cities in the foreground of knowledge production and informed, responsible policy-making.

In reformulating and extending urban knowledge to meet the policy ambitions of cities, nations, and the multilateral system, a more extensive and robust urban science has to better address urban complexity and difference. The new knowledge outputs will also need to be legible so that evidence and analysis can more effectively guide (and evaluate) urban decision-makers in the critical decades ahead. There is a clear political and practical imperative in coming to terms with the universal challenges and opportunities embodied in the dynamics of the urban transition. Nuanced locally specific study is clearly imperative to inform action, and no two cities are the same. But, a common global urban register or vision that is understood by a range of stakeholders is what will change mindsets and galvanize collective action at the scale required to ensure a more sustainable urban planet. The intellectual challenge is thus a task of informing, critiquing, and revising the methods and modes of urban thinking – to collectively improve urban life for all. Doing this requires not only working with varied stakeholders but also coming to grips with missing data and complex urban dynamics. No single discipline or scholar or laboratory can achieve this alone – not least as there is a critical need to incorporate many more urban points into the overall theorizing of the city. Collaboration is essential.

Finally, divergent views are inevitable in building cross-disciplinary multi-stakeholder pathways for an ever-more urbanized age ahead. While consensus is unlikely (and may not be desirable) it should be possible to identify, based on robust research, the major issues facing the urban planet. To this end, there are four overarching intellectual tensions that inform this volume.

- First is the idea that while the Anthropocene already entails a fundamentally urban way of life and urban identity (Ljungqvist et al. 2010; Barthel et al. 2010), biophysical impact is not the only respect in which cities will shape the future – far from it.

- Second is that while specialist knowledge needs to be valued and extended, there is an imperative for new forms of urban knowledge, where cities are located in a global framing and approached from an interdisciplinary and systems perspective.

- Third is that although twenty-first-century urbanism requires a particular focus on the global south, all cities and regions can and must innovate to transform from their currently unsustainable trajectories.

- Fourth is that at the same time that researchers have to maintain critical independent views, the present is a critical time for urban scholars and policy-makers to work together to achieve the major transitions and transformations that are needed.

References

Acuto, M., and Parnell, S. (2016). Leave No City Behind, *Nature*, 352(6288): 873.

Bai, X., McPhearson, T., Cleugh, H., Nagendra, H., Tong, X., Zhu, T., and Zhu, Y.G. (2017). Understanding Urban-Environmental Linkages: Conceptual and Empirical Advances, *Annual Review of Environment and Resources*, 42(1): 215–240.

Barnett, C., and Parnell, S. (2016) Ideas, Implementation and Indicators: Epistemologies of The post-2015 Urban Agenda, *Environment and Urbanization*, 28(1): 87–98.

Barthel, S., Sörlin, S., and Ljungkvist, J. (2010). Innovative Memory and Resilient Cities: Echoes from Ancient Constantinople, in Sinclair, P., Nordquist, G., Herschend, F., and Isendahl, C. (eds.), *The Urban Mind: Cultural and Environmental Dynamics*, Uppsala: Uppsala University, pp. 391–405.

Batty, M. (2013). *The New Science of Cities*, Cambridge, MA: MIT Press.

Biermann, F., Bai, X., Bondre, N., Broadgate, W., Chen, C.T.A., Dube, O.P., Erisman, J.W., Glaser, M., van der Hel, S., Lemos, M.C., and Seitzinger, S. (2016). Down to Earth: Contextualizing the Anthropocene. *Global Environmental Change,* 39: 341–350.

Braun, B. (2005). Environmental Issues: Writing a More-than-Human Urban Geography, *Progress in Human Geography,* 29 (5): 635–650.

Brenner, N., and Schmid, C. (2014). Planetary Urbanization, in Brenner, N. (ed.) *Implosions/ Explosions: Toward a Study of Planetary Urbanization.* Berlin: Jovis, pp. 160–163.

Clark, G., (2016). Global Cities: A Short History. Washington, DC: Brookings Institution Press.

Schaer, F. (2012). Urban World: Cities and the Rise of the Consuming Class. New York: McKinsey Global Institute.

Elmqvist, T., Redman, C. L., Barthel, S., and Costanza, R. 2013. History of Urbanization and the Missing Ecology, in, Elmqvist, T., Bai, X., Frantzeskaki, N., Griffith, C., Maddox, D., McPhearson, T., et al. (eds.), Urbanization, Biodiversity and Ecosystem Services: Challenges and Opportunities. The Netherlands: Springer Open, pp.13–30. DOI 10.1007/978-94-007-7088-1_2.

Erixon Aalto, H., and Ernstson, H. (2017). Of Plants, High Lines and Horses: Civics and Designers in the Relational Articulation of Values of Urban Natures. *Landscape and Urban Planning,* 157: 309–321.

Ernstson, H., Lawhon, M., and Duminy, J. (2014) Conceptual Vectors of African Urbanism: "Engaged Theory-Making" and "Platforms of Engagement." *Regional Studies,* 48 (9): 1563–1577.

Ernstson, H., and Sörlin, S. (eds.) (2018). *Grounding Urban Natures: Histories and Futures of Urban Ecologies*, Cambridge, MA: MIT Press, in review.

Florida, R. (2002) *The Rise of the Creative Class.* New York: Basic Books.

Gandy, M., (2013) Marginalia: Aesthetics, Ecology, and Urban Wastelands, *Annals of the Association of American Geographers*, 103 (6): 1301–1316.

Glaeser, E. (2011). *Triumph of the City: How Our Greatest Invention Makes Us Richer, Smarter, Greener, Healthier, and Happier.* Harmondsworth: Penguin.

Lachmund, J. (2011). The Making of an Urban Ecology. Biological Expertise and Wildlife Preservation in West Berlin, in Brantz, D., and Dümpelmann, S. (eds.), *Greening the City. Urban Landscapes in the Twentieth Century.* Charlottesville/London: University of Virginia Press, pp. 204–227.

Heynen, N.C., Kaika, M., and Swyngedouw, E. eds., (2006). *In the Nature of Cities: Urban Political Ecology and the Politics of Urban Metabolism* (Vol. 3), London: Taylor & Francis.

Heynen, N., (2014) Urban Political Ecology I: The Urban Century, *Progress in Human Geography*, 38 (4): 598–604.

Hinchliffe, S., and Whatmore, S., (2006) Living Cities: Towards a Politics of Conviviality, *Science as Culture*, 15 (2): 123–138.

Hinchliffe, S., (2008) Reconstituting Nature Conservation: Towards a Careful Political Ecology, *Geoforum*, 39 (1): 88–97.

Hodson, R. (2016) Urban Health and Well-Being, *Nature*, 531: 7594.

International Energy Agency (IEA), 2008. *World Energy Outlook 2008*. Paris: International Energy Agency.

Ljungkvist, J., Barthel, S., Finnveden, G., and Sörlin, S. (2010). The Urban Anthropocene: Lessons for Sustainability from the Environmental History of Constantinople, in Sinclair, P.J.J., Nordquist, G., Herschend, F., and Isendahl, C. (eds.), *The Urban Mind: Cultural and Environmental Dynamics*. Uppsala University: Department of Archaeology and Ancient History, pp. 367–390.

Lwasa, S. (2010). Adapting Urban Areas in Africa to Climate Change: The Case of Kampala, *Current Opinion in Environmental Sustainability*, 2(3): 166–171.

McPhearson, T., Pickett, S.T.A., Grimm, N., Niemelä, J., Alberti, M., Elmqvist, T., et al. (2016). Advancing Urban Ecology Toward a Science of Cities, *BioScience*, 66(3):198–212.

McPhearson, T., Parnell, S., Simon, D., Gaffney, O., Elmqvist, T., Bai, X., et al. (2016b) Scientists Must Have a Say in the Future of Cities, *Nature*, 538: 165–166.

McPhearson, T., Parnell, S., Simon, D., Gaffney, O., Elmqvist, T., Bai, X., et al. (2016c). Building Urban Science to Achieve the New Urban Agenda, *The Nature of Cities*, www.thenatureofcities .com/2016/10/24/building-urban-science-to-achieve-the-new-urban-agenda/

Melosi, M.V. (1993) The Place of the City in Environmental History, *Environmental History Review*, 17: 1–23.

Melosi, M.V. (2010) Humans, Cities, and Nature: How Do Cities Fit in the Material World?, *Journal of Urban History*, 36 (1): 3–21.

Mitlin, D., and Satterthwaite, D. (2013) *Urban Poverty in the Global South: Scale and Nature*. London: Routledge.

Nagendra, H. (2016) *Nature in the City: Bengaluru in the Past, Present and Future*. New Delhi: Oxford University Press.

Parnell, S., and Robinson, J. (2017). The Global Urban: Difference and Complexity in Urban Studies and the Science of Cities, in Hall, S., and Burdett, R. (eds.) *Handbook of Social Science*. London: Routledge, pp. 13–31.

Robinson, J. (2016). Thinking Cities through Elsewhere: Comparative Tactics for a More Global Urban Studies, *Progress in Human Geography*, 40(1): 3–29.

Rosen, C., and Tarr, J. (1994) The Importance of an Urban Perspective in Environmental History, *Urban History*, 20: 299–310.

Rosenzweig, C., Solecki, W., Hammer, S.A., and Mehrotra, S. (2010). Cities Lead the Way in Climate-Change Action, *Nature*, 467(7318): 909–911.

Sedrez, Lise. (2005). *The "Bay of All Beauties": State and Environment in Guanabara Bay, Rio de Janeiro, Brazil, 1875-1975*. Ann Arbor, MI: University Microfilms.

Seto, K., Güneralp, B., and Hutyra, L. (2012). Global Forecasts of Urban Expansion to 2030 and Direct Impacts on Biodiversity and Carbon Pools, *Proceedings of the National Academy of Sciences*, 109: 16083–16088.

Seto, K.C., and Ramankutty, N. (2016). Hidden Linkages between Urbanization and Food Systems. *Science*, 352: 943–945.

Sharan, A. (2014). *In the City, Out of Place: Nuisance, Pollution and Urban Dwelling in Modern Delhi, c.1850-2000*. Oxford: Oxford University Press.

Shao, M., Tang, T., Zhang, Y., and Li, W. (2006) City Clusters in China: Air And Surface Water Pollution, *Frontiers of Ecology and the Environment*, 4: 353–361.

Simon, D. (ed.) (2016). *Rethinking Sustainable Cities: Accessible, Green and Fair*. Bristol: Policy Press.

Sukopp, H. (2002). On the Early History of Urban Ecology in Europe. *Preslia, Praha* 74: 373–393.

Swyngedouw, E. (1996). The City as a Hybrid: On Nature, Society and Cyborg Urbanization, *Capitalism Nature Socialism*, 7 (2): 65–80.

Swyngedouw, E. (2004). *Social Power and the Urbanization of Water: Flows of Power*. Oxford: Oxford University Press.

United Nations (2014). *World Urbanization Prospects: The 2014 Revision*, New York: United Nations Department of Economic and Social Affairs.

United Nations (2015) *Transforming Our World: The 2030 Agenda for Sustainable Development*. New York: United Nations.

Warren-Rhodes, K., and Koenig, A. (2001). Escalating Trends in the Urban Metabolism of Hong Kong: 1971–1997, *AMBIO: A Journal of the Human Environment*, 30(7): 429–438.

Wang, T., Müller, D.B., and Graedel, T.E. (2007) Forging the Anthropogenic Iron Cycle. *Environmental Science & Technology* 41(14): 5120–5129.

Watson, V. (2009) Seeing from the South: Refocusing Urban Planning on the Globe's Central Urban Issues, *Urban Studies*, 46: 2259–2275.

Zalasiewicz, J., et al. (2017). Scale and Diversity of the Physical Technosphere: A Geological Perspective, *Anthropocene Review*, 4(1): 9–22.

Part I

Dynamic Urban Planet

Chapter 1: Global Urbanization

Perspectives and Trends

Dagmar Haase, Burak Güneralp, Bharat Dahiya, Xuemei Bai, and Thomas Elmqvist

1.1 Perspectives on Urbanization

Urbanization is one of the most important global change processes. As the share of people in, and the footprint of, urban areas continue to grow globally and locally, understanding urbanization processes and resulting land use – both their patterns and intensity – is increasingly important with respect to natural resource use, sociodemographics, health, and global environmental change (Seto and Reenberg 2014). For decades, urban studies have been grappling with the question of how to define "urban"; the definition of urban includes comparatively straightforward official definitions, such as those that use the administrative unit with a set minimum number of inhabitants (McIntyre et al. 2000), but, in some cases, it also includes such factors as population density, built-up area (urban morphology), commuting density, travel distance (Nilsson et al. 2014), and proportion of workforce engaged in nonagricultural economic activities (Census of India 2011). In spite of this variety, official definitions do not accurately represent the urban in all its diversity. Even scholarly studies tend to adopt one or a subset of many perspectives in understanding the urban as a phenomenon, from the most well-understood demographic perspective (Kazepov 2005) to relatively more recently formulated or reformulated perspectives based on space (Angel 2010; Seto et al. 2011); urbanity (Boone et al. 2014); material and energy flows (Kennedy et al. 2007; Bai 2016); teleconnections (Seto et al. 2012); network and power hierarchies (Sassen 2001); ecology (Grimm et al. 2008); social ecology (Elmqvist et al. 2013); and urban policy and governance (Bai et al. 2010). Building an integrated systems approach in urban science and practice has also been called for (Bai et al. 2016; McPhearson et al. 2016).

Here, we will elaborate on a subset of these perspectives and discuss their roles in improving our understanding of the urban and urbanization processes.

Note that some of the perspectives are covered in other chapters; for example, urban material energy flows are addressed in Chapter 4, urban ecology and cities as complex systems in Chapter 1.2, and urban policy and governance in several chapters and provocations in Parts II and III.

1.1.1 The Demographic Perspective

The first cities appeared many millennia ago (Kazepov 2005; Childe 1950). Since then, urbanization dynamics evolved substantially in time and space, but the most fundamental ingredient remained the same: people. In 1800, only 3 percent of the world's population lived in cities, but this figure rose to 47 percent by the end of the twentieth century. In 1950, there were 83 cities with populations that exceeded 1 million; by 2010, this number had risen to more than 460.

There is a linkage between demographic transition and urbanization in the form of a systematic trend whereby less developed economies tend to be more rural and to have higher birth rates (Lesthaeghe 2010). As the economy of a country develops, more of its population resides in urban areas with an accompanying fall in intrinsic birth rates (Lesthaeghe 2010); this can also be observed for the demographic (fertility) behavior of migrants (Milewski 2010) (see also Chapter 6). Thus, for example, rapidly growing African cities can be viewed as being in the early stages of this transition, while cities in Europe or the United States can be seen as reaching the later stages.

If we use the administrative definition of the urban, the most urbanized regions worldwide are North America (82 percent), Latin America and the Caribbean (80 percent), Europe (74 percent), and Oceania (71 percent) (UN 2014). In contrast, Africa and Asia remain mostly rural, with 41 percent and 49 percent of their respective populations living in urban areas. In particular, Nigeria, Ethiopia, Tanzania, and Kenya in Africa, and China, India, Indonesia, and Myanmar in Asia feature large rural populations. Regions that are less urbanized, such as Africa and Asia, are currently urbanizing faster than those with an already high share of urban population (Dahiya 2012b). Notwithstanding the current level of urbanization or the growth rate of their cities, all regions are expected to continue urbanizing over the coming decades.

Today, as in the past, the majority of the world's cities have been growing with a population growth rate of ≥1 percent up to >5 percent per year (Oswalt and Rieniets 2006; UN-Habitat 2016). However, there have always been cities and conurbations exhibiting negative net growth rates (Haase and Schwarz 2016; Figure 1.1). There are approximately 350–400 shrinking cities worldwide, most of them in the post-industrialized Western world, namely Europe and the United States, but also in Japan (Haase 2014). Urban shrinkage is by no means a new phenomenon: Several cities whose history goes back millennia – such

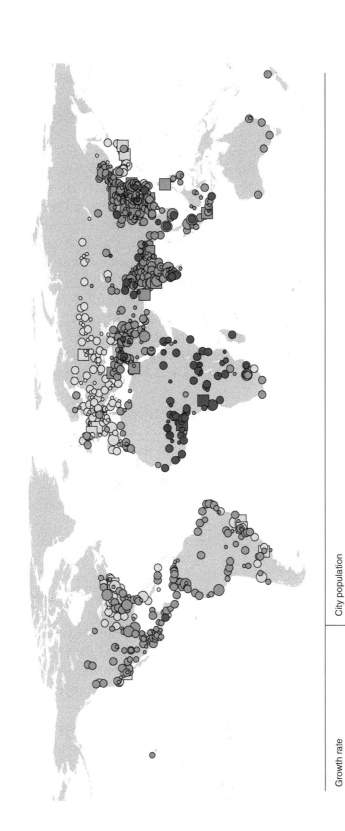

Figure 1.1 Growth rates of urban agglomerations by size class, 2014–2030. Source: Jerker Lokrantz/Azote, modified after World Urbanization Prospects, Population Division, UN 2014.

as Rome, the first megacity on the planet (Haase 2014), and Istanbul, capital of four empires over a span of two millennia (Necipoğlu 2010) – have undergone several cycles of growth and shrinkage.

Over the next few decades, urbanization will continue, particularly in Asia and Africa. According to the most recent estimates from the United Nations, two out of three inhabitants in 2050 will live in urban areas (UN 2014). Most of this urban growth will take place in Asia and the West African urban belt, with population growth rates of 3–5 percent per year (UN 2014a). However, global data also show that the growth rate of the urban population in the developing world is expected to fall from 3–5 percent per year to under 2 percent per year in 2030 (UN-Habitat 2010a, 2014). The UN predicts that, by 2050, 65 percent of populations in developing countries and nearly 90 percent of populations in developed countries will live in urban areas (UN 2014).

In many parts of the world, the physical expansion of urban areas has been faster than urban population growth (Angel et al. 2011a, 2011b), suggesting declining densities. Studies have also reported an accelerated decline in average household size over the past decades (Haase et al. 2013; Liu et al. 2003). Consequently, on the one hand, most cities in developed countries have been facing an increase in per capita living space, definitely one of the many factors significantly influencing the spatial (built space) growth of cities. On the other hand, such decline in household size in developing countries has exacerbated the lack of urban housing stock, which results in large slum populations, the global total of which were estimated at 862.6 million people in 2013 (UN-Habitat 2010a and 2010b). However, in some East Asian cities (particularly in China) and in Europe, significant increases in urban-built densities have also been observed over the last decade (Frolking et al. 2013).

1.1.2 Aging of the Urban Planet

Global population aging, including urban aging, is a process known as the "demographic transition," in which first mortality, then fertility decline. Decreasing fertility coupled with increasing life expectancy has been reshaping the age structure of the populations in most regions of the planet by shifting relative weight from younger to older age groups (Lesthaeghe 2010). In less developed regions, the aging index is 23; that is, we currently count 23 people older than 60 years of age for every 100 children younger than 15 years old. By 2050, the aging index is projected to almost quadruple, reaching 89 (UN 2017). Over the same period, in the developed world, the aging index is projected to increase from 106 to 215. The only exception to this trend is Africa, where, compared to all the other regions of the world, the aging index is forecasted to remain under 50 through 2050 (Figure 1.2). In cities, where women

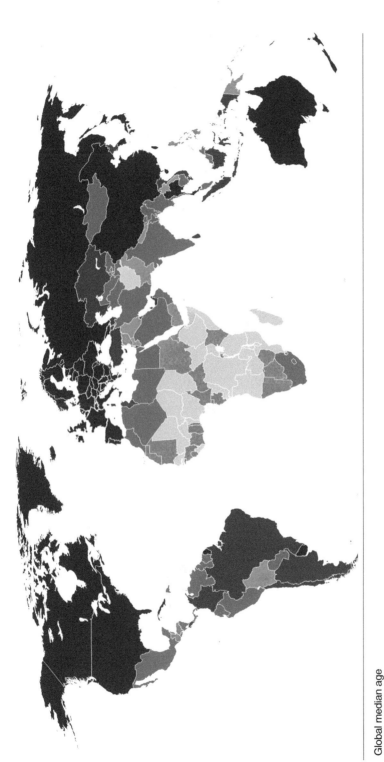

Global median age

Years: 14–20 ■ 20–25 ■ 25–30 ■ 30–35 ■ 35–40 ■ 40+ ■ No data

Figure 1.2 Median age by country for 2015. A youth bulge is evident for Africa and to a lesser extent for South and Southeast Asia and Central America.
Source: Jerker Lokrantz/Azote, modified after UN Factbook.

are comparatively more educated, financially more independent, give birth later and where single-parent families are much more common, these trends are stronger.

There is another difference between urban aging in the developed, affluent urban areas and in the less developed, less affluent urban areas: Although the highest proportions of elderly persons are found in more developed cities, this age group is growing considerably more rapidly in the poorer and less affluent parts of the urban world, such as China and Thailand. As a consequence, older populations will increasingly be concentrated in less developed regions. Regardless of these trends, in both affluent and less affluent cities, older women generally greatly outnumber older men (UN 2017), as women tend to outlive men.

1.1.3 The Spatial Perspective

Global urbanization is a physical phenomenon as much as it is a demographic one. Although there has recently been an increase in attention given to global spatial patterns of urbanization, we have few theoretical explanations for the spatial configuration of large urban areas across regions and countries (Lynch 1961). Whatever theoretical knowledge on urban form exists has originated in urban planning and architecture, with an emphasis on intra-urban patterns and shapes (Jabareen 2006).

This trend, however, may be slowly changing. Over the past few years, several studies have shed light on the global patterns of actual built-up urban land and how it changed over the last four decades. A subset of these studies presents a "window into the future" (Fragkias et al. 2013: p. 418). Estimates of global urban land range from 0.2 percent to 2.4 percent of the terrestrial land surface (Potere and Schneider 2007; World Bank 2015). What is clear is that urban land is not equally distributed across the world due to geographic, climatic, and resource-related opportunities and constraints. Urban expansion over the last 30 years has been greatest along coastlines and low-lying coastal zones (Seto et al. 2011). Current urban hotspots are situated on the coastlines of South Asia, Southeast Asia, Southeast China, the United States' East Coast, Western Europe, Japan, West Africa, and the Atlantic coast of Latin America. With regard to coastal flood risks, nearly all of the 10 largest megacities are in developing countries. With regard to the value of property and infrastructure assets' exposure to coastal flood risks, a global ranking of megacities includes eight from Asia: Miami, Guangzhou, New York, Kolkata, Shanghai, Mumbai, Tianjin, Tokyo, Hong Kong, and Bangkok (Nicholls et al. 2008). Indeed, a recent study found that, at the turn of the twenty-first century, 11 percent of all urban land (over 70,000 km²) was located within low-elevation coastal zones

(Güneralp et al. 2015), defined as "the contiguous area along the coast that is less than 10 m above sea level" (McGranahan et al. 2007: p. 17). In addition, emerging coastal metropolitan regions in Africa and Asia are expected to have larger areas exposed to flooding than those in developed countries.

There is wide variability in terms of the spatial configuration of urban areas across different geographies around the world. An analysis of the similarities and differences in urban form and growth across 25 midsized cities from different geographical settings and levels of economic development revealed that although all 25 cities are expanding, those outside the United States do not exhibit the dispersed spatial forms characteristic of North American cities (Schneider and Woodcock 2008). There is a diversity of urban landscapes around the world with significant differences in spatial configuration among individual cities. However, there also seems to be a scale effect: While there is a tendency for increased landscape heterogeneity at individual-city scale, urban landscapes are increasingly becoming homogeneous at the global scale (Jenerette and Potere 2010). Though a variety of socioeconomic and biophysical factors influence the spatial growth of cities and their relative influence varies from region to region (Seto et al. 2012), it is claimed that globalization leads to a proliferation of similar urban forms across different geographies (Leichenko and Solecki 2005). At least one study found that income, in interaction with city size, appears to have a pronounced effect on urban growth, particularly in relatively smaller cities (Jenerette and Potere 2010). Importantly, the emerging urban agglomerations in the developing world appear to be more compact than their counterparts in Europe and North America (Huang et al. 2007).

Urbanization is arguably the most significant form of land-use and land-cover change because it has considerable effects on the pattern, dynamics, and functionality of ecosystems (Elmqvist et al. 2013). The process of urbanization can be clearly observed along the rural-urban gradient – that is, the ideal typical transect that links the urban (built, populated) and the rural (open, vegetated), which displays a typical configuration of population density, coverage of built-up area, respective impervious cover, and demographic structure, including lifestyles and travel behavior (Haase and Nuissl 2010). Along the rural-urban gradient, an increasing amount of land consumption – namely the transformation of green spaces to built-up areas, described as landscape urbanization, in contrast to demographic urbanization (Bai et al. 2011) – has been reported by many authors on the basis of field research and statistical data analysis (including McDonnell et al. 1997; Luck and Wu 2002; Lewis and Brabec 2005; Irwin and Bockstael 2007; Weng 2007; Yu and Ng 2007; Schwarz 2010). Likewise, the transformation along the rural-urban gradient has been detected by analysis of satellite imagery (including Lausch et al. 2015).

In regard to those cities whose populations are stagnating or declining, Scheuer et al. (2016) show a similar phenomenon at work for the age of built-up urban land and its relative variability; they identified "mature" and "expanding" urbanization along a polynomial fit for all large cities across the globe. Their study therefore suggests that growing and shrinking cities lie along a continuum – in what appears to be a cyclic process – of demographic transition, economic development, and urbanization (Scheuer et al. 2016).

1.1.4 Re(new)ed Perspectives

Urbanization is a multifaceted phenomenon, with profound changes in land, socioeconomics including consumption patterns, institutions, and environment (Friedmann 2006; Bai et al. 2014). This diversity provides fertile ground for introduction of new – or renewed – conceptualizations to characterize the urban and different urbanization processes. In one of the more recent such conceptualizations, Boone et al. (2014: p. 313) proposed the concept of "urbanity," defined as "the magnitude and qualities of livelihoods, lifestyles, connectivity, and place that create urban-ness of intertwined human experiences and land configurations". The concept of urbanity emerges from of a growing consensus that the classic urban versus rural classification to categorize land is insufficient for planning, research, and analysis. Importantly, the concept of urbanity underscores a continuum which can be applied beyond the administrative boundaries of cities, and therefore can extend to multiple dimensions, including livelihoods, land uses, and economies. Urbanity can also be used to understand how land-use changes in nonurban areas are connected to underlying urbanization dynamics. In this way, urbanity is closely tied to another recent conceptual framework in land-use science: urban land teleconnections (ULTs). The ULT concept seeks to uncover the linkages between land-use change and underlying urbanization dynamics (Seto et al. 2012).

ULTs "refer to the distal flows and connections of people, economic goods and services, and land use change processes that drive and respond to urbanization" (Seto et al. 2012: p. 1). ULTs express that the linkages between urban land-use change and the ecosystem resources consumed by urbanites are not exclusively formed over short distances, nor are they exclusively place based. Rather, these linkages include many processes that urbanites influence in distant locations (Seto et al. 2012). ULTs allow us to shed light on rural land-use changes and migration that are driven by distal urban functions. For example, local or regional shifts in dietary preferences and consumption styles driven by urbanization and increasing incomes are reinforced globally, but also have impacts on distal places through information and material linkages. Thus, ULTs link decisions, actions, and land changes at both urban and rural ends of a continuum (Güneralp et al. 2013). "Telecoupling," a similar but broader concept, refers to the system-level interactions among different human and natural processes across a range of spatial and temporal scales as, for instance, in the case of urban water system (Deines et al. 2015). These systemic interactions have enormous implications for quality of life, economy, sustainability, and social equity in both urban and rural areas.

Despite being grounded in specific locations, cities can also be described as global entities or functional units whose influence reach far beyond their immediate vicinity. The concept of "global cities" considers some cities to be key nodes in the global economic, communication, and financial system (Sassen 2001). The global cities concept originates from social sciences – especially from urban studies – and follows the idea that global urbanization can be understood as a phenomenon that is largely created, facilitated, and enacted in strategic geographic locations. These locations, in turn, emerge as a consequence of a hierarchical network of the global system of finance, transport, money flows, and trade (Sassen 2001, 2008; see Figure 1.3).

Given the multifaceted nature of cities in a globally interconnected world and the sustainability challenges they face, an integrated systems perspective is required in urban research and practice (see, for example, Güneralp and Seto 2008). The current framework of cities as social-technological systems is too narrow and should be complemented by a view of cities as complex social-ecological-technological systems, as has recently advanced within urban ecology and social-ecological systems perspectives (Elmqvist et al. 2013). This advance is critical given that the continuum of urbanity includes many characteristics and processes other than the particular density of people or land area covered by human-made structures. Bai et al. (2016) call for the radical redesign of urban institutional structure and processes along with financing of systems approaches in urban governance and the creation of stronger systemic integration among science, policy, and practice. McPhearson et al. (2016) call for moving urban ecology towards an integrated urban science. A recent example of integrating different urban disciplines is a study attempting to build a conceptual bridge between the large body of empirical works on urban metabolism to urban ecosystem research through identifying eight energy and material flow characteristics of urban ecosystems (Bai 2016).

1.2 Urbanization Trends around the World

Throughout history, urban areas have shown immense variety and variability across different cultures and geographies, and even within the same cultural or geographical sphere. The earliest cities in Mesopotamia, the Indus Valley, and

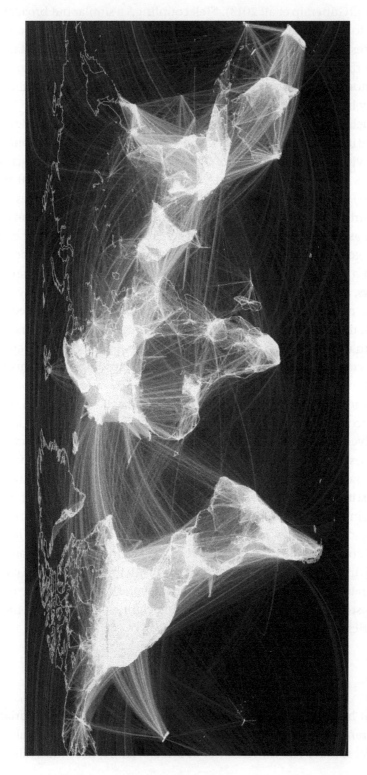

Figure 1.3 Facebook connections worldwide. Source: Jerker Lokrantz/Azote, modified after Facebook www.facebook.com/.

the Mediterranean region were highly compact in area, but a few were characterized by sizeable populations and densities. For example, Rome, in its heyday in the early third century CE, had 1.5 million inhabitants, a population count the city did not attain again until the 1930s (Davis 1955). The pre-medieval and medieval cities of Europe and Asia are typical examples of compact cities with midrise houses and high population densities. Regions with younger urbanization, such as North America, tend to develop less compact cities as a whole (Angel 2010).

Particularly in the developed world, post–World War II motorization, poor planning, and market failures led to urban sprawl, which is defined broadly as "excessive spatial growth of cities" (Brueckner 2000: p. 161) or, more specifically, as spatial growth of cities that creates forms of suburban development that lack accessibility and open space (Ewing 1997). As a spatio-temporal process, urban sprawl can be seen as a low-density expansion or "leapfrog development" of large urban areas into the surrounding rural landscape (Kasanko et al. 2006; Bengston et al. 2005). To give an example, from 1990 to 2006, urban land and associated infrastructure across Europe grew at an annual rate of about 1,000 km², which is equivalent to the entire area of the German capital of Berlin. Nevertheless, the most prominent case of this kind of urban growth has been the expansion of the cities in the United States in post–World War II era (Batty et al. 1999; Brueckner 2000).

The development of large suburbanized peripheries around historically compact European cities (Haase and Nuissl 2010) came to be known as the "Zwischenstadt" – a settlement form in between the urban and the rural (Sieverts 2003), which is mainly composed of detached houses and industrial, commercial, and retail sites that dominate the urban-to-rural interface (Meeus and Gulinck 2008; Nilsson et al. 2014). Conversely, rapidly growing urban areas in Asia and Africa display many rural features in their peri-urban spaces, including various forms of gardening and farming (McGee 1991). This type of growth is distinctly different than suburbanization seen in North America or Europe; such peri-urban spaces in East and Southeast Asia are called "desakota" after the Indonesian words "desa" and "kota" – "village" and "city," respectively.

Particularly after 1990, a considerable proportion of European cities, but also many cities in Japan, started losing population following significant fertility drops and out-migration; they were shrinking (Haase et al. 2013). Another prominent case of shrinkage – the US case – is less clearly related to fertility drops; rather, there have been large population shifts internal to the United States due to the disintegration of economies that were based on manufacturing and heavy industry in some regions, such as the Rust Belt and to the economic boom in others. Shrinkage today is ongoing, but it is accompanied by regrowth, with a return of the predominantly young and educated population to the city centers (Kabisch et al. 2010) (see Section 1.2.1 for more on urban shrinkage).

The cities in the developing world have also been differentiating over the last three decades. Whereas many millions of urban residents, who are typically concentrated in "informal" or squatter settlements in both inner and outer parts of these cities (Angel et al. 2011b; UN-Habitat 2010b; UN-Habitat 2014b), still face significant hardships and lack access to many urban amenities, affluent centers of innovation have also been developing and have been accompanied by increasing wealth, often in the same cities. These apparent contradictions are the most visible in rapidly growing cities of China, Brazil, India, Indonesia, Mexico, and South Africa, where the most affluent households often spatially segregate themselves from the poor majority in gated communities. Still, over the past few decades, declining urban population densities appear to be a hallmark of contemporary urbanization in most parts of the world (Angel et al. 2011a), a phenomenon that needs further investigation.

1.2.1 "Antipodes" of Urbanization: Urban Shrinkage

While rapid urban growth is presenting challenges for urban planners and policy-makers in certain parts of the world, in others, a contrasting phenomenon is presenting a completely different set of challenges: urban shrinkage. Urban shrinkage is characterized by many facets such as population loss; declining industrial and other economic activities accompanying underuse of buildings and urban infrastructure; declining population densities; vacant housing; fiscal constraints; and an increase in derelict land and brownfields as a consequence of land abandonment. A. Haase et al. (2012), D. Haase (2012), and Rink and Kabisch (2009) define urban shrinkage as a phenomenon of massive population loss in cities that results from a specific interplay of (1) economic (such as the Rust Belt of the United States), (2) financial, (3) demographic, (4) environmental, and (5) political changes or disruptions (such as in the former socialist countries in Europe) (Figure 1.4). Particularly prominent examples are the systemic changes that occurred across Central and Eastern Europe, including eastern Germany, after 1990, coupled with the introduction of a market economy (Moss 2008). Temporary shrinkage might also result from environmental disasters, such as Hurricane Katrina, which devastated the city of New Orleans in 2005, causing the city to lose a considerable part of its population; however, the population increased by 10 percent since 2010. Other examples of this hazard-driven shrinkage include Fukushima, Japan, or Pripjat in the Ukraine, where nuclear accidents led to massive or complete losses of the urban population; in these cases, a return is far from obvious.

Population decline
- · −10 to −24%
- · −25 to −49%
- ● −50 to −74%
- ● −75 to −100%

Figure 1.4 Regions of urban shrinkage in the world. Source: Kabisch et al. 2010.

Another reason for urban shrinkage is demographic change – namely low fertility and massive out-migration. The current processes determining urban shrinkage in Central and Eastern Europe have emerged in the form of the post-Soviet transition decline of traditional heavy industries. This decline induced general economic crises, unemployment, out-migration to other prospering regions, subsequent declines in fertility, and increases in population aging (D. Haase et al. 2012). Furthermore, widespread suburbanization in the peri-urban zones around shrinking cities leads to more residents abandoning the city and, eventually, to the development of "donut-cities," such as those in eastern Germany after 1990 (Couch et al. 2005) or Detroit in the United States.

Since about 2000, a new trend following peri-urbanization has been observed in some parts of the world: A number of cities in Germany, Central and Eastern Europe, and formerly shrinking parts of the eastern United States are no longer experiencing a loss in their population, but are regaining inhabitants. Positive migration balances are mainly based on intraregional in-migration and a considerable decline in out-migration (Kabisch et al. 2010). People are increasingly opting to stay in the city, even as suburbanization progresses. Concurrently, a discourse about a comeback of urban living – dubbed "reurbanization" – as a future scenario for a number of major cities in eastern Germany has come to the fore (D. Haase et al. 2008; Rink et al. 2012). Reurbanization is also currently being discussed in the United Kingdom and other European countries (Buzar et al. 2007; Colomb 2007) as well as in the United States (Cheshire 2006).

Reurbanization is a recent trend seen in cities that underwent a period of urban stagnation and decay (Wolff et al. 2017) followed by a new cycle of the demographic transition, economics, and urbanization. Reurbanization is characterized by a range of socio spatial processes not unlike gentrification, since taking advantage of the increasing affordability of real estate within inner city areas seems to be the main impetus. Its focus is clearly on the household dimension, as reurbanization processes are driven by households representing a range of socioeconomic groups (Kabisch et al. 2010).

Another recent trend, "Cittaslow," or "slow towns," originated and developed a firm foothold in Europe but is gradually being adopted in other parts of the world as well (Park and Kim 2016). Cittaslow is a network of 182 towns aiming to contribute to local urban development and thus to improve their quality of life (Hatipoglu 2015). The main goal of the Cittaslow approach is to broaden the philosophy of slow food to local communities and to the government of towns, applying the concepts of eco-gastronomy and local/traditional food production to the practice of everyday life. Municipalities which join the Cittaslow association are motivated by the idea of an urban area where humans are still protagonists of the slow and healthy succession of seasons. Cittaslow also means facilitating rich traditions of arts and craft in urban spaces with squares, theaters, shops, cafés, and restaurants, surrounded by unspoiled cultural landscapes. Other hallmarks of Cittaslow cities are spontaneity of religious rites and respect for traditions through the joy of slow and quiet living (see a review about urban cultural ecosystem services by Kabisch et al. 2014). Clearly, Cittaslow is a concept for affluent urban areas characterized by slow or no (population) growth. It is also, however, increasingly adopted by small towns and cities as an alternative to sustainable tourism development (Hatipoglu 2015; Park and Kim 2016). The Cittaslow approach is complemented by other similarly inspired ideas across the world, such as the "Life-based-City" (see the provocation by Cecilia Herzog in Chapter 21).

1.3 Future Trends of Urbanization

Current observations and statistical trends (UN 2014) suggest that the urbanization process will continue for the next few decades, further tilting the global demographic balance towards cities and towns. The UN projects that the world's urban population, almost 4 billion in 2015, will grow by about 75 percent until 2050, bringing the urban population up to 6.3 billion (2014). We must expect a highly uneven urban population development in less affluent regions due to segregation of the relatively fewer rich among many poor households – a pattern that we already observe in many fast-growing African megacities. Moreover, a larger number of future urbanites will concentrate in either medium-sized cities – most likely in Europe and parts of Africa and Asia – or megacities (defined as having a population of at least 10 million) mostly in Asia. This form of population concentration will put pressure on rural hinterlands and natural resources located within smaller city-regions and mega-urban areas (UN 2014).

Even more dramatic increases in population are forecasted for urban (built-up) land. In their middle-of-the-road scenario, Angel et al. (2011a, 2011b) forecasted that global urban land cover would be nearly 1.3 million km² by 2030 and 1.9 million km² by 2050, increases of 110 percent and more than 210 percent, respectively, since 2000. Seto et al. (2012) forecast that there will be a 185 percent increase in global urban land cover, with areas having a high probability of urban expansion amounting to 1.2 million km² from 2000 to 2030; urban expansion in Asia is expected to account for nearly half of this increase. More recently, Güneralp et al. (2017) projected that in all regions around the world, urban population densities will continue to decline with significant consequences for building energy use. They forecast that even if it is assumed that urban areas do not grow to be as geographically expansive as they have over the past few decades, urban population densities around the world are likely to continue to decline. For example, in North America, urban population densities overall are expected to decline from 2,100 capita per km² in 2010 to between 1,000 and 2,000 capita per km² in 2050. Comparatively, in South Asia, urban population densities are expected to decline from about 19,000 capita per km² to between 4,800 and 17,600 capita per km² over the same period.

Scenario analysis can be a powerful approach to studying the relative influence of different demographic, economic, technological, and environmental trajectories on the growth and spatial configuration of urban areas. The European Union's project, PLUREL (Peri-Urban Land Use Relationships), is a good example of this approach (Nilsson et al. 2015). Among the total of four scenarios they considered, a "Hypertech" scenario is likely to see small- and medium-sized towns becoming even more prominent, leading to increased peri-urbanization of rural areas. In a "Peak Oil" scenario, most people attempt to return to large cities because high transport costs will limit commuting distances. In their "Self-Reliance" scenario, considerable budgets will be spent on adaptation to climate change; people gravitate towards living in small, self-supporting communities. In the fourth scenario, where urbanized areas "Fragment," cities become more dispersed and more segregated as younger migrants inhabit city centers, while older residents escape to enclaves outside the city. Across all future scenarios that researchers explored in the project, urban expansion will continue at rates that are higher than those of any other land use (Boitier et al. 2008).

1.4 Towards a Synthesis: A Typology of Urbanization?

Spatial-temporal typologies of urbanization have been studied intensively by geographers, economists, and other social scientists for many decades (Haase and Nuissl 2010). The major factors that are thought to influence the aforementioned processes and types of urbanization are related to economic competition between different land uses/users (Thünen 1826; Alonso 1964) or between social/ethnic groups (Burgess 1925; Hoyt 1939; Harris and Ullmann 1945). More recent models regard the changing concentration of population in an urban area/agglomeration as key, and formulate a sequence of four phases of urban development: urbanization, suburbanization, desuburbanization, and reurbanization (Berg et al. 1982; Champion 2001; Kabisch and Haase 2011). Others approached the dynamics and transformation of urban development based on complex systems theory (Wilson 1976), the theorem of fractal development represented by means of cellular automata (White and Engelen 1993; Batty 2008) or systemic self-organization (Portugali 2000).

The multifaceted nature of urban areas and urbanization defies sweeping cat-
egorizations. Nevertheless, scholars have proposed several typologies of urban
areas; most are grounded in specific geographies based on their various characteristics, such as peri-urban areas (Gonçalves et al. 2017; von der Dunk et al.
2011); city-industry dynamics (Hatuka and Ben-Joseph 2017); urban energy use
(Creutzig et al. 2015); urban green infrastructure (Koc et al. 2016); urban form
(Jabareen 2006; Gil et al. 2012); metropolitan land-use patterns (Cutsinger and
Galster 2006); national urban policy (Holland 2015); urban planning theories
(Yiftachel 1989); and urban conflicts (Trudelle 2003). For example, a rare attempt
to develop a formal typology of urban areas across the world proposed four city
types based on the rates and patterns of their spatial growth (Schneider and
Woodcock 2008): low-growth cities with modest rates of infill development
(residential densification); high-growth cities with rapid, fragmented development; expansive-growth cities with extensive dispersion at low population
densities; and frantic-growth cities with extraordinary land conversion rates at
high population densities. Another attempt at a formal, global urban topology,
based on design concepts, proposes a different set of types of sustainable urban
forms (Jabareen 2006): the neo-traditional development, the urban contain-
ment, the compact city, and the eco-city. These limited-scope typologies and
the collective body of work on the similarities and differences in urbanization
trends around the world suggest that a broad typology of contemporary urbanization may be possible (see this volume's concluding chapter, "Synthesis").

1.5 Challenges and Opportunities of Urbanization Heading into the Twenty-First Century

Where will we stand at the end of the twenty-first century regarding urbanization? At 99 percent urbanites on earth? At 10 percent global urban land
cover? These scenarios may seem preposterous, but they reflect an increasing
realization that urban areas play increasingly influential roles in global change
processes. It is this realization that led the United Nations General Assembly
in September 2015 to adopt a full-fledged Sustainable Development Goal (or
SDG) with a specific urban focus, SDG 11 (see https://sustainabledevelopment
.un.org). The focus of SDG 11 is to "make cities and human settlements inclusive, safe, resilient, and sustainable." While the various targets under SDG 11
are laudable, moving towards them means considerable effort and creativity
will be needed to overcome the challenges urban areas face today. One potential caveat of SDG 11 in this respect is its apparent overreliance on techno-man-
agerial approaches and institutional arrangements (Caprotti et al. 2017). While
metrics, indicators, and evaluation systems – all hallmarks of "smart cities"

initiatives – can have their uses, they are not a panacea for the full spectrum of contemporary urban challenges. The issues revolving around the availability and veracity of the data that are needed to operationalize these metrics, indicators, and evaluation systems aside, there is a need to complement – and even contextualize – those data by approaches that heed political aspects and realities of urban challenges.

The challenges that urban areas will increasingly have to grapple with in the future involve climate change, access to basic services to secure human life, such as drinking water, food, clean air, healthcare (including basic sanitation requirements); and resilience to disasters (Dahiya 2012a, 2016); resilience is also listed among other SDGs to be met by 2030. By 2025, the annual rate of change of urban population is expected to be about 2 percent in developing regions and 0.5 percent in developed regions (UN-Habitat 2013), including extremely rapidly growing urban areas in the West African Belt and Asia, and shrinking cities in Europe, Russia, and the US Rust Belt (Dahiya 2012a; Haase 2013). This will result in an increasing number of affluent, stagnating, or shrinking cities mainly in developed countries, and less affluent, fast growing cities mainly in developing countries. Both trends create enormous challenges in terms of infrastructure management and local governance, as nearly 37 percent of the world's urban population currently lives in slums under inequitable conditions, and lack access to many urban amenities.

The notions of "circular urbanization," "circular migration," or "floating population," all of which describe rural residents who come to cities to work but can be mobile, moving between the urban and the rural, further complicate the picture (Overseas Development Institute 2006; UN-Habitat 2010b). For example, the floating population in all of China's cities amounts to 260 million individuals (UN-Habitat 2016). To accommodate such different trajectories of urbanization and types of cities, new approaches in urban policy and governance are needed. These approaches should take into account the spatial, temporal, and institutional scales inherent to urban governance. Furthermore, they need to be designed to empower urban stakeholders and to enhance public participation (Bai et al. 2010; Dahiya 2012b, 2014). To this list of challenges one can add promoting a fine-grained mix of housing types and providing attractive public realms, green-blue spaces, pedestrian-friendly streetscapes, and efficient, accessible public transportation, all of which are put forward by proponents of such urban design movements as New Urbanism.

Sustainable urbanization strategies need to focus on pro-poor dwelling developments, improved resource utilization, and better access to local economies to reduce unemployment and poverty as well as poverty-driven migration. New approaches of urban governance must be flexible to address emerging challenges effectively; for example, conceptual frameworks of urban planning may be more useful than an actual detailed plan, preparation of which often lags behind on-the-ground developments. Such an approach should also address formalization and regularization of land tenure, which represents a huge problem, especially in the cities of developing countries. Linkages among urban, peri-urban, and rural areas require improved coordination between urban governance and regional, national, and even international development planning. None of these challenges are insurmountable, and the very fact that there is an SDG – however imperfectly formulated – that directly addresses them raise hopes that they will be effectively tackled in the near future by urban and national governments.

Acknowledgments

We would like to thank the editors of the book for their inspiring ideas, intense discussion, and critical comments on earlier versions of this chapter, which helped to improve this piece of work tremendously. Dagmar Haase thanks the AXA Fund and the Royal Swedish Academy of Agriculture and Forestry Stockholm for generous financial support.

References

Alonso, W. 1964. *Location and Land Use: Toward a General Theory of Land Rent*, Cambridge, MA: Harvard University Press.

Angel, S. 2010. *The Atlas of Urbanization*. Lincoln Institute.

Angel S., Parent, J., Civco, D.L., Blei, A., and Potere, D. 2011a. The Dimensions of Global Urban Expansion: Estimates and Projections for All Countries, 2000–2050. *Progress in Planning*, 75: 53–107. DOI: 10.1016/j.progress.2011.04.001

Angel, S., Parent, J., Civco, D.L., and Blei, A.M. 2011b. *Making Room for a Planet of Cities*. Policy Focus Report/Code PF027, Lincoln Institute of Land Policy.

Bai, X. 2016. Eight Energy and Material Flow Characteristics of Urban Ecosystems. *Ambio*, 45(7): 819–830.

Bai, X., Chen, J. and Shi, P. 2011. Landscape Urbanization and Economic Growth in China: Positive Feedbacks and Sustainability Dilemmas. *Environmental Science & Technology*, 46: 132–139.

Bai, X., McAllister, R.R., Beaty, R. M. and Taylor, B. 2010. Urban Policy and Governance in a Global Environment: Complex Systems, Scale Mismatches and Public Participation. *Current Opinion in Environmental Sustainability*, 2: 129–135.

Bai, X., Shi, P., and Liu, Y. 2014. Society: Realizing China's Urban Dream. *Nature*, 509: 158.

Bai, X., Surveyer, A., Elmqvist, T., Gatzweiler, F.W., Güneralp, B., Parnell, et al., 2016. Defining and Advancing a Systems Approach for Sustainable Cities. *Current Opinion in Environmental Sustainability*, 23: 69–78.

Batty, M. 2008. The Size, Scale, and Shape of Cities, *Science*, 319: 769–771.

Batty, M., Xie, Y., and Sun, Z. 1999. The Dynamics of Urban Sprawl. CASAWorking Paper Series, Paper 15, University College London, Center for Advanced Spatial Studies (CASA), London.

Bengston, D.N., Potts, R.S., Fan, D.P., and Goetz, E.G. 2005. An Analysis of the Public Discourse about Urban Sprawl in the United States: Monitoring Concern about a Major Threat to Forests. *Forest Policy and Economics*, 7 (5): 745–756.

Berg, L. van den, Drewett, R., Klaassen, L., Rossi, A. and Vijverberg, C.H.T. 1982. *Urban Europe. A Study of Growth and Decline*. Oxford: Pergamon Press.

Boitier, B., Da Costa, P., Le Mouel, P. and Zagame, P. 2008. Calculation of Land Use Price and Land Use Claims for Agriculture, Transport and Urban Land Use at National Level. PLUREL Deliverable D1.1.2., www.plurel.net/images/D112.pdf.

Bloom, D.E., Canning, D., and Fink, G. 2008. Urbanization and the Wealth of Nations. *Science*, 319: 772–775.

Boone, C., Redman, C.L., Blanco, H., Haase, D., Koch, J., Lwasa, S., Nagendra, H., Pauleit, S., Pickett, S.T.A, Seto, K.C, and Yokohari, M. 2014. Reconceptualizing Land for Sustainable Urbanity, in Seto K., and Reenberg, A. (eds.) *Rethinking Global Land Use in an Urban Era*. Strüngmann Forum Reports, vol. 14, Julia Lupp, series editor. Cambridge, MA: MIT Press.

Brinkhoff, T. 2012. The Principal Agglomerations of the World, http://www.citypopulation.de

Brueckner, J.K. 2000. Urban Sprawl: Diagnosis and Remedies. *International Regional Science Review*, 23(2): 160–171.

Burgess, E.W. 1925. The Growth of the City: An Introduction to a Research Project, in Park, R.E., Burgess, E.W., and McKennzie, R., (eds.) *The City*. Chicago: University of Chicago Press, pp. 47–62.

Buzar, S., Ogden, P.E., Hall, R., Haase, A., Kabisch, S., and Steinfuhrer, A. 2007. Splintering Urban Populations: Emergent Landscapes of Reurbanisation in Four European Cities. *Urban Studies*, 44(4): 651–677.

Caprotti, F., Cowley, R., Datta, A., Broto, V.C., Gao, E., Georgeson, L., Herrick, C., Odendaal, N., and Joss, S. 2017. The New Urban Agenda: Key Opportunities and Challenges for Policy and Practice. *Urban Research & Practice*, 1–12.

Census of India 2011. Census Terms: Implication of Terms Used in Indian Censuses. http://censusindia.gov.in/Data_Products/Library/Indian_perceptive_link/Census_Terms_link/censusterms.html

Champion, T. 2001. *Urbanization, Suburbanization, Counterurbanisation, Reurbanisation*, in Paddison, R., (ed.) *Handbook of Urban Studies*. London: Sage, pp. 143–161.

Chen, M.A. 2012. The Informal Economy: Definitions, Theories and Policies. WIEGO Working Paper No. 1. Cambridge, MA, USA: Women in Informal Employment: Globalizing and Organizing (WIEGO).

Cheshire, P. 2006. Resurgent Cities, Urban Myths and Policy Hubris: What We Need to Know. *Urban Studies*, 43: 1231–1246.

Childe, V.G. 1950. The Urban Revolution. *Town Planning Review*, 21: 3–17.

Colomb, C. 2007. Unpacking New Labour's 'Urban Renaissance' Agenda: Towards a Socially Sustainable Reurbanisation of British Cities? *Planning, Practice & Research*, 22: 1–24.

Couch, C., Karecha, J., Nuissl, H., and Rink, D. 2005. Decline and Sprawl: An Evolving Type of Urban Development – Observed in Liverpool and Leipzig, *European Planning Studies*, 13(1): 117–136.

Creutzig, F., Baiocchi, G., Bierkandt, R., Pichler, P.-P., and Seto, K.C., 2015. Global Typology of Urban Energy Use and Potentials for an Urbanization Mitigation Wedge. *Proceedings of the National Academy of Sciences*, 112(20): 6283–6288.

Cutsinger, J., and Galster, G. 2006. There Is No Sprawl Syndrome: A New Typology of Metropolitan Land Use Patterns. *Urban Geography*, 27(3): 228–252.

Dahiya, B. 2012a. 21st Century Asian Cities: Unique Transformation, Unprecedented Challenges. *Global Asia*, 7(1): 96–104.

Dahiya, B. 2012b. Cities in Asia, 2012: Demographics, Economics, Poverty, Environment and Governance. *Cities*, 29(2): S44–S61. DOI: 10.1016/j.cities.2012.06.013

Dahiya, B. 2014. Southeast Asia and Sustainable Urbanization. *Global Asia*, 9(3), 84–91.

Dahiya, B. 2016. ASEAN Economic Integration and Sustainable Urbanization. *Journal of Urban Culture Research*, 12: 8–14. DOI: 10.14456/jucr.2016.10

Davis, K. 1955. The Origin and Growth of Urbanization in the World. *American Journal of Sociology*, 60(5): 429–437.

Dearden, J., Jones, M.W., and Wilson, A. 2015. DynaMoVis: Visualization of Dynamic Models for Urban Modeling, *The Visual Computer*, 31(6–8): 1079.

Deines, J.M., Liu, X., and Liu, J. 2015. Telecoupling in Urban Water Systems: An Examination of Beijing's Imported Water Supply, Water International, DOI: 10.1080/02508060.2015.1113485

Elmqvist, T.M., Fragkias, M., Güneralp, B., et al. (eds.) 2013. *Global Urbanization, Biodiversity and Ecosystem Services: Challenges and Opportunities*. Springer.

Ewing, R. 1997. Is Los Angeles-Style Sprawl Desirable? *Journal of the American Planning Association*, 63(1): 107–126.

Fragkias, M., Güneralp, B., Seto, K.C., and Goodness, J. 2013. A Synthesis of Global Urbanization Projections, in T. Elmqvist, M. Fragkias, J. Goodness, B. Güneralp et al. (eds.) *Urbanization, Biodiversity and Ecosystem Services: Challenges and Opportunities*., Springer Netherlands, pp. 409–435.

Friedmann, J. 2006. Four Theses in the Study of China's Urbanization. *International Journal of Urban and Regional Research*, 30: 440–451.

Frolking S., Milliman, T., Seto, K.C., and Friedl, M.A. 2013. A global Fingerprint of Macro-Scale Changes in Urban Structure from 1999 to 2009. *Environmental Research Letters*, 8, 024004. DOI: 10.1088/1748–9326/8/2/024004

Frontline 2013. Dholavira: The Harrappan hub. Frontline. www.frontline.in/arts-and-culture/heritage/the-harappan-hub/article4840474.ece

Gil, J., Beirão J.N., Montenegro, N. and Duarte J.P. 2012. On the Discovery of Urban Typologies: Data Mining the Many Dimensions of Urban Form. *Urban Morphology* 16(1): 27–40.

Gonçalves, J., Gomes M.C., Ezequiel S., Moreira, F. and Loupa-Ramos, I. 2017. Differentiating Peri-Urban Areas: A Transdisciplinary Approach towards a Typology. *Land Use Policy*, 63: 331–341.

Grimm, N.B., Foster D., Groffman P., Morgan Grove J., Hopkinson C.S., Nadelhoffer K.J., et al. 2008. The Changing Landscape: Ecosystem Responses to Urbanization and Pollution across Climatic and Societal Gradients. *Frontiers in Ecology and the Environment* 6(5): 264–272.

Güneralp, B., Zhou Y., Ürge-Vorsatz D., Gupta M., Yu S., Patel P.L., et al. 2017. Global Scenarios of Urban Density and Its Impacts on Building Energy Use through 2050. Proceedings of the National Academy of Sciences.

Güneralp B., Güneralp, I. and Liu, Y. 2015. Changing Global Patterns of Urban Exposure to Flood and Drought Hazards. *Global Environmental Change*, 31, 217–225.

Güneralp, B., Seto, K.C. and Ramachandran, M. 2013. Evidence of Urban Land Teleconnections and Impacts on Hinterlands. *Current Opinion in Environmental Sustainability*, 5(5): 445–451.

Güneralp, B., and Seto, K.C. 2008. Environmental Impacts of Urban Growth from an Integrated Dynamic Perspective: A Case Study of Shenzhen, South China. *Global Environmental Change*, 18: 720–735.

Haase, A., Rink, D., and Großmann, K., 2012. Urban Shrinkage as a Challenge for Modelling Human-Environmental Interaction, paper presented at the 6th International Congress on Environmental Modelling and Software (iEMSs), Leipzig, Germany, July 1–5.

Haase, D. 2014. The Nature of Urban Land Use and Why It Is a Special Case, in Seto, K., and A. Reenberg, (eds.) *Rethinking Global Land Use in an Urban Era. Strüngmann Forum Reports*, vol. 14, Julia Lupp, series editor. Cambridge, MA: MIT Press.

Haase, D. 2013. Shrinking Cities, Biodiversity and Ecosystem Services, in: T. Elmqvist, M. Fragkias, B. Güneralp, et al. (eds.) *Global Urbanization, Biodiversity and Ecosystem Services: Challenges and Opportunities*. Springer, pp. 253–274.

Haase, D., and Nuissl, H. 2010. The Urban-to-Rural Gradient of Land Use Change and Impervious Cover: A Long-Term Trajectory for the City of Leipzig. *Land Use Science*, 5(2): 123–142.

Haase, D., and Schwarz, N. 2016. Urban Land Use in the Context of Global Land Use, in K.C. Seto, William, D. Solecki, and C. Griffith (eds). *The Routledge Handbook of Urbanization and Global Environmental Change*. London New York: Routledge Taylor & Francis, pp. 50–63.

Haase, D., Haase, A., Bischoff, P., and Kabisch, S. 2008. Guidelines for the 'Perfect Inner City' Discussing the Appropriateness of Monitoring Approaches for Reurbanisation. *European Planning Studies*, 16(8): 1075–1100, DOI: 10.1080/09654310802315765.

Haase, D., Kabisch, N., Haase, A., Kabisch, S., and Rink, D. 2012. Actors and Factors in Land Use Simulation – The Challenge of Urban Shrinkage. *Environmental Modelling and Software*, 35: 92–103.

Haase, D., Kabisch, N., and Haase, A. 2013. Endless Urban Growth? On the Mismatch of Population, Household and Urban Land Area Growth and Its Effects on the Urban Debate. *PLoS ONE*, 8(6): e66531. DOI:10.1371/journal.pone.006653.

Harris, C.D., and Ullmann, L.E. 1945. The Nature of Cities, *Annals of the American Academy Political and Social Science*, 242, 7–17.

Hatipoglu, B. 2015. "Cittaslow": Quality of Life and Visitor Experiences. *Tourism Planning & Development*, 12(1): 20–36.

Hatuka, T., and Ben-Joseph, E. 2017. Industrial Urbanism: Typologies, Concepts and Prospects. *Built Environment*, 43(1): 10–24.

Holland, B. 2015. Typologies of National Urban Policy: A Theoretical Analysis. *Cities*, 48: 125–129.

Hoyt, H. 1939. *The Structure and Growth of Residential Neighbourhoods in American Cities*, Washington, DC: Federal Housing Administration.

Huang, J., Lub, X.X., and Sellers, J.M. 2007. A Global Comparative Analysis of Urban Form: Applying Spatial Metrics and Remote Sensing. *Landscape and Urban Planning*, 82: 184–197.

Irwin, E.G. 2010. New Directions for Urban Economic Models of Land Use Change: Incorporating Spatial Dynamics and Heterogeneity. *Journal of Regional Science*, 50(1): 65–91.

Irwin, E.G., and Bockstael, N.E. 2007, The Evolution of Urban Sprawl: Evidence of Spatial Heterogeneity and Increasing Land Fragmentation, *PNAS*, 104(52): 20672–20677.

Jabareen, Y.R. 2006. Sustainable Urban Forms: Their Typologies, Models, and Concepts. *Journal of Planning Education and Research*, 26(1): 38–52.

Jenerette, G.D. and D. Potere 2010. Global Analysis and Simulation of Land-Use Change Associated with Urbanization. *Landscape Ecology*, 25(5): 657–670.

Kabisch, N., and Haase, D. 2011. Diversifying European Agglomerations: Evidence of Urban Population Trends for the 21st Century. *Population, Space and Place*, 17: 236–253.

Kabisch, N., Haase, D., and Haase, A. 2010. Evolving Reurbanization? Spatio-Temporal Dynamics Exemplified at the Eastern German City of Leipzig. *Urban Studies*, 47(5) 967–990.

Kabisch, N., Qureshi, S., and Haase, D. 2014. Urban Nature: Human-Environment Interactions in Urban Green Spaces – Contemporary Issues and Future Prospects. *Env Impact Ass Review*, 50: 25–34.

Kasanko, M., Barredo, J.I., Lavalle, C., McCormick, N., Demicheli, L., Sagris, V., and Brezger, A. 2006. Are European cities becoming dispersed? *Landscape and Urban Planning*, 77 (1–2), 111–130.

Kazepov, Y. (ed). 2005. *Cities of Europe. Changing Contexts, Local Arrangements and the Challenge to Urban Cohesion*, Blackwell, Oxford.

Kaza, N., Towe, Ch., and Ye, X. 2011. A Hybrid Land Conversion Model Incorporating Multiple End Uses. *Agricultural and Resource Economics Review*, 40(3): 341–359.

Kennedy, C., Cuddihy, J. and Engel-Yan, J. 2007. The Changing Metabolism of Cities. *Journal of Industrial Ecology*, 11(2): 43–59.

Koc, C.B., Osmond, P., and Peters, A. 2016. A Green Infrastructure Typology Matrix to Support Urban Microclimate Studies. Procedia Engineering, pp. 183–190

Lausch, A., Blaschke, T., Haase, D., Herzog, F., Syrbe, R.U., Tischendorf, L., Walz, U. 2015. Understanding and Quantifying Landscape Structure – A Review on Relevant Process Characteristics, Data Models and Landscape Metrics. Ecol. Modell. 295, 31–41. http://dx.doi .org/10.1016/j.ecolmodel.2014.08.018.

Leichenko, R.M. and Solecki, W.D. 2005. Exporting the American Dream: The Globalization of Suburban Consumption Landscapes. *Regional Studies*, 39(2): 241–253.

Lesthaeghe, R.J. 2010. The Unfolding Story of the Second Demographic Transition. *Population and Development Review*, 36(2): 211.

Liu J., Daily, G.C., Ehrlich, P., and Luck, G.W. 2003. Effects of Household Dynamics on Resource Consumption and Biodiversity. *Nature*, 421: 530–532.

Luck, M., and Wu, J. 2002, A Gradient Analysis of Urban Landscape Pattern: A Case Study From the Phoenix Metropolitan Region, Arizona, USA, *Landscape Ecology*, 17, 327–339.

Lutz, W., and K.C. Samir. 2010. Dimensions of Global Population Projections: What Do We Know about Future Population Trends and Structures? *Philosophical Transactions of the Royal Society B: Biological Sciences* 365(1554): 2779–2791.

Lynch, K. 1961. The Pattern of the Metropolis. *Daedalus* 90(1): 79–98.

McGee, T.G. 1991. The emergence of desakota regions in Asia: expanding a hypothesis, in Ginsburg, N., Koppel, B., and McGee, T.G. (Eds.), *The Extended Metropolis: Settlement Transition in Asia*. University of Hawaii Press, Honolulu, pp. 3–26.

McGranahan, G., Balk, D. and Anderson, B. 2007. The Rising Tide: Assessing the Risks of Climate Change and Human Settlements in Low Elevation Coastal Zones. *Environment and Urbanization* 19, 17. DOI: 10.1177/0956247807076960.

McIntyre, N.E., Knowles-Yánez, K., and Hope, D. 2000. Urban Ecology as an Interdisciplinary Field: Differences in the Use of "Urban" between the Social and Natural Sciences, *Urban Ecosystems*, 4: 5–24.

McPhearson, T., Pickett, S.T., Grimm, N.B., Niemelä, J., Alberti, M., Elmqvist, T., et al., 2016. Advancing Urban Ecology toward a Science of Cities. *BioScience*, p.biw002.

Meeus, S.J., and Gulinck, H. 2008. *Semi-Urban Areas in Landscape Research: A Review*. *Living Reviews in Landscape Research*, 2, www.livingreviews.org/lrlr-2008–3.

Milewski, N. 2010. Fertility of Immigrants. *A Two-Generational Approach in Germany*. Berlin/ Heidelberg: Springer.

Moss, T. 2008. 'Cold Spots' of Urban Infrastructure: 'Shrinking' Processes in Eastern Germany and the Modern Infrastructural Ideal. *International Journal of Urban and Regional Research*, 32 (2), 436–451.

Necipoğlu, G. 2010. From Byzantine Constantinople to Ottoman Konstantiniyye. In *From Byzantion to İstanbul 8000 years of a capital* (pp. 262–277). Istanbul: Sabancı University, Sakıp Sabancı Museum.

Nicholls, R.J., Hanson S., Herweijer C., Patmore N., Hallegatte S., Corfee-Morlot J., Chateau J., and Muir-Wood R., 2008. Ranking Port Cities with High Exposure and Vulnerability to Climate Extremes: Exposure Estimates, OECD Environment Working Papers, No 1. Paris, France: OECD Publishing.

Nilsson K., Nielsen T. S., Aalbers C., Bell S., Boitier B., Chery J-P, Fertner C., Groschowski M., Haase D., Loibl W., Pauleit S., Pintar M., Piorr A., Ravetz J., Ristimäki M., Rounsevell M., Tosics I., Westerink J., Zasada I. 2014. Strategies for Sustainable Urban Development and Urban-Rural Linkages, Research brief, March 2014, European Journal of Spatial Development.

Oswalt P., and Rieniets T. (eds.) 2006, *Atlas of Shrinking Cities*. Hatje: Ostfildern.

Overseas Development Institute, 2006. Internal Migration, Poverty and Development in Asia: Briefing Paper 11. London: Overseas Development Institute.

Park, E. and S. Kim 2016 The Potential of Cittaslow for Sustainable Tourism Development: Enhancing Local Community's Empowerment. *Tourism Planning and Development* 13(3): 351–369.

Parker, D.C., Manson, S.M., Janssen, M.A., Hoffmann, M.J., and Deadman, P. 2003. Multi-agent systems for the simulation of land-use and land-cover change: A review. *Annals of the American Association of Geographers,* 93: 314–337.

Popkin, B.M. 2006. Global Nutrition Dynamics: The World Is Shifting Rapidly toward a Diet Linked with Noncommunicable Diseases. *The American Journal of Clinical Nutrition,* 84: 289–98.

Portugali, J. 2000, *Self-Organisation and the City*, Berlin: Springer.

Potere, D., and Schneider, A. 2007. A Critical Look at Representations of Urban Areas in Global Maps. *GeoJournal,* 69: 55.

Redman, C.L. 2014. Should Sustainability and Resilience Be Combined or Remain Distinct Pursuits? *Ecology and Society,* 19(2), 37. http://dx.doi.org/10.5751/ES-06390-190237.

Rink, D. 2009. Wilderness: The nature of urban shrinkage? The debate on urban restructuring and restoration in Eastern Germany. *Nature and Culture,* 3 (1): 275–292.

Rink, D., and Kabisch, S., 2009. The Ecology of Shrinkage: Introduction, *Nature and Culture,* 4 (3): 223–230.

Rink D., Haase A., Grossmann K., Couch C., and Cocks M. 2012. From Long-Term Shrinkage to Regrowth? A Comparative Study Of Urban Development Trajectories of Liverpool and Leipzig. *Built Environment,* 38 (2): 162–178.

Robinson, D., Brown D., Parker D., Schreinemachers P., Janssen M., Huigen M., et al. 2007. Comparison of Empirical Methods for Building Agent-Based Models in Land Use Science. *Journal of Land Use Science* 2(1), 31–55.

Sassen, S. 2001. *The Global City*: New York, London, Tokyo:Princeton University Press.

Sassen, S. 2008 *Territory, Authority, Rights: From Medieval to Global Assemblages.* Princeton, NJ: Princeton University Press.

Scheuer, S., Haase, D., and Volk, M. 2016. On the Nexus of the Spatial Dynamics of Global Urbanization and the Age of the City. *PLoSONE,* 11(8): e0160471. DOI:10.1371/journal. pone.0160471.

Schneider, A., and Woodcock, C.E. 2008. Compact, Dispersed, Fragmented, Extensive? A Comparison of Urban Growth in Twenty-Five Global Cities Using Remotely Sensed Data, Pattern Metrics and Census Information. *Urban Studies,* 45(3): 659–692.

Schwarz, N., Haase, D., and Seppelt, R. 2010. Omnipresent Sprawl? A Review of Urban Simulation Models With Respect to Urban Shrinkage, *Environment and Planning B,* 37: 265–283.

Seto, K.S., Reenberg, A., Boone, C.C., Fragkias, M., Haase, D., Langanke, T., et al. 2012. *Teleconnections and Sustainability: New Conceptualizations of Global Urbanization and Land Change.* PNAS, www .pnas.org/cgi/doi/10.1073/pnas.1117622109.

Seto, K., and Reenberg, A. (eds.) 2014. *Rethinking Global Land Use in an Urban Era.* Strüngmann Forum Reports, vol. 14, Julia Lupp, series editor. Cambridge, MA: MIT Press.

Seto, K.C., Fragkias, M., Güneralp, B., Reilly, M.K. 2011. A meta-Analysis of Global Urban Land Expansion, *Plos One* 6(8): e23777. DOI: 10.1371/journal.pone.0023777

Sieverts, T. 2003, *Cities Without Cities: An Interpretation of the Zwischenstadt*, London: Spon Press.

Simmonds, D., Waddell, P., and Wegener, M. 2013. Equilibrium versus Dynamics in Urban Modelling. *Environ Plann B* 40(6), 1051–1070. DOI: 10.1068/b38208

Thünen von, J.H. 1966. (C.M. Wartenberg, trans.) 1826, Der Isolierte Staat (Hamburg: Perthes) in, P. Hall (ed.) *The Isolated State: an English Edition of Der Isolierte Staat*, Oxford, New York: Pergamon Press.

Trudelle, C. 2003. Beyond Social Movements: A Relational Typology of Urban Conflicts. *Cahiers de Geographie du Quebec*, 47(131): 223–242.

UN-Habitat 2009. *State of the World's Cities 2012. Harmonious Cities*. London, UK and Sterling, VA, USA: Earthscan for and on behalf of the United Nations Human Settlements Programme (UN-Habitat).

UN-Habitat 2010a. 2010/11 *State of the World's Cities Report, "Bridging the Urban Divide"*. Nairobi, Kenya: United Nations Human Settlements Programme (UN-Habitat).

UN-Habitat 2010b. *The State of Asian Cities 2010/11*. Fukuoka: United Nations Human Settlements Programme(UN-Habitat).

UN-Habitat 2013 *State of the World's Cities 2012/2013: Prosperity of Cities*. New York, USA: Routledge for and on behalf of the United Nations Human Settlements Programme(UN-Habitat).

UN-Habitat 2014. *The State of African Cities 2014. Re-imagining sustainable urban transitions*. Nairobi, Kenya: United Nations Human Settlements Programme(UN-Habitat).

UN-Habitat 2016. Goal 11: Make Cities Inclusive, Safe, Resilient and Sustainable. www.un.org/sustainabledevelopment/cities/

UN 2014. World Urbanization Prospects: The 2014 Revision. United Nations Department of Economic and Social Affairs/Population Division. http://esa.un.org/unpd/wup/.

UN 2017. World Population Prospects. www.un.org/development/desa/publications/world-population-prospects-the-2017-revision.html

Van Delden, H., 2009. Integration of Socio-Economic and Bio-Physical Models to Support Sustainable Development, in B. Anderssen et al. (Eds), *18th IMACS World Congress – MODSIM09 International Congress on Modelling and Simulation*. Cairns, Australia.

Vertovec, S. 2007. Super-Diversity and Its Implications. *Ethnic and Racial Studies*, 30(6): 1024–1054.

Von Der Dunk, A., Grêt-Regamey A., Dalang, T. and Hersperger, A.M. 2011. Defining a Typology of Peri-Urban Land-Use Conflicts – A Case Study from Switzerland. *Landscape and Urban Planning* 101(2): 149–156.

Weng, Y.-C. 2007. Spatiotemporal Changes of Landscape Pattern in Response to Urbanization, *Landscape Urban Planning*, 81: 341–353.

White, R., and Engelen, G. 1993. Cellular Automata and Fractal Urban Form: a Cellular Modeling Approach to the Evolution of Urban Land-Use Patterns, *Environment Planning A*, 25, 1175–1199.

Wilson, A.G. 1976. Catastrophe Theory and Urban Modelling: An Application to Modal Choice, *Environment Planning A*, 8, 351–356.

Wolff, M., Haase, A., Haase, D., Kabisch, N. 2017. The Impact of Urban Regrowth on the Built Environment. *Urban Studies*. In press.

World Bank 2015. *East Asia's Changing Urban Landscape: Measuring a Decade of Spatial Growth*. Washington, DC: The World Bank. DOI: 10.1596/978–1-4648–0363-5

Yiftachel, O. 1989. Towards a New Typology of Urban Planning Theories. *Environment & Planning B: Planning & Design*, 16(1): 23–39.

Yu, X.J., and Ng, C.N. 2007. Spatial and Temporal Dynamics of Urban Sprawl Along Two Urban Rural Transects: A Case Study of Guangzhou, China. *Landscape Urban Planning*, 79: 96–109.

Chapter 2: Embracing Urban Complexity

Marina Alberti, Timon McPhearson, and Andrew Gonzalez

2.1 Cities in the Context of the Anthropocene

In this chapter, we argue for the need to take a complex systems approach to understand urbanization and its impacts based on its key variables and drivers: agents, emergence, self-organization, and criticality. A complex systems approach will necessitate a shift from viewing cities only as social-technological systems to viewing them also as social-ecological systems and, even further, as complex social-ecological-technological systems, or SETs (McPhearson et al. 2016a; Depietri and McPhearson, 2017), involving the interactions and coevolution of social systems, living systems, and built systems.

Cities are one of the most distinctive features of the Anthropocene – a new geologic epoch characterized by the dominant influence of humanity on the environment – yet one of the least understood Earth systems. Philosophers have been curious about how cities emerge and function since the first appearance of human settlements 10,000 years ago, but both formal conceptualization and study of urban systems are more recent (Geddes 1915; Mumford 1961; Park 1925; Lynch 1961; Forrester 1969; Jacobs 1969; Hall 1998). Over the last century, scholars in a broad array of disciplines have advanced various theories to explain urban dynamics. Such theories have evolved separately, in discrete domains, for more than a century, and strongly reflect a view of humans and natural systems as essentially separated from each other. Conceptualizations have commonly preceded attempts to study such systems empirically. The emergence of a new urban ecology beginning in the late 1990s represents the first significant attempt to integrate a diversity of approaches from a broad set of disciplines to advance understanding of cities as complex, coupled human-natural systems (Pickett et al. 1999; Grimm et al. 2000; Alberti et al. 2003; Grimm et al. 2008; Alberti 2016; Bai 2016; McPhearson et al. 2016a).

Earlier theories of cities have been useful for describing a variety of urban phenomena, but cannot provide a general explanation of how cities emerge, persist, or collapse. The development of complexity theory has enabled scholars to begin asking such questions and making sense of various aspects of city function and dynamics. Cities across the globe exhibit unique patterns visible from space (Figure 2.1), reflecting diverse socioeconomic and biophysical characteristics, as well as their history and stage of development (Bai and Imura 2000; Bai 2003). Yet, the emerging patterns hint at universal principles of emergence, growth, and evolution of cities. We can ask: What do cities have in common, regardless of their geographical location and size? And which elements are specific to historical or geographic circumstance? Are there underlying mechanisms and universal laws of urban evolution (Bettencourt et al. 2007; Batty 2008)? As urban scientists have introduced mathematical rigor to the exploration of common urban properties across the world's cities and high resolution data have become increasingly available, we begin to discover new insights for planning and policy-making. Yet the application of complex models and empirical explorations remain at an early stage (McPhearson et al. 2016b). Urban ecology advances the need of a science of cities as coupled human-natural systems.

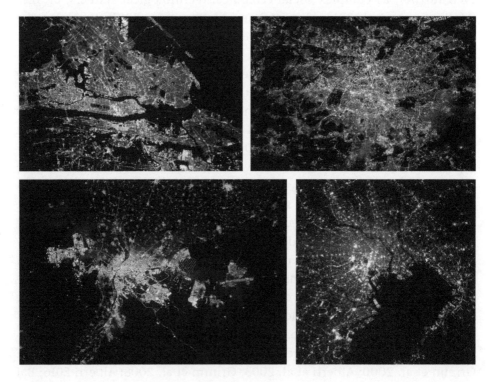

Figure 2.1 Cities' patterns from space. NASA City Night Lights 1) New York City, 2) Paris, 3) Cairo, and 4) Tokyo.

2.2 The City as a Complex System

As major drivers of global change, cities have a prominent role in enabling the Earth's transition to sustainability (see Chapter 1). Understanding the complex dynamics linking urban changes to social-ecological-technical change is critical to gaining new insights for the future of ecological and human well-being.

2.2.1 Agents

Cities are characterized by complex interactions among multiple heterogeneous agents and components across multiple scales. Agents are members of households, individual businesses, real estate developers, local and regional governments, nonprofit organizations, and academic institutions that make a variety of decisions affecting resources and land use. These agents are highly heterogeneous within and across cities and their decisions. Empirical evidence suggests that household residential location choices (Waddell 2013) or landscape management practices (Polsky et al. 2014) are influenced by their diverse characteristics, perceptions, and preferences. These decisions directly and indirectly affect the biophysical system through land conversion, exploitation of resources, and generation of emissions and waste. Businesses make decisions about production, location, and management practices. Members of households make choices about employment, residential location, housing type, travel mode, and other activities. Real estate developers make decisions about housing development and redevelopment. Governments shape urban resource flows and environmental impacts about investing in infrastructures and services, as well as adopting policies and regulations that influence agents' interactions and the decisions they make (Bai 2016). Decisions are made at the individual, community, city, and regional levels through both economic and social institutions.

2.2.2 Emergence

In cities and urbanizing regions, agents interact dynamically within communities and through social networks, economic markets, and many public institutions (including governmental and other nonprofit and nongovernmental organizations), giving rise to emergent properties. It is through these multiple interactions across time and space that urban agents generate observable emergent physical (for example, sprawl), behavioral (for example, travel), social (for example, neighborhood segregation), economic (for example, income, real estate values), ecological (for example, biodiversity), and environmental (for example, atmospheric pollution) patterns.

Urban segregation and inequality are examples of emergent patterns result-ing from dynamic interactions among many agents and social groups and their residential choices which, in turn, are simultaneously influenced by personal preferences, job markets, land and real estate markets, and public policies and investments (Box 1.1). Emerging contemporary patterns of urban segregation are far more complex than typically represented by the average center-periph-ery pattern of early urbanization. In Brazilian cities, for example, Feitosa (2010) shows how political and socioeconomic changes that occurred in the 1980s significantly altered the patterns of urban segregation and the dynamic inter-actions that govern urban spatial configurations. The poor were not able to afford dwellings in the "legal city" or to build houses in irregular settlements (do Rio Caldeira 2000; Torres et al. 2002). Instead, they initiated the prolif-eration of *favelas* in central areas even closer to wealthy neighborhoods. The emergent pattern challenges the spatial duality and socioecological homoge-neity of urban spaces – the traditional allocation of affluent families in central neighborhoods, with poor families pushed to the peripheries – by diffusing and intermixing *favelas* located in different regions of the city, including those closer to wealthy neighborhoods (Torres et al. 2002).

Multiple feedback mechanisms between urban segregation and individ-ual choices reinforce such patterns. Urban segregation has consistently led to negative consequences for the lives of urban inhabitants by reinforcing social exclusion, concentration of poverty, limited access to natural resources, environmental degradation, and greater exposure to environmental risks. As a result, segregation and institutionalized inequality substantially affects the capacity of cities to contribute to social and economic development (Sabatini et al. 2001; Torres et al. 2003).

2.2.3 Self-Organization

As cities grow, they increase in complexity, yet such complexity is not fully guided or managed by an outside source; this development is self-organizing. In self-organizing systems, patterns and organization develop through interac-tions internal to the system. In *Self-Organization and the City*, Portugali (2002) introduces the notions of stability and instability across scales. Building on the example of urban segregation, the emergence of slums can be seen as the emergence of instability pockets essential to ensure global stability of the urban system (Portugali 2000; Barros and Sobriera 2002). But a more in-depth exam-ination uncovers the emergence of slums – traditionally considered to be and defined as "informal settlements" – as a complex socioecological phenomenon: the social production of habitat resulting from social exclusion (Zárate 2016).

Complexity and self-organization pose challenges to the dominant planning paradigm. Despite the increasing attention of planning scholarship to resilience science, planning practice has just begun to incorporate resilience principles and to move away from a steady-state approach and a view of planning as an outside agent controlling and directing urban change. There is an inherent tension between the self-organization properties of complex socio-ecological systems and the idea of planning towards a desirable societal goal. Transforming such tension towards a novel planning paradigm might be key to advancing both the discipline and the practice. Self-organization has important implications for the way systems evolve (Jorgenson 1997; Phillips 1999). Yet, various theories draw different conclusions. Phillips (1999) suggests that the key question is how divergent self-organization and patterns are linked to instability and chaos, and how, together, they affect system evolution. The extent to which cities are self-organized and how this drives system dynamics is critical to understanding how to intervene in this complexity to achieve desirable goals for urban societies.

2.2.4 Criticality

Self-organized systems are at a critical state – a state in which perturbations are propagated over long temporal or large spatial scales (Bak 1996). Such systems exhibit scale-invariance characteristic of the critical point (or attractor towards which a system tends to evolve) of a phase transition. An example is a sand pile in which local interactions result in frequent, small avalanches and infrequent large ones. In such systems, transitions can be triggered by external forces or internal changes in system feedbacks. Such "phase transitions" may be triggered by unpredictable external events, but often they result from endogenous underlying processes that maintain their stability and resilience.

There is increasing evidence indicating that major transitions in financial systems and ecosystems are typically preceded by gradual change in internal processes until they reach a threshold: a small external perturbation can trigger a domino effect that propagates through the system and causes a shift to a new state (Sheffer et al. 2013).

There are several documented examples of regime shifts in ecological systems: in lakes, coral reefs, oceans, and forests (Scheffer et al. 2001). The literature also documents examples of regime shifts in human societies both in prehistoric human societies, such as Easter Island (Flenley and King 1984), and more recent examples across multiple regions of the world (Kinzig et al. 2006). But how the coupling between human and environmental systems adds to such complex dynamics is not fully understood (Liu et al. 2007). In such systems, further nonlinearities affect the interactions between external and internal conditions and drive the system to a critical threshold that might cause a regime shift and/or system reorganization (Holling 1973).

Hurricanes Sandy and Katrina clearly illustrate the unexpected shocks cities are likely to face in the next decades; both storms were a result of increasing climate extremes driving fast variables (that is, storm formation) and interacting with the slow, variable processes of wetland loss; increased human and infrastructure vulnerabilities associated with land cover change (that is, coastal development); transportation, housing, and energy sector vulnerabilities; and the build-up of system complexity over time (Sanderson et al. 2016; Blum and Roberts 2009).

2.2.5 Biodiversity and Urban Areas as Socioecological Systems

Emergent patterns of biodiversity in cities illustrate the complex socioecological dynamics of urban ecosystems. Humans are affecting the abundance and distribution of species across the planet, and these impacts are projected to increase in this century (Pereira et al. 2010; Pimm et al. 2014). The expansion of cities will triple urban land cover by 2030, compared to 2000, and will occur in areas of significant biodiversity hotspots (Seto et al. 2012; see also Section 1). The future of urban biodiversity will depend on how cities spread, but also on socioecological interactions and on how habitat is preserved within cities. Attention to habitat size and connectivity will maintain not only species, but ecosystem processes *and* the evolutionary processes that allow adaptation and diversification within cities (Loreau et al. 2003).

Urbanization transforms the biophysical structure of the landscape, which contributes to biodiversity change both directly within cities (McKinney 2008; Elmqvist et al. 2013; Aronson et al. 2014) as the expanding built environments alter habitat quality and connectivity, and at much larger scales as it indirectly drives habitat loss through trade demands for food and resources (Seto et al. 2012). Cities also constitute habitat for many species. Many anthrophilic species do well in urban environments, and trends in the diversity of these species may increase as urban land cover increases (Aronson et al. 2015).

Aronson et al. (2014) compared 54 cities and found that the density of bird and plant species (number of species per km²) in cities has declined substantially: only 8 percent of native bird and 25 percent of native plant species are currently present compared with estimates of nonurban densities of species. Aronson et al. (2014) found that the density of species in cities and the loss of density of species was best explained by land cover and city age rather than by nonanthropogenic factors (such as geography and climate).

Beninde et al. (2015) conducted a meta-analysis of the factors mediating intra-urban bird, insect, and plant species richness across 75 cities worldwide. Their focus was on within-habitat species richness as opposed to city-scale species richness. They found that habitat patch areas and corridors (connected linear strips of habitat) have the strongest positive effects on species richness, along with vegetation structure. Large habitat patches of greater than 50 hectares in size are necessary to prevent the loss of area-sensitive species in cities. They only analyzed data for corridors from two cities, but the effects were marked for multiple taxa. Functional connectivity is vital to increasing the effective area of urban habitat, so networks of corridors are likely to help biodiversity conservation in cities (Rayfield et al. 2015; Albert et al. 2017).

Our most complete data on urban biodiversity are from European and North American cities. We expect to find similar patterns of biodiversity change in cities in Asia and Africa, but monitoring is required to establish whether similar patterns of change will be observed over the coming century. Widespread adoption and implementation of a common indicator set, such as the City Biodiversity Index (Kosaka et al. 2013), will further foster comparisons across cities. Biodiversity is integral to the ecosystem services that benefit people in urban environments (such as microbial diversity, which influences human immune system health (Rook 2013); as such, these monitoring programs would also reveal how changes in biodiversity affect the quality of ecosystem services.

2.2.6 Adaptation and Eco-Evolutionary Dynamics of Biodiversity

Evidence that cities drive microevolutionary change poses new challenges for the study of urban sustainability (Palkovacs et al. 2012; Alberti 2015; Alberti et al. 2017a). By examining more than 1,600 observations of phenotypic change in species across the globe, Alberti et al. (2017a) were able to detect a clear urban signal. Examples of phenotypic changes driven by urbanization have been documented for many species of birds, fish, plants, mammals, and invertebrates (Yeh and Price 2004; Carlson et al. 2011; Haas et al. 2010; Cheptou et al. 2008; Jacquemyn et al. 2012; Alberti et al. 2017b). Humans in cities affect species composition and their functional roles by selectively determining phenotypic trait diversity and causing organisms to undergo rapid evolutionary change. Changes in individuals, populations, and communities have cascading effects on ecosystem functions and human well-being, including biodiversity, nutrient cycling, seed dispersal, food production, and human health (Alberti 2015).

Several scholars of urban ecology are exploring the link between phenotypic change and their effects on ecosystem functions in urbanizing regions

(Marzluff 2012; Donihue and Lambert 2014; Alberti 2015; Alberti et al. 2017a). The emergence of eco-evolutionary feedbacks on contemporary time scales (Pimental 1961; Schoener 2011) might affect ecosystem productivity and stability of cities (Matthew et al. 2011). For example, the physical structure of estuarine and coastal environments is maintained by a diversity of organisms, particularly dune and marsh plants, mangroves, and seagrasses. Evolution in traits underlying their ecosystem-engineering effects has potentially significant functional impacts on coastal cities' resilience. Other examples of ecosystem functions relevant to both ecosystem and human well-being include nutrient cycling and primary productivity regulated by consumers' traits, which control their demand for resources. Understanding the mechanisms by which human agency affects evolutionary feedback is critical to anticipating future evolutionary trajectories in cities.

2.2.7 Resilience

One important attribute of a complex system is resilience, which, for cities, can be translated to the ability to maintain human and ecosystem functions simultaneously over the long-term (Alberti and Marzluff 2004; see also Chapter 7). In cities, ecological and human functions are interdependent. Urban sprawl can cause rapid shifts in the quality of natural habitat, from a well-connected natural land cover to a state in which the natural land cover is greatly reduced and highly fragmented (Dupras et al. 2015). Sprawl is a dynamic gradient of urban land cover that results when urban dwellers and real estate developers operate without taking into account the full social and ecological costs of providing human services to low-density development (Alberti and Marzluff 2004).

Patterns of urban development and infrastructure play a key role in maintaining the capacity of urban regions to adapt in the face of urban growth and environmental change. For example, we know that urban sprawl drives loss of forest cover and natural habitat and threatens biodiversity (Elmqvist et al. 2013). The amount of impervious surface and the density of roads is associated with loss of ecological integrity of streams, and hydrological changes associated with urbanization and shoreline hardening increase the vulnerability of coastal cities to floods. Yet, we do not know how different urban forms, densities, land-use mix, and types of infrastructures affect the diverse ecological processes that affect ecological conditions and human well-being. Nor do we fully understand the trade-offs associated with different housing or infrastructure alternatives (Alberti 2010). New patterns of urbanization pose additional challenges to characterizing mismatches between supply and demand of ecological goods and services that require cross-boundary and cross-scale considerations (Kremer et al. 2016; McPhearson et al. 2015).

Resilience in urbanizing regions depends on variable biophysical and socioeconomic conditions as well as stage of urban development; resilience in a city and its surrounding region is highly affected by its infrastructure. Cities provide unique opportunities to rethink and establish novel, integrated infrastructure systems such as, sustainable energy systems that rely on renewable energy sources (Kammen and Sunter 2016). Technological developments, in turn, have the potential to influence future urban trajectories. Using two cases of large hydraulic works in the Dutch delta, van Staveren and van Tatenhove (2016) illustrate how past technological interventions can profoundly shape the direction in which deltas develop.

2.3 Urban Social-Ecological-Technical Systems and Innovation

Advancing social-ecological conceptual frameworks for understanding complex dynamics of urbanization requires explicitly representing the built infrastructure and technological components of urban systems (Ramaswami et al. 2012; McPhearson et al. 2016a; Depietri and McPhearson, 2017) and the relative change in urban metabolism that their development implies (Kennedy et al. 2007; Kennedy et al. 2009). More recent studies attempt to provide conceptual bridges between urban metabolism and urban ecosystem studies (Bai 2016). Cities depend on larger-scale built infrastructures (such as electric power, water supply, and transportation networks) that sustain flows of resources over large distances. The new, emerging patterns of urbanization (including city regions, urban corridors, and mega-regions) result from the evolution of technology and generate new demand for infrastructure systems that require further technological innovation. Urban regions operate as hubs of global and regional flows of people, capital, services, and information that drive the global economy (Sassen 2012). Yet, the rapid socioeconomic and environmental changes cities are both causing and experiencing pose new challenges to infrastructure systems, exacerbated by the inability of many cities to keep pace with rapid urban growth and the lack of appropriate institutional and governance structures to respond to emergent problems.

Transitions in complex systems pose great challenges to system stability and resilience, but are also an important source of novelty and transformation (Alberti 2016). While cities are often associated with poverty concentration, slum proliferation, and social and environmental problems, they have also traditionally been the centers of economic growth and innovation. Urban areas house 54 percent of the global population and generate more than 70 percent of global GDP (UN-Habitat 2016). Empirical data across many cities show that close interactions among diverse people in cities foster collaborative creativity and the capacity to innovate. Recent studies have explored the relationships between important measures of outputs from socioeconomic processes in cities and population size, providing ample evidence that important properties of cities of all sizes increase, on average, faster (socioeconomic superlinearity) or slower (material infrastructure sublinearity) than city population size (Bettencourt 2013). Bettencourt et al. (2010) found that income and innovation change in a consistently *super*linear manner (with exponent β ~1+ 1/6) in response to growth, showing increasing returns, while infrastructure responds *sub*linearly (β ~ 1–1/6), suggesting economies of scale in material infrastructure relative to population growth (Figure 2.2).

To explain why the emergent patterns observed in cities are a special case of complex natural systems, Bettencourt (2013) compares cities to stars. Cities attract people and accelerate social interaction and social outputs in a manner that is analogous to the way in which stars compress matter and burn brighter and faster with increased size. Social interactions – efficient social networks, embedded in space and time, that evolve – make the city a new phenomenon in nature. Yet, in spite of a city's fast pace and rapid evolution, achieving sustainability depends not only on the ability to innovate, but also on the type of innovation that is performed.

As centers of innovation, cities have the potential to play a prominent role in reorienting patterns of urbanization and infrastructure towards

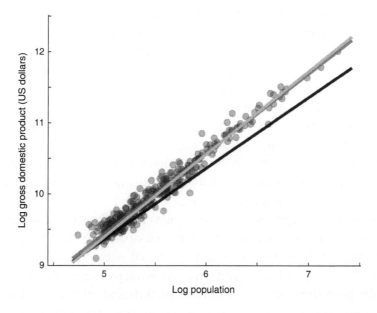

Figure 2.2 The scaling of gross domestic product as a function of city population. Source: Bettencourt 2013.

sustainability – for example, through integrated renewable energy systems (McPhearson et al. 2016c). Yet, innovation and novelty are part of a tightly coupled system of socioeconomic and environmental drivers mediated by both built infrastructure and technological systems. For example, the generation and adoption of efficient technologies (including those that relate to energy, water, and CO_2 emissions) are driven by a complex interplay between increasing social interactions (such as social networks), the quality of urban ecosystems, and increasing environmental changes (such as extreme climatic events), but also by the vulnerability and resilience of the city to these changes. In cities, the built infrastructure and natural infrastructure play critical roles in reducing vulnerability, mitigating hazards, and responding to disasters. Technological innovation and its diffusion depend on socioeconomic conditions, urban development policies, and institutional capacity. Scholars have begun to explore the relationships between emerging novel governance and management systems and socioecological innovation (Walker et al. 2004; Chapin et al. 2010; Folke et al. 2010; Westley et al. 2011; Olsen et al. 2014). Furthermore, the importance of these factors can vary across cultures and biomes.

Recent work by international organizations focused on improving slum conditions and preventing their formation is reflected by a decrease from 39

Box 2.1 The Complexity of Slums

Slum settlements are an example of a complex urban phenomenon with significant implications for the sustainability of an urban planet. Across the globe today, one in eight people (approximately 881 million) lives in slums, and this number is expected to increase in the near future (UN-Habitat 2016). According to the UN, the number of slum dwellers continues to increase, despite the decline in the *proportion* of the urban population residing in slums. Slums are a challenge to sustainable transitions for humanity: they increase poverty and demands on basic services in urban areas, threaten human health, and exert stresses on the environment. Spontaneous settlements typically occur in the most environmentally vulnerable areas, and their lack of proper sanitation and waste management systems are major sources of both environmental pollution and the spread of infectious diseases.

Among the various informal settlements associated with rapid urbanization, slums are a particularly challenging and urgent global phenomenon due to the perpetual poverty, deprivation, and sociospatial exclusion of slum dwellers, and due to their impacts on the overall prosperity of the cities in which they exist.

percent to 30 percent of urban populations living in slums in developing countries between 2000 and 2014. Yet, absolute numbers of people living in slums
continue to rise as a result of rapid urbanization and overall global population
growth, as well as the failure of cities to provide appropriate housing and manage growth. Transforming slums into sustainable urban settlements requires
a new understanding of slums as complex phenomena emerging from the
interactions of multiple forces and the recognition of these emergent settlements not as "informal," but as a "social production of habitat" – a definition
intended to describe people producing their own habitat: dwellings, villages,
neighborhoods, and even large parts of cities (Zárate 2016).

Both the emergent patterns of informal settlements and their evolution
reflect the interaction of multiple factors and contrasting forces: population
growth; rural-to-urban migration; weak governance; economic vulnerability
and underpayment for labor; displacement caused by conflict, natural disasters
and climate change; and, significantly, the lack of affordable housing options
for the urban poor as governments increasingly disengage from a direct role in
provision of housing. The complex interaction of these diverse factors often
causes the housing sector to become susceptible to domination by speculative
forces that tend to benefit affluent urban residents (UN-Habitat 2015).

For example, by comparing the current patterns of urban segregation to the
traditional center-periphery pattern in Brazilian cities, Feitosa (2010) shows that
complex interactions among bottom-up and top-down processes and mechanisms operate at multiple scales. A new pattern of segregation has resulted
from the political and socioeconomic changes of the 1980s, superimposed
on the typical center-periphery pattern that separates the wealthy from poor
urban dwellers (do Rio Caldeira 2000; Lago 2000; Torres et al. 2002). The slowing of the Brazilian economy during the 1980s and a corresponding decline in
per capita income led to an impoverishment of the population and an increase
in social inequalities. The simultaneous establishment of the Federal Law for
Urban Land Parceling (6766/79), which regulates the minimal requirements
for development of urban settlements and was intended to improve access to
infrastructure and public facilities of the periphery, promoted a larger social
diversity in areas that were only occupied by the lower classes (do Rio Caldeira
2000; Lago 2000) while increasing the number of urban dwellers unable to
afford the "legal city" or even to build their own dwellings in "irregular" settlements (Feitosa 2010). Together, these factors prompted the emergence of *favelas*, the Brazilian slums found throughout various regions of the city, even in
close proximity to wealthy neighborhoods (Torres et al. 2002).

What characterizes slums, from an urban complex dynamic perspective,
is not location, but the living conditions experienced inside them. A slum,
according to UN-Habitat, is a settlement in which the inhabitants suffer

one or more of the following "household deprivations": lack of access to an improved water source, lack of access to improved sanitation facilities, lack of sufficient living area, lack of housing durability, and lack of security of tenure (UN-Habitat 2011). The persistence of slums is the result of a reinforcing mechanism or positive feedback. Increased poverty and lack of basic infrastructure and services, together with a degraded and unhealthy environment, drive the emergence, persistence, and growth of slums both in developing and developed countries. Actions to improve slum living conditions require promoting policies and incentives that operate simultaneously on multiple levels, linking urban planning, financing, and legal and livelihood components from the bottom up. Transition to a sustainable future for urban slums implies acknowledgment of the self-organizing nature of such phenomena and the opportunities inherent in this self-organization for reorienting urban slums towards urban sustainability.

2.4 Complexity of Coupled Human-Natural Systems

Over the last three decades, complexity theory has provided a new basis for understanding how myriad local interactions among multiple agents can generate simple behavioral patterns and ordered structures. Cities are nonequilibrium systems; random events produce system shifts, discontinuities, and bifurcations (Krugman 1993, 1998; Batty 2005), and patterns emerge from complex interactions that take place at the local scale, suggesting that urban development self-organizes (Batten 2001). Emergent patterns are often scale-invariant and fractal, indicating that the emergent morphology of cities results from self-organizing processes operating at the local scale (Batty and Longley 1994; Allen 1997).

Understanding the complex relationships between patterns of urban development and the processes that maintain ecosystem function and resilience in urban areas requires a new framework to uncover the mechanisms that determine the relationship dynamics of urban ecosystem services and their roles in maintaining resilience of urbanizing regions (McPhearson et al. 2015). Urban systems are hybrid ecosystems and several types of new hybrid functions may emerge from these interactions. For example, barrier islands in urbanizing estuaries are part of a tightly coupled system of human and ecosystem processes; they perform the hybrid function of protecting estuary biodiversity and controlling coastal flooding (Alberti 2016).

The rapid advancement of computer power, together with the remarkable emerging availability of high-resolution social and ecological data, provides unprecedented opportunities to reframe our questions (Figure 2.3). Instead

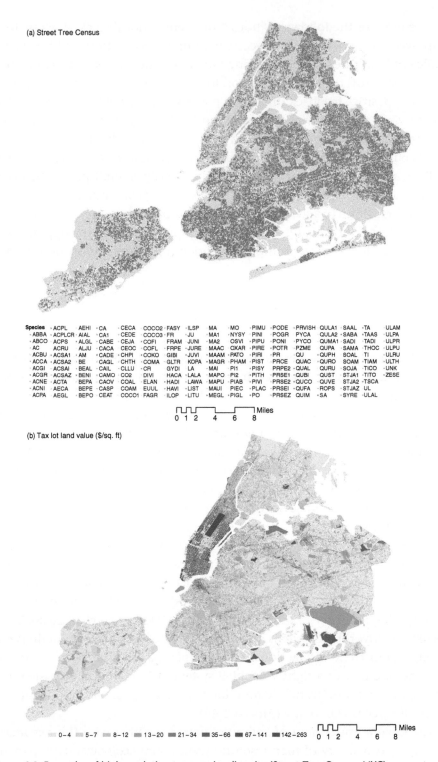

Figure 2.3 Examples of high-resolution tree species diversity (Street Tree Census, NYC), property values (Assessor data, NYC), and energy intensity (Energy consumption, NYC).

(c) Source energy-use intensity (kBtu/sq. ft)

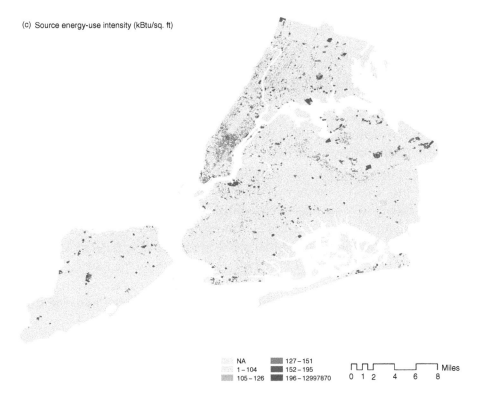

NA		127–151		
1–104		152–195		
105–126		196–12997870		

0 1 2   4   6   8   Miles

Figure 2.3 (cont)

of asking how patterns of human settlements and activities affect social and ecosystem processes, we can ask: How do humans, interacting with their bio-physical environment, generate emergent phenomena in urbanizing ecosystems, and how do these patterns selectively amplify or dampen human and ecological processes and functions? Cities are coupled human-natural systems in which people are dominant agents with a new capacity to redefine the rules of nature's game (Alberti 2016). Although extensive urban research has focused on the dynamics of urban systems and their ecology, efforts to understand urban systems in an integrated manner are relatively recent and are only beginning to address the processes and variables that couple human and ecological functions (McPhearson et al. 2016a; Bai 2016).

Scholars of both urban development and ecology have begun to recognize the importance of explicitly considering human and ecological processes in studying urban systems. Yet building an integrated approach to advancing such understanding challenges scholars from different disciplines to revise fundamental assumptions in their disciplines with regard to humans and ecosystems.

2.5 Insights for Urban Planning from Complexity Science

To navigate the transition towards a sustainable urban future, it is necessary that we understand cities as integrated social, economic, and physical systems in more precise and predictive ways. This requires quantitative models of the internal structures of cities and of the interactions between cities and the Earth's natural environments that account for the processes of human development and economic growth, as well as their feedbacks on patterns of urban development. It also poses new challenges and offers insights for rethinking planning theory to more effectively contribute to urban governance in an era of global change (Wilkinson 2012). Emerging socioecological innovations across world cities indicate possible pathways to set new trajectories for the future of our urban planet. By developing and analyzing qualitative scenarios combined with modeling grounded in new empirical analysis, we can begin to assess strategies and uncover transformational pathways for cities to transition to more desirable and sustainable futures (McPhearson et al. 2017).

How can we plan in the face of complexity? What can we learn from complexity science that will help guide urban design and planning? An initial series of questions directs planners towards new perspectives on problem definitions: How do we define the problem? What are the boundaries of the system? What is the spatial scale of the analysis? What is the time horizon? What are the components (ecological, social, political, economic) within the system? What are the connections and feedbacks (physical, biogeochemical, biotic, social, economic, political)? What are the drivers? What is controllable? Where are the control points? What is known? What is ambiguous or uncertain? What might plausibly be changed? What information do we need to assess alternative problem solving strategies?

Complexity science provides new tools to conceptualize the city and urban regions as complex systems (Bettencourt 2013) and indicates key principles to guide their planning and management (Ahern 2013; Alberti 2016):

1.   *Diversity and modularity*: Create and maintain diverse development patterns and modular infrastructure systems that support diverse human and ecosystem functions under different conditions and uncertain scenarios.

2.   *Self-organization:* Focus on maintaining self-organization and increasing the capacity of coupled human-natural systems to adapt instead of aiming to control change and to reduce uncertainty.

3.   *Uncertainty*: Expand the ability to consider uncertainty and surprise in urban decision-making by designing strategies and built infrastructure systems that are robust to the most divergent plausible futures.

4. *Adaptation*: Create options for learning through experimentation, and opportunities to adapt through flexible policies and strategies that mimic the diversity of environmental and human communities.

5. *Transformation*: Expand the institutional capacity for change through transformative learning by challenging assumptions and actively reconfiguring problem solving.

2.5.1 Conclusion

The increasing pressure from climate change (Rosenzweig et al. 2010), rapid urbanization (UN 2014), and the rapid development of infrastructure to prepare for these changes all pose new challenges to urban decision-makers to make important investment decisions while navigating complexity (McPhearson et al. 2016b). Tackling complexity and uncertainly in urban systems is challenging and will require new evidence, approaches, and tools. It will demand a new level of collaboration among ecologists, geographers, sociologists, political scientists, economists, planners, designers, and other disciplines to advance the field of urban ecology into a new urban science (McPhearson et al. 2016a; Alberti 2017). To meet this demand, scholars will need to be able to identify examples of new practices that highlight opportunities for improving urban resilience and sustainability at the local and global scales (McHale et al. 2015).

❧ References

Ahern, J. 2013. Urban Landscape Sustainability and Resilience: The Promise and Challenges of Integrating Ecology with Urban Planning and Design. *Landscape Ecology* 28(6):1203–1212. doi: 10.1007/s10980-012-9799-z.

Albert, C., Rayfield, B., Dumitru, M., and Gonzalez, A. 2017. Applying Network Theory to Prioritize Multi-Species Habitat Networks That Are Robust to Climate and Land-Use Change. *Conservation Biology* 31(6): 1383–1396. doi: 10.1111/cobi.12943.

Alberti, M., 2010. Maintaining Ecological Integrity and Sustaining Ecosystem Function in Urban Areas. *Current Opinion in Environmental Sustainability*, 2(3):178–184. DOI: 10.1016/j.cosust.2010.07.002.

Alberti, M. 2015. Eco-Evolutionary Dynamics in an Urbanizing Planet. *Trends in Ecology and Evolution*, 30 (2):114–126.

Alberti, M. 2016. *Cities That Think like Planets: Complexity, Resilience, and Innovation in Hybrid Ecosystems*. Seattle: University of Washington Press.

Alberti, M. 2017. Grand Challenges in Urban Science. *Frontiers in Built Environment* 3: 6. doi:10.3389/fbuil.2017.00006.

Alberti, M., and Marzluff, J. 2004. Ecological Resilience in Urban Ecosystems: Linking Urban Patterns to Human and Ecological Functions. *Urban Ecosystems* 7: 241–265. doi: 10.1023/B:U ECO.0000044038.90173.c6.

Alberti, M., Marzluff, J.M., Shulenberger, E., Bradley, G., Ryan, C., and Zumbrunnen, C. 2003. Integrating Humans into Ecology: Opportunities and Challenges for Studying Urban Ecosystems. *BioScience* 53(12):1169–1179. doi: 10.1641/0006-3568(2003)053[1169:IHIEOA]2.0.CO;2.

Alberti, M., Marzluff, J., and Hunt, V.M. 2017. Urban Driven Phenotypic Changes: Empirical Observations and Theoretical Implications for Eco-Evolutionary Feedback. *Philosophical Transactions of the Royal Society B: Biological Sciences* 372(1712): 20160029. doi:10.1098/rstb.2016.0029.

Alberti, M., Correa, C., Marzluff, J., Hendry, A., Palkovacs, E.P., Gotanda, K., et al. 2017. Global Urban Signatures of Phenotypic Change in Animal and Plant Populations. *Proceeding of the National Academies of Science* 114(34): 8951–8956. doi: 10.1073/pnas.1606034114.

Allen, P.M. 1997. *Cities and Regions as Self-Organising Systems: Models of Complexity*, Taylor and Francis, London.

Aronson, M.F.J., La Sorte, F.A., Nilon, C.H., Katti, M., Goddard, M.A., Lepczyk, C.A., et al. 2014. A Global Analysis of the Impacts of Urbanization on Bird and Plant Diversity Reveals Key Anthropogenic Drivers. *Proc. Biol. Sci.* 281, 20133330. doi: 10.1098/rspb.2013.3330.

Aronson, M.F.J., Handel, S.N., La Puma, I.P., and Clemants, S.E. 2015. Urbanization Promotes Non-Native Woody Species and Diverse Plant Assemblages in the New York Metropolitan Region. *Urban Ecosystems* 18: 31–45. doi: 10.1007/s11252-014-0382-z.

Bai, X. 2003. The Process and Mechanism of Urban Environmental Change: An Evolutionary View. *International Journal of Environment and Pollution* 19(5): 528–541.

Bai, X. 2016. Eight Energy and Material Flow Characteristics of Urban Ecosystems. *Ambio* 45: 819. doi: 10.1007/s13280-016-0785-6.

Bai, X., and Imura, H. 2000. "A Comparative Study of Urban Environment in East Asia: Stage Model of Urban Environmental Evolution." *International Review for Environmental Strategies* 1(1): 135–158.

Bak, P. 1996. *How Nature Works: The Science of Self-Organized Criticality*. New York: Springer.

Barros, J., and Sobriera, F. 2002. City of Slums: Self-Organisation across Scales. UCL Working Paper 55. ISSN 1467–1298.

Batten, D.F. 2001. Complex Landscapes of Spatial Interaction. *The Annals of Regional Science* 35(1):81–111.

Batty, M. 2005. *Cities and Complexity: Understanding Cities through Cellular Automata, Agent-based Models, and Fractals*. Cambridge, MA: MIT Press.

Batty M. 2008. The Size, Scale, and Shape of Cities. *Science* 319: 769–771.

Batty, M., and Longley, P.A. 1994. *Fractal Cities: A Geometry of Form and Function*. London: Academic Press.

Beninde, J., Veith, M., and Hochkirch, A. 2015. Biodiversity in Cities Needs Space: A Meta-Analysis of Factors Determining Intra-Urban Biodiversity Variation. *Ecology Letters* 18(6): 581–592. doi: 10.1111/ele.12427.

Bettencourt, L.M.A., and West, G. 2010. A Unified Theory of Urban Living. *Nature* 467: 912–913. doi:10.1038/ 467912a.

Bettencourt, L.M.A., Lobo, J., Helbing, D., Kuhnert, C., and West, G.B. 2007. Growth, Innovation, Scaling, and the Pace of Life in Cities. *Proceedings of the National Academy of Sciences* 104(17): 7301–7306. doi:10.1073/pnas.0610172104.

Bettencourt, L.M.A. 2013a. The Kind of Problem a City Is. SFI WORKING PAPER: 2013-03-008.

Bettencourt, L.M.A. 2013b. "The Origins of Scaling in Cities." *Science* 340 1438–1441.

Blum, M.D., and Roberts, H.H., 2009. Drowning of the Mississippi Delta Due to Insufficient Sediment Supply and Global Sea-Level Rise, *Nature Geoscience* 2(7): 488–491.

Carlson, S.M., Quinn, T.P., and Hendry, A.P. 2011. Eco-Evolutionary Dynamics in Pacific Salmon. *Heredity* 106(3): 438–447. doi:10.1038/hdy.2010.163.

Chapin, F. S., III, Carpenter, S.R., Kofinas, G.P., Folke, C., Abel, N., and Clark, W.C., et al. 2010. Ecosystem Stewardship: Sustainability Strategies for a Rapidly Changing Planet. *Trends in Ecology and Evolution* 25: 241–249.

Cheptou, P.O., Carrue, O., Rouifed, S., and Cantarel, A. 2008. Rapid Evolution of Seed Dispersal in an Urban Environment in the Weed *Crepis sancta*. *Proceedings of the National Academy of Sciences* 105: 3796–3799.

Depietri, Y., and McPhearson, T. 2017. Integrating the Grey, Green, and Blue in Cities: Nature-Based Solutions for Climate Change Adaptation and Risk Reduction, in N. Kabisch, H. Korn, J. Stadler, and A. Bonn (eds.), *Nature-Based Solutions to Climate Change in Urban Areas*, Springer International Publishing. doi: 10.1007/978-3-319-56091-5.

do Rio Caldeira, T. P. 2000. *City of Walls: Crime, Segregation, and Citizenship in São Paulo*. University of California Press.

Dupras, J., Alam, M., and Revéret, J.P. 2015. Economic Value of Greater Montreal's Non-Market Ecosystem Services in a Land Use Management and Planning Perspective. *The Canadian Geographer/Le géographe canadien* 59(1): 93–106. doi: 10.1111/cag.12138.

Elmqvist, T., Fragkias, M., Goodness, J., Güneralp, B., Marcotullio, P.J., McDonald, R.I., et al., (eds). 2013. *Urbanization, Biodiversity and Ecosystem Services: Challenges and Opportunities*. Dordrecht: Springer. doi:10.1007/978-94-007-7088-1.

Feitosa, F.F. 2010. Urban Segregation as a Complex System: An Agent-Based Simulation Approach. *Ecology and Development Series No. 70*. Göttingen: Cuvillier Verlag. www.zef.de/fileadmin/web-files/downloads/zefc_ecology_development/eds_70_Feitosa.pdf.

Flenley, J.R., and King, S.M. 1984. Late Quaternary Pollen Records from Easter Island. *Nature* 307: 47–50.

Folke, C., Carpenter, S.R., Walker, B., Scheffer, M., Chapin, T., and Rockström, J. 2010. Resilience Thinking: Integrating Resilience, Adaptability and Transformability. *Ecology and Society* 15(4): 20.

Forrester, J.W. 1969. *Urban Dynamics*. Pegasus Communications.

Geddes, P. 1915. *City in Evolution*. London: Williams and Norgate Ltd.

Grimm, N.B., Grove, J.M., Pickett, S.T.A., and Redman, C.L. 2000. Integrated Approaches to Long-Term Studies of Urban Ecological Systems. *BioScience* 50 (7): 571–584.

Grimm, N.B., Faeth, S.H., Golubiewski, N.E., Redman, C.L., Wu, J., Bai, X., and Briggs, J.M. 2008. Global Change and the Ecology of Cities. *Science* 319(5864): 756–760.

Haas, T.C., Blum, M.J., and Heins, D.C. 2010. Morphological Responses of a Stream Fish to Water Impoundment. *Biology Letters* 6(6). doi: 10.1098/rsbl.2010.0401.

Hall, P. 2000. Creative Cities and Economic Development. *Urban Studies* 37(4): 639–649.

Holling, C.S. 1973. Resilience and Stability of Ecological Systems. *Annual Review of Ecology and Systematics* 4(1): 1–23. doi: 10.1146/annurev.es.04.110173.000245.

Jacobs, J. 1969. *The Life of Cities*. Random House.

Jacquemyn, H., De Meester, L., Jongejans, E., and Honnay, O. 2012. Evolutionary Changes in Plant Reproductive Traits Following Habitat Fragmentation and Their Consequences for Population Fitness. *Journal of Ecology* 100: 76–87.

Jorgensen, B., 1997. *The Theory of Dispersion Models*. CRC Press.

Kammen, D.M., and Sunter, D.A., 2016. City-Integrated Renewable Energy for Urban Sustainability. *Science* 922–928.

Kennedy, C., Cuddihy, J., and Engel-Yan, J. 2007. The Changing Metabolism of Cities. *Journal of Industrial Ecology* 11(2): 43–59. doi: 10.1162/jie.2007.1107.

Kinzig, A.P., Ryan, P., Etienne, M., Allison, H. , Elmqvist, T., and Walker, B.H. 2006. Resilience and Regime Shifts: Assessing Cascading Effects. *Ecology and Society* 11(1): 20.

Kosaka, Y., and Xie, S.P. 2013. Recent Global-Warming Hiatus Tied to Equatorial Pacific Surface Cooling. *Nature* 501(7467): 403–407. doi:10.1038/nature12534.

Kremer, P., Hamstead, Z., Haase, D., McPhearson, T., Frantzeskaki, N., Andersson, E., et al. 2016. Key Insights for the Future of Urban Ecosystem Services Research. *Ecology and Society* 21(2): 29. doi: 10.5751/ES-08445-210229.

Krugman, P. 1993. First Nature, Second Nature, and Metropolitan Location. *Journal of Regional Science* 33(2): 129–144. doi:10.1111/j.1467-9787.1993.tb00217.x.

Krugman, P. 1998. What's New about the New Economic Geography? *Oxford Review of Economic Policy* 14 (2):7–17.

Lago, L.C. 2000. *Desigualdades e Segregação na Metrópole: o Rio de Janeiro em Tempos de Crise*. Revan/ Fase: Rio de Janeiro.

Liu J, Dietz, T., Carpenter, S.R., Alberti, M., Folke, C., Moran, E., et al. 2007. Complexity of Coupled Human and Natural Systems. *Science* 317(5844): 1513–1516.

Loreau, M., Mouquet, N., and Gonzalez, A. 2003 Biodiversity as Spatial Insurance in Heterogeneous Landscapes. *Proceedings of the National Academy of Sciences* 100: 12765.

Lynch, K. 1961. The Patterns of the Metropolis. *Daedalus* 90:79–98.

Marzluff, J.M. 2012. Urban Evolutionary Ecology. *Studies in Avian Biology* 45, 287–308.

Matthews, B., Narwani, A., Hausch, S., Nonaka, E., Peter, H., Yamamichi, M., and Sullam, K.E. 2011. Toward an Integration of Evolutionary Biology and Ecosystem Science. *Ecology Letters* 14: 690–701. doi:10.1111/j.1461–0248.2011.01627.x.

McHale, M.R., Pickett, S.T.A., Barbosa, O., Bunn, D.N., Cadenasso, M.L., Childers, D.L., et al. 2015. The New Global Urban Realm: Complex, Connected, Diffuse, and Diverse Social-Ecological Systems. *Sustainability* 7 (5): 5211–5240.

McKinney, M.L. 2008. Effects of Urbanization on Species Richness: A Review of Plants and Animals. *Urban Ecosystem* 11:161–176.

McPhearson, T., Iwaniec D., and Bai, X. 2017. Positives Visions for Guiding Urban Transformations toward Desirable Futures. *Current Opinion in Environmental Sustainability* (Invited for Special Issue), in press.

McPhearson, T., Pickett, S.T.A., Grimm, N., Niemelä, J., Alberti, M., Elmqvist, T., et al. 2016a. Advancing Urban Ecology Toward a Science of Cities. *BioScience* 66(3): 198–212. doi:10.1093/biosci/biw002.

McPhearson, T., Haase, D., Kabisch, N., and Gren, Å. 2016b. Advancing Understanding of the Complex Nature of Urban Systems. *Ecological Indicators* 70: 566–573. http://dx.doi.org/10.1016/j.ecolind.2016.03.054.

McPhearson, T., Parnell, S., Simon, D., Gaffney, O., Elmqvist, T., Bai, X., et al. 2016c. Scientists Must Have a Say in the Future of Cities. *Nature* 538:165–166.

McPhearson, T., Andersson, E., Elmqvist, T., and Frantzeskaki, N. 2015. Resilience of and through Urban Ecosystem Services. *Ecosystem Services* (Special Issue) 12: 152–156, doi: 10.1016/j.ecoser.2014.07.012.

Mumford, L. 1961. *The City in History*. New York. Harcourt.

Olsson, P., Galaz, V., and Boonstra, W.J. 2014. Sustainability Transformations: A Resilience Perspective. *Ecology and Society* 19(4): 1. http://dx.doi.org/10.5751/ES-06799-190401.

Palkovacs, E.P. Kinnison, M.T., Correa, C., Dalton, C.M., and Hendry, A.P. 2012. Fates Beyond Traits: Ecological Consequences of Human-induced Trait Change. *Evolutionary Applications* 5: 183–191. doi: 10.1111/j.1752–4571.2011.00212.x.

Park, R.E., and Leggewie, C. 1925. *The City*.

Pereira, H.M., Leadley, P.W., Proença, V., Alkemade, R., Scharlemann, J.P., Fernandez-Manjarrés, J.F., et al. 2010. Scenarios for Global Biodiversity in the 21st Century. *Science* 330(6010): 1496–1501. doi: 10.1126/science.1196624.

Phillips, J.D., 1999. Divergence, Convergence, and Self-Organization in Landscapes. *Annals of the Association of American Geographers* 89(3):466–488. doi: 10.1111/0004–5608.00158.

Pickett, S.T.A., Wu, J., and Cadenasso, M.L. 1999. Patch Dynamics and the Ecology of Disturbed Ground: A Framework for Synthesis, in L.R. Walker, (ed.) *Ecosystems of the World: Ecosystems of Disturbed Ground*. Amsterdam: Elsevier Science, pp. 707–722.

Pimentel, D. 1961. Animal Population Regulation by the Genetic Feedback Mechanism. *The American Naturalist* 95: 65–79.

Pimm, S.L., Jenkins, C.N., Abell, R., Brooks, T.M., Gittleman, J.L., Joppa, L.N., Raven, P.H., Roberts, C.M., and Sexton, J.O. 2014. The Biodiversity of Species and Their Rates of Extinction, Distribution, and Protection. *Science* 344(6187): 1246752. doi: 10.1126/science.1246752.

Polsky, C., Grove, J.M., Knudson, C. Groffman, P.M., Bettez, N., Cavender-Bares, J., et al. 2014. Assessing the Homogenization of Urban Land Management with an Application to U.S. Residential Lawn Care. *Proceedings of the National Academy of Sciences USA* 111(12): 4432–4437.

Portugali, J. 2000. Spatial Cognitive Dissonance and Socio-spatial Emergence in a Self-Organizing City, in *Self-Organization and the City*. Berlin, Heidelberg: Springer, pp. 141–173.

Ramaswami, A., Chavez, A., and Chertow, M. 2012. Carbon Footprinting of Cities and Implications for Analysis of Urban Material and Energy Flows. *Journal of Industrial Ecology* 16(6): 783–785. doi: 10.1111/j.1530-9290.2012.00569.x.

Rayfield, B., Pelletier, D., Dumitru, M., Cardille, J., and Gonzalez, A. 2015. Multi-Purpose Habitat Networks for Short-Range and Long-Range Connectivity: A New Method Combining Graph and Circuit Connectivity. *Methods in Ecology and Evolution* 7: 222–231.

Rook, G.A. 2013. Regulation of the Immune System by Biodiversity from the Natural Environment: An Ecosystem Service Essential to Health. *Proceedings of the National Academy of Sciences USA* 110: 18360–18367.

Rosenzweig, C., Solecki, W., Hammer, S.A., and Mehrotra, S. 2010. Cities Lead the Way in Climate-Change Action. *Nature* 467(7318): 909–911. doi:10.1038/467909a.

Sabatini, F., Caceres, G., and Cerda, J. 2001. Residential Segregation in Main Chilean Cities: Tendencies from the Past Three Decades and Possible Frameworks for Action. *EURE* (Santiago) 27(82): 21–42.

Sanderson, E.W., Solecki, W.D., Waldman, J.R., Parris, A.S. (eds.) 2016. *Prospects for Resilience. Insights from New York City's Jamaica Bay*. Washington, DC: Island Press.

Sassen, S., 2012. Interactions of the Technical and the Social: Digital Formations of the Powerful and the Powerless. *Information, Communication & Society* 15 (4): 455–478.

Scheffer, M., Carpenter, S., Foley, J.A., Folke, C., and Walker, B. 2001. Catastrophic Shifts in Ecosystems. *Nature* 413(6856): 591–596.

Schoener, T.W. 2011. The Newest Synthesis: Understanding the Interplay of Evolutionary and Ecological Dynamics. *Science* 331(6016): 426–429. doi:10.1126/science.1193954.

Seto, K.C., Güneralp, B., and Hutyra, L.R. 2012. Global Forecasts of Urban Expansion to 2030 and Direct Impacts on Biodiversity and Carbon Pools. *Proceedings of the National Academy of Sciences* 109(40): 16083–16088. doi: 10.1073/pnas.1211658109.

Sheffer, E., Hardenberg, J., Yizhaq, H., Shachak, M., and Meron, E. 2013. Emerged or Imposed: A Theory on the Role of Physical Templates and Self-Organisation for Vegetation Patchiness. *Ecology Letters*, 16(2): 127–139. doi: 10.1111/ele.12027.

van Staveren, M. F., and van Tatenhove, J. P. M. 2016. Hydraulic Engineering in the Social-Ecological Delta: Understanding the Interplay Between Social, Ecological, and Technological Systems in the Dutch Delta by Means of "Delta Trajectories." *Ecology and Society* 21(1):8. http://dx.doi.org/10.5751/ES-08168-210108.

Torres, H.G., Marques, E.C., Ferreira, M.P., and Bitar, S. 2002. Poverty and Space: Pattern of Segregation in São Paulo. Paper presented at Workshop on Spatial Segregation and Urban Inequality in Latin America, Austin, Texas, 15–16 Nov 2002.

Torres, H.G., Marques, E.C., Ferreira, M.P., and Bitar, S. 2003. Pobreza e Espaço: Padrões de Segregação em São Paulo. *Revista do IEA* 17(47):13–42.

UN-Habitat. 2011. *State of the World's Cities, UN Habitat*. http://mirror.unhabitat.org/pmss/listItem-Details.aspx?publicationID=3387&AspxAutoDetectCookieSupport=1.

UN-Habitat Urban Data. 2015. *City Equity Index*. http://urbandata.unhabitat.org/.

UN-Habitat. World Cities Report 2016. *Urbanization and Development: Emerging Futures.* May. https://unhabitat.org/wp-content/uploads/2014/03/WCR-%20Full-Report-2016.pdf.

Walker, B., Holling, C.S., Carpenter, S.R., and Kinzig, A. 2004. Resilience, Adaptability and Transformability in Social–Ecological Systems. *Ecology and Society* 9(2): 5.

Westley, F., Olsson, P., Folke, C., Homer-Dixon, T., Vredenburg, H., Loorbach, D., et al. 2011. Tipping Toward Sustainability: Emerging Pathways of Transformation. *AMBIO* 40:762–780.

Wilkinson C. 2012. Social-Ecological Resilience: Insights and Issues for Planning Theory *Planning Theory* 11(2): 148–169.

Yeh, P.J., and Price, T.D. 2004. Adaptive Phenotypic Plasticity and the Successful Colonization of a Novel Environment. *The American Naturalist* 164 (4): 531–542. doi:10.1086/423825.

Chapter 3: Understanding, Implementing, and Tracking Urban Metabolism Is Key to Urban Futures

Abel Chávez, Chris Kennedy, Bin Chen, Marian Chertow, Tim Baynes, Shaoqing Chen, and Xuemei Bai

3.1 Introduction

Eighty percent of the world's population is expected to live in urban areas by 2050 and will demand a high density of infrastructure in order to meet human development aspirations. Occupying nearly 3 percent of the total global land surface, cities are also the centers for nearly 80 percent of the global domestic product, or GDP (UNEP 2012) (see Chapter 6). Meanwhile, cities are also global catalysts for 50 percent of solid wastes, 75 percent of natural resource consumption, and between 60 and 80 percent of greenhouse gas, or GHG, emissions (UNEP 2012). These functions present a plethora of infrastructure-related opportunities for efficiency integration, as infrastructure provides access to essential goods and services that are linked to human development and health. Yet, infrastructure, while essential, is also the source of many environmental problems caused through direct and indirect emissions. It is estimated that present-day infrastructure is responsible for 122 gigatonnes (Gt) CO_2, with developed countries owning a per capita infrastructure footprint five times larger than their developing country counterparts (Müller et al. 2013). Moreover, Müeller and colleagues estimate that if all infrastructure needs are met using typical Western technologies, the environmental impact would amount to 350 Gt CO_2, or seven times the current global GHG emissions of 50 Gt CO_2.

Urbanization will continue to be the stimulus for new infrastructure; although global average annual urbanization rates in 2050 are projected to occur at half of today's rate (from 2 percent today to 1 percent in 2050), urbanization in *less-developed regions* will occur at an annual rate of change of approximately 1.5 percent, while it will occur at a rate of *more-developed regions* at a rate of 0.25 percent, leading to a continued high demand for infrastructure in developing regions. What is not as clear, and what is often overlooked, is where the impacts of urbanization will be most observed. And while large urban agglomerations, for a host of reasons, are often centers of research about urbanization phenomena, we should also consider the suite of smaller urban areas that are in the midst of substantial transformations of their own. Of the global urban population, most – 51 percent – of urban dwellers reside in communities of less than 500,000 inhabitants (see Figure 3.1). Moreover, by 2030, almost 40 percent of the global urban population will be located in communities of less than 300,000 inhabitants, many of which will demand infrastructure and whose activities may incur substantial environmental impacts, if not adequately designed. Thus, in the face of urbanization and infrastructure development, it is imperative that we understand the effects that urbanization and associated infrastructure development can have on the material and energy demands associated with cities and communities everywhere. Such an understanding may trigger efficiency gains related to the services that infrastructure provides. One way to understand and measure changes in efficiency gains is through the concept of "urban metabolism."

In this chapter, we discuss the concept of urban metabolism and how it has been and can be used to understand the resource flows and environmental impacts associated with cities. Even though in this chapter we loosely adopt the commonly used nomenclature of urban metabolism to represent all communities, it is important to note that urban and rural communities alike, have

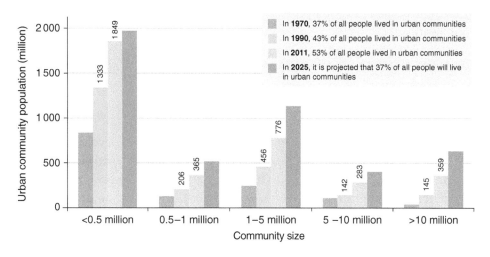

Figure 3.1 Urban population by community size for cities of five unique sizes. Note that smaller cities/communities of 500,000 inhabitants or less will continue to house the majority (approximately 50 percent) of the world's urban population. Source: Jerker Lokrantz/Azote, modified after Chávez (2017).

associated metabolic flows; some scholars have begun articulating the concept of community metabolisms (Chávez 2017) and rural metabolisms (Haas and Krausmann 2015). Thus, the urban metabolism framework is a form of modeling and assessing community processes, whether individually or in aggregation, to gain greater understanding of material and energy flows associated with communities. Since the seminal work of Abel Wolman (1965), many lines of research inquiry about urban metabolism have been undertaken, and some cities have adopted the concept to study their own resource flows associated with material and energy in their aims to integrate efficient, sustainable, and resilient material and energy flows. As we will show later in this chapter, urban metabolism analysis has also undergone its own transitions in terms of its definition of the urban boundary – early studies took a strictly "boundary-limited perspective," whereas the latest studies define the boundary to include a community's hinterlands, encompassing the supply chains associated with a community. The chosen definition of boundary has substantial impacts on the scope of resilience that must be incorporated to hedge against resource shocks.

We will begin by presenting an overview of research focusing on urban metabolism. Then, recalling that urban metabolism is ultimately concerned with measuring material and energy stocks and flows, we will describe some of the conceptual and methodological advances that have emerged from the urban metabolism foundation. Next, we will present how communities have and might consider incorporating the metabolism framework for sustainable and resilient system development. Last, we will comment on the challenges that lie ahead.

3.2 Urban Metabolism: Material and Energy Flows

3.2.1 A Historical Perspective and Updated Understanding

Urban metabolism is a socionatural metaphor originally developed in the 1960s by Abel Wolman as a form to study city-scale material and energy flows. Though various concepts central to urban metabolism have been present since the nineteenth century, Wolman's work (1965), in which he attempted to quantify the material and energy flows for a hypothetical US city of one million people, organizes them under one idea: a city's metabolism, which he defined as "all the materials and commodities needed to sustain the city's inhabitants at home, at work and at play" (Wolman 1965). Since then, there has been an intensification of urban metabolic research yielding several new questions and novel understanding of city metabolic flows. Figure 3.2 represents a modern urban metabolism concept.

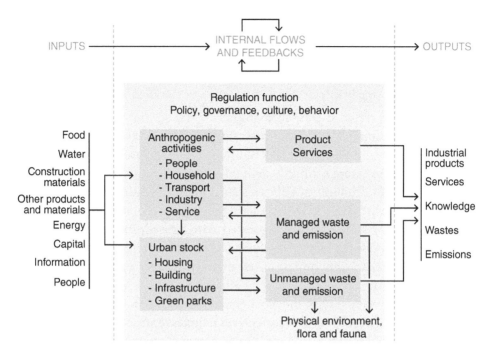

Figure 3.2 Conceptual diagram of urban metabolism. A proportion of the resources that flow into cities become urban stock, while others enable and drive various anthropogenic functions and eventually produce intended or unintended outputs that stay within the system boundary or are exported beyond the boundary, with various impacts on the physical environment, flora and fauna, and associated ecological processes. Urban metabolism is shaped and regulated by factors such as urban policy, urban governance, culture, and individual behaviors. Source: Jerker Lokrantz/Azote, modified after Bai (2016).

Building on Wolman's foundation, the 1970s produced the first set of actual urban metabolism case studies. Under the UNESCO Man and Biosphere Program, researchers applied urban metabolism approaches in Brussels (Duvigneaud and Denaeyer-De Smet 1977), Hong Kong (Newcombe et al. 1978) and Tokyo (Hanya and Ambe 1976). After a hiatus in the 1980s, interest in urban metabolism reemerged in the 1990s with research by Stephen Boyden and Peter Newman for Australian cities (Boyden et al. 1981; Newman 1999); in Austria and Switzerland with work by Peter Baccini and Paul Brunner (Baccini and Brunner 1991); and with work by French ecologist Herbert Girardet (Girardet 1992). As more studies emerged, Kennedy et al. (2007) conducted a comparison of the metabolisms of eight metropolitan regions, identifying metabolic processes that potentially undermine the sustainability of cities, including changing groundwater levels, build-up of toxic materials, exhaustion of local materials, heat islands, and accumulation of nutrients. Barles completed a metabolic assessment for Paris (Barles 2009) and later explored the relation of urban metabolism to sustainable urban development (Barles

2010). Standardized and quantitative urban metabolism models also emerged from this work (Niza et al. 2009). In this body of work, we observe a progression of urban metabolism research based on increasing understanding of coverage, scale, links to socioeconomic contexts, and spatial and temporal variations of metabolic flows (Bai 2016).

From the first urban metabolism studies to today's cross-cutting research, urban metabolism has witnessed much transformation. Earlier, urban metabolism studies developed and applied methods that measured "economy-wide" material flows that were primarily defined by a community's physical boundary. These studies, including Wolman's 1965 work, considered water and fuel inputs coupled with outputs such as sewage and air pollutants. With time, the scope of economy-wide activities expanded to include additional inputs such as land, food, and building materials, along with a set of emerging socioeconomic indices by which to benchmark cities' metabolic flows (see Newman 1999, for example). More recently, a growing amount of research has examined the metabolisms associated with biogeochemical fluxes due to their substantially higher resource intensities, even though such fluxes represent only a small portion of a city's material flows. Flows of nitrogen and phosphorus, for instance, have been shown to merit additional research because their impacts transcend a city's boundaries (Baker et al. 2001; Metson et al. 2015; Lin et al. 2016; Cui et al. 2015). Finally, as the understanding of the true inputs and outputs associated with a typical community has evolved, so has the collective understanding of what "economy-wide" means. Early urban metabolism studies frequently adopted a purely boundary-limited definition (that is, a purely jurisdictional definition) of a community and accounted for direct flows only. However, more recent applications of the urban metabolism approach conform with global standards, which call for the inclusion of indirect or embodied flows. For example, Chester et al. (2012) were one of the first research teams to couple the concept of urban metabolism with life cycle analysis, offering twofold benefits: providing a robust perspective on a community's metabolism while assisting in avoiding the shifting of burdens or responsibilities to other communities.

The usefulness of urban metabolism studies increased with the recognition that they provided the necessary activity data required to conduct greenhouse gas inventories for cities (Kennedy et al. 2009, 2010). Some studies have used the urban metabolism framework to develop measures of resource efficiency in cities (Baccini and Oswald 2008; Zhang and Yang 2007; Browne et al. 2009). Bai (2007) emphasizes the importance of policy and regulations in regulating metabolic flows. Other applications of urban metabolism include the development of sustainability indicators, mathematical modeling for policy analysis, and use as a basis for design (Newman 1999; Kennedy et al. 2011; Chávez and Ramaswami 2013).

The literature on urban metabolism has increased substantially in the past decade. A search using Scopus, a database of peer-reviewed literature, showed that the number of papers on urban metabolism increased from about two per year in 2000 to about 50 per year in 2014 (Kennedy 2015). This is encouraging for efforts to make collection of metabolism data a mainstream activity for cities (Kennedy and Hoornweg 2012). Included among the later literature are spatially disaggregated studies within cities, studies about life cycle extensions of urban metabolism, and various studies considering particular components of the urban metabolism; for instance, moving away from the early work's limited focus on specific flows, bulk, and boundary-limited scope, more recent work has measured above- and below-ground infrastructure-related material flows (see Tanikawa and Hashimoto 2009, for example) as well as delving into cross-cutting, multidisciplinary, and life-cycle-based research (see Kennedy 2015 and Chávez and Ramaswami 2013). The study of urban metabolism now includes increasingly broader interdisciplinary contexts, engaging urban planners, engineers, political scientists, ecologists, and industrial ecologists, among others (Castán Broto et al. 2012; Newell and Cousins 2014).

Textbooks by Ferrão and Fernández (2013) and Baccini and Brunner (2012) provide extensive details on the urban metabolism. Literature reviews on urban metabolism include those by Kennedy et al. (2011), Holmes and Pincetl (2012), Zhang (2013), Bai (2016), and Beloin-Saint-Pierre et al. (2016). Weisz and Steinberger (2010) discuss the challenges of reducing material and energy flows in cities. Kennedy (2012) provides a simple mathematical model broadly linking the quantity and performance of infrastructure stocks to urban metabolism.

On a more conceptual level, Bai (2016) argues that the approach and empirical findings of urban metabolism studies have the potential, although not fully realized, to contribute significantly to the understanding of cities as human dominant, complex socioecological systems. In an attempt to build conceptual bridges between urban metabolism studies, which views the city as an organism, and urban ecosystem studies, which view cities as an ecosystem, Bai (2016) identified eight urban ecosystem characteristics that urban metabolism research reveals: energy and material budget and pathways; flow intensity; energy and material efficiency; rate of resource depletion, accumulation, and transformation; self-sufficiency or external dependency; intrasystem heterogeneity; intersystem and temporal variation; and regulating mechanisms and governing capacity.

3.2.2 Urban Boundaries

One of the cross-cutting questions in all of the urban studies is where to draw the boundary around a city, recognizing that the boundary itself has most likely changed over time. Drawing the boundary too narrowly carries the risk of insufficient recognition of the "urban system." Drawing it too broadly can dilute the unique elements of the urban core. Because researchers approach urban issues from so many different disciplinary directions, many overlapping approaches and tools arise that can lead to confusion and need to be sorted out.

Recent iterations of urban metabolism have redefined the definition of "economy" to extend the urban boundary beyond the traditional boundary-limited approach, which has allowed for the inclusion of linkages between cities and their hinterlands – where the hinterland itself can vary between regional to global (for example, Pichler et al. 2017). While still considered urban metabolism, said studies yield a footprint such as ecological, water, or carbon footprints. Moreover, these footprints can include industrial and/or supply-chain impacts further up the chain of production, but can also be focused on consumption-based footprints involving households and governments in cities, which are the "final consumers" of what has been produced whether locally or imported from outside (Chávez and Ramaswami 2013; Ramaswami et al. 2012). For example, in a study looking at consumption-based (that is, household) GHG emissions, Lin et al. (2013) found that up to 70 percent of GHGs can be attributed to regional and national activities beyond the urban boundaries that support household consumption (see Pichler et al. 2017).

Expanding the boundary of a city, and thus the scope of urban metabolism research, from purely boundary-limited to including the hinterlands is captured by transboundary footprinting. The method of transboundary footprinting recognizes that there are often key infrastructural facilities, such as power plants, landfills, and airports, that may not be within the city limits, but nevertheless are part of what keeps the city operating and producing, and which could be counted as part of the city's overall environmental impact. Both transboundary footprinting and urban metabolism use material flow accounting and analysis and can trace an array of substances through the system under study (Zhang 2013). Some have suggested the addition of life cycle accounting to further analyze external supply relationships to match specific urban areas and the places on which they depend (Pincetl et al. 2012).

One particular greenhouse gas, carbon dioxide (symbolized as CO_2), is the focus of a great deal, but not all, of urban metabolism and transboundary footprinting studies. Indeed, there is a peer-reviewed and robust protocol for city-scale greenhouse gas inventorying in cities called the Global Protocol for Community-Scale Greenhouse Gas Emission Inventories, or GPC, that is increasingly being adopted. It is a joint project by ICLEI, the World Resources Institute, and the C40 Cities Climate Leadership Group, with additional collaboration by the World Bank, UNEP, and UN-Habitat. As a global reporting standard, the GPC enables cities and communities to consistently measure and report greenhouse gas emissions and to develop climate action plans and low-emission urban development strategies while using coupled production and consumption-based approaches (ICLEI 2016).

Finally, urban metabolism helps a city understand the physical basis of what occurs within its boundaries by measuring its inputs and outputs. There are many more social, political, and economic elements to examine beyond cities and their hinterlands, but urban metabolism is an essential aspect for understanding important biophysical interactions.

3.3 Global and National Trends in Material and Energy Flows

Our knowledge of historical resource use trends gives us an imperfect guide to the future. This knowledge is imperfect because a number of countries are entering an unprecedented phase of socioeconomic maturity, while others are poised to undertake rapid urban development. The latter have the opportunity to avoid the resource-intensive path taken by the developed world in the twentieth century, but this outcome is far from certain.

Globally, trends in material and energy flows present interesting metabolic challenges. Overall, when resource use is divided by the number of people on Earth, as of 2010, each person yearly demands 10 tons of materials. Using the standardized System of National Accounts, UNEP (2016) illustrates the vast disparities in material use between economies in the Global North and those in the Global South. In North America and Europe, each person requires approximately 20 and 14 tons, respectively – far exceeding material demand across other economies. Regional contexts offer critical insights into understanding these material flows at finer scales.

Several studies have looked closely at physical material flows at the scale of disaggregated world regions. Using distinct methodological approaches, Krausmann et al. (2009), Schaffartzik et al. (2014), and Wiedmann et al. (2015) each examined global scale material flows that uncovered parallel trends by material type (that is, minerals, ores, fossil energy, biomass, etc.). Others have examined flows for specific regions: Gierlinger and Krausmann (2012) studied the United States; Weisz et al. (2006) studied Europe; Krausmann et al. (2011) studied Japan; Russi et al. (2008) studied some of Latin America; Gonzalez-Martinez and Schandl (2008) studied Mexico; and Giljum (2004) studied Chile. And while these several studies illustrate that the overall rate of material flows is accelerating, the following important dimensions merit careful understanding.

Until 2000, Japan's total energy needs were generally always rising, but since then there has been a persistent decline. Europe's total primary energy demand has declined more than 8 percent since 2005 (3 percent between 2013 and 2014) (EEA 2015). While Africa and South Asia are entering a phase of industrialization that will likely lead to an increase in construction, some contend that China's construction of residential buildings will plateau after 2035. Although China is expected to add another 225 million urban dwellers, its national population will peak and start to decline in the next 10 years, which could influence the direction of China's urban expansion (for example, driving lower-density development or new settlements). The centrality of China's construction and manufacturing sectors is likely to be replaced over the next 15 years with more service-oriented production (NBSC 2016; Magnier 2016); this has broad implications for material and energy flows from the buildings sector (You et al. 2011; Hu et al. 2010).

To highlight some of the material and energy flow challenges facing China, between 2011 and 2013 China consumed more cement (6.6 Gt) than the United States did between 1901 and 2000 (4.5 Gt) (Smil 2014). This rate far exceeded prior expectations (Fernández 2007), and it is uncertain if this trend can persist. The International Energy Agency (IEA) estimates that although China will remain the largest producer and consumer of coal and overtake the United States in oil consumption, it will require 85 percent less energy to produce each future unit of economic growth (that is, energy/GDP will decrease by 85 percent) (OECD/IEA 2015). Accounting for six main construction materials used in urban residential buildings in Beijing from 1949 to 2008, Hu et al. (2010) report that a total of 510 million tons of material were imported into the city, of which 470 million tons (or 92.5 percent) were retained in new stocks, that is, built environment and infrastructure; 33 percent of those new stocks emerged between 2003 and 2008.

Since record-keeping began, the United States has had the world's largest total primary energy supply, a trend that had been increasing until 2009, when China took over this rank. The United States has since seen a decline in both per capita and overall energy needs (OECD/IEA 2014) and there has been a similar decrease in domestic material consumption (UNEP 2016).

From a global urban perspective, Africa and India combined will add more than one billion *new* urban residents by 2040 (UNDESA 2014). To provide electricity for these residents, India's power sector needs to quadruple by 2040; this will likely lead India to becoming the world's biggest importer of coal. In developing countries, urbanization will demand materials to create infrastructure, vehicles, and buildings. China has experienced a rapid expansion of builtup urban area, which is both driving and driven by economic growth in and around the cities (Bai et al. 2011), with the built-up urban area growing much faster than the urban population (Bai et al. 2014). Müller et al. (2013) estimate that if the developing world proceeds to construct its new cities with the same

intensity and type of infrastructure we see in developed countries, the potential carbon cost is more than a third of the world's cumulative carbon budget to
2050 (if we seek to restrain global warming to 2°C above preindustrial averages).

While the direct material needs of the developing world will enlarge and
those of the developed world might stabilize – and possibly even decouple
from economic activity – it is important to be wary of *indirect* material needs
embodied in trade. The overall material footprints of Japan, the United States,
and the United Kingdom are all more than 150 percent greater than their direct
domestic material consumption (Wiedmann et al. 2015). For residence and
service-oriented urban centers that typically import energy and energy-intensive materials and goods, consumption-based approaches, such as input-output footprints, may yield higher energy-use estimates compared to territorial
accounting, though the opposite may be true in net-producing urban centers
(Chávez and Ramaswami 2013). However, in the end, this may continue to follow the trajectory presented by Bristow and Kennedy (2015) (see Figure 3.3),
who portray a strong linear relationship between global energy use and global
urban population.

Meanwhile, as we collectively enhance data collection and analysis methods
for measuring aggregate and global level material flows, one paramount challenge to robust assessments is likely to persist going forward. Data-rich economies, mostly those in the Global North (also known as "OECD economies"),
are the epicenter of most comprehensive material flow and metabolic studies;
these studies continue to provide important insights for the planning of new
communities. Conversely, communities in the Global South are often restricted

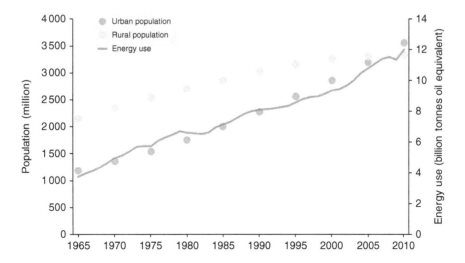

Figure 3.3 Global energy use for urban and rural population, 1965 to 2010. Source: Jerker
Lokrantz/Azote, modified after Bristow and Kennedy (2015).

from further metabolic assessments due to their limited available data. Samples of studies show that research-community partnerships are employing a suite of novel data techniques to be able to inform local communities of important challenges, including e-waste in Nigeria (Nnorom and Osibanjo 2008); energy, material, and greenhouse gases for Delhi, India (Chávez et al. 2012); and food consumption for Manila, Philippines (Chakraborty et al. 2016). However, some obvious gaps exist, which elevate the potential for successful open-source data efforts to fill them (see Chapter 11).

3.3.1 Drivers of Material and Energy Flows

Global drivers of material use have generally been linked to both per capita income and per capita consumption (UNEP 2016). At a more granular scale, researchers have proposed various characteristics of cities that drive urban material and energy flows; these driving characteristics can generally be categorized as natural environmental, socioeconomic, urban function and integration energy system characteristics, and urban form (GEA 2012). The global energy assessment indicates that the natural environment relates to attributes of geographic location, climate, and resource endowments, while socioeconomic drivers typically relate to household characteristics, economic structure, and demography.

As of 2010, a study of the material and energy flows of the world's 27 megacities showed that electricity use per capita is also strongly related to urban area per capita. The authors found that the underlying cause of this relationship was the increase in building floor space. As cities sprawl, there is more room for bigger buildings, which consume more electricity. Building floor area per capita also influences heating fuel use in cities, although heating degree days (a measure of coldness below a base of 18°C room temperature) is the dominant driver (Kennedy et al. 2010, 2015).

Researchers have also observed a high level of correlation between drivers. Kennedy et al. (2015) illustrated high correlation ($r^2 > 0.7$) between urbanized area per capita and electricity use, transportation fuel use, and water consumption (Table 3.1; all per capita). There is also, however, a strong correlation ($r^2 = 0.8$) between GDP per capita of the metropolitan region and urbanized acre per person. Hence, GDP has medium to strong correlation with electricity, transportation, and water use. Many of the variables are interrelated, and overall, cities appear to develop more consumptive metabolisms as they become wealthy and spread out. These findings agree with previous studies, which established that when reporting metabolic energy and carbon flows from cities, one should carefully normalize by the appropriate metrics, namely economic metrics such as GDP for production-based flows, and population metrics for

Table 3.1 Simple univariate correlation matrix between per capita parameters for 27 of the world's megacities as of 2010

Correlations	Electricity cons.	Heating and indust. fuel	Transp. fuel	Water cons.	Solid waste	Heating degree days	Area per pers.	GDP
Electricity consumption (MWh)	–							
Heating and industrial fuel (GJ)	0.40	–						
Transportation fuel (GJ)	0.61	0.70	–					
Water consumption (kL)	0.51	0.51	0.69	–				
Solid waste production (t)	0.44	0.23	0.57	0.45	–			
Heating degree days	0.45	0.59	0.50	0.17	0.27	–		
Area (km²) per person	0.78	0.60	0.79	0.72	0.68	0.42	–	
GDP ($)	0.68	0.41	0.68	0.46	0.55	0.58	0.80	–

consumption-based flows (Ramaswami and Chávez 2013). Additional studies observe changing patterns of metabolic flows across the income axis. For example, in a study looking at phosphorus metabolism through food consumption in Chinese cities, Li et al. (2012) observed an increasing trend of overall phosphorus flow in and out of cities, while an inverted U shape described the share of phosphorus remaining within the urban boundaries. Taking a longitudinal perspective, Cui et al. (2015) conclude that the quantity, configuration, and efficiency of phosphorus metabolism through cities can change drastically in response to changes in consumer and producer behavior, as well as in socioeconomic structure. All of the drivers, trends, and outcomes discussed in this section have directional impact on urban metabolism.

3.4 Theory for Measuring Urban Material and Energy Flows

This chapter has introduced a number of urban metabolism frameworks and models to assist with measuring urban-scale material and energy flows. Baynes and Wiedmann (2012) present a robust set of approaches often used in urban metabolism, such as transboundary footprinting, input-output consumption-based approaches, and complex systems science. One additional approach is a network-oriented method termed "ecological network analysis," or ENA, which presents a set of strong tools for examining structure and function of ecosystem flows (Patten 1978; Finn 1976; Fath and Patten 1999). ENA is a variant of economic input-output analysis (Leontief 1951). ENA has been used to model various metabolic flows, including energy, carbon, water, and others, in a range of cities (Zhang et al. 2010; Liu et al. 2011; Chen et al. 2015). The most notable benefit of the network approach is that it can provide information about relationships between urban sectors in a holistic way, in which both direct and indirect (remote) interactions can be captured.

Increasingly, current research has been striving for urban metabolism data that includes both in-boundary activities and out-of-boundary (or life cycle) impacts (Chen et al. 2014). Input-output models (Smith and Morrison 2006) and life cycle analysis (Pincetl et al. 2012) have been utilized to include activities that occur "upstream" and "downstream" of the city in the framework of urban metabolism. With their embodied material and energy inputs for urban growth, they are both capable of assessing the footprints of cities. Recent work integrating input-output and life cycle data with ENA is promising for assessing and regulating urban sectors to mitigate resource overuse and unintended emissions (Chen and Chen 2015, 2016). Novel integrations could assist metabolic understanding of cities.

Future theoretical frameworks can consider integrating multiple metabolic lenses into understanding the complexities of cities. For example, considering the multiple possibilities for parceling cities into territorial, production, and consumption footprints (see Chávez and Ramaswami 2013) can help us gain a stronger appreciation for the metabolisms of cities and the relevant approaches for maximizing their respective material and energy flows.

3.4.1 Efficient, Sustainable, and Resilient Metabolisms

Creating efficient, sustainable, and resilient metabolism models, while challenging, is imperative in our rapidly expanding and urbanized world. Resource use is increasing, many production systems are peaking, and the consumption and demand for goods and services are at unprecedented highs. Methods and principles of industrial ecology, such as those mentioned in Section 3.3 (material and energy flow analysis and life cycle footprinting), as well as others (dematerialization, recyclability, urban industrial symbiosis, and so forth) (Chertow et al. 2016), can become the cornerstones for assisting the range of stakeholders who are integrating and implementing three vital characteristics – efficiency, sustainability, and resilience – into community metabolisms. While sometimes perceived as interchangeable, these three attributes are unique in the following ways:.

Efficiency concerns the quantity of inputs to produce an output. Typically, an efficient metabolism is characterized by relatively low levels of material use and energy flows to achieve a standard level of output. Examples of key indicators for measuring and tracking efficiency in community metabolisms are electricity per economic or sector output, energy per sector output, or material inputs per waste generation.

Sustainability in urban metabolism addresses the impacts associated with the material and energy flows of a particular system. Sustainability can be measured via environmental (such as CO_2 per sector or CO_2 per GDP), economic (such as income, energy use, and energy-use intensity), and social (such as education and public health) indicators (see Katehi et al. 2016).

Resilience of metabolism relates to the capacity of a particular flow, or to the entire metabolism, for recovery after a disruption. While linkages between metabolism and resilience are ripe for new lines of inquiry, their coupling with disciplinary extensions can yield a practical suite of options for metabolisms to absorb or mitigate against shocks. Industrial ecology – and, specifically, supply-chain analysis – has the potential to reveal key areas of material substitutability, helping inform alternate material uses should system disruptions occur. Example of key indicators of resilience may include metrics for diversity, alternatives among inputs, and measuring impacts from shocks (see Chapter 7).

3.4.2 Gaps in Current Understanding

To embark on and successfully complete effective metabolism assessments requires a wide array of local- and community-level data. It is true that many communities have rich data collection and processing teams. Cities such as New York City, Tokyo, Berlin, and Mexico City have robust data caches, which facilitate metabolism assessments. Many data-rich cities have, coupled with rich secondary data found in the literature. Anecdotally, we note that cities with rich data are often megacities or larger urban centers located in Annex 1 countries (see UNFCCC 2014 for country classifications). Meanwhile, cities in non-Annex 1 countries and/or smaller communities do not display these benefits; in most instances, they are data poor.

Beyond larger urban areas in Annex 1 countries and/or megacities, most communities do not have easily or publicly accessible data to complete vital metabolism assessments that would enhance community and infrastructure planning. As we illustrate using Figure 3.1, much of the world's projected population growth will occur in communities under 500,000 habitants – all of which require substantial and effective planning in order to achieve efficient, sustainable, and resilient metabolisms. Understanding the intricacies of metabolic demands is necessary and imperative – it is also a gap that reasonable data can help close. As an example of this problem, completing coupled and detailed production and consumption footprints that compare cities in the Global North (Annex 1) and in the Global South (non-Annex 1) has proven to be impossible with the current state of data (UCCRN 2016). Should data limitations prevent a community from actively embarking on and a creating efficient, sustainable, and resilient metabolisms?

Given the vast differences in data availability and community development stages, understanding the material needs of communities in relation to their development may yield novel understandings for a sustainable and resilient future. Thus, classifying communities into three broad types may provide new lines of inquiry for the research community. Communities that are unbuilt (*rapidly growing*), built (*mostly stable*), and unbuilding (*shrinking*) each have distinctive attributes in terms of their metabolic flows. We posit that Type A, unbuilt communities, include many of the small(er) communities throughout the Global South that are currently experiencing rapid rates of population and GDP growth. These communities have a very high demand for materials and are poised for styles of planning that can avoid a negative infrastructural and material legacy. Type B, built communities, are the *mostly stable* communities of North America, Europe, Japan, and Australia, where rates of growth (as indicated by GDP) are not bulging as those elsewhere are. These economies are experiencing an increased level of efficiency in material use per GDP, an outcome likely driven by their primarily service-based economic structure. Type C – unbuilding communities that are shrinking and depopulating – are a phenomenon currently observed in the United States' Rust Belt (see Schilling and Logan 2008)) and Europe's east (see Bontje 2004). As shrinking communities transition from materials-intense outputs towards tertiary sector production, they may well be poised for exemplary green infrastructure development.

Box 3.1 Beijing case study

Innovative Policies and Levers: Exemplary Case Studies

Beijing, the capital of China, has one of the largest gross domestic products, or GDPs of Chinese cities (350 billion USD in 2014) and is home to more than 20 million people. Beijing is also the leading city of the Jing-Jin-Ji economic region, the development of which has a substantial impact across the entire country. With a fast-growing population and expanding urban areas, Beijing has an increasingly high demand for energy and resources from Jing-Jin-Ji and the rest of city operations, raising a significant challenge to supplying energy for the city sustainably.

Taking Beijing's 2012 energy use as an example, the three major sources are reported as coal (37 percent), diesel oil (16 percent) and gasoline (14 percent) (Chen and Chen 2015). Meanwhile, energy flow analysis shows that the most energy-consuming components of Beijing at this time were manufacturing (45 percent of total direct energy consumption), services (29 percent), and transportation (16 percent). Using input-output analysis, researchers found that the total energy embodied in Beijing's supply chains associated with urban sectors was almost seven times higher than its direct energy use within the urban boundary. Since Beijing is also in a severe water shortage, it is important that we take both energy use and water consumption into consideration, together.

The resilience and sustainability (or lack thereof) of coupled energy and water metabolism has been a central problem for fast-growing cities such as Beijing. By applying network resilience metrics to urban systems, some scholars hope to show efficiency gains and how stable an urban system can be while facing both energy and water challenges. The resilience of energy-water coupled systems in Beijing is lower than that of natural ecosystems in general (Chen and Chen 2016). The relationships among urban sectors are altered by the competition of energy and water flows. It is clear that coordinated regulation of different metabolic flows in cities, particularly in megacities (for example, Beijing), is essential for more sustainable and rational development.

3.5 Conclusions

Throughout this chapter, we have presented several motivations for the increased use of urban metabolism as a governing framework for understanding the materials and energy flows associated with cities. While the methodological foundations for adopting urban metabolism may have matured through research, development of a typological framework could greatly benefit its scalability and cross-city applicability. Having an urban metabolism typology can help uncover nuanced city details that, in turn, can lead to inquiry and understanding for metabolic flows as they relate to various types of cities. Typological development has seen some momentum recently.

A typology can simply be described as a form of classification, separation, or presentation that segments groups based on a number of key features. For example, a rudimentary typology for cities can adopt a scale based on affluence from less affluent to more affluent. Alternatively, a typology can examine city growth and adopt a scale from rapidly growing to no growth, or even to shrinking. While these are only some of the several typological options, the few early urban metabolism typologies have accounted for added complexities. For example, Chávez and Ramaswami (2013) propose a typology based on a city's import and export of GHG emissions to classify three types of cities – net consumer, balanced, and net producer. Another effort, rooted in Saldivar-Sali (2010), is led by Massachusetts Institute of Technology's Urban Metabolism team, which has developed a typology that uses four independent variables (climate, GDP, population, and density) to reveal clusters (or groups) of cities in terms of eight dependent variables (energy, electricity, fossil fuel, industrial and construction minerals, biomass, water, and domestic material). The opportunities to build on the early work to bring added understanding to urban metabolic flows continues.

3.5.1 Future of and Opportunities Surrounding Urban Material and Energy Flows

Tools based on urban metabolism have witnessed several iterations and many transitions since early research in the 1960s. Analysis that was initially boundary limited by bulk mass flows has transitioned to robust life cycle assessment approaches with the ability to examine from the jurisdictional boundary across the complete supply chain into a city's hinterland(s) – which often include multiple economies in multiple countries (Pichler et al. 2017). Additionally, the early studies quantified the total physical flows for a limited number of sectors, such as energy or waste. Over time, however, urban metabolism studies have expanded in sectors to include transportation, buildings, materials, and others – as well as economic, social, and environmental indicators. Moreover, recent studies including a full*er* set of metabolic flows can provide estimates beyond non-visual material uses, such as those associated with underground infrastructures in cities. The latest estimates of urbanization and urban resource (material and energy) demands increase the need for deeper understanding across communities and their metabolisms.

The creation and use of typologies can help establish more robust understanding of urban metabolisms. Although some attempts have been made in the recent past which can serve as foundations for future typological frameworks, there are additional research opportunities for developing an overarching typology for urban metabolism. Completing such a typology could help drive efficiency, sustainability, and resilience for communities of all sizes everywhere, while merging urban metabolism typologies with global community standards that are being developed in parallel. Such products can also help reduce the knowledge gaps related to sharing best practice and forging partnerships across communities of similar clusters (or types).

Several unknowns and opportunities for new lines of inquiry remain within the analytical field of urban metabolism. For example, it is understood that we are becoming more material inefficient at the global level; in other words, the global economy now requires more material inputs per unit GDP than it once did. Our continuing global shift to materially inefficient economies, which are experiencing unprecedented transformations, contributes to this worldwide trend of increasing resource use and inefficiency. However, due to data limitations, we are still uncertain how these global trends transpire at local, community scales. Are there significant and important differences between the material requirements in subnational economies, for example? The emerging opportunities for integrating material efficiencies, especially in rapidly growing communities, may be many.

As we consider the future of urban metabolism, we can look back at its origins, appreciate its present, and innovate towards the future. From urban global population projections and the strength of GDP emerging from cities, to the expansive opportunities for efficiency resulting from natural resource use and waste and emissions output, communities face plenty of opportunities and challenges. Considering that the bulk of future urban growth is projected to occur in cities of less than 500,000 inhabitants, the questions surrounding material and energy needs for developing high-quality livelihoods will continue to evolve. Many data gaps remain, inhibiting our nuanced understanding of urban metabolism, and these gaps slow the channelling of necessary resources to their required uses in cities. As researchers, practitioners, policy-makers, and interested citizens, it is up to us to continue employing, deploying, and innovating urban metabolism approaches to increase our understanding of resource flows across the urban boundary – and to implement genuinely resilient systems.

🌍 *References*

Baccini, P., and Brunner, P.H., (1991). *Metabolism of the Anthroposphere*. Berlin: Springer Verlag.

Baccini, P. and Brunner, P.H. (2012). *Metabolism of the Anthroposphere: Analysis, Evaluation, Design*, 2nd edition, London: MIT Press.

Bai, X. (2007). Industrial Ecology and the Global Impacts of Cities. *Journal of Industrial Ecology*, 11(2), 1–6.

Bai, X., Schandl, H., Douglas, I., Goode, D., Houck, M., and Wang, R. (2011). *Urban ecology and industrial ecology. In The Routledge Handbook of Urban Ecology*. Routledge, New York.

Bai, X., P. Shi, and Y. Liu. (2014). Society: Realizing China's Urban Dream. *Nature* 509: 158.

Bai, X. (2016). *Eight energy and material flow characteristics of urban ecosystems*. Ambio, 45: 819–830.

Baker, L.A., Hope, D., Xu, Y., Edmonds, J., and Lauver, L. (2001). Nitrogen Balance for the Central Arizona-Phoenix (CAP) Ecosystem. *Ecosystems*, 4: 582–602.

Barles, S. (2009). Urban Metabolism or Paris and Its Region. *Journal of Industrial Ecology*, 13(6): 898–913.

Barles, S. (2010) Society, Energy and Materials: The Contribution of Urban Metabolism Studies to Sustainable Urban Development Issues. *Journal of Environmental Planning and Management*, 53(4): 439–455.

Baynes, T.M., and Wiedmann, T. (2012). General Approaches for Assessing Urban Environmental Sustainability. *Current Opinion in Environmental Sustainability*, 4: 458–464.

Beloin-Saint-Pierre, D., Rugani, B., Lasvaux, S., Mailhac, A., Popovici, E., Sibiude, G., et al. (2016). A Review of Urban Metabolism Studies to Identify Key Methodological Choices for Future Harmonization and Implementation. *Journal of Cleaner Production*, 163: S223–S240.

Bontje, M. (2004). Facing the Challenge of Shrinking Cities in East Germany: The Case of Leipzig. *GeoJournal*, 61: 13–21.

Boyden, S., Millar, S., Newcombe, K., and O'Neill, B. (1981). *The Ecology of a City and its People: The Case of Hong Kong*. Australian National University Press, Canberra.

Bristow, D., and Kennedy, C.A. (2015). Why Do Cities Grow? Insights from Non-equilibrium Thermodynamics at the Urban and Global Scales, *Journal of Industrial Ecology*, 19(2): 211–221.

Browne, D., O'Regan, B., and Moles, R. (2009). Assessment of Total Urban Metabolism and Metabolic Inefficiency in an Irish City-Region. *Waste Management*, 29(10): 2765–2771.

Castán Broto, V., Allen, A., and Rapoport, E. (2012). Interdisciplinary Perspectives on Urban Metabolism. *Journal of Industrial Ecology*, 16(6): 851–861.

Chakraborty, L.B., Sahakian, M., Rani, U., Shenoy, M., and Erkman, S. (2016). Urban Food Consumption in Metro Manila: Interdisciplinary Approaches Towards Apprehending Practices, Patterns, and Impacts. *Journal of Industrial Ecology*, 20(3): 559–570.

Chávez, A. (2017). Key Drivers and Future Trends of Urban Carbon Emissions, in S. Dhakal and M. Ruth (eds.), *Creating Low Carbon Cities*. Cham: Springer.

Chávez, A., and Ramaswami, A. (2013). Articulating A Trans-Boundary Infrastructure Supply Chain Greenhouse Gas Emission Footprint for Cities: Mathematical Relationships and Policy Relevance. *Energy Policy*, 54: 376–384.

Chávez, A., Ramaswami, A., Dwarakanath, N., Ranjan, R., and Kumar, E. (2012). Implementing Trans-Boundary Infrastructure-Based Greenhouse Gas Accounting for Delhi, India: Data Availability and Methods. *Journal of Industrial Ecology*, 16(6): 814–828.

Chen, S.Q., Chen, B., Fath, B.D. (2014). Urban Ecosystem Modeling and Global Change: Potential for Rational Urban Management and Emissions Mitigation. *Environmental Pollution*, 190:139–149.

Chen, S.Q., and Chen B. (2016). Urban Energy-Water Nexus: A Network Perspective. *Applied Energy*, 184: 905–914.

Chen, S.Q., and Chen, B. (2015). Urban Energy Consumption: Different Insights from Energy Flow Analysis, Input-Output Analysis and Ecological Network Analysis. *Applied Energy*, 138: 99–107.

Chen, S.Q., Chen, B., and Su M.R. (2015). Non-Zero-Sum Relationships in Mitigating Urban Carbon Emissions: A Dynamic Network Simulation. *Environmental Science & Technology*, 2015; 49 (19): 11594–11603.

Chertow, M., J. Zhu, and V. Moye. (2016). Positive Externalities in the Urban Boundary: the Case of Industrial Symbiosis. In K. Seto, W. Solecki, and C. Griffith, (eds.) *Handbook on Urbanization and Global Environmental Change*. London: Routledge International Handbooks.

Chester, M., Pincetl, S., and Allenby, B. (2012). Avoiding Unintended Tradeoffs by Integrating Life-Cycle Impact Assessment with Urban Metabolism. *Environmental Sustainability*, 4: 451–457.

Cui, S., Xu, S., Huang, W., Bai, X., Huang, Y., and Li, G. (2015). Changing urban Phosphorus Metabolism: Evidence from Longyan City, China. *Science of The Total Environment*, 536, 924–932.

Duvigneaud, P., and Denaeyer-De Smet, S. (1977). L'Ecosystéme Urbs, in L'Ecosystéme Urbain Bruxellois, in Productivité en Belgique. In Duvigneaud, P., Kestemont, P. (eds.), *Traveaux de la Section Belge du Programme Biologique International*, Belgium: Duculot-Gembloux, pp. 581–597.

EEA (2015) Indicators – Primary energy consumption by fuel. Available at www.eea.europa.eu/data-and-maps/indicators/primary-energy-consumption-by-fuel-6/assessment.

Fath, B.D., and Patten, B.C. (1999). Review of the Foundations of Network Environ Analysis. *Ecosystems*, 2: 167–179.

Fernández, J.E. (2007) Resource Consumption of New Urban Construction in China. *Journal of Industrial Ecology* 11: 99–115.

Ferrão, P., and Fernández, J.E. (2013). *Sustainable Urban Metabolism*. Cambridge: MIT Press.

Finn, J.T. (1976). Measures of Ecosystem Structure and Function Derived from Analysis of Flows. *Journal of Theoretical Biology*, 56: 363–380.

GEA (2012). Urban Energy Systems. in T.B. Johansson, A. Patwardhan, N. Nakicenovic, and L. Gomez-Echeverri (eds). *Global Energy Assessment: Toward a Sustainable Future*. Cambridge, UK and New York, NY: Cambridge University Press, pp, 1307–1400.

Gierlinger, S., and Krausmann, F. (2012). The Physical Economy of the United States of America: Extraction, Trade and Consumption of Materials from 1870 to 2005. *Journal of Industrial Ecology*, 16 (1): 365–377.

Giljum, S. (2004). Trade, Materials Flows, and Economic Development in the South: The Example of Chile. *Journal of Industrial Ecology*, 8(1–2): 241–261.

Girardet, H., (1992). *The Gaia Atlas of Cities*. London: Gaia Books Limited.

Gonzalez-Martinez, A.C., and Schandl, H. (2008). The Biophysical Perspective of a Middle Income Economy: Material Flows in Mexico. *Ecological Economics*, 68: 317–327.

Haas, W. and Krausmann, F. (2015). Rural Metabolism: Material flows in an Austrian village in 1830 and 2001. Institute of Social Ecology, Social Ecology Working Paper 155, Vienna.

Hanya, T., and Ambe, Y., (1976). A Study on the Metabolism of Cities, in *Science for a Better Environment*. Tokyo: HSEC, Science Council of Japan, pp. 228–233.

Holmes, T., and Pincetl, S. (2012). *Urban Metabolism Literature Review*. Berkeley: UCLA Institute of the Environment – Center for Sustainable Urban Systems.

Hu, D., You, F., Zhao, Y., Yuan, Y., Liu, T., Cao, A., et al.s (2010). Input, Stocks and Output Flows of Urban Residential Building System in Beijing city, China from 1949 to 2008. *Resources, Conservation and Recycling*, 54(12): 1177–1188.

ICLEI. (2016). The Global Protocol for Community-Scale Greenhouse Gas Emission Inventories (GPC). Available at www.iclei.org/our-activities/our-agendas/low-carbon-city/gpc.html.

Katehi, L. et al. (2016). "Pathways to Urban Sustainability: Challenges and Opportunities for the United States", The National Academies Press – Washington, DC. DOI: https://doi.org/10.17226/23551.

Kennedy, C. (2012). A Mathematical Model of Urban Metabolism, in M.P. Weinstein and R.E. Turner (eds.), *Sustainability Science: The Emerging Paradigm and the Urban Environment*. London: Springer, pp. 275–292.

Kennedy, C., Steinberger, J., Gasson, B., Hillman, T., Havránek, M., Hansen, Y., et al. (2009). Greenhouse Gas Emissions from Global Cities. *Environmental Science and Technology*, 43: 7297–7302.

Kennedy, C., Steinberger, J., Gasson, B., Hillman, T., Havránek, M., Hansen, Y., et al. (2010). Methodology for Inventorying Greenhouse Gas Emissions from Global Cities. *Energy Policy*, 37(9): 4828–4837.

Kennedy, C.A. and Hoornweg, D. (2012). Mainstreaming Urban Metabolism. *Journal of Industrial Ecology*, 16(6): 780–782.

Kennedy, C.A. Pincetl, S. and Bunje, P. (2011). The Study of Urban Metabolism and Its Applications to Urban Planning and Design. *Journal of Environmental Pollution*, 159 (8–9): 1965–1973.

Kennedy, C.A., Cuddihy, J. and Engel Yan, J. (2007). The Changing Metabolism of Cities, *Journal of Industrial Ecology*, 11(2): 43–59.

Kennedy, C.A., I. Stewart, A. Facchini, I. Cersosimo, R. Mele, B. Chen, et al. (2015). Energy and Material Flows of Megacities, *Proceedings of the National Academy of Sciences*, 112 (19): 5985–5990.

Kennedy, C.A., (2015). Industrial Ecology and Cities, in R. Clift and A. Druckman (eds.), *Taking Stock of Industrial Ecology*. Berlin: Springer-Verlag, pp. 69–86

Krausmann, F., Gingrich, S., Eisenmenger, N., Erb, K-H., Haberl, H., and Fischer-Kowalski, M. (2009). Growth in global material use, GDP and population during the 20th century. *Ecological Economics*, 68: 2696–2705.

Krausmann, F., Gingrich, S., and Nourbakhch-Sabet, R. (2011). The Metabolic Transition in Japan: A Material Flow Account for the Period From 1878 to 2005. *Journal of Industrial Ecology*, 15(6): 877–892.

Leontief, W.W. (1951). *The Structure of American Economy, 1919–1939: An Empirical Application of Equilibrium analysis*. New York: Oxford University Press.

Li, G. L., Bai, X., Yu, S., Zhang, H., and Zhu, Y.G. (2012). Urban Phosphorus Metabolism through Food Consumption. *Journal of Industrial Ecology*, 16(4): 588–599.

Lin, T., Yu, Y., Bai, X., Feng, L., and Wang, J. (2013). Greenhouse Gas Emissions Accounting of Urban Residential Consumption: A Household Survey Based Approach. *PloS one*, 8(2): e55642.

Lin, T., Wang, J., Bai, X., Zhang, G., Li, X., Ge, R. and Ye, H. (2016). Quantifying and Managing Food-Sourced Nutrient Metabolism in Chinese Cities. *Environment International*, 94: 388–395.

Liu, G.Y., Yang, Z.F., Chen, B., and Zhang, Y. (2011). Ecological Network Determination of Sectoral Linkages, Utility Relations and Structural Characteristics on Urban Ecological Economic System. *Ecological Modelling* 222: 2825–2834.

Magnier, M. (2016). As Growth Slows, China Highlights Transition From Manufacturing to Service. *The Wall Street Journal, January* 19, 2016.

Metson, G.S., Iwaniec, D.M., Baker, L.A., Bennett, E.M., Childers, D.L., Cordell, D., et al. (2015). Urban Phosphorus Sustainability: Systemically Incorporating Social, Ecological, and Technological Factors into Phosphorus Flow Analysis. *Environmental Science & Policy*, 47: 1–11.

Müller, D.B., Lui, G., Løvik, A.N., Modaresi, R., Pauliuk, S., Steinhoff, F.S. and Brattebø, H. (2013). Carbon Emissions of Infrastructure Development. *Environmental Science and Technology*, 47 (20): 11739–11746.

NBSC. (2016). China Statistical Yearbook 2014. China's National Bureau of Statistics. Available at www.stats.gov.cn/tjsj/ndsj/2014/indexee.htm.

Newcombe, K., Kalma, J., Aston, A. (1978). The Metabolism of a City: The Case of Hong Kong. *Ambio* 7: 3–15.

Newell, J.P. and Cousins, J.J. (2014). The Boundaries of Urban Metabolism: Towards a Political–Industrial Ecology. *Progress in Human Geography*, 39(6): 702–728.

Newman, P. (1999). Sustainability and Cities: Extending the Metabolism Model. *Landscape and Urban Planning*, 44: 219–226.

Niza S., Rosado L. and Ferrão, P. (2009). Urban Metabolism: Methodological advances in Urban Material Flow Accounting Based on the Lisbon Case Study. *Journal of Industrial Ecology*, (13 – 3): 384–405.

Nnorom, I.C. and Osibanjo, O. (2008). Electronic Waste: Material Flows and Management Practices in Nigeria. *Waste Management*, 28: 1472–1479.

OECD/IEA (2014). *Energy Balance of OECD Countries*. Paris: International Energy Agency.

OECD/IEA (2015). *World Energy Outlook*. Paris: International Energy Agency.

Baccini, P., and Oswald, F. (2008) Designing the Urban: Linking Physiology and Morphology, in Hadorn, G.H. et al. (eds.) *Handbook of Transdisciplinary Research*. Dordrecht: Springer.

Patten, B.C. (1978). Systems Approach to the Concept of Environment. *The Ohio Journal of Science* 78: 206–222.

Pichler, P.P., Zwickel, T., Chávez, A., Kretschmer, T., Seddon, J., and Weisz, H. (2017). Reducing Urban Greenhouse Gas Footprints. *Nature, Scientific Reports*, 7: 14659.

Pincetl, S., Bunje, P., and Holmes, T. (2012) An Expanded Urban Metabolism Method: Towards a Systems Approach for Assessing the Urban Energy Processes and Causes. *Landscape and Urban Planning* 107: 193–202.

Ramaswami, A., Chávez, A., and Chertow, M. (2012). Carbon Footprinting of Cities and Implications for Analysis of Urban Material and Energy Flows. *Journal of Industrial Ecology*, 16 (6): 783–785.

Ramaswami, A. and Chávez, A. (2013). What Metrics Best Reflect the Energy and Carbon Intensity of Cities? Insights from Theory and Modeling of 20 US Cities. *Environmental Research Letters*, 8(3): 1–11.

Russi, D., Gonzalez-Martinez, A.C., Silva-Macher, J.C., Giljum, S., Martínez-Allier, J., and Vallejo, M.C. (2008). Material Flos in Latin America: A Comparative Analysis of Chile, Ecuador, Mexico, and Peru, 1980–2000. *Journal of Industrial Ecology*, 12(5/6): 704–720.

Saldivar-Sali, A. (2010). A Global Typology Of Cities: Classification Tree Analysis of Urban Resource Consumption. Master's Thesis. Massachusettes Institute of Technology (MIT).

Schaffartzik, A., Mayer, A., Gingrich, S., Eisenmenger, N., Loy, C., and Krausmann, F. (2014). The Global Metabolic Transition: Regional Patterns and Trends of Global Material Flows, 1950–2010. *Global Environmental Change*, 26: 87–97.

Schilling, J., and Logan, J. (2008). Greening the Rust Belt. *Journal of the American Planning Association*, 74 (4): 451–466.

Smil, V. (2014). *Making the Modern World: Materials and Dematerialisation*. Wiley: West Sussex.

Smith, P., and Morrison, W.I. (2006). *Simulating the Urban Economy: Experiments with Input-Output Techniques*. New York: Routledge.

Tanikawa, H., and Hashimoto, S. (2009). Urban Stock Over Time: Spatial Material Stock Analysis Using 4d-GIS. *Building Research & Information*, 37(5–6): 483–502.

UCCRN (2016). Urban Energy Supply Sector: Challenges and Opportunities for Low-Carbon, Resilient and Just Cities. Chapter 8 in *Climate Change and Cities: Second Assessment Report of the Urban Climate Change Research Network (ARC3-2)*.

UNEP (2012). Global Initiative for Resource Efficient Cities: Engine to Sustainability. UNECE Green Economy Seminar, September 26, Soraya Smaoun.

UNDESA (2014). World Urbanization Prospects. http://esa.un.org/unpd/wup.

UNEP. (2016). *Global Material Flows and Resource Productivity*. An Assessment Study of the UNEP International Resource Panel. H. Schandl, M. Fischer-Kowalski, J. West, S. Giljum, M. Dittrich, N. Eisenmenger, et al. Paris, United Nations Environment Programme.

UNFCCC. (2014). Parties and Observers. United Nations Framework Convention on Climate Change. http://unfccc.int/parties_and_observers/items/2704.php.

Weisz, H., Krausmann, F., Amann, C., Eisenmenger, N., Erb, K-H., Hubacek, K., and Fischer-Kowalski, M. (2006). The Physical Economy of the European Union: Cross-Country Comparison and Determinants of Material Consumption. *Ecological Economics*, 58: 676–698.

Weisz, H., and Steinberger, J.K. (2010). Reducing Energy and Material Flows in Cities. *Current Opinion in Environmental Sustainability*, 2: 185–192.

Wiedmann, T.O., Schandl, H., Lenzen, M., Moran, D., Suh, S., West, J., and Kanemoto, K. (2015). The Material Footprint of Nations. *Proceedings of the National Academy of Sciences* 112: 6271–6276.

Wolman, A. (1965). The Metabolism of Cities. *Scientific American* 213(3): 179–190.

You, F., Hu, D., Zhang, H., Guo, Z., Zhao, Y., Wang, B., and Yuan, Y. (2011). Carbon Emissions in the Life Cycle of Urban Building System in China – A Case Study of Residential Buildings. *Ecological Complexity*, 8(2): 201–212.

Zhang, Y. (2013). Urban Metabolism: A Review of Research Methodologies. *Environmental Pollution*. 178: 463–473.

Zhang, Y., and Yang, Z. (2007). Eco-Efficiency of Urban Material Metabolism: A Case Study in Shenzhen, China. *Acta Ecologica Sinica*. 27 (8): 3124–3131.

Zhang, Y., Yang, Z.F., and Fath, B.D. (2010). Ecological Network Analysis of an Urban Water Metabolic System: Model Development, and a Case Study for Beijing. *Science of The Total Environment*, 408: 4702–4711.

Chapter 4: Live with Risk While Reducing Vulnerability

Patricia Romero-Lankao, Olga Wilhelmi, and Mikhail Chester

4.1 Introduction

Urban areas can play a key role in the transformation that is required in humankind's ways of understanding and responding to climate and sustainability challenges. These new ways, however, will require bringing together urban planners, social scientists, business leaders, engineers, and other diverse knowledge and power domains – an undertaking that creates its own set of seemingly intractable complications. As documented by scholars studying diverse fields of human endeavor, from scientific inquiry to governmental planning and private or public sector construction of infrastructure, one of the most difficult problems in creating change lies in moving people beyond the mental models, ways of knowing, tools, and analytical systems they learn during their academic training and professionalization.

Scholarship on urban risk and vulnerability offers an example of this trend. While research on risk and vulnerability has grown considerably in recent years, it has consisted primarily of case studies based on the assumption that both risk and vulnerability depend on context. Often, scholars and practitioners offer conflicting theories and conceptualizations that tend to shed light only on certain aspects of the problem, while other areas remain in the dark. This trend has implications for politics, equity, and sustainability. For instance, the vast majority of epidemiological studies on health risks from heat waves quantify the relationship between heat waves and health outcomes, while controlling for age and other factors. However, these studies omit underlying historical processes of sociospatial segregation (such as land-use development) that explain urban populations' differentiated access to green areas, air conditioning, health services, and other assets and options – and thus, their differentiated exposure to temperature, capacity to adapt to heat stress, and ability to mitigate heat risks. The development of approaches that can explain these differences may help us move towards cohesive and policy-relevant narratives.

This chapter starts with a brief discussion of existing definitions and approaches to the interactions between urbanization, urban risk, and vulnerability. We outline the necessary components of an interdisciplinary understanding of how environmental and societal processes, such as global warming and urbanization, contribute to intra- and interurban inequalities in vulnerability to heat waves, floods, droughts, and other climatic hazards. We highlight some of the mechanisms by which vulnerability and risk are shaped by the dynamics of urbanization, acting on urban centers as places with unique social and environmental histories, opportunities, and constraints. We close with some remarks on ways forward for reducing risk and enhancing populations' capacity, within and across urban areas, to deal with risk.

4.2 Conceptualizing Urbanization, Urban Vulnerability, and Risk

Before exploring the influence of urbanization and urban areas on risk, we will briefly consider the conceptualizations of "urbanization," "urban," and "risk." Urbanization dynamics and the urban areas they produce are altering forests, open spaces, agricultural lands, wildlife, energy, food, and water resources and, consequently, are altering risks in complex and accelerating ways. These changes not only threaten the quality of life that urban and rural residents have come to expect, but they also offer opportunities for innovative risk mitigation and adaptation options. Urban-regional infrastructure systems that facilitate critical services, such as the delivery of water and energy and the provision of mobility and shelter, have enabled the growth of urban areas, populations, and activities, but have often resulted in detrimental environmental impacts.

4.2.1 Urbanization and the Environment

Determining the impacts caused by urban areas is difficult, as little agreement exists about the definition of urbanization and urban areas (Marcotullio et al. 2014). We define "urbanization" as a series of interconnected development processes or dynamics that shift how humans interact with each other and the environment to create risks (Romero–Lankao et al. 2014b). These processes include:

- Particularly in middle- and low-income countries, an increasing number of people living in urban areas;

- Processes of stabilization and even population shrinkage related to post-industrialization and deindustrialization, particularly in high-income countries;

- Changes in lifestyles and cultures (living on coasts, for example) that motivate people to live in hazard-prone areas;

- Economic shifts from primary activities, such as agriculture, to manufacturing and services, which compete for access to water, land, and ecosystem services;

- Changes in the patterns of land use of urban areas and associated infrastructure that affect shifts in resource use and hazard risk;

- The ecological and physical transformations implied by these processes.

At the local level, the effects of urbanization can exacerbate the climate changes affecting urban populations. These effects, such as the urban heat island, or UHI, effect, might amplify the outcomes of global climate change (Ntelekos et al. 2010). UHI refers to increased temperatures in urban areas compared to their rural surroundings, driven by human activities and alterations of land surface characteristics and their thermal properties. The UHI effect, which varies across and within cities, often in relation to affluence and urban planning, can increase human health risks differently across the urban-rural gradient (Miao et al. 2009). These variations are mostly due to physical and socioeconomic factors, such as land cover patterns, city size, and the ratio of impervious surfaces to areas covered by vegetation or water (Grimm et al. 2008; Harlan and Ruddell 2011). Also of importance are intra-urban sociospatial inequalities in access to air conditioning and green and open space. Based on these differences, lower socioeconomic and ethnic minority groups are more likely to live in warmer neighborhoods with greater exposure to heat stress and higher vulnerability (Harlan et al. 2007). In summary, urbanization dynamics entails shifts in land use, infrastructure, economic activity, demographic structure, and lifestyle. The patterns of interactions between society and the environment have created differences in risk and vulnerability within and across urban areas.

4.2.2 Urban Areas

Notwithstanding the importance of urban areas, scholars and communities of practice disagree about what defines urban areas. Some define urban areas as a specific form of human association or settlement that can be characterized based on criteria of population size, physical form, and economic function. Others define cities as growth machines that tend elite interests, induce social inequality and injustice, and deteriorate the environment. Yet, others conceive of cities as socioecological systems (or SES) of interacting biophysical and socioeconomic components whose dynamic organization and management have many consequences for sustainability and resilience. As such, urban areas shape the level of environmental pressure populations exert on ecosystems and their natural resource base, and shape the vulnerability of urban populations to climatic and environmental hazards. Recent scholarship has pointed to the relevance of urban infrastructure as the sociotechnical system defining the material – and mostly unsustainable – metabolism of city regions (Monstadt 2009; Smith and Stirling 2010; McFarlane and Rutherford 2008). Metabolism refers to the flows of materials and energy through cities and regions (see Chapter 3). Infrastructure is a physical manifestation of metabolism and is deeply embedded in societal and political imaginations of how a city shall function. As infrastructure has become increasingly complex in terms of physical interconnectedness and the institutions and rules that govern it, the mechanisms by which we can significantly transform infrastructure to make it more sustainable have become less clear.

However, while the SES concept is useful, it is too abstract to yield an operational understanding of lower level system urban interactions. Therefore, we suggest a definition of "urban areas" as socioecological systems (Folke et al. 2005; Ostrom et al. 2007), with five dynamic development domains: sociodemographic, economic, technological, ecological, and governance (SETEG) (Arup 2014; Romero-Lankao and Gnatz 2016). These development domains reflect processes of change affecting risk and people's vulnerabilities. The sociodemographic domain includes a set of factors conditioning people's preferences for living in risk-prone areas based on lifestyles (including the aesthetic desirability of location); on social practices of living, commuting, or eating; or on lack of options. The economic domain shapes differences in wealth creation and inequality in access to assets and options (such as insurance) to respond to floods, water scarcity, and other hazards. The technological domain involves knowledge of techniques, processes, and so forth that can be embedded in machines, infrastructures, and the built environment, and can shape risk of environmental impacts, such as those that arise from lack of green areas to mitigate risks from floods and heat waves. Technology also offers options to retrofit or introduce "green" infrastructure or hazard protection measures, or to improve house quality and design in order to keep people protected (see Section 4.3 and Figure 4.1). The ecological domain, defined by such factors as topography, temperature, and precipitation, affects an urban area's endowment of natural resources, ecosystem services, susceptibility to and capacity to mitigate droughts, floods, and heat waves. The governance domain affects patterns of urban growth, land-use regulations, and proactive or reactive risk mitigation and adaptation responses.

Figure 4.1 A flooded house in Mexico City. Floods are major contributors to infrastructure and housing damage among poor populations in cities. Source: Patricia Romero-Lankao et al. 2014a.

4.2.3 Urban Vulnerability and Resilience

Human experience of the environment in terms of risks and threats constitutes a key theoretical foundation of vulnerability research (Blaikie et al. 2014). Studies on urban vulnerability portray it as the degree to which a city, a population, infrastructure, or an economic sector (that is, a system of concern) is susceptible to and unable to cope with and adapt to the adverse effects of hazards or stresses, such as heat waves, storms, and political instability (Field et al. 2012). Urban vulnerability is a relational concept. Besides referring to a system or group sensitivity to heat waves, floods, and other hazards, it is also a relative property defining the capacity of that system or group to adapt to and cope with those hazards.

Vulnerability is a function of exposure, sensitivity, and capacity (Adger 2006; Field et al. 2014). "Exposure" is the presence of populations, infrastructure, or economic, social, or cultural assets in places that could be adversely affected. "Sensitivity" refers to factors, such as age or preexisting medical conditions that determine susceptibility to hazards. "Capacity" is the potential of a population or a system to modify its features and behavior to respond to existing and anticipated hazards. Capacity relates to the unequally distributed pool of resources, assets, and options that governmental, private, and nongovernmental urban actors can draw on to manage environmental risks, while pursuing the lives and development goals they value. In a study of urban heat waves, for example, Wilhelmi and Hayden (2010) adopted this definition and proposed a people- and place-based vulnerability framework. This framework integrates quantitative and qualitative data and focuses on social and behavioral elements of capacity, including social networks, knowledge, attitude, and practices; household resources; and access to existing risk reduction programs.

For the most part, scholarship on urban vulnerability consists primarily of case studies and analyses based on incompatible theories and paradigms that can be grouped in three traditions: "vulnerability as impact" or top-down (the most commonly applied approach); "inherent or contextual vulnerability"; and "urban resilience"(Patricia Romero-Lankao and Qin 2011).

"Vulnerability as impact" scholars conceive population vulnerability as an outcome (for example, a health impact or property damage) from exposure to heat waves, floods, and other hazards (O'Neill 2005). Thanks to this body of research, we have learned that the relationship between people's exposure to extreme temperature and mortality has a *V* or *J* shape, with mortality generally increasing both above and below some temperature threshold. These scholars have also examined the role of specific individual- and city-level characteristics (such as green areas) in modifying the temperature-mortality relationship. Furthermore, through epidemiological studies, we are able to state with some confidence that the elderly and people with preexisting medical conditions are particularly sensitive to extreme heat, and that higher levels of education in a population are associated with decreased risk of mortality. However, by looking at populations at the city level, urban vulnerability as impact studies fail to encompass intra-urban inequalities. For example, they do not examine what specific populations and places are at risk, to what they are vulnerable, and how and why they are differentially affected; whether they possess necessary skills, awareness, and assets to be able to adapt; and how their choices are constrained by the sociodemographic, economic, technological, ecological, and governance domains in which they operate.

The above questions *are* addressed by "inherent or contextual vulnerability" scholars, who examine the influence of historical patterns of sociospatial segregation on differences in populations' capacity to draw on income, education, social networks, and other resources to respond to hazards and to mitigate risk. Earlier approaches, rooted in geography, natural hazards, and livelihoods research, had already pointed out that hazards disproportionately affect poor and marginalized populations and those living in hazard-prone geographic areas (Moser 1998; Burton 1993; Hewitt 1983). Contextual studies shed light on the role of equity and affluence, the two faces of the urban development coin; on the capacity of upper income, privileged populations to live in lower density, greener, and cooler neighborhoods and, hence, to be more able to adapt to extreme heat, floods, and other hazards (Harlan et al. 2007). Structural disadvantages at the neighborhood level, such as concentrated affluence, formality, or commercial vitality, play a fundamental role in health and quality of life outcomes, such as heat wave mortality; fires from illegal connections to the electricity grid; or morbidity associated with exposure to hazardous materials (Hayden et al. 2011; Qin et al. 2015). For example, a study in neighborhoods of Buenos Aires, Argentina; Bogota, Colombia; Mexico City, Mexico; and Santiago, Chile found that low-income and informal neighborhoods are more at risk because they lack high-quality housing and easy access to jobs, and have precarious electrical connections. As stated by informants in Buenos Aires,

> Most of the families are hanging from the electrical network ... and these are bad connections, and the houses are made of wood and are very precarious. We have had several fires. Yes, in those cases we've had evacuees here" (Respondent from the Caritas NGO working in San Fernando, Buenos Aires). (Romero-Lankao et al. 2014a)

More integrative analytical approaches have emerged in recent years. The natural hazards and human ecology approaches to societal vulnerability have been increasingly expanded to include the concepts of complex human-natural system resilience to climate change (Hewitt 1983). Other approaches expanded the concepts of physical and place-based vulnerability to social factors, especially those related to coping and adaptive capacities, institutions, and governance systems (Adger 2006; Turner 2010; Romero-Lankao and Qin 2011). "Urban resilience" offers an example of integrative approaches.

While dozens of definitions of resilience exist, scholars tend to conceive of it as the ability of a system or population to absorb disruptions, persevere, self-organize, learn, and adapt. The notion of capacity is fundamental to connecting the analytic with the normative dimensions of urban resilience. This concept helps us in analyzing the unequally distributed pool of resources, assets, and options that populations and decision-makers can draw on to manage risks, while pursuing the lives and development goals they value. It also helps connect the underlying SETEG domain contexts that give rise to those resources and to explain inequalities in exposure and vulnerability. Urban resilience is related to normative and ethical principles such as the unequally distributed resources that individuals and organizations have (or potentially have) to effectively mitigate and adapt to the hazards and stresses they encounter.

Resilience has one of its two main roots in mathematics, physics, and engineering, where it is defined as the capacity of a system to "bounce back" or return to a steady-state equilibrium after such stressors as floods, political turmoil, or a banking crisis. In the second main root we find an ecological, or "bounce-forward" approach, in which resilience is defined according to how much disturbance an urban community or system can adapt to while remaining within critical thresholds, after which it can move to another regime. In this "safe-to-fail" paradigm, resilience is conceived of as the ability of cities and communities to change, adapt, and, crucially, transform in response to both internal and external hazards and pressures (Davoudi et al. 2012; Gunderson 2001; Ahern 2011).

Cities as diverse as Dhaka, Bangladesh, and Boulder, Colorado, in the United States are such examples of this capacity to bounce forward. After 1991, when a hurricane hit Bangladesh, killing at least 138,000 people and leaving 10 million people homeless, people undertook efforts – promoted by local authorities, the national government, and international organizations – to decrease the risks faced from tropical cyclones. These efforts included the development of an early warning system and the construction of public shelters to host evacuees; Cyclone Sidr, which hit Bangladesh in 2007, subsequently tested these infrastructural developments. Although between 8 and 10 million Bangladeshis were exposed to Sidr – perhaps the strongest cyclone to hit the country since 1991 – there were approximately 32 times fewer deaths (4,234 people lost compared to approximately 138,000), illustrating Bangladesh's capacity to learn and adapt (UN-Habitat 2011).

The unprecedented flood of September 11–18, 2013, in Boulder, Colorado – which killed 10 people, resulted in 18,000 evacuees, and caused the destruction of 688 homes, and damages to an additional 9,900 homes – brought into sight many of the interdependencies between urban risk and resilience (MacClune et al. 2014). Although Boulder was exposed to a flood estimated to be between a 25-year and 100-year magnitude (that is, a flood big enough to occur only once every 25 or 100 years), the city's Greenways Program allowed green areas to mitigate flood damage. Impact damages were also conditioned on historic development pathways and social, political, and economic factors. Apartments impacted by sewage upwelling, for instance, had been below-grade and frequently were occupied by lower-income families and university students. Although Boulder's utility staff was aware of the need to upgrade the sewage drainage system, the cost of such an improvement was prohibitively high. Combined with a fear of potential litigation, these factors led the city to either inaction or minimal action, which increased citywide vulnerability to the floods. Six out of seven key roads that follow creeks up mountain canyons in Boulder failed, leaving affected populations isolated and unable to leave flood-damaged areas. Yet, even amidst the near chaos and extensive damages wrought by the flood, strong preexisting relationships and a culture of cooperation among city and county governmental and nongovernmental actors were key assets that sped up response and enabled effective recovery through learning from previous experiences, such as the Four Mile Fire of 2010.

4.3 A System Approach to Risk

In recent years, scholars and practitioners have focused on the interface of urban areas and risk – how urban populations and actors from the private, public, and social sectors, including the institutions and infrastructure they create, affect the environment – and vice versa, encompassing how environmental impacts feedback and affect the social fabric of a city. To understand the risks and the challenges that cities face in reducing them, we need a system analysis of the interactions between multiple development and environmental domains. Yet, when it comes to understanding risk in cities, there is comparatively less knowledge about the interactions between the different SETEG domains shaping risks.

The concept of risk is characterized by differences in definition and scope (Renn 2008). Risk can be defined, for example, as the probability of occurrence of a hazard, such as a flood or landslide, multiplied by the consequences if the event occurs (Field et al. 2014). We define "urban risk" as the potential for uncertain outcomes, such as economic loss and mortality, where something of value such as lives, livelihoods, or property is at stake. Risk results from the interaction of the vulnerability and exposure of populations, assets, and economic activities to hazards, such as floods and heat waves (Figure 4.2). Urban populations are frequently exposed to multiple hazards. These hazards can be one-offs, extreme events of short duration – such as storms or landslides – often striking with little warning. They can also be slow-onset events (such as century-long increases in urban average temperatures), as well as a range of subtle, everyday threats that are the product of a variety of factors (for example, UHI). Hazards can result from broader drivers, such as climate change and climate variability (including sea-level rise and weather extremes), from regional environmental degradation (mudslides resulting from land-use changes induced by urbanization, for instance), and from broader social changes such as globalization, urbanization, and political turmoil that affect the well-being, wealth, and feasibility of urban populations' livelihoods (Figure 4.2).

While the majority of place-based studies focus on the links between urbanization and hazard exposure, or examine the interactions between exposure and sensitivity, fewer studies explicitly characterize or analyze the capacity of the affected populations to perceive and adapt to hazards (Morss et al. 2005; Hayden et al. 2011; Romero-Lankao et al. 2016). Scholarship suggests that there is a clear value of deepening analysis of capacity, which needs to be complemented by a wider understanding of how adaptive behavior and practices are likely to be socially and institutionally structured, and economically constrained and modified over time (Few 2012).

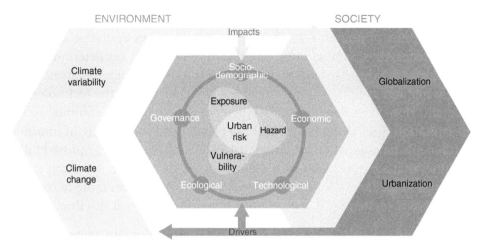

Figure 4.2 Urban risk. This conceptual diagram shows urban risk not only as a result of hazard exposure and vulnerability, but also as shaped by five interacting development domains: sociodemographic, economic, technological, ecological, and governance. These domains operate within a wider context of interactions between environment and society. Source: Romero-Lankao and Gnatz 2016 modified after Field et al. 2012. Design Jerker Lokrantz/Azote.

4.3.1 The Multiple Domains of Urban Risk

Understanding urban risk requires analyzing the complex, context-specific, and nuanced interactions between sociodemographic, economic, technological, ecological, and governance domains shaping hazard, exposure, and vulnerability (Figure 4.2).

Sociodemographic: There is increasing evidence that a population's capacity to mitigate and adapt to risks is not strictly an artifact of its intrinsic individual factors, such as age or preexisting medical conditions. Structural dynamics of the sociodemographic domain, such as the younger or older age population balance of cities, which is related to shifts to service-oriented economies, can make certain populations more sensitive to particular hazards, with the elderly being more sensitive to extreme temperatures. Because women experience unequal access to assets and decision-making processes, and are most often responsible for household needs, women can be more exposed and vulnerable to such hazards as indoor pollution.

Economic: Citywide economic vigor and advantages may enhance the effectiveness of urban safety nets by determining the city's capacity to respond to risks through avenues such as charitable organizations, churches, businesses, social services, and more formal social networks (Browning et al. 2006). Beyond that, in cities around the world, the dynamics of uneven economic growth shapes social inequality, thus influencing all dimensions of risk and urban populations' vulnerabilities. These dynamics create and perpetuate

the relative differences in vulnerability between poor and wealthy populations. Because of uneven economic development, cities as diverse as Mexico
City, Buenos Aires, Santiago, and Mumbai have deficits in key determinants of
capacity, such as health services and education, as well as high-quality housing
and water and sanitation infrastructure – key elements of the technological
domain. However, context-specific differences also exist. For example, access
to sanitation in Mumbai is low, with 35 percent of people living in informal
settlements having sanitation, and revolves around the use of improved toilet
facilities that are not shared with other households. In Latin American cities,
access to single-family toilets is relatively higher, and relates more to connection to sewage systems (Chatterjee 2010; Romero-Lankao et al. 2014b and 2016).

Technologic: Particularly in urban contexts, this domain materializes in
water, energy, sanitation, and other infrastructure areas that shape availability of and access to resources and services that define populations' capacities
to respond. Technology shapes response capacity because infrastructure unequally mitigates or amplifies people's resilience to climatic and non-climatic
threats. However, the mechanisms by which infrastructures unequally shape
risk are context-specific and result from economic and political processes of
investment, which privilege some technologies, sectors, and places over others.
For instance, in cities of developing countries, such as Mumbai, the proportion
of people with access to reliable electricity tends to be much higher (80.8 percent) than the proportion with access to water (61 percent) (Romero-Lankao et
al. 2016). Three reasons explain why, historically, economic compulsions led
to a fast expansion of Mumbai's electricity distribution network and not of the
water network (Zérah 2008). While public policies facilitated investments in
electricity, public investments in water and sanitation suffered from competition with other priorities. Once an electricity grid is constructed, the cost of
individual connection is marginal, while the costs of extending connections
to the water distribution network and transporting water are high. Hence, in
contrast with electricity, the spread of the water network correlates with the
spread of formal housing development. Because over half of Mumbai's population lives in informal settlements, its water distribution is also one of its most
profound expressions of social inequality and differentiated vulnerability.

Ecological or environmental: This domain refers to the biophysical, climatic, ecological, and hydrological factors (such as topography and precipitation) affecting an area's susceptibility to hazards, such as floods. New insight
into how this domain interacts with the technological to affect urban populations' ability to mitigate risk and protect themselves from hazards is emerging,
as illustrated by research on extreme heat. A number of studies have shown
that having a low income, advanced age, preexisting health conditions,
social isolation, linguistic isolation, limited access to healthcare, and working

outdoors increase an urban population's vulnerability to heat (Harlan et al. 2013; Hondula et al. 2015; O'Neill 2005). Yet, limited but increasing knowledge exists of how ecological and built environmental services can mitigate or exacerbate this vulnerability. Consider two scenarios. In the first, a vulnerable person lives in an older structure of poor heat-protective design (with low-quality insulation and inexpensive doors that absorb a large amount of incoming solar radiation, for example) and has to spend more on electricity to keep their unit running to cool the living space. In the second, the same person lives in a newer structure with modern energy codes and central air conditioning. We could hypothesize that the person in the second scenario is less vulnerable given that their residence offers protective features against the hazard. Similar hypotheses could be developed for tree shading, xeriscaping, material use, and a plethora of other factors related to ecological and built environmental services.

In Phoenix, Arizona, in the United States, we have observed that, over time, households with higher incomes have been able to afford to plant and shade their properties in a way that may reduce their vulnerability to heat (Jenerette et al. 2011). Related questions exist about the built environment. As we have mentioned, air conditioning is a critical protective measure; those without air conditioning, those who are unable to afford to use it; or those who have inefficient air conditioning may be more vulnerable to heat (Fraser et al. 2016). Yet home (private) air conditioning represents only a fraction of the heat refuge space that we experience. We spend a good deal of our day in publicly cooled spaces, whether those be our offices or shopping areas. A comparison between Los Angeles and Phoenix shows that the mixed land uses of Los Angeles, coupled with its gridded roadway network, make obtaining access to publicly cooled spaces easier than in Phoenix (Fraser et al. 2016). Additionally, the thermal characteristics of residential and nonresidential buildings can make air conditioning more costly. Thus, as buildings have gotten newer, their ability to retain cooled air for a longer period has also improved (Nahlik et al. 2016). However, it is possible that affording to live in a newer building requires one to have a relatively high income. As we advance our understanding of vulnerability to climate change, it will become more and more important to understand not only the effects of social, ecological, and technological factors, but – perhaps more importantly – how these factors interact.

Governance: This domain shapes risk inequalities through the legacies of political decisions and policies around urban land-use planning and investments in infrastructures and services; through some of the mechanisms of social exclusion (by class and race, for example); and through decisions made about where to locate energy, water, and other infrastructure networks. In many cities of low- and middle-income countries, growth of both low-income informal housing and higher-income gated communities often occurs in areas that provide ecosystem services (such as wetlands or forests providing flood protection and water infiltration) or are prone to storm surges, landslides, and floods. Still, while some forms of growth in risk-prone areas enjoy state sanction, others are criminalized. In these cases, informal status becomes both a source of stigmatization that disempowers populations living in informal neighborhoods *and* a systemic determinant of lack of access to land tenure, high-quality housing, infrastructure, services, and other assets and options to mitigate risks and/or to adapt (Box 4.1) (Roy 2009).

Box 4.1 Informality, risk, and vulnerability

In urban areas of middle- and low-income countries, large sections of the population work within the informal economy or are living in housing that was constructed informally. As such, they face the possibility that governments may forcibly remove them from sites deemed to be vulnerable to risks – and away from their means of livelihood. They may also be moved simply because other actors want the land they occupy for more profitable uses. Informality is a state of regulatory flux, where land ownership, land use and purpose, access to livelihood options, job security, and social security cannot be fixed and mapped according to any prearranged sets of laws, planning instruments, or regulations (Roy 2009; McFarlane 2012). This leads to an ever-shifting relationship between the legal and the illegal, the legitimate and the illegitimate, and the authorized and the unauthorized. Informality can create advantages and disadvantages along lines of sociospatial stratification. For instance, informality becomes the site of considerable state power when some forms of growth in risk-prone areas enjoy state sanction while others are unauthorized and criminalized. Informal status becomes a systemic determinant of lack of access to assets and options to mitigate risks and/or to adapt. Conversely, the regular, legal, or formal status of a source of livelihood, neighborhood, and/or settlement provides security from eviction; formal recognition becomes an incentive to invest in more structural adaptation actions (such as house improvements to effectively prevent fires and respond to floods). Obtaining formal status not only is a requirement for infrastructure and service provision for urban populations, but also helps to prevent stigmatization and disempowerment. Studies of informal settlements in Buenos Aires found that their residents tended to be stigmatized. As suggested by a respondent in Greater Buenos Aires: "There were times that services would not come in the neighborhood because it was considered a red (dangerous, insecure) zone" (Romero-Lankao et al. 2014a: 5). This study documented that similar arguments are frequently offered as reasons not to provide services in Bogota, Colombia; Mexico City, Mexico; Mumbai, India; and Santiago, Chile (Romero-Lankao et al. 2014a).

4.3.2 The Relevance of Scale

Urban risk depends on scale. Hazards and adaptation capacities, and their domains and drivers, vary through time and across households, neighborhoods, and city regions (Figure 4.3). For example, a family with a two-level house may only have enough economic resources to move its belongings to the upper part of the house when faced with a flood (as happens in many coastal cities, such as Mumbai and Buenos Aires). This action, however, is not as effective a long-term response at the city and region levels as the construction of flood protection infrastructure, or the implementation of urban policies that strengthen the asset base of low-income groups, can be.

While we need citywide studies to compare patterns and differences in risk and vulnerability across urban areas, they can obfuscate the importance of understanding how variation in SETEG factors can contribute to people's vulnerability. While we are accustomed to seeing maps of variations in socio-economic conditions, such as income, ecological services and physical infra-structure can also vary significantly across a city. Consider the metropolitan

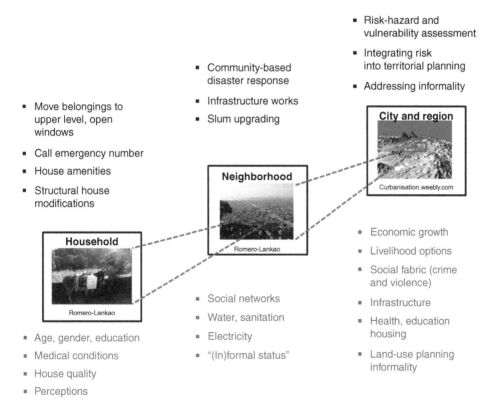

Figure 4.3 Capacity and actual responses vary across scale, that is, across a household, neighborhood, and city region. Source: Romero-Lankao et al. 2014a.

area of Phoenix, Arizona, where residential structures constructed in the middle of the twentieth century dominate the city's downtown core, while its outlying regions – largely constructed from 1990 onward – use modern energy codes and thermally preferable materials, which protect people from extreme temperatures. These examples highlight the importance of assessing vulnerability at neighborhood scales, where we can capture the largest differences in the underlying SETEG factors.

One of the challenges in understanding urban risk and vulnerability is our ability to assess spatial heterogeneity of social and environmental characteristics in a changing urban landscape. While prior research offers theoretical and methodological conceptualizations of vulnerability in cities, many studies do not explicitly connect vulnerability concepts to actions we can take to reduce vulnerability to weather hazards and to improve overall quality of life. Observing, mapping, and modeling human behavior, social practices, and decision-making in the context of climatic and meteorological hazards are intricate research problems. Whether people take protective measures during a hurricane event such as evacuating, or alter daily routines or go to air conditioned places, to prevent heat-related illnesses, action is influenced by a combination of individual characteristics and capacities, such as risk perception, social capital, and access to resources – which vary across space and over time (Riad et al. 1999).

Determining the differential vulnerabilities and adaptive capacities at a neighborhood to household level is essential to reducing negative outcomes from hazards (Morss et al. 2011). Smit and Wandel (2006: 282) note that "in the climate change field, adaptations can be considered as local or community-based adjustments to deal with changing conditions within the constraints of the broader economic-social political arrangements." This highlights the importance of scale as internal to the system, indicating that what occurs at the household level also affects the community, which is in turn influenced by the citywide and macroscopic forces that shape the ability of individuals to adapt to or cope with challenging conditions. Previous research on extreme heat, for example, emphasizes the variability within cities, especially in terms of differences among households and communities, on adaptive capacity (Uejio et al. 2011; Harlan et al. 2013). At the individual level, factors such as advanced or very young age, preexisting medical conditions, and disability contribute to higher vulnerability, while exposure and capacity vary among neighborhoods. In Indian and Latin American cities, researchers have found that low-income neighborhoods have relatively more precarious working, housing, and living conditions than in middle-income neighborhoods, and inhabitants still rely on neighbors and family to respond to disruptions. Households in higher-income neighborhoods are able to move beyond coping to undertaking structural building modifications to withstand floods and extreme temperatures. However, it is common for a low proportion of households across socioeconomic statuses to have strong social networks on which to fall back to mitigate risks and adapt (Romero-Lankao et al. 2014a; Romero-Lankao et al. 2016).

Vulnerability studies also highlight the importance of sociodemographic factors such as social practices, perceptions, and behavior at an individual or household scale (Hayden et al. 2011; Morss et al. 2005; Qin et al. 2015). Knowledge, attitudes, and practices (KAPs), as well as social capital, household resources, and access to community programs that reduce hazard risk, play important roles in minimizing vulnerability. For example, insofar as it relates to hurricane risk, KAP can substantially influence individual and collective responses, though the literature recognizes gaps in our knowledge about the links between perceptions and actions (Pidgeon and Butler 2009; Pidgeon and Fischhoff 2011). People rely on knowledge, media coverage, local weather patterns, and their perceptions of organizations to create their personal views of reality (Dessai and Sims 2010). Natural hazards research has examined how perception of risk is determined by prior experience, knowledge, proximity to a hazard, and demographic characteristics, (Botzen et al. 2009; Lindell and Hwang 2008), finding that prior experience may either increase *or* decrease perception of risk, depending on local context and other sociobehavioral characteristics (Riad et al. 1999). Studies of evacuation decisions after Hurricanes Hugo and Andrew concluded that a simple warning is often not enough. Instead, individuals and communities require a multifaceted and tailored approach. For example, Hayden et al. (2011) illustrate that extreme heat vulnerability is nuanced and may be offset by information that is not readily captured through demographic data, such as important social ties and reliance on neighbors for help during emergencies. These connections among households at a neighborhood level may provide a degree of protection in the event of a weather hazard.

Work in cities from low- and middle-income countries shows the nuanced ways in which socioeconomic status determines the extent to which urban populations rely on their networks and which sources of information they rely on to respond to extreme events such as floods, storm surges, and heat waves. In Mumbai, for instance, a low percentage of households relies on more formal social networks, such as political organizations). Although wealthier, more resilient households had more frequently participated in social networks as safety nets, more vulnerable household groups were more likely to fall on personal support during extreme emergencies (Romero-Lankao et al. 2016). In Latin American cities, people with higher socioeconomic status were more likely to rely on individual means, such as by searching the Internet for state-supplied hazard information, while people with lower socioeconomic status relied on neighborhood networks and personal knowledge to respond to floods, landslides, and other hazards. These varied results point to the need to understand the importance both of scale (Figure 4.3) and of context-specific combinations of vulnerability attributes at play within and across urban households and neighborhoods.

4.4 Looking Forward: Critical Pathways for Reducing Risk and Vulnerability

Research on urban vulnerability and risk has grown considerably in recent years. Still, it is characterized by differences in conceptualizations and scope. More narrowly focused studies have helped identify many of the numerous parts of the risk puzzle. However, we still lack a cohesive picture of the dynamic whole created by the interaction of these parts. Through the application of more integrated approaches and frameworks, such as the examples in this chapter, scholars and communities of practice working across traditions, disciplines, and framings might be able to create an integrative knowledge that will aid in the design and implementation of more sustainable risk mitigation and adaptation actions and policies.

Decision-makers and stakeholders involved in designing and implementing risk mitigation and adaptation actions need to consider not only the multiple local hazards to which a population is exposed, but also the set of SETEG domains that shape differentiated vulnerabilities and adaptive capacities of populations. These factors arise from household, neighborhood, and citywide processes and from the larger, countrywide social and environmental drivers that may support or undermine the capacity to respond. Both urbanization and climate change are two such large forces; they are simultaneously fueled by local conditions and the imperatives of individual lives and livelihoods, hopes for a better life, and challenges to pursuing that life. In order to understand the whole, we need to pull it apart and look at its hazard exposure, sensitivity, and capacity facets; to understand these parts, we must look back and see the whole. It is only through such iterative approaches that we may hope to understand urban vulnerability and risk.

We must recognize that cities – like people, ecosystems, infrastructure, and governing bodies – are complex. Therefore, the context-specific and dynamic interactions between the urban system SETEG domains leads to emergent behaviors that we still struggle to understand. We must recognize this complexity when developing strategies that reduce climate and environmental change risk. We need to be acknowledged that solutions that target a single system domain are likely to lead to effects in the others, including outcomes that we may not have experienced in the past. In an increasingly urban world with greater hazards ushered in by climate and environmental change, scholars, decision-makers, and communities need to bring together their knowledge systems in search of integrative and socially relevant solutions.

✿ References

Adger, W.N. 2006. Vulnerability. *Global Environmental Change* 16 (3): 268–281.

Ahern, J. 2011. From Fail-Safe to Safe-to-Fail: Sustainability and Resilience in the New Urban World. *Landscape and Urban Planning* 100 (4): 341–343.

Arup, R.P.A. 2014. Resilience – Sustainable Cities – Siemens. WCMS3PortletPage. http://w3.siemens .com/topics/global/en/sustainable-cities/resilience/Pages/home.aspx?stc=wwzcc120526.

Blaikie, P., T. Cannon, I. Davis, and B. Wisner. 2014. *At Risk: Natural Hazards, People's Vulnerability and Disasters*. Abingdon: Routledge.

Botzen, W.J.W., J.C.J.H. Aerts, and J.C.J.M. Van Den Bergh. 2009. Dependence of Flood Risk Perceptions on Socioeconomic and Objective Risk Factors. *Water Resources Research* 45 (10), DOI: 10.1029/2009WR007743

Browning, C.R., D. Wallace, S.L. Feinberg, and K.A. Cagney. 2006. Neighborhood Social Processes, Physical Conditions, and Disaster-Related Mortality: The Case of the 1995 Chicago Heat Wave. *American Sociological Review* 71 (4): 661–678.

Burton, I. 1993. *The Environment as Hazard*. New York: Guilford Press.

Chatterjee, M. 2010. Slum Dwellers' Response to Flooding Events in the Megacities of India. *Mitigation and Adaptation Strategies for Global Change* 15 (4): 337–353.

Davoudi, S., K. Shaw, L.J. Haider, A.E. Quinlan, G.D. Peterson, C. Wilkinson et al. 2012. Resilience: A Bridging Concept or a Dead End? 'Reframing' Resilience: Challenges for Planning Theory and Practice Interacting Traps: Resilience Assessment of a Pasture Management System in Northern Afghanistan Urban Resilience: What Does It Mean in Planning Practice? Resilience as a Useful Concept for Climate Change Adaptation? The Politics of Resilience for Planning: A Cautionary Note: Edited by Simin Davoudi and Libby Porter. *Planning Theory & Practice* 13 (2): 299–333.

Dessai, S., and C. Sims. 2010. Public Perception of Drought and Climate Change in Southeast England. *Environmental Hazards* 9 (4): 340–357.

Few, R. 2012. Health Behaviour Theory, Adaptive Capacity and the Dynamics of Disease Risk. *Climate and Development* 4 (4): 301–310.

Field C.B., M. van Aalst, N. Adger, D. Arent, J. Barnett, R. Betts, et al. 2014. Technical Summary, in Field, C.B., V.R. Barros, D.J. Dokken, K.J. Mach, M.D. Mastrandrea, T.E. Bilir et al. (eds.), *Climate Change 2014: Impacts, Adaptation, and Vulnerability. Part A: Global and Sectoral Aspects. Contribution of Working Group II to the Fifth Assessment Report of the Intergovernmental Panel on Climate Change*. Cambridge: Cambridge University Press, pp 35–96.

Field, C.B., V. Barros, T.F. Stocker, and Q. Dahe. 2012. *Managing the Risks of Extreme Events and Disasters to Advance Climate Change Adaptation: Special Report of the Intergovernmental Panel on Climate Change*. Cambridge: Cambridge University Press.

Folke, C., T. Hahn, P. Olsson, and J. Norberg. 2005. Adaptive Governance of Social-Ecological Systems. *Annual Review of Environmental Resources* 30: 441–473.

Fraser, A.M., M.V. Chester, D. Eisenman, D.M. Hondula, S.S. Pincetl, P. English, and E. Bondank. 2016. Household Accessibility to Heat Refuges: Residential Air Conditioning, Public Cooled Space, and Walkability. *Environment and Planning B: Planning and Design*, 44(6): 1036–1055. 0265813516657342.

Grimm, N.B., S.H. Faeth, N.E. Golubiewski, C.L. Redman, J. Wu, X. Bai, and J.M. Briggs. 2008. Global Change and the Ecology of Cities. *Science* 319 (5864): 756–760.

Gunderson, Lance H. 2001. *Panarchy: Understanding Transformations in Human and Natural Systems*. Washington, DC: Island Press.

Harlan, S.L., A.J. Brazel, G. Darrel Jenerette, N.S. Jones, L. Larsen, L. Prashad, and W.L. Stefanov. 2007. In the Shade of Affluence: The Inequitable Distribution of the Urban Heat Island. *Research in Social Problems and Public Policy* 15: 173–202.

Harlan, S.L., J.H. Declet-Barreto, W.L. Stefanov, and D.B. Petitti. 2013. Neighbourhood Effects on Heat Deaths: Social and Environmental Predictors of Vulnerability in Maricopa County, Arizona. *Environmental Health Perspectives (Online)* 121 (2): 197–204.

Harlan, S.L., and D.M. Ruddell. 2011. Climate Change and Health in Cities: Impacts of Heat and Air Pollution and Potential Co-Benefits from Mitigation and Adaptation. *Current Opinion in Environmental Sustainability* 3 (3): 126–134. doi:10.1016/j.cosust.2011.01.001.

Hayden, M.H., H. Brenkert-Smith, and O.V. Wilhelmi. 2011. Differential Adaptive Capacity to Extreme Heat: A Phoenix, Arizona, Case Study. *Weather, Climate, and Society* 3 (4): 269–280.

Hewitt, K. 1983. *Interpretations of Calamity from the Viewpoint of Human Ecology*. Boston: Allen & Unwin Inc.

Hondula, D.M., R.C. Balling Jr, J.K. Vanos, and M. Georgescu. 2015. Rising Temperatures, Human Health, and the Role of Adaptation. *Current Climate Change Reports* 1 (3): 144–154.

Jenerette, G.D., S.L. Harlan, W.L. Stefanov, and C.A. Martin. 2011. Ecosystem Services and Urban Heat Riskscape Moderation: Water, Green Spaces, and Social Inequality in Phoenix, USA. *Ecological Applications* 21 (7): 2637–2651.

Lindell, M.K., and S.N. Hwang. 2008. Households' Perceived Personal Risk and Responses in a Multihazard Environment. *Risk Analysis* 28 (2): 539–556.

MacClune, K., Allan, C., Venkateswaran, K., and Sabbag, L. 2014. *Floods in Boulder: A Study of Resilience*. http://i-s-e-t.org/resources/case-studies/floods-in-boulder.html.

Marcotullio, P.J., S. Hughes, A. Sarzynski, S. Pincetl, L.S. Peña, P. Romero-Lankao, D. Runfola, and K.C. Seto. 2014. Urbanization and the Carbon Cycle: Contributions from Social Science. *Earth's Future*, August(2): 496–514, doi:10.1002/2014EF000257.

McFarlane, C. 2012. Rethinking Informality: Politics, Crisis, and the City. *Planning Theory & Practice* 13 (1): 89–108.

McFarlane, C., and J. Rutherford. 2008. Political Infrastructures: Governing and Experiencing the Fabric of the City. *International Journal of Urban and Regional Research* 32 (2): 363–374.

Miao, S., F. Chen, M.A. LeMone, M. Tewari, Q. Li, and Y. Wang. 2009. An Observational and Modeling Study of Characteristics of Urban Heat Island and Boundary Layer Structures in Beijing. *Journal of Applied Meteorology and Climatology* 48 (3): 484–501.

Monstadt, J. 2009. Conceptualizing the Political Ecology of Urban Infrastructures: Insights from Technology and Urban Studies. *Environment and Planning. A* 41 (8): 1924–1942.

Morss, R.E., O.V. Wilhelmi, M.W. Downton, and E. Gruntfest. 2005. Flood Risk, Uncertainty, and Scientific Information for Decision Making: Lessons from an Interdisciplinary Project. *Bulletin of the American Meteorological Society* 86 (11). 1593–1601.

Morss, R.E, O.V. Wilhelmi, G.A. Meehl, and L. Dilling. 2011. Improving Societal Outcomes of Extreme Weather in a Changing Climate: An Integrated Perspective. *Annual Review of Environment and Resources* 36 (1): 1–25.

Moser, C.O.N. 1998. The Asset Vulnerability Framework: Reassessing Urban Poverty Reduction Strategies. *World Development* 26 (1): 1–19.

Nahlik, M.J, M.V. Chester, S.S. Pincetl, D. Eisenman, D. Sivaraman, and P. English. 2016. Building Thermal Performance, Extreme Heat, and Climate Change. *Journal of Infrastructure Systems*, 23(3): 04016043.

Ntelekos, A.A., M. Oppenheimer, J.A. Smith, and A.J. Miller. 2010. Urbanization, Climate Change and Flood Policy in the United States. *Climatic Change* 103 (3–4): 597–616. doi:10.1007/s10584-009-9789-6.

O'Neill, M.S. 2005. Disparities by Race in Heat-Related Mortality in Four US Cities: The Role of Air Conditioning Prevalence. *Journal of Urban Health: Bulletin of the New York Academy of Medicine* 82 (2): 191–197. doi:10.1093/jurban/jti043.

Ostrom, E., M.A. Janssen, and J.M. Anderies. 2007. Going beyond Panaceas. *Proceedings of the National Academy of Sciences* 104 (39): 15176–15178.

Pidgeon, N., and C. Butler. 2009. Risk Analysis and Climate Change. *Environmental Politics* 18 (5): 670–688.

Pidgeon, N., and B. Fischhoff. 2011. The Role of Social and Decision Sciences in Communicating Uncertain Climate Risks. *Nature Climate Change* 1 (1): 35–41.

Qin, H., P. Romero-Lankao, J. Hardoy, and Angélica R.-H. 2015. Household Responses to Climate-Related Hazards in Four Latin American Cities: A Conceptual Framework and Exploratory Analysis. *Urban Climate* 14 (1): 94–110.

Renn, O. 2008. *Risk Governance: Coping with Uncertainty in a Complex World*. London: Earthscan.

Riad, J.K., F.H. Norris, and R. Barry Ruback. 1999. Predicting Evacuation in Two Major Disasters: Risk Perception, Social Influence, and Access to Resources. *Journal of Applied Social Psychology* 29 (5): 918–934.

Romero-Lankao, P., and D.M. Gnatz. 2016. Conceptualizing Urban Water Security in an Urbanizing World. *Current Opinion in Environmental Sustainability* 21: 45–51.

Romero-Lankao, P., D.M. Gnatz, and J. Sperling. 2016. Examining Urban Inequality and Vulnerability to Enhance Resilience: Insights from Mumbai, India. *Climatic Change*.

Romero-Lankao, P., S. Hughes, H. Qin, J. Hardoy, A. Rosas-Huerta, R. Borquez, and A. Lampis. 2014a. Scale, Urban Risk and Adaptation Capacity in Neighbourhoods of Latin American Cities. *Habitat International* 42 (0): 224–235. doi:10.1016/j.habitatint.2013.12.008.

Romero-Lankao, P., Gurney, K.R., Seto, K.C., Chester, M., Duren, R.M., Hughes, S., Hutyra, L.R., Marcotullio, P., Baker, L., Grimm, N.B., and Kennedy, C., 2014b. A Critical Knowledge Pathway to Low-Carbon, Sustainable Futures: Integrated Understanding of Urbanization, Urban Areas, and Carbon. *Earth's Future*, 2(10): 515–532.

Romero-Lankao, P., and H. Qin. 2011. Conceptualizing Urban Vulnerability to Global Climate and Environmental Change. *Current Opinion in Environmental Sustainability* 3 (3): 142–149. doi:10.1016/j.cosust.2010.12.016.

Roy, A. 2009. Why India Cannot Plan Its Cities: Informality, Insurgence and the Idiom of Urbanization. *Planning Theory* 8 (1): 76–87.

Smit, B., and J. Wandel. 2006. Adaptation, Adaptive Capacity and Vulnerability. *Global Environmental Change* 16 (3): 282–292.

Smith, A., and A. Stirling. 2010. The Politics of Social-Ecological Resilience and Sustainable Socio-Technical Transitions. *Ecology and Society* 15 (1): 11.

Turner, B.L. 2010. Vulnerability and Resilience: Coalescing or Paralleling Approaches for Sustainability Science? *Global Environmental Change* 20 (4): 570–576.

Uejio, C.K., O.V. Wilhelmi, J.S. Golden, D.M. Mills, S.P. Gulino, and J.P. Samenow. 2011. Intra-Urban Societal Vulnerability to Extreme Heat: The Role of Heat Exposure and the Built Environment, Socioeconomics, and Neighborhood Stability. *Health & Place* 17 (2): 498–507.

UN-Habitat. 2011. *Cities and Climate Change: Global Report on Human Settlements*.

Wilhelmi, O.V., and M.H. Hayden. 2010. Connecting People and Place: A New Framework for Reducing Urban Vulnerability to Extreme Heat. *Environmental Research Letters* 5 (1): 014021.

Zérah, M.-H. 2008. Splintering Urbanism in Mumbai: Contrasting Trends in a Multilayered Society. *Geoforum* 39 (6): 1922–1932.

Chapter 5: Harness Urban Complexity for Health and Well-Being

Franz W. Gatzweiler, Jo Ivey Boufford, and Anna Pomykala

5.1 Introduction to Global Health Challenges

To improve global health and well-being for cities, three global realities must be considered: the demographic shift related to aging of the population, the epidemiologic shift from infectious to noncommunicable diseases as the major threats to health, and climate change – which is changing disease patterns and quality of life, as well as, for some cities, creating serious challenges to their physical infrastructure. All of these critical challenges to health around the world converge in cities and the rapid rate of urbanization worldwide make attention to urban health a critical component of sustainable development.

The number and size of cities is expanding in all regions of the world, with China positioned as the world's largest urban nation (see Chapter 1.1). Rapid urbanization is already presenting challenges to all countries, but its pace and scale are greatest in low- and middle-income countries, not only because of the rise of megacities (those with populations over 10 million), but primarily due to the rapid development of midsized cities of 250,000 to 500,000 inhabitants.

While the rapid rise in the world's population of people aged 60 years or older is a public health triumph, it adds an additional challenge to advancing the health of people in cities: in the next four decades, 21 percent of the population will be over 60 years old, though the rate of increase of this demographic will still be higher in developed countries than in developing ones. Creating urban environments that support active, healthy aging, and health-promoting conditions for all ages is critical to preventing unsustainable pressures on health and social service systems and to maintaining a healthy workforce and active, engaged citizens.

The epidemiologic shift towards noncommunicable diseases, or NCDs – including primarily cardiovascular disease, or CVD; diabetes; cancer; and pulmonary disease – has made NCDs the number one cause of death globally, with a disproportionate impact in low- and middle-income countries and their already fragile healthcare systems. Deaths from NCDs are projected to increase

77 percent between 1990 and 2020, growing from 28.1 million to 49.7 million deaths annually (Report of the Obesity Working Group 2013). The rise in NCDs is tied to globalization and urbanization, as well as the aging of the population.

The environmental impacts of urbanization – increasing energy use and related greenhouse gas emissions, soil degradation, biodiversity loss, and severe water stress – have also had tremendous health consequences: In 2012, approximately seven million people died prematurely as a result of exposure to air pollution (WHO 2014), making air pollution the world's single largest environmental health risk.

In order for cities to evolve as engines for national economic development and as hubs for technological innovation, social progress, and environmental sustainability, city leaders must respond to these challenges with evidence-based policies and programs that can promote the health of urban residents. For example, when plans for the built environment (including housing, land use, and transport) include consideration of their health impacts, cities can facilitate healthy choices in terms of food, exercise, and social engagement; address the physical and mental health issues linked to NCDs, infectious diseases, violence, road accidents, unemployment, poverty, and natural disasters; and maximize the resilience of its residents. In contrast, a failure to address the health of people living in cities can place urban residents at serious health, economic, and security risks. Since healthy people are critical to social and economic development, addressing the health impacts of urbanization must be central to national, regional, and local sustainable development agendas.

5.2 Determinants of Urban Health

Health experts now know that there are broader and more important determinants of health than the availability of medical care (Figure 5.1), which has often been the major focus of global and national health policy attention and investment (Dahlgren and Whitehead 1991; Woolf et al. 2007). Age, sex, and genetic makeup, as well as other "constitutional factors" such as ethnicity, influence people's health, as does access to quality health care. But other factors, including safe natural and built environments (housing, transportation, parks, and urban design), and the socioeconomic environment (the availability of education, jobs, and social support) can prevent or exacerbate risky health behaviors (such as diet, exercise, tobacco use, and unhealthy alcohol and drug use). In addition, the public policies and political environment that shape these environments, including the societal impact of racism, have far greater impacts on health than the environments alone. These can be modified to affect the health of entire populations.

Figure 5.1 Broad determinants of health. Urban health experts now know that the built, physical, social, and economic environments are crucial factors in maintaining and improve health. Source: Jerker Lokrabtz/Azote.

Because cities are the places with the highest human population densities and concentrations of physical, social, and economic infrastructure, they pose challenges to and yet provide opportunities for action on these variables to improve the health and well-being of the majority of the world's population. The multifactorial nature of these challenges calls for a multisectoral approach to governance and for an approach that is inclusive – involving multiple stakeholders and communities in identifying and solving priority problems themselves. A systems approach to such governance, along with a commitment to decisions that advance health and health equity, will be critical to urban health and, therefore, to global health.

5.3 A Conceptual Framework for a Systems Approach to Urban Health and Well-Being

Figure 5.2 aims to explain how urban health and well-being emerges and is further changed by urban systems functions. Because the city is an open system, it is also influenced by processes outside the urban system (see Chapter 1.2).

In identifying the various goods and services that urban systems provide, this framework also supports action based on the evidence that the key factors influencing urban health are primarily located outside the traditional health-care system. Table 5.1 concentrates more deeply on the components of "urban

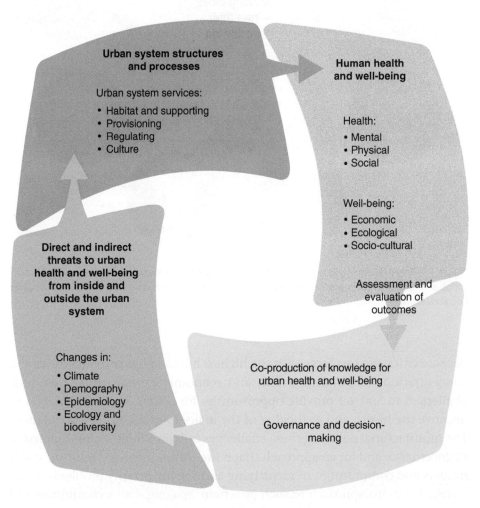

Figure 5.2 Urban health and well-being emerges as an outcome of urban system structure and processes and change factors from outside the system. Source: Jerker Lokrantz/Azote.

Table 5.1 Urban system goods and services and examples of health benefits and risks

Type of urban system service	Description of urban system services	Examples of health benefits and risks
Habitat and supporting	These are physical spaces and infrastructure for living and working in the city. Green (such as parks), blue (such as lakes), and gray (such as roads and buildings) environments are created to provide basic needs, including shelter, waste management, water treatment and sanitation, production of goods, and energy provision. Habitat functions make the city a livable place by providing the hardware that enables material, energy, and data flows, thereby facilitating urban metabolisms.	Housing-related health risks: • Allergies and asthma occur as a result of the accumulation of indoor pollutants and dampness • Infectious diseases spread • Increases or disruptions of immune system regulation by the microbiome of the built environment exaggerate or suppress inflammation • Respiratory and cardiovascular diseases arise from indoor air pollution • Risk of airborne infectious diseases rises because of inadequate ventilation • Illness arises, driven by temperature extremes • Risks of home injuries exist Health benefits from urban green space: • Urban heat is reduced • Greenhouse gas emissions are offset • Storm water is attenuated • Urban residents are provided with spaces for physical activity and social interaction • Exposure to microbiota occurs, which educates the human immune system

Table 5.1 (cont)

Type of urban system service	Description of urban system services	Examples of health benefits and risks
Provisioning	These include goods and services provided by the urban system – some of which can be exchanged on markets, provided by the public, or coproduced. Goods include food, water, manufactured goods, medicines, computers, and books, among many others. Services include access to and use of roads, communication and other public infrastructure, security, waste management, health care and education systems, and disaster response and emergency systems. The provision and production of goods and services can be organized publicly, privately, or in public-private combinations.	<ul><li>Obesity increases due to unhealthy urban food environments</li><li>Urban farmers markets increase healthier food choices</li><li>Pharmaceuticals and medicines are accessible</li><li>Public health facilities are accessible</li><li>Transport and communication infrastructure can improve social networks</li><li>Social determinants of health</li><li>Health insurance</li><li>Hospitals</li><li>Clean water</li><li>Sanitation facilities</li></ul>
Regulating	These are benefits derived from having a system of rules and regulations in place, by means of which the urban system is governed (in the social space) and managed (in the economic and technological space). Regulating services include institutional infrastructure, which determines social interactions and other urban metabolic outcomes, such as regulating access to public places and services, markets and businesses, traffic, the collection and use of data, the implementation of food safety protocols, and the application of environmental standards in the urban economy. Formal and informal rules, norms, and conventions are part of the urban institutional environment.	<ul><li>Policing and public safety</li><li>Enforcement of traffic rules and road safety</li><li>Food safety standards and controls</li><li>Disease control regulations</li><li>Hygiene regulations/standards</li><li>Medical law</li><li>Public health law</li><li>Construction regulations</li><li>Standards in the control of hazardous substances</li><li>Environmental regulations</li></ul>

Type of urban system service	Description of urban system services	Examples of health benefits and risks
Cultural	These are benefits created in urban sociocultural spaces; they include social spaces and liberties for economic and political innovation; exchange of ideas; creativity from exposure to cultural diversity and different forms of cultural expression; recreation and leisure; space for spiritual enrichment; and places to do art and undertake cognitive development. Examples include cultural events, religious places, "Heimat" (sense of belonging), exhibitions, libraries, cultural heritage values (such as historical places), and cultural diversity.	• Culture is a key component in health maintenance and promotion (Napier et al. 2014) • Cultural diversity in healthcare systems increases inclusion of minorities • Cultural competence can improve quality of health care; culturally adapted health care can improve patient understanding and health outcomes • Culture's dictation of female and male roles that limit women's mobility and ability to seek health care

system services," drawing on the processes described in Figure 5.2. Habitat and supporting services provide space and infrastructure to meet the basic needs of life. These are the preconditions for energy and information flows, such as houses, roads, marketplaces, water pipes, sanitation infrastructure, and telephone lines. Provisioning services provide products and energy for consumption and production. Regulation services generate benefits from governing interactions and exchange processes. Cultural services generate nonmaterial benefits for cognitive and knowledge development. Understanding the interconnections of these systems and aligning them to produce health is the challenge for a "Health in All Policies"[1] governance of a city and can be facilitated by a systems approach to identifying the problem and exploring solutions.

5.4 A Systems Approach to Some Common Urban Health Challenges

5.4.1 Transportation

The following examples reveal the breadth of interconnected urban health problems related to complex interrelations between transportation (Figure 5.3), food security (Figure 5.4), and public health as examples of a systems approach to common urban health problems.

Increased road use by private vehicles, for instance, takes advantage of and eventually wears down an intact road infrastructure. Urban planning that

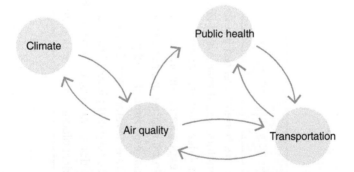

Figure 5.3 Simplified interconnections between urban transportation, air quality, climate change, and public health. Source: Jerker Lokrantz/Azote, modified after Lung (2014).

---

[1] "'Health in All Policies' is an approach to public policies across sectors that systematically takes into account the health implications of decisions, seeks synergies, and avoids harmful health impacts in order to improve population health and health equity." (The Helsinki Statement on Health in All Policies 2013, p.2)

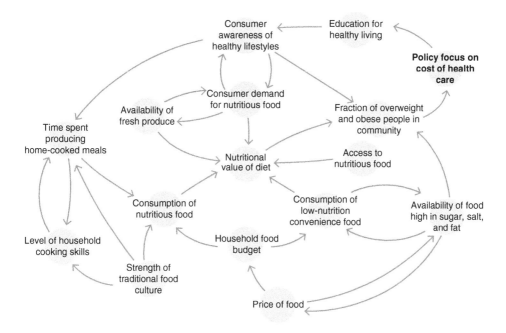

Figure 5.4 Dynamic relationships between variables for food security and the proportion of obese people in urban communities. Source: Jerker Lokrantz/Azote, modified after Proust and Newell (2016).

favors the use of cars can lead to increased air pollution and road traffic injuries, as well as contribute to a reduction in physical activity, with implications for public health and heath care costs from obesity, cardiovascular disease, chronic and acute pulmonary disease, and certain cancers. In contrast, positive health impacts can be expected from reducing the amount of private cars on roads and improving public transport infrastructure (Lung 2014).

5.4.2 Access to Affordable, Nutritional Foods

Today, the prevailing rates of weight- and diet-related chronic diseases, such as diabetes and hypertension, are increasing in every region, but especially in low- and middle-income countries. Population growth, rising incomes, urbanization, and globalization are some of the major drivers of changes in dietary patterns (Figure 5.4). Estimates suggest that by 2030, the number of overweight and obese people will have increased from 1.33 billion in 2005 to 3.28 billion, around one-third of the projected global population (GPAFS 2016).

Urban food security refers to the access to, availability of, and use of food. This includes production, distribution, safety, and quality of food, but it often ignores the nutritional value of diets and individual choices. The Food and Agriculture Organization, or FAO, defines food security as a "situation that exists when all people, at all times, have physical, social and economic access to sufficient, safe and nutritious food that meets their dietary needs and food preferences for an active and healthy life" (FAO 2015). Food insecurity has substantial negative impacts on the physical and mental health of adults and children and is a major problem for many urban populations.

Food insecurity can also exist in communities where sufficient food is not available and/or where diets are not nutritious or safe. These low-quality diets contain insufficient calories, vitamins, and minerals or contain too many calories and too much saturated fat, salt, and sugar. The risk that poor diets pose to mortality and morbidity is now greater than the combined risks of unsafe sex and alcohol, drug, and tobacco use. To achieve healthier diets, food systems must focus on quality and on making the healthy and affordable food choice the easy choice.

To improve diets, healthy eating must be the easiest available choice; likewise, to reduce obesity, physical activity must be desirable and accessible. No single intervention can address the many factors (as identified in Figure 5.2) that contribute to obesity. Priorities for policy-makers include addressing drivers of caloric overconsumption within the food system; supporting access to healthy and affordable foods, especially in low-income communities; incentivizing production of fresh produce; establishing public procurement guidelines that support these producers; developing workplace/school setting interventions that promote healthy eating and physical activity; and providing nutrition education that is culturally appropriate (Libman et al. 2016).

An example of a successful intersectoral partnership for obesity control is the Ensemble Prévenons l'Obésité Des Enfants (Together Let's Prevent Childhood Obesity), or EPODE, an international network that aims to connect a network of stakeholders that takes a "whole community approach" to reducing obesity in a particular locale by coordinating action across school-based interventions, parent and community engagement, municipal support for environmental changes (such as new sports facilities), and media coverage (Report of the Obesity Working Group 2013).

A school meal initiative to improve child nutrition and school enrollment rates that incorporated procurement rules addressed multiple local needs – for fresh, high-quality food as well as a stable market for small local producers. Similarly, the UN World Food Programme's Home Grown School Feeding Program, as implemented in the municipality of Campinas in São Paulo, Brazil, transitioned the community from unpopular and low-quality processed foods to broadly approved, high-quality fresh vegetables, fruits, and meats when regulations were added that required 30 percent of the national school food budget to be spent on food sourced directly from family farmers in the local region served by the school (Otsuki 2011).

As these examples illustrate, a systems approach offers an exciting framework for multisectoral definitions of problems and problem solving that incorporates evidence-based solutions for promoting health in urban planning, housing, transportation, food systems, education, and other sectors. Indeed, researchers have applied a systems science approach to other health issues such as obesity, and this technique is a growing area of interest for public health scholars.[2]

In addition to exploring the complex interconnectedness of system variables that determine urban health, the systems approach, as developed by the Urban Health and Wellbeing programme of the International Council for Science, integrates human health concerns into questions about urban system function. It also addresses knowledge creation in science and society in order to harness urban complexity by solving complicated, wicked types of problems, and the different types of knowledge needed to solve them (ICSU 2011; Gatzweiler et al. 2016).

Accordingly, for society, a systems approach to urban health and well-being means scientists coproducing knowledge for urban health in collaboration with affected communities, government agencies, and civil society organizations; recognizing how different urban system functions and modes of urban life are connected to particular health and well-being outcomes; raising awareness and educating the public and policy-makers on interrelated issues of health and well-being; creating demand and opportunities for entrepreneurship, business, and civil society engagement for health and well-being; and creating networks of like-minded system thinkers and agents of change for improving health and the quality of life in cities.

For science, a systems approach means:

1. The development of new conceptual models that incorporate dynamic relations of the processes leading to health in urban settings. These conceptual models must be specific to a given research problem or question; the development of these models may involve input from stakeholders as well as scientists, as appropriate to the research problem and context.

2. The use of systems tools and formal simulation models, such as agent-based models, systems dynamic models, or other systems modeling tools, to better understand the functioning of the integrated urban health system or to predict changes to health under various hypothetical interventions.

---

[2] See, for example, The Columbia University Systems Science Program, a joint venture between the Mailman School of Public Health and the School of Engineering and Applied Sciences (SEAS), http://engineering.columbia.edu/breaking-down-complex-systems-public-health.

3. The integration of various sources and types of data (including spatial, visual, quantitative, and qualitative data) in the conceptual models and/or the formal simulation models as well as the identification of important data gaps that need to be filled in order to advance understanding of how the system works.

5.5 Governance to Advance Urban Health and Well-Being

Effective, inclusive, and representative "government" – including the institutional means to ensure provision of infrastructure – requires goods and services to address urban health problems. Such a government must also be able to engage other stakeholders to achieve agreement on the nature of the problem, potential solutions, and how to measure success. Alignment on aspects of a given problem and its solution is often referred to as "governance." An extensive literature shows that effective government is part of good governance and both are important determinants of urban health; particularly important is a strong public health infrastructure that can work cooperatively to examine potential risks and benefits to health policies, programs, and investments across sectors.

This need for broad-based action underlies a governance framework for health called a "Health in All Policies" approach, which reflects the importance of a public policy focus on the broader determinants of health, such as housing, transportation, built and natural environments, education, and economic development to create communities that actually support and permit healthier behaviors. The complexity of these determinants and their solutions further requires the input of a broad range of stakeholders beyond healthcare providers, such as community-based organizations, academia, business, and the media. The public health system can help to catalyze actions that bring the many stakeholders in urban health together to systematically consider the health implications of decisions, to seek synergies, and to avoid harmful health impacts to improve population health and health equity.[3]

The World Health Organization's recent *Global Report on Urban Health: Equitable, Healthier Cities for Sustainable Development* devotes its third section to the need for a renewed focus on urban governance to achieve the Sustainable

---

[3] WHO: Health in All Policies: Framework for Country Action http://apps.who.int/iris/bitstream/10665/112636/1/9789241506908_eng.pdf?ua=1.

Development Goals globally, as well as to achieve healthier cities in countries (WHO 2016). Since local governments may have responsibility for multiple functions that affect health (including land use, roads and transportation, and environmental protection), governance for healthy and sustainable cities requires an integrated approach across agencies and sectors that facilitates meaningful community participation. Empowering citizens with information is key to their involvement in decision-making on urban health initiatives, especially to ensure sustainable action on health inequities. Data sharing and transparency are also important for enabling civil society, government, and the private sector to work together effectively. With rapid urbanization constraining government capacity to provide quality services, the private sector serves an increasingly important role as a partner in meeting the needs of urban residents. Above all, the report emphasizes the importance of adopting a "Health in All" approach to policy and decision-making processes across city governments, with health equity as a core value.

An example of governance for health that addresses one of the important urban health challenges of aging is the Age-Friendly New York City Initiative. Using the WHO age-friendly framework[4] that promotes healthy aging using a life-course approach to help cities plan for the needs of older adults. The WHO identified eight domains of age-friendliness that, if addressed through improvements to policies, practices, and programs, can reverse or slow the disability trajectory.

One comprehensive example is the Age-Friendly New York City Initiative (hereinafter Age-Friendly NYC), a public-private initiative that brings key people from multiple sectors and government agencies together to improve the lives of older adults by changing their physical and social environments to promote the maintenance of independence and active engagement of older persons in the life of the city. Launched in 2007, Age-Friendly NYC is a partnership between a nongovernmental organization – the New York Academy of Medicine – and local government offices, including the Office of the Mayor of the City of New York and the New York City Council. Age-Friendly NYC attracted the support of local policy-makers during the global financial crisis because of several factors: the number of older persons in New York City was projected to grow by 40.7 percent within the next 20 years; this subpopulation would be one of the most diverse groups of older persons in the world; and older people live in all parts of the city and vote and shop locally, thus they are engines for community economic development. A mayor-appointed Age-Friendly Commission, with representatives from business, city government, NGOs, and the private sector, oversees the initiative, which includes input

---

[4] www.who.int/ageing/projects/age_friendly_cities_programme/en/.

from older persons via public hearings held across the city. Mayor Michael Bloomberg also mobilized 22 city agencies around the initiative, asking them to examine the programs and capital investments already planned over the next five years to determine how they might be changed if the needs of older persons were taken into account. The result was a report with 59 city government commitments that continue to be tracked by the commission, which has also promoted complementary private sector activities.

One area in which Age-Friendly NYC has had a visible impact is in addressing transportation challenges faced by older adults that decrease their ability to leave their homes, to engage actively in their communities, and to exercise and access healthy food. Solutions are aimed at creating "Complete Streets"; these provide for safe and active movement for all users by improving the safety of seniors and other pedestrians, as well as all road users in New York City. Aspects of Complete Streets include bus shelters with seating and signage, paid for by advertising; school buses repurposed during the school day for grocery store trips; benches installed with older adult input; and improvements to streets and signage in neighborhoods with the most pedestrian accidents, including extending pedestrian crossing times, altering curbs and sidewalks, restricting vehicle turns, and narrowing roadways. When all of these improvements are implemented, officials expect an estimated 10 percent reduction in pedestrian fatalities among older people.

Lessons learned in creating and implementing cross-sectoral strategies for age-friendly cities are equally applicable to efforts to prevent NCDs, where there is increasing evidence that incidents over a lifetime seem to make individuals more vulnerable to premature morbidity and mortality. Approaches that change the environment will have a broader impact than efforts to change individual behavior and should be a priority for city action. Initiatives that can address more than one need are more likely to gain and sustain the support of political leaders. Low-cost and no-cost interventions can have a tremendous impact on health and may be easy to incorporate into existing plans and activities. Because the determinants of health are affected by all sectors, planning for health should leverage financial resources from within and outside the health sector; partnerships outside of government and public engagement are key to sustainability.

5.6 Conclusions

As we have gained information about and understanding of the multiple determinants of health, we have found that the systems approach to urban health and well-being permits individuals charged with and concerned about improving the health of cities to better develop strategies that identify the multisectoral origins of the problem; encourages research for solutions that advance health; and engages effectively with multiple stakeholders to increase the likelihood of sustainable implementation of new initiatives.

We must remember to keep inequity at the forefront of any discussion of urban policies. Since cities are the locus of vast inequities of opportunity, compounded by poverty, race, ethnicity, gender, age, and migration status, urban dwellers bear the consequences of unplanned urbanization differently than nonurban residents, with adverse impacts falling disproportionately on the vulnerable and poor (see, for example, Marmot 2015). Moreover, in cities, concentrations of deprivation often exist at the neighborhood level. This phenomenon emphasizes the importance of identifying problems, creating appropriate solutions, and tracking progress in partnership with local communities, which are the experts on their neighborhood. The evidence clearly indicates that locally owned solutions are critical to achieving and sustaining a community's health (see Cummins et al. 2007; Kershaw et al. 2015).

Ultimately, the effective governance of cities in general – and, specifically, of cities seeking to achieve goals of health and well-being – depends on political will. As we move to engage political officials at the city level, we must first understand that they may not be familiar with the evidence for the multiple determinants of health, and may still see the solution to achieving health as primarily an issue of assuring access to health care and strengthening personal healthcare systems. Further, as national governments increasingly move to identify their own models for local government and the decentralization of authority, it is important to understand whether local government entities have the authority to address such problems and, even where such authority *does* exist, whether they have the basic information systems and infrastructure to solve them. A systems approach to these challenges can help to facilitate understanding and action to improve the health and well-being of people in cities, and to achieve the Sustainable Development Goals for improved health for all.

Acknowledgments

We thank Indira Nath, Pierre Ritchie, Anthony Capon, Carlos Dora, Yong-Guan Zhu, Ilene Speizer, Gérard Salem, Luuk Rietvald, Ana Diez Roux, José Siri, Saroj Jayasinghe, Christl A. Donnelly, Keisuke Hanaki, Hany M. Ayad, and Susan Parnell for constructive comments and contributions to the chapter.

🌐 *References*

Cummins, S., Sarah Curtis, Ana V. Diez-Roux, Sally Macintyre. 2007. Understanding and Representing "Place" in Health Research: A Relational Approach. *Social Science and Medicine*, 65(9): 1825–1838.

Dahlgren, G., and M. Whitehead. 1991. *Policies and Strategies to Promote Social Equity in Health*. Stockholm: Institute for Futures Studies.

FAO (Food and Agriculture Organization of the United Nations). 2015. *The State of Food Insecurity in the World 2015, Meeting the 2015 International Hunger Targets: Taking Stock of Uneven Progress*. FAO, Rome.

Gatzweiler, F.W., H.M. Ayad, J.I. Boufford, A. Capon, A.V. Diez Roux, Ch. Donnelly, K. Hanaki, S. Jayasinghe, I. Nath, S. Parnell, L. Rietveld, P. Ritchie, G. Salem, I. Speizer, Y. Zhang, and Y.-G. Zhu. 2016. *Advancing Urban Health and Wellbeing in the Changing Urban Environment. Implementing a Systems Approach*. Hangzhou, Singapore: Zhejiang University Press and Springer.

GPAFS (Global Panel on Agriculture and Food Systems for Nutrition). 2016. *Food Systems and Diets: Facing the Challenges of the 21st Century*. London: Global Panel.

ICSU. 2011. *Report of the ICSU Planning Group on Health and Wellbeing in the Changing Urban Environment: A Systems Analysis Approach*. Paris: International Council for Science.

Kershaw, K.N., T.L. Osypuk, D.P. Do, P.J. De Chavez, and A.V. Diez Roux. 2015. Neighborhood-Level Racial/Ethnic Residential Segregation and Incident Cardiovascular Disease: The Multi-Ethnic Study of Atherosclerosis. *Circulation*, 131(2): 141–148.

Libman, K., L. Beatty, M. Fiedler, S. Abbot, D. Green, and L. Weiss. 2016. Food and Nutrition, Hard Truths about Eating Healthy. Data Brief "City Voices: New Yorkers on Health," The New York Academy of Medicine. www.nyam.org/media/filer_public/cb/46/cb469439-6d28-4a74-ac07-c98aab837cf7/cityvoicesnutritionfinal7-16.pdf.

Lung, C.S.-C. 2014. Using a Systems Approach to Design Green Transportation System for Better Urban Health under Climate Change. Research, November 6-8, 2nd International UGEC Conference Urban Transition and Transformations Science, Synthesis & Policy, Taipei, Taiwan.

Marmot, M. 2015. The Health Gap: The Challenge of an Unequal World, *The Lancet* 386(10011): 2442–2444.

Napier, D., C. Ancarno, C.B. Butler, J. Calabrese, A. Chater, H. Chatterjee, et al., Culture and Health, *The Lancet*, 384(9954): 1607–1639.

Otsuki, K. 2011. Home-Grown Food in Schools for a Green Economy. United Nations. https://unu.edu/publications/articles/home-grown-food-in-schools-for-a-green-economy.html.

Proust, K., and B. Newell. 2016. Urban Sub-System Influence Diagrams, Designing Health Places: Systems Thinking and the SDGs. United Nations University-Int Inst Global Health, Urban Thinkers Campus, Kuching, Sarawak.

Report of the Obesity Working Group. 2013. Strategic Action to Combat the Obesity Epidemic, Shiriki Kumanyika, Kimberly Libman and Ana Garcia, World Innovation Summit for Health, Doha, Qatar.

The Helsinki Statement on Health in All Policies 2013. 8th Global Conference on Health Promotion, Helsinki, Finland, June 2013. http://apps.who.int/iris/bitstr eam/10665/112636/1/9789241506908_eng.pdf?ua=1.

Woolf, S.H., R.E. Johnson, R.L. Phillips, and M. Philipsen. 2007. Giving Everyone the Health of the Educated: An Examination of Whether Social Change Would Save More Lives Than Medical Advances. *American Journal of Public Health*, 97(4): 679–683.

World Health Organization (WHO) 2014. 7 Million Premature Deaths Annually Linked to Air Pollution. Press release. www.who.int/mediacentre/news/releases/2014/air-pollution/en/.

World Health Organization (WHO) 2016. Global Report on Urban Health: Equitable, Healthier Cities for Sustainable Development. World Health Organization and UN-Habitat. www.who .int /kobe_centre/measuring/urban-global-report/en/.

Chapter 6: Macroeconomy and Urban Productivity

Michael Cohen and Lena Simet

6.1 Introduction: Cities as the Locus of Productivity, Value Creation, and Income Generation

In the twenty-first century, cities offer the potential of economic opportunity. Historically, as an increasing share of the total population of a country's population lives in urban areas, GDP has increased (World Bank 2009). As displayed in Figure 6.1, this is more than an accidental correlation: It reflects the clear relationship between the efficiencies and productivity of agglomeration economies and location. Agglomeration, when accompanied by growing density and proximity, allows the reduction of costs of production of goods and services and growing consumption by an ever-wealthier urban labor force. The process of value creation itself is a quintessential process of bringing factors of production together in time and space.

Economies of scale can generate higher productivity as shown in studies in Brazil, which concluded that productivity increased roughly 1 percent for every 10 percent increase in the number of workers employed in an industry or in a city. This very large increase means that by growing from a city of 1,000 workers to one with 10,000 workers, productivity would increase by a factor of 90 (Spence et al. 2009). Thus, over time, aggregate economic growth is closely associated with the urban percentage of total population. Historically, "very few countries have reached income levels of US$10,000 per capita before reaching about 60 percent urbanization" (Spence et al. 2009: 3). All high-income countries are 70 to 80 percent urbanized (Spence et al. 2009).

In 2016, all countries generated more than half of their GDP in urban-based economic activities (Cohen 1991). Projections for future economic growth in all countries demonstrate that the trend towards greater concentration of economic activity will occur in urban areas of all sizes. Even in the rare case of countries in which urbanization occurred without growth, a pattern that Spence et al. (2009: 8) call "pathological urbanization," there is little evidence that urbanization exacerbated poverty.

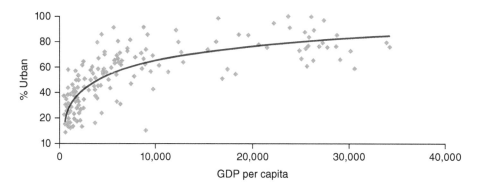

Figure 6.1 The relationship between per capita GDP and urbanization across countries (1996 dollars). Source: Jerker Lokrantz/Azote, modified after Spence et al. (2009).

Productivity is a highly localized phenomenon. Location, in turn, greatly impacts a person's opportunities. The country, region, city, and neighborhood in which a person grows up affect that person's income mobility, living standard, and quality of life. The stark divide between rich and poor countries is therefore a highly localized issue, too. We then have to ask ourselves, what factors encourage some cities to prosper and others to decay? More importantly, what can be done to change it? How can gaps between labor productivity be reduced, and how can labor from low-productivity activities flow to high-productivity activities?

This chapter attempts to respond to these questions in the light of the adoption of the New Urban Agenda, the outcome document of the Habitat III conference held in 2016, which is set to guide the urbanization efforts of the next 20 years.

6.2 Productivity Enhancing and Constraining City Characteristics

In 1991, the World Bank identified four major constraints on urban productivity – infrastructure deficiencies, regulatory effects, weak local governments, and the absence of urban finance institutions (Cohen 1991) – that help to answer our motivating questions.

While the weaknesses of urban infrastructure have been observed all over the world, a comparative study from Lagos, Jakarta, and Bangkok concludes that small- and medium-sized enterprises spent from 35, to 20, to 12 percent of gross fixed investments, respectively, to provide water supply; electricity; solid waste collection and disposal; and worker transport in cities where these services were largely unreliable and frequently unavailable (Anas et al.

1996). It was thus no surprise that these firms had limited profits and did not grow to be very large. These heavy "infrastructure taxes" constrained firm size and employment growth. In this way, infrastructure deficiencies undermine economic productivity. These direct impacts are accompanied by other negative externalities from infrastructure failure, such as the traffic problems in Bangkok, flooding in Jakarta, or air pollution in Mexico City, each of which has generated citizen action and political demands for remedial action.

The second major constraint to urban productivity is *costly regulation*. While many forms of regulation are essential for public safety, whether in the form of fire laws or environmental protections, some forms of regulation greatly increase the cost of urban economic activity. A 1989 study of the housing sectors in Kuala Lumpur and Bangkok found that, while Malaysia is much richer than Thailand, Bangkok produced better and cheaper housing than Kuala Lumpur. The answer to this puzzle lay in the 55 steps and three years required to obtain a building permit in Kuala Lumpur – delays that amounted to about 3 percent of GDP. Regulations imposed heavy taxes on households and firms hoping to start new construction (Hannah et al. 1989). Colonial housing regulations in former British colonies in West Africa had similar effects. When apartheid ended in South Africa in 1994, builders had to complete 24 steps to obtain necessary permits. The number has now been reduced to nine.

These constraints do not exist in an institutional vacuum. A third important constraint on urban productivity *is the many institutional, technical, and financial weaknesses of local government.* In many cases, national governments keep local governments closely constrained, dependent on monthly or annual financial transfers that are conditional on fulfilling national objectives and policies. The financial constraints to local governments are clear in the low percapita amounts of budgetary resources available for local spending.

It follows, then, that local governments fail to maintain local infrastructure or social services, while at the same time providing notably slow and inefficient services to urban residents in such matters as renewing drivers' licenses. Moreover, local governments should be given the institutional capacity to introduce policies that improve the welfare of their citizens by, for instance, adjusting the local minimum wage to the high costs of living in some cities.

A fourth constraint is *the lack of urban finance institutions to finance long-term, durable assets*, such as infrastructure or housing. While cities need long-term finance for these important assets, most developing countries lack robust financial sectors to provide the quantity of finance needed on reasonable terms. This dearth of financial resources contributes to the presence of infrastructure deficiencies and the slow rate of investment in public goods.

Taken together, these four constraints – identified more than 20 years ago – continue to be relevant in explaining why cities are not more productive than they already are. While these local constraints are the basis for enhancing or reducing productivity levels, exogenous factors might be just as influential. The following section will shed light on the influence of global exogenous forces and how they affect urban economic performance.

6.3 Urban Areas as Sites of Impact of Global Economic Change

The position of urban economic activities in macroeconomic performance becomes increasingly complicated as we consider the multiple and shifting impacts of global economic processes. The global economic crisis, which began in 2008–2009 generated diverse impacts in cities, including the initial freezing of credit, reduced demand for manufactured goods and exports, growing unemployment, lost incomes, reduced public revenues, and contracting local economies. These impacts were well recorded in the Asian financial crisis of 1997 and in Argentina after the crisis of 2001–2002, and have been noted in the ongoing European recession.

The process of urban economic contraction is very painful and also very visible. As public and private spending declines, street vendors and service purveyors lose demand for their services. As sales decline, so do tax revenues, which finance public expenditures.

Studies of Latin American economies in the 1990s showed that when economic growth occurred, the urban poor benefited. But when recession hit, the poor fell farther than the rich, and they stayed down for a longer time (Morley 1998). The worsening income distribution in Latin American countries the resulted cannot be easily separated from the patterns of volatility that have affected the region. This is also exacerbated by drastic reductions in the flow of important cash remittances that have dwarfed any official aid to Latin America (Terry 2005).

Cities can be expected to continue to feel the impact of global economic crises, leaving deep footprints on the urban social fabric and the physical conditions of urban areas. Within the public sector, there is an obvious need for expenditures to provide basic services and to operate and maintain urban infrastructure, but these are challenged by low levels of public investment and the lack of credit. These shortages of funds have serious effects on the quantity and quality of public goods in cities. Both the reduced level and the changing composition of public expenditures have been observed within regions and for the world as a whole (World Bank 2009).

6.4 The Urbanization of Poverty, Productivity, and Rising Inequalities

As cities have generated higher incomes, they have also become the preferred destinations of migrants, whether from rural areas or from other countries (Harris and Todaro 1970). In 1970, about half of urban growth in developing countries could be attributed to migration, the other half to natural increase. By 1990, that ratio had shifted towards 70 percent from natural increase and 30 percent from migration (Preston 1990; see Chapter 1). While in most countries of Latin America, the Middle East, and East Asia, the large population shifts to urban areas have already occurred, newer accelerated international migration – by Syrian refugees to Europe in 2015–2016, for example – has added new demographic pressures to receiving cities and countries.

Though we reached a tipping point in 2008 when the world's total population became more than half urban, this shift has not led to a deceleration in urbanization; rather, new projections for the 2015–2030 period predict another two billion residents will be added to cities. That number is equivalent to adding about 70 million people per year, or the population of Pittsburgh or Hanoi every week.

While people in cities generally live at higher income levels than in rural areas, this massive demographic transformation is also reflected in what has been called "the urbanization of poverty" (Martine 2012). For example, in Latin America, a region that experienced economic growth rates of about 5 percent on average from 2005 to 2007, more than 350 million people continue to live on less than $3,000 a year, and 120 million are living on less than $2 a day.

Moreover, increasing numbers of the world's urban population live in slums. The Millennium Development Project estimated this number of people at 924 million in 2003. Projections suggest that the additional two billion urban residents expected to move into cities by 2030 will live in poor housing conditions that lack a clean water supply and sanitation, as well as other infrastructure services such as drainage, solid waste collection, and electricity. To this we must add significant deficits in essential social services, such as schools and clinics, as well as increasing levels of air pollution and congestion.

Poor living conditions also contribute to lowering the productivity of the urban labor force. Poor sanitary conditions create health problems, which reduce physical strength and the number of days people are capable of earning wages. High-density settlements with large numbers of unemployed youth are frequently the sites of violence and despair. Often, these slums are located on dangerous sites that are highly vulnerable to flooding and other natural disasters. Slums become the loci of cumulative vulnerabilities, creating scenarios in which it is difficult even for educated youth to overcome their living environments (UN-Habitat 2003).

Two primary conclusions can be drawn from this discussion. First, urban areas are the places of economic and social opportunity, including higher incomes, jobs, and upward mobility. Yet, the combination of rapid demographic growth, growing demand for essential urban infrastructure and social services, and inadequate resources to deliver these services creates severe challenges for urban governance. Local governments are increasingly unable to satisfy the scale and complexity of demands coming from urban civil society.

While many exogenous forces contribute to urban poverty and inequality, public policies can directly contribute to their reduction. Developments and challenges in two dimensions are critical to this endeavor: 1) productivity, unemployment, and inequality and 2) the informal sector.

6.4.1 Productivity, Unemployment, and Inequality

Much of the period spanning the 1990s to the present has been dominated by a policy and strategic focus on macroeconomic management, heavily influenced by arguments for liberalization of the "Washington Consensus" and the *unproven belief* that growth over time will reduce unemployment. This perspective supported the view that state intervention in employment issues was inefficient, harkening back to the New Deal or state-backed programs in the former Soviet Union or in China. Such beliefs have had a lasting and negative impact on efforts to strengthen the abilities of municipalities to address urban employment and underemployment by developing unrealistic expectations from the private sector, and by side-stepping the public sector – that is, city government – rather than working to strengthen its areas of comparative advantage for job creation.

For these reasons, we should be surprised that the past decades have been marked by increasing inequality. Although aggregate economic growth and local productivity have increased, wages have stagnated, and structural inequality of both income and wages has become a social and economic concern (Bivens and Mishel 2015).

In 17 out of 22 OECD countries, inequality has increased since 2000 (OECD 2015). Industrialized countries are currently experiencing levels of inequality not seen since the nineteenth century, and many developing countries have become more unequal over the past decade. Asia, the region that experienced the highest growth rates in the world (with a GDP growth rate of about 7 percent) and the largest reduction in poverty ever recorded in history (from 54 percent living in poverty in 1990 to 21.5 percent living in poverty in 2010), is also the region in which the rich-poor divide is widening most quickly (OECD 2015).

Piketty's (2014) ground breaking historical analysis of inequality offers an explanation for this surge in inequality. The present state of affairs, which he refers to as "patrimonial capitalism," favors capital owners and "rentiers" over the working population. According to his analysis, the reason for this scenario is the rate of return on capital (r), which has increased at a much greater level than the rate of economic growth (g): in mathematic terms, $r > g$. For the last 300 years, the rate of return on capital has increased at a steady rate of about 5 percent, while g, conversely, has shown severe fluctuations and lower growth rates. As wealth grows faster than economic output, economic growth is accumulated in the hands of a few, increasing the wealth gap between the famous 1 percent and the rest of society.

Piketty (2014) stresses that conditions vary across countries, depending on the level of government intervention in the market. Figure 6.2 displays the relationship between GDP per capita and the Gini coefficient – a measure of inequality – in selected countries in Latin America and the Caribbean. The relationship illustrated here confirms Piketty's theory, revealing that there is no clear link between these two variables. Mexico and Brazil, for example, have similar levels of income per capita, yet starkly contrasting levels of inequality (Mexico's Gini is .45; Brazil's reached .57 in 2010).

Among many developed countries, there is increased concern about a *productivity-pay gap*, where wage growth has fallen greatly behind productivity growth. The case of the United States is particularly striking. Figure 6.3 presents the cumulative growth in net productivity of the total economy and inflation-adjusted average compensation of workers in the private sector since 1948. In the decades following World War II, hourly compensation of workers increased in tandem with economy-wide productivity. After 1973, however, hourly wages stagnated for the majority of US workers, while productivity continued to rise. This trend became even more severe after 2000, after which a

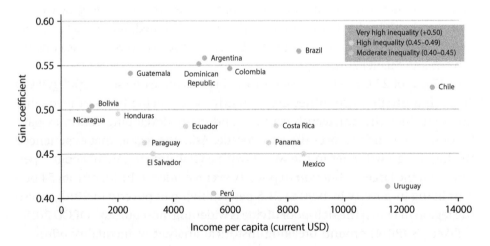

Figure 6.2 The relationship between income per capita (current USD) and Gini coefficient in Latin American countries. Source: Jerker Lokrantz/Azote, modified after UN Habitat (2014).

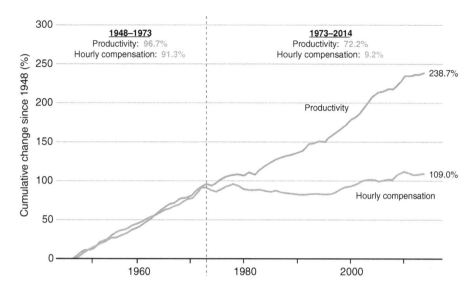

Figure 6.3 Cumulative change in productivity (orange) and hourly compensation (green) in the United States between 1945 and 2015. Source: Jerker Lokrantz/Azote, modified after EPI (Bivens and Michel 2015).

mere 1.8 percent of the net productivity growth of 21.6 percent was translated into compensation for workers.

According to the Economic Policy Institute's Bivens and Michel (2015), the central driver of this productivity-pay gap is inequality, inequality of compensation, and the falling share of income allocated to workers relative to capital owners, which confirms Piketty's theory of $r > g$, where rate of return on capital has become greater than the rate of economic growth.

Because cities play an important role in national economic development and productivity growth, the next logical step provoked by these patterns is to consider possible implications of these national trends on urban areas, and to identify how urban areas impact developments on a national level.

In a study of 220 metropolitan areas in the United States, Hsieh and Moretti (2015) found that the most productive cities, including New York and San Francisco, are not contributing to national GDP growth as one might expect. The New York metropolitan area serves as a prime example. It ranks among the top 20 most productive metropolitan areas in the United States (Parilla and Muro 2017). According to Hsieh and Moretti's analysis, however, the New York metropolitan region was only responsible for 5 percent of the country's aggregate output growth. While cities like New York are more productive and offer higher nominal wages, these pull factors are offset by extremely high costs for housing, which present constraints to worker mobility and a spatial misallocation of labor across the country.

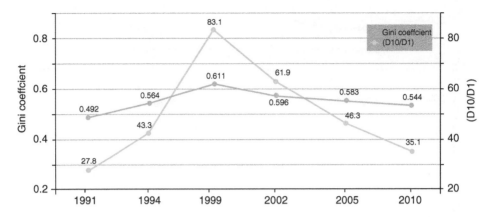

Figure 6.4 Changes in the Gini coefficient, as well as the differential between the salaries earned by the richest and the poorest 10 percent (a metric called D10/D1) in Bogotá between 1991 and 2010. Source: Jerker Lokrantz/Azote, modified after UN-Habitat (2014).

The case of Colombia's capital, Bogotá, is a more positive example of shared economic growth. After the 1998 crisis, both Colombia and Bogotá experienced economic recovery; in 2007, Bogotá's GDP grew by approximately 7 percent (UN-Habitat 2014). As depicted in Figure 6.4, the economic growth occurred in tandem with a constant reduction in the city's Gini coefficient, as well as a reduction in the differential between the salaries earned by the richest and the poorest 10 percent of the population. A study by UN-Habitat (2014) finds that this reduction in income inequality is a result of structural changes and the introduction of local social policies aimed at reducing inequality, including a wide provision of public services. Even in times of economy recovery from the 2008 crisis, when economic growth slowed significantly, inequality in Bogotá continued to decrease, falling below the national urban Gini coefficient.

In sum, increased urban productivity does not always go hand in hand with more equitable income distribution and better working conditions. This is not to say that economic growth and the generation of inequalities are inextricably linked, but rather point to the importance of national and local government efforts to limit increases in inequality.

6.4.2 The Informal Sector

The informal economy is widespread and increasing in size in most parts of the world, especially in low- and middle-income countries, where it accounts for half to three-quarters of all nonagricultural employment (Chen 2010; ILO 2013). Informal employment comprises about 65 percent of nonagricultural employment in developing Asia, 51 percent in Latin America, 48 percent in

North Africa, and 72 percent in sub-Saharan Africa; in these regions, this labor force produces between 20 and 40 percent of GDP.

How the informal sector fits into and develops within individual regions and countries varies considerably. Asia has felt the impacts of globalization, with its effects on capital and labor flows, movement of technology, and wage rates, most intensely. The East Asian financial crisis of 1997–1998 affected the small-scale sector, weakening the demand for locally produced products while increasing interest rates and reducing purchasing power. Bank credit became scarce at a time when input prices for energy and other raw materials increased. At the macro-level, economists nonetheless assumed that local economies were relatively sheltered from this regional crisis. Some observers with their feet on the ground wrote about "the geography of change" in this period (Amin and Robins 1990), raising questions about the resilience or vulnerability of the urban and local economies to external shocks.

Many studies on the informal sector have argued that there is a negative correlation between the size of the informal sector and the growth rate of per capita GDP, as is illustrated in the downward sloping trend line in Figure 6.5 (Slonimczyk 2014).

In contrast, other studies (for example, Heintz 2006) point out that the correlation between informality and slow growth of GDP does not necessarily imply causality. In fact, slow growth could explain a certain degree of informality, rather than the other way around. Rather than perceiving the formal and informal sectors as conflicting, the two economies may work in symbiosis. In an era of globalization and outsourcing, many key components and services used by the formal sector are outsourced to the informal economy.

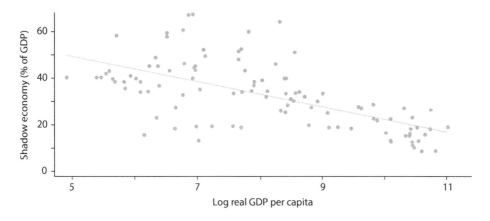

Figure 6.5 The relationship between GDP per capita and the shadow economy as a percentage of total GDP on a global average. Source: Jerker Lokrantz/Azote, modified after Slonimczyk (2014).

The perception of the informal sector as a pool of potential entrepreneurs whose wealth creation capacity is constrained by a regulatory burden sidesteps the fact that most workers in the informal economy are engaged in disguised employment relationships (Chen 2006). This alternate vision views the informal economy as linked, in a dynamic and often subservient relationship, with the formal economy, and indicates that efforts to "formalize" the informal economy are doomed to failure without addressing the broader dynamics that stimulate job creation in the larger economy – formal and informal, rural as well as urban.

Heintz (2006: 5) recognizes the growing importance of urban informal employment "as rapid urbanization continues and the growth of formal job opportunities lags behind the expansion of the urban labor force." He further argues that "municipal regulations frequently fail to recognize urban informal activities as legitimate."

The International Labour Organization (ILO 2013) argues that the root of the informal economy problem is the inability of economies to create sufficient numbers of quality jobs. Employment growth in the formal segment of the economy in most countries has lagged behind the growth of the labor force, trends that are likely to continue in the future (ILO 2008). Even in China, where the rates of economic growth and poverty reduction have been remarkable, the informal economy is growing.

Workers in the informal economy are not only disproportionally affected by global economic forces, but also by changing climate patterns. In turn, the informal economy can, and already does, play a crucial role in greening the urban economy and contributing to climate resilience. Brown et al. (2014) encourage local governments to collaborate with the informal sector in achieving more inclusive and green economies.

6.5 Imagining the Future of Urban Productivity

According to a recent OECD (2015) report, global economic growth is projected to slow in most countries. While the OECD considers structural changes, it misses to explore the potential of cities in fostering productivity growth. The Habitat II Agenda of 1996 recognized that urban economies are a prerequisite for improved living conditions and sustained national development. Whether and to what degree economic growth will be sustained over the next decades will therefore depend greatly on the increase of productivity, more specifically, urban productivity. Identifying challenges and opportunities of cities can therefore inform urban agendas for sustained growth in the future.

6.5.1 Future Challenges

The pace of urbanization combined with a lack of institutional capacity presents a major challenge for cities in the developing world. As fiscal powers continue to concentrate at the national level, local governments lack the resources to manage and accommodate the growth of cities. Lagos exemplifies this challenge. Estimates suggest that 2,000 new people arrive in the city daily; it is expected to double in size by 2031 (Obioma 2013). How can a city possibly cope with such a population increase? This challenge manifests itself particularly in increasing demand for infrastructure and access to basic services, including public transportation, water, sanitation, electricity, and access to health care and education. Yet, if urban growth continues to be unplanned and underfinanced, informal settlements will continue to proliferate and overcrowding will become worse, which could lead to the creation and spread of new and old diseases.

Cities in upper-income countries face major challenges regarding their infrastructure, too, as they find infrastructure aging and in desperate need of repair. Especially in large and growing cities, existing systems built in the early phases of industrialization are coming under increasing strain. Insufficient maintenance and expansion efforts limit the transport possibilities within cities, affecting productivity and growth. In the case of New York City, estimates suggest that approximately $47 billion is needed over the next five years to bring the city's aging infrastructure to a state of good repair (Forman 2014). The neglect of public infrastructure will pose a financial and logistical challenge to the city and its capacity for future growth.

Second, adapting to the changing patterns of demographics will present a growing challenge for cities everywhere. Low fertility rates and a declining and aging population pose a particular challenge to cities in Europe and Northeast Asia (see also Chapter 5). This demographic shift places a major burden on the public welfare system and decreases the likelihood of productivity growth; it will further increase the stress on public infrastructure services, too. Shrinking cities negatively affect economic growth, as vacant buildings reduce the capital value of real estate and create a diminishing tax base; financing public sector services, such as schools and hospitals, requires a strong tax base.

Cities in developing countries face demographic challenges, too, yet they are very different in kind than the cities in the developed world. In the developing world, the very young will constitute the majority of the population living in cities. In Uganda, for example, close to 50 percent of the national population is currently below the age of 14, and a mere 5 percent of the population is older than 55 (Indexmundi 2017). If these young people are not successfully absorbed into the labor market, pathological urbanization processes are unlikely to contribute to sustained urban productivity growth, but are likely to exacerbate urban poverty, social and political instability, and emigration of the highly skilled members of the labor force.

This brings us to the next challenge: changing migration patterns. An increasing number of people are fleeing conflict, economic stresses, and climate change hazards in their home countries, and are seeking new homes in cities within developed countries. Strict labor protection laws in the recipient countries often prevent migrants from working in the formal sector, who find themselves either working in activities in the informal sector or as recipients of public assistance programs. If not accounted for, a large influx of migrants increases local pressures on land and housing, and can increase the costs of living in cities. Countries that migrants are fleeing from are also left with challenges, including the emigration of members of a highly skilled labor force. This so-called brain drain reduces the potential of local productivity. Overall, when highly skilled migrants are legally constrained from contributing to high-productivity activities in their recipient countries, the global urban productivity frontier is diminished.

Rising inequalities in wages and wealth present another major challenge for the future of urban productivity. High inequality, paired with distorted land and housing prices, results in spatial misallocations of labor away from high-productivity and into low-productivity cities. Inequality disproportionately affects women, minority groups, and lower-income earners, reinforcing differences among classes, genders, and races. While inequality is on the rise in cities of developed countries, inequality levels in cities across Africa, Asia, and Latin America continue to be the highest in the world and are increasing in many cities. If unaddressed, inequality levels could reach new thresholds, reducing the labor productivity potential of a large share of the world's population.

Finally, cities across the world are encountering increasing pressures from global market economies. Cities that have managed to become one of these "global cities" now find themselves with high productivity levels, yet benefits are often captured by a global elite and seldom trickle down to the local workforce. In particular, those employed in the non-tradable sector experience stagnating wages, resulting in increasing polarization of income and wages. Cities that are not one of the "global players" are confronted with declining industries and emigration of skilled labor.

6.5.2 Opportunities

While pessimists are absorbed by these challenges, leading to predictions of economic slowdown in the foreseeable future, optimists believe in the human capacity to find creative ideas for future adaptation, turning challenges into opportunities for future growth. Nobody can predict the future of urban pro-ductivity with perfect accuracy. However, judging from the obstacles ahead, preventing these challenges from turning into crises is increasingly important.

For instance, cities experiencing an aging population could strategically incorporate newly arriving migrants into local labor markets to counter their negative population growth, ensuring sustained future economic growth that, in turn, is required to finance local infrastructure services. Wage-led growth could be an equitable strategy for recovery in economic downturns, as wage growth can support demand via consumption expenditures, and can induce higher-productivity growth. Changes in functional income distribution also have important supply side effects.

Moving towards a green economy could have tangible and considerable effects on productivity and economy growth. UNEP suggests that transitioning to a green economy does not only generate wealth and gains in natural capital, but it also produces a higher rate of GDP growth (UNEP 2011). The structural change from extractive capitalism towards a more sustainable system could create new jobs, especially for vulnerable communities. This requires reedu-cating and re-skilling the labor force, and must include those outside of the formal economy.

In addition, the role that cities and local governments can play in foster-ing urban productivity has yet to be realized. A great divergence between cit-ies within the same country can be traced back to effective versus destructive policies at the local level. Yet, effective policy-making at the local level alone cannot overcome the challenges that lie ahead. Aside from enabling national policies, the international level is crucial in and of itself, too. Especially in a globalizing world in which cities are deeply embedded in and affected by global dynamics, international collaboration in addressing future challenges is key. According to Piketty for example, the introduction of a progressive global tax on capital is the only way to address patrimonial capitalism and increasing wealth inequality.

Considering the level of international collaboration needed to implement such an endeavor, the years 2015 and 2016 should be contributing to optimism rather than pessimism. In September 2015, more than 150 world leaders came together to adopt the Sustainable Development Goals; in October of 2016, a series of member states reconvened at the Habitat III conference to envision the future of cities. Still, achieving the necessary levels of structural change in the way our world operates will require more than international, high-level conferences that result in commitments without actions, or agendas that will be rapidly forgotten. Local and national governments must be held account-able for their commitments, their misallocation of public resources, and the maldistribution of increased returns on productivity.

In cities across the world, imbalances of labor markets, increasing costs of housing, and a lack of pro-poor policies are damaging. Astronomical levels of income inequality in cities point to institutional and structural failures in income distribution, which must be addressed to ensure inclusive urbanization. Considering Piketty's findings on the state of today's capitalism, a more progressive tax on wealth and a fundamental adjustment for the financial system will be necessary to make today's economy socially equitable and ecologically sustainable. To reduce inequalities, we need accountable institutions, effective social programs, and strong links between the various levels of government in addition to stable economies and productivity growth.

Perhaps we should depart from using efficiency and productivity as the main metrics for judging the performance of urban areas and urbanization, and reintroduce moral philosophy into the equation, as Hausman and McPhearson (2006) suggest. Extensive public transfers and improvements to fiscal policy fostered better social cohesion in many Latin American countries, reducing poverty and widening access to both public services and opportunities at the national level. These strong national institutions must be recreated at the local level to address growing threats of urban inequality. A higher minimum wage, improved overtime thresholds, strengthening workers' collective bargaining rights, and stronger employment protection legislation would not only improve the situation of the working poor, it would also help reduce the wage gap between men and women, and between minority and non-minority workers. After all, the values of ethics, liberty, justice, and equality influence the outcomes of economics, and therefore could help economies work more effectively.

🌐 *References*

Amin, Ash, and Kevin Robins. 1990. The Re-Emergence of Regional Economies? The Mythical Geography of Flexible Accumulation. *Environment and Planning D: Society and Space* 8 (1): 7–34.

Anas, Alex, Kyu Sik Lee, and Gi-Taik Oh. 1996. Costs of Infrastructure Deficiencies in Manufacturing in Indonesia, Nigeria, and Thailand. Policy Research Working Paper 1604. Washington DC: The World Bank.

Bivens, Josh, and Lawrence Mishel. 2015. *Understanding the Historic Divergence between Productivity and a Typical Worker's Pay: Why It Matters and Why It's Real*. Washington DC: Economic Policy Institute (Instituto De Políticas Económicas).

Parilla, Joseph and Mark Muro. 2017. Understanding US Productivity Trends from the Bottom-Up. Brookings Institution, www.brookings.edu/research/understanding-us-productivity-trends-from-the-bottom-up/

Brown, Donald, Gordon McGranahan, and David Dodman. 2014. Urban Informality and Building a More Inclusive, Resilient and Green Economy. *Habitat International*. 53(April): 97–105.

Chen, Martha Alter. 2006. *Rethinking the Informal Economy: Linkages with the Formal Economy and the Formal Regulatory Environment.* Vol. 10. United Nations University, World Institute for Development Economics Research.

Chen, Marty. 2010. Informality, Poverty and Gender: Evidence from the Global South, in, Sylvia Chant (ed.), *The International Handbook of Gender and Poverty: Concepts, Research, Policy.* Cheltenham: Edward Elgar, pp. 463–471.

Cohen, Michael A. 1991. *Urban Policy and Economic Development: An Agenda for the 1990s.* Washington, DC: The World Bank.

Forman, Adam. 2014. Desperately needed Infrastructure Improvements Must Be Given Dedicated Funding. *Gotham Gazette.* July 22. www.gothamgazette.com/index.php/opinion/5151-needed-infrastructure-improvements-must-get-dedicated-funding-forman

Hannah, Lawrence, Alain Bertaud, Stephen Malpezzi, and Stephen Mayo. 1989. Malaysia: The Housing Sector; Getting the Incentives Right. World Bank Sector Report 7292. Washington, DC: The World Bank.

Hausman, Daniel M., and Michael S. McPherson. 2006. *Economic Analysis, Moral Philosophy and Public Policy.* Cambridge: Cambridge University Press.

Harris, John R., and Michael P. Todaro. 1970. Migration, Unemployment and Development: A Two-Sector Analysis. *The American Economic Review* 60 (1): 126–142.

Heintz, James. 2006. Growth, Employment, and Poverty Reduction. Discussion paper prepared for the workshop "Growth, Employment, and Poverty Reduction," held at the Department for International Development, 17 March.

Hsieh, Chang-Tai, and Enrico Moretti. 2015. *Why do Cities Matter? Local Growth and Aggregate Growth.* Chicago: Kreisman Working Papers Series in Housing Law and Policy No. 30. https://ssrn.com/abstract=2693282 or http://dx.doi.org/10.2139/ssrn.2693282

Indexmundi. 2017. *Uganda Demographics Profile 2017.* www.indexmundi.com/uganda/demographics_profile.html.

ILO. 2013. *Women and Men in the Informal Economy: A Statistical Picture (second edition).* Geneva: International Labour Organization.

ILO. 2008. *World of Work Report 2008. Income Inequalities in the Age of Financial Globalization.* Geneva: International Labor Organization.

Slonimczyk, Fabián. 2014. "Informal Employment in Emerging and Transition Economies." IZA World of Labor.

Martine, George. 2012. *The New Global Frontier: Urbanization, Poverty and Environment in the 21st Century.* London: Earthscan.

Morley, Samuel A. 1998. La pobreza en tiempos de recuperación económica y reforma en América Latina: 1985–1995, in *Política macroeconómica y pobreza en América Latina y el Caribe.* Madrid: Mundi-Prensa, pp. 47–70.

Obioma, Chigozie. 2016. Lagos Is Set to Double in Size in 15 Years. how Will My City Possibly Cope? The Guardian. www.theguardian.com/cities/2016/feb/22/lagos-population-double-size-how-cope?CMP=fb_a-cities_b-gdncities.

Organisation for Economic Co-operation and Development. *In It Together: Why Less Inequality Benefits All*. Paris: OECD Publishing, 2015. http://dx.doi.org/10.1787/9789264235120-en

Piketty, Thomas. 2014. Capital in the Twenty-First Century. Cambridge: Harvard University Press.

Preston, Samuel H. 1990. Urban Growth in Developing Countries: A Demographic Reappraisal. *Population and Development Review* 5 (2): 195–215.

Spence, Michael, Patricia Clarke Annez, and Robert M. Buckley. 2009. *Urbanization and Growth*. Commission on Growth and Development. Washington, DC: The World Bank.

Terry, Donald F. 2005. *Beyond Small Change: Making Migrant Remittances Count*. Washington, DC: Inter-American Development Bank.

UNEP. 2011 Towards a Green Economy: Pathways to Sustainable Development and Poverty Eradication. www.unep.org/greeneconomy. St-Martin-Bellevue, France: United Nations Environment Programme.

UN-Habitat. 2003. The Challenge of Slums: Global Report on Human Settlements 2003. *Management of Environmental Quality: An International Journal* 15(3): 337–338.

UN Habitat. 2014. *Construction of More Equitable Cities*. Nairobi: UN-Habitat, CAF, Avina.

World Bank. 2009. *Geography, Reshaping Economic. World development report*. Washington, DC: The World Bank.

Part II

Global Urban Sustainable Development

Chapter 7: Rethinking Urban Sustainability and Resilience

David Simon, Corrie Griffith, and Harini Nagendra

This chapter provides a critical review of the evolution, framings, and disciplinary underpinnings of narratives and discourses around two core concepts in this field – namely urban sustainability and resilience – over the last few decades. It further assesses the recent contributions and limitations of these approaches both conceptually and operationally with respect to an urbanizing world. Both terms entered the lexicon in relation to profound societal challenges of our time and were only subsequently applied to more specific contexts, including urban areas. Therefore, our account starts by surveying this broad canvas in order to contextualize the more detailed assessment of urban sustainability and resilience debates that follows. Strategically, this discussion introduces Part 2 on account of both the central importance of these twin concepts and the need to understand some of the diverse ways that they now find expression in key current urban challenges.

7.1 The Evolution of Urbanization and Sustainability Thinking

Following *Silent Spring*, Rachel Carson's (1962) landmark study of the effects of excessive pesticide use on bird life and food webs in the United States, international concern for humans' impact on the environment and the unsustainability of resource-intensive, consumerist lifestyles increased steadily. This concern was spurred by a series of industrial and shipping accidents that caused major pollution disasters, as well as other disparate strands in the 1960s. Consequently, the United Nations convened its landmark Conference on the Human Environment in Stockholm in 1972, for which three other classic texts in the sustainability canon were published from rather different perspectives on the need to live within resource constraints and in harmony with ecological principles. These were the Club of Rome's *Limits to Growth* (Meadows et al. 1972), Barbara Ward and René Dubos' *Only One Earth* (1972), and *The Ecologist* magazine's *A Blueprint for Survival* (1972). A key outcome of the Stockholm summit was the establishment of two specialist agencies, the United Nations Environment Programme (UNEP) and the UN Centre for Human Settlements (now the UN Human Settlements Programme, or UN-Habitat), to address environmental conservation and sustainability concerns in general and the complex challenges of urban development and sustainability, respectively.

Stockholm was also the first in what has become established as a regular series of global environmental sustainability summits, most notably the UN Conference on Environment and Development, or UNCED, in Rio de Janeiro in 1992; the World Summit on Sustainable Development, also called WSSD or "Rio+10" in Johannesburg in 2002; and the UN Conference on Sustainable Development, also called UNCSD or "Rio+20," held again in Rio in 2012. In parallel, the more specific annual UN Framework Convention on Climate Change (UNFCCC) Conferences of the Parties, and equivalent initiatives on other conventions and treaties have helped to focus attention and political negotiations, not always very successfully, on issues of sustainability. In addition, innumerable NGOs and other agencies operating at all spatial scales and from diverse philosophical and theoretical positions have emerged to create an immensely diverse ecosystem of environmentalisms, some of which advocate particular versions of sustainable development, while others argue for "deep" or other ecological environmentalism that is implicitly or explicitly antidevelopmental (compare with Giddens 2011; Bond 2012; Middleton et al. 1993; Death 2010).

Essentially, therefore, sustainable development has become successfully mainstreamed, to the stage that world political and religious leaders across the spectrum profess at least rhetorical commitment to the objective at summits and in policy statements, even if their actions are less than fully aligned with or even directly contradictory to this aim. Having become a "sloganized" concept, for want of a better term – and with which all wish to be associated, since it is universally considered to be a good thing – sustainability has inevitably lost its original progressive (or even radical and subaltern) purchase in relation to poverty reduction, redistribution, and environmental justice, for instance. The Brundtland Report's popularization of sustainable development came in response to a concern about limits to economic growth and associated environmental problems (WCED 1987), but there has always been disagreement over interpretation of the concept, including the extent to which it could be both a goal and a process, and how the economic, social, and environmental dimensions could be reconciled (WCED 1987; Simon 1989). Even now, most official policies and programmes constitute examples of "weak" sustainable development, comprising modest reform or regulatory measures, accompanied by much "greenwashing" to ensure minimal change to business as usual.

"Strong" sustainable development initiatives involving more substantive changes to current practices and lifestyles are generally associated with radical or progressive NGOs, grassroots movements, and the like, although some private firms are perhaps emerging as strong pioneers now that the green economy is seen increasingly to make business sense (for example, Zorrilla 2002; Simon 2003; Weiss and Burke 2012).

Although it had earlier origins – and, indeed, one can usefully understand sustainability in the context of the longer perspective of urban history (Lumley and Armstrong 2004; Douglas 2013) – direct concern with applying sustainability principles to urban contexts gained rapid momentum after the UNCED summit in Rio in 1992. The specific instrument of urban sustainability intervention has been Local Agenda 21 (LA21), the urban component of Agenda 21, one of the two principal outcomes of the UNCED summit. Local Agenda 21 required local governments worldwide to formulate a sustainability plan for their towns and cities via a consultative process. The International Council for Local Environmental Initiatives (now known as ICLEI- Local Governments for Sustainability), an international NGO established in 1990, was commissioned to oversee implementation of LA21.

Inevitably, progress in urbanizing the sustainability agenda has varied greatly by world region and even within individual countries. Even in high-income countries, it initially proved quite challenging to gain the political will of elected councillors and to engage citizens beyond small, environmentally aware and already engaged minorities, while town planners and engineers grappled with the necessary revisions of planning and building codes and materials, infrastructural provision, and even funding models. Initially, at least, the geographical concentration of wealth; industry; energy-intensive, elite lifestyles; and emissions – and the vested interests they represent – in large urban areas were widely perceived to provide formidable obstacles to major change (for example, see Pugh 1996).

The international community also recognized that urban areas in low- and lower-middle income countries would be unable to implement LA21 unaided. Local resource and revenue constraints, a lack of perceived relevance, the immediate basic needs deficits that demanded priority attention, and the rural orientation of official development assistance programmes at the time represented a severe combination of constraints (see Pugh 2000). Consequently, ICLEI came to focus much of its attention on devising specific measures that would be appropriate and acceptable in such countries. The Human Settlements Programme of the London-based International Institute of Environment and Development, long headed by David Satterthwaite, has also played a consistent and invaluable role in engaged thinking, writing, and advocacy around urban sustainability challenges in the Global South, not least in influencing policy within UN-Habitat (for examples, see Satterthwaite 1993, 1997; Parnell 2016; see also Chapter 9). Satterthwaite's (1997) paper remains important for clearly highlighting the fallacy that cities could become sustainable as urban islands, without sustainability in the wider territories and societies of which they form integral parts.

Programmes, organizations, and agendas developed under the banner of sustainability have grown steadily in number since the late twentieth century, and also across world regions and at multiple scales – from the level of the city or neighborhood to much broader global initiatives (Du Pisani 2007). UN-Habitat's twin series of biennial publications, *Global Report on Human Settlements*, and *State of the World's Cities* (and the latter's continental companion reports) reflect how that agency's thinking and programming on urban sustainability have evolved since the 1990s. Since its establishment in its current form in 2004, United Cities and Local Governments, the global association of subnational governments, has also played a prominent role in galvanizing urban sustainability actions, not least on climate change and the Urban Sustainable Development Goal, by its membership.

7.2 Urban Resilience: Evolution, Scope, Application, and Challenges

As with its counterpart term, "sustainability," the application of the term "resilience" to socioecological systems gained prominence in relation to discussions of broader issues of conservation (Folke 2006); both have been relatively recently applied to urban systems. Originally developed for application in fields as diverse as mathematics, engineering, materials science, and psychology (Olsson et al. 2015), researchers later applied resilience to ecological systems theory via mathematical models of population ecology (Bodin and Wiman 2004). People later broadened the concept of resilience to include issues of human drivers and responses to ecological change, and eventually to the consideration of the adaptive management of coupled social-ecological systems. In contrast to sustainability, the idea of resilience places greater emphasis on issues of coupled system dynamics that can lead to nonlinear feedbacks and to slow, as well as abrupt, system changes. Resilience keeps at its core the acceptance and management of constant change, uncertainty, and "unknowability," that is, the impossibility of achieving definite knowledge about system trajectories in complex social-ecological systems.

With the rapid acceleration of urban growth and its associated challenges, exacerbated by global environmental and climate change, resilience has become an increasingly visible term in discussions of urban planning and policy (Meerow et al. 2016). Resilience has found favor among widely divergent groups of actors, in large part because of the fuzziness and malleability of the term that enables it to act as a "boundary object" (Brand and Jax 2007), representing different things to different sets of players. Yet the fuzziness of the term also generates challenges for operationalization of resilience planning, making it difficult to develop clear metrics and indicators of resilience that can be monitored over time. For instance, resilience, in the urban planning context, has been defined variously as a goal, as a desired outcome, and as a process, making progress difficult to grasp or measure.

Like sustainability, resilience is fundamentally a normative concept (Strunz 2012), although not always explicitly defined as such. Most discussions around urban sustainability implicitly assume resilience to be a desirable property, although this has been increasingly criticized by research that addresses problems such as urban inequity (such as Vale and Campanella 2005). In contrast to sustainability, the concept of resilience (and its counterpart, vulnerability) implies a greater emphasis on urban processes, including adaptive capacity to maintain dynamic equilibria and transformation to alternative desired social-ecological states. The goal of such planning has typically been geared towards achieving specific outcomes in response to global challenges, such as climate change (Romero-Lankao and Dodman 2011). Some critics (for example, Olsson et al. 2015) argue that a fundamental dissonance exists in the way resilience is framed in the natural sciences, as a desirable system property, and in the social sciences, where the resilience of certain sociocultural norms that perpetuate inequity and power imbalances may be inherently problematic, requiring transformation and system change rather than resilience and the perpetuation of the status quo.

In recent years, the importance of resilience planning in an era of increased uncertainty has also gained ground, leading some scholars to propose the idea of cities that accept concepts of disturbance and change as fundamental to urban planning (Ahern 2011). Planning for resilience in an era of change requires the effective incorporation of typical characteristics of twenty-first century urban centers, including challenges of social, ecological, and economic diversity; balancing modularity with teleconnected networks (Seto et al. 2012); and redundancy with efficiency. A city with a diverse economy and reduced socioeconomic inequities can be expected to rebound more quickly from disasters as compared to a city with a specialized, narrow economic base with strong economic and social hierarchies, for example (Campanella 2006).

Finally, the protection and restoration of urban ecosystems is a historically neglected component of resilience planning that is now gaining significant traction across the globe (McPhearson et al. 2015). Cities with functioning, diverse, interconnected, multifunctional ecosystems exhibit greater resilience to natural disasters such as tornadoes and floods (Ahern 2011). Urban ecosystems thus provide cost-effective approaches to increasing the capacity of urban landscapes to deal with uncertainties and shocks that are typically more robust compared to anthropogenic, engineered solutions (Ernstson et al. 2010). Further, given their multifunctionality, urban ecosystems provide diverse services in cities, acting to increase human well-being. Urban green and blue spaces constitute public goods that increase the quality of the environment (including air and water) and, as commons, provide food, fodder, and fuel wood to many urban residents, particularly in cities of the Global South. Thus, urban ecosystems increase the resilience of residents to food shortages in times of crisis, providing common pool resources accessed by all, but in particular used by disadvantaged sections of society, such as practitioners of ecosystem-based livelihoods and urban migrant laborers (Colding and Barthel 2013; Nagendra 2016). Urban social movements, drawing on a wide base of urban cultural and social diversity, can be especially important in acting as a buffer against the problematic trends of privatization of urban green spaces witnessed in many cities. In this context, urban ecosystems connect the social and the ecological, providing an important motivation for social and community action that cuts across sociocultural and economic barriers, facilitates social entrepreneurship, and maintains feedback loops that contribute to the renewal of social capital in cities from Bogotá – where a gradient of ecological networks has been suggested as a way to connect wild habitats to built spaces (Andrade et al. 2013) – to Cape Town, where a proposed urban biosphere reserve has the potential to address ecological goals of biodiversity conservation as well as social goals of inclusion and poverty alleviation (Krasny et al. 2013).

7.3 Global Sustainability through Urbanization and Environmental Change

Whether or not it is an oxymoronic concept, as often claimed, sustainability pervades today's politics, research, and practice in efforts to meet human development goals without compromising the resources and environment that sustain the economic goods and services needed to support them (see Section 7.1). However, in reality, the three pillars that underpin traditional sustainability thought (economic, social, and environmental) are rarely approached together, resulting in fragmented research perspectives and policies. Efforts have tended to focus on economic and environmental dimensions, with less focus on the social; however, more holistic interpretations of sustainability are emerging that focus on urbanization and cities as key components of this process (see Bina 2013; Seto et al. 2012, Pickett et al. 2013; Steele et al. 2015).

"Ecosystem services," "well-being," and "low-carbon" are just some of the new ideas and concepts that have moved the sustainable development discourse forward (Bina 2013), increasingly in the urban context.

Moreover, the importance of a better understanding of urbanization processes, interactions, and feedbacks with other systems for global sustainability has become increasingly clear over the last decade. Urban environmental change research has expanded the place-based approach associated with traditional urban studies to address the temporal and spatial interactions that urbanization, a social-ecological process itself, has with other biophysical systems (Sánchez-Rodríguez et al. 2005; Seto et al. 2016). Knowledge and actions that deal with these interactions are critical for a modern agenda towards a more equitable and healthy world. Any hope of achieving global sustainability in holistic terms requires that we understand the connections between urban processes, natural resources, land change, human migration, financial flows, and technology transfers and innovation with environmental change in this broader context (Seto et al. 2012; Pincetl 2016).

The next section briefly reviews salient areas within urbanization and global environmental change (GEC) research and practice that have added to sustainability and resilience thinking over the last decade.

7.4 Urban Adaptation and Mitigation within Sustainability and Resilience

The connections between urbanization and GECs, including the more frequent consequences of climate-related disasters and greater climate uncertainty, have increased the need to climate-proof and adapt urban areas to potential risks (Richards and Bradbury 2007; Thornbush et al. 2013). Concerned parties have traditionally focused on the impacts in rural areas, since damage therein was often more extreme, causing concern over potential damage to natural resources and disruption of agricultural systems (Birkmann et al. 2010). However, attention to urban areas grew rapidly following numerous weather extremes and reports thereafter, highlighting existing gaps in our understanding of the unique urban challenges related to adaptation (Commission on Climate Change and Development 2009). These challenges are attributed to cities' regional and global connectivity and their diverse characteristics, including their population size and density, stage within their respective development processes, and variances in hard and soft infrastructure. Particularly within low- and middle-income countries, where cities are often rapidly urbanizing, exposure to disease and other health problems became cause for deep concern and inquiry into urban coping capacity in the context of nonexistent or substandard development infrastructure, such as weak water and sanitation systems; high concentrations of urban poverty, including slums and informal settlements; and weak social and political institutions (Birkmann et al. 2010).

In the last decade, as more frequent and often more severe occurrences of extreme events – including intense rains and flooding, hurricanes and storm surges, and heat waves – persisted, so did the emergence of urban adaptation responses, prompting research on multiscale responses within urban areas (that is, at the individual, neighborhood, community, or city levels) (Bicknell et al. 2009). A number of research advancements followed, including the identification and assessment of the diversity of actions and comprehensive adaptation strategies in cities across regions (Carmin et al. 2012), the urban governance and institutional capacities to pursue adaptation (Anguelovski and Carmin 2011; Aylett 2015), and more nuanced understandings of drivers of vulnerability and risk in various urban populations (Garschagen and Romero Lankao 2015). In the latter case, resilience theory has provided a lens or tool to approach climate change adaptation and to manage social-ecological systems (Garschagen 2011; Section 7.2). Today, "resilience" is often used in the same manner as "adaptation"; that is, building urban resilience often implies building urban adaptive capacity to stresses and shocks from climatic events. Efforts to create urban resilience "toolkits" through disciplinary integration have grown in recent years, along with attempts to codesign comprehensive city strategies with the involvement of multiple stakeholders (Solecki et al. 2011).

On the other side of the coin, mitigation actions, like adaptive actions, are often implemented locally in cities as part of national efforts to reduce GHG emissions. In aggregate, aggressive urban mitigation actions could have profound global impacts (Seto et al. 2014). Since the 1992 Kyoto Protocol and events thereafter, such as Rio+20 and the 2015 UNFCCC summit in Paris (COP 21) (see Section 7.1), many nations have committed to reducing their emissions footprints as part of broader sustainability efforts. This has translated given impetus to cities, where the majority of emissions occur and where the majority of efforts to curb them are undertaken. Many cities have created baseline GHG emissions inventories and sustainability portfolios that include consumption- and production-based efforts to reduce emissions. Some of these efforts include municipal and residential emissions reductions through improving energy efficiencies in built infrastructure, encouraging alternative modes of transportation, and increasing efficiencies in water treatment and distribution; promoting urban food production, composting and recycling, and reduction in water use; and integrating green infrastructure and tree planting into the urban landscape for carbon sequestration. These and myriad other efforts and innovations have been tailored to cities' individual needs and cultural, geographical, and economic characteristics (Seto et al. 2014; Simon 2016). "Low-carbon" cities are a new trend found in the discourse of mitigation that people are employing in urban environments worldwide. Such cities are increasingly being touted as having capabilities to transform sociotechnical and governance systems (Bulkeley et al. 2011) through the redesign and recon-figuration of energy infrastructures. Personnel at ICLEI, the World Bank, and the World Wildlife Fund in China, among others, for example, are pursuing a low-carbon agenda wherein "a low-carbon city recognizes its responsibility to act. It pursues a step-by-step approach towards carbon neutrality, urban resilience and energy security, supporting an active green economy and stable green infrastructure" (ICLEI 2016). Such actions represent what some refer to as the emergence of a low-carbon urban transition. However, both actual progress and the extent to which urban adaptation or resilience and carbon reduction efforts are integrated with broader development goals are unclear and remain in need of further research.

7.5 Integrating Adaptation, Mitigation, and Urban Development for an Equitable Future

Urban system complexity and dynamics across scales are not new to the under-standing of urban sustainability, but approaches often continue to oversim-plify the interactions of urban systems with other socioeconomic, geopolitical, and environmental processes. Urbanization and GEC research foster multidi-mensional perspectives that transcend the short term and cross spatial scales, but they would benefit from further disciplinary integration to build new the-ories and methods. Such knowledge, for example, would be useful for cities to better operationalize adaptation to and mitigation of the negative impacts of climate and other environmental change, and could strengthen the social dimension in the sustainability narrative (Sánchez-Rodríguez 2008).

   As a term, sustainability has often been used to bridge mitigation and adap-tation; it has been well documented that to achieve long-term urban sustaina-bility, efforts to promote urban resilience to climate change that are inclusive of both adaptation and mitigation strategies must be bundled with broader development policies and plans (Leichenko 2011). Research continues to stress the importance of integrating the two often conceptually distinct strands of sustainability and mitigation/adaptation (Golubchikov 2011; Dodman 2009; Thornbush et al. 2013), as findings show that adaptation actions (such as greater use of air conditioning as urban temperatures rise) can sometimes have an inverse effect on mitigation (a proportional higher energy use and GHG emissions) – known as maladaptation.

The idea that integral components of long-term urban sustainability and global sustainability include justice and equity is emerging within urban responses to climate change. This shift arises from our recognition that, first, the responsibility for climate change is not equally distributed, meaning that some nations and cities are doing more with respect to mitigation and reducing emissions than others. Second, climate change does not affect all people equally or in the same ways, as some populations, and groups within populations, are more vulnerable due to historically rooted, political-economic relationships and processes that are not beneficial for all (Steele et al. 2015). Recent inquiry into the relationship between climate justice principles in urban policy development has found remarkable differences in both mitigation and adaptation policies in terms of distributional and procedural justice in cities of both the Global North and South (Bulkeley et al. 2012).

Further research into vulnerability, equity, and social justice could help frame policies with fair or just outcomes through a greater understanding of existing inequality or where/how future inequality might occur. Resilience theory that incorporates governance, institutional processes, and organizational structures could add to the understanding of the existing strengths and constraints of governments, institutions, and organizations in different sociocultural contexts, yielding more successful integration of concepts of resilience and transformation in sectoral policies, urban planning, and design (Garschagen 2011). Emerging eco-social justice perspectives are also broadening the sustainability agenda by increasing attention to the needed integration between environmental change, social change, human vulnerability or resilience, and biodiversity loss in the city (Steele et al. 2015).

Ultimately, the call to transform our cities and to push the "urbanization transition" along more sustainable trajectories is urgent, but challenging. To be successful, it requires understanding context and leverage points for change, which will require continued analysis of urbanization processes (including drivers, interactions, and outcomes) that occur at multiple scales (see Part III, "Urban Transformations to Sustainability"). Research approaches that frame urbanization as an opportunity for global sustainability, wherein principles of equity and justice are centralized, hold promise for achieving such transformations.

◎ References

Ahern, J. (2011). From Fail-Safe to Safe-To-Fail: Sustainability and Resilience in the New Urban World. *Landscape and Urban Planning* 100(4): 341–43.

Andrade, G.I., Remolina, F., and Wiesner, D. (2013). Assembling the Pieces: A Framework for the Integration of Multi-Functional Ecological Main Structure in the Emerging Urban Region of Bogotá, Colombia. *Urban Ecosystems* 16: 723–739.

Anguelovski, I., and Carmin, J. (2011). Something Borrowed, Everything New: Innovation and Institutionalization in Urban Climate Governance. *Current Opinion in Environmental Sustainability* 3: 169–175.

Aylett, A. (2015) Institutionalizing the Urban Governance of Climate Change Adaptation: Results of an International Survey, *Urban Climate* 14(1) December: 4–16

Bicknell, J., Dodman, D., and Satterthwaite, D. (eds.). (2009). *Adapting Cities to Climate Change: Understanding and Addressing the Development Challenges*. London: Earthscan.

Bina, O. (2013). The Green Economy and Sustainable Development: An Uneasy Balance? *Environment and Planning C: Government and Policy* 31: 1023–1047.

Birkmann, J., Garschagen, M., Kraas, F., and Quang, N. (2010). Adaptive Urban Governance: New Challenges for the Second Generation of Urban Adaptation Strategies to Climate Change. *Sustain Science* 5(2):185–206

Bodin, P., and B. Wiman. (2004). Resilience and Other Stability Concepts in Ecology: Notes on Their Origin, Validity, and Usefulness. *ESS Bulletin* 2.2: 33–43.

Bond, P. (2012) *Politics of Climate Justice: Paralysis Above, Movement Below*. Durban: UKZN Press.

Brand, F.S., and Jax, K. (2007). Focusing the Meaning (s) of Resilience: Resilience as a Descriptive Concept and a Boundary Object. *Ecology and Society* 12: 23. www.ecologyandsociety.org/vol12/iss1/art23/

Bulkeley, H., Carmin, J., Castán Broto, V., Edwards, G.A.S., and Fuller, S. (2013). Climate Justice and Global Cities: Mapping the Emerging Discourses. *Global Environmental Change*, 23(5): 914–925. DOI: 10.1016/j.gloenvcha.2013.05.010.

Bulkeley, H., Castán Broto, V., Hodson, M., and Marvin, S. (2011). *Cities and Low Carbon Transitions*. Abingdon, Oxon: Routledge.

Campanella, T.J. (2006). Urban Resilience and the Recovery of New Orleans. *Journal of the American Planning Association* 72(2): 141–146.

Carmin, J., Nadkarni, N., and Rhie, C. (2012). *Progress and Challenges in Urban Climate Adaptation Planning: Results of a Global Survey*. Cambridge, MA: DUSP/MIT.

Carson, R. (1962). *Silent Spring*. New York: Houghton Mifflin [later also Penguin Modern Classic]

Colding, J., and Barthel, S. (2013). The potential of 'Urban Green Commons' in the resilience building of cities. *Ecological Economics* 86:156–66.

Commission on Climate Change and Development (2009). Governance Gaps in *Closing the Gaps: Disaster Risk Reduction and Adaptation to Climate Change in Developing Countries, Commission on Climate Change and Development*, Stockholm: Commission on Climate Change and Development, pp. 24–33.

Death, C. (2010). *Governing Sustainable Development*. London and New York: Routledge.

Dodman, D. (2009). Blaming Cities for Climate Change? An Analysis for Urban Green-House Gas Emissions Inventories. *Environment and Urbanization*, 21(1): 185–201.

Douglas, I. (2013). *Cities: An Environmental History*. London and New York: I.B. Tauris.

Du Pisani, J.A. (2007). Sustainable Development – Historical Roots of the Concept, *Environmental Sciences*, 3(2): 83–96, DOI:10.1080/15693430600688831

Ernstson, H., van der Leeuw, S.E., Redman, C.L., Meffert, D.J., Davis, G., Alfsen, C., and Elmqvist, T. (2010). Urban Transitions: On Urban Resilience and Human-Dominated Ecosystems *Ambio* 39(8): 531–545.

The Ecologist, (1972). *A Blueprint for Survival*. London: The Ecologist Magazine.

Folke, C. (2006). Resilience: The Emergence of a Perspective for Social–Ecological Systems Analyses. *Global environmental change* 16(3): 253–267.

Garschagen, M., (2011). Resilience and Organisational Institutionalism from a Cross-Cultural Perspective: An Exploration Based on Urban Climate Change Adaptation in Vietnam. *Natural Hazards (2013)* 67: 25–46 DOI 10.1007/s11069-011-9753-4.

Garschagen, M., and Romero Lankao, P. (2015). Exploring the relationships between urbanization trends and climate change vulnerability. *Climatic Change*, 133 (1): 37–52. doi:10.1007/s10584-013-0812-6.

Giddens, A. (2011). *The Politics of Climate Change*, 2nd edn. Cambridge: Polity.

Golubchikov, O. (2011). *Climate Neutral Cities: How to Make Cities Less Energy and Carbon Intensive and More Resilient to Climatic Challenges*. Geneva: United Nations Economic Commission for Europe (UNECE).

ICLEI (2016, March 4). *Low-Carbon City*.

Krasny, M.E., Lundholm, C., Shava, S., Lee, E., and Kobori, H. (2013). Urban Landscapes as Learning Arenas for Biodiversity and Ecosystem Services Management, in Elmqvist, T., Fragkias, M., Goodness, J., Güneralp, B., Marcotullio, P.J., and McDonald, R.I., et al. (eds.) *Urbanization, Biodiversity and Ecosystem Services: Challenges and Opportunities*. The Netherlands: Springer, pp. 629–664.

Leichenko, R. (2011). Climate Change and Urban Resilience. *Current Opinion in Environmental Sustainability*. 3: 164–168.

Lumley, S., and Armstrong, P. (2004). Some of the Nineteenth Century Origins of the Sustainability Concept, *Environment, Development and Sustainability* 6(3): 367–378.

McPhearson, T., Andersson, E., Elmqvist, T., and Frantzeskaki, N. (2015). Resilience of and through Urban Ecosystem Services. *Ecosystem Services* 12: 152–156.

Meadows, M., Meadows, M., Randers, J., and Behrens, W. (1972). *The Limits to Growth*. London: Pan Books.

Meerow, S., Newell, J.P., and Stults, M. (2016). Defining Urban Resilience: A Review. *Landscape and Urban Planning* 147: 38–49.

Middleton, N., O'Keefe, P., and Moyo, S. (1993). *Tears of the Crocodile: from Rio to reality in the Developing World*. London: Pluto.

Nagendra, H. (2016). *Nature in the City: Bengaluru in the Past, Present, and Future*. Delhi: Oxford University Press.

Olsson, L., Jerneck, A., Thoren, H., Persson, J. and O'Byrne, D. (2015). Why Resilience Is Unappealing to Social Science: Theoretical and Empirical Investigations of the Scientific Use of Resilience. *Science Advances* 1(4), p.e1400217, DOI: 10.1126/sciadv.1400217.

Parnell, S. (2016). Defining a Global Urban Development Agenda, *World Development* 78: 529–540. http://dx.doi.org/10.1016/j.worlddev.2015.10.028.

Pickett, S.T.A., Cadenasso, M.L., McGrath, M. (eds.) (2013). *Resilience in Ecology and Urban Design: Linking Theory and Practice for Sustainable Cities*. New York: Springer.

Pincetl, S. (2016). Urban Precipitation: A Global Perspective, in K.C. Seto, W.D. Solecki, and C.A. Griffith (eds.) *The Routledge Handbook of Urbanization and Global Environmental Change*. London and New York: Routledge, pp. 152–168.

Pugh, C. (ed.) (1996). *Sustainability, the Environment and Urbanization*. London: Earthscan.

Pugh, C. (ed.) (2000). *Sustainable Cities in Developing Countries*. London: Earthscan.

Richards, J., and Bradbury, S. (2007). Sustainability is not only about carbon emissions. *Building Engineer* 82(9): 40.

Romero-Lankao P, and Dodman D. (2011). Cities in Transition: Transforming Urban Centers from Hotbeds of GHG Emissions and Vulnerability to Seedbeds of Sustainability and Resilience: Introduction and Editorial Overview. *Current Opinion in Environmental Sustainability* 3(3): 113–120.

Sánchez-Rodríguez, R. (2008). Urban Sustainability and Global Environmental Change: Reflections for an Urban Agenda in G. Martine, G. McGranahan, M. Montgomery and R. Fernández-Castilla (Eds.), *The New Global Frontier Urbanization, Poverty and Environment in the 21st Century*. London and Sterling, VA: Earthscan, pp. 149–164.

Sánchez-Rodríguez, R., Seto, K. C., Simon, D., Solecki, W. D., Kraas, F., and Laumann, G. (2005). Science Plan Urbanization and Global Environmental Change Project (IHDP Report No. 15). Bonn: International Human Dimensions Programme on Global Environmental Change.

Satterthwaite, D. (1993). The Impact on Health of Urban Environments. *Environment and Urbanization*, 5 (2): 87–111.

Satterthwaite, D. (1997). Sustainable Cities or Cities That Contribute to Sustainable Development? *Urban Studies* 34 (10): 1667–1691.

Seto, K.C., Solecki, W.D., and Griffith, C.A. (eds.) (2016). *The Routledge Handbook of Urbanization and Global Environmental Change*. London and New York: Routledge.

Seto K.C., S. Dhakal, A. Bigio, H. Blanco, G.C. Delgado, D. Dewar, et al. (2014). Human Settlements, Infrastructure and Spatial Planning in Edenhofer, O., R. Pichs-Madruga, Y. Sokona, E. Farahani, S. Kadner, K. Seyboth, et al. (eds.) *Climate Change 2014: Mitigation of Climate Change*. Contribution of Working Group III to the Fifth Assessment Report of the Intergovernmental Panel on Climate Change. Cambridge: Cambridge University Press.

Seto, K.C., Reenberg, A., Boone, C.G, Fragkias, M., Haase, D., Langanke, T., et al. (2012). Urban Land Teleconnections and Sustainability. *Proceedings of the National Academy of Sciences*, 109(20): 7687–7692.

Simon, D. (1989). Sustainable Development: Theoretical Construct or Attainable Goal? *Environmental Conservation* 16(1): 41–48.

Simon, D. (2003). Dilemmas of Development and the Environment in a Globalising World: Theory, Policy and Praxis, *Progress in Development Studies* 3(1): 5–41.

Simon, D. (2016) Green cities: from tokenism to incrementalism and transformation, in Simon, D. (ed.) Rethinking Sustainable Cities: Accessible, green and fair. Bristol: Policy Press.

Solecki, W., R. Leichenko, and K. O'Brien. (2011). Climate Change Adaptation Strategies and Disaster Risk Reduction in Cities: Connections, Contentions, and Synergies. *Current Opinion in Environmental Sustainability* 2011 (3): 35–141.

Steele, W., Mata, L., and Fuenfgeld, H. (2015). Urban climate Justice: Creating Sustainable Pathways for Humans and Other Species. *Current Opinion in Environmental Sustainability* 2015(14): 121–126.

Strunz, S. (2012). Is Conceptual Vagueness an Asset? Arguments from Philosophy of Science Applied to the Concept of Resilience. *Ecological Economics 76*: 112–118.

Thornbush, M., O. Golubchikov, and S. Bouzarovski (2013) Sustainable Cities Targeted by Combined Mitigation–Adaptation Efforts for Future-Proofing. *Sustainable Cities and Society*, 9: 1–9.

Vale, L.J., and Campanella, T.J. (2005). *The Resilient City: How Modern Cities Recover from Disaster*. New York: Oxford University Press.

Ward, B., and Dubos, R. (1972). *Only One Earth*. Harmondsworth: Penguin.

Weiss, T. and Burke, M.J. (2012). Legitimacy, Identity and Climate Change: Moving from International to World Society? *Third World Quarterly* 32(6): 1057–1072.

World Commission on Environment and Development (WECD) (1987). *Our Common Future*. Oxford: Oxford University Press.

Zorrilla, C. (2002). Reflections on Sustainability from the Trenches. *Development* 45(3): 54–58.

Chapter 8: Indicators for Measuring Urban Sustainability and Resilience

David Gómez-Álvarez and Eduardo López-Moreno with Edgardo Bilsky, Karina Blanco Ochoa, and Efrén Osorio Lara

8.1 Introduction

Due to the unprecedented growth and emergence of urban areas around the world, urbanization is one of the most significant trends of the twenty-first century. By 2030, 60 percent of the world's population is expected to live in cities, and by 2050, nearly 70 percent (UN-Habitat 2015). The acceleration of the urban phenomenon poses unexpected and motley challenges for contemporary societies, which are in need of new metrics to measure the dimensions circumscribing today's urbanization.

Urban indicators offer an overall snapshot of the city in order to determine intra-urban variations and areas that require greater attention from policy-makers. In terms of policy use and analysis, urban indicators play a key role in creating good policies for three main reasons: first, they highlight relevant issues that should be considered throughout the design and implementation of public policies; second, they are effective tools for policy-makers to set concrete targets for urban policies (OECD 2000); and third, they can help to assess the performance of the policies implemented by local, regional, and national authorities.

New metrics require a shift in the conceptualization and understanding of city progress, moving well beyond traditional economic metrics towards more comprehensive and holistic perspectives that position both human and environmental well-being at their cores. The shortcomings and inadequacies of conventional economic indicators as development standards reveal that urban well-being can no longer be equated with economic progress. Thus, a paradigmatic transformation that moves away from this traditional perspective towards new measurements of development becomes fundamental.

This chapter addresses the importance and value of urban indicators and their contribution to the design of better informed, sound policies. It briefly reviews the evolution of different developments in measuring and under-standing cities, demonstrating that models based on classical economics have been insufficient. The New Urban Agenda, the Paris Agreement, and the 2030 Development Agenda – embodied in the urban Sustainable Development Goal (SDG) 11 (see Chapters 7 and 9) – require the introduction of new and innovative sets of indicators. We must use such tools in analyzing current urbanization patterns through multidimensional approaches to improve the difficult task of managing cities and to refine policy-making in accordance with the SDGs. This work seeks to demonstrate the value of urban data as an essential tool for the formulation of better informed policies at local, national, and international levels. Such data provide useful information that allows for strategic decision-making oriented towards the mitigation of both direct and indirect consequences of urbanization in diverse contexts and city sectors.

The next section presents the evolution of measurement tools, emphasizing the main characteristics and contributions of each generation of indicators. Thereafter, the chapter provides a discussion of the importance of local and regional government empowerment for meeting the 2030 Development Agenda and concludes by emphasizing the need for greater efforts to design better measurement instruments to fill the gaps in existing sets of urban indicators.

8.2 The Need for Urban Indicators

In many parts of the world, urban phenomena and processes of urbanization remain poorly documented, understood, and measured. Many cities around the world are suffering from inadequate urban data, leading to an information crisis that is undermining their capacity to develop effective urban policies (Muhammad 2001). Too often, the existing data that cities have are not adequately detailed, documented, or harmonized, or are not available and accessible for critical issues relating to urban growth and development.

Further, numerous cities lack a sustained or systematic appraisal of urban problems, such as loss of public space, environmental impact, and land consumption. Due to the inadequacy of existing measurement tools along with urban data deficiencies in these cities, there is little internal appreciation of what their own policies and programs are achieving (Muhammad 2001). This impedes appropriate monitoring and assessment, as well as an accurate formulation of public policies. Even in countries with a strong monitoring culture and data collection practices, the development of a coherent and reliable set of indicators for urban areas is not a simple task (Wong 2006).

The arrival of the 2030 Development Agenda, along with the SDGs, marks a turning point with great potential to fill the urban data vacuum in the upcoming years. According to the monitoring framework proposed by the "Urban SDG," embodied in SDG 11, which calls on us to "make cities and human settlements inclusive, safe, resilient and sustainable," accurate urban data and metrics enable cities to make decisions about the best policies and means to track urban progress, while also documenting a city's performance in terms of policy outcomes and achievements (UN-Habitat 2015). The assessment and monitoring of the effects of urban dynamics are frequently used as tools in urban planning for guaranteeing a more sustainable development path. Therefore, a monitoring framework oriented towards improving the difficult task of administering and managing cities in accordance with the 2030 Development Agenda is a fundamental precondition to meeting the SDG targets.

Furthermore, according to the Organisation for Economic Co-operation and Development, or OECD, "Indicators are needed to monitor and evaluate the impact of compact city policies. They will make it possible to benchmark progress and establish future goals. In particular, internationally comparable indicators can help policy makers analyze their policy performance from a wider perspective and improve their policy actions" (OECD 2012: 80). In this regard, urban indicators are crucial tools for providing objective evidence of prevailing conditions and changes over time (Muhammad 2001) associated with complex urban phenomena, yet they must also be able to evolve as the world becomes more urbanized. It will become increasingly important to develop a greater amount of meaningful urban indicators that aim for a broader depiction of urban dynamics.

8.3 The Evolution of Measuring and Monitoring Cities: What Has Been Done?

To date, there have been several attempts to measure a city's progress towards sustainable urban development. Diverse actors and stakeholders working at different scales have immersed themselves in the difficult task of defining a set of indicators covering the totality of the urban picture in order to assess the state of urban development across nations. However, due to the increasing need to measure a broader conception of human and societal well-being, both global and local efforts to develop urban indicators have moved beyond economic growth as a metric for progress towards a comprehensive and integral understanding of human and ecological welfare. This has meant a change from a national income accounting system to a more localized and people-centered approach (Wong 2014).

The initial attempts to measure and assess urban development through standardized metrics were carried out by supranational organizations such as the World Bank, the UN, and the OECD, among others. They focused on developing isolated and sectoral indicators that would monitor and collect information from the national level, leading to an incomplete depiction of urban dynamics. More recently, national efforts through domestic statistical agencies have also collected data at the national and subnational levels within certain countries. Both public and private subnational and local efforts have also collected data in a decentralized fashion, which, under certain circumstances, could be more reliable.

In the context of the Post-2015 Development Agenda, former UN Secretary General Ban Ki-moon pointed out that we need to "look beyond the confines of economic growth that have dominated development policy and agendas for many years" (UN-Habitat 2013: iii). Current urban indicators should "examine how cities can generate and equitably distribute the benefits and opportunities associated with prosperity, ensuring economic well-being, social cohesion, environmental sustainability, and a better quality of life in general" (ibid.). In addition, the OECD has emphasized that "the measurement of sustainable development requires drawing together indicators from the three dimensions of sustainable development, the economy, the environment and society. The two primary aims are to form a coherent picture of sustainable development trends and to provide information that is relevant to policy questions" (OECD 2000: 7).

In this spirit, during the 2016 World Economic Forum in Davos, the leaders of international organizations and institutions that have traditionally relied on economic metrics to measure development argued that GDP is not a good way to assess national economic health and that a new measure is urgently required which better assesses the dynamics that have emerged as a result of urbanization processes. (Thomson 2016). This echoes longstanding critiques by social activists, progressive economists, and some international agencies. The current GDP-based approach emerged as the result of a long process of empirical and conceptual evolution, which began early in the twentieth century when Simon Kuznets introduced GDP in the 1930s. Since then, the design and the development of concepts, metrics, and monitoring frameworks have been a constant around the world.

After analyzing the main urban indicators, one can distinguish three main generations in their evolution over time. These generations attempt to quantify a greater number of urban dynamics components in order to better measure and understand complex urban phenomena, each conceived from diverse contexts, frameworks, and international consensus regarding the conceptualization of development. The first generation is based on classical economic indicators as a metric for city progress; the second generation is characterized by the use and design of thematic indicators based on a broader understanding of development, which is embodied in the Millennium Development Goals, or MDGs; the third generation corresponds to the current set of indicators that address more holistically and comprehensively the new conceptualization of city prosperity contained in the 2030 Development Agenda and the SDGs (Figure 8.1).

It is important to emphasize that their evolution through successive generations does not mean that indicators from the first and second generations are now useless, obsolete, or invalid due to their antiquity. What this evolution demonstrates is ongoing progress in the increasing complexity and improvement of urban indicators to offer a broader approach to urban dynamics. Indeed, first-generation indicators continue to be used in different contexts, not least as updates to long time series, and demand remains for some data used in them. Not all are amenable to incorporation into newer generation indicators, but having some basic data is preferable to none. In Sections 8.3–8.5, we will explain in further detail each generation of indicators and their respective main characteristics. We will also provide some examples of urban indicators that best illustrate each generation.

First Generation

- Conventional economic metrics to measure progress: macroeconomic approach
- Atomistic, unidimensional, and simplistic perspective
- Isolated indicators such as population, GDP, city sprawl
- Examples: UN World Urbanization Prospects; World Bank World Development Indicators Series

Second Generation

- Thematic and sectoral urban indicators: assessment of new dimensions of urban dynamics
- Broader understanding of development
- First attempt to measure and assess at the local level
- Millenium Development Goals as guidelines towards urban development
- Lack of a territorial approach
- Examples: Global City Indicators Program – World Bank; Global Urban Indicators – UN-Habitat; Urban Governance Index – UN-Habitat; The Cities Data Book – Asian Development Bank

Third Generation

- Holistic, integral, comprehensive, and multidimensional monitoring frameworks: human and ecological well-being at the core
- New conceptualization of city prosperity: city's subjective well-being
- 2030 Development Agenda and SDGs as guidelines towards sustainable urban development
- Synergy among indicators rather than isolation
- New actors and stakeholders involved in designing monitoring frameworks
- Examples: World Council on City Data; City Prosperity Index – UN-Habitat; Better Life Index – OECD

Figure 8.1 The evolution of urban indicators

8.4 First Generation of Urban Indicators

Over most of the past century, our understanding of city dynamics was very limited, due in part to data sparseness and deficiencies. The main indicators to measure progress and development were economic metrics with a macro-perspective, which only addressed three main dimensions of the city: the economic dimension, through GDP; the demographic dimension, through population count; and the size dimension, through city sprawl. In this manner, people measured cities using isolated indicators that reflected only a small piece of the city puzzle. Even basic attempts to understand urban dynamics through population size are problematic, in part because of the diverse institutions carrying them out. Urban indicators that emerged within this first generation illustrate the urban reality with an atomistic, unidimensional, and simplistic approach. Because these indicators were based on economics, they were not useful for explaining subjective urban issues such as well-being in terms of quality of life. Furthermore, the monitoring frameworks of this generation lack local contextualization. They have a generic and objective quantitative nature, and they serve only for comparative exercises.

The first attempt to develop urban indicator sets by a supranational organization occurred during the 1960s when the World Bank launched the first World Development Indicators Series, which aimed to monitor city achievements by the international development goals of that time (Wong 2006, 2014). These series continue to be published annually, with each year's report focusing on a specific aspect of development (World Bank 2016) to reflect development's increasing breadth and complexity.

8.5 Second Generation of Urban Indicators

The arrival of the new millennium marked a watershed moment in assessing cities. As the world became increasingly urbanized and global challenges more complex – or, at least, were becoming recognized as such – the year 2000 provided a unique opportunity to reverse the unsustainable evolution of cities. Great enthusiasm and optimism surrounded the introduction of the MDGs, a suite of eight goals that established measurable, universally agreed-upon objectives oriented towards the achievement of progress in "developing countries" in areas such as income, poverty, access to improved sources of water, primary school enrollment, and child mortality (UNDP 2016).

However, the arrival of the second generation of urban indicators in 1992, the year when *Agenda 21* was launched at the United Nations Conference on

Environment and Development, or UNCED (see Chapter 7), preceded the MDG innovation. Authors of the Agenda stressed that as "the need for information arises at all levels, from that of senior decision-makers at the national and international levels to the grass-roots and individual levels" (UN 1992), it is crucial to bridge data gaps and improve information availability in order to ensure better decision-making based on increasingly sound information. As a result, the sectoralization of indicator sets, linked to the narrowing of aims to target specific policy questions (OECD 2000), and the application of greater attention to local dimension of cities became the most visible trends among the second generation of urban indicators. These trends necessitated a shift from the conventional macroeconomic perspective towards a broader approach to urban dynamics that included new dimensions, themes, and methods to measure and assess city performance.

During this period, people realized that cities could no longer be measured and understood as the sum of income, population, and city sprawl; the accelerated urbanization phenomenon required the introduction of new dimensions into the city equation in order to obtain a broader picture of urban dynamics. Thus, the indicator sets that emerged paid greater attention to human and ecological well-being. Some examples of international urban indicator sets that clearly illustrate the main characteristics and the approach of this generation are *The Global City Indicators Program*, designed by the World Bank; *The Cities Data Book*, developed by the Asian Development Bank; and *Global Urban Indicators* and *Urban Governance Index*, both created by UN-Habitat (Box 8.1).

Box 8.1 International urban indicator sets of the second generation

Source: OECD (2012: 85–86), citing OECD (2011), "Urban Environmental Indicators for Green Cities: A Tentative Indicator Set," paper presented to the Working Party on Environmental Information, internal working document.

The Global City Indicators Program (GCIP) is a decentralized, city-led initiative that enables cities to measure, report on, and improve their performance and quality of life, facilitate capacity building, and share best practices through an easy-to-use web portal. The GCIP aims to help cities monitor performance and quality of life by providing a framework to facilitate consistent and comparative collection of city indicators. The GCIP also aims to enhance city government accountability to the public and has a strong focus on the performance of cities' public services, including those for water supply, wastewater, and solid waste. The World Bank initiated the GCIP in 2008 and is now run by the Global City Indicators Facility, based at the University of Toronto, which oversees the development of indicators and

---

Box 8.1 (cont)

helps cities to join the program. As of 2015, 255 cities across 82 countries were participating in the program, up from some 125 just four years earlier.

The **Cities Data Book (CDB)** is a comprehensive set of urban indicators formulated in 2001 by the Asian Development Bank to improve urban management and performance measurement. The broad categories of the environment-related indicators are the same as those found in other indicator sets (water, wastewater, solid waste, noise, and so forth), but the CDB's indicators go into greater detail on specific concerns addressed by this institution (for example, the wide range of methods of sewage disposal in Asian cities).

The **Global Urban Indicators (GUI)** database was established to monitor progress on the implementation of the UN-Habitat Agenda. The database covers 236 cities across the globe, including those from the OECD countries. As a whole, however, the indicators focus strongly on the concerns of cities in developing countries. In 1996 and 2001, the program produced two main databases, GUI Databases I and II, containing data for 1993 and 1998, respectively; these were presented at the Habitat II and Istanbul +5 conferences. The next Global Urban Indicators database (III) will continue to address the key Habitat Agenda issues, with a specific focus on the MDGs and, particularly, Target 11 on the improvement of slum dwellings. Altogether, there are 42 key and complementary indicators in the GUI dataset in total.

Websites:

GCIP: www.cityindicators.org/Default.aspx

CDB: www.adb.org/publications/urban-indicators-managing-cities

GUI: http://unhabitat.org/books/global-urban-indicators-database/

8.6 Third Generation of Urban Indicators

Since the 2030 Development Agenda launched in September 2015, a strong commitment to achieving a more holistic form of urban prosperity and development emerged among the majority of nations around the world (Wong 2014). A shift in the paradigms of development, subjective well-being, and city prosperity towards a broader, multidimensional understanding of these aspects led to the arrival of a third generation of urban indicators. The publication of the *State of the World's Cities 2012/2013: Prosperity of Cities* (UN-Habitat

2013) marked an inflection point between the second and third generations. It triggered significant discussion among the international community that translated into the introduction of a new, multidimensional conceptualization of city prosperity, materialized in the City Prosperity Index, or CPI.

The conception of the CPI comes with a strong assertion of the vitality and transformative dynamics of cities, and thus their importance in what is now the urban age (UN-Habitat 2013, cited in Wong 2014), for new types of cities that achieve a sustainable path of development. In this regard, SDG 11 recognizes urbanization as a transformative force for development which, if effectively steered and deployed, can help the world to overcome many of its major global challenges (UN-Habitat 2015). City prosperity is currently understood in terms of a more integrated and holistic approach than in the past, which seeks to promote collective well-being, public goods, and overcoming the dangers posed to cities in a context of rapid urbanization. The CPI estimates prosperity through different interlinked dimensions: productivity, infrastructure development, quality of life, equity and social inclusiveness, environmental sustainability, and governance. Arriving at a third generation of urban indicators such as the CPI meant

> a fresh approach to prosperity, one that is holistic and integrated and which is essential for the promotion of a collective well-being and fulfillment of all. This new approach does not only respond to the crises by providing safeguards against new risks, but it also helps cities to steer the world towards economically, socially, politically and environmentally prosperous urban futures. (Clos, quoted in UN-Habitat 2013: iv)

The introduction of a third generation of urban indicators also meant the emergence and immersion of new actors and stakeholders in the difficult task of designing and developing innovative, holistic, and integral sets of indicators to measure and assess urban dynamics. Such diversification of actors implied a fundamental change in the structure of the conventional architecture of the global monitoring framework of our century (see Box 8.2). An example that clearly illustrates the emergence of this trend is the appearance of the World Council on City Data (WCCD) an independent international organization that hosts a network of innovative cities committed to improving services and quality of life using open-city data. It also provides a consistent and comprehensive platform for standardized urban metrics (WCCD 2016). Currently, the WCCD offers a new set of 100 urban indicators that comprise 17 dimensions of urban dynamics based on the first international standard on city data, ISO 37120.

The recent adoption of the Social Progress Index at the local level among some cities around the world is another example that clearly demonstrates the diversification of sources of urban data as well as the broadening of the

---

Box 8.2 The experience of Jalisco in designing comprehensive urban dictators

MIDE Jalisco (MIDE stands for "to measure" in Spanish) is a comrehensive monitoring system of the Jalisco State Government, Mexico, that includes over 300 indicators of results and performance; this allows citizens to follow the state's evolution in real time. Through MIDE Jalisco, the press, academics, decision-makers, and the general public have access to all of the indicators as open-source data. MIDE Jalisco is being unfolded into different subsystems, both sectoral and territorial, to monitor specific policy and geographic areas in depth. MIDE Guadalajara Metropolitana is an initiative to create the first subsystem designed for the city level, powered by Jalisco State Government together with the nine metropolitan municipalities that comprise Guadalajara Metropolitan Area, with the technical support of UN-Habitat and the WCCD. MIDE Guadalajara Metropolitana will be the first urban and metropolitan indicators platform in Mexico and Latin America to integrate the latest generation of indicators.

---

dimensions measured during the current generation of urban indicators. The Social Progress Index is a framework designed to measure the diverse elements of social progress, to document progress, and to encourage interventions to enhance human well-being (Social Progress Index 2015).

8.7 Towards a Fourth Generation of Urban Indicators

Despite efforts to measure and assess urban dynamics through more holistic indicators, our understanding of cities is still limited in four different ways: most reports tend to have partial global geographical coverage of specific regions; many tend to focus on measurement at the national level; they often provide a small depiction of a particular aspect of urban dynamics (Wong 2014); and most lack a territorial, "geo-localized" approach.

Although we have witnessed huge progress in the development of urban data, as of 2017, there is no single set of indicators or monitoring frameworks that covers the full range of issues included in the broad agenda of urban dynamics. In fact, despite progress in many Western countries, even the economic output of cities remains elusive, as data collection for this information is lacking in most countries. These limits to our current measurement tools affect our ability to assess trade-offs among alternative policy choices accurately (OECD 2000). For this reason, the increasing necessity of relying on more robust, coherent, and flexible frameworks of indicators to analyze the performance of cities has been placed at the core of the global agenda. The current version of the CPI is a useful starting point (Sands 2014), but it is not enough. For instance, even though the CPI theoretically accepts the importance of governance, there is no clear definition of what CPI means with regards to urban and land governance, or how to measure it. The prevailing limitations of currently available sets of urban indicators remind us that we need to keep moving forward towards a fourth generation. As Wong says, "There are still significant knowledge gaps in the framing and operationalization of prosperity" (2014).

A fourth generation of urban indicators should provide a broader, people-centered approach; alongside the existing monitoring frameworks, this generation of indicators should also include a strong territorial dimension into city analysis as a key factor that could enhance the accuracy in estimating urban governance. This means the adoption of a more localized approach of development at the city level, in order to provide a more contextualized interpretation of urban dynamics.

8.8 What We Have Learned from Monitoring Cities

A significant lesson we have learned is that most governments and stakeholders involved in the design of monitoring frameworks for urban dynamics adopt a citywide approach by finding synergies among indicators. The implementation of "isolated targets without a comprehensive approach to the city may undermine the very basic principle of sustainability" (UN-Habitat 2015: 5). Given that cities are immensely diverse, measuring accurately and, even more so, using data comparatively in the contexts of global indicators and indices, is extremely difficult. The challenges – and burdens – of data collection and reporting are also greater in smaller cities and towns than in their larger counterparts. Therefore, urban indicators need to be scale- and context-sensitive to accommodate smaller urban areas, not just large cities and metropolises.

Experience has shown us the importance of paying special attention to the local level, which is closest to the population. Local governments and administrations are "essential institutional building blocks ... mechanisms, and process, through which public goods and services are delivered to citizens and through which citizens can articulate their interests and needs, mediate their differences, and exercise their rights and obligations" (UNDP 2009: 5). Thus, building and strengthening institutional capabilities at international, national, and local levels are crucial requirements for contemporary societies. Meeting these needs should be addressed with greater impetus since "decentralized governance, carefully planned, effectively implemented and appropriate managed, can lead to significant improvement in the welfare of people at the local level, the cumulative effect of which can lead to enhanced human development" (UNDP 2004: 2).

In the context of the 2030 Development Agenda, cities and metropolises play a key role since urbanization and city growth have been recognized internationally as transformative forces for development. Thus, the empowerment of local and regional authorities becomes essential for meeting SDG 11. The implementation of the urban SDG should lead to greater coordination among national and local stakeholders, providing higher levels of participation for local authorities in the difficult task of collecting, analyzing, and validating data and information for better urban governance.

8.9 Localizing the 2030 Development Agenda: The Empowerment of Local and Regional Governments[1]

Alongside communities and private sector actors, the essential role that local and regional governments (LRGs) play in delivering the 2030 Development Agenda has been recognized during a number of official events throughout the recent transition from the MDGs to the SDGs. It has been noted on several occasions that the achievement of the SDGs depends heavily on coordination among local governments and other stakeholders involved; global challenges have to be met with local responses (Wong 2014; Simon et al. 2016). The localization of the 2030 Development Agenda should not be seen solely as a technical agenda of implementation at the local level, but also as a political agenda that empowers local actors and puts decision-making, data production, and analysis and solutions provision at levels closer to the citizens. This would imply not only gathering different types of data, but also doing things differently, providing diverse sets of competences and resources to different actors and administrations.

This agenda is most clearly embodied in SDG 11, which is local by design – that is, meant to be embraced and delivered by subnational urban governments. The inclusion of an explicitly urban goal in the SDGs is an important achievement and is a testament to the successful advocacy, throughout 2013–2014 of, among others, the Global Taskforce of Local and Regional Governments and its partners, which is a coordination mechanism bringing together the major international networks of local governments to undertake joint advocacy

---

[1] The following note is extracted and slightly modified from Global Taskforce (2014). See also Lucci (2015).

relating to international policy processes.[2] As argued during the *#Urban SDG Campaign*, an urban goal should mobilize and empower LRGs and urban actors, contribute to integrating the different dimensions of sustainable development (economic, social, environmental) and the spatial design of cities, strengthening the linkages between urban and rural areas, and transforming urban challenges into opportunities. However, SDG 11 does not take a holistic approach to urban development. Key urban concerns, including local governance, are not addressed, while other key urban responsibilities are partially included under other goals.

More generally, to be achievable, a majority of the goals and targets will need strong involvement of LRGs in both urban and rural areas (see Simon et al. 2016). This is why it is important to discuss what we mean by "localization." Localizing the 2030 Development Agenda often refers to at least two dimensions: 1) the definition and implementation of the targets and indicators at the local level and 2) the monitoring and evaluation process.

With respect to the first dimension, it is obvious that subnational governments have responsibilities (either direct responsibilities or those shared with central government or in partnership with other stakeholders) for achieving targets and service provision in the majority of the areas related to the SDGs (Cities Alliance 2015; González et al. 2011; UCLG 2014). The scope of subnational governments' work is clearly linked to alleviating poverty; securing nutrition; ensuring health and education; promoting gender equality; managing water, sanitation, urban planning, public transport, waste, and energy resources; promoting local economic development and decent jobs; fighting climate change; and increasing communities' resilience.

However, localizing the Post-2015 Agenda can also refer to monitoring progress at the subnational level (irrespective of whether LRGs have competency in that specific area). This can help to assess inequalities within countries and support better decision-making and resource allocation at all levels, as well as enabling local communities and civil society organizations to hold their governments accountable. In this spirit, the UN's Inter-Agency and Expert Group (IAEG) reports out of the UN made suggestions for geographical disaggregation of data for most outcome-based targets (United Nations 2013). This should include, for example, urban/rural and regional breakdowns and, where possible disaggregation at lower levels, such as municipalities, urban agglomerations, or marginal areas, such as slums.

---

[2] The **Global Taskforce of Local and Regional Governments** is a coordination mechanism set up in 2013 at the initiative of UCLG President and Mayor of Istanbul Kadir Topbaş. It brings together the major international networks of local governments (22) to undertake joint advocacy relating to international policy processes, particularly the climate change agenda, the Sustainable Development Goals and Habitat III. See www.gtf2016.org/

These two approaches to localization are complementary. Ideally, subnational governments should define a specific subset of goals and targets where they have direct responsibilities and set up the level of indicators, contributing to their delivery and achievement. But this will also require stronger coordination and partnership between different levels of government, as is required for effective, multilevel governance. National governments should encourage local authorities to identify and adopt concrete commitments that might help to achieve the SDGs. When it comes to monitoring progress at subnational levels, local and regional governments could focus on monitoring for vulnerable areas and communities. They could even focus on the gaps in performance within their respective areas of jurisdiction – for example, in slums versus in the local average – to clearly identify spatial inequalities. However, data constraints are generally more pronounced at local levels than at the national level. In many cases, where data are based on survey information, it is difficult to disaggregate indicators beyond rural/urban and regional breakdowns. It is particularly difficult to have adequate source data for vulnerable populations (such as slum dwellers). This has obvious resource and capacity implications in terms of data collection, and would require the support of national statistics offices.

There is consensus that local and regional governments should play a crucial role in implementing and monitoring most of Agenda 2030. Localizing the SDGs means providing adequate targets and indicators to measure their impact at the territorial level, and proposing strategies and tools to facilitate the efficient involvement of LRGs in the implementation process. However, besides the need to improve mechanisms to obtain reliable local data, the implementation process needs strong and empowered local and regional governments. Thus, processes oriented to facilitate enabling environments for LRGs should be prioritized. Supporting decentralization processes, both political and fiscal, through strengthening institutional and operational capacities to deliver basic services and sound public policies; developing new forms of governance that enable multilevel partnerships; and insisting on multi-stakeholder approaches, are important conditions for allowing the localization of the development agenda.

8.10 Conclusions

Our analysis demonstrates that as the world moves into the urban age, new challenges and opportunities regarding the current monitoring frameworks for cities have emerged (UN-Habitat 2013). For instance, urban indicators offer a useful tool that contributes in several ways to mitigating the negative effects of urbanization on contemporary societies. We have also demonstrated the evolution of attempts to develop better urban indicators and monitoring frameworks. The elastic nature of the main characteristics and sets of indicators that comprise each generation illustrates that urban indicators have evolved in parallel with conceptualizations of development, well-being, and prosperity. Empirical evidence over the years has demonstrated that classical economic metrics are insufficient standards with which to measure and understand current urban dynamics.

However, we have not yet reached the finishing line; at present, we are undergoing a transitional process towards a fourth generation of more comprehensive and holistic sets of urban indicators in which several stakeholders are involved. The emerging monitoring frameworks do somehow respond to the urgent need to fill the urban information vacuum through a broader and multidimensional understanding of city prosperity. Yet, important limitations still prevail among such attempts to measure and understand urban dynamics. Cities need to keep moving forward in the difficult task of designing better measurement instruments. In the context of increasing urbanization, it is crucial to incur the costs of developing such measurement instruments as an investment in better understanding cities, and hence becoming capable of mitigating the problems and challenges that harm our planet. In this regard, the development of better and new urban indicators should be at the core of the urban agenda. This effort must include a focus on how data to support such indicators will be collected to build global datasets and by whom – city networks, researchers, or others – particularly in light of shifting political realities or other barriers that might complicate such efforts, thereby creating gaps in the process.

Building and strengthening institutional capabilities of cities is also an essential task that must be addressed in every single society. Local and regional authorities have a central role to play in meeting the 2030 Development Agenda and in "contributing to national and global recovery" (Ban Ki-moon, quoted in UN-Habitat 2013: iii). A fourth generation of more people-centered and territorialized indicators will provide the necessary means to creating better-informed policies and designing sound development plans for the future.

🌐 References

Cities Alliance, 2015. *Sustainable Development Goals and Habitat III: Opportunities for a Successful New Urban Agenda*. Discussion Paper No. 3. www.citiesalliance.org/sites/citiesalliance.org/files/Opportunities%20for%20the%20New%20Urban%20Agenda.pdf.

Global Taskforce, 2014. *How to Localize Targets and Indicators of the Post-2015 Agenda*, November 14, www.uclg.org/sites/default/files/localisation_targets_indicator_web.pdf.

González, A., Donnelly, A., Jones, M., Klostermann, J., Groot, A., and Breil, M. 2011. Community of Practice Approach to Developing Urban Sustainability Indicators. *Journal of Environmental Assessment Policy and Management* 13 (4): 591–617.

Lucci, P. 2015. *Localising' the Post-2015 Agenda: What Does It Mean in Practice?* ODI, January. www.odi.org/publications/8992-localising-post-2015-agenda-does-mean-practice.

Muhammad, Z.B. 2001, Development of Urban Indicators: A Malaysian Initiative, in J. J. Pereira, and I. Komoo (eds.) *Geoindicators for Sustainable Development.* Kuala Lumpur: Institute for Environment and Development: Universiti Kebangsaan Malaysia, pp. 17–32.

OECD, 2012. *Compact City Policies: A Comparative Assessment*, OECD Green Growth Studies, OECD Green Growth Studies. Paris: OECD Publishing.

OECD, 2000. *Frameworks to Measure Sustainable Development.* Paris: OECD Publishing.

Sands, G. 2014. Measuring the Prosperity of Cities. *Habitat International*, 45 (1): 1–2.

Social Progress Index. 2015. *Social Progress Index 2015.* www.socialprogressimperative.org/data/spi.

Simon, D., Arfvidsson, H., Anand, G., Bazaaz, A., Fenna, G., and K., Foster, et al. 2016. Developing and Testing the Urban Sustainable Development Goal's Targets and Indicators – A Five-City Study. *Environment and Urbanization* 28: 49–63.

Thomson S., 2016. GDP a Poor Measure of Progress, say Davos Economists, *World Economic Forum*, last modified January 23, www.weforum.org/agenda/2016/01/gdp

UCLG, 2014. *Basic Services for All in an Urbanizing World*, 3rd Global Report on Local Democracy and Decentralization. Oxon; New York: Routledge.

UNDP, 2016. *A New Sustainable Development Agenda*, www.undp.org/content/undp/en/home/sdgoverview.html

UNDP, 2009. *A User's Guide to Measuring Local Governance.* Oslo, Norway: UNDP Oslo Governance Center.

UNDP, 2004. *Decentralized Governance for Development: A Combined Practice Note on Decentralization, Local Governance and Urban/Rural Development*, www.undp.org/content/dam/aplaws/publication/en/publications/democratic-governance/dg-publications-for-website/decentralised-governance-for-development-a-combined-practice-note-on-decentralisation-local-governance-and-urban-rural-development/DLGUD_PN_English.pdf.

UN-Habitat, 2015. *Sustainale Cities and Communities: SDG GOAL 11 Monitoring Framework.* New York: UN-Habitat.

UN-Habitat, 2013. *State of the World's Cities 2012/2013 Prosperity of Cities.* Nairobi: United Nations Human Settlements Programme.

United Nations, 2013, *A New Global Partnership: Eradicate Poverty and Transform Economies Through Sustainable Development. The Report of the High-Level Panel of Eminent Persons on the Post-2015 Development Agenda*, New York: United Nations Publications. www.un.org/sg/management/pdf/HLP_P2015_Report.pdf.

WCCD, 2016. *World Council on City Data*, www.dataforcities.org/

Wong, C. 2014. A Framework for 'City Prosperity Index': Linking Indicators, Analysis and Policy. *Habitat International*, 45: 3–9.

Wong, C. 2006. *Quantitative Indicators for Urban and Regional Planning: The Interplay of Policy and Methods*. London: Routledge.

World Bank, 2016. *World Development Reports: Digital Dividends*, Washington, DC: International Bank for Reconstruction and Development/The World Bank. www-wds.worldbank.org/external/default/WDSContentServer/WDSP/IB/2016/01/13/090224b08405ea05/2_0/Rendered/PDF/World0developm0000digital0dividends.pdf.

Chapter 9: The UN, the Urban Sustainable Development Goal, and the New Urban Agenda

Andrew Rudd, David Simon, Maruxa Cardama, Eugénie L. Birch, and Aromar Revi

9.1 Evolving International Conceptions of the Urban

Since its establishment 70 years ago in the ashes of World War II, the international multilateral system's conception of "the urban" has evolved significantly. This reflects both the maturation of the original United Nations (UN) and Bretton Woods institutions and the subsequent establishment of new, more specialized institutions in the 1970s to respond to the rise of environmental and human settlements challenges on international agendas and priorities. Of particular relevance in this context are the UN Environment Programme, or UNEP, and the UN Human Settlements Programme, or UN-Habitat (formerly the United Nations Centre for Human Settlements, or UNCHS). Both of these programs are symbolically headquartered in Nairobi as part of an initiative to give the UN a more global physical footprint.

The importance of having a UN agency devoted entirely to human settlements issues, albeit focused on what the UN vocabulary still resolutely refers to as "developing countries," should not be underestimated. UN-Habitat's orientation was expanded to include the transitional economies of Eastern and Central Europe after the end of the Cold War, and though its governing council and reporting cover all five UN regions, its policy advice and capacity development are only now becoming more global. Initially, its effectiveness was hampered by its classification as a "Centre" – without the status of a UN implementing agency, it had to work through UNEP for strategic and budgetary purposes. This constraint was eased when it achieved programme status in 2002 (UN-Habitat 2015). Nevertheless, rather than leading such innovations, the UN's urban conceptions and approaches to tackling the principal problems of fast-growing cities in poor countries have generally lagged behind changes fomented on the ground, in NGO thinking, and in the research literature.

To wit, notwithstanding numerous dramatic demographic shocks with important and often long-term urban consequences, such as the mass displacements of World War II and the partition of India and Pakistan in 1947, as well as accelerating rural-urban migration and growing refugee settlements in decolonizing and newly independent states during the 1950s and 1960s, the dominant conception of urbanization by governments and international agencies was as a temporary, largely negative phenomenon. This perspective was strongly influenced by erstwhile colonial policy in late nineteenth- and early twentieth-century European settlement colonies, which maintained that indigenous populations had been predominantly rural before the European conquest, and where urban areas were established to serve the settler populations and imperial purposes rather than indigenous needs. The reality of long-standing, large-scale, and sophisticated indigenous urban cultures in many previously conquered indigenous polities from Meso-America through North and West Africa and the Middle East to South and Southeast Asia was somehow erased from such constructs.

The policy response to this perception comprised concerted efforts to keep rural dwellers in rural areas and agriculturally productive, while passively seeking to lessen cities' impact on the environment. This proved ineffective almost everywhere, and rapid net migration continued. The conventional solution of state-funded mass housing in high-density apartment blocks in Latin America and a mixture of single-sex worker "hostels" and small "matchbox" family houses in East and southern Africa became increasingly unaffordable to city authorities and national governments, many of which ceased such practices after independence.[1] Moreover, residents found them alienating (and often alien) social environments, with many sociocultural problems and considerable un- and underemployment where industrialization was not occurring or was expanding only slowly. This resulted in a widespread spatial mismatch between need and availability of housing, services, and employment (Gilbert and Gugler 1992).[2]

Innovative research, pioneered by Walter Mangin and John Turner in Latin American cities in the 1960s, demonstrated that working with the urban

---

[1] Later, governments experimented with other urban housing models, including tenant-purchase and site-and-service schemes, often through development cooperation funding. Some of these were strategically located close to business and industry (and have more recently experienced revitalization through public-private partnerships). While some governments were experimenting, however, the private sector took over the lion's share of housing provision without the benefit of much planning guidance from public authorities.

[2] A signal exception has been the very high-density high-rise apartment blocks in Singapore and Hong Kong, in particular, where such social "pathologies" have not emerged and these urban designs appear to have been quite readily assimilated. This has never been adequately explained but cultural acceptability is likely to be important. Shane (2011) provides fuller coverage.

poor to address their housing and livelihood needs was far more effective in facilitating urban integration than large-scale, top-down public sector housing delivery. Despite opposition from many quarters, especially among governments and national elites, such work spawned a sea change in attitudes, with the first World Bank-funded site-and-service scheme launched in Dakar, Senegal, in 1970, and a veritable flourishing of various self-help and aided self-help experiments and programs through the 1970s and 1980s (see Turner 1980; Moser and Peake 1987; Rodwin 1987; Amis and Lloyd 1990; Gilbert and Gugler 1992; Aldrich and Sandhu 1995). In many cases, these schemes were peripherally located and poorly integrated into the overall urban fabric – though, in retrospect, they were surprisingly resilient to changing urban environments. Despite their varied success, they ultimately did little to address the ongoing urbanization pressures, which became increasingly differentiated in space and time at different scales – both subnational and regional – in accordance with economic cycles and official policies.

Reflecting the changing perceptions, Habitat I, the first global summit on the topic in Vancouver in 1976, was far more positive about urbanization. Its outcome document is often even bullish on the prospects of human settlements. Nevertheless, it states that "[r]ural backwardness ... contribute[s] to uncontrolled urban growth," leading ultimately to "intolerable psychological tensions due to overcrowding and chaos." As a consequence, it urges the UN to "give priority to improving the rural habitat." This was said to "enable the greatest possible number of scattered and dispersed rural settlements to derive the benefit from basic services" which would "help to reduce the migration to urban areas" (United Nations 1976).

In 1996, Habitat II, the second major global housing and shelter convention, held in Istanbul, posed participatory planning and management as a solution to these persistent processes and failed official policies (UN-Habitat 1996). That it took over 25 years from the first World Bank site-and-service scheme to gain prime position in the global agenda demonstrates the duration of policy lag. Nevertheless, this, too, was a limited response that failed to get to grips with rapid urban growth and the turmoil caused by the financial crisis just two years later. This change in the economy saw rising unemployment and government fiscal deficits, which in turn precipitated reduced subsidies for housing and other basic needs and social provisions (see, for example, Satterthwaite 1997).

As evidence of the human cost and development reverses of the economic crisis mounted, world leaders adopted the eight Millennium Development Goals, or MDGs, at a special UN summit in late 2000. Heralded as another landmark by recognizing poverty as the principal impediment to development and committing resources to tackling it via a series of annually reportable targets and indicators, they applied only to poor countries. Although no MDG addressed urban issues directly, a few targets and indicators on slums and water and sanitation had urban relevance and implications. However, the underlying framing of urbanization amounted to a reversion to mid-twentieth century perspectives, in terms of which it is defined principally as a housing crisis, and the UN's role is thus restricted to treating its primary symptom: the slum.

UN-Habitat (2010a: 16) defines slums as comprising households "lacking one or more of the following: improved water; improved sanitation; sufficient living area; durable housing; and secure tenure." Hence, the proportion of an urban area's population living in slums constitutes the proportion of such slum households. This definition has been widely criticized as too limiting, pejorative, and prone to statistical misrepresentation. This critique arises because when one or more of the "urban deprivations" is relieved, the house(hold) in question is recorded as having been lifted out of slum conditions – which is often not the case, despite the improvements. Nor does such an improvement address the actual drivers of slum formation. However, the human rights-based definition of "adequate housing" is broader, and adds the key dimension of location (vis-à-vis employment, hence mobility) and cultural adequacy.

The recent adoption of the 2030 Agenda for Sustainable Development thus represents a decisive shift in approach, from reactive to ambitiously proactive. The New Urban Agenda was adopted by the UN heads of government at Habitat III in Quito, Ecuador, in October 2016, symbolizing the UN's recognition of urbanization as a permanent driver of development with potentially positive impacts on people and the planet. How the 2030 Agenda is ultimately linked to the New Urban Agenda – particularly in terms of monitoring and indicators – during their simultaneous implementation remains to be seen, since the two documents have no appreciable formal connection.

It is worth pointing out that, amid the inevitable focus on evolving institutional perspectives, the examples cited above of Turner and Mangin in relation to low-income housing policy remind us that the roles of key individuals in shaping international institutions and their agendas should not be overlooked (compare with Weiss et al. 2005; Parnell 2016).

In September 2015, after an unprecedented consultative process geared towards designing the successor to the MDGs[3], the 193 nations of the UN unanimously adopted the 2030 Agenda for Sustainable Development (Figure 9.1)[4]. At its core are 17 global Sustainable Development Goals, or SDGs, and their 169 targets. The SDGs are much more ambitious than the MDGs in that they address the challenges of the entire world, not just low- and middle-income

---

[3] www.un.org/millenniumgoals/
[4] https://sustainabledevelopment.un.org/post2015/transformingourworld

Figure 9.1 UN Summit Adopts Post-2015 Development Agenda. A view of the General Assembly Hall following the adoption of the post-2015 development agenda by the UN summit convened for that purpose. Source: UN Photo/Cia Pak, New York, 2015

countries. The inclusion of SDG 11 represents broad international consensus to legitimize sustainable urban development as a transformational driver for human development.

SDG 11 is no minor victory for urban sustainability stakeholders – including practitioners, local and regional governments, and their networks, as well as national governments, science and academia, philanthropy, and the private sector – that actively engaged in the three-year intergovernmental process that produced the Agenda. Throughout this time, they confronted the possibility that the urban dimension might be merged with other goal areas, such as infrastructure or sustainable consumption and production, or simply become mainstreamed across other SDGs (with the likely diminution or disappearance of its spatial aspect). It is worth highlighting that 2015 saw the adoption not only of the 2030 Agenda, but also of the Sendai Framework for Disaster Risk Reduction 2015–2030,[5] the Addis Ababa Action Agenda on financing for development,[6]

---

[5] http://www.unisdr.org/we/coordinate/sendai-framework
[6] http://www.un.org/esa/ffd/wp-content/uploads/2015/08/AAAA_Outcome.pdf; http://www.un.org/esa/ffd/publications/aaaa-outcome.html.

and the Paris Agreement on Climate Change[7]; these three acknowledge the potential, consequences, and responsibilities, respectively, that are inherent in urban development.

With its fate now secure, SDG 11 has renewed the MDG imperative of ensuring basic living conditions for human dignity (Target 11.1) but has also raised a host of new, twenty-first-century issues. Target 11.2 is a call to action on urban transport provision, which has major implications for access to economic opportunities, household expenditures, greenhouse gas emissions, and health. SDG 11 also addresses air pollution and waste as key challenges to be tackled at the urban scale (11.6) and emphasizes the improvement of community resilience to disaster (11.5). Moreover, cities and human settlements are recognized as worthy of cultural and natural heritage safeguarding. Among the targets that address means of implementation for SDG 11, we find a clarion call for the use of integrated policy and planning (11.b), as well as a focus on building sustainable and resilient buildings in least-developed countries (11.c).

Three other targets under SDG 11 merit special attention. The unprecedented focus of SDG 11 on urban planning and land use (Target 11.3), public and green space (Target 11.7), and national and regional development planning (11.a) make SDG 11 uniquely spatial compared to all other SDGs. These three essential enablers of development are largely unaddressed in the other, predominantly space-blind SDGs. By contrast, the focus of SDG 11 on the wider built environment gives long-overdue attention to the preeminently path-determinant role of physical configuration.

Target 11.3 represents broad international consensus that spontaneous, unplanned urban expansion too often yields inefficiency, increased emissions, and segregation. Nevertheless, it is still difficult for governments to fully apprehend the far-reaching impacts of spatial planning and its numerous benefits and co-benefits, including higher-level outcomes such as efficiency, productivity, amenity, and resilience. Favorable settlement patterns enable these; unfavorable ones not only do not enable them, but ultimately lock a city into rigid, inefficient patterns that are often very expensive and difficult to retrofit. Good spatial planning will likely have positive spillover effects outside of SDG 11, including strengthened food systems and expanded access to services and utilities. Target 11.3 also qualifies planning as a discipline that must be participatory. It can help governments and citizens alike understand the far-reaching impacts of urban form, so that they can engage in the planning process more meaningfully (Rudd et al. 2017). In so doing, they can address a number of critical questions: Where should development be located? Which pattern(s) will

---

[7] http://newsroom.unfccc.int/unfccc-newsroom/finale-cop21/

it embody? How will it balance process and outcome to yield both social and environmental sustainability?

Target 11.7 responds to research that shows public and green space disappearing in unplanned cities. At the same time, existing public space in planned cities is being commercialized, exacerbating socioeconomic fragmentation (UN-Habitat 2013, 2015). Both situations are weakening cities' capacities to provide basic services equitably and efficiently, suggesting the need for both a qualitative and quantitative approach: cities, particularly fast-growing ones, should first secure an adequate proportion of public space; additionally, cities can take measures to improve the amenities, accessibility, greenness, and safety of existing public space. Scholars and practitioners are left with crucial open questions, such as: How can policy-makers optimally use the information provided by geospatial technology? How to best influence the norms that regulate the private ownership of land?

SDG 11 also acknowledges cities as developmental drivers beyond their administrative boundaries. The goal's promotion of urban-rural linkages (Target 11.a) signals a reinvigorated desire from the international community to move from a dichotomous conception of urban and rural development to one of mutually reinforcing, synergistic development across the rural-urban continuum. However, such a concept remains quite difficult to translate into tangible policies at all levels of government. Cities still require concrete legislative, spatial, and financing solutions that extend beyond the provision of agricultural goods to urban centers and the control of urban expansion into rural areas.

The 2030 Agenda pledges that no one should be left behind in any nation. This universality leaves us with the corollary challenge of being sufficiently specific for relevance and impact in diverse local contexts. Significantly different levels of development, governance structures, and capacities among the world's cities mean that some SDG 11 targets appear to be much more applicable to certain urban contexts than others. A "locally relevant" policy-science interface may help translate the universal SDG 11 targets into national and subnational action programs (Simon et al. 2016).

The universality of the 2030 Agenda, achieved through intergovernmental negotiations, has meant a trade-off with ambition as well as some glaring omissions. SDG 11 does not even pay lip service to cities' status as engines of economic development, innovation, and job creation. It also avoids the issue of governance, including decentralization and access to finance at subnational levels. Achieving sustainable cities will surely require strategic frameworks and plans that are integrated into all levels of government and policy-making. UN language speaks of the integrated character of the 2030 Agenda, particularly the way it targets the social, economic, and environmental dimensions of sustainability on equal footing. If the implementation of SDG 11 succeeds in integrating all three dimensions, it can accelerate the pace of achievement of many other SDGs. Conversely, if SDG 11 implementation is interlinked with other urban-critical SDGs – especially poverty (SDG 1), health (SDG 3), and inequality (SDG 10); water and sanitation (SDG6) and energy (SDG7); employment and economic growth (SDG8) and infrastructure (SDG9); sustainable consumption and production (SDG12) and climate change (SDG13); and accountable and inclusive institutions (SDG16) – their achievement can help overcome some of the omissions within SDG 11 itself.

Maximizing balanced gains across all three dimensions of sustainability will depend on effective interlinkages. This notion is familiar to urbanists and many local and regional governments that are accountable to the public and accustomed to integrated planning and management, but governments have not put it into practice widely, nor have developing institutional frameworks commonly embedded it into their thinking. This is why national urban policies are a twenty-first century "must-have" (UN-Habitat 2014; Parnell and Simon 2014). Such policies can integrate long-term visions with strategic approaches, and, when crafted in collaboration with all levels of government, can reflect the needs and assets of a country, its regions, and its cities. Progress has been slow: only nine countries have implemented national urban policies to date (UN-Habitat 2016). Nevertheless, SDG 11 and the New Urban Agenda offer unparalleled opportunities for countries to adopt them.

In multilateralism, technical rigor is not immune to political negotiation, but that should not tarnish the historic milestone that is the adoption of SDG 11. It is a powerful plan of action that will certainly promote and incentivize urban sustainability all over the world. Undoubtedly, the task ahead is complex and the solutions are not always clear. Nonetheless, that which three years ago was little more than the dream of a few fringe urbanists is now an undeniable victory that must be leveraged to create a global implementation plan across stakeholders and disciplines. The SDGs represent a common denominator, but one that is a floor for urban action, not a ceiling.

9.2 Metrics and the Impact of the Urban SDG

Determining the impact of SDG 11 and the urban dimension of other SDGs relies heavily on the choice of metrics to assess their implementation. Experts generally adopt a conceptual framework to guide and anchor the choices underlying a set of performance metrics. Such a framework helps define and refine a common vision, encourages the creation and regular updating of information, underlines and reinforces progress (or demonstrates the weaknesses, failings, and false assumptions) of a given policy or program, and supports a wider public understanding of the enterprise under consideration (Hak et al. 2007). Although many evaluation techniques exist (such as quasi-randomized studies, case studies, benchmarks, surveys, and questionnaires), the use of indicators has become the commonly accepted approach in assessing sustainable development (Hak et al. 2007; Bell and Morse 2008; Chapter 8, this volume).

To review: An indicator is a simple measure that signals whether a policy or program is on target to reach a predetermined goal. By contrast, benchmarks, while related, are predetermined milestoness. Many types of indicators exist. They range from a single figures derived from several inputs (as in the broadly accepted gross national product, or GDP) to systems of multiple indicators (as in the approach employed by the MDGs, which associated 48 indicators with its 8 goals and 18 targets). The monitoring of the SDGs will implicitly use the goals and their targets as a conceptual framework and will take the multiple indicator system approach, such that there are indicators under consideration.

Figure 9.2 illustrates the place of indicators in public policy. Employed correctly, indicators not only serve to gauge progress, but are valuable tools with which to communicate to the public. While indicators have limitations, scholars and practitioners in policy areas continue to advance the work of testing selected indicators against policy goals and actual behavior, consulting users about indicator improvement, and sharpening the data that underlie indicators to achieve uniformity and comparability (Birch et al. 2011).

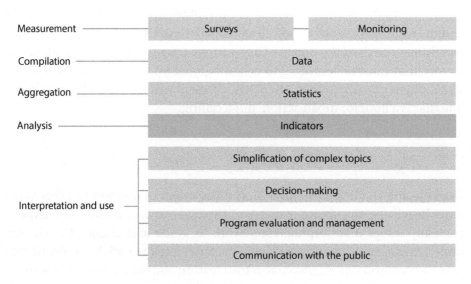

Figure 9.2 The place of indicators in public policy

In the case of SDG 11, the agreed upon conceptual framework holds that cities are systems of systems (for example, housing, transportation, and environment), places of agglomeration (that is, clustering of people and their activities), and nexuses of sustainable development. The underlying assumption is that the transformational potential of cities lies in the equitable and efficient planning and managing of land to foster the provision of urban systems that maximize the benefits and minimize the costs of agglomeration. Current knowledge holds that certain techniques tend to support this approach. They include mixing land uses, adaptively reusing buildings, crafting walkable neighborhoods linked to each other and beyond with public transportation, and reinforcing ecosystem services with green and blue patches and corridors.

According to the conceptual framework of SDG 11, achieving sustainable urban development suggests the use of a series of indicators premised on the advantages of agglomeration (United Nations, Economic and Social Council 2015). Such a series starts with a base figure that measures the alignment of land consumption with population growth to mark necessary and sufficient conditions for equitable and efficient service provision and to support agglomeration. This land efficiency indicator, or LES, is most simply expressed as a ratio: the rate of land consumption to the rate of population growth. While the LES is a new type of indicator that calls for the use of geographic information systems in tandem with traditional demographic data collection methods, the technology is now sufficiently developed to be employed widely.

A land-use efficiency ratio is diagnostic rather than prescriptive; desirable ratios should be determined locally, based on the cost of services, customs, and land availability. However, a baseline of 1:1 would indicate that the growth rates for land use and population are in equilibrium. A baseline of 2:1 would signal that a place is becoming less dense because land consumption would have occurred at twice the rate of population increase. Conversely, a 1:2 ratio would indicate more dense land development with less land being used to accommodate a growing population. Notably, the corrective in places where land is viewed as a seemingly limitless resource would be to address uncontrolled, fragmented, and/or sprawling development patterns; the remedy in places where land supply is constrained would be to release, allocate, and/or prepare sufficient land to accommodate growth (see Atlas of Urban Expansion 2016). Thus, this indicator is a gross measure that "takes the temperature" of a place, showing an overall trend. It warns decision-makers of potential issues – issues that would require more nuanced analysis to inform policy-making. Nevertheless, global trends all point to a general decline in land-use efficiency – that is, a movement towards sprawl – which tends, overall, to correlate with undesirable socioeconomic and environmental effects.

At a minimum, then, the LES alerts decision-makers to the general nature of growth in their communities, which can guide deeper probes to explore the location, direction, and character of land consumption. These issues include ascertaining whether developments are on disaster-prone or vulnerable land; whether they are contiguous or fragmented; whether they are moving towards existing nearby centers; and whether metropolitan mobility is increasing or decreasing. Answers to these and other questions will enable decision-makers to craft policies to affect the place and timing of future development. Such answers might also help urban residents better understand the short- and long-term trade-offs involved in configuration-based planning and contribute to more educated decision-making (Rudd et al. 2017).

The LES also works with other indicators associated with the SDG 11 targets to expose interrelated policy choices, especially those addressing housing (proportion of people living in slums), transportation (proportion of people having access to public transportation), public space (the average share of the built-up area of cities that is open space for public use), and the environment (percentage of urban solid waste regularly collected). Working in tandem with related policy choices is useful because of the thresholds of socioeconomic viability that urban agglomeration can help other sectors meet. If, for example, the LES demonstrates less dense settlement patterns, instituting a citywide, technologically advanced waste management system may be economically unfeasible until the municipality employs land-use policies to promote the required density for such a management system to work. Conversely, if the LES shows excessive density, then looking into instituting corrective policy for public space provisions would likely be in order.

Finally, decision-makers can employ the LES and the other indicators for SDG 11 to assist in the achievement of the total suite of SDGs. For example, with its focus on the provision of public transport infrastructure, the indicator for Target 11.2 will almost certainly result in lower per capita rates of energy use and emissions production, thus accelerating the achievement of SDG 7 and SDG 13 on energy and climate. Likewise, the indicator for Target 11.1, which addresses slums, indirectly calls for dwellings composed of durable materials and with access to water and sanitation, which will contribute to the achievement of SDG 3 on health. Similarly, the land-use efficiency measure adds to an understanding of land-use patterns and thus could serve efforts to protect peri-urban agriculture and habitat, consequently supporting SDGs 2 and 15, which are concerned with food and biodiversity.

While a clear conceptual framework must underlie the metrics of any effective indicator system, such a framework is critical to the measurement of equitable and efficient planning and managing of land. This is particularly the case if cities aim to maximize the benefits and minimize the costs of agglomeration.

Urban spatial configuration plays a highly deterministic role and portends many spillover effects in the economic, social, and environmental dimensions of urban sustainability. In connection with this the LES is the fundamental indicator because it gauges the relationships between land consumption and population. The LES and other associated SDG 11 indicators on housing, transportation, resilience, cultural and environmental heritage, environment, and public space form a holistic approach to implementing SDG 11 and are ultimately supportive of other SDGs in important ways.

9.3 Implementation and the Future

Much of the world is currently underprepared to implement SDG 11, be it at the city, provincial, national, or global scale. This is a serious challenge facing the global urban community. Except for a handful of countries and a somewhat larger cohort of cities, the constitutional and legal mandates; institutional capacities; and human and financial resources required to implement these universal goals are at best weak, and – at worst – confused and contradictory. Moreover, such parameters are often missing at the city level. These shortcomings will need to be addressed by the early 2020s if the SDGs are to be delivered by 2030.

Even more challenging for many countries is the prospect of having to implement *all* the SDGs in urban areas, from poverty; health and education; basic services; employment; and prosperity to safety; rule of law and institutional strengthening; and partnerships (Kanuri et al. 2016). The first step in enabling the achievement of the SDGS is the recognition that most countries – and almost all cities, even in high-income countries or countries scoring highly on the Human Development Index – are "developing," in that they are far from achieving many of the universal economic, social, and environmental targets agreed in the 2030 Agenda (Sachs et al. 2016; Revi 2016). There is much to be done over the next few years to improve the coverage and quality of the SDG goals, targets, and indicators through an iterative process of innovation and testing, capacity building, financing, monitoring, and evaluation. Once this process is undertaken, rapid, flexible, and multi-stakeholder problem solving will ultimately be required to implement them (Kanuri et al. 2016; Simon et al. 2016). In short, this will be an interlinked local, national, and global effort.

However, sectorally organized national governments are generally not only unwilling to share power and resources with cities, but even struggle simply to *imagine* integrated, cross-sectoral planning and delivery (Parnell 2016). In stark contrast, joint planning and delivery are parts of the daily lives of most mayors, as well as local and regional urban leaders, who are naturally able to see the value of the SDGs clearly (New School 2015). A local-to-national convergence along these lines will require active dialogue between cities, a partnership among various levels of government, and the recognition that citizens lie at the heart of the implementation agenda. The New Urban Agenda outlines the need to address integrated action across all the SDGs, sectors, and levels of governance if we are to ensure that no one and no place is left behind (Revi 2016; UN-Habitat 2016). The reality of the Habitat III process – and that it happens only once every two decades – has provided a fillip to a clear agreement on these foundational questions (United Nations 2016).

Since the answers to these questions have political implications, they require high-level approval by UN member states, similar to that required for the SDGs; this approval occurred in December 2017, when the General Assembly endorsed the New Urban Agenda after its adoption in Quito[8]. Its implementation will proceed in a series of processes that will extend to 2018 and beyond. The New Urban Agenda confirms the linkages between its implementation and that of the SDGs.[9] On the international stage, important next steps for the SDGs are (1) agreeing on national and subnational monitoring systems that will ultimately move through the High-level Political Forum, thereby providing a formal role for local and regional governments, (2) committing to a reimagined global, regional, and national architecture for financing urban infrastructure, (3) delineating a clear operational division of labor among key UN agencies and stakeholders – including UN-Habitat, other UN and multilateral agencies, development finance institutions, bilateral aid agencies, and new private sector and other nongovernmental players, (4) continuing the mobilization of local and regional governments – in partnership with the enterprise sector; universities and knowledge institutions; movements; and trade unions – towards the implementation of SDG 11, and (5) engaging citizens (especially youth) so that they take charge of key choices and actions (Kanuri et al. 2016).

Effective SDG implementation depends on a set of five minimum enabling conditions (Kanuri et al. 2016). First, a facilitatory constitutional, legal, and regulatory environment must exist to enable local and regional governmental stakeholders to contribute to implementation. Second, a multilevel national urban and settlements policy framework must be in place to permit planning, implementation, and monitoring at multiple levels (see Section 9.1). Third, the institutional capacities of stakeholders – and of agents of change at the

---

[8] A/71/L.23, 23 December 2016. http://habitat3.org/wp-content/uploads/New-Urban-Agenda-GA-Adopted-68th-Plenary-N1646655-E.pdf.

[9] See New Urban Agenda, paragraph 164. We stress that the follow-up to and review of the New Urban Agenda must have effective linkages with the follow-up to and review of the 2030 Agenda for Sustainable Development to ensure coordination and coherence in their implementation.

appropriate levels of subsidiarity to the country and regional context – must be commensurate to the task. Fourth, appropriate mechanisms of local and domestic financing (linked to regulatory and institutional capacities) must be available to direct financial flows into infrastructure, services, housing, and buildings at both regional and city levels. Fifth, an open and flexible institutional environment must exist to enable key stakeholders from community groups, private enterprises, media, and research organizations to interact, focus on problem solving and implementation, and learn from one another.

These five minimum conditions will require nurturing in a variety of contexts related to history, culture, political economy, and the spatial specificity of urban systems. A clear definition and partitioning across the rural-urban continuum may help provide clarity on roles, institutional jurisdictions, policy frameworks, and financing, so that implementation can take center stage. Subsidiarity may not be possible until city, regional, and national governments and other stakeholders build a culture of trust and partnership. This is a complex and often contentious process of political and economic discovery, as new institutional structures, interest groups, and blocks of winners and losers will emerge. Addressing both horizontal (that is, across sectors) and vertical (that is, across levels) governance could have constitutional, legal, and regulatory implications, depending on the national context.

In many contexts, implementation will also hinge on strengthening and developing urban economic systems. This will likely include reducing the risk of lending to cities, increasing municipal authorities' local revenue generation capacities, and addressing employment, informality, worker skills, and productivity. Preemptively addressing land and labor market concerns and building integrative and participatory planning processes will pay off over the medium- and long run. All the same, the capacity to address emergent shocks – ranging from conflict and economic cycles to disasters and climate change – remains low, and this will require a concerted effort to build resilience. Ultimately, the monitoring and evaluation frameworks for both the SDGs and New Urban Agenda will need to enable the localization of action, the tracking of impact using citizen participation and open big data, and the aggregation of results for reporting at the national level.

In spite of the considerable enthusiasm that the SDG, COP 21, and Habitat III processes have generated, it is important to remember that the global urban community is still in its adolescence in terms of local and collective action (Parnell 2016). It would do well to learn from the experience of more mature global constituencies, such as those of health, education, and agriculture, to avoid disciplinary fragmentation and enable the localization of the entire 2030 Agenda. Indeed, localization concerns more SDGs than SDG 11. But the inverse is also true: urbanization is also about more than localization in two key ways.

First, as the 20 years between Habitat II and Habitat III have taught us, urbanization is more than governance. Space- and place-based strategies must underpin all of our efforts to shape cities and human settlements. Second, urbanization is wider than the local scale. A focus on the subnational and national scales – as units of spatial inquiry and as levels of governmental intervention – are as important as the local in delivering urban outcomes.

That the 2030 Agenda, Sendai Framework, Addis Ababa Action Agenda, Paris Agreement, and now the New Urban Agenda have happened under UN auspices represents a noteworthy breakthrough. These agreements indicate a validation by the UN of a more universal, proactive approach to sustainable development in general, and urban development in particular. While this approach and the various frameworks and agendas supporting it implicate a much wider range of actors than the UN itself, a full discussion of those actors is beyond the scope of this chapter. Suffice it to say that for these agendas' aims to be realized, the UN will increasingly have to embrace this full range of actors. As the UN is inherently constrained by its accountability to national governments – and, thus, by competing national interests – this expanded configuration is particularly important. Promisingly, the unprecedented level of consultation with non-UN entities in the formulation of the 2030 Agenda suggests a major shift in modality.

As the world implements the 2030 Agenda, immediate results may be rare and difficult to sustain. However, there are positive signs from some countries – and a moderate number of cities and towns – that are ready to take the plunge to test and further SDG implementation (GLTF et al. 2016; Simon et al. 2016). Building trust, sharing, resources and experiences sharing, and deepening the sense of solidarity and common purpose of key actors and stakeholders at local, regional, national, and global scales will be essential.

References

Aldrich, B., and Sandhu, R. (eds.) (1995) *Housing the Urban Poor*. London: Zed Books.

Amis, P., and Lloyd, P. (eds.) (1990) *Housing Africa's Urban Poor*. Manchester and New York: Manchester University Press for the International African Institute.

Atlas of Urban Expansion (2016) http://atlasofurbanexpansion.org/cities.

Bell, S., and S. Morse (2008) *Sustainability Indicators, Measuring the Immeasurable?* 2nd Edition. London: Earthscan.

Birch, E. A. Lynch, A., Andreason, S., Eisenman, T., Robinson, J. and Steif, K. 2011. Measuring U.S. Sustainable Urban Development. Penn IUR White Paper on Sustainable Urban Development. http://penniur.upenn.edu/uploads/media/measuring-u-s-sustainable-urban-development .original.pdf.

Gilbert, A. and Gugler, J. (1992) *Cities, Poverty and Development: Urbanization in the Third World.* Oxford and New York: Oxford University Press.

GLTF, UN Habitat and UNDP (2016) Roadmap for localizing the SDGs: Implementation and Monitoring at subnational level. https://unhabitat.org/roadmap-for-localizing-the-sdgs-implementation-and-monitoring-at-subnational-level/.

Hak, T., Moldan, B., and Dahl, A. (2007) *Sustainability Indicators; A Scientific Assessment.* Washington, DC: Island Press.

Kanuri, C., Revi, A., Espey, J. and Kuhle, H. (2016) *Getting Started with the SDGs in Cities: A Guide for Stakeholders*, Sustainable Development Solutions Network (SDSN). http://unsdsn.org/wp-content/uploads/2016/07/9.1.8.-Cities-SDG-Guide.pdf.

Moser, C.O.N., and Peake, L. (eds.) (1987) *Women, Human Settlements and Housing.* London and New York: Tavistock.

New School (2015) Cities Deliver Sustainable Development. http://livestream.com/TheNewSchool/cities-deliver-sustainable-development

Parnell, S., (2016) Defining a Global Urban Development Agenda, *World Development* 78: 529–540. http://dx.doi.org/10.1016/j.worlddev.2015.10.028.

Parnell, S. and Simon, D. (2014) National Urbanization and Urban Strategies: Necessary But Absent Policy Instruments in Africa, in Parnell, S., and Pieterse, E. (eds.) *Africa's Urban Revolution.* London: Zed Books, pp. 237–256.

Revi, A. (2016) The New Urban Agenda as an implementation scaffolding for the 2030 Development Agenda in Proc. German Habitat Forum. www.german-habitat-forum.de/assets/bmz_german-habitat_160808.pdf.

Rodwin, L. (ed.) (1987) *Shelter, Settlement and Development.* London: Allen and Unwin.

Rudd, A., Malone, K., and Bartlett, M. (2017) Participatory Urban Planning in Russ, A. and Krasny, M. (eds.), *Urban Environmental Education Review.* Ithaca: Cornell University Press.

Sachs, J., Schmidt-Traub, G., Kroll, C., Durand-Delacre, D. and Teksoz, K. (2016) An SDG Index and Dashboard. New York: Bertelsmann Stiftung and Sustainable Development Solutions Network (SDSN). www.sdgindex.org.

Satterthwaite, D. (1997) Can U.N. Conferences Promote Poverty Reduction? A Review of the Istanbul Declaration and the Habitat Agenda. Comparative Urban Studies Occasional Paper 14. Washington, DC: Woodrow Wilson International Center for Scholars.

Sendai Framework for Disaster Risk Reduction 2015–2030, www.unisdr.org/files/43291_sendaiframeworkfordrren.pdf.

Shane, D.G. (2011) *Urban Design Since 1945: A Global Perspective.* Hoboken and Chichester: John Wiley & Sons.

Simon, D., Arfvidsson, H., Anand, G., Bazaaz, A., Fenna, G., K. Foster, et al. (2016) Developing and Testing the Urban Sustainable Development Goal's Targets and Indicators – A Five-City Study. *Environment and Urbanization*, 28(1): 49–63.

Transforming our World – The 2030 Agenda for Sustainable Development www.un.org/ga/search/view_doc.asp?symbol=A/RES/70/1&Lang=E.

Turner, A. (1980) (ed.) *The Cities of the Poor*. London: Croom Helm.

UN-Habitat (1996) The Habitat Agenda: Istanbul Declaration on Human Settlements http://unhabitat.org/wp-content/uploads/2014/07/The-Habitat-Agenda-Istanbul-Declaration-on-Human-Settlements-2006.pdf.

UN-Habitat (2010a) Chapter 1: Development Context and the Millennium Agenda, in *The Challenge of Slums: Global Report on Human Settlements 2003 – Revised and updated version*. Nairobi: UN-Habitat. http://unhabitat.org/wp-content/uploads/2003/07/GRHS_2003_Chapter_01_Revised_2010.pdf.

UN-Habitat (2010b) *State of the World's Cities: Bridging the Urban Divide*. Nairobi: UN-Habitat.

UN-Habitat (2013) *Streets as Public Spaces and Drivers of Urban Prosperity*. Nairobi: UN-Habitat.

UN-Habitat (2014) *The Evolution of National Urban Policies*. Nairobi: UN-Habitat.

UN-Habitat (2015) History, Mandate and Role in the UN System. http://unhabitat.org/about-us/history-mandate-role-in-the-un-system/.

UN-Habitat (2016) *Global State of National Urban Policies Report*. Nairobi: UN-Habitat.

United Nations (1976) The Vancouver Declaration. http://unhabitat.org/the-vancouver-declaration-on-human-settlements-from-the-report-of-habitat-united-nations-conference-on-human-settlements-vancouver-canada-31-may-to-11-june-1976.

United Nations (2016) HABITAT III New Urban Agenda. http://habitat3.org/wp-content/uploads/New-Urban-Agenda-GA-Adopted-68th-Plenary-N1646655-E.pdf.

UN Conference on Housing and Sustainable Urban Development Habitat III (2015) Issues Paper #11 – Public Space, Habitat III, New York. www.habitat3.org/the-new-urban-agenda/issue-papers.

Weiss, T., Carayannis, T., Emmerij, L. and Jolly, R. (2005) *UN Voices: The Struggle for Development and Social Justice*. Bloomington and Indianapolis: Indiana University Press.

United Nations, Economic and Social Council (2015) Report of the Inter-Agency and Expert Group on Sustainable Development Goal Indicators. E/CN.3/2016/2/Rev.1 (TBC), http://unstats.un.org/unsd/statcom/47th-session/documents/2016–2-IAEG-SDGs-E.pdf.

Chapter 10: Utilizing Urban Living Laboratories for Social Innovation

Sandra Naumann, McKenna Davis, Michele-Lee Moore, and Kes McCormick

10.1 Introduction

Cities have long been recognized as potential hubs of knowledge, social and cultural diversity, jobs, education, public services, and infrastructure (see Scott 1997; Kong 2007; Sassen 2011). Alongside these opportunities, however, cities also face a changing climate, reduced availability of raw materials and natural resources, and dwindling physical space for the built environment. These challenges are accompanied by increasing disparities in income and resultant social inequalities; mounting threats to human health, well-being, and food security; growing refugee and migration influxes; and demographic changes (for example, Coutard et al. 2014; Zhou 2000). These concerns and associated governance challenges increase the urgency for new socially, ecologically, and culturally sensitive approaches to urban development. Such approaches need not only to reduce human vulnerability and environmental footprints, but also to build social cohesion and support ecological sustainability, cultural integration, and the establishment of a shared identity between citizens within a just system of distribution and access to urban resources and wealth (Duxbury et al. 2016).

Conventional public sector models for urban governance are often unexpected or too overstretched to adequately respond to the severity, urgency, and complexity of the outlined challenges (Kieboom 2014). Against this framework and a growing movement for citizen participation in governance processes (for example, Lowndes et al. 2001; Bai et al. 2010; Rosol 2010), many actors are working to transform urban governance to ensure that a greater diversity of voices are accounted for in decision-making processes and urban initiatives. One of the many ways in which urban actors have begun to (re)organize is via the creation of "urban living laboratories," or simply "urban living labs." Such labs exist across North and South America, Africa, Asia, Oceania, and Europe, many of which are connected through an open network organized by the European Network of Living Labs, or ENoLL (see http://openlivinglabs.eu/).

While a shared definition of urban living labs has not yet been agreed upon, they are generally understood to involve collaborative research and urban development activities undertaken alongside the intended end users, exploiting experimental platforms and/or approaches in real time. This both fosters the generation of social and technical innovations and allows for ongoing, continuous analysis to take place so that the lessons learned throughout can be applied to the relevant initiative, as well as to other urban contexts (Voytenko et al. 2016; Mulder 2012; Schliwa and McCormick 2016). In the urban context and in relation to this chapter, urban living labs enable citizens and urban actors to create experimental spaces and arenas outside the prevailing governance system as a means to generate novel solutions and engage new actors, collaborations, ideas, and funds.

This chapter explores the role of urban living labs in supporting social and governance innovations that are the subject of social innovation scholarship. That is, this exploration considers how well the practice of creating urban governance innovation aligns with the surrounding theory on the topic. Although different strands of literature have emerged around the concept of social innovation and have varying perspectives and definitions of the term, we draw on a definition rooted in complex systems thinking (see, for example, Westley et al. 2006; Westley 2013). We understand social innovation to be any initiative (including products, processes, programs, projects, policies, or platforms) that challenges and – ultimately – fundamentally alters the defining routines, resource and authority flows, or beliefs of the broader social system in which it was introduced (Westley and Antadze 2010). In the urban governance sphere, social innovations could entail, for example, innovative social-ecological programs or policies, social finance models, new governance modes, and/or novel forms of cooperation, participation, and partnerships that alter the distribution of authority or knowledge and resource flows (Gonzaléz and Healey 2005; Geobey et al. 2012; Klievnik and Jannsen 2014). Despite urban living labs being intended as an experimental space and a platform for generating social and governance innovation, theoretical examinations and practical analysis of the intersection of social innovation theory and urban living lab practices are limited.

This chapter contributes to this discussion by introducing a brief history of urban living labs and the governance challenges they are intended to address, and subsequently exploring whether urban living labs hold potential as a new forum for urban governance innovation experiments to support positive transformative change. We begin by reflecting on two recent cases, a living lab in

Malmö, Sweden, and the Helle Oase lab in Berlin, Germany, building on current literature to deepen our discussion. Recognizing that urban living labs are
a relatively new phenomenon and social innovation processes take many decades, this discussion aims to provide a starting point to improve understanding of how different forms of urban living labs are emerging to address current
urban challenges and to explore whether these can serve as a platform for
social innovations that are likely to lead to systemic change. Such an analysis
can contribute to the development of new research questions and hypotheses.
Finally, the potential approaches for integrating new social arrangements that
emerge from urban living labs within existing urban governance structures are
discussed.

10.2 Limitations of Existing Governance Approaches to Cope with Emerging Urban Challenges

Cities often experience governance challenges similar to those faced at the
international, national, and regional levels. Consequently, urban areas are
forced to grapple with growing inequality and structural injustices and the
restructuring of governing agencies and economies underpinned by neoliberal,
market-based approaches (Jessop 2002) that largely fail to deliver "the promised efficiency, voice and service integration gains" for city dwellers (Warner
2012). Further challenges include short-term political leadership cycles, competing priorities, budgetary concerns, and an often aging infrastructure that
is ill-suited to a changing climate (Birkmann et al. 2010). In parallel, as Bishop
and Davis (2002) argue, discontent among citizens about these types of issues
has created a strong pressure for all levels of government to adopt participatory
processes that ensure a fair and democratic inclusion of previously marginalized voices, enhance transparency and accountability, and improve the management of public services (Grindle 2007). However, participation processes
themselves are rife with challenges and may still leave citizen expectations
unmet (Bishop and Davis 2002; Irvin and Stansbury 2004).

This combination of factors has led to both a practical and political need for cities to transform their governance frameworks. While opinions and approaches
for how best to accomplish this goal are diverse, it is widely acknowledged that
such changes require significant shifts in mindsets, partnership constellations,
and approaches to governing urban spaces and relationships (for example, Bos
et al. 2015; Seitzinger et al. 2012). Resultant governance structures would thus
need to be able to contend with complex socioecological systems, the demands
and needs of the respective urban populations, and the multiscale issues and
interests contained therein.

While some cities have emerged as leaders for creating new and adaptive governance structures and processes which move beyond interests at the local government level, these cases remain limited (examples include the Cities for Climate Change Protection Programme and the Covenant of Mayors for Climate and Energy in the European Union). Where these initiatives of strong leadership and action by cities do exist, they are often undertaken in the absence of, or in direct conflict with, the respective national governments (see Parker and Rowlands 2007).

Although governance transitions face a high risk of failure and require innovation and experimentation to be successful, their potential to address current environmental and societal shortcomings can be significant. In this context, some cities have exhibited an openness to becoming arenas for experimentation and social innovation (Bulkeley and Castán Broto 2013) and serve as a reference for generating knowledge about the emergence, development, and institutionalization of innovation for sustainable urban development (Schneidewind and Scheck 2013; Evans and Karvonen 2014). Urban living labs have emerged as one form of experimental space for social innovation.

10.3 Innovation Pathways for Cities and the Role of Urban Living Labs

Starting mostly as research and development spaces for information and communications technology, the concept of living labs has been credited to William J. Mitchell of MIT (Quak et al. 2016). The concept gradually expanded and drew on interactive processes with diverse actors to address a range of sustainability issues. While literature on the subject is beginning to flourish alongside the growing prevalence of cities being described as laboratories for social innovation, further in-depth exploration of living labs remains limited (Evans and Karvonen 2011, 2014; König 2013; Nevens et al. 2013; Schneidewind and Scheck 2013; McCormick et al. 2013).

Urban living labs have continued to evolve; they are now appearing all over the world and are taking on a new scope (see Box 10.1). More recently, living labs have been used as a tool to reinterpret, challenge, and improve urban governance to better address issues of sustainability. Recent initiatives involve, for example, urban stakeholders developing and testing new technologies, governance arrangements, and ways of living (Bulkeley and Castán Broto 2013). Although urban living labs' physical manifestation may be attached to a defined space, the concept relates more to an approach: intentional collaborative experimentation between researchers, citizens, companies, and local governments (Schliwa and McCormick 2016).

Box 10.1 Global examples of urban living labs

The **Siyakhula Living Lab in South Africa** aims to develop and field-test a prototype of a simple, cost-effective, robust telecommunications platform to reach out to marginalized and semi-marginalized communities. Beyond technology and infrastructure provisioning, the lab provides information and communications technology skills development and training, as well as advice and blueprints for networking and software service provisioning (see http://siyakhulall.org/).

The **Lots of Green program in Youngstown, Ohio, United States**, aims to support and empower local citizens to improve vacant lots and design green spaces to mitigate high rates of violent crime and low property values. Lab members successfully tested two types of vacant lot interventions on crime: a cleaning and greening "stabilization" action and a "community reuse" action mostly involving community gardens (Kondo et al. 2016).

The **LivingLab Shanghai, China**, is an educational platform promoting innovation for generating societal construction of knowledge that bridges top-down and bottom-up social innovation processes in a real-world context by involving relevant stakeholders. The lab also develops alternative approaches and solutions to complex problems for sustainability in an environment that includes both megacity challenges and nearby rural areas that are resource limited (see www.openlivinglabs.eu/livinglab/livinglab-shanghai).

The **Adelaide Living Laboratory, Australia**, comprises three property development sites and engages stakeholders to provide pathways for low-carbon living in Adelaide with both local and national significance. The lab focuses on (1) cocreation; (2) integrated energy, water, waste, and transport precinct modeling; (3) energy demand management solutions; and (4) the value proposition for investment in low-carbon development (Berry and Davidson 2015).

Five key attributes characterize urban living labs (Voytenko et al. 2016; Quak et al. 2016; Evans and Karvonen 2014). First, *geographical embeddedness* implies that the labs are embedded in the urban context. *Experimentation and learning* mean that they involve testing, experimenting, and reflexive learning processes, while *participation and user involvement* outline the involvement of multiple partners from different sectors and engagement of users and citizens. Fourth, *leadership and ownership* refer to the labs having a leader or coordinator that shapes the design of the activities. Finally, *evaluation and refinement* refer to continuous evaluation or assessment that feeds back into improvements, refinements, and learning within the labs.

Researchers are increasingly categorizing urban living labs within frameworks and typologies based on their use of a variety of methods and metrics to support the generation of innovation and learning. For example, Leminen et al. (2012) proposed four types of living labs to capture the range of approaches being employed in cities around the world: utilizer-driven, enabler-driven, provider-driven, and user-driven living labs. These types are defined by the dominant actor in the initial phase of the lab or by the principal promoter of innovation activities later on. They differ in terms of activities, structure, organization, and coordination. *Utilizers* are often companies applying the living labs approach for product-service system development, *enablers* are often but not exclusively local governments representing the public sector, *providers* are mainly research institutions and universities that in some cases host living labs on university campuses (for example, Robinson et al. 2013), and, finally, *users* are people or grassroots organizations that often initiate living labs. This basic framework draws attention to the key role played by the leading actor or coordinator in designing and implementing urban living labs.

In the following sections, we investigate two different urban living labs and draw on the literature to complement these findings and frame them within wider theoretical discussions. Our first case is an *enabler-driven* platform in Malmö, Sweden that focuses primarily on improving the energy efficiency and liveability of existing apartment buildings, reducing greenhouse gas emissions, and increasing social well-being. The second case represents a *user-driven* initiative utilizing collaborative urban gardening to improve social cohesion in a socially deprived neighborhood in Berlin, Germany. We analyze aspects such as the motivations, existing social perceptions and understandings, as well as the aims, objectives, and approaches for each initiative. This also includes a discussion of the actors involved and institutional structures, impacts, benefits and limitations, and future outlooks. The two examples provide contrasting approaches of urban living labs, with the Malmö case being platform-based and city-led and the Berlin case being project-based and citizen-led (see Table 10.1). Given their small-scale spheres of activity and early stages of development, the case study findings are, to some degree limited in their ability to clarify the connection and interlinkages mentioned; nevertheless, they serve to highlight indicative trends and conclusions for further research and actions at the city level.

Table 10.1 Characteristics of the selected urban living labs

Name	Location	Challenges addressed	Focus	Type of urban lab	Actors involved
Malmö Innovation Platform	Malmö, Sweden	Rejuvenating southeast Malmö (area shaped by former shipping industry)	Improving the energy efficiency and livability of existing apartment buildings	Platform-based, city-led, enabler-driven	City of Malmö, Region Skåne, universities, entrepreneurs, building owners, residents, schools, and so forth
Helle Oase	Berlin, Germany	Lack of common green space in a low strata and densely populated area	Urban gardening and social cohesion	Initiative-based, community-led, user-driven	Local residents; supporters, including: district office, local youth group, nature protection association, medicinal school

Case Study 1 Malmö Innovation Platform – Improving the Energy Efficiency and Liveability of Existing Apartment Buildings

A coastal city in the south of Sweden, Malmö, struggled economically in the early post-industrialization years following the collapse of the ship building industry in the 1980s, which led to a range of other social challenges. Recently, however, the City of Malmö has actively worked to address major societal challenges and to increase the sustainability of the city (McCormick and Kiss 2015) by supporting a diverse range of innovative projects initiated by the city, citizens, businesses, associations, and academia.

One of these initiatives involves the Malmö Innovation Platform. The City of Malmö assumes the main leadership role in the platform, but is supported by a partnership-based steering group when making major decisions. The steering group consists of the City of Malmö, Region Skåne, Lund University, Malmö University, the Swedish University for Agricultural Sciences, Media Evolution, EoN (an energy company), and MKB (a housing company). Sixteen business organizations participate in the platform, including representatives of the real estate, construction and design, energy services and information technology, and consultancy and innovation sectors.

The platform currently focuses on the renovation of existing apartment buildings in low-medium income areas in the southeast of Malmö as part of the city's larger efforts towards sustainable development (McCormick and Kiss 2015). The area faces a multitude of cultural, social, and economic challenges, including the need to renovate many homes originally constructed as part of Sweden's "Million Homes Program" in the 1960s. The infrastructure no longer meets efficiency standards, and the overall liveability of these places has become a concern. The initiative pilots and develops new technologies, services, business concepts, and local jobs while also experimenting with different organizational and collaborative setups between businesses, the municipality, and academia for supporting the renovation of buildings (McCormick and Kiss 2015).

The platform brings together diverse actors, creates space for discussion on urban (re)development, and supports the creation and implementation of urban experiments, which aim to break away from the "business as usual" paradigm. Initiatives are designed to reorganize and restructure relationships inside Malmö and between the key actors in the platform (see Table 10.2). The platform does not carry out projects or innovations itself, but instead supports their initiation and implementation by bringing together individuals from different organizations and providing starter funds for idea development. Participants share experiences and knowledge gained from the supported projects via the platform, where those experiences are evaluated and, ideally, utilized in new projects (McCormick and Kiss 2015). Platform participants are also attempting to embed technical experiments in a broader discussion about the social organization of the city and the flows of authority and resources.

Ownership of the initiatives is shared by the companies participating in the platform. A key motivation for companies to engage is the enabling of new partnerships and opportunities. All companies invest time and resources into the activities. At the project level, participation goes beyond the partners in the platform and encompasses residents and local organizations, such as schools, community groups, and housing associations.

Table 10.2 Examples of projects supported by the Malmö Innovation Platform

Projects	Description
District heating	EoN (an energy company) performs renovations to district heating systems in existing apartment buildings to test if significant improvements can be made and what benefits for residents might be achieved
Every drop	MKB (a housing company) aims to reduce hot-water usage in apartments by influencing behavior; MKB transfers saved funds into local schools, thereby strengthening the local community and the schools
Recycling centers with maker-spaces	VA Syd (a waste management company) and Malmö University test the potential to combine local recycling centers by reusing materials and "waste" in shared maker-spaces
Local jobs	Trianon (a building owner) puts demands on building companies by including a "social clause" in their building contracts requiring the employment of local people in renovation and building projects

10.3.1 Impacts, Benefits, and Limitations

The Malmö Innovation Platform initially focused less on results and more on identifying the key questions for socioeconomic development in the city, and on developing and enabling collaborative processes, which are challenging to evaluate. To date, the main impact of the platform is the creation of a meeting space for diverse urban stakeholders in which they can share perspectives on challenges, understand the problems from different perspectives, and feed this new knowledge into the process of developing innovative solutions. The platform also serves to integrate projects or experiments which were previously considered as discrete units, by highlighting the lessons learned and using these to inform the development of new initiatives. The convening and coordinating function is necessary, but is in itself is not a governance innovation that transforms the existing urban governance regime. Thus, questions remain whether this is sufficient to lead to a governance innovation.

The Malmö Innovation Platform has initiated over 50 projects since its inception. While its ambitions are clear, a need remains to better structure evaluation processes to ensure that the platform meets its own objectives. Although companies clearly use the platform to test creative solutions and learn from successes and failures, the transferability of the initiatives is difficult to assess. Moreover, it is challenging to determine if this platform supports a step away from "business as usual" or whether it reinforces a pattern of creative elite experimentation which has often led to challenges associated with gentrification (Peck 2005). A key aspect going forward will be to continue to develop the platform so it remains relevant and useful for participating partners and for marginalized communities who are currently not represented by the partnership in the long term.

10.3.2 Outlook and Future Directions

The second phase of the Malmö Innovation Platform began in 2016 and will broaden the geographic scope of the lab across the entire city. It will attempt to tackle many of the barriers identified in the first phase, such as financing new projects (through the provision of some funding for pilot projects) and better connecting citywide visions with experiments and collaborative activities cutting across the government, businesses, community, and academia.

As part of this development, the Sustainable City Accelerator has been established to support innovative players from all sectors in the application of new sustainable urban development solutions. The accelerator will purportedly support the analysis of challenges around Malmö, establish partnerships with the key stakeholders, owners, and clients; develop ideas and solutions of a technical, social, digital, and organizational character; and test and implement solutions in the physical urban development in the city. Innovators from the private, public, and voluntary sectors as well as academia will be able to use the accelerator as an arena for the development of ideas and collaborations. Thus far, however, the discussions have utilized a positive framing about "diversity" and "collaboration" without widely acknowledging the power asymmetries and ways in which such lab processes may disadvantage those without technical knowledge about building construction or about technological innovation.

Case Study 2 Helle Oase, Berlin, Germany – Creating Social Cohesion through Collective Gardening

Helle Oase is a 4,000-square-meter urban permaculture garden for local residents initiated in 2012 in Berlin, Germany. It is the only urban garden in the city and is located in a prefabricated housing (Plattenbau) estate in Berlin-Hellersdorf, which is a densely populated and highly developed area. The area is also known for its low social strata, high unemployment (particularly among young people), and low incomes. The initiative provides an opportunity for collective gardening, creates an open and positive space for the community, and acts as a meeting point for residents. The citizen garden is a multifunctional space containing not only cultivated plots and fruit trees, but also a sitting area for gardeners, a playground, hammocks, a soccer field, and walkable pathways.

Berlin-Hellersdorf is characterized by large and monotonous prefabricated housing estates, resulting in a comparably dense residential area. As is often the case in urban areas, this community is disconnected from food production processes and nature and lacks agricultural land. A centrally located area of fallow land offered a great opportunity to create a place where residents could stay and spend time with their previously unknown neighbors, thereby also gaining a sense of stability and calm to counteract their often troubled daily lives (Albrecht and Lohr 2015).

Inspired by British urban gardening projects, Helle Oase was initiated by a single individual with support from a core group of other local residents. In order to build a sense of community and to strengthen social cohesion among the residents in the area, these founders emphasized stimulating and maintaining social interactions. Albrecht and Lohr (2015) found that there is a very high level of cooperation through shared norms and values within the project. These repeated social interactions have helped to build trust and enable participants to build a shared identity.

The garden is open to everyone, regardless of an individual's socioeconomic background or ability to participate regularly. Participants are, however, asked to abide by some basic common principles. For example, the burden of work and harvest is to be shared equally. Moreover, any occurring problems are encouraged to be solved in a conflict-free manner.

Helle Oase is supported by a vital network, which is spread across different bureaucratic levels and types of institutions and organizations, including the district office, a local youth group and a nature protection association, a medicinal school, the larger neighborhood, and the core group of residents. The physical area is formally owned by a state-owned real estate agency (Berlin Liegenschaftsfond), but Helle Oase holds the user management rights on a temporary basis. Communication between the gardeners is managed via weekly face-to-face meetings, time spent working together in the garden, and a website. Moreover, the Helle Oase core group interacts with the neighboring community via online and personal invitations to garden parties, informal talks with passers-by, workshops, and employee-friendly gardening hours. The initial funding for Helle Oase was provided by a national European Social Fund program, which ended in 2014, creating the need for alternative financing via a donation platform.

10.3.3 Impacts, Benefits, and Limitations

Although from the outside it may appear to be a simple urban gardening initiative, the Helle Oase is an urban living lab because of its creation of a garden that aims to serve as an experimental space to reveal and test new paths and means for creating social cohesion within a socially deprived area. It also enforces reflexive learning processes by applying simple but common principles in the newly created, common green space.

In addition to the production of low-value physical goods (food, flowers, and herbs), the Helle Oase provides social and educational benefits. For example, the garden serves as a vital and attractive community space; creates a sense of community and group spirit; evokes a high level of identification with the project; increases social cohesion and earned social capital through an open and constructive process to solve problems and make joint decisions; and enhances the process of mutual learning. Finally, the garden creates a high level of cooperation and trust among the participants and serves as an educational tool for spreading knowledge about sustainable gardening. Further, Helle Oase contributes to ecological sustainability and has a positive impact on biodiversity. It is worth noting that these benefits might be restricted to some individuals, or may not be able to be fully explored due to the limited number of actively participating gardeners, or potential conflicts in sharing or stealing the harvest, or vandalism in the relaxation area (Albrecht and Lohr 2015).

The user-driven Helle Oase lab may not have the capacity to change established routines and enable broader societal transformation to the political or authoritative system, but it is nevertheless noteworthy given its emphasis on trust and cooperation building. These processes often require long periods to progress. However, larger transformation processes to improve social cohesion and build social capital (particularly in socially deprived areas) require political support throughout the city. Such action could significantly contribute to the development of new urban community models that are driven by local residents and local interest groups. For these reasons, the Helle Oase case is highly relevant within social innovation discourse, as it represents a valuable example of the many grassroots initiatives appearing in cities across the world.

10.3.4 Outlook and Future Directions

Initiatives such as Helle Oase can provide cost-efficient and viable socioecological solutions to problems associated with densely populated built areas, such as low social strata, unemployment, lack of social cohesion and community sensibility, heterogeneity of citizens, and high crime rates. Conversely, such labs require a relatively high level of social commitment by motivated local residents and the ongoing support of local and regional actors. Regular financial support as well as long-term management (or even property) rights to use open spaces in the community are also key to ensure its sustainability.

This initiative has the potential to be replicated or transferred to other densely populated built areas. Helle Oase has not yet produced follow-up initiatives within Berlin, in part because of the established, vital urban gardening scene which already exists in Berlin. Key challenges looking towards the future include the temporary nature of the contract with the district office, insecure financial support (European funding for Helle Oase ended in 2014; the organization has since relied mainly on donations), and the need for more engaged participants across which the workload associated with the initiative can be better distributed.

10.4 Bridging the Gap between Public Policy, Governance, Urban Living Labs, and Social Innovation

These two illustrative and distinct cases demonstrate that urban living labs can provide a protected space for experimentation and for forming creative collaborations that can, in turn, foster different approaches to resolving societal problems. While these developments potentially lay the foundation on which social innovation processes can emerge, our analysis demonstrates their failure to propel true systemic change in ways coherent with the provided definition of social innovation. In this regard, neither of the case studies has led to any fundamental changes in the defining resource and authority flows or beliefs of the broader social system in which they were introduced. Reasons for these failures may link to the infancy of these initiatives, the lack of political support, and insufficient integration into existing structures (in the Berlin case), or the lack of connecting technical innovations to create new social opportunities (in the Malmö case).

We therefore highlight the need for additional research on the relationship of urban living lab initiatives to overall urban governance. In particular, the following aspects are suggested to be pursued: whether the existing lab forms are truly fostering governance innovations that will create large-scale systemic change, and what the critical success factors and realistic timespan entail. More specifically, there remains a pressing need to answer the questions: How can newly created social arrangements be integrated within existing (political) governance structures to maximize effectiveness in responding to current urban challenges and turn into social innovations that enable true changes within existing governance systems? Can such successful experimental initiatives developed in urban labs move from small-scale, niche positions to a broader scale? What conditions would be required to facilitate such a move? Although the evidence from the case studies and available literature has provided only insufficient answers to these multifaceted issues to date, an array of interesting insights can be discussed in light of existing literature and pursued further in future research in this field.

For social innovations to emerge, develop, and stabilize, a set of coalition-building opportunities for actors and certain framework parameters must be present (such as the institutional context, welfare regime context, and local political culture) (Cattacin and Zimmer 2016). In this context, urban living labs may offer a platform and a flexible approach to start building such coalitions and to increase connectivity among different actors within the urban area, which will be necessary for more systemic transformative changes (see Westley et al. 2006; Westley 2013). Those innovations that do emerge may be integrated into existing governance systems with various degrees of difficulty. While the Helle Oase still requires strong support and political will at the municipal level, the Malmö Innovation Platform has already been promoted by the local government, demonstrating that different organizational configurations may create better access to the political will that can inevitably be necessary for addressing complex challenges. However, this hypothesis requires further testing with additional cases.

Moreover, existing urban governance scholarship has determined that governance regimes embedded in a federal system or in systems applying the subsidiarity principle are likely to facilitate the greatest emergence and sustainability of social innovations because the local level is in a position to address social challenges independently.[1] Cattacin and Zimmer (2016) found that local self-government and cooperation with nonstate actors such as civil society organizations show a higher level of openness and likelihood for social innovations. In this context, it is promising to see that urban governance increasingly involves nongovernmental actors from civil society and private businesses – a practice in line with the core features of urban living labs (Gerometta et al. 2005). The Malmö Innovation Platform represents, for example, a new interface and form of cooperation between the city and nonstate actors, and is actively engaging with partners to enable sustainability interventions. Such new partnerships and modes of governance can also facilitate significant

---

[1] Through cross-national comparative research (77 social innovation cases in 20 European cities), the WILCO (Welfare Innovations at the Local Level in Favour of Cohesion) project examined how local welfare systems affect social inequalities and favor social cohesion with a special focus on the missing link between innovations at the local level and their successful transfer and implementation to other settings. See http://www.wilcoproject.eu

sharing of knowledge and cultivation of learning processes. In this context, both cases from Malmö and Berlin reveal that urban living labs do not necessarily challenge the existing governance structures. Rather, the experiments act as learning platforms for new urban knowledge, which may eventually inform systemic governance change.

In European cities, Brandsen et al (2016). found that initiatives that remain separate from or insufficiently integrated into urban policies are potentially limited in their expected impacts and ability to address current societal challenges. Social innovations that both complement existing urban development strategies and can contribute to making the respective cities more dynamic and attractive are more likely to be accepted, supported by local governments, and integrated into local welfare administrations securing their sustainability (García-Sánchez and Prado-Lorenzo 2009). However, even in these cases, it is not guaranteed that true impacts on the system will occur.

Innovative initiatives focusing on vulnerable groups living on the fringes of urban society and dealing with social inequities are unfortunately accorded less attention under urban development strategies and political agendas, and are commonly affected by budget cuts. In the specific case of Helle Oase – and as revealed by Ewert (2016) – public funding for innovative capital may diminish in the near future for social innovations, emphasizing the need to develop and establish a new system to enable cooperation between the political administrative system and social innovations. These conditions may also weaken the capacity of cities to integrate such new developments thoroughly into public policies, thereby diminishing their potential to transform into social innovations. Research on urban living labs needs to continue to track whether urban living lab initiatives continue to rely on existing governance mechanisms, such as funding from local governments, or whether they turn to using their platforms themselves to create innovative approaches to financing their initiatives. A host of critiques could emerge from either of those approaches, and the risk is that neither leads to transformative changes responding to identified needs.

Overall, there seems to be a trend of shifting from a hierarchical model of governance to a heterarchical, more participatory structure in cities (Hohn and Neuer 2006). This progression may enable a better horizontal integration of new, nonpublic actors that can provide services for urban society at a large scale. In this context, it is essential that the involved actors recognize each other's roles in the creation of a workable urban society (Cattacin and Zimmer 2016) by creating respect, trust, and even responsibilities and power. Gerometta et al. (2005) go further and suggest that the state should instead adopt an enabling and stimulating role, maintaining responsibility for central problems of societal welfare while promoting an environment for civil society organizations and the private sector to fuel social innovations and contribute to sustainable urban development. The Malmö Innovation Platform illustrates how such a vision can be achieved, given its strong support from the local city government and its function as a connector of entrepreneurs, property owners, and local residents who want to pursue sustainable urban transformation processes. However, this approach can neglect to confront the potential asymmetrical power dynamics existing in urban areas, requiring that we be more specific when talking about how this represents system transformation, not just a perpetuation of governing approaches that have created inequalities in the first place. Therefore, further research is needed to assess the potential of government-led urban living labs.

The integration of emerging social innovative initiatives and arrangements into existing governance structures to respond effectively to current urban problems remains a challenging endeavor. Nevertheless, we can highlight a few promising outcomes. The capacity of civil society and its networks to develop and establish solutions to current societal challenges and to contribute to more sustainable, liveable, and cohesive cities – as well as to the urban governance arrangements that promote them – should be acknowledged by state and city governments. Making explicit use of self-organization and civil society initiatives (Gerometta et al. 2005) as part of the official urban development agenda and respective action plans, as well as providing room for experimentation, such as through urban living labs, can not only enrich the urban development agenda, but can also contribute to its achievement.

Further actions to enable social innovations and their integration into existing structures may entail a transfer of responsibilities and power to non-state actors and enable a thorough and equal participation of civil organizations across all social strata (for example, ensuring everyone is equipped with voting rights) in local policy processes. The examples of initiatives in Malmö and Berlin do not suggest a transfer of power, but rather attempts to better engage local communities. There is, however, an underlying question of power dynamics. Overall, frequent dialogue and exchange between private companies and business, civil society, and city government should take place (for example, via round tables) to inform public and legal decision-making and strategic decisions at the state and city levels. Urban living labs are a platform for such dialogue and collaborative activities that can span multiple organizations and sectors. Still, urban living labs should try to embed their practices in the systems that they seek to change, should rethink current modes of governing in urban systems, and should approach public authorities to discuss the integration and uptake of their activities (Kieboom 2014).

10.5 Outlook

The outlined case studies offer a small taste of the wide variety of urban living labs and their potential to tackle various societal challenges, including environmental, economic, cultural, and social issues. There remains a clear need to consider how localized, discrete initiatives such as urban living labs amount to larger, system-level change or to transformations in urban governance arrangements (that is, social innovations) and what the critical success factors behind them are. Although urban living labs have proliferated across the world in recent years and have proven to be a valuable and innovative approach to developing new products and platforms for convening and coordinating, it remains too early to determine whether the additive effects of the diversity of technical innovations and collaborative approaches will equate to the change necessary to achieve urban sustainability. However, the examples and literature presented in this chapter suggest considerable potential for urban living labs to contribute to the development of more sustainable cities, increased social justice, and the development of a system which is better prepared to handle future societal and environmental challenges.

References

Albrecht, S., and Lohr, K. 2015. Taking Elinor to the Gardens. Analysing Collective Action Variations in Urban Gardening. www.youtube.com/watch?v=3YhBpQoyZ3M

Bai, X., McAllister, R.R., Beaty, R.M., and Taylor, B. 2010. Urban Policy and Governance in a Global Environment: Complex Systems, Scale Mismatches and Public Participation. *Current Opinion in Environmental Sustainability*, 2(3): 129–135.

Berry, S., and Davidson, K. 2015. Adelaide Living Laboratory Value Proposition: Literature Review. University of South Australia. Report for CRC Low Carbon Living

Birkmann, J., Garschagen, M., Kraas, F., and Quang, N. 2010. Adaptive Urban Governance: New Challenges for the Second Generation of Urban Adaptation Strategies to Climate Change. *Sustainability Science*, 5(2): 185–206.

Bishop, P., and Davis, G. 2002. Mapping Public Participation in Policy Choices. *Australian Journal of Public Administration*, 61(1): 14–29.

Bos, J.J., Brown, R.R., and Farrelly, M. 2015. Building Networks and Coalitions to Promote Transformational Change: Insights from an Australian Urban Water Planning Case Study, *Environmental Innovation and Societal Transitions*, 15: 11–25.

Brandsen, T., Cattacin, S., Evers, A., and Zimmer, A. 2016. Introduction in Brandsen, T., S. Cattacin, A. Evers, and A. Zimmer (eds.), *Social Innovations in the Urban Context*. Cham, Heidelberg, New York, Dordrecht, London: Springer Open, pp. 3–20.

Bulkeley, H., and Castán-Broto, V.C. 2013. Government by Experiment? Global Cities and the Governing of Climate Change. *Transactions. Institute of British Geographers*, 38: 361–375.

Cattacin, S., and Zimmer, A. 2016. Urban Governance and Social Innovations in Brandsen, T., S. Cattacin, A. Evers, and A. Zimmer (eds.), *Social Innovations in the Urban Context*. Cham, Heidelberg, New York, Dordrecht, London: Springer Open, pp. 21–30.

Coutard, O., Finnveden, G., Kabisch, S., Kitchin, R., Matos, R., Nijkamp, P., et al. 2014. Urban Megatrends: Towards a European Research Agenda: A Report by the Scientific Advisory Board of the Joint Programming Initiative Urban Europe. www.arrs.gov.si/sl/medn/urbana/inc/JPI-Urban-Europe-Megatrends-Report.pdf

Duxbury, N., Hosagrahar, J., and Pascual, J. 2016. Why Must Culture Be at the Heart of Sustainable Urban Development? UCLG. www.acpculturesplus.eu/sites/default/files/2016/02/19/agenda_21_for_culture_why_must_culture_be_at_the_heart_of_sustainable_urban_development.pdf

Evans, J., and Karvonen, A. 2011. Living Laboratories for Sustainability: Exploring the Politics and Epistemology of Urban Transition in H. Bulkeley, V. Castán Broto, M. Hodson, and S. Marvin (eds.), *Cities and Low Carbon Transitions*. Routledge, London: 126–141.

Evans, J., and Karvonen, A. 2014. "Give Me a Laboratory and I Will Lower Your Carbon Footprint!" – Urban Laboratories and the Pursuit of Low Carbon Futures. *International Journal of Urban and Regional Research*, 38 (2): 413–430

Ewert, B. 2016. Poor But Sexy? Berlin as a Context for Social Innovation in Brandsen, T., S. Cattacin, A. Evers, and A. Zimmer (eds.), *Social Innovations in the Urban Context*. Cham, Heidelberg, New York, Dordrecht, London: Springer Open, pp. 143–160.

García-Sánchez, I. and Prado-Lorenzo, J. 2009. Decisive Factors in the Creation and Execution of Municipal Action Plans in the Field of Sustainable Development in the European Union. *Journal of Cleaner Production*, 17(11): 1039–1051.

Gerometta, J., Häussermann, H., and Longo, G. 2005. Social Innovation and Civil Society in Urban Governance: Strategies for an Inclusive City. *Urban Studies*, 42(11): 2007–2021.

Geobey, S., Westley, F. R., and Weber, O. 2012. Enabling Social Innovation through Developmental Social Finance. *Journal of Social Entrepreneurship*, 3(2): 151–165.

González, S., and Healey, P. 2005. A Sociological Institutionalist Approach to the Study of Innovation in Governance Capacity. *Urban Studies*, 42 (11): 2055–2069

Grindle, M.S. 2007. *Going Local. Decentralization, Democratization, and the Promise of Good Governance*. Princeton: Princeton University Press.

Hohn, U., and Neuer, B. 2006. New Urban Governance: Institutional Change and Consequences for Urban Development. *European Planning Studies*, 14(3): 291–298.

Irvin, R.A., and Stansbury, J. 2004. Citizen Participation in Decision Making: Is It Worth the Effort?. *Public Administration Review*, 64(1): 55–65.

Jessop, B. 2002. Liberalism, Neoliberalism, and Urban Governance: A State–Theoretical Perspective. *Antipode*, 34(3): 452–472.

Kieboom, M. 2014. Lab Matters: Challenging the Practice of Social Innovation Laboratories. Amsterdam: Kennisland. Licensed under CC-BY.

Klievink, B., and Janssen, M. 2014. Developing Multi-Layer Information Infrastructures: Advancing Social Innovation through Public-Private Governance. *Information Systems Management* 31: 240–249

Kondo, M., Hohl, B., Han, SH., and Branas, C. 2016. Effects of Greening and Community Reuse of Vacant Lots on Crime. *Urban Studies*, 53(15): 3279–3295, DOI: 10.1177/0042098015608058

Kong, L., 2007. Cultural Icons and Urban Development in Asia: Economic Imperative, National Identity, and Global City Status. *Political Geography*, 26(4): 383–404.

König, A. 2013. Conclusion: A Cross-Cultural Exploration of the Co-Creation of Knowledge in Living Laboratories for Societal Transformation across Four Continents, in König, A. (ed.) *Regenerative Sustainable Development of Universities and Cities – The Role of Living Laboratories.* Cheltenham: Edward Elgar.

Leminen, S., Westerlund, M., and Nyström, A.G. 2012. Living Labs as Open-Innovation Networks. *Technology Innovation Management Review*, September: 6–11.

Lowndes, V., Pratchett, L. and Stoker, G. 2001. Trends in Public Participation: Part 1–Local Government Perspectives. *Public Administration*, 79(1): 205–222.

McCormick, K., Anderberg, S., Coenen, L., and Neij, L. 2013. Advancing Sustainable Urban Transformation. *Journal of Cleaner Production*, 50: 1–11. doi:10.1016/j.jclepro.2013.01.003

McCormick, K. and Kiss, B. 2015. Learning through Renovations for Urban Sustainability: The Case of the Malmö Innovation Platform. *Current Opinion in Environmental Sustainability*, 16: 44–50.

Mulder, I., 2012. Living Labbing the Rotterdam Way: Co-Creation as an Enabler for Urban Innovation. *Technology Innovation Management Review*, 2(9): 39.

Nevens, F., Frantzeskaki, N., Gorissen, L., and Loorbach, D. 2013. Urban Transition Labs: Co-Creating Transformative Action for Sustainable Cities. *Journal of Cleaner Production*, 50: 111–122. doi:10.1016/j.jclepro.2012.12.001

Parker, P., and Rowlands, I. H. 2007. City Partners Maintain Climate Change Action Despite National Cuts: Residential Energy Efficiency Programme Valued at Local Level. *Local Environment* 12.5: 505–517.

Peck, J. 2005. Struggling with the Creative Class. *International Journal of Urban and Regional Research*, 29(4):740–770.

Quak, H., Lindholm, M., Tavasszy, L. and Browne, M. 2016. From Freight Partnerships to City Logistics Living Labs–Giving Meaning To The Elusive Concept Of Living Labs. *Transportation Research Procedia*, 12: 461–473.

Robinson, J., Berkhout, T., Cayuela, A., and Campbell, A. 2013. Next Generation Sustainability at the University of British Columbia: The University as Societal Test-Bed for Sustainability, in König, A. (ed.) *Regenerative Sustainable Development of Universities and Cities: The Role of Living Laboratories*, Cheltenham: Edward Elgar, pp. 27–48. DOI 10.4337/9781781003640.00009

Rosol, M. 2010. Public Participation in Post-Fordist Urban Green Space Governance: The Case of Community Gardens in Berlin. *International Journal of Urban and Regional Research*, 34(3): 548–563.

Sassen, S. 2011. *Cities in a World Economy*. Washington, DC: Sage Publications.

Schliwa, G., and McCormick, K. 2016. Living Labs: Users, Citizens and Transitions, in Evans, J., Karvonen, A. and Raven, R. (eds.), *The Experimental City*, London: Routledge, pp. 163–178.

Schneidewind, U., and Scheck, H. 2013. Die Stadt als "Reallabor" für Systeminnovationen, in Rückert-John, J. (ed.), *Soziale Innovation und Nachhaltigkeit*. Wiesbaden: Springer Fachmedien., pp. 229–248. http://dx.doi.org/10.1007/978-3-531-18974-1_12

Scott, A.J. 1997. The Cultural Economy of Cities. *International Journal of Urban and Regional Research*, 21(2): 323–339.

Seitzinger, S.P., Svedin, U., Crumley, C.L., Steffen, W., Abdullah, S.A., Alfsen, C., et al. 2012. Planetary Stewardship in an Urbanizing World: Beyond City Limits. *Ambio*, 41(8): 787–794

Voytenko, Y., McCormick, K., Evans, J., and Schliwa, G. 2016. Urban Living Labs for Sustainability and Low Carbon Cities in Europe: Towards a Research Agenda. *Journal of Cleaner Production*, 123 (2016): 45–54

Warner, M.E. 2012. Privatization and Urban Governance: The Continuing Challenges of Efficiency, Voice and Integration. *Cities*, 29: S38–S43.

Westley, F.R., and Antadze, N. 2010. Making a Difference: Strategies for Scaling Social Innovation for Greater Impact. *The Innovation Journal: The Public Sector Innovation Journal*, 15(2): 2.

Westley, F.R., Zimmerman, B., and Patton, M.Q. 2006. *Getting to Maybe: How the World Is Changed*. Toronto: Vintage Canada.

Westley, F.R. 2013. Social Innovation and Resilience: How One Enhances the Other. *Stanford Social Innovation Review*, 11(3): 6–8.

Zhou, X. 2000. Economic Transformation and Income Inequality in Urban China: Evidence from Panel Data. *American Journal of Sociology*, 105(4): 1135–1174.

Chapter 11: Can Big Data Make a Difference for Urban Management?[1]

Ulrich Mans, Sarah Giest, and Thomas Baar

11.1 Introduction

The term "big data" has emerged as a powerful technology trend affecting many aspects of life. Since the early days of big data applications in science and various commercial sectors, the term has come to refer to the exponential increase in the volume and variety of data available, as well as the availability of new tools and approaches to process ever more complex data. Reflecting its global impact on societies, the United Nations speaks of a "Data Revolution" (UN IAEG 2014). Within several domains, big data are already being applied with success. The increased availability of consumer data, for example, provides new opportunities for business and commercial enterprises to develop targeted advertisements and increase revenues (Mayer-Schönberger and Cukier 2013). Big data have facilitated major scientific breakthroughs in various academic disciplines including healthcare, environmental studies, and physics (Krumholz 2014; Bryant et al. 2008). In the public policy realm, the collection and processing of personal data has already transformed intelligence and surveillance practices (Lyon 2014). Law enforcement is another field that has experienced a growing number of experiments in data-driven innovations, such as fraud detection, crime fighting, and violence (Technopolis et al. 2015).

Given the above-average connectivity in urban areas, cities lie at the heart of the trend towards data-driven approaches for confronting societal challenges (Barber 2013; Thakuriah et al. 2015). With more than half of the world's population residing in cities and more than 90 percent of the population growth through 2050 expected to occur in urban areas, there is increased pressure to look for data-driven solutions in the urban context (Pfeffer et al. 2015). This holds particularly true for cities in the Global South, where urban sprawl represents a

---

[1] An earlier version of this chapter was presented at the International Studies Association Annual Conference in March 2016, in Atlanta, Georgia, United States.

major impediment to sustainable development. Since the 1970s, low-income cities have experienced a 325 percent population increase. In Latin America alone, 110 million people out of 558 million urbanites live in slums, or so-called no-go areas, where basic municipal utility and service delivery remain scarce (de Boer 2015; Muggah 2015; see also Chapters 7, 8, and 9). In this context, recent studies emphasize that "cities … are unable to respond to the needs of their growing populations faced with rising violence, crime, and poverty" (Mancini and Súilleabháin 2016: III). Urban scholars argue that many cities are set to struggle with income and social inequality; youth unemployment; homicide and criminal violence; poor access to key services; high concentrations of, or preexisting, violence; and exposure to environmental threats (Muggah and Diniz 2013).

To date, most big data applications in the urban context have centered on the quick wins of managerial practices. For example, data analytics are being used in a variety of urban policy sectors, such as public health or infrastructure improvements. These schemes are often driven by cost-saving considerations (Batty 2013), while there is much less movement vis-à-vis the underlying dynamics of urban life and policies aimed at improving social cohesion. Applications are also mostly occurring in OECD countries, where data generation to date is still much more meaningful than in data-poor regions: Using mobile phone records to improve public transport, for example, is only viable once a certain threshold of mobile phone users and representation across the population has been reached. Such an effort makes sense in affluent cities, but not (yet) in urban agglomerations where the digital infrastructure and connectivity are more nascent. At the same time, there is an increasing number of experiments in the developing world, where new data sources are being collected and analyzed for the public good (Bellagio Big Data Workshop Participants 2014).

This chapter aims to contribute to this emerging discourse about how big data can improve urban policy-making, and focuses on the role that this technology can play in building more inclusive cities in the Global South. The authors highlight the need for urban authorities to invest in additional resources as well as meaningful knowledge transfer mechanisms that are in line with the concept of "mobile urbanism." This is particularly important in low-income cities, where policy-makers are driven by the desire to address urban violence and to build more inclusive cities across different constituencies.

11.2 Managing the City in a Digital Age

Data in the urban context can be used in various ways and are applicable to diverse settings. An analysis of 58 initiatives worldwide, performed by Technopolis, the Oxford Internet Institute, and Centre for European Policy

Studies in 2015, shows that the most widespread use of data relates to agenda setting and/or problem analysis. The same study found that open data were commonly used for transparency, accountability, and increasing participation, whereas administrative and statistical data were used for implementation and monitoring purposes (Technopolis et al. 2015). To understand these applications, we clustered them into three dimensions: *data, processes*, and *community*.

11.2.1 Dimensions of Big Data in the Urban Context

First, big data are about the availability of *data* as a source of information and, ultimately, knowledge. The proliferation of information and communication technologies has led to a data surge. Datasets have become so large and complex that traditional tools and approaches are often inadequate for processing them. While the volume of data that is becoming available is an issue, three additional challenging characteristics of the new complexities of digital data streams are velocity (speed of data streams); variety (unstructured versus structured data streams); and veracity (quality of data) (Soubra 2012). Some have added a number of other Vs, *such* as *viability*, for contexts in which reliable data collection is extremely difficult (Mans and Baar 2014).

Second, big data relate to the development of new tools and practices in order to collect, analyze, and work with this digital information (Mayer-Schönberger and Cukier 2013). King (2013) argues that big data are about the *processes* through which we can generate knowledge. Challenges include capturing, verifying, cleaning, storing, sharing, searching, analyzing, visualizing, and presenting the data. In order to infer information and knowledge from data, new disciplines and practices have started to emerge. Such data sciences are producing highly automated approaches, such as machine learning and pattern recognition. In many instances, however, the interpretation of data is unlikely to be taken over by automatic processes; there are growing concerns about the limitations to technically mediated solutions (see, for example, Latonero et al. 2017). Instead, there is a need for hybrid sets of skills that combine human and machine intelligence for supporting policy decisions.

Third, the growing interest in big data has created a new *community* around digital pioneers, which represents a paradigmatic shift in how a diverse set of stakeholders interacts (Letouzé et al. 2015). In a hyper-connected world, the design and implementation of data-driven innovations are incredibly complex and lead to a shift of existing power balances: data sources are becoming more decentralized and analytical tools more accessible to the wider public. As a result, there are limits to the level of "control" that public authorities have over what happens within local policy networks. At the national level, we already see a myriad of citizen networks starting to engage in decision-making processes through data-driven innovations.[2] We also observe a growing number of professionals in the public policy domain that are warming up to the possibilities that data can bring for improving service delivery to citizens (see Chapter 10). In other words, policy-making in a digital age calls for a more active involvement of new (often loosely connected) stakeholders – such as civil society, private enterprises, or private citizens that hold or produce relevant data (WEF 2015a) – which are able to collect, process, validate, and interpret these newly available types of data.

Big data should therefore be understood as a phenomenon bringing together a large variety of stakeholders that individually or collectively engage in the processes that determine how data are collected and used for, among other things, policy goals. Here, it is important to differentiate between data-driven and data-informed policy. Rather than relying on data alone, the term "data-informed policy" refers to decisions that include data as just one factor, coupled with more qualitative judgments about context and potential risks.

The following section presents the academic discourse on knowledge management in cities that applies in the context of data-driven innovation. The subsequent sections look at the different data types that shape the Data Revolution landscape and reflect on their potential benefits. We base this reflection on two case studies that highlight the intricacies of knowledge transfer for effective integration of data-driven innovation into urban policy development: data-informed policy.

11.2.2 Addressing the Urban Knowledge Gap

With the emergence of a large variety of data streams that offer (real time) information on what happens in the city, urban authorities around the world have started to explore new opportunities for improving traffic oversight, service delivery, or crime fighting. At the same time, there are limitations to data-driven innovation. Major barriers are the lack of capacity to apply the insights derived from big data and the inability to effectively inform decision-making using big data in specific cases. To date, many local governments are not equipped for using big data; therefore, capacity-building is considered a pressing challenge (van Edwijk et al. 2015; Giest 2017).

Recent literature offers various models for gaining knowledge on urban dynamics, and how to operationalize these for improved and better-informed decision-making. On the one hand, knowledge management is discussed as

---

[2] Examples include the Kenyan citizen engagement platform, *Ushahidi* (see: https://www.ushahidi .com/), or Latin American initiatives such as *Chequeado* (see: http://chequeado.com).

a city-specific issue; on the other, there is a discourse on knowledge transfer between cities. Both play a crucial role in understanding the dynamics of data use for urban policy-making.

The Learning City 1: Policy Transfer versus Mobile Urbanism

For city-to-city knowledge transfer, there are two slightly different conceptual models of how knowledge is transferred. First, there is the political science understanding of "policy transfer," which describes an unstructured market of policy ideas that are adopted, transferred, or emulated to maximize reform goals (Peck and Theodore 2010). Put differently, policy transfer is a process in which "knowledge about how policies, administrative arrangements, institutions and ideas in one political setting (past or present) is used in the development of policies, administrative arrangements, institutions and ideas in another political setting" (Dolowitz and Marsh, 2000: 5). The idea of policy transfer has increasingly been paired with the concept of learning in order to understand better how the information that is being transferred is shaped and used in the local context. This, in turn, has led to a discussion about different forms of learning, depending on the political pressure on, as well as the capacity of, policy-makers to adopt new ideas (Giest 2016). Cohen and Levinthal (1990) highlight that "learning capabilities involve the development of the capacity to assimilate existing knowledge" (quoted in Giest 2016: 130). Learning also plays a role in related policy transfer models, such as Municipal International Cooperation (MIC) and city twinning. These are collaboration schemes among two or more cities aiming to transfer knowledge based on a formal relationship. By definition, MIC takes the form of a collaborative effort between local governments to stimulate knowledge exchange between their staff members, often on previously identified topics (van Edwijk et al. 2015). MIC tends to serve broader political goals, such as strengthening democracy and enabling city diplomacy relations, than city twinning. The idea of city twinning builds on a similar idea. Here, cities in distinct geographical and political areas are paired, mainly between North American or European cities and African or South American cities (Muggah 2014).

Next to policy transfer, there is a more recent approach referred to as "policy mobility" or "mobile urbanism." This approach highlights the translational, networked, and multiscalar nature of urban policy (McCann and Ward 2011). The main difference vis-à-vis policy transfer is that mobile urbanism includes a broader set of actors, going beyond policy-makers and bureaucrats to include players who can come from anywhere inside or outside the city. Examples include local policy-makers who use best practice cases from other places and global communities that are adapted to the local context. Here, practitioners emphasize the need to balance local impacts on the one hand and global flows of knowledge on the other (Dicken et al. 2001; McCann and Ward 2010).

When discussing urban policies in a digital age, the high degree of "mobility" of ideas is particularly relevant to data-driven innovation. Technology advances are fast paced, and if innovative solutions in a given city have proven successful, these can travel quickly to inspire policy-makers in other cities that face similar challenges. At the same time, this knowledge/policy transfer is often a highly political one, as there are struggles related to which policies are being framed as successes, thus empowering certain cities at the expense of others (Robinson 2006; McCann and Ward 2010).

The Learning City 2: Knowledge Management within Cities

Before policies can travel between cities, the research and practice communities within a city play a crucial role in developing successful measures when it comes to introducing new routines and innovative practices (Mans and Meerow 2012). For big data applications, in particular, policy-makers are largely dependent on external advice and input from scientific institutions, technology companies, or related sets of experts to inform or guide decision-making. Knowledge or information management can thereby take various forms. In the urban context, researchers highlight the role of local citizens and their participatory role in the process of developing localized types of knowledge (Hordijk and Baud 2006; Mancini and Súilleabháin 2016). With respect to big data applications in policy development, local governments have often relied on data collected by other actors in the city, or even at the national level. "The result," they note, "is a highly fragmented and dispersed set of local level data" (Hordijk and Baud 2006: 675). In addition, local knowledge is crucial for understanding how to account for biases in big data (that is, representativeness of the local community) and how to provide the required context for analysis (Taylor 2015). These necessities lead to an emphasis on building networks that connect the relevant stakeholders to enable a more critical reflection and improved understanding of the data, informed by local and contextual knowledge. As a report by the Aspen Institute (2012: 11) points out,

> [The integration of data-driven innovation in policy development] will require training a cadre of individuals and intermediary organizations to understand neighborhoods as well as statistics and using "data coaches" to community groups. To be effective data coaches, individuals and organizations must be responsive to communities and their priorities, get better at "translation work" that allows them to interpret data and present it in forms that are useful to practitioners, and develop tools and strategies that make it easier for practitioners to use data for self-evaluation and decision-making.

It is not enough to develop an infrastructure for transferring information and data. Cities need to invest proactively in a strategy that connects citizens and policy-makers to foster data-driven innovation. City authorities need to put in place a new type of digital communications environment and adequate mechanisms when integrating data-driven innovation as part of their operations and policy-making. Such changes can take the form of individuals, institutions, and/or technologies, as well as through importing models from other cities (Komninos 2002; Fuggetta 2012). In this process, it is important to account for the speed of innovation in data-related technology: it is increasingly difficult to keep a sufficiently up-to-date overview of all relevant developments, even if there are enough resources for a dedicated team of experts. Instead, city authorities increasingly have to rely on hybrid, international networks of experts that share best practices as these emerge from pilot projects around the globe (Verhulst 2016).

11.3 Towards More Inclusive Cities? Tackling Inequality and Violence with Data

How can big data help policy-makers build more inclusive cities in the Global South? There are many ways to approach this question; for the purposes of this chapter, we focus on the possibilities that are emerging for tackling inequality and violence. We first present five categories of data streams, and then present the possible impact these could have on both challenges. Even though using big data to accomplish inclusivity goals is a relatively nascent field, we present some insights from published case studies on reducing violence in cities within Colombia and South Africa to highlight recent developments in the use of data and the knowledge transfer mechanisms involved.

11.3.1 (New) Types of Data Streams

When looking at the opportunities and challenges that come with the Data Revolution, it is useful to distinguish between various categories of additions to the data landscape that have entered (or are likely to enter) the city's policy realm. It is important to note that much of the big data discourse addresses the emerging possibilities of *data analytics* and new computational methodologies to handle increasingly large databases. For example, technology advances in the fields of real-time dashboards, automated visualizations, machine learning, and artificial intelligence have generated much interest in this regard. However, it is useful to move beyond the analytics, and instead to define the new *types* of data streams that are likely to shape the way decision-making is undertaken.

Many of the more radical, data-driven innovations are inspired by new types of data that have thus far not been collected by city authorities. In this context, Rigobon (2016) refers to "designed" and "organic" data streams, which emphasize that what data will be collected has traditionally been decided beforehand and has subsequently been collected according to a predefined scheme (through surveys, questionnaires, and/or administrative records, for example). The main difference between these traditional data collection regimes and big data collection is that new data streams increasingly come in the form of unstructured data. In the following, we introduce five types of data streams that can help to navigate today's data landscape: public datasets, citizen reporting, open web data, digital breadcrumbs, and remote sensing.

Public Datasets

Although public datasets do not necessarily constitute a new type of data stream, digitization and the availability of new analytical capacities lead to an increased uptake of these data in policy-making processes. Data sources for policymaking now include, a.o. "real-time sensor data, public administration data (including open data), data from statistical offices, commercially traded data and several types of targeted or ad-hoc data" (Technopolis et al. 2015: n.p.). In addition, we observe the promotion of open data in the public sector and among NGOs, which leads to increased free availability of these datasets in machine-readable formats. The digital divide is still a major limiting factor in this form of data collection. Governments in non-OECD countries are generally much more reluctant – and less able – to make datasets publicly available.[3] Questions remain regarding the extent to which digital technologies can improve the collection of data in the developing world, and how much of this additional data will be made available for urban authorities (or other third parties) as a consequence.[4]

Citizen Reporting

With access to mobile devices and the Internet on the rise, connecting to citizens is becoming cheaper, faster, and more reliable. This connectivity can be used for survey techniques based on Short Message Service (SMS), online feedback forms, and so forth. Collecting data in this way is often conducted through digital platforms, which can be run by public entities, private or

---

[3] As part of its Global Open Data Index, Open Knowledge International provides an overview and comparative ranking on open government data (OKI 2014).

[4] In January 2017, the first UN World Data Forum took place in Cape Town, South Africa. At the meeting, national statistics officials and data and technology experts held numerous meetings to discuss how to apply new data technologies to monitor progress on the Sustainable Development Goals.

community organizations, or as a joint effort. In various Kenyan cities for example, the NGO Sisi ni Amani applied SMS-based citizen reporting in order to reduce ethnic tensions across communities (Parker 2011; Trujillo et al. 2013); other examples include violence monitoring at several protest sites in Bangkok throughout 2014, "in order to better understand the situation and track relevant developments" (Elva 2014: n.p.). Further, the Nairobi police have been experimenting with the use of cell phones to reach out to slum inhabitants in Mathare (Frilander et al. 2014). Even in such underserved areas of the city, mobile phone ownership is nearly universal, and approximately 50 percent of these devices are Internet enabled, which makes direct, real-time communication with citizens a possibility (whether by police or other public services agencies). Still, particular challenges can arise with regard to the validity and representativeness of the information provided by respondents in this style of big data collection (van der Windt, 2012).

Open Web Data

Online content has long been readily available in the form of websites, news archives, event reporting, and blog posts. This includes online platforms such as Global Dataset of Events, Language, and Tone (GDELT) or Armed Conflict Location & Event Data Project (ACLED) that provide event data,[5] or simply search engine tools that are available to any online reader.[6] New developments include a) an increasing number of methodologies making it possible to "scrape" the content of websites automatically without human oversight and b) the emergence of social media as an additional form of open web data. Popular platforms including Facebook, Twitter, Instagram, YouTube, and LinkedIn, as well as many other social platforms, offer various degrees of access to their customers' data.

To be clear, the latter is a peculiar form of "open" data. Many of these sources are available to the general public, yet access to them is controlled by private entities. Depending on the aims and privacy restrictions that come with the use of this type of data stream, it is possible to derive relevant insights from what is posted online. These insights can be used for assessments of political preferences and social topics of interest extrapolated from Twitter messages (UN Global Pulse 2014), to verify flood damage across urban settlements using multiple social media platforms (Quaggiotto 2014), or to analyze social patterns in relation to security/crime issues in the context of cities (Pfeffer et al. 2015). It is also to possible establish knowledge of social and political networks

---

[5] www.gdelt.org and www.acleddata.com
[6] See, for example, www.forbes.com/sites/kalevleetaru/2015/09/28/is-the-black-lives-matters-movement-fading-a-data-driven-look-at-web-searches-and-television/.

based on this data (O'Callaghan et al. 2014; Bozdag et al. 2014). It is likely that many of today's possibilities will evolve in the coming years. The key question is which open online data streams can be employed to gain relevant insights for users, and to what extent machine-readable is access granted?

Digital Breadcrumbs

The more people are connected to or work with digital technologies, the more they leave traces of what they do in their daily lives (Pentland 2012). This includes any type of consumption in digital form (supermarket purchases, cell phone airtime vouchers, or financial transfers). Even though this type of data is not necessarily representative, it can reach far beyond the middle class. For example, refugees receive vouchers in the form of e-cards that register what, when, and where people buy goods (WFP 2017; Flaemig et al. 2017). To date, the most powerful form of these "breadcrumbs" are mobile phone data. There are a number of interesting experiments with cell phone data, for example, to detect crime hotspots in London (Bogomolov et al. 2015) and understanding social ties across different communities in the Ivory Coast (Bucicovschi et al. 2013). Also, mobile phone data have been used in Afghanistan to determine changes in movement patterns after micro-violence, such as improvised explosive device (IED) explosions (World Bank 2014), and to develop new poverty monitoring methodologies in Senegal (Pokhriyal et al. 2015). However, digital breadcrumbs come with major caveats.

On the one hand, these types of data streams are often proprietary and not accessible without prior negotiations with a commercial party, such as telecom providers or financial service providers. Second, the clients of these services do not generally know about (or consent to) their data being used (this is different, for example, than social media content, for which a certain degree of consent can be assumed). Even though analysis of digital breadcrumbs is generally done on an aggregated level without substantial risks of privacy infringements, full privacy does not exist: Most datasets that include personal data carry the risk that individuals can be reidentified (Berens et al. 2016; OCHA 2016). Currently, standards for data sharing and data use simply do not exist to a degree that makes all stakeholders comfortable with experimentation with these types of datasets. However, sector-specific data use guidelines and related frameworks that help create trust and form new data collaboratives are likely to emerge over time (WEF 2015b; IDRG 2015; GovLab 2016).

Remote Sensing Data

Satellite images are a well-known source of data that are usually expensive, but are increasingly accessible, even for smaller organizations. This technology is based on sensors that have been placed in orbit, made possible only via monetary investments. The affordability of remote sensing has risen in part because common sensors are being placed nearly everywhere, from closed circuit television cameras to air quality sensors, track-and-trace devices in vehicles, and sensors required for the Internet of Things (for example, sensors in refrigerators, street lights, and so forth). An interesting example is the ability, through remote sensing, to "measure the quantity, timing, and locations of gunfire incidents with greater accuracy than do reported crime or 911 call data through sensors" (Carr and Doleac 2016: 4). This technology, called "Shotspotter," is currently applied in the United States (ibid.). Shotspotter's physical manifestation is a connected system of audio sensors on top of buildings that detects the sounds of gunfire and analyzes them for accuracy. If Shotspotter confirms the sound of gunfire, the program responds by sending a message to local police with the location of the shots fired. The data produced by Shotspotter – date, time, location, single/multiple gunshots – are publicly available.

Likewise, in the geospatial arena, the emergence of drones as a new type of cheap sensor increasingly impacts the way environmental data can be collected or verified. In disaster areas, for example, drones are already being used for quick damage assessments, and a growing number of experiments are underway to use drone-mounted cameras in the fields of agriculture or environmental protection in urban areas (see, for example, Meier 2014). Affordable, high-resolution satellite imagery enables people to retrieve information about hard-to-reach places and conflict areas. For example, "Amnesty International requested the assistance of the Geospatial Technologies and Human Rights Project of the American Association for the Advancement of Science to investigate the veracity of reports of human rights violations stemming from the escalating conflict in Aleppo, Syria" (Amnesty International n.d.: n.p.).

These five types of data streams can have different applications in different contexts. Looking at the innovation landscape today, we see a number of cases that address aspects of urban violence, that is, policing, law and order, and related challenges. Examples of more structural approaches that use data-driven innovations to reduce inequality throughout the city are less common.[7] This is not a surprise, as many questions remain about the extent to which new data streams can complement classical data sources, especially in a developing country. Data are generally biased towards the digital haves and have-nots; we need to develop methodologies that make new data streams both representative and reliable. Table 11.1 gives an overview of the possible uses of these five new types of data streams for both the reduction of violence and inequality in urban contexts.

---

[7] Exceptions include http://masschallenge.org/startups/2016/profile/ubuntucapital.

Table 11.1 Possible uses for data in creating more inclusive cities

	Examples of data application	
Type of data stream	Reducing violence	Reducing inequality
Public datasets (Census and administrative data on policing, education, healthcare, and so forth)	Data from police reports can be matched with other data streams such as SMS-based surveys.	Census data can be used in combination with social media content to understand public perceptions among youth, for example, on unemployment.
Citizen reporting (SMS-based surveys, online reporting platforms, and so forth)	Police departments can collect information from citizens on crime-related incidents in a given area.	Local perceptions of major issues in a given area can be collected by public authorities and/or local community-based organizations.
Open web data (Online content, social media, and so forth)	Social media can be used to identify hate speech towards a given group; it can also be used for outreach purposes to encourage citizens to avoid certain areas or not to engage in violence.	Social media content can be collected and analyzed in order to determine major problems in certain areas or to encourage civic engagement.
Digital breadcrumbs (Consumer data, mobile phone data, and so forth)	Aggregated mobile phone data can show where people move at night, giving clues about relative safety in certain urban areas.	Aggregated consumer data (for example, airtime vouchers) can reveal major changes in the socioeconomic situation of certain areas.

Remote sensing		
(Satellite imagery, sensor networks, Internet of Things, and so forth)	Audio sensors can detect gunshots in real time and provide clues about the deterioration of security in a given area.	Air- or water-quality sensors can detect problems with the quality of public goods.

As discussed in the previous section, any of these applications requires a meaningful dialogue between those who work with the technology and those with contextual expertise regarding the location in which it will be applied. We are at the very beginning of the Data Revolution – much remains unexplored and untested; indeed, the use of new data streams in formulating city policies is far from mainstream. City authorities tend to start with existing data rather than tapping into new data streams. Moving forward, we need to improve our understanding of the underlying dynamics of knowledge transfers insofar as they relate to data-driven innovation. While still evolving, two examples, from Cali and Cape Town, highlight some of the lessons learned about knowledge transfer mechanisms that support data-informed policy.

11.3.2 Reducing Violence with Data Knowledge: Cali and Cape Town

Cali – Colombia, and Cape Town – South Africa are two cities that have shifted towards data-informed policy in connection to reducing violence. We identify some of the opportunities and challenges that are connected to this shift. Generally speaking, the availability of additional data has led some cities to take a more evidence- and/or data-based approach towards violence; Colombia has become an especially popular research example (see Gaviria 2000; Bourguignon et al. 2002; Cotte Poveda 2012).

In Latin America, several cities – including Bogotá, Cali, Medellín, San Pablo, and Recife – have been able to reduce violent incidents dramatically using policies that harness big data. The programs stem from a mixture of models used in the United States and evidence for what works in the targeted cities in Latin America (Ojea 2014). This has also led to new revelations about the root causes of violence. For example, for a long time, the US lens on crime, in combination with substantial media coverage of drug-related crimes, led officials in Cali to believe that drug dealers were the biggest cause of homicides in the city

(Velasco 2015). Using recent and local statistics, however, officials learned that "homicide victims and aggressors were predominantly young, unemployed males who had low levels of education, came from the poorer sectors of the city and were frequently involved in gang fights" (Velasco 2015: 3). In other words, drug traffic was still part of the equation, but was only indirectly responsible for violence. The crime figures in this case largely came from an online platform called "The Monitor," which interactively maps the distribution of murder by country, year, age of victim and, where available, gender, and type of weapon. The online database draws on statistics from the United Nations Office for Drugs and Crime, government offices, health institutes, and policy records, as well as a detailed, city-level breakdown for Latin America. However, streamlining such information is challenging, since Latin American countries have different ways of defining crime and differ in the way they collect information. The Inter-American Development Bank is currently in the process of standardizing violence indicators (Velasco 2015).

Cape Town has also moved towards a more comprehensive approach for tackling violence based on quantitative and qualitative data. This shift was facilitated by the Violence Prevention through Urban Upgrading (VPUU) not-for-profit initiative, which works with local and national governments and includes international groups with stakeholder expertise in developing such measures. The VPUU applied a combination of high-quality, research-based documentations, monitoring, and evaluation surveys, as well as databases of police-reported robberies over a ten-year period (Cassidy et al. 2015), as well as incorporating census data and information from the South African Index of Multiple Deprivation. The researchers subsequently geolocated the data to specific areas through the use of mobile phones that were distributed to the community (Cassidy et al. 2015). In this way, citizen reporting, digital breadcrumbs, secondary databases, and qualitative information were gathered to inform potential policy changes. These changes have led officials to focus increasingly on infrastructural causes for violence, such as lighting, improved public spaces, and safer public transportation, after-school activities, and an improved education system (WCG 2011; Cassidy et al. 2015).

In both cities, a diverse set of stakeholders initiated policy changes to incorporate big data. Cali's mayor, Dr. Rodrigo Guerrero, introduced weekly meetings of the heads of all departments connected with law enforcement (Rosenberg 2014). Those meetings involved officials from "the police, judiciary and forensic authorities, members of the Institute for Research and Development in Violence Prevention and Promotion of Social Coexistence (CISALVA) at the University of Valle, cabinet members responsible for public safety, and the municipal statistics agency" (Velasco 2015: 6). The meetings were an attempt to pool contextual knowledge on violence in combination with the data to make sense of the status quo and to discover possible improvements to initiatives. In Cape Town, as in Cali, the goal was a more comprehensive approach to violence. Here, changes involved the inclusion of stakeholders in public health, criminal justice, education, and social development sectors, and active participation and partnership of citizens and civil society more broadly (WCG 2013; Cassidy et al. 2015).

Both cities also faced political obstacles, including changes in local government, funding, and knowledge sharing among local stakeholders. For Cali, these challenges were twofold: first, the national government was unwilling to provide additional financial support to data-driven innovation. The city needed money to support more policing in risk-prone areas, during holidays and paydays, as well as after 2 a.m. – days and times during which violence had been shown to increase. In addition, because Colombian mayors can serve only one term, newly implemented measures could be, and were, overturned by the new mayor. After Mayor Guerrero's term (1992–1995), the murder rate rose again (Rosenberg 2014). In Cape Town, measures suggested by VPUU were unpopular with the government because they targeted areas where the political opposition was in charge. According to Cassidy et al. (2015), this not only resulted in limited implementation, it further posed a threat to the research process, since it compromised the availability and validity of evaluative data from community stakeholders and drove an overreliance on administrative data. Ultimately, crime data can also be uncomfortable for mayors and governments, especially before elections, since better recording and more accurate data often lead to higher reported crime rates that might hurt political ambitions.

Overall, both cities are increasingly incorporating data-informed policies into their measures against violence and have, over the course of establishing these initiatives, involved a range of stakeholders who can provide more contextual perspectives. In the years to come, additional data tools could lead to more accurate and complete data on crime and violence trends in cities. However, as the examples have also shown, there is a political component that can slow down or even hinder the use of big data.

11.3.3 Discussion

Our examples from South Africa and Colombia show that data-informed policy is largely shaped through joint efforts of national and local governments as well as local communities and law enforcement agencies. These case studies also indicate that data are only one piece of the larger puzzle when targeting violence in cities; issues remain surrounding political and collaborative aspects. To guide future paths for data use in the context of urban policy in the Global South, we believe there are two overarching lessons summarized by these cases.

Data-Informed Policy-Making

First, using big data is accompanied by risks of drawing misleading conclusions, such as assumptions about causes of violence that are drawn from public datasets, but do not apply to a specific region. Data analytics cannot simulate the complex picture of potential interactions of different policy domains, such as crime and infrastructure, or the dynamics among social groups in certain neighborhoods (Bollier 2010). The research community is skeptical of claims of universal urban experiences, stressing that contextual particularities and local experiences within places are important (Brenner and Schmid 2015; Thakuriah et al. 2015). It follows that conclusions drawn in cities with high crime rates do not automatically apply to other cities with similar statistics, but different local contexts. The example of Cali has shown that officials were too quick to assume that drug-related crime was driving up the homicide numbers when drug trafficking had only an indirect effect. However, the challenge is to strike an appropriate balance between automated analysis and contextual interpretation now that data are becoming more widely used.

The Politics of Data-informed Policy

Second, data can be political. When utilizing the information gained from data, political obstacles emerge in two ways. Data can bring to the surface insights that are uncomfortable to political stakeholders. Cape Town exemplifies a city uncooperative in data collection efforts, either because proposed data collection efforts were connected to regions in the hands of the political opposition or because data collection initiatives were branded as campaigns against the government (Consortium on Crime and Violence Prevention 2015). Furthermore, collaboration across political constituencies might prove difficult. Based on the insights from Cali and Cape Town, cross-stakeholder engagement emerges as a key dimension for deploying data-based initiatives in cities. Such engagement has been achieved in the form of regular meetings of heads of departments (Cali) or by involving citizens in data collection (Cape Town). Underlying this collaboration is the notion of trust – trusting that the data are put to good use by government, as well as trust in local stakeholders by the government. Moving towards more data-informed policies, city stakeholders will have to find meaningful ways to create mutual trust.

The elements discussed in this chapter call for a more thorough understanding of how advances in data-driven innovation could translate into new forms of urban policy-making – and how collaboration between various stakeholders and actors can be supported from the beginning to avoid inappropriate technology and policy designs. Much remains to be done to support decisions about which policies to adopt and when to be cautious in applying data-informed policy. From a research perspective, future studies should give clues about the interplay of additional, more detailed data being collected and the political repercussions this might have. If new data streams enable more accurate, but also more problematic, numbers for certain issues such as violence and poverty, the political opposition might outweigh the societal benefits that data-driven innovations provide. Overcoming these obstacles requires alignment between different stakeholders within the city, as well as paying attention to the timing and circumstances within which data-informed policies are developed.

References

Amnesty International (n.d.) *Satellite Imagery Analysis for Urban Conflict Documentation: Aleppo, Syria*, AAAS. www.aaas.org/aleppo.

Aspen Institute (2012) Developing and Using Data and Evidence to Improve Place-Based Work. Proceedings from a meeting convened by the Aspen Institute Roundtable on Community Change with support from The Annie E. Casey Foundation, New York, September 8–9, 2011. https://assets.aspeninstitute.org/content/uploads/files/content/images/rcc/Sept%202011%20 Data%20Meeting%20Proceedings%20FINAL%206%206%2012.pdf

Barber, B. (2013) *If Mayors Ruled the World: Dysfunctional Nations, Rising Cities*. New Haven, CT: Yale University Press.

Batty, M. (2013) Big Data, Smart Cities and City Planning. *Dialogues in Human Geography*, 3(3): 274–279.

Bellagio Big Data Workshop Participants (2014) *Big Data and Positive Social Change in the Developing World: A White Paper for Practitioners and Researchers*, Oxford: Oxford Internet Institute. www .rockefellerfoundation.org/uploads/files/c220f1f3-2e9a-4fc6-be6 c-45d42849b897-big-data-and.pdf.

Berens, J.B., Mans, U., and Verhulst, S. (2016) Comparing and Mapping Responsible Data Approaches. TheGovLab and Center for Innovation, Leiden University.

de Boer, J. (2015) Resilience and the Fragile City. *Stability: International Journal of Security and Development*. 4(1): p.Art. 17. doi: http://DOI.org/10.5334/sta.fk.

Bogomolov, A. Lepri, B., Staiano, J., Letouze E., Oliver, N., Pianesi, F., and Pentland, A. (2015) Moves on the Street: Classifying Crime Hotspots Using Aggregated Anonymized Data on People Dynamics. *Big Data*, 3(3): 148–158.

Bollier, D. (2010) The promise and peril of Big Data, Aspen Institute, available online: www.emc .com/collateral/analyst-reports/10334-ar-promise-peril-of-big-data.pdf.

Bourguignon, F., Nunes, J., and Sanchez, F. (2002) What Part of the Income Distribution Matter for Explaining Crime? The case of Colombia. Working Paper, DELTA ENS.

Bozdag, E., Gao, Q., Houben, G.J., and Warnier, M. (2014) Does Offline Political Segregation Affect the Filter Bubble? An Empirical Analysis of Information Diversity for Dutch and Turkish Twitter Users. *Computers in Human Behavior*, 41: 405–415.

Bryant, R., Katz, R.H., and Lazowska, E.D. (2008) Big-Data Computing: Creating Revolutionary Breakthroughs in Commerce, Science and Society. http://cra.org/ccc/wp-content/uploads/sites/2/2015/05/Big_Data.pdf.

Bucicovschi, O., Douglass, R.W., Meyer, D.A., Ram, M., Rideout, D., and Song, D. (2013) Analyzing Social Divisions Using Cell Phone Data, in Blondel, V., de Cordes, N., Decuyper, A., Devlisse, P., Raguenez, J. and Smoreda, Z. (eds.), *Mobile Phone Data for Development*. Cambridge, MA: Netmob, pp. 42–54.

Brenner N. and Schmid C. (2015) *Towards a New Epistemology of the Urban City* 1(2–3): 151–182.

Cohen, W.M. and Levinthal, D.A. (1990) Absorptive Capacity: A New Perspective on Learning and Innovation. *Administrative Science Quarterly*, 35(1): 128–152.

Carr, J. and Doleac, J. (2016) The Geography, Incidence, and Underreporting of Gun Violence: New Evidence Using ShotSpotter Data. Brookings Research Paper, April 2016.

Cassidy, T., Ntshingwa, M., Galuszka, J., and Matzopoulos, R. (2015) Evaluation of a Cape Town Safety Intervention as a Model for Good Practice: A Partnership between Researchers, Community and Implementing Agency. *Stability: International Journal of Security and Development*. 4(1): p.Art. 27. doi: http://DOI.org/10.5334/sta.fi.

Consortium on Crime and Violence Prevention (2015) Dialogue on Safety and Security: Insights from Cape Town. Key Points from the Third International Dialogue on Safety and Security Cape Town, February 25–27, 2015. https://igarape.org.br/wp-content/uploads/2015/10/SafetySecurityDialoguesReport.pdf.

Cotte Poveda, A. (2012) Violence and Economic Development in Colombian Cities: A Dynamic Panel Data Analysis. *Journal of International Development*, 24: 809–827.

Dicken, P., Kelly, P.F., Olds, K., and Wai-Chung Yeung, H. (2001) Chains and Networks, Territories and Scales: Towards a relational framework for analysing the global economy. *Global Networks*, 1: 89–112. doi:10.1111/1471–0374.00007.

Dolowitz, D., and Marsh D. (2000) Learning From Abroad: The Role of Policy Transfer in Contemporary Policy Making. *Governance*, 13 (1): 5–24.

van Edwijk, E., Baud, I., Bontenbal, M., Hordijk, M., van Lindert, P., Nijenhuis, G., and van Westen, G. (2015) Capacity Development or New Learning Spaces through Municipal International Cooperation: Policy Mobility at Work? *Urban Studies*, 52 (4): 756–774.

Elva Community Engagement [Elva] (2014) Monitoring Violence in Bangkok. https://elva.org/case-studies.

Flaemig, T., Sandstrom, S., Caccavale, O.M., Bauer, J-M., Husain, A., Halma, A., and Poldermans, J. (2017) *Using Big Data to Analyse WFP's Digital Cash Programme in Lebanon*. Humanitarian Practice Network. http://odihpn.org/blog/using-big-data-to-analyse-wfps-digital-cash-programme-in-lebanon.

Frilander, M., Lundine, J., Kutalek, D., and Likaka, L. (2014) *New Technologies for Improving Old Public Security Challenges in Nairobi*. Igarapé Institute. http://issat.dcaf.ch/mkd/content/download/49277/782313/file/NE-15_New-technologies-in-Nairobi_4th_june.pdf.

Fuggetta, A. (2012) 3+1 Challenges for the Future of Universities, *The Journal of Systems and Software*, 85: 2417–2424.

Gaviria, A. (2000) Increasing Returns and the Economic Evolution of Violent Crime: The Case of Colombia. *Journal of Development Economics*, 61: 1–25.

Giest, S. (2016) Overcoming the Failure of 'Silicon Somewheres': Collective Learning in Innovation Networks. *Policy and Politics*. 45(1): 39–54 doi.org/10.1332/030557316X14779412013740.

Giest, S. (2017) Big Data Analytics for Mitigating Carbon Emissions in Smart Cities: Opportunities and Challenges. *European Planning Studies*, 25(6): 941–957 (doi: 10.1080/09654313.2017.1294149).

GovLab (2016) Data Collaboratives: Exchanging Data to Improve People's Lives, GovLab (blog). http://thegovlab.org/datacollaboratives.

Hordijk, M. and I. Baud. (2006) The Role of Research and Knowledge Generation in Collective Action and Urban Governance: How Can Researchers Act as Catalysts? *Habitat International*, 30: 668–689.

International Data Responsibility Group [IDRG] (2015) International Data Responsibility Group: Putting People First in a Digital Age. www.responsible-data.org.

King, G. (2013) Big Data is Not About The Data! Talk at the New England AI Meetup, 5/14/2013. http://gking.harvard.edu/files/gking/files/evbase-neai_0.pdf.

Komninos, N. (2002) *Intelligent Cities: Innovation, Knowledge Systems, and Digital Spaces*. London and New York: Routledge.

Krumholz, H.M. (2014) Big Data and New Knowledge in Medicine: The Thinking, Training, and Tools Needed for a Learning Health System. *Health Affairs*, 33 (7): 1163–1170.

Latonero, M., Kleinman, M., and Hiatt, K. (2017) Tech Folk: 'Move Fast and Break Things' Doesn't Work When Lives Are at Stake, *The Guardian*, February 2017. www.theguardian.com/global-development-professionals-network/2017/feb/02/technology-human-rights.

Letouze, E., Vinck, P., and Kammourieh, L. (2015) The Law, Politics and Ethics of Cell Phone Data Analytics. Data-Pop Alliance publication. http://datapopalliance.org/wp-content/uploads/2015/04/WPS_LawPoliticsEthicsCellPhoneDataAnalytics.pdf.

Lyon, D. (2014) Surveillance, Snowden, and Big Data: Capacities, Consequences, Critique. *Big Data & Society*, July–December: 1–13.

Mans, U., and Baar, T.J. (2014) *Defining Peace Informatics*. www.peaceinformaticslab.org/learn-more.html.

Mans, U. and Meerow, S. (2012) Role of Local Governments in Promoting Renewable Energy Businesses. ICLEI Policy Paper.

Mancini F. and Súilleabháin A.Ó. (eds.) (2016) *Building Resilience in Cities under Stress*. New York: International Peace Institute.

McCann, E. and Ward, K. (2010) Relationality / Territoriality: Toward a Conceptualization of Cities in the World. *Geoforum* 41 (2), 175–184.

McCann, E. and Ward, K. (2011) *Mobile Urbanism*. Minneapolis: University of Minnesota Press.

Meier, P. (2014). *Digital Humanitarians: How Big Data is Changing the Face of Humanitarian Response*. Boca Raton: CRC Press.

Mayer-Schönberger, V. and Cukier, K. (2013) *Big Data: A Revolution That Will Transform How We Live, Work, and Think*. Boston: Houghton Mifflin Harcourt.

Muggah, R. (2014) How Are Some Fragile Cities Tackling Their Worst Problems? [TED Talk]. www.npr.org/2016/01/08/462282897/how-are-some-fragile-cities-tackling-their-worst-problems.

Muggah, R. (2015) A Manifesto for the Fragile City. *Journal of International Affairs*, 68 (2): 19–36.

Muggah, R. and Diniz, G.M. (2013) Digitally Enhanced Violence Prevention in the Americas. *Stability: International Journal of Security and Development*. 2(3): p.Art. 57. DOI: http://doi.org/10.5334/sta.cq.

O'Callaghan, D., Prucha, N., Greene, D., Conway, M., Carthy, J., and Cunningham, P. (2014) Online Social Media in the Syria Conflict: Encompassing the Extremes and the In-Betweens, Proceedings of the 2014 International Conference on Advances in Social Network Analysis and Mining (ASONAM 2014).

OCHA Think Brief [OCHA] (2016) Building Data Responsibility into Humanitarian Action. United Nations Office for the Coordination of Humanitarian Affairs. www.unocha.org/sites/unocha/files/Building%20data%20responsibility%20into%20humanitarian%20action.pdf

Ojea, V. (2014) Latin America Accounts for More than 30% of the World's Homicides. The World Bank, March 5. www.worldbank.org/en/news/feature/2014/02/11/en-america-latina-sufre-mas-del-30-de-los-homicidios-mundiales

Open Knowledge International [OKI] (2014) Tracking the State of Government Open Data. http://index.okfn.org.

Parker, P. (2011) Sisi Ni Amani 'Peacemapping' in Kenya. www.insightonconflict.org/blog/2011/09/kenya-peacemapping.

Peck, J. and Theodore, N. (2010) Mobilizing Policy: Models, Methods, and Mutations. *Geoforum*, 41(2): 169–174.

Pentland, A. (2012) Reinventing Society in the Wake of Big Data. *Edge*, August 30. www.edge.org/conversation/reinventing-society-in-the-wake-of-big-data.

Pokhriyal, N., Dong, W., and Govindaraju, V. (2015) Virtual Networks and Poverty Analysis in Senegal. D4D Netmob, Conference Paper.

Pfeffer, K., Verrest, H. and Poorthuis, A. (2015) Big Data for Better Urban Life? – An Exploratory Study of Critical Urban Issues in Two Caribbean Cities: Paramaribo (Suriname) and Port of Spain (Trinidad and Tobago). *The European Journal of Development Research*, 27(4): 505–522.

Quaggiotto, G. (2014) Using Twitter to Get Ground Truth on Floods: An Interview with Floodtags Founder Jurjen Wagemaker, *UN Global Pulse Blog*, November 19. www.unglobalpulse.org/blog/using-twitter-get-ground-truth-floods-interview-floodtags-founder-jurjen-wagemaker.

Rigobon, R. (2016) Keynote Speech at the Annual Bank Conference on Development Economics 2016: Data and Development Economics, June 20, 2016, Washington, DC.

Robinson, J. (2006) *Ordinary Cities: Between Modernity and Development*. Abingdon and New York: Routledge.

Rosenberg, T. (2014) Colombia's Data-Driven Fight against Crime. *New York Times*. https://opinionator.blogs.nytimes.com/2014/11/20/colombias-data-driven-fight-against-crime/

Soubra, D. (2012) The 3 Vs that Define Big Data. *Data Science Central*, July 5, 2012. www.datasciencecentral .com/forum/topics/the-3vs-that-define-big-data.

Taylor, L. (2015) Big Data and Urban Governance, in Gupta, J., Pfeffer, K., Verrest, H., and Ros-Tonen, M. (eds.) *Geographies of Urban Governance*. Cham: Springer International.

Technopolis, Oxford Internet Institute and Centre for European Policy Studies (2015) Data for Policy: A Study of Big Data and Other Innovative Data-Driven Approaches for Evidence-Informed Policymaking. www.technopolis-group.com/data-policy-innovative-data-driven-approaches-evidence-informed-policymaking/.

Thakuriah, P., Tilahun, N., and Zellner, M. (2015) Big Data and Urban Informatics: Innovations and Challenges to Urban Planning and Knowledge Discovery. In Proceedings of NSF Workshop on Big Data and Urban Informatics, 4–32. https://urbanbigdata.uic.edu/proceedings/

Trujillo, H.R., Elam, D., Shapiro, G., and Clayton, M. (2013) The Role of Information and Communication Technology in Preventing Election-Related Violence in Kenya, 2013. *Perspectives on Global Development and Technology*, 13(1–2):, 111–128.

UN Global Pulse (2014) Using Twitter to Understand the Post-2015 Global Conversation, Global Pulse Project Series, no.6, 2014. www.unglobalpulse.org/sites/default/files/UNGP_ProjectSeries_Post2015_Priorities_2014_0.pdf.

UN IAEG (2014) A world That Counts: Mobilizing the Data Revolution for Sustainable Development. www.undatarevolution.org/wp-content/uploads/2014/12/A-World-That-Counts2.pdf.

Van der Windt, P. (2012) From Crowdsourcing to Crowdseeding: The Cutting Edge of Empowerment, in Livingstone, S. and Walter-Drop, G. (eds.). *Bits and Atoms: Information and Communication Technology in Areas of Limited Statehood*, Oxford: Oxford University Press, pp. 144–155.

Velasco, R. (2015) Big Data Are Reducing Homicides in Cities across the Americas. *Scientific American*, October 1, 2015.

Verhulst, S. (2016) Corporate Social Responsibility for a Data Age, *Stanford Social Innovation Review* (February). https://ssir.org/articles/entry/corporate_social_responsibility_for_a_data_age? platform=hootsuite.

Western Cape Government [WCG] (2011) *Western Cape's Draft Strategic Plan*. South Africa: WCG.

Western Cape Government [WCG] (2013), *Integrated Violence Prevention Policy Framework*. South Africa: WCG.

World Bank (2014) Big Data in Action for Development: World Bank Publication 2014. http://live .worldbank.org/sites/default/files/Big%20Data%20for%20Development%20Report_final%20 version.pdf.

World Economic Forum [WEF] (2015) *Global Agenda Council on Data-driven development*. WEF Publication (webpage). www.weforum.org/communities/global-agenda-council-on-data-driven-development.

World Economic Forum [WEF] (2015B) Data-Driven Development: Pathways for Progress (January 2015). http://digitalprinciples.org/wp-content/uploads/2015/05/WEFUSA_DataDriven Development_Report2015.pdf.

World Food Programme [WFP] (2017) Cash-Based Transfer. http://www1.wfp.org/cash-based-transfers.

Chapter 12: Collaborative and Equitable Urban Citizen Science

Karen MacClune, Kanmani Venkateswaran, Bolanle Wahab, Sascha Petersen, Nivedita Mani, Bijay Kumar Singh, and Ajay Kumar Singh

12.1 Introduction

Conventional science is usually conducted in a remote location, abstracted from day-to-day conditions and needs. Even when it produces useful outputs, those outputs are rarely effectively communicated to those who could put them to best use. "Citizen science" is increasingly providing powerful alternatives to this approach.

Though citizen science often evokes images of, for example, school children measuring rainfall, we see it as a much larger field. Citizen science can range from crowd-sourcing information to participatory monitoring and action research, to collaboration between the general public and professional scientists, and to highly informed public science interests funded by citizens.

The common threads of citizen science are:

1. Citizen science functions as a check and balance on information. In places where information is controlled by governments or the private sector and there is limited access or manipulation, citizen science can increase access to information or provide alternative information.

2. Citizen science operates at different scales. It is often granular and/or collected by hundreds or thousands of people and can, therefore, provide very different information from what is available through conventional channels, allowing for investigations that have not previously been possible.

3. Citizen science is grounded locally and relates to issues that people see and/or experience on a daily basis. This relevancy aids in community ownership of the results and makes them more actionable.

4. Citizen science cultivates an informed and engaged citizenship. Participants understand the value of science and see themselves as an integral part

of that science. Ideally, this translates to a more informed public and greater citizen engagement in influencing science-policy decisions.

These differences between citizen science and conventional science mean that citizen science can generate unexpected – and sometimes very different – knowledge. That knowledge can lead to transformative change in how processes are undertaken and in how people act.

Citizen science is supporting the growth of new scientific endeavors in powerful ways, particularly as technology has progressed and virtual networks have expanded, increasing scientific literacy and inclusivity (Bonney et al. 2009; Connors et al. 2012). Yet, it is not clear that citizen science is being used to its fullest potential. Indeed, Mueller and Tippins (2012: 3) argue that citizen science has largely been top-down:

> The key point is that it does not matter whether or not individuals engage in citizen science projects focused on mammals, birds, weather, climate change, flora, or invasive species. The participants primarily serve to collect data for scientists rather than to collaborate with scientists, democratize protocol and equipment, assess ideas, and work in relation to others.

For this reason, we are encouraged to see the emergence of a new type of citizen science, one based on equitable collaboration. In this citizen science, citizens are engaged as equal players in the scientific process, contributing their local, grounded perspectives, knowledges, understandings, needs, and aspirations in an ongoing and iterative process. This is related to but different from action research, which is either initiated by researchers to solve an immediate problem or is an iterative learning and doing process. Action research doesn't necessarily engage citizens. Citizen science empowers citizens to act, and makes science directly responsive to their needs and interests. Therefore, citizen science is especially important for urban-focused science, in which a multitude of diverse perspectives and knowledges need to be captured. This chapter explores several case studies from urban areas in which citizens were engaged in equitable collaboration, and how this led to new learning and action.

12.2 Types of Citizen Science

There are two types of commonly practiced citizen science; one is focused on data collection, while the other both collects data and conducts its own analysis of that data.

12.2.1 Citizen Science as a Data Collection Mechanism

This type of citizen science involves large groups of citizens, often distributed over wide geographical areas, to collect data. This structure allows for collection of information at a geographic scale and at a level of detail that has never previously been possible. For example, in the United States, the Community Collaborative Rain, Hail and Snow Network, or CoCoRaHS, is a national project that enlists a community-based network of volunteers to measure and record precipitation data. Project staff map, analyze, and disseminate the resulting information. These results are ultimately used by a wide variety of organizations and individuals, ranging from scientists to city utilities, from emergency managers to students. CoCoRaHS's goals are to generate and disseminate accurate precipitation data with substantially greater granularity than traditional methods have permitted, to increase community awareness about weather, to build collective awareness of climate, and to develop citizens' skills in scientific data collection (see www.cocorahs.org).

However, this project largely perpetuates a one-way flow of data. Citizens provide data to scientists, who then undertake the analysis and dissemination. There is no direct tie back to the citizen data collectors in ways that impacts their lives. Such a structure is fairly typical of crowd-sourced data projects. Still, this form of crowd-sourcing data does combine the capacities of traditional science with the capacities of communities to collect extensive data while raising citizen awareness about science.

12.2.2 Citizen Science as a Citizen Scientific Analysis

A less common form of citizen science involves citizens in the analysis of the data they collect and, therefore, establishes a more direct interface with scientists. Citizen science of this form frequently arises either due to a lack of information and data that citizens want to address, or over questions about the validity of existing scientific knowledge. While this method allows citizens to engage more with the analysis of data and advocate for themselves and their needs, they do not have control over how the data are ultimately used in decision-making processes.

Communities in Thailand, for example, began research of this type in the early 2000s in response to the controversial Pak Mun Dam on the Mun River, the largest tributary of the Mekong River. The Pak Mun Dam was built in 1994 by the Thai government and the World Bank and had immediate adverse impacts on the environment, including fisheries, as well as the livelihoods of local residents who depended upon them. The Assembly of the Poor, a strong people's movement, formed to protest dam operations and impacts. In response, the

Thai government agreed to open the dam's gates to restore natural flows, and to conduct studies on impacts to fisheries and communities. To ensure that people's concerns were heard, Living River Siam, a nongovernmental organization, developed a research method for communities to conduct their own scientific studies. In what has become known as "Thai Baan" research, Pak Mun villagers systematically documented how the dam had affected their lives and the fisheries on which they depended (Herbertson 2012).

Although both the conventional and citizen science studies clearly documented highly damaging impacts on ecosystems and livelihoods, the Thai government chose to continue dam operations. Dramatic declines in fisheries have continued. Nevertheless, the network of Thai communities and NGOs emerged strong and unified after the experience; the Assembly of the Poor continues to support people who were affected by development projects; and interest in Thai Baan research continues to grow. In 2004, a similar effort by villagers combining Thai Baan research and political pressure convinced the Thai government to preserve the Khon Pi Luang rapids on the Mekong River. This illustrates how citizen science can help citizens to understand the sociopolitical environment and players involved in an issue and to take action in ways that will achieve change.

12.2.3 The Limitations of These Two Models

Both citizen science as data collection mechanism and citizen science as analysis have favorable attributes for citizens and the environment and, in many cases, encourage more locally grounded actions. However, they are also top-down – the citizens involved do not have control over how the data are used, nor are they included in associated decision-making and/or planning processes. This is problematic for a number of reasons.

First, top-down science does not necessarily produce scientific knowledge that is "usable" in the local context. Usable science is knowledge that is produced through integrated processes that meet constituent needs (Lemos and Morehouse 2005). One of the most effective and powerful ways to produce usable science is through the coproduction of knowledge. This refers to an iterative process (Dilling and Lemos 2011), involving both scientists and citizens, where different values, experiences, and information – which are all partial, imperfect, and situated in their local contexts (Haraway 1988; Harding 2011) – are brought together to produce a common knowledge or solution to a local problem. This situated, common knowledge accounts for the range of needs and capacities that should be considered when producing and using science (Dilling and Lemos 2011).

Second, scientist-driven citizen science projects do not necessarily engage meaningful public participation. Such projects tend to focus on one frame (for example, an ecological frame) and "[draw] participants into thinking they are doing something scientific when what they are doing does not nearly capture the integrated nature of science, culture, and consequences" (Mueller and Tippins 2012: 6). Citizens are unlikely to gain an understanding or see the value of science – or to function as checks and balances for traditional scientific knowledge – if they are not engaging with the myriad factors (social, cultural, political, economic, technological, physical) that influence the results of science and its associated actions.

Third, the exclusion of citizens from processes that determine how citizen science data are used can dis-incentivize citizen ownership of local solutions. Citizen ownership of initiatives is important, particularly if those initiatives are aimed at responding to local problems and/or generating local outcomes. Citizen ownership can incentivize communities to sustain action over the long term and, eventually, to institutionalize the changes needed to achieve initiative goals within their communities (Shediac-Rizkallah and Bone 1998; Simpson et al. 2003;). Such ownership can create real transformation. Mueller and Tippins (2012) suggest that participation in science needs to be democratized to ensure that diverse voices are engaged in dialogue based on mutual trust and respect. The experience should also be allowed to shape participants' futures based on their needs and based on the locally embedded scientific knowledge that they are instrumental in creating. Not only will this create a more informed public, but it will also generate a public that is critical and engaged in influencing science-policy decisions.

12.2.4 A Third Type of Citizen Science: Equitable Collaboration

A third type of citizen science based on equitable collaboration needs to emerge; in some places, it is already emerging. To produce science that is embedded in the local context, and to promote environmental and social justice, citizens need to be given more power within scientific processes. This type of citizen science requires scientific processes to be codesigned and knowledge to be coproduced by scientists and citizens (Colston et al. 2015). Such engagement can both contextualize and customize external scientific knowledge and learning so that it can both be translated into action that is locally owned and can inform international "expert" knowledge in ways that make that knowledge more relevant.

Standout challenges of undertaking citizen science of this type in urban, as compared to rural, environments include a greater diversity of stakeholders required to provide the needed contextualization and customization, an increase in complexity, and less social cohesion, all of which can make it difficult to identify and engage stakeholders. Capturing this complexity is critical in urban-focused science and action, and further illustrates the importance of pursuing citizen science based on equitable collaboration in urban settings.

The following urban citizen science case studies emphasize what successful projects in these areas can look like. They explore how the engagement of citizens from the outset influenced the process and outcome of the studies and produced benefits for everyone involved.

12.3 Case Study One: The Odo-Osun Natural Spring Project, Ibadan, Nigeria

Oke-Offa Babasale is an unplanned, high-density, low-income residential community in Ward 10, Ibadan North-East local government area, or IbNELGA, of Ibadan, Nigeria (Figure 12.1). A spring has been the major source of water to the community for drinking and other domestic uses year-round for over 80 years (Adewoye 1995). The spring is located within a densely built community and is accessible from the nearest road only by a network of foot paths running between residential buildings. Prior to the development of the spring, the water supply situation in the community was poor. Women and children (ages 8 to 16 years old) spent hours scouting for water, and there was a high incidence of waterborne diseases, typhoid fever, and cholera (Odo-Akeu Spring Water Development Project Working Group 1996; SIP-TSU n.d.).

The **Odo-Osun Community Spring Water Development Project**, or OCSWDP, was designed to provide 20 to 50 liters per person per day of clean and hygienic water to the people of Oke-Offa Babasale community and adjoining areas for an affordable fee. By improving the environment of a heavily polluted and underutilized natural spring, the project sought to enhance and sustain the community's access to safe water.

The process of collaboration and integration evolved in stages through series of consultation and communication as follows:

- The Oke-Offa Babasale Community conducted a situation analysis, identified problems related to the spring, and consulted the UN-Habitat sponsored Sustainable Ibadan Project-Technical Support Unit, also called SIP-TSU, for assistance;

- SIP-TSU conducted a joint diagnostic survey of the environment and the quality of spring water with community leaders and representatives of other stakeholders;

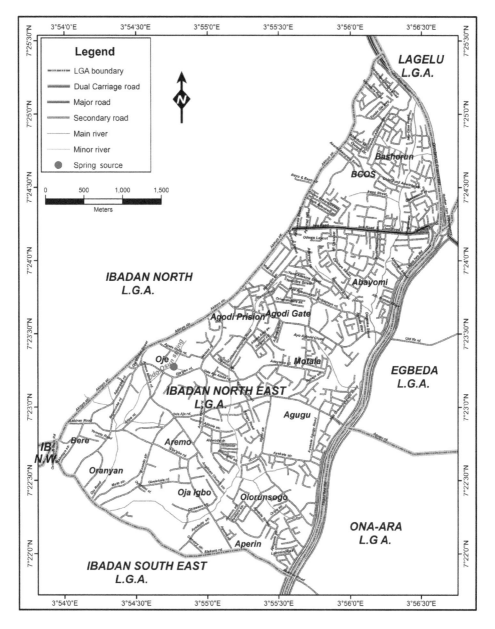

Figure 12.1 Odo-Osun Spring in Ibadan North-East local government. Source: CNES/Airbus DS, DigitalGlobe/Esri, @OpenStreetMap.

- SIP-TSU and other stakeholders communicated results using video documentation, print, and electronic media;

- New water infrastructure was designed in consultation with SIP-TSU, representatives of the community, and other stakeholders;

- A cost estimate was prepared and roles assigned to identified stakeholders;

- Resources were mobilized, a project management committee was established, and a bank account was opened; and

- Project implementation and design of a framework for operation took place between 1995 and 1997.

The SIP-TSU provided overall technical guidance and advice and assisted the community in establishing the 16-member Odo-Osun Spring Water Development Working Group, which served as the think-tank committee for the project. A respected community leader, Chief David Adewoye, coordinated the working group; it drew its membership from the community, Oyo State Department of Rural Development, Ibadan North-East LG Council, UNICEF, SIP, academia, and the private sector.

The collaboration ensured an equal partnership, based on consensus, in critical decision-making. Each side contributed time, material, financial resources, and human resources, though in varying proportions. Conventional scientists scaled up the community's traditional method of increasing water yield from natural springs, brooks, and streams by introducing a concrete storage tank fitted with hand pumps and taps for easy and hygienic collection of water. The community members managing the project were taught how to fix simple faults in the pumps while plumbing artisans within the community could replace damaged pipes and taps.

The Odo-Osun project has resulted in a number of benefits, including increased access to hygienic water; less time spent by women and children scouting for water; improved attendance of children at school; project accountability and probity; an example of effective multi-stakeholder collaboration; capacity building for community members on water system construction and repair; improved sanitation in the vicinity of the spring; improved health and reduction in waterborne diseases among the people of the community; sustainable natural resource protection and conservation; more time for women to pursue socioeconomic activities; and a good lesson in integration of citizen science and formal science (Figure 12.2).

However, these benefits were not achieved without effort. The project was faced with some challenges, including:

- Community members initially found the pay-as-you-draw water scheme, implemented to pay for project costs and ongoing maintenance, to be alien. Many residents protested the user fees, resisted payment, and forcefully drew water.

Figure 12.2 Odo-Osun spring in 2010. Source: Grace Oloukoi.

- Community members were slow to understand the sustainability-related and cost-recovery implications of self-financing the service delivery, operations, and maintenance of a community-based resource.

- A fence, erected around the spring to prevent pollution and vandalization of pumps and taps, was seen as limiting the previous 24-hour access.

- There were complaints against the management committee about composition of the committee, lack of information, poor communication, and over-protection of the spring.

To resolve the conflict, project participants applied indigenous approaches (Wahab and Odetokun 2014). The SIP-TSU, acting as facilitator and mediator, consulted with and mobilized representatives of Oke-Offa Babasale community, including the youth, women, and project development stakeholders, to attend a series of meetings over five months to resolve the grievances. At the end, the project put in place a more robust, inclusive project management structure composed of the representatives of each zone, the elders, youth, women, and an auditor.

The citizen-initiated OCSWDP, realized through multi-stakeholder collaboration, earned international recognition as an ambassador project on New Solutions for Sustainable Cities during the Stockholm Partnership for Sustainable Cities final event held in Stockholm, June 4–7, 2002. This project has demonstrated how citizen science can be integrated with formal science to enhance the quality of a community-based water resource, to increase a community's access to potable water, and to promote sustainable water delivery. The project experienced some challenges from the integration of the two sciences, but these were resolved using the extant indigenous approaches to conflict resolution within the community.

12.4 Case Study Two: Using City Stakeholder-Defined Extreme Weather Thresholds to Customize Climate Projections, United States

The Climate Thresholds Project is designed to enlist city stakeholders and climate scientists to codevelop climate projection data customized specifically to city needs. Started in 2014, the project is funded by the National Oceanic and Atmospheric Administration's Sectoral Applications Research Program and is led by Adaptation International, with support from the Southern Climate Impacts Planning Program, the Climate Assessment for the Southwest, Atmos Research, and ISET-International. The project is partnering with four cities of various sizes, capacities, and resources with a diversity of climate challenges: Boulder, Colorado; Miami, Oklahoma; Las Cruces, New Mexico; and San Angelo, Texas.

Many communities around the world are already vulnerable to extreme weather events. As climate conditions change, many of these vulnerabilities may get worse or increase in frequency, magnitude, and/or intensity. Communities already know from experience when weather goes from being a nuisance to a problem for their citizens, city operations, natural resources, and other things that matter to the community. To develop effective community responses to future change, it is essential to utilize local experience and knowledge to identify critical thresholds for extreme weather events and to understand how these events may be altered in the future as the climate changes.

To be truly useful for local decision-making, climate information needs to be as specific as possible for that community. For many communities, generic thresholds for extreme weather events are insufficient to connect people with climate impacts and catalyze actions. The Climate Thresholds Project is piloting and testing a methodology for: (1) engaging citizens to identify critical thresholds for extreme weather events specific to their communities; (2) using these thresholds to analyze localized climate projections to community-specific needs; and (3) supporting community stakeholders to take new actions in response to identified risks.

The core of the methodology is a series of community workshops in each city called Shared Learning Dialogues – participatory, multisector workshops where new information is introduced and explored collectively. This approach addresses two major challenges in building resilience and adaptive responses to climate change: 1) translating scientific information into forms useable by stakeholders; and 2) generating buy-in and developing practical solutions that include a variety of stakeholders who operate in different ways, with different tools and contexts, and from different interests (Randolph 2011).

Equally essential is clear information about changing climate and extreme weather conditions and the associated impacts and risks that the city will face. To date, projections of climate change have generally been provided in one of two ways: one-size-fits-all national or regional reports and datasets; or locally tailored, external, expert-driven, desktop studies. Even the best of these generally fails to present information in ways that relate to local, on-the-ground issues and needs. The Shared Learning Dialogue approach works to address this disconnection between information holders and information users by bringing them both into the dialogue and allowing both sides to learn (Tyler and Moench 2012). It also recognizes that information users have unique local experience that is invaluable in developing meaningful knowledge for the community.

In each city, stakeholders involved in the Shared Learning Dialogues include city and county staff; emergency management personnel; medical and mental health professionals; utility representatives; local, state, and federal researchers; and local and state decision-makers, as well as project staff and scientists. This diversity allows participants to look beyond their traditional job duties and identify areas of common interest or particular problematic climate and extreme weather events. For example, in Las Cruces, key concerns included extreme heat, extreme cold, extreme wind and dust, flooding, and city water demand, with specific questions related to each. Following the Shared Learning Dialogue, the project team worked with participants to narrow these concerns down to specific, quantifiable indicators that localized global climate models can project with medium-high confidence. Table 12.1 gives examples of participant questions and their associated thresholds.

Many of the thresholds identified in Las Cruces are similar to those in the other three cities – high maximum temperatures, high nighttime temperatures,

Table 12.1 Las Cruces, NM, stakeholder-identified extreme weather thresholds

Category	Problem	Question	Threshold
Extreme heat	High heat	How will summer temperatures change?	Number of days per year with maximum temperatures above 100°F (El Paso airport closes the short runway) Nighttime temperatures greater than 85°F for two or more days (temperatures start becoming a human health problem)
Humidity	Evaporative cooling	How will the effectiveness of evaporative cooling change in the future?	90°F or more and 35 percent relative humidity or more
Extreme cold	Freezing conditions	Will more freeze events occur, like in 2011? How could freezing conditions change?	Maximum daily temperatures below 32°F for two or more days Number of nights of hard freeze (28°F)
Precipitation	Flooding	How might flooding change in the future?	2.5 in. per day precipitation events (similar to event on August 1, 2006) Three or more consecutive days of precipitation of 1 in. or more each day
Water resources	Municipal water usage	How will temperatures affect water demand?	The occurrence of three or more days of 100°F or higher temperatures combined with no precipitation
Wind	Dust storms	How will the frequency of dust storms change?	Years with similar temperature and precipitation conditions to 2003 and 2011 (calendar years)

increased frequency of flooding – but the exact numbers vary, fitting the local environments of each city. Other thresholds – the effectiveness of evaporative cooling and frequency of dust storms – are particular to Las Cruces.

The workshop discussions in each city have been strongly influenced by the diversity and the multisectoral views represented. Discussions have ranged from the potential climate impacts on agriculture and how they could change local culture, to explorations of the various types of climate action that will be needed and how to achieve these through local code changes, to how to educate and influence funding agencies and political entities to begin building support for acting more broadly.

The questions that city stakeholders are asking about how future climate will affect them, their operations, and the things they care about are focused and insightful. They have gone far beyond disseminating generic climate projection information. They are grappling with a broad range of possible impacts that could result from changing climatic conditions and are deciding what they can start doing today to mitigate or adapt to those impacts. These questions span departments and disciplines – the county transportation department is talking with the city sustainability officer, the police chief, and the state senator's office staff about what their issues are and how they can work together to solve challenges. The results are dramatically more proactive than is typically achieved in a more traditional, top-down climate modeling project.

This project clearly falls into the third category of citizen science focused on equitable collaboration. The ultimate users of the information are not only those identifying thresholds, but are also those coproducing knowledge about why those thresholds are important and how to incorporate the new information they have gleaned into decision-making processes. From a scientific perspective, the results are equally expansive. Project staff are being pushed to identify resources for city players that can help them generate urban heat island maps, understand the potential impacts of climate change on crops, and explore how to distinguish between natural variability and changing climatic conditions. The questions that city stakeholders are asking make it clear how much more could be done to make climate projection information actionable and are generating exciting new avenues for scientific exploration.

12.5 Case Study Three: Adversity to Advantage in Gorakhpur, India

Climate change is threatening food production systems and, therefore, the livelihoods and food security of millions of people who depend on agriculture in India. Consistent warming trends and more frequent and intense extreme weather events have been observed in recent decades, and climate change projections show consistent temperature increases and erratic precipitation trends. Farmers must adapt to these changing conditions to build resilient livelihoods.

People involved in agriculture tend to be among the poorest urban residents, and the poorest of all tend to be women farmers. Yet the women farmers of Mahewa ward of Gorakhpur city, in eastern Uttar Pradesh, have been adopting innovative and resilient agricultural practices. These practices have sustained their farming – especially vegetable cultivation – in an area that is acutely waterlogged.

Mahewa ward is situated in a low-lying area on the southwestern periphery of Gorakhpur city (Figure 12.3) where residents have particularly poor socioeconomic status. Located near a wholesale vegetable market, the majority of the farmers of Mahewa ward grow vegetables to sustain their livelihoods. Waterlogging and weather uncertainties – such as late monsoons, intense rains, and drought – adversely impact the vegetable farming in the area. Farming in such challenging conditions has been successful only because of the synergy between scientific methods adopted by the farmers and the application of citizen science.

Gorakhpur Environmental Action Group, or GEAG, formed under the Asian Cities Climate Change Resilience Network initiative, began promoting resilient agriculture with small, marginal, and women farmers in 2010. Their underlying strategy is to make farming economically viable and to demonstrate new, climate-resilient farming techniques.

To engage with farmers, GEAG set up and facilitated a neighborhood committee on Climate Resilient Agriculture, or CRA. The CRA committee provides a platform for farmers to share their agriculture-related problems and to find solutions. Since the platform meets monthly at the ward level, it is easy for women farmers to access, participate, and learn new methods of farming. This platform has been instrumental in scaling up new techniques to other farmers.

One of the key agricultural practices promoted by GEAG in the CRA committee has been *dhaincha* (*Sesbania aculeate*; Figure 12.4) farming. Dhaincha is a leguminous crop that is tolerant of high saline and waterlogged conditions. It is popularly and scientifically known for its green manuring attributes; scientists recommend it as a measure to reclaim alkaline soils that have been induced by waterlogging. GEAG's past experiences had shown that dhaincha survives very well in waterlogged conditions.

The farmers who grew dhaincha for a year saw additional potential uses for the crop. They began using the hard, semi-woody stem of dhaincha as the base for climber crops in a multitier cropping system. This unique method of crop combination (dhaincha with vegetable crops) helps reduce the impacts of

Figure 12.3 Mahewa ward, Gorakhpur, India. Source: map provided by GEAG.

Figure 12.4 Dhaincha (center). Source: photo by GEAG.

waterlogging on the vegetable crops and, simultaneously, increases soil fertility when the farmers plough dhaincha back into the soil after the vegetable crop is harvested. Farmers also began using dhaincha as fuel and as fodder for livestock. In the CRA committee meetings, successes were shared and expanded.

Dhaincha farming has improved the incomes of local farmers. Table 12.2 shows the income of Ms. I.D., a farmer in Mahewa ward, who sowed dhaincha along with sponge gourd on a quarter of an acre of land. With an input cost of Rs. 1250 (18.75 USD), she earned profits worth Rs. 7750 (116.50 USD).

Dhaincha is very popular in the urban environment. The intervention started with 10 farmers; now, more than 500 farmers have adopted it. The farmers are also promoting this technique in farmer field schools, meetings, in farmers' fairs, and so forth. Word-of-mouth popularity has produced much recognition and adoption of the crop. Farmers have also started using it as a "trap crop," as it provides protection against pests and insects.

Equitable collaboration between GEAG and the farmers improved the dhaincha farming model substantially. The resulting model delivers sustainable social and economic benefits to poor farmers, enabling them to increase their incomes and improve the quality of their lives. Such local innovations are attracting large numbers of other farmers who are facing similar problems farming in waterlogged contexts and are experiencing deteriorating soil health. Today, this citizen science initiative, acting in synergy with conventional science, is helping approximately 800 farmers in this flood-affected region.

Table 12.2 Cost-benefit ratio of dhaincha cultivation

Crop	Cropping area (acres)	Input cost (in Indian rupees)	Total production (quintals)	Output cost (in Indian rupees)	Net profit	Cost-benefit ratio
Dhaincha	0.25	50	5.0	2000	1950	1:39
Sponge gourd		1200	7.0	7000	5800	1:5
Total		1250	12.0	9000	7750	

12.6 Discussion

All three case studies fall into our third category of citizen science, which focuses on equitable collaboration. In all three cases, scientists worked with citizens to coproduce knowledge about how information could be best used locally. This process was facilitated by boundary organizations that have links to the community and experts. Likewise, in all three cases, the outside experts learned how extensively their information needed to be tailored to be adapted for local action.

These case studies illustrate several elements that we believe should be at the foundation of citizen science if it is to reach its full potential:

1. Coproduction of knowledge, as illustrated in the dhaincha farming study

2. Meaningful participation, as illustrated in the climate thresholds study

3. Citizen ownership of solutions, as illustrated in the Odo-Osun study

We note that, in addition to these three elements, monitoring and evaluation is a growing area of donor interest and an undertaking that supports the development of strong science, particularly science focused on producing change. As such, we see monitoring and evaluation as fundamental to citizen science and an area in which citizen science could grow considerably. However, a detailed exploration of monitoring and evaluation, insofar as it can help support and develop citizen science, is beyond the scope of this chapter.

The dhaincha farming case study illustrates the benefits of coproduction of knowledge. GEAG brought top-down information on green manuring with dhaincha into Mahewa ward, but it was the women farmers, working together and with GEAG, who quickly realized dhaincha could also be used to address other issues they were having – trouble growing vegetable crops in waterlogged soils and lack of fuel and fodder. By customizing the top-down information with bottom-up knowledge of local needs and capacities, highly useful science was created. The credibility, legitimacy, and saliency of this knowledge to the local community is evident in the rapid uptake and continued development of this crop by other farmers, and in the economic impacts it is having on farmers' lives.

The climate thresholds case study illustrates the value of meaningful participation. Climate projection data have been available in the United States for well over a decade, yet governments, agencies, organizations, and businesses are only just beginning to take action to mitigate climate emissions or to adapt to anticipated climate change impacts. Action, where taken, still tends to be highly focused within one or a few sectors. In this case study, the use of Shared Learning Dialogues to convene highly diverse, multidisciplinary groups significantly changed the content of the dialogue in all four project cities. Participants' thinking became substantially broader, opportunities for cross-sectoral collaboration were identified, and local stakeholders began actively exploring the depths of internal and external expert knowledge in the room. This is only possible when participants feel they are engaged as equals, such that their knowledge, perspective, and opinions matter.

Finally, the Odo-Osun case study illustrates the value of citizen ownership of solutions. Many of the issues identified as challenges for the Odo-Osun project are typical of development projects worldwide – conflict over who is involved, over access, and over cost. The other common cause of project failure is selection of technology that cannot be maintained by those using it. By keeping the community at the heart of this project, technologies the community could maintain were preserved, and the challenges were addressed.

All three types of citizen action explored in this chapter – citizen data collection, citizen analysis, and equitable collaboration – are valuable. Citizen data collection is changing the nature of information available to conventional science and is making new analyses possible. Similarly, citizen analysis is challenging the conventional knowledge base and provides much broader sets of data and assessments in the conducted areas. Nonetheless, we believe the real power of citizen science lies in the third area – equitable collaboration. The three case studies we have explored here demonstrate the different cultures, problems, and solutions that are present in urban settings; still, the core method of equitable collaboration used in all three cases has contributed to the success of all three projects, has led to learning both for the citizens and scientists involved, and, through co-development of project focuses and goals, has produced valuable outcomes for the citizens who participated in the work.

12.7 Opportunities Moving Forward

Citizen science is changing the scientific process in powerful ways, and its full potential has yet to be tapped. However, to add value, citizen science needs to be done well, which takes time and funding. If we are to invest our time and money, where should we focus to make our investment as influential as possible?

Some of the opportunities we see include:

- **Scale**: Citizen science can help bridge the micro- versus macroscale gap. Conventional knowledge, particularly outside the developed world, is generally only available at a macroscale, and, frequently, it is stuck there due to a lack of finer-scale data. Increasingly, citizen science can help us to close that gap, informing the macroscale picture with microscale detail.

- **Framing**: Many of the data that can be easily captured by citizens aren't data that scientists can use. We need to explore ways to take what can be captured easily and to give it value.

- **Techniques**: Local knowledge, such as changes in distribution of indicator species, is not easily crowd-sourced. We need more research into what communities know and how this could support, or challenge, conventional science; how citizens can capture this information and feed it into conventional science; and how we can incentivize citizen participation.

- **Validation**: Science typically requires verifiable information rather than perception, myth, or ideology. Yet, citizen-collected data are often based on perception, and in the context of vastly differing lived experiences for citizen scientists and conventional scientists. These perceptions are an important part of how fact is interpreted and provide valuable information about existing needs, values, and constraints. While perceptions are difficult to validate, collaborative engagement between citizens and conventional science can help bridge the gap between formal and informal ways of knowing and create a knowledge that is valid and relevant for a given context.

- **Ownership and action**: Increased coproduction of science can lead to high feelings of ownership and high levels of action based on the research results. Refining techniques for building ownership and fostering action will assist in scaling coproduction up and out.

Overall, citizen science is supporting the growth of new science endeavors in exciting ways, particularly as technology has progressed and virtual networks have expanded, increasing scientific literacy and inclusivity of contributors. But, it is not being utilized to its full potential. In this chapter, we have identified the value and opportunities for conducting citizen science that is more equitable and collaborative as a means of narrowing the gap between knowledge and action, particularly in urban settings. We know there are multiple organizations that have been practicing this type of science for years, as illustrated by the studies explored here. We hope this chapter inspires more organizations to embrace citizen science, both for the benefit of citizens, for the benefit of research, and for the benefit of the positive change it can affect for us all.

References

Adewoye, D. (1995). A Brief Address on Odo-Akeu Community Development Association. Address presented to stakeholders on Odo-Akeu Spring Water Development Project at the weekly meeting of the Association on September 6.

Bonney, R., Cooper, C.B., Dickinson, J., Kelling, S., Phillips, T., Rosenberg, K.V., and Shirk, J. (2009). Citizen Science: A Developing Tool for Expanding Science Knowledge and Scientific Literacy. *BioScience*, 59(11): 977–984.

Colston, N.M., Vadjunec, J.M., and Wakeford, T. (2015). Exploring the Entry Points for Citizen Science in Urban Sustainability Initiatives. *Current Opinion in Environmental Sustainability*, 17: 66–71.

Connors, J.P., Lei, S., and Kelly, M. (2012). Citizen Science in the Age of Neogeography: Utilizing Volunteered Geographic Information for Environmental Monitoring. *Annals of the Association of American Geographers*, 102(6): 1267–1289.

Dilling, L., and Lemos, M.C. (2011). Creating Usable Science: Opportunities and Constraints for Climate Knowledge Use and Their Implications for Science Policy. *Global Environmental Change*, 21(2): 680–689.

Haraway, D. (1988). Situated Knowledges: The Science Question in Feminism and the Privilege of Partial Perspective. *Feminist Studies*, 14(3): 575–599.

Harding, S. (2011). *The Postcolonial Science and Technology Studies Reader*. Durham, NC: Duke University Press.

Herbertson, K. (2012). Citizen Science Supports a Healthy Mekong. *International Rivers*, retrieved from www.internationalrivers.org/resources/citizen-science-supports-a-healthy-mekong-7759.

Lemos, M.C., and Morehouse, B.J. (2005). The Co-Production of Science and Policy in Integrated Climate Assessments. *Global Environmental Change*, 15(1): 57–68.

Mueller, M.P., and Tippins, D. (2012). The Future of Citizen Science. *Democracy and Education*, 20(1), Article 2.

Odo-Akeu Spring Water Development Project Working Group (1996). Proposal for Technical and Financial Assistances for the Development of Odo-Akeu Spring Water at Babasale in Ibadan North-East Local Government. Unpubl. report by SIP Technical Support Unit.

Randolph, J. (2011). *Creating the Climate Change Resilient Community*, in B.E. Goldstein (ed.) *Collaborative Resilience: Moving Through Crisis to Opportunity*, Cambridge, MA: MIT Press, pp. 127–148.

Shediac-Rizkallah, M.C., and Bone, L.R. (1998). Planning for the Sustainability of Community-Based Health Programs: Conceptual Frameworks and Future Directions for Research, Practice and Policy. *Health Education Research*, 13(1): 87–108.

Simpson, L., Wood, L., and Daws, L. (2003). Community Capacity Building: Starting with People Not Projects. *Community Development Journal*, 38(4): 277–286.

SIP-TSU (2015). Executive Summary on Odo-Osun Natural Spring Project at Oke-Offa Babasale, Ibadan, in Ibadan North-East Local government area of Oyo State. Unpubl. report by SIP Technical Support Unit.

Tyler S., and Moench M. (2012). *A Framework for Urban Climate Resilience. Climate and Development*, 4(4): 311–326.

Wahab, B. and Odetokun, O. (2014). Indigenous Approaches to Housing-Induced Domestic Conflict Management in Ondo City, Nigeria. *Journal of Sustainable Development*, 7(4): 28–46. http://dx.doi.org/10.5539/jsd.v7n4p28.

Part III

Urban Transformations to Sustainability

Chapter 13: Sustainability Transformation Emerging from Better Governance

Patricia Romero-Lankao, Niki Frantzeskaki, and Corrie Griffith

13.1 Urban Governance and Transformations

Urbanization and urban areas are profoundly altering the relationship between society and the environment at accelerated rates, affecting our chances to create livable, sustainable, and just societies worldwide. Urban areas are key sources of resource use and pollutants globally. For instance, they emit up to 70 percent of global greenhouse gas, or GHG, emissions (Romero-Lankao et al. 2014). However, both resource use and GHG emissions within a city are not often under the remit of local governments; rather, they are the responsibility of national governments, the private sector, and other actors. At the same time, urban populations, economic activities, infrastructure, and services are vulnerable to an array of negative environmental impacts, such as mortality from extreme heat and damages from hurricanes, storm surges, and flooding. Furthermore, environmental issues are cross-scale issues. This means that urban areas are affected by actions beyond their boundaries, and urban uses of natural resources, GHG emissions, and risks create effects far outside the demarcations of city limits (see Chapters 3 and 4). Hence, these issues are not only local governmental concerns, but require a diversity of actors across sectors and jurisdictions to network and create coalitions for climate and environmental governance to sustainably manage the use of water, energy, and other resources; to mitigate GHG emissions; and to adapt to and mitigate environmental risks.

The complex nature of environmental and climate challenges associated with the current Anthropocene era cannot be suitably dealt with by the modest and fragmented responses that are most common in urban areas worldwide. Incremental reform may prove inadequate; instead, we may require transformative responses that alter core elements of urban systems, such as energy, water, and land-use regimes *and* influence multiple interconnected domains, such as sociodemographics, economics, technology, environment, and governance itself, with their basic power relations, worldviews, and market structures (Park et al. 2012). The study of transformation in response to environmental change is established among scholars and communities of practice. However, it is critical to focus on the value this knowledge can add to existing environmental policy and governance in urban areas, which are both key drivers of environmental change and sources of solutions. Transformation is a concept deeply embedded in the human narrative. It conveys the notion of systemic, essential, and radical change that can affect an array of fundamental urban socioecological system domains such as sociodemographics, the economy, technology, ecology, and governance regimes (Folke et al. 2005; Romero-Lankao and Gnatz 2013; Geels and Schot 2007; Patterson et al. 2016). For instance, can the concept of transformation play a normative role in helping us purposefully move cities towards sustainability and resilience? Or should it be confined to an ex-post analysis of change in cities? And why should we focus on cities?

Many actions and strategies will be needed to trigger such transformative processes, from coordinated action by governments to innovation in the private sector, experimentation, and pressure from civil society. This is where the questions around the role of governance in shaping transformations towards urban sustainability and resilience become paramount. Are we mostly interested in understanding the links between governance and the politics of change? Are we looking into governance as part of the problem and engaging with transformations in existing city governance regimes? Is our emphasis on governance that creates the conditions for transformation to emerge, or on actively fostering transformation processes? (Patterson et al. 2016) What exactly must be transformed; why, how, by whom, and in whose interest; and, what factors drive or trigger the necessary transformations?

Rather than suggesting the most appropriate range of responses needed to achieve transformational actions and policies, this chapter sets the stage for Part III and builds on previous work to identify both opportunities and challenges that city officials and private and civil society actors face in their efforts to develop governance solutions that support sustainable and resilient urban development. This chapter will start with the definition of key terms (for example, urban governance), and of main approaches to the governance factors shaping change towards more sustainable and resilient development pathways (Section 13.2). Many actions and strategies have been introduced to address sustainability and resilience concerns (for example, urban water management and transportation). In Section 13.3, we will briefly describe different types of actions seeking to mitigate or prevent risk and to adapt to existing and possible environmental threats and disruptions. Mitigation refers to actions aimed at reducing resource use and environmental impacts and risks; adaptation refers to actions aimed at managing these impacts, before or after they are experienced (Field et al. 2014). The following sections describe the nature of the actor-networks involved in designing and implementing actions (Section 13.4), and the opportunities, barriers, and limits that multilevel governance poses to local climate and environmental policy (Section 13.5).

13.2 Multilevel Governance and Transformations

Interest in transformations towards sustainability and resilience has grown considerably in recent years among researchers and communities of practice globally. For instance, it has been addressed in debates around the Sustainable Development Goals (SDGs, see Part II). It is one of the themes of Future Earth's Sustainability Research Platform. And it has become a key component of IPCC assessment efforts (Field et al. 2014). Urban governance and politics are critical to understanding and shaping these transformations for many reasons: Governance can offer both barriers and opportunities to transitioning towards urban sustainability and resilience; further, these transformations are inherently contested and political (Patterson et al. 2016; Romero-Lankao et al. 2016).

Urban governance takes place within broad socioeconomic and political contexts, with actors and institutions at multiple scales shaping the effectiveness of urban actions and responses. In particular, urban environmental governance comprises formal and informal rules, rule-making systems, and actor-networks across sectors and jurisdictions, both in and outside of government, that are established to steer cities towards sustainable resource management, environmental change mitigation and adaptation, and transitions along alternative development paths (Biermann et al. 2010).

Below, we review the main strands of literature that engage with the influence of governance in actions and strategies seeking to transition urban areas towards more sustainable and resilient development pathways. These include theories of sociotechnical transitions (Geels and Schot 2007; Rutherford and Coutard 2014) and socioecological transformability, political ecology perspectives (for example, sustainability pathways and transformative adaptation; Lawhon and Murphy 2012) and a growing body of scholarship on experimentation. These approaches provide significant, albeit partial, visions of urban transformations that aid in the understanding of the barriers and opportunities associated with the practice of urban sustainability and resilience transitions. For instance, sociotechnical transitions theory sheds light on some of the processes shaping changes in environmental management regimes, while political ecology approaches illuminate the influence of power relations among actors with different values and interests in shaping social change.

13.2.1 Sociotechnical and Socioecological Theories of Transformation

Sociotechnical transitions theories, also called STTs, examine the multilevel processes through which socioecological and technical systems experience transformations. STTs define transformations as shifts to systemically different sociotechnical regimes of resource use and relationships with the environment (Smith and Stirling 2010; Geels and Schot 2007; Rutherford and Coutard 2014). Transformation is conceived as a series of far-reaching changes along different domains: technological, governance, economic, sociocultural, and environmental. It includes a broad range of actors and unfolds over substantial periods (50 years or longer, for example). Examples include the transition from cesspools to sanitation, from telephone to cellphone, and from internal-combustion to electric vehicles. Within the transitions literature, there is a fast-growing body of work on urban transformations. This work has evolved from situating "urban" simply as the context of new empirical examination of transition experiments to investigating urban patterns of transformation as unique to the understanding of contemporary transitions.

A *sociotechnical regime* organizes social practices and structures relationships among private, governmental, and nongovernmental actors, whose understandings of priorities, appropriate actions, and technologies are intertwined with the expectations and skills of users, with institutional arrangements, and with physical infrastructures providing energy, water, and materials. A regime is "dynamically stable" and imposes a logic and direction for incremental sociotechnical and socioecological change along established pathways of development, which, in turn, create path dependency or lock-in. Electricity and urban water management provide conspicuous examples of lock-in due to the endurance of their material structures and the sturdy techno-institutional interrelationships associated with them. While regimes are dynamically stable, they are constantly subject to drivers and pressures that can lead to their destabilization and transformation. Some of these drivers and pressures are:

Innovations and experimentations, or proactive changes such as new technologies, social experiments, and governmental or grassroots initiatives. Innovations can contribute to structural or fundamental changes in cultures, structures, practices, and relations between actors. Experimentation can nurture new technologies and create new institutions and new governance processes.

Conflict and contestation of actions around access to, use of, or redistribution of natural resources, assets, and decisions, with resulting social and environmental implications (for example, on water quality and availability, social inequality, and livelihoods); and,

Environmental impacts and triggers in the form of natural resource depletion and scarcity, disasters, or changes in risk tolerance resulting from shifts in economic, cultural, and/or political dynamics (Romero-Lankao and Gnatz 2013).

Governance and governmental policies frequently exert an influence on transitions through *transition management*, which includes insights from complex systems and governance approaches (Loorbach and Rotmans 2010). Transition management conceives socioecologic systems, such as urban areas, as complex and adaptive. Management in this context appears as a reflexive and evolutionary governance process (Markard et al. 2012).

Socioecological systems literature has engaged with the question of how adaptive governance can enhance or foster adaptability of cities as socioecological systems. The concept of resilience, originated in ecology, is fundamental to this approach, which focuses on how much stress and disturbance an urban system can adapt to while remaining within critical thresholds before it moves to another regime (Carpenter and Brock 2008). In this perspective, urban resilience is conceived as the ability of complex socioecological systems, such as cities and urban communities, to change, adapt, and – crucially – to transform in response to both internal and external stresses and pressures (Davoudi et al. 2012; Ahern 2011). Governance of cities plays two roles within this approach. In the first one – governance for navigating change – both short-term and long-term actions seek to shield cities from hazards and disruptions, and to provide urban communities and actors with the capacity to respond to change and uncertainty. In the second role – governance for transformation – actions and policies are envisioned and implemented that create new urban systems when current conditions render existing systems unviable (Folke et al. 2005).

13.2.2 Experimentation

As noted above, innovations or experimentations can destabilize sociotechnical regimes and drive transformative change. Experimentation is a process for instigating sustainability transitions, particularly within cities, with many cases showing impacts on governance dynamics, for example from experimentation in the urban water sector (Ferguson et al. 2013; Poustie et al, 2016), in urban mobility (Späth and Rohracher 2012), and in urban energy (Castan-Broto and Bulkeley 2013). Experimentation includes lighthouse projects that have great symbolic value for urban planning and development, such as the Floating Urbanization pilot project, the Floating Pavilion in the City Ports of Rotterdam, or the eco-district Hammerby in Stockholm. Experimentation can come in the form of open-ended labs that test, or, cocreate new approaches or solutions to urban challenges, such as increasing community cohesion or facilitating urban regeneration through coproduced urban agendas, as well as through urban projects that can set transformative processes in motion. Experiments can be facilitated by local governments, established by public-private partnerships, or self-organized by civil society and citizens themselves, from the grassroots. Recent scholarship showcases the importance of creating both physical and institutional space for experimentation processes to take place (Castan-Broto and Bulkeley 2013; Bulkeley et al. 2016; Frantzeskaki et al. 2014, 2017; Nevens et al. 2013; Loorbach et al. 2017).

Experimentation has, in many cases, evolved into the preferred governance tool for addressing complex urban problems. This may explain the observed proliferation of experimentation as a way of governing cities for climate change across Europe, Latin America, and Asia. In particular, the empirically based research on sustainability transitions, focused on smart cities, resilient or sustainable cities, and water-scarce cities, showcases that there is merit in trial experiments and new solutions in cities. These processes create a base of evidence for effective urban solutions that tackle local manifestations of climate change. Experimentation is not limited to climate change concerns; it can also address issues of inequality and accessibility to health care, services, and education. Future urban research will need to examine how experiments addressing urban sustainability challenges contribute to urban agendas for development and what impact they have on contemporary urban dynamics in ecological, social, economic, and political domains of cities.

While there is a recognized need for new approaches to deal with political and social challenges to secure sustainable and livable urban futures, experiments and new forms of governance can enable positive transitions to urban sustainability. However, these innovations are not always welcomed by communities or by political institutions. The controversies, contestations, and conflicts that come along with experimentation are also important ingredients in the governance of urban transformations (Chapters 14 and 15). Alongside these tensions, the current manifestations of governance practices and processes need to be revised and adapted to allow institutional space for actors driving urban transformation and experimentation, which act as lighthouses for new pathways to sustainability (Chapter 16).

13.2.3 Critical Theories of Transformation

Sociotechnical transition theories have helped elucidate the barriers to and options for transformations through the interplay between governmental and private actors, social practices, and institutions. By focusing on urban resilience as an ability to bounce forward, socioecological system theories have shed light on cities' and urban actors' capacity to change, adapt, and – crucially – to transform in response to hazards and disruptions. However, sociotechnical transition theories, which have focused mostly on Europe and the United States, have little to say about how transitions may play out differently in the cities of middle- and low-income countries (Bulkeley et al. 2010). Similarly, scholars have suggested that socioecological system theories cannot be uncritically applied in the process of trying to understanding how social domains function. In this view, urban groups and communities have the capacity to cope, or adapt, to stresses and disruptions, but these capabilities are also shaped by social, political, and cultural processes. Socioecological approaches have often been criticized for being deterministic and for omitting the role of different levels of agency and power in creating or preventing transformational movement away from previous system phases and cycles. As illustrated by many scholars, pro-growth coalitions, unabated by powerless local authorities and civil society organizations, pose challenges to navigating towards more sustainable and resilient pathways of urban development (Fernández et al. 2016; Romero-Lankao et al. 2015).

To address these concerns, sustainability pathways approaches seek to understand transformations in ways that are sensitive to the deeply political, contested nature of urban sustainability and resilience issues (Robinson and Cole 2015; Bendor et al. 2015). This is achieved by taking into consideration diverse views of and aspirations for what desirable sustainable solutions are, and consider mechanisms to navigating trade-offs and side effects of the proposed transformative solutions. Cultural values, as well as economic and political considerations, play key roles in defining sustainability and resilience goals; acceptable risks to livelihood, property, and other things urban actors value; and outcomes. Because this perspective assumes that both sustainability and resilience are contested, dynamic, and uncertain, it puts institutions and values at the center of efforts to understand and navigate transformations towards sustainability and resilience in cities.

Political ecology scholars have criticized STTs as providing a narrow lens for viewing the processes shaping (limiting, fostering) change, with their emphasis on infrastructures, users, experiments, and technological innovations (Lawhon and Murphy 2012). Political ecology scholars suggest that STTs do not take into consideration that corporate and state leaders, scientists, and innovators of all sorts do not always hold progressive, fair, and/or environmentally friendly values and interests. For political ecology scholars, both cooperation and conflict are inherent features of decision-making in general, and transition management in particular (Lawhon and Murphy 2012). This is so because environmental policies that can aid in transition essentially revolve around who benefits and who bears the risks of actions, with a clear set of winners and losers. For example, large-scale power generation and trans-basin water imports can be a desirable means of dealing with energy and water scarcity for some urban elites and benefiting populations within a city, but these changes can be highly undesirable for people and places that bear the stress and hardship implied by these actions. Therefore, it is essential to ask, in the governance of any transition process: what actors and places are at stake; with whom and where power resides; what social and environmental consequences of decision-making are at play; and whose voices and narratives remain unheard?

13.3 Responses and Actions Developed and Implemented in Urban Areas

Many actions are being developed and implemented worldwide with the purpose of providing urban sustainability solutions that address issues such as water and energy management, flood mitigation, other environmental protections (air quality), and cleaner and affordable transportation systems, to name a few. It is increasingly clear that ensuring the future sustainability of the planet requires that these strategies and plans address the consequences of a changing and uncertain climate. Such impacts manifest differently, are experienced uniquely in urban areas (and, at even finer resolutions, are experienced differently among different urban populations), and must be dealt with accordingly – in specific ways that are embedded in the sociopolitical and economic realities that characterize an urban space at local scales.

Urban climate responses include climate change mitigation and adaptation actions, also called resilience actions. These responses range from short to long term, from local to regional, and vary widely in their effectiveness and outcomes. They also include the following domains:

1. Understanding the problem: For instance, if the goal is to mitigate GHG emissions, an inventory will provide a baseline against which mitigation targets can be assessed. A focus on reducing vulnerability will require assessments of the damage to property, disease, and loss of livelihoods that urban populations may face under a changing climate.

2. Incremental responses: For example, mitigation actions focused on municipal government buildings and vehicle fleets are the most common approaches used by city officials worldwide. It is also very common among cities to start with adaptation actions that build on ongoing disaster risk management (Barrero 2013).

3. Broader, longer-term responses that seek to change urban form, institutions, and social practices are equally important. Examples of these include:

a.   Infrastructural investments that: (i) decrease vehicle kilometers trav-
eled, foster mixed-use development, improve destination accessibility,
and reduce distance to transit. These goals are achieved by concentrating
development and, hence, reducing energy use by vehicles and the stress
associated with driving (Hamin and Gurran 2009); (ii) discourage growth
in risk-prone areas and protect or restore ecosystem services such as water
infiltration, flood protection, and temperature regulation. These actions
may help create synergies between mitigation and adaptation by influencing resource use and emissions, and by fostering the resilience of people
and places;

b.   Actions that build capacity by enhancing the resources and options
afforded to populations from diverse socioeconomic groups to use environmentally friendly sources of energy, food, or water, and to adapt to
environmental threats, such as those induced by climate change;

c.   Actions that reduce exposure to environmental and climate threats, or
that mitigate risk (such as dikes and barriers, or multiple-use green ways).

4.   *Transformative responses* that create shifts in energy, water, transportation,
and land-use regimes, growth ethos, production and consumption practices,
and worldviews(Field et al. 2014). Some of these actions target the underlying
drivers of resource use, emissions, and vulnerability, such as a shift from centralized electricity fueled by fossil fuels to decentralized, rooftop solar energy,
or a focus on integrating environmental and local disaster risk management
concerns with an inclusive and pro-poor urban development agenda, as exemplified by Manizales (see Chapter 15). As such, transformative actions hold the
potential to promote a more systemic shift towards sustainable and resilient
urban development (Shaw et al. 2014; Burch et al. 2014).

This section reviews some of the climate responses (with a focus on adaptation or resilience efforts) that occur in cities of multiple regions and typologies, setting the stage for the following section, which analyzes the governance
and decision-making processes and structures that have enabled – or constrained – their development and implementation. Our brief description of
these responses provides useful entry points to juxtapose global problems and
local solutions or vice versa, and the multiscale governance processes involved.
Such actions are diverse in nature and scope, can range from small- to larger-scale
efforts, and include a variety of tools and approaches for implementation.

Actions to increase adaptive capacity to threats – including, but not limited to, climate-induced flooding from heavy rainfall events or storm surges,
heat waves, or water scarcity and drought – ultimately affect urban areas and
populations, but how and at which scale they are developed can vary. Urban

households and communities, for example, have long implemented measures to adapt to changing environmental conditions and specific threats by drawing on local knowledge, consistent with sociocultural practices. These are numerous and particularly common in low-income and developing nations where large-scale poverty exists and the institutional capacities to adapt are much weaker. Examples of adaptation practices include innovation in water collection and retention in times of drought, changing precipitation patterns, or saline intrusion; adaptation to agricultural practices through altering the timing and types of crop grown; tree and vegetation planting for storm water absorption or heat mitigation; and the construction of pole or stilt housing in flood prone, high-risk urban areas. It is still unclear how to scale up adaptation actions and institutionalize them within local and regional policies, and in doing so, if the adaptation actions are appropriate for these larger scales. Conversely, more comprehensive and thoughtful decision-making efforts that include a range of urban stakeholders can also reduce cases of maladaptation that occur due to ad hoc coping strategies and actions that sometimes conflict with broader socioeconomic and environmental conditions (Schaer 2015).

Adaptation to climate threats is as complex as the urban system, and it is proportionately challenging to develop and implement at the city or regional level, requiring approaches that are multidimensional and include actors at multiple scales. Citywide adaptation and risk mitigation responses often employ a range of approaches that can include either soft or hard infrastructure measures, or a combination of both, to adapt to specific climate change impacts. For example, to mitigate effects of the microclimate in cities (such as urban heat island), cities are beginning to utilize cool pavements (light-colored surfacing or permeable pavements); cool roofs (often categorized as "white," "blue," or "green" roof strategies to differentiate the approaches); increasing vegetation abundance; and reducing waste heat (Gartland 2012). Coastal cities, often plagued by extreme flooding due to sea level rise, storm surges, and hurricanes, may utilize hard engineering approaches such as sea walls or levees, or turn towards nature-based solutions or ecosystem-based adaptations, including restoring natural wetlands or mangrove ecosystems to buffer the effects of extreme wind and flooding. These "softer," ecosystem-based approaches, which are viewed as more cost efficient, comprehensive, and multifunctional by design, have gained popularity as a response to the negative associations of "hard" adaptations, which are prone to being inflexible, costly, and inadequate for addressing a range of interests or perspectives of the problem the action seeks to address.

13.4 Multilevel Actor-Networks

As indicated in our introduction, environmental – and particularly climate – changes are socially and environmentally pervasive phenomena. Therefore, they challenge actors from different sectors and jurisdictions to create multilevel governance networks and coalitions. Rather than being homogeneous, these groups frequently hold different values and interests, create shifting alliances, and have varying levels of power. This heterogeneity poses challenges for coherent and legitimate urban climate change governance, as actor-networks play multiple and changing roles in urban environmental governance: some provide energy, food, and water resources; others function as facilitators of interactions within and between cities; and yet others define dominant environmental discourses more broadly. The climate change arena offers examples of the relevance of actor-networks, with many urban actors independently committing to mitigation and adaptation, even in the absence of national climate change policies. Furthermore, some actors from the private sector are addressing climate change within their own companies, or are forming partnerships to achieve a common goal. The myriad of actors involved means that, in many cases, suboptimal outcomes will be created.

Actors and their governance arrangements operate in a complex web of interactions, a pattern that had been captured using the notion of *interplay*. The concept of interplay sheds light on the interdependence of institutional arrangements at varying (vertical interplay) and similar (horizontal interplay) levels of organization (Young 2002). These interdependences create policy challenges. The actors involved in the governance of environmental change in cities frequently have very diverse mandates, operate at different time scales, and use different expertise or understanding of the climate issue. For instance, in Cape Town, South Africa and Mexico City, Mexico, officials have pursued climate change mitigation, but the effectiveness of their actions has been constrained by differences in ruling parties and political cultures that constrain structured interactions and collaborations (Holgate 2007; Romero-Lankao 2007). In larger urban areas as diverse as New York, Mexico City, Dakar, and Buenos Aires, which comprise two or more local and state authorities, each authority can act only within its boundaries. This means that the overall impact of their policies may be limited unless there is horizontal collaboration among neighboring authorities, or an overarching strategic metropolitan authority exists to ensure citywide action (Solecki et al. 2011).

For diverse reasons frequently related to authoritarian culture or jurisdictional boundaries, environmental authorities seldom interact with development authorities, and tiers of government seldom collaborate. Priorities in urban planning are dominated by economic concerns, with environmental concerns frequently taking the back seat. As a result, the design and implementation of a sustainability plan depends on strong administrative leadership, as well as on whether the commitment of the various implementing actors is guaranteed and how long-term decisions are made.

Actor-networks have appeared that link city officials, private sector actors, community organizations, and academics, to create more coordinated, international approaches to sustainability and resilience challenges such as those posed by climate change (Betsill and Bulkeley 2004; Andonova 2010). ICLEI's Partners for Climate Protection program and the C40 are examples of increasingly important global networks that influence responses to sustainability challenges (Andonova 2010) by providing financial resources as well as opportunities for learning and sharing experiences, tools, and lessons. Notwithstanding the promise of these networks, the interactions among participant actors and the effectiveness of their actions are constrained by the wide differences in jurisdictional remit, organizational culture and structure, and political context.

Actors and actor-networks vary in the extent to which they can influence the framing of sustainability issues, the governance of climate and environmental change, and the resources to implement actions. This inequality is best illustrated by the fact that those urban populations that are most vulnerable to climate change are often not those who are responsible for the majority of GHG emissions. Climate and environmental change also have the potential to exacerbate existing societal inequalities in terms of income distribution; access to resources and options to pursue livelihoods; and capacity to effectively respond to environmental and social threats (Romero-Lankao et al. 2015). A growing body of research reveals that climate and environmental change governance strategies and actions can create or recreate (un)just decision-making processes and outcomes or result in an (in)equitable distribution of risks and resources (Hughes 2013).

13.5 Multilevel Governance Poses Opportunities and Barriers to Local Policy

While city officials are at the forefront of acting on global environmental challenges such as climate change, existing scholarship points to a variety of opportunities, barriers, and limits to the implementation of coordinated and cross-sectoral actions. Many environmental and climate plans need to be holistic and comprehensive; yet, the siloed, shorter-term nature of decision-making poses political, cultural, and professional challenges to horizontal and vertical coordination between actors, who usually are scattered across sectoral agencies, utilities, and city-administrative departments (Kern et al. 2008), and work on short planning horizons.

Scholarship has also found that the expertise required to address sustainability challenges frequently remains concentrated in environmental departments. This makes cross-sectoral and cross-jurisdictional coordination within the organizational hierarchy of city government particularly challenging, as environmental bodies usually have limited remit over and capacity to implement actions in key development areas, such as energy, transportation, land planning, and finance (Kern et al. 2008; Romero-Lankao et al. 2015).

Fragmentation in governance systems is driven by more than the physical separation of actors. The implementation of climate and environmental policies is also constrained by a multitude of formal and informal institutional barriers, such as the varied visions, values, interests, and decision-making power of involved actors (Agrawala et al. 2011). Addressing fragmentation as a cross-sectoral planning concern is fundamental if unwanted trade-offs are to be avoided and potential synergies created (Wejs 2014).

Other factors – such as leadership, legal frameworks, scientific information, leadership, the ability to self-organize and mobilize knowledge, and support for the implementation of sustainable solutions – also shape urban actors' capacity to implement effective actions. While the influence of each factor varies with context, a key area for future analysis are the conditions under which the inadequacies of different combinations of factors function as barriers to effective urban governance. Here, we will briefly touch on some of these.

The legal context in which urban governance takes place plays a key role in determining the extent to which climate and environmental actions, regulations, and programmatic priorities are legitimized, incentivized, prioritized, or demonized. Legal frameworks can also mediate the relationship between decision-makers, the private sector, and the broader public as they provide political structures (or not) for participatory planning and decision-making according to prevailing political norms and cultures. For instance, absent or inappropriate laws dealing with climate adaptation and mitigation can be a hurdle to investments in "climate-proofed" technologies or warning systems. However, it can take a lot of time and energy to change legal frameworks, as this entails complex negotiations across sectors and national to local political levels of decision-making.

The creation of and access to new, city-specific, socially relevant scientific information and local knowledge is fundamental for effective decision-making, particularly in the arena of climate change, where climate projections, GHG inventories, and vulnerability assessments are vital for setting baselines against which progress towards mitigation and adaptation targets can be evaluated.

The availability, communication, and use of information are essential for effective governance. These are not mere technical exercises of collection and insertion of information into the policy process; rather, they are politically determined by power relationships between levels of government, and between government, the private sector, and grassroots actors (Romero-Lankao et al. 2015). Problems of access to usable information are particularly substantial. For instance, an international survey on climate change policies shows that, for 40 percent of surveyed cities, lack of information on the local impacts of climate change is a major challenge to climate change planning and implementation (compared to the 27 percent who report being challenged by a lack of data on GHG emissions)(Aylett 2013a).

Behind the efforts of many cities that are taking steps to address climate change and other sustainability concerns lies the work of leaders, often termed *policy champions*, who frame climate and other concerns as policy issues and put them onto the political agenda (Betsill and Bulkeley 2007). Effective leadership strategies comprise the capacity to leverage resources from national and international networks, to create and promote the right framings of complex issues (such as climate mitigation as a means to save money and promote green growth), to create collective consensus, and to institute a shared understanding about the policy direction of a city (Cashmore and Wejs 2014). For instance, scholarship has found that leadership from a mayor, from senior elected officials, or from senior managers is a fundamental enabler of successful climate mitigation strategies (Aylett 2013b). However, for the leadership of individuals to persist, it must be complemented by legal and regulatory changes, by investments in institution building (Hughes and Romero-Lankao 2014), and by a strong civil society (see, for example, Manizales).

13.6 Concluding Remarks

While local governments face many obstacles, they also possess a variety of instruments and policy options for governance, such as land-use planning, transportation systems, building codes, and closer ties to constituents working on the ground. These instruments can help strengthen and trigger action by other levels of government and by private and civil society actors. The level of independence and capacity to govern sustainability and resilience varies across urban areas, but there are still many potential and often untapped possibilities available to urban actors to create effective actions. Urban actors vary in their levels of leadership, access to information, legal mandates, and financial resources. Thus, most innovative approaches will unavoidably need to consider both bottom-up and top-down strategies that can help nurture innovations and experiments to achieve sustainable, effective, and fair urban environmental governance.

The remaining chapters in this section look closely at the governance of environmental change and transformations through different forms of experimentation. They examine the actors driving experimentation to shed light on the conditions, momentum, and institutional contexts in which experimentations operate and how they affect the dynamics of urban change. The authors also engage with the conflicts and contestations arising from dominant interests vested in space accessibility and use in cities, all of which are related to different narratives and perceptions about what desirable and inclusive development looks like in cities.

🌐 References

Agrawala, S., M. Carraro, N. Kingsmill, E. Lanzi, M. Mullan, and G. Prudent-Richard. 2011. Private Sector Engagement in Adaptation to Climate Change. OECD Environment Working Paper.

Ahern, J. 2011. From Fail-Safe to Safe-to-Fail: Sustainability and Resilience in the New Urban World. *Landscape and Urban Planning* 100 (4): 341–43.

Andonova, L.B. 2010. Public-Private Partnerships for the Earth: Politics and Patterns of Hybrid Authority in the Multilateral System. *Global Environmental Politics* 10 (2): 25–53.

Aylett, A. 2013a. Networked Urban Climate Governance: Neighborhood-Scale Residential Solar Energy Systems and the Example of Solarize Portland. *Environment and Planning C: Government and Policy* 31 (5): 858–75.

Aylett, A. 2013b. The Socio-Institutional Dynamics of Urban Climate Governance: A Comparative Analysis of Innovation and Change in Durban (KZN, South Africa) and Portland (OR, USA). *Urban Studies* 50 (7): 1386–1402.

Barrero, L.S.V. 2013. The Bioplan: Decreasing Poverty in Manizales, Colombia, through Shared Environmental management, in S. Bass, H. Reid, D. Satterthwaite, and P. Steele (eds.), *Reducing Poverty and Sustaining the Environment. The Politics of Local Engagement*, Earthscan: London, pp. 44–77.

Bendor, R., J. Anacleto, D. Facey, S. Fels, T. Herron, D. Maggs, R. Peake, J. Robinson, M. Robinson, and J. Salter. 2015. Sustainability in an Imaginary World. *Interactions* 22 (5): 54–57.

Betsill, M., and H. Bulkeley. 2007. Looking Back and Thinking Ahead: A Decade of Cities and Climate Change Research. *Local Environment* 12 (5): 447–56.

Betsill, M.M., and H. Bulkeley. 2004. Transnational Networks and Global Environmental Governance: The Cities for Climate Protection Program. *International Studies Quarterly* 48 (2): 471–93.

Biermann, F., M.M. Betsill, J. Gupta, N. Kanie, L. Lebel, D. Liverman, H. Schroeder, B. Siebenhüner, and R. Zondervan. 2010. Earth System Governance: A Research Framework. *International Environmental Agreements: Politics, Law and Economics* 10 (4): 277–98.

Bulkeley, H., V. Castán Broto, M. Hodson, and S. Marvin. 2010. *Cities and Low Carbon Transitions*. Vol. 35. Routledge.

Bulkeley, H., L. Coenen, N. Frantzeskaki, C. Hartmann, A. Kronsell, L. Mai, et al., Urban Living Labs: Governing Urban Sustainability Transitions, *Current Opinion in Environmental Sustainability* 22: 13-17.

Burch, S., A. Shaw, A. Dale, and J. Robinson. 2014. Triggering Transformative Change: A Development Path Approach to Climate Change Response in Communities. *Climate Policy* 1-21.

Castan-Broto, V. and H. Bulkeley. 2013. A survey of urban climate change experiments in 100 cities. *Global Environmental Change* 23 (1): 92-102.

Carpenter, S.R., and W.A. Brock. 2008. Adaptive Capacity and Traps. *Ecology and Society* 13 (2): 40. www.ecologyandsociety.org/vol13/iss2/art40/

Cashmore, M., and A. Wejs. 2014. Constructing Legitimacy for Climate Change Planning: A Study of Local Government in Denmark. *Global Environmental Change* 24: 203-12.

Davoudi, S., K. Shaw, L. Jamila Haider, A.E. Quinlan, G.D. Peterson, C. Wilkinson, Hartmut Fünfgeld, D. McEvoy, L. Porter, and S. Davoudi. 2012. Resilience: A Bridging Concept or a Dead End? 'Reframing' Resilience: Challenges for Planning Theory and Practice Interacting Traps: Resilience Assessment of a Pasture Management System in Northern Afghanistan Urban Resilience: What Does It Mean in Planning Practice? Resilience as a Useful Concept for Climate Change Adaptation? The Politics of Resilience for Planning: A Cautionary Note: Edited by Simin Davoudi and Libby Porter. *Planning Theory & Practice* 13 (2): 299-333.

Ferguson, B., N. Frantzeskaki, and R. Brown. 2013. A Strategic Program for Transitioning to a Water Sensitive City, *Landscape and Urban Planning* 117: 32-45.

Fernández, I.C., D. Manuel-Navarrete, and Robinson T.-S. 2016. Breaking Resilient Patterns of Inequality in Santiago de Chile: Challenges to Navigate Towards a More Sustainable City. *Sustainability* 8 (8): 820. doi:10.3390/su8080820

Field C.B., M. van Aalst, N. Adger, D. Arent, J. Barnett, R. Betts, et al. 2014. Technical Summary, in Field, C.B., V.R. Barros, D.J. Dokken, K.J. Mach, M.D. Mastrandrea, and T.E. Bilir, et al. (eds.), *Climate Change 2014: Impacts, Adaptation, and Vulnerability. Part A: Global and Sectoral Aspects. Contribution of Working Group II to the Fifth Assessment Report of the Intergovernmental Panel on Climate Change*. Cambridge: Cambridge University Press, pp. 35-94.

Folke, C., T. Hahn, P. Olsson, and J. Norberg. 2005. Adaptive Governance of Social-Ecological Systems. *Annual Review of Environment and Resources* 30: 441-73.

Frantzeskaki, N., J. Wittmayer, and D. Loorbach 2014. The Role of Partnerships in 'Realizing' Urban Sustainability in Rotterdam's City Ports Area, the Netherlands, *Journal of Cleaner Production*, 65: 406-417. http://dx.doi.org/10.1016/j.jclepro.2013.09.023.

Frantzeskaki, N., V. Castan-Broto, L. Coenen, and D. Loorbach (eds.). 2017. *Urban Sustainability Transitions*, New York: Routledge.

Gartland, L.M. 2012. *Heat Islands: Understanding and Mitigating Heat in Urban Areas*. Routledge.

Geels, F.W., and J. Schot. 2007. Typology of Sociotechnical Transition Pathways. *Research Policy* 36 (3): 399-417.

Hamin, E.M., and N. Gurran. 2009. Urban Form and Climate Change: Balancing Adaptation and Mitigation in the U.S. and Australia. *Habitat International, Climate Change and Human Settlements*, 33 (3): 238–245. doi:10.1016/j.habitatint.2008.10.005.

Holgate, C. 2007. Factors and Actors in Climate Change Mitigation: A Tale of Two South African Cities. *Local Environment* 12 (5): 471–484. doi:10.1080/13549830701656994.

Hughes, S. 2013. Justice in Urban Climate Change Adaptation: Criteria and Application to Delhi. *Ecology and Society* 18 (4): 48.

Hughes, S., and P. Romero-Lankao. 2014. Science and Institution Building in Urban Climate-Change Policymaking. *Environmental Politics* 23 (6): 1023–1042. doi:10.1080/09644016.2014.921459.

Kern, K., and G. Alber. 2008. Sustainable Energy, and Climate Policy. 2008. Governing Climate Change in Cities: Modes of Urban Climate Governance in Multi-Level Systems. *Competitive Cities and Climate Change* 171.

Lawhon, M., and J.T. Murphy. 2012. Socio-Technical Regimes and Sustainability Transitions Insights from Political Ecology. *Progress in Human Geography* 36 (3): 354–78.

Loorbach, D., and J. Rotmans. 2010. The Practice of Transition Management: Examples and Lessons from Four Distinct Cases. *Futures* 42 (3): 237–246.

Loorbach, D., N. Frantzeskaki, and F. Avelino. 2017. Sustainability Transitions Research: Transforming Science and Practice for Societal Change, *Annual Review of Environment and Resources*, 42: 599–626, doi.org/10.1146/annurev-environ-102014-021340.

Markard, J., R. Raven, and B. Truffer. 2012. Sustainability Transitions: An Emerging Field of Research and Its Prospects. *Research Policy* 41 (6): 955–967.

Nevens, F., N. Frantzeskaki, D. Loorbach, and L. Gorissen. 2013. Urban Transition Labs: Co-Creating Transformative Action for Sustainable Cities, *Journal of Cleaner Production* 50: 111–122.

Park, S.E., N.A. Marshall, E. Jakku, A.-M. Dowd, S.M. Howden, E. Mendham, and A. Fleming. 2012. Informing Adaptation Responses to Climate Change through Theories of Transformation. *Global Environmental Change* 22 (1): 115–126.

Patterson, J., K. Schulz, J. Vervoort, S. van der Hel, O. Widerberg, C. Adler, M. Hurlbert, K. Anderton, M. Sethi, and A. Barau. 2016. Exploring the Governance and Politics of Transformations Towards Sustainability, *Environmental Innovation and Societal Transitions* 24: 1–16.

Poustie, M., N. Frantzeskaki, and R. Brown. 2016. A Transition Scenario for Leapfrogging to a Sustainable Urban Water Future in Port Vila, Vanuatu, *Technological Forecasting and Social Change*, 105(April): 129–139. doi:10.1016/j.techfore.2015.12.008

Robinson, J., and R.J. Cole. 2015. Theoretical Underpinnings of Regenerative Sustainability. *Building Research & Information* 43 (2): 133–143.

Romero-Lankao, P. 2007. How Do Local Governments in Mexico City Manage Global Warming? *Local Environment* 12 (5): 519–535.

Romero-Lankao, P., and D.M. Gnatz. 2013. Exploring Urban Transformations in Latin America. *Current Opinion in Environmental Sustainability* 5 (3–4): 358–367. doi:10.1016/j.cosust.2013.07.008.

Romero-Lankao, P., D.M. Gnatz, O. Wilhelmi, and M. Hayden. 2016. Urban Sustainability and Resilience: From Theory to Practice. *Sustainability* 8 (12): 1224. doi:10.3390/su8121224

Romero-Lankao, P., K. Gurney, K. Seto, Mikhail Chester, R.M. Duren, S.H., L.R. Hutyra, et al. 2014. A Critical Knowledge Pathway to Low-Carbon, Sustainable Futures: Integrated Understanding of Urbanization, Urban Areas and Carbon. *Earth's Future* 2 (10): 515–532. doi:10.1002/2014EF000258.

Romero-Lankao, P., J. Hardoy, S. Hughes, A. Rosas-Huerta, R. Borquez, and D.M. Gnatz. 2015. Multilevel Governance and Institutional Capacity for Climate Change Responses in Latin American Cities, in *The Urban Climate Challenge Rethinking the Role of Cities in the Global Climate Regime. Cities and Global Governance*. Routledge, pp. 179–204.

Rutherford, J., and O. Coutard. 2014. Urban Energy Transitions: Places, Processes and Politics of Socio-Technical Change. *Urban Studies* 51 (7): 1353–1377.

Schaer, C. 2015. Condemned to Live with One's Feet in Water? A Case Study of Community Based Strategies and Urban Maladaptation in Flood Prone Pikine/Dakar, Senegal. *International Journal of Climate Change Strategies and Management* 7 (4): 534–551.

Shaw, A., S. Burch, F. Kristensen, J. Robinson, and A. Dale. 2014. Accelerating the Sustainability Transition: Exploring Synergies between Adaptation and Mitigation in British Columbian Communities. *Global Environmental Change* 25: 41–51.

Smith, A., and A. Stirling. 2010. The Politics of Social-Ecological Resilience and Sustainable Socio-Technical Transitions. *Ecology and Society* 15 (1): 11. www.ecologyandsociety.org/vol15/iss1/art11/

Solecki, W., R. Leichenko, and K. O'Brien. 2011. Climate Change Adaptation Strategies and Disaster Risk Reduction in Cities: Connections, Contentions, and Synergies. *Current Opinion in Environmental Sustainability* 3 (3): 135–141. doi:10.1016/j.cosust.2011.03.001.

Späth, P., and H. Rohracher 2012. Local Demonstrations for Global Transitions—Dynamics across Governance Levels Fostering Socio-Technical Regime Change Towards Sustainability. *European Planning Studies.*, 20: 461–479.

Wejs, A. 2014. Integrating Climate Change into Governance at the Municipal Scale: An Institutional Perspective on Practices in Denmark. *Environment and Planning C: Government and Policy* 32 (6): 1017–1035.

Young, O.R. 2002. The Institutional Dimensions of Environmental Change: Fit, Interplay, and Scale. MIT Press.

Chapter 14: To Transform Cities, Support Civil Society

Niki Frantzeskaki, Adina Dumitru, Julia Wittmayer, Flor Avelino, and Michele-Lee Moore

14.1 Introduction

Civil society's current engagement in providing and fostering sustainability practices and services illustrates that civil society's role has expanded beyond advocacy, and that some civil society organizations aim to address the challenge of inclusivity via sustainability innovations. While some civil society organizations may provide basic services that are no longer met by a changing welfare state, others may play a critical role in changing unsustainable social, ecological, economic, and cultural patterns. In part, the different configurations of civil society visible today have emerged in response to social movements, and grassroots initiatives (Tomozeiu and Joss 2014; Williams et al. 2014; Warshawsky 2015).

Civil society organizes itself in collectives, networks, and nested hubs; mobilizes resources (people, ideas, and funds); and arrives to the wider public through its attempts to put sustainability into practice. For those affected by significant urban challenges, who thus become interested in transforming our cities and societies district by district and community by community, the sense of change that civil society brings can often be seen as a sign of hope that humanity can, collectively, steer away from a deeper crisis or trap. But at the same time, the activities of civil society can create systems where governments can avoid or limit their responsibility in taking daring action to deal with the structural, persistent problems behind these unsustainability crises.

We follow Androff (2012) and Belloni (2001) in understanding civil society as a broad notion, encompassing grassroots organizations, community-based organizations, advocacy groups (such as NGOs), coalitions, professional associations, and other organizations that operate between the state, individuals, and the market. This heterogeneity means that civil society includes various institutional logics, and it crosses the boundaries between formal and informal, public and private, for-profit and nonprofit. With civil society's initiatives and social innovation networks proliferating across Europe, it is relevant to consider what is understood by civil society, its role in sustainability transitions, and how this role evolves and changes in different socioeconomic and socio political contexts, across sectoral domains (such as energy, food, mobility, built environment, and education), and across spatial scales (local, regional, national).

Sustainability transitions are about deep, radical change towards sustainability in ways of thinking, doing, and organizing (Frantzeskaki and de Haan 2009), as well as in ways of knowing and relating (Loorbach et al. 2017). As such, the roles that actors assume and actively pursue in the course of a sustainability transition relate to their capabilities to mobilize resources and creativity and to exercise power for transformative action (Wittmayer and Rach 2016). Current sustainability transitions research has identified that not only is the role of civil society changing, but so are the forms of civil society participation in such transitions. Specifically, the adoption of new roles for civil society actors has led to a transformation of their relationships and forms of engagement with other actors (state actors, market-based actors, and so on). However, in the field of sustainability transitions research, studies on civil society have mostly been focused on the phenomena of community energy (Seyfang et al. 2013, 2014; Hargreaves et al. 2013; Smith et al. 2015) and the role of civil society and social movements in energy transitions more generally (Smith 2012, Seyfang and Haxeltine 2012).

Invigorating the role of civil society in sustainability transitions in sectors other than energy will further contribute to clarifying the importance of such sectoral contexts and add to debates on human-environment interactions in sustainability science. With civil society encompassing and representing a wide array of interests, values, and behaviors, a further examination and conceptualization of its evolving roles is needed. This will shed light on the social and economic dimensions of sustainability, as well as uncover the tensions between these and the environmental dimension of sustainability at local and global levels (Miller 2015).

14.2 The Nature of Civil Society

If we are to understand how civil society develops and how it participates in sustainability transitions, we need to have a clearer articulation of what civil society is. Some argue it encompasses grassroots and community-based organizations, advocacy groups (such as NGOs), coalitions, professional associations, and other organizational forms (Androff 2012; Belloni 2001); for other authors in sustainability transition studies civil society refers to all organizations that are not part of the state. One thing that is agreed in the literature is that the state and civil society are different, with civil society being autonomous from the state. The border between the two is not a "hard" border, meaning it is sometimes difficult to decide whether an organization is part of civil society or the state. In some cases, civil society confronts the state (therefore NGOs are sometimes described *as* civil society; think, for example, of Greenpeace campaigns against deep drilling or nuclear power stations), while in other cases, civil society works alongside the state (for example, in the areas of health). A more recently expressed view is that civil society can be understood as a battleground where those competing for power (both the state and civil society *organizations*) confront each other. At the next level down, a battle for hegemony also takes place *within* civil society organizations. As Räthzel et al. (2015: 160) write, there is a need "to investigate civil society as a 'force-field' in which multiple inter- and intra-relationships interact. While state and civil society organizations may oppose each other, and occupy dual positions in the space of civil society, they are present within each other."

The discourses and practices of community-by-community transformation performed by civil society hold the potential to consider afresh how civil society can initiate and support sustainability transitions while responding to citizen demands for more direct participation in decision-making and more control over defining collective courses of action. We argue that civil society performs a new function in society: civil society is altering deep-seated societal values and beliefs in urban areas towards more sustainable ones, creating and establishing social-ecological and economic literacy and putting knowledge into action for sustainability (Moore and Westley 2011). Such profound change creates the conditions for demand and acceptability of sustainability policies.

14.3 The Roles of Civil Society in Urban Sustainability Transitions

The roles of civil society and the ways in which it interacts with other actors are diverse. In order to capture the recent shifting roles and new forms of civil society, we base our analysis on empirical case study work about civil society in urban sustainability transitions from five research EU-funded projects: ARTS, GLAMURS, GUST, InContext, and TRANSIT. Researchers across these five European research projects convened in a workshop in Rotterdam, the Netherlands, to investigate the role of civil society in sustainability transitions. During the workshop, a wide diversity of empirical cases also informed the discussion and deepened the questions on how to systematically conceptualize the roles of civil society in sustainability transitions and how to search for new evidence.

The case presentations and debates at the workshop allowed researchers with an in-depth knowledge of specific case studies to identify the recurrence of three different roles civil society organizations play and three categories of dangers they face in their interactions with state institutions and actors. This initial inductive analytical framework was then used to orient a thorough literature review, intended to systematize a larger pool of analyzed cases in urban sustainability transitions in Europe. The review covered articles from 2010 to 2015, along with some key additional references from earlier years. Even though many publications were identified (860 papers in total) and thoroughly reviewed, in this chapter, we emphasize those that take a critical perspective on the interactions and interdependencies between civil society and urban systems of provisioning and governance (81 papers). The conceptualized roles are novel to the fields of urban governance and sustainability transitions as a result of our work for this chapter and a related positioning paper (Frantzeskaki et al. 2016).

This chapter characterizes three major roles for civil society as being central to the success of moving towards sustainability transitions. First, local initiatives by civil society can *pioneer and model new practices that can then be picked up by other actors* (for example, policy-makers), eventually leading to incremental or radical changes in our practices and ways of organizing things. Civil society can therefore be an integral part of, and driver for, such transformations; by establishing new connections in the system, it may trigger wider change. Second, civil society can *also fill the void left by a changing welfare state*, thereby safeguarding and serving social needs, but doing so in new ways. Last, it can act *as a hidden innovator – innovating in the shadows, disconnected from public or market actors* – through initiatives that may contribute to sustainability, yet remain disconnected from wider society. There are challenges with each of these roles; we will discuss each in turn below.

14.4 Civil Society as Pioneer, Model, and Driver for Sustainability Transitions

In the last decades, we have witnessed increasing skepticism about the ability of dominant institutions (such as national governments and large businesses) to support transformations, and a growing distrust of their interest in adopting a social agenda alongside economic and political agendas (Birch and Whittam 2008). Given the understanding and local knowledge that civil society has gained in urban contexts through people's direct experience of systemic problems, once initiated, civil society actors' efforts can lead to a fast-paced realization of new ideas and new approaches for more socially, culturally, and ecologically responsible governance (Aylett 2010, 2013). Their proximity to local urban contexts, flexibility (due to operating on the fringes of complex bureaucratic settings), and elasticity allow for transformative innovation to be created and seeded by and through civil society. Civil society organizations have the knowledge and capacity to bring about projects that directly contribute to sustainability, showcasing and gathering evidence in favor of their feasibility as legitimate alternatives. Aylett (2013: 862) argues that "community organizations can show the feasibility of alternative practices" and points out the direct impact civil society has in providing evidence of "what works" for sustainability.

Civil society is generally concerned with ensuring that marginalized voices are heard by decision-makers and can participate in ongoing debates on solutions and governance for sustainability transitions (Calhoun 2012). As such, civil society can advocate for more radical and progressive ideas, rather than "returning to old ideals" (Calhoun 2012). The radicalism of innovation that civil society creates is also shaped "by the attempt to sustain local levels of organization (including local culture as well as social networks) that make possible ... relatively effective collective action" (Calhoun 2012: 12). Beyond acting as advocates, though, civil society organizations are often modeling the innovations themselves, and rapidly experimenting and adapting ideas to the local context, which, if successful, can contribute to altering ways of doing, organizing, and thinking (cultures, structure, and practices) (Boyer 2015; Burggraeve 2015; Bussu and Bartels 2014; Calhoun 2012; Carmin et al. 2003; Cerar 2014; Christmann 2014; Creamer 2015; Foo et al. 2014; Forrest and Wiek 2015; Fuchs and Hinderer 2014; Garcia et al. 2015; Kothari 2014; Magnani and Osti 2016; Seyfang and Smith 2007; Seyfang and Longhurst 2013; Seyfang et al. 2014; Somerville and McElwee 2011; Touchton and Wampler 2014; Verdini 2015; Zajontz and Laysens 2015; Walker et al. 2014; Warshawsky 2014; Wagenaar and Healey 2015).

If we zoom in to the workings of sustainability transition initiatives led by civil society, we see that they can provide empirical ground or proof of concept for new market forms (such as shared economy, or economy of the common good (Felber 2015), or for new economic structures (such as co-management, cooperatives, and alternative currencies (Orhangazi 2014; Riedy 2013; Walljasper 2010) by responding to a market need in a socially, culturally, and ecologically responsible and value-creating way, or in a socially structured way (Somerville and McElwee 2011). As such, civil society organizations can gain both direct and indirect in market structures as well as in business organizations "through other stakeholders ... via increasing consumer awareness" (Harangozo and

Zilahy 2015). An example of an initiative led by a socially driven enterprise is the Impact Hub Rotterdam, a "locally rooted, globally connected social enterprise with the ambition to connect, inspire and support professionals within and beyond the public, private and third sectors working at 'new frontiers' to tackle the world's most pressing social, cultural, and, environmental challenges." (Impact Hub Rotterdam 2015). Essentially, Impact Hub Rotterdam offers access to a working space and to a community of people working on meaningful ideas related to sustainability. Rather than competing, its members (mainly social entrepreneurs themselves) are supportive of one another, as it is in everybody's interest that all members have maximum impact in shaping the world more sustainably (Wittmayer et al. 2015). In this way, the Impact Hub stretches standard ideas of how a company *ought* to be run, and demonstrates how companies *could* operate, as everybody is invited to co-shape the structures, space, and content of the Impact Hub and how a company relates to its immediate surroundings. The Impact Hub Rotterdam is connected to a global network of Impacts Hubs and, at the same time, is firmly rooted in a disadvantaged neighborhood of Rotterdam and aims to add value to these immediate surroundings by engaging in partnerships with local government, welfare organizations, and schools.

Civil society organizations not only alter ways of organizing, but also alter practices that relate to urban lifestyles. By connecting evidence on environmental degradation and impact from the global scale to local practices, civil society organizations have been able to target ways of living and consuming in cities. Being linked to a community of practice via creating stronger ties with others enforces citizens' efforts towards leading a low-carbon lifestyle (Howell 2013). Examples that illustrate this point emerge from civil society organizations in cities that have focused on food production, distribution, and consumption (Laestadius et al. 2014). Miazzo and Minkjan (2013) show how food can be an instrument of invention and inspiration for more sustainable lifestyle choices, as well as an entry point for holistic understandings of how lifestyles connect local to global solutions and challenges. Food-centered/food-focused civil society initiatives around the Global North partake in city making and in urban regeneration projects. As Miazzo and Minjan (2013: n.p.) note, "locally based food production, processing, distribution and consumption initiatives are supporting social equity and improving economic, environmental and social outcomes." Food initiatives can be instrumental in creating urban planning synergies with local governments and in altering planning practices and approaches to include social interests, ideas, and innovations. As such, they can influence how urban regeneration may be designed and implemented, and may contribute to the creation of institutional spaces needed to revitalize local economies.

One of the main findings of the GLAMURS project has been that living more authentic lifestyles and experiencing more meaningful connections to others, especially around food production and consumption, are among the main motivations for starting and joining sustainability grassroots initiatives (Dumitru et al. 2016). An example of one food cooperative that brings together fulfillment of such motivations, as well as contributing to altering urban planning policies in the city of Rome and enhancing their own model of land stewardship, is the Cooperativa Romana Agricoltura Giovani, or Coraggio, one of the case studies selected in GLAMURS. The cooperative joins together women and men (farmers, agronomists, chefs, architects, day workers, anthropologists, and educators) with a passion for sustainable agriculture, healthy food production, and environment and landscape preservation. It is committed to developing an urban agricultural model that is healthy, organic, and multifunctional. Overall, Coraggio's aim is to replace degraded concrete buildings in the neighborhood with a new way of living based on environmental concerns, on respecting the dignity of labor, and on the social value and meaning of agriculture. Coraggio carried out a public debate with the Rome Municipality to obtain the concession of public lands to young farmers who can create public, multifunctional farms capable of producing food as well as services (agricultural training and experimentation, didactics, workshops, urban gardening, food services, restoration, green tourism, and outdoor sports). This transfer of lands was successful, and farmers have been managing it since 2015.

In Rotterdam, the civil society-led initiative "Uit je eigen stad" (From your own city) has emerged because of individuals desiring access to locally produced food for local consumption and the removal of middlemen in the food market. The initiative is based on a farm that also has an adjacent restaurant and market, all of which were built on vacant space in the former city harbor of Rotterdam. The civil society organization holds seminars and information days on how urban dwellers can grow their own food in the city and how to celebrate vegetarian cuisine; it has grown into a learning hub not only for urban citizens but also for smaller-scale urban farming initiatives in the city of Rotterdam. The "Uit je eigen stad" initiative contributed not only to the rethinking of vacant space in the city harbor area, but also in reimagining life in an industrial city during its slow transition to post-industrialization. The first five years of operation have positioned the founders in a diversifying and upscaling pathway; in response, the initiative has now connected and collaborates with multiple food entrepreneurs. It is prime example of successfully establishing sustainable local food production with traditional methods, with hydroponics and aquaponics that reuse waste nutrients, and with a fully operational restaurant as a circular organic food initiative.

Many cities face challenge of segregation when less affluent neighborhoods with higher proportions of low-skilled individuals who have little education and find it difficult to remain employed become socially and economically separated (Zwiers and Koster 2015; van Eijk 2010). Civil society initiatives in these neighborhoods often respond to socioeconomic needs, including providing individuals with new skills to integrate them in society and the job market. Gorissen et al. (2017) further illustrate that civil society initiatives contribute to establishing new local markets and repurposing existing, but unused, infrastructure for sustainable services and jobs.

An example of a civil society organization performing this function is Cultural Workplace, a foundation in Rotterdam. It originated from a one-year project by the Museum Rotterdam, which focused on creating encounters between inhabitants by renting a former shop-space in the middle of the neighborhood. Some of the interactions of residents were recorded as "modern heritage," for example, through a radio programme. The project reached "unusual suspects" and, subsequently, a core group of those individuals stood up to continue and even broaden the purpose of the initiative, which now also includes a range of skills training workshops.

Civil society organizations also play a facilitating role between individual citizens and local and state institutions because they are trusted by individuals, employ "locally legitimate mechanisms" in mediation and communication (Stephenson 2011), and serve as a buffer of first responses from and to individuals in the event of a market failure. They thus serve as empowering contexts, enabling the seeking of new courses of action (Stephenson 2011) and working as vehicles for individual political engagement (Androff 2012; cf. Belloni 2001). Civil society organizations do not operate in isolation; rather, they interact in many ways with dominant government and market logics. This raises questions concerning the distance they establish from the "centers of power" and whether they can be truly transformative. Tension occurs when civil society actors need to decide whether they strictly adhere to their core values and try to fit in while transforming dominant structures, or make compromises to make their organization adaptable to the system in which it operates (Seyfang and Smith 2007: 593).

14.5 Civil Society as a Self-Organizing Actor

Civil society operates as a self-organizing actor to meet social needs that have not historically been provided by the state or the market (Androff 2012; Barber 2013; Belloni 2001; Bonds et al. 2015; Brunetta and Caldarice 2014; Caraher and Cavicchi 2014; Célérier and Botey 2015; Christiansen 2015; Desa and Koch

2014; Devolder and Block 2015; Ferguson 2013; Flint 2013; Foo et al. 2014; Franklin 2013; Hasan and Mcwilliams 2015; Kothari 2014; Krasny et al. 2014; Mehmood 2016; Riedy 2013; Sagaris 2014; Sonnino 2014; Staggenborg and Ogrodnik 2015; Warshawsky 2015). They establish self-help dynamics (Bacq and Janssen 2011; Horsford and Sampson 2014) and contribute to new social orders of active citizens (Riedy 2013). Local civil society can counterbalance neoliberal policies and, in this way, reflect "renewed forms of democracy, solidarity and embrace of difference" (Williams et al. 2014: 2799).

When advocating or protecting common interests, issues, or values, civil society (organizations) can be aligned with or can be seen as forming a social movement. From the perspective of urban politics and urban governance, "social movements, nonviolent actions, and civic protest are not just efforts at reforming democracy, they are democracy in action" (Barber 2013). Androff (2012: 298) addresses the democratic role of civil society for advocating social justice issues, including human rights issues that are neither influenced nor framed by political agendas in a so-called truth-seeking mission that "counters the propaganda, misconceptions, myths and untruths that are often used to create a climate of fear and intimidation and can help in reducing the stereotypes, dehumanization and discrimination that often accompany violence and injustice." An interesting example in this regard is the participatory budgeting initiative – a participatory democracy practice – in the Indische Buurt, a neighborhood of Amsterdam. Here, the initiative of citizens aiming to understand and increase their say in municipal budgeting united with the initiative of a local government for more budget transparency, together making "for more budget transparency and accountability on the local level and strengthens participatory democracy by increasing the awareness, knowledge and influence of citizens in the neighborhood about and on the municipal budget" (Wittmayer and Rach 2016). The citizen-led initiative was based on a Brazilian practice of budget monitoring aiming to increase transparency and legitimacy of budgets based on ideas of human rights, social justice, and democracy. A fair distribution of public resources is considered key in this respect. Civil society organizations also restore the ability of local communities to connect with different urban stakeholders – not only with the local government but also with businesses – establishing multiplicity in connections and possible collaborations (Harangozo and Zilahy 2015).

Another noteworthy example of a citizen initiative providing a space that promotes social contact and intergenerational exchange while people are having fun and acquiring new skills is the network of Repair Cafes in Schiedam, Delft, and The Hague, chosen as case studies in the GLAMURS project. Repair Cafés are free, accessible meeting places where people gather to fix broken objects by sharing knowledge of and experience with repairing things, as well as to simply have a good time with other people. One of the main aims of Repair Cafés is to reduce the amount of waste that our society produces by extending the lifetime of objects, while also teaching people that broken items can often be repaired. The Repair Cafés have also fulfilled an important social function by offering a pleasant environment in which people can meet and bolster or strengthen social contacts. Repair Cafés also provide low-cost repair options for people that cannot afford to go to regular repair venues. Martine Postma, a journalist, started the first Repair Café in Amsterdam. Based on the success of the first Repair Café, people have set up many Repair Cafés within and outside the Netherlands since 2009. In March 2016, there were over one thousand Repair Cafés in 24 different countries; their number is still growing. Postma is still actively involved in the national Repair Café Foundation and currently works on the diffusion of Repair Cafés around the world.

With the ability to articulate social needs and to experience and express the way new practices and approaches can contribute to desirable urban situations, civil society furthers the capacity to self-organize and for citizens to serve their own needs. As such, local civil society can also establish the "capacity to act," or even counterbalance neoliberal policies and, in this way, can reflect "renewed forms of democracy, solidarity and embrace of difference" (Williams et al. 2014). An example of self-organization contributing to changes in policy is the reopening of a community center in a disadvantaged neighborhood of Rotterdam by a local action group. Beginning in 2011, the local community center had been closed due to several municipal and organizational choices, such as the decision of the local municipality not to include resources for the center in a newly issued tender for welfare work. The action group investigated possibilities for reopening the center, including intensive lobbying with different organizations, launching a petition, and acquiring and disseminating information regarding ownership structure financial obligations, and neighborhood needs. Beginning in 2012, the action group formed a foundation and unofficially reopened the center, taking on all daily tasks on a voluntary basis, notwithstanding ongoing negotiations with the municipality regarding rent and exploitation, which were not settled until 2015.

This act of self-organization did not happen in a vacuum – additional initiatives in Rotterdam were trying to achieve the same goal. Civil society organizations and their networks create polycentric arrangements via co-provision of services (Healey 2015; Holden et al. 2015) and by supporting more economically resilient communities, or communities "consisting in economies of specialisation and flexibility" (Giammusso, 1999). However, such patterns blur civil society organizations' functions with those of a retreating welfare state, and put them at risk of becoming stretched until their innovative potential, flexibility, and elasticity disappear in the face of existing demands.

14.6 Civil Society as Hidden Innovator

Civil society acts as a hidden innovator that contributes to sustainability while often remaining disconnected from other spheres of social life (Bacq and Janssen 2011; Célérier and Botey 2015; Desa and Koch 2014; Doci et al. 2015; Dowling et al. 2014; Feola and Nunes 2014; Forrest and Wiek 2015; Fraser and Kick 2014; Garcia et al. 2015; Hasan and McWlliams 2015; Healey 2015; Healey and Vigar 2015; Horsford and Sampson 2014; Napawan 2016; Staggenborg and Ogrodnik 2015; Romero-Lankao 2012; Viitanen et al. 2015; Zhang et al. 2015). In accordance with this mode of operation, civil society often innovates with the "rules in use" rather than with the "rules of the game," meaning that they address lower-level institutions and their informal counterparts, and prioritize applying results in practice, then manifesting contrasts with existing policies and other types of formal institutions. This pattern of action is often reinforced by the public engagement and stewardship programs cities have in place for planning and by the governance of regeneration programs (Shandas and Messer 2008).

Researchers increasingly note the desire of civil society initiatives to remain below the radar, because, they explain, exposure comes at the expense of time and effort not spent on pursuing their founding mission. It therefore challenges the (perhaps naïve) notion that civil society wants to be discovered. The reluctance of civil society actors to become visible can be viewed in a few ways: (a) it could be the result of negative experiences, in which they have been instrumentalized by others, or, (b) it could be an expression of a desire to step away from wider society and pursue one's own aspirations and ideas "far from the maddening crowd" (Androff 2012; cf. Belloni 2001). In such cases, do alternative pathways that rely on civil society maintaining its original, alternative status would work better for citizens and cities?

A clear case of citizen initiatives striving to create an alternative to existing consumerist and accelerated lifestyles are the Romanian ecovillages studied in GLAMURS: Stanciova Ecovillage, Aurora Community, and Armonia Brassovia. These types of communities are notable among other sustainability-related lifestyle initiatives because they require their members to undergo a more radical, across-the-board transition to new lifestyle choices, consumption habits, and time-use patterns. They are usually built on the principles of permaculture, downshifting, and a sharing economy. Promoting a safe space for experimentation with a different lifestyle is present in these initiatives. This does not necessarily mean that they are invisible (as they are very open to contacts with other such initiatives and a diversity of societal actors), but it does mean they exert efforts to protect the boundaries of their experimental spaces.

If we extend our scope of analysis to the food domain, one illustrative example of a hidden pioneer enhancing a short supply chain of organic food is Zocamiñoca, a cooperative of responsible consumption in the city of A Coruña (region of Galicia, Spain) whose main objective is to facilitate access to organic products. The initiative promotes short food distribution circuits and the consumption of healthy, locally sourced food products, while also striving to assure a sustainable livelihood for local organic producers. They actively promote a change in consumption habits towards local, seasonal, and organic products. Beyond such consumption patterns, they actively encourage local participation through a structure of working groups on different sustainability themes centered on food. With more than 300 members, they have become a hub for innovative and participatory activities focused on food, and represent a place where members experience a change towards slower, sustainable lifestyles that spill over into other lifestyle domains. They promote new values of trust and strive to embed them in norms governing the relationships between producers and consumers, joined by a set of common goals and a locally embedded, common identity (Dumitru et al. 2016).

At the same time, civil society can be a medium for local people to participate towards a common mission or vision (Androff 2012; Feola and Nunes 2014). Arentsen and Bellekom (2014) point out that community energy initiatives, for example, are "seedbeds of innovation" in their aim to hybridize and embed sustainable energy practices and in their questioning of dominant energy practices and institutions, yet, they have little impact on wider institutional transformations or shifts. Schools of social innovation say that social innovation is a product of networks, groups, and formal and informal organizations rather than of "hero entrepreneurs" (Bacq and Janssen 2011). Likewise, civil society can be legitimized and supported by programs for community participation and activation when they are instrumentalized for active engagement rather than for passive consultation, and when the resulting synthesis incorporates ideas and innovative practices (Shandas and Messer 2008).

Thus, via active engagement of civil society in local programs and projects of urban regeneration, civil society can play a role in establishing a sense of place that is also transformative in the sense that it incorporates new ways of sustainable thinking, living, and practicing. Still, it remains unknown what the position civil society organizations can functionally occupy between overexposure and remaining in the shadows, and the effects that these different positions have on achieving transformations.

14.7 Unintended Effects of the Three Roles

Within the European Union, civil society initiatives can be used by neoliberal agendas to support their narratives on decentralization and retreat of the state (Blanco et al. 2014). As it recognizes that neoliberalism is contested (Newman 2014), civil society may unintentionally be supporting the argument of a "self-servicing" society that does not require governmental support for basic services, such as elderly care and education (Ferguson 2013). National and local governmental agencies responsible for social policy and welfare policy cut offs can use the presence and activities of civil society as justifications for the reductions of welfare state programs. We also observe a new surge of community-based initiatives, and that the state is increasingly calling upon "the community" to take over public services and responsibilities. This is especially apparent in discussions on welfare state reform such as the "Big Society" – as a part of which governments are reorganizing their responsibilities and tasks vis-à-vis their citizens (Scott 2010; Jordan 2012; Tonkens et al. 2013). Such reductions in government support come with a caveat: by relying on civil society for service delivery, there is a risk of deepening social inequalities between and within communities, given their uneven capacities to self-sustain and self-organize. By relying on "the community" in this way, the state further neglects structural injustice and masks ineffective governance by empowering civil society at the outset, and by reassigning responsibility from government onto local actors (Williams et al. 2014). What strategies civil society organizations use to resist such abdication of responsibility, while simultaneously assuring they have the resources to operate, is still an open empirical question.

Further, civil society activities can be structured as political responses to injustice or to deeply marginalized systems of provision. As political expressions, they can also be exclusive or provoke conflict. These facets position civil society as a politicized actor, often stigmatized as the troublemaker rather than seen as the whistle-blower for market failures. In view of the way large-scale infrastructure projects are planned in cities, the question remains how social needs and voids of services are being accounted for in such plans, and how to balance the risk of co-opting of civil society by utilizing it for municipal ends with the risk of ignorance or avoidance of civil society when designing such large service delivery plans (Meng et al. 2014).

As responsibility is reassigned to civil society, the state can hamper civil society organizations through complex and weighty bureaucratic procedures which can be challenging for organizations with minimal resources allocated for formulating responses (Blanco et al. 2014; Borzel and Risse 2010; Engelke et al. 2015; Fisher et al. 2012; Fraser and Kick 2014; Ferguson 2013; Giammusso 1999; Hajer 2016; Semino 2015; Williams et al. 2014). Furthermore, if state policies and programs intervene by establishing or incentivizing civil society organizations to serve existing political agendas (Tomozeiu and Joss 2014; Griffin 2010), these organizations may be viewed as the "visible hand of the state," which, in turn, may demoralize and delegitimize individuals working to create bottom-up civil society organizations, and may affect local democratic politics to a wider extent. The overexposure resulting from such utilization of civil society organizations by the state can leave these actors exhausted and erode their mission (Bonds et al. 2015; Busa and Garder 2014; Creamer 2015; Felicetti 2013; Foo et al. 2014; Giammusso 1999; Griffin 2010; Holden et al. 2015; Moss et al. 2014; Peck et al. 2013; Semino 2015; Shannon 2014; Tomozeiu and Joss 2014; Williams et al. 2014; Warshawsky 2015).

14.8 A New Urban Research Agenda Considering Civil Society's Roles

Here, we formulate a few reflections for a new research agenda based on our account of the roles of civil society in emerging sustainability transitions. We propose five overarching future directions below.

Identify conditions that enable civil society to play a transformational role in cities. Intermediary organizations can help to create links between initiatives and government structures. However, in some cases, these are not needed, as initiatives can interact directly with governments and businesses (for instance, through leaders that link different organizations). This intermediate space can exist and might not need to be institutionalized in the form of lead offices, formal projects, or organizations. However, an intermediate space can be important for the spread of initiatives, and is a place where radical, bottom-up initiatives that operate only on the fringe of the system and top-down, dominant actors in the existing system can meet. Intermediary actors are therefore organizations and bridging actors that span several groups, such as, for example, living labs.

For example, in urban areas where segregation takes a socio spatial form, initiatives will tend to operate more in those communities where needs are greatest. Their presence will thus signal the hot spots of social and economic unsustainability while also, at least on some occasions, provide an excuse for welfare state program reforms to exclude areas from support due to the presence of self-organized communities. This argument implies a trade-off: while there is effectiveness in welfare measures when they are targeted spatially, since this enables their inclusion in policy mixes of urban regeneration, as Zwiers and Koster (2015) argue, universal welfare programs for income support and re-skilling for socioeconomic integration "generate the broadest base of support." Civil society organizations can indicate which urban localities or "which types of urbanity" are most vulnerable to social and economic segregation and can create an evidence-based for local welfare redistribution that has a systemic impact on urban poverty. When operating in this way, civil society (organizations) can radically alter welfare distribution approaches and transform cities towards social resilience.

Adopt a dynamic understanding of the role of civil society and use empirical designs that can capture their fluid nature in cities. While the emergence of civil society organizations is routinely hailed as a positive wave of change, we need to break away from romanticizing inclinations, and empirically investigate the different roles that civil society actors play in complex configurations of interactions and diverse agendas. Additional cross-case study analyses and meta-analyses, rather than in-depth, single case study research, would contribute to understanding both the bright and the dark sides of civil society roles today.

Understand and assess the true diversity of civil society in the present context. Civil society has a fluid and flexible nature that enables it to operate outside immobilizing constraints. This fluidity also leads to the existence of a wide variety of actors, who experience tensions with other actors and within their own groups. To avoid overly simplified typologies, civil society actors should be incorporated into research cycles so that they are embedded more deeply in sustainability transitions, to allow for a new understanding of the diversity of urban civil society and its multiple roles.

Conceptualize and empirically explore the dynamic interactions between urban civil society actors and other actors and elements in the contexts in which they are embedded. Rich conceptualizations of contexts that include geographical scale, as well as trends in cultural values, and perceptions of roles of different actors, are still largely missing from the literature on civil society. Examining the multiplicity of interactions beyond the dichotomy of collaboration and conflict will deepen the understanding of actors' impact and enable a response to contextual conditions, as well as an understanding of the impact of context on sustainability transitions. Future empirical research should identify the conditions under which civil society may play a transformational role versus those that mainly lead it to perpetuating the status quo.

Encourage knowledge coproduction about the impacts of social agency and the relationship to urban transitions. As Haapio (2012) notes, there is no urban society that can achieve sustainability on its own, so partnership work across multiple actors will bring about new solutions to deal with societal and ecological challenges. In an increasing specialized and globalized world, knowledge exists in multiple forms and is the property of different actors. Research must turn to new modes of producing knowledge in cooperation and cocreation with other actors (Frantzeskaki and Kabisch 2016). Including civil society actors in research design and cycles, as proposed earlier, will position them as local experts, contributing their knowledge and practices to local innovations rather than being involved solely in engagement and in raising awareness, when the capacity of civil society (organizations and actors) allows for this level of contribution (Laestadius et al. 2014).

Acknowledgments

This article is based on research carried out as part of the Accelerating and Rescaling Sustainability Transitions Project ("ARTS" Project) funded by the European Union's Seventh Framework Programme (FP7) (grant agreement 603654), the Transformative Social Innovation Theory ("TRANSIT") project, which is funded by the European Union's Seventh Framework Programme (FP7) (grant agreement 613169), the GLAMURS Project funded by the European Union's Seventh Framework Programme, and the JPI Urban Europe funded Project GUST (Governance of urban sustainability transitions). The views expressed in this article are the sole responsibility of the authors and do not necessarily reflect the views of the European Union.

☙ *References*

Aylett, A. (2010), Conflict, Collaboration, and Climate Change: Participatory Democracy and Urban Environmental Struggles in Durban, South Africa. *International Journal of Urban and Regional Research*, 34: 478–495.

Aylett, A. (2013), Networked Urban Climate Governance: Neighborhood-Scale Residential Solar Energy Systems and the Example of Solarize Portland, *Environment and Planning C: Government and Policy*, 31: 858–875.

Androff, D. (2012), Can Civil Society Reclaim Truth? Results from a Community-Based Truth and Reconciliation Commission. *The International Journal of Transitional Justice*, 6: 296–317.

Arentsen, M., and Bellekom, S. (2014), Power to the People: Local Energy Initiatives as Seedbeds of Innovation?, *Energy, Sustainability and Society*, 4:2, www.energsustainsoc.com/content/4/1/2

Bacq, S., and Janssen, F. (2011) The Multiple Faces of Social Entrepreneurship: A Review of Definitional Issues Based on Geographical and Thematic Criteria, *Entrepreneurship & Regional Development: An International Journal*, 23:5–6: 373–403, DOI: 10.1080/08985626.2011.577242

Barber, B.R. (2013), *If Mayors Ruled The World: Dysfunctional Nations, Rising Cities*. Yale University Press.

Blanco, I., Griggs, S. and Sullivan, H. (2014), Situating the Local in the Neoliberalisation and Transformation of Urban Governance, *Urban Studies*, 51(15): 3129–3146

Belloni, R. (2001), Civil Society and Peace Building in Bosnia-Herzegovina, *Journal of Peace Research*, 38(2): 163–180.

Birch, K., and Whittam, G. (2008): The Third Sector and the Regional Development of Social Capital, *Regional Studies*, 42:3: 437–450

Bonds, A., Kenny, J.T. and Wolfe, R.N. (2015), Neighborhood Revitalization without the Local: Race, Nonprofit Governance, and Community Development, *Urban Geography*, 36:7: 1064–1082, DOI: 10.1080/02723638.2015.1049479

Borzel, T.A., and Risse, T., (2010), Governance without a State: Can It Work? *Regulation and Governance*, 4; 113–134. DOI:10.1111/j.1748–5991.2010.01076.x

Boyer, R.H.W. (2015), Grassroots Innovation for Urban Sustainability: Comparing the Diffusion Pathways of Three Ecovillage Projects, *Environment and Planning A*, 45: 320–337.

Burggraeve, R. (2015), Volunteering and Ethical Meaningfulness. *Foundations of Science*, 20(2): 1–4.

Busa, J.H., and Garder, R. (2014), Champions of the Movement or Fair-Weather Heroes? Individualization and the (A)Politics of Local Food. *Antipode*. http://dx.doi.org/10.1111/anti.12108.

Bussu, S., and Bartels, K.P.R. (2014), Facilitative Leadership and the Challenge of Renewing Local Democracy in Italy, *International Journal of Urban and Regional Research*, 38(6): 2256–2273, DOI:10.1111/1468–2427.12070

Brunetta, G., and Caldarice, O. (2014), Self-Organization and Retail-Led Regeneration: A New Territorial Governance within the Italian Context, *Local Economy*, 29(4–5): 334–344.

Calhoun, C. (2012), *The Roots of Radicalism: Tradition, the Public Sphere, and Early Nineteenth-Century Social Movements*, Chicago: University of Chicago Press.

Caraher, M., and Cavicchi, A. (2014), Old Crises on New Plates or Old Plates for a New Crises? Food Banks and Food Insecurity. *British Food Journal*, 116(9): 1382–1391.

Carmin, J., Hicks, B., and Beckmann, A. (2003), Leveraging Local Action: Grassroots Initiatives and Transboundary Collaboration in the Formation of the White Carpathian Euroregion, *International Sociology*, 18:4: 703, DOI: 10.1177/0268580903184004

Célérier, L., and Botey, L.E.C. (2015), Participatory budgeting at a community level in Porto Alegre: a Bourdieusian interpretation, *Accounting, Auditing & Accountability Journal*, 28(5): 739–772, dx.doi.org/10.1108/AAAJ-03-2013-1245.

Cerar, A. (2014), From Reaction to Initiative: Potentials of Contributive Participation, *Urbani izziv*, 25(1). DOI: 10.5379/urbani-izziv-en-2014-25-01-002

Christiansen, L.D. (2015), The Timing and Aesthetics of Public Engagement: Insights from an Urban Street Transformation Initiative, *Journal of Planning Education and Research*, 35(4): 455–470.

Christmann, G.B. (2014), Investigating Spatial Transformation Processes: An Ethnographic Discourse Analysis in Disadvantaged Neighbourhoods. *Historical Social Research*, 39(2): 235–256. DOI: http://dx.doi.org/10.12759/hsr.39.2014.2.235-256

Creamer, E. (2015), The Double-Edged Sword of Grant Funding: A Study of Community-Led Climate Change Initiatives in Remote Rural Scotland, *Local Environment*, 20:9: 981–999, DOI: 10.1080/13549839.2014.885937.

Desa, G., and Koch, J.L. (2014), Scaling Social Impact: Building Sustainable Social Ventures at the Base-of-the-Pyramid, *Journal of Social Entrepreneurship*, 5:2: 146–174, DOI: 10.1080/19420676.2013.871325.

Devolder, S., and Block, T. (2015), Transition Thinking Incorporated: Towards a New Discussion Framework on Sustainable Urban Projects, *Sustainability*, 2015, 7: 3269–3289; DOI:10.3390/su7033269.

Doci, G., Vasileiadou, E., and Petersen, A.C. (2015), Exploring the Transition Potential of Renewable Energy Communities, *Futures*, 66: 85–95.

Dowling, R., McGuirk, P., and Bulkeley, H. (2014), Retrofitting Cities: Local Governance in Sydney, Australia, *Cities*, 38: 18–24.

Dumitru, A., Garcia-Mira, R., Diaz-Ayude, A., Macsinga, I., Pandur, V., and Craig, T. (2016), GLAMURS Deliverable 4.2, GLAMURS: EU SSH.2013.2.1–1. Grant agreement no:613169.

Engelke, H., Mauksch, S., Darkow, I.L., and von der Gracht, H.A. (2015), Opportunities for Social Enterprise in Germany – Evidence from an Expert Survey, *Technological Forecasting and Social Change*, 90: 635–646.

Felber, C. (2015), *Change Everything: Creating an Economy for the Common Good*, ZED Books.

Felicetti, A. (2013), Localism and the Transition Movement, *Policy Studies*, 34(5–6): 559–574, DOI: 10.1080/01442872.2013.862449

Feola, G., and Nunes, R. (2014), Success and Failure of Grassroots Innovations for Addressing Climate Change: The Case of the Transition Movement, *Global Environmental Change*, 24: 232–250.

Fisher, D.R., Campbell, L.K., and Svendsen, E.S. (2012), The Organizational Structure of Urban Environmental Stewardship, *Environmental Politics*, 21:1: 26–48, dx.doi.org/10.1080/09644016.2011.643367

Flint, R.W. (2013), *Practice of Sustainable Community Development, A Participatory Framework for Change*, Berlin: Springer.

Ferguson, N. (2013), *The Great Degeneration, How Institutions Decay and Economies Die*. Penguin Publishers.

Foo, K., Martin, D., Wool, C., and Polsky, C. (2014), The Production of Urban Vacant Land: Relational Placemaking in Boston, MA Neighborhoods, *Cities*, 40: 175–182.

Forrest, N., and Wiek, A. (2015), Success Factors and Strategies for Sustainability Transitions of Small-Scale Communities – Evidence from a Cross-Case Analysis, *Environmental Innovation and Societal Transitions*, 17: 22–40.

Franklin, S. (2013), Role, Class, and Community Organizing in Support of Economic Justice Initiatives in the Twenty-First Century, *Community Development Journal*, DOI:10.1093/cdj/bst035

Frantzeskaki, N., and de Haan, H.(2009), Transitions: Two Steps from Theory to Policy, *Futures*, 41: 593–606.

Frantzeskaki, N., and Kabisch, N. (2016), Designing a Knowledge Co-Production Operating Space for Urban Environmental Governance – Lessons from Rotterdam, the Netherlands and Berlin, Germany, *Environmental Science and Policy*, 62: 90–98.

Frantzeskaki, N., Dumitru, A., Anguelovski, I., Avelino, F., Bach, M., Best, B., et al. (2016), Elucidating the Changing Roles of Civil Society in Urban Sustainability Transitions, *Current Opinion in Environmental Sustainability*, 22: 41–50.

Fraser, J.C., and Kick, E.L. (2014), Governing Urban Restructuring with City-Building Nonprofits, *Environment and Planning A*, 46: 1445–1461.

Fuchs, G., and Hinderer, N. (2014), Situative Governance and Energy Transitions in a Spatial Context: Case Studies from Germany, *Energy, Sustainability and Society*, 4:16.

Garcia, M., Eizaguirre, S., and Pradel, M. (2015), Social Innovation and Creativity in Cities: A Socially Inclusive Governance Approach in Two Peripheral Spaces of Barcelona, *City, Culture and Society*, 6: 93–100.

Giammusso, M., (1999), Civil Society Initiatives and Prospects of Economic Development: The Euro-Mediterranean Decentralized Co-Operation Networks, *Mediterranean Politics*, 4:1: 25–52, DOI: 10.1080/13629399908414674

Gorissen, L., Spira, F., Meyers, E., Velkering, P., and Frantzeskaki, N. (2017), Moving Towards Systemic Change? Investigating Acceleration Dynamics of Urban Sustainability Transitions in the Belgian City of Genk, *Journal of Cleaner Production*, Article in Press

Griffin, L. (2010), Governance Innovation for Sustainability: Exploring the Tensions and Dilemmas, *Environmental Policy and Governance* 20(6): 365–369.

Haapio, A. (2012), Towards Sustainable Urban Communities, *Environmental Impact Assessment Review*, 32: 165–169.

Hasan, S., and McWilliams, C. (2015), Civil Society Participation in Urban Development in Countries of the South: The Case of Syria, *International Planning Studies*, 20(3): 228–250, DOI: 10.1080/13563475.2014.984663

Hajer, M. (2016), in Brugmans, G., van Dinteren, J., and Hajer, M., (eds), IABR-2016- The Next Economy.

Harangozo, G., and Zilahy, G. (2015), Cooperation between Business and Non-Governmental Organizations to Promote Sustainable Development, *Journal of Cleaner Production*, 89: 18–31.

Hargreaves, T., Hielscher, S., Seyfang, G., and Smith, A. (2013). Grassroots Innovations in Community Energy: The Role of Intermediaries in Niche Development. *Global Environmental Change*, 23(5): 868–880.

Healey, P. (2015), Citizen-Generated Local Development Initiative: Recent English Experience, *International Journal of Urban Sciences*, 19(2): 109–118. DOI: 10.1080/12265934.2014.989892

Healey, P., and Vigar, G. (2015), Creating a Special Place: The Ouseburn Valley and Trust in Newcastle, *Planning Theory & Practice*, 16(4): 565–567, DOI: 10.1080/14649357.2015.1083153

Holden, M., Li, C., and Molina, A., (2015), The Emergence and Spread of Ecourban Neighbourhoods around the World, *Sustainability*, 7: 11418–11437; DOI:10.3390/su70911418

Horsford, S.D., and Sampson, C. (2014), Promise Neighborhoods: The Promise and Politics of Community Capacity as Urban School Reform, *Urban Education*, 49(8): 955–991. DOI: 10.1177/0042085914557645

Howell, R.A. (2013), It's Not (Just) "The Environment, Stupid!" Values, Motivations, and Routes to Engagement of People Adopting Lower-Carbon Lifestyles, *Global Environmental Change*, 23: 281–290.

Jordan, B. (2012), Making Sense of the 'Big Society': Social Work and the Moral Order, *Journal of Social Work*, 12(6): 630–646.

Kothari, A. (2014), Radical Ecological Democracy: A Path Forward for India and Beyond, *Development*, 57(1): 36–45. DOI:10.1057/dev.2014.43

Krasny, M.E., Russ, A., Tidball, K.G., and Elmqvist, T. (2014), Civic Ecology Practices: Participatory Approaches to Generating and Measuring Ecosystem Services in Cities, *Ecosystem Services*, 7: 177–186.

Laestadius, L.I., Neff, R.A., Barry, C.I., and Frattaroli, S. (2014), "We Don't Tell People What To Do": An Examination of the Factors Influencing NGO Decisions to Campaign for Reduced Meat Consumption in Light of Climate Change, *Global Environmental Change*, 29: 32–40.

Loorbach, D., Frantzeskaki, N., and Avelino, F. (2017), Sustainability Transitions Research: Transforming Science and Practice for Societal Change, *Annual Review of Environment and Resources*, 42(November).

Magnani, N and Osti, G. (2016), Does Civil Society Matter? Challenges and Strategies of Grassroots Initiatives in Italy's Energy Transition, *Energy Research and Social Science*, 13: 148–157.

Mehmood, A. (2016), Of Resilient Places: Planning for Urban Resilience, *European Planning Studies*, 24(2); 407–419, http://dx.doi.org/10.1080/09654313.2015.1082980

Meng, M., Koh, P.P., Wong, Y.D., and Zhong, Y.H. (2014), Influences of Urban Characteristics on Cycling: Experiences of Four Cities, *Sustainable Cities and Society*, 13: 78–88.

Miazzo, F., and Minkjan, M. (eds.) (2013), *Farming the City, Food as a Tool for Today's Urbanization*. The Netherlands: CITIES.

Miller, T.R. (2015), *Reconstructing Sustainability Science, Knowledge and Action for a Sustainable Future*, Earthscan.

Moore, M., and Westley, F. (2011). Surmountable Chasms: Networks and Social Innovation for Resilient Systems. *Ecology and Society*, 16(1): 5. www.ecologyandsociety.org/vol16/iss1/art5/

Moss, T., Becker, S., and Naumann, M. (2014), Whose Energy Transition Is It, Anyway? Organization and Ownership of the Energiewende in Villages, Cities and Regions, *Local Environment*, 20(12): 1547–1563, DOI: 10.1080/13549839.2014.915799

Napawan, N.C. (2016), Complexity in Urban Agriculture: The Role of Landscape Typologies in Promoting Urban Agriculture's Growth, *Journal of Urbanism: International Research on Placemaking and Urban Sustainability*, 9(1): 19–38, DOI:10.1080/17549175.2014.950317

Newman, J. (2014), Landscapes of Antagonism: Local Governance, Neoliberalism and Austerity, *Urban Studies*, 51(15): 3290–3305.

Orhangazi, O. (2014), Contours of Alternative Policy Making in Venezuela, *Review of Radical Political Economics*, 46: 221.

Peck, J., Theodore, N., and Brenner, N. (2013), Neoliberal Urbanism Redux? *International Journal of Urban and Regional Research*, 37(3): 1091–1099. DOI:10.1111/1468-2427.12066

Räthzel, N., Uzzell, D., Lundstrom, R., and Leandro, B. (2015), The Space of Civil Society and the Practices of Resistance and Subordination, *Journal of Civil Society*, 11(2): 154–169.

Riedy, C. (2013), Waking Up in the Twenty First Century, *On the Horizon*, 21(3): 174–186.

Romero-Lankao, P. (2012), Governing Carbon and Climate in the Cities: An Overview of Policy and Planning Challenges and Options, *European Planning Studies*, 20(1): 7–26.

Shandas, V. and Messer, W.B. (2008) Fostering Green Communities through Civic Engagement: Community-Based Environmental Stewardship in the Portland Area, *Journal of the American Planning Association*, 74(4): 408–418

Sagaris, L. (2014), Citizen Participation for Sustainable Transport: The Case of "Living City" in Santiago, Chile (1997–2012), *Journal of Transport Geography*, 41, 74–83.

Scott, M. (2010), Reflections on the Big Society, *Community Dev J*, 46(1): 132–137

Shannon, J. (2014), Food Deserts: Governing Obesity in the Neoliberal City. *Progress in Human Geography*, 38(2): 248–266.

Semino, S.M. (2015), Governmental Promotion of Social Cohesion and Its Effect on Local Civil Society Organizations: How These Institutions Respond to the Inclusion of Vulnerable Groups as Active Citizens, *Social Policy and Society*, 14(2): 189–201, doi:10.1017/S1474746414000207

Seyfang, G., and Smith, A. (2007), Grassroots Innovations for Sustainable Development: Towards a New Research and Policy Agenda. *Environmental Politics*, 16 (4): 584–603. doi:10.1080/09644010701419121

Seyfang, G., and Haxeltine, A. (2012) 'Growing Grassroots Innovations: Exploring the Role of Community-Based Social Movements in Sustainable Energy Transitions', *Environment and Planning C*, 30(3): 381–400.

Seyfang, G., Hielscher, S., Hargreaves, T., Martiskainen, M., Smith, A. (2014) A Grassroots Sustainable Energy Niche? Reflections on Community Energy in the UK, *Environmental Innovation and Societal Transitions*, 13: 21–44. DOI: 10.1016/j.eist.2014.04.004

Seyfang, G., Longhurst, N. (2013) Desperately Seeking Niches: Grassroots Innovations and Niche Development in the Community Currency Field, *Global Environmental Change*, 23(5): 881–891. DOI: 10.1016/j.gloenvcha.2013.02.007

Seyfang, G., Park, J.J., and Smith, A. (2013), A Thousand Flowers Blooming? An Examination of Community Energy in the UK. *Energy Policy* 61: 977–989.

Seyfang, G., and Smith A. (2007), Grassroots Innovations for Sustainable Development: Towards a New Research and Policy Agenda, *Environmental Politics*, 16(4): 584–603.

Smith, A. (2012) Civil Society in Sustainable Energy Transitions in Verbong, G. and Loorbach, D. (eds.) *Governing the Energy Transition: Reality, Illusion or Necessity?* Routledge Studies in Sustainability Transitions. New York: Routledge, pp. 180–202.

Smith, A., Hargreaves, T., Hielscher, S., Martiskainen, M., and Seyfang, G. (2015). Making the Most of Community Energies: Three Perspectives on Grassroots Innovation. *Environment and Planning A*, 0308518X15597908.

Somerville, P., and McElwee, G. (2011), Situating Community Enterprise: A Theoretical Exploration, *Entrepreneurship & Regional Development: An International Journal*, 23(5–6): 317–330, DOI: 10.1080/08985626.2011.580161

Sonnino, R. (2014). The New Geography of Food Security: Exploring the Potential of Urban Food Strategies. *The Geographical Journal*. http://dx.doi.org/10.1111/geoj.12129.

Staggenborg, S., and Ogrodnik, C. (2015), New Environmentalism and Transition Pittsburgh, *Environmental Politics*, 24(5): 723–741, http://dx.doi.org/10.1080/09644016.2015.1027059.

Tomozeiu, D., and Joss, S. (2014), Adapting Adaptation: The English Eco-Town Initiative as Governance Process. *Ecology and Society*, 19(2): 20. http://dx.doi.org/10.5751/ES-06411-190220.

Tonkens, E., Grootgegoed, E., and Duyvendank, J.W. (2013), Introduction: Welfare State Reform, Recognition and Emotional Labour, *Social Policy and Society*, 12(3): 407–413.

Touchton, M., and Wampler, B. (2014), Improving Social Well-Being through New Democratic Institutions, *Comparative Political Studies*, 4(10): 1442–1469, DOI: 10.1177/0010414013512601

Van Eijk, G. (2010), *Unequal Networks. Spatial Segregation, Relationships and Inequality in the City*, Amsterdam: IOS press.

Verdini, G. (2015), Is the Incipient Chinese Civil Society Playing a Role in Regenerating Historic Urban Areas? *Evidence from Nanjing, Suzhou and Shanghai, Habitat International*, 50: 366–372.

Viitanen, J., Connell, P., and Tommis, M. (2015), Creating Smart Neighborhoods: Insights from Two Low-Carbon Communities in Sheffield and Leeds, United Kingdom, *Journal of Urban Technology*, 22(2): 19–41, DOI: 10.1080/10630732.2014.971537

Walker, J.S., Koroloff, N., and Mehess, S.J. (2014), Community and State Systems Change Associated with the Healthy Transitions Initiative, *Journal of Behavioral Health Services and Research*, 254–271, DOI: 10.1007/s11414-014-9452-5

Wagenaar, H., and Healey, P. (2015), The Transformative Potential of Civic Enterprise, *Planning Theory & Practice*, 16(4): 557–585, DOI: 10.1080/14649357.2015.1083153

Warshawsky, D.N. (2014), Civil Society and Urban Food Insecurity: Analyzing the Roles of Local Food Organization in Johannesburg, *Urban Geography*, 35(1): 109–132, DOI: 10.1080/02723638.2013.860753

Warshawsky, D.N. (2015), The Devolution of Urban Food Waste Governance: Case Study of Food Rescue in Los Angeles, *Cities*, 49: 26–34.

Williams, A., Goodwin, M., and Cloke, P. (2014), Neoliberalism, Big Society, and progressive localism, *Environment and Planning A*, 46: 2798–2815.

Wittmayer, J.M., Avelino, F., and Afonso, R. (eds.) (2015), WP4 CASE STUDY Report: Impact Hub. TRANSIT: EU SSH.2013.3.2–1 Grant agreement no: 613169

Wittmayer, J.M. and Rach, S. (2016), Participatory Budgeting in the Indische Buurt; Chapter 5 of TRANSIT Case Study Report Participatory Budgeting. TRANSIT: EU SSH.2013.3.2–1 Grant agreement no: 613169

Zajontz, T. and Laysens, A. (2015), Civil Society in Southern Africa – Transformers from Below? *Journal of Southern African Studies*, 41(4): 887–904, DOI: 10.1080/03057070.2015.1060091

Zhang, Z., Skitmore, M., de Jong, M., Huisingh, D., and Gray, M. (2015), Regenerative Sustainability for the Built Environment from Vision to Reality: An Introductory Chapter, *Journal of Cleaner Production*, 109: 1–10.

Zwiers, M., and Koster, F. (2015), The Local Structure of the Welfare State: Uneven Effects of Social Spending on Poverty within Countries, *Urban Studies*, 52(1): 87–102.

Chapter 15: Governing Urban Sustainability Transformations

The New Politics of Collaboration and Contestation

Sarah Burch, Sara Hughes, Patricia Romero-Lankao, and Heike Schroeder

15.1 The Urban Politics of Sustainability Transformations

In December 2015, at the Twenty-First Conference of the Parties to the United Nations Framework Convention on Climate Change, 195 countries adopted an ambitious, global climate change agreement that is the first to assign binding commitments to both developing and developed countries. The Paris Agreement, which entered into force on November 4, 2016, aims to limit average warming to "well below" 2°C (potentially 1.5°C), and further highlights the depth of the climate change mitigation and adaptation challenge. Climate change and our collective responses to it represent just one dimension of the broader and more complex project of sustainability: an interwoven set of environmental, social, and economic goals that are contested, evolving, and rooted in a particular place and time. The varied and systems-oriented nature of sustainability is illustrated by the diversity of the Sustainable Development Goals, which were adopted in New York in 2015 and set out an agenda for transformation by 2030.

Calls for transformation have increasingly permeated sustainability and climate change scholarship (Burch et al. 2014; Kates et al. 2012; Westley et al. 2011), with varying foci that include the implications for governance (Biermann et al. 2012; Stirling 2014), climate change adaptation (Kates et al. 2012), urban spaces (McCormick et al. 2013; Romero-Lankao and Gnatz 2013), and the related notion of sustainability transitions (Avelino et al. 2016; Patterson et al. 2016). Even so, the idea of transformation is evolving: depending on the disciplinary bent, empirical domain, and even geographic context of the inquiry, the definition of transformation, and the boundaries of the system being transformed, may shift. For the purposes of this chapter, we understand transformations to be nonlinear changes, including "radical shifts, directional turns or step changes in normative and technical aspects of culture, development or risk management" (Pelling et al. 2015: 113) that may pertain to climate change adaptation, mitigation, or some other dimension of sustainability. These changes may be intentional and managed, or unexpected (Folke et al. 2010; O'Brien 2012), but they always represent a fundamental rethinking of how a system (such as a city, sector, or level of government) should or could function.

The challenge of sustainability transformations intersects with the powerful, inexorable forces of urbanization that nations at all stages of industrialization and socioeconomic development are experiencing. It is clear that urban spaces present a multitude of opportunities for, and obstacles to, sustainability: cities produce approximately 70 percent of global energy-related greenhouse gas emissions (O'Brien 2012); maintain crucial (and potentially vulnerable) infrastructure; influence poverty, affordability, and social services; and shape the consumption of resources such as water and energy through their design and governing institutions. This intersection has sparked interest, in both scholarly and policy circles, in the drivers, dynamics, and sociopolitical implications of innovation at the urban scale. Not solely the domain of government, transforming cities requires the active participation of civil society (see Chapter 14), research communities, and the private sector (Johnson et al. 2015). These actors have roles that may change over the course of an urban sustainability transition (Fischer and Newig 2016), suggesting that strategies to engage them must also shift over time and space.

Despite significant interest, private sector and civil society actors are often under-engaged and underrepresented in climate change and sustainability decisions, with especially limited engagement on issues of climate change adaptation (UN-Habitat 2011). This clashes with the reality that the private sector maintains control over significant sources of emissions and urban land development, and also holds potential for creating and implementing innovative adaptation and mitigation solutions. Small businesses, for instance, may be powerful leverage points, with the potential to shift demand, innovate technologically and organizationally, and collaborate with government. This is especially important in the Global South, given governance limitations and capacity barriers.

Introducing new forms of action and innovation has implications for the urban politics of sustainability transformations. While the broadest possible definition of politics is often taken to refer to "all of the activities of co-operation and conflict" that emerge as humans make decisions about the creation and distribution of resources (Leftwich 1983: 11, as cited by Avelino et al. 2016: 557), we consider politics to involve interactions through which the identity of actors is shaped, their legitimacy established, and their values articulated in the public realm. Transformations in urban spaces, therefore, will bring to light tensions within the process of collective action, especially given the ever-widening array of actors that hold sway over the multilevel governance of societal challenges. Such collaborative work is necessary, but is not politically neutral or uncontested (Bulkeley et al., 2014). As a result, a challenge for urban transformations will be finding ways to negotiate and resolve (or accept) differences in order to reach collaborative outcomes. Collaboration and its challenges also present an opportunity to offer a more nuanced reckoning of power (Avelino and Rotmans, 2011; Avelino and Wittmayer, 2016) in urban systems.

In this chapter, we particularly emphasize that these politics of collaboration are not confined to city hall, but rather play out in efforts to mobilize and coordinate diverse sets of resources in cities. This diffusion of power beyond the traditional realm of governmental actors has implications for the transparency and legitimacy of decision-making. We begin this chapter by collecting conceptual and theoretical tools that have emerged to understand the role of both collaboration and contestation[1] in transitions towards sustainable futures. We explore promising experiments in urban sustainability transformations that have, in turn, shaped local politics and models of governance. We pay particular attention to the capacity of local governance actors to respond to identified sustainability challenges, the networks of interaction they form among themselves and beyond, and the scale of transformation that takes place over time. We elaborate on how new partnerships among public and private actors can deliver on multiple priorities simultaneously, addressing social, economic, and environmental concerns, while also offering opportunities to elicit, explore, and negotiate values. Ultimately, we seek to understand how sustainability transformations are reshaping urban politics more broadly, and are, in turn, revealing new governance questions.

15.1.1 The Role of Collaboration and Contestation in Planting the Seeds of Urban Sustainability Transformations

The explosion of interest in pathways to carbon neutrality and deeper sustainability has led to a variety of framings with at least one dimension in common: regardless of the language used, sustainability and climate change scholars are increasingly exploring examples of policy- and decision-making at the urban scale that offer the promise of accelerated action. Novelty, experimentation, innovation, and transformation surface repeatedly in disciplines (or domains

---

[1] We view collaboration and contestation not as diametrically opposed processes, but rather two dynamics that often simultaneously occur in urban spaces as various actors work together to navigate sustainability transitions.

of scholarship) including public policy, urban and political geography, technology studies, entrepreneurship, social-ecological systems, resilience, and multilevel governance. With the particular goal of unearthing the implications of urban sustainability transitions for the politics and contestation of collaboration, this section explores clusters of research that cross these domains. We focus on the parallel ideas of sustainability transitions and transformations, urban living laboratories, climate change experiments, and sustainability entrepreneurship or innovation.

15.1.2 Sustainability Transitions: Adding Politics, Institutions, and Actors to the Study of Technological and Social Innovation

The diverse domain known as transitions theory has made a key contribution to the study of technological innovation by making explicit the web of social practices and institutional structures that enmesh particular technologies. In acknowledging that sustainable technologies (such as renewable energy systems, building design, and transportation infrastructure) are nested within multiple intersecting sets of rules, and sustained by habitual behaviors that are rooted in values, it becomes clear that transitions are not under the direct control of any single actor (or even any set of actors). As such, there is no single transition trajectory: sustainability represents a set of values that change over time and space, and are likely to be deeply contested.

Transitions theory has coalesced to comprise four strong strands of research (Sarzynski 2015): active intervention in sustainability pathways through *transition management* (Markard et al. 2012); the *multilevel perspective* focusing on the interplay of rules, actors, and technologies at three levels: the niche, regime, and landscape (Rotmans et al. 2001; Smith et al. 2005); cultivation of radical innovations through *strategic niche management* (Geels 2002, 2005a, 2005b; Rip and Kemp 1998); and an examination of the institutional and organizational changes that comprise *technological innovation systems* (Geels and Schot 2008; Kemp and Rip 2001). These domains are interwoven, share traits such as the contextualization of a technology within the underlying sociopolitical and economic fabric, and often explicitly consider the deeply normative and contested goal of sustainability. Transitions theory is most often applied in highly industrialized contexts, but needs to be carefully adapted to urban areas of middle- and low-income countries, where authoritarian states depending on foreign aid and revenues from the global commodities market constrain collaboration options (Lawhon and Murphy 2012; Romero-Lankao and Gnatz 2013). Politics runs throughout all aspects of transitions, acting variously as an enabler of, or barrier to, progress along a particular pathway (Meadowcroft 2011).

Increasingly, calls are being made to add a distinctly spatial perspective to the study of sustainability transitions, which would help build understanding of the diversity of pathways that transitions can follow (given the variety of institutions, resources, and actors present in different places) (Hekkert et al. 2007). Emerging strands of transitions scholarship include calls for a deeper analysis of the politics of these transitions (Coenen et al. 2012), the power dynamics that give rise to particular transition pathways, and the realities of the Global South, where authoritarian and often failing or predatory states define different governance architectures that shape transformations (Meadowcroft 2009, 2011).

Explorations of governance in the transitions literature seek to overcome the failures that have emerged from rigid, hierarchical, fragmented, conventional, top-down, government-centric approaches by moving towards systems-based, flexible, and participatory strategies that foster social learning through governance (Lawhon and Murphy 2012; Romero-Lankao and Gnatz 2013). Urban sustainability transitions can be triggered by regulatory, political, and environmental shifts (Pickett et al. 2013). Key features in a sustainable city include the use of bottom-up management and decision-making, approaching top-down decision-making through a more holistic lens, explicitly addressing the norms and values that shape urban behavior, and creating incentives for the participation of a diverse range of actors in key decisions (van der Brugge and van Raak 2007).

As climate change and sustainability are increasingly recognized as the domain of fluid, multi-actor and multilevel governance, rather than tasks most suited to traditional hierarchical government, transitions theory provides key insights into how sustainability plays out in practice in the urban context. The interplay among an ever-widening array of actors (see, for example, Farla et al. 2012) in the sustainability space offers opportunities for conflicting values to be elicited, negotiated, and put into practice (that is, through policy decisions, technological innovations, and evolving behaviors). Tensions inevitably arise throughout this process, which raises the need for participatory processes (an issue to which we will return later in this chapter) that can account for unequal distribution of power and varying perceptions of legitimacy.

15.2 From Transition to Transformation: A Semantic or Substantive Shift?

The term "transformation" has been gaining traction since the launch of the global research network Future Earth, the Intergovernmental Panel on Climate Change, or IPCC, Special Report on Managing the Risks of Extreme Events and

Disasters to Advance Climate Change Adaptation (Hughes et al. 2013), and the subsequent IPCC Fifth Assessment Report (2012, 2014). This term has been employed and understood differently in various disciplines. For some urban ecologists, for instance, a transformation can be thought of as "radical changes in the form, metabolism, economy and demography of urban ecosystems themselves" (see for example, Revi et al. 2014). To those who employ social-eco-logical or complex adaptive systems approaches, transformation might be defined as "physical and/or qualitative changes in form, structure, or meaning making" (see for example, Revi et al. 2014, citing Pickett et al. 2013) or non-linear changes in fundamental dimensions of a social-ecological system such as culture, development, or risk management (O'Brien 2012). Indeed, thresh-old behavior is increasingly being noted in key earth systems (Folke et al. 2010; Nelson et al. 2007; Pelling 2011), suggesting the need for a transformation in underlying development pathways (Rockstrom et al. 2009; Steffen et al. 2007) or development paradigms, including deeply held values, governance regimes, and patterns of behavior (Burch et al. 2014).

Given the diverse set of "objects" of transformation, metrics may be particu-larly challenging to find, and will inevitably be subjective (that is, change rel-ative to some previous state, as viewed by a particular group or individual who is shaped by their own values and context). With this subjectivity in mind, in looking for examples of transformation (or potential for transformation), we might evaluate the extent to which power relations have shifted, development priorities have changed, or new identities have developed (following Pelling et al. 2015) – issues that are central to the urban political domain. As such, we hypothesize that examples of partnerships or policies that target the root causes of unsustainable development pathways, rather than simply the symptoms, might be more likely to have transformative effects. Examples might include targeting a shift in business models (from solely profit-driven to focused equally on creating social benefit) rather than marginally reducing corporate green-house gas emissions through energy efficiency. Small-scale, local experiments may plant the seeds of these transformations (see the case study sections in this chapter), but other sociopolitical and economic conditions must be present to encourage these seeds to grow into systemic or global changes.

Transformations towards sustainability in the urban context focus atten-tion on the planning and governance dimensions of change, placing a strong emphasis on strategies and policies that trigger radical change in multiple urban systems (such as transportation, lifestyle and consumption, resource management, and others) (Westley et al. 2011). In urban spaces, the pursuit of a fundamental shift in the underlying development pathway opens up the possibility of designing policies that address climate change mitigation, adap-tation, and broader sustainability goals (such as biodiversity, water quality, and social equity) simultaneously (McCormick et al. 2013). This is new territory, however, and may require urban actors to conduct "experiments" in sustainability before considering strategies for scaling these initiatives up and out, with broader urban, national, and global effects. Given the complexity of urban systems and the varied nature of the sustainability challenge, many urban sustainability experiments involve the participation of a wide variety of actors, with social learning and knowledge mobilization as explicit goals.

15.3 Collaboration and Contestation in Urban Living Labs: Moving from Experiment to Transformation

Prevalent in transitions, transformations, and climate governance scholarship is a recurring theme: The process of shifting development pathways is messy, involving networks of actors, each with their own motivations, capacities, and ways of understanding the challenges at hand. As such, collaboration among these actors becomes a crucial enabler of the types of adaptive governance that are required in the context of complex social-ecological systems (Pahl-Wostl et al. 2007). The specific character of this collaboration, including the ways that participants are equipped to engage (see for example, Burch et al. 2010; Burgess et al. 2005), and the scale at which the collaboration plays out (Burch et al. 2014), shape the pace and nature of the sustainability transition.

Urban Living Labs, or ULLs, are emerging as a form of collective urban governance that may address some of the challenges associated with path dependency, distributed authority, and varying legitimacy identified by scholars studying transformations to sustainability (Burch et al. forthcoming, see also Chapter 10). ULLs are considered a form of experiment that fosters learning in a place-explicit (urban) context with multiple actors to develop innovative, scalable sociotechnical interventions to generate a sustainable future (Westley et al. 2011). Key characteristics of ULLs identified include geographical embeddedness; experimentation and learning; participation and user involvement; leadership and ownership; and evaluation and refinement (Bulkeley et al. 2015). The agency of multiple actors is underexplored in current ULL literature, as it is in the broader field of sustainability transitions (Voytenko et al. 2016). Of the many actors who participate in sustainability transitions, small firms (or small- and medium-sized enterprises) represent an example of the value of collaboration and network-building in these urban experiments. This collaboration, however, is not a uniformly smooth or homogenous process: indeed, drawing together multiple actors with divergent motivations (and, in some cases, proprietary knowledge that is closely held) can create messy processes in which goals, and the pathways to achieving them, are disputed.

Participation in innovation networks allows small firms access to sophisticated technology and technological expertise, risks and costs sharing, access to additional market knowledge, fostering a critical mass of companies to advance certain topics and set the agenda, transferring knowledge between partners, and the ability to help develop industry standards (Coenen et al. 2012; Markard et al. 2012). The idea behind these networks is that all participants jointly formulate problems and issues and use each other's experiences and knowledge to generate new ideas and different solutions. The forum for dialogue created by a network, where managers can meet in an atmosphere of trust to discuss problems and solutions that arise in their daily activities, is what many managers of small enterprises need in order to enhance their sense of "security" and reduce their uncertainty when they decide to tackle complex environmental issues (Bos-Brouwers 2010; Hansen and Klewitz 2012). Successful collaborative efforts embrace three interconnected types of work – *conceptual, relational*, and *action driven* – that together build a healthy "learning ecology" for systemic change (or transformation). The most important member organizations to include in collaborative networks are those who represent the aspects and stakeholders of the problem being explored, and that wider exploration of these aspects is encouraging system-change progress (Halila 2007).

For networks to be innovative, diversity among members is paramount. Diverse views, backgrounds, and interests of members allow the network to generate more creative, innovative solutions to issues and challenges. A diversity of views gives way to more fruitful collective learning, which in itself is an essential foundation for whole-system innovation. Network convenors must ensure the network has the resources it needs to do its work over time (Senge et al. 2007). A bottom-up process where members may exercise their influence and bring new ideas into play has proven to be effective at harnessing member ideas and giving them life, leading to common goals and, subsequently, common visions (Loorbach and Wijsman 2013; Svendsen and Laberge 2005). Results from sustainability-oriented networks can be highly diverse, including product innovations (Lehmann 2006; Loorbach and Wijsman 2013), process innovations (Loorbach 2010; Loorbach and Wijsman 2013), implementation of standardized environmental initiatives (Svendsen and Laberge 2005), and the self-development of sustainability-oriented certifications reflecting the priorities of the network (Halila 2007).

Despite what we know about the value of networks, the diffusion of authority to actors beyond the state, and the potential to exploit synergies between various development and environmental priorities, it is quite likely that transformations can only be recognized with the benefit of hindsight (Lehmann 2006). At most, we can identify strategies or approaches that plant the seeds of transformation, or hold transformative *potential*. As introduced above, these seeds could include efforts to institutionalize or embed sustainability priorities in organizational structures and practices, social learning that mobilizes information about successes and failures across niches, and multiscale governance approaches that reveal and capitalize on synergies while avoiding trade-offs.

Taken together, the literatures presented in this chapter suggest a number of characteristics of the multi-actor partnerships focused on sustainability experiments, which might most successfully navigate the tensions between collaboration and contestation. These include (1) partnerships that address the root causes of unsustainability rather than simply the symptoms; (2) participatory processes that equip actors to engage meaningfully, addressing unequal distribution of communicative power and technical knowledge; and (3) efforts that address conceptual, relational, and action-driven types of work. We propose that these characteristics have the potential to generate a more fruitful, legitimate, and transparent brand of sustainability politics in urban spaces.

In practice, sustainability experiments are being carried out in a multitude of contexts, each of which illustrates different dimensions of the dynamics of collaboration in urban spaces. In the sections that follow, we pick up the themes explored above (namely the incremental versus transformative potential of experiments, the importance of meaningful inclusion of a diverse array of actors, and the political dynamics of change) in three case studies from very different parts of the world: New York City, in the United States; London, in the United Kingdom; and Manizales, in Colombia. A robust set of qualitative or quantitative metrics of transformation have not yet been thoroughly tested in empirical settings, so we seek to explore the possibility that these cases are experimenting with strategies that address the root causes of unsustainable development, and may have ripple effects beyond the local scale.

15.4 The Politics of Urban Collaboration in Practice

Case Study 1 Reconciling Conflicting Viewpoints through a New Politics of Collaborative Regulation in New York City

In 2007, New York City, under the leadership of Mayor Michael Bloomberg, released PlaNYC, a plan for the city that aimed, in part, to reduce the city's GHG emissions by 30 percent by the year 2030. The plan was the city's response to projected population growth and the looming threat of changing temperatures, rainfall patterns, and sea level rise. While there are a range of sector-specific targets and initiatives discussed in the plan

---

(for example, waste, transportation, housing), they claim that "collectively these initiatives all address our greatest challenge: climate change" (see for example, Bos et al. 2013; Burch et al. 2014; Geels and Schot 2007).

One way that PlaNYC proposes to achieve this GHG reduction goal is by making the city's buildings more energy efficient and sustainable. New York City's buildings account for approximately 75 percent of the city's GHG emissions due to dense development and relatively accessible public transportation. Reducing energy use in buildings is therefore an important goal, but presents two significant challenges. First, the vast majority of the city's buildings are privately owned, so reducing energy use requires coordinating and motivating thousands of individual building owners. The second challenge is that 85 percent of the buildings that will be in the city in 2030 (when the city needs to meet its GHG emissions reduction target) have already been built. This means that energy conservation measures will have to take place by retrofitting existing buildings, which is often more difficult than building energy efficient buildings from the start. Given these parameters, the city needed a way to target energy use in existing, privately owned buildings to meet its ambitious GHG targets.

To reduce energy use in existing buildings, the city sought to update building codes to incorporate energy efficiency technologies and best practices. This is a firmly regulatory approach to reducing GHG emissions, which city governments often shy away from in fear of industry backlash. One reason New York City has been able to require systematic changes to how the city's buildings use energy is through the use of a collaborative approach to regulation. Based on interviews with decision-makers, managers, and key stakeholders in the city, city documents, and prior scholarly work, we show that the city government used *institutionalized collaborative work* as a strategy to help overcome the challenges of conflicting views and different starting points in relation to the city's climate change goals.

While the goal of energy efficiency might appear to fall squarely within the incrementalism category, the collaborative process followed in this case has the potential to create ripple effects across other urban systems (which could be considered an early indicator of transformation). In 2008, Mayor Bloomberg and City Council Speaker Quinn charged the Urban Green Council (the New York chapter of the US Green Buildings Council) with convening the Green Codes Task Force. The task force and its support network was composed of city managers, environmental groups, technical experts, and representatives from the private sector. Funding for the task force was provided by the Mertz Gilmore Foundation and the New York Community Trust, and meetings were hosted by the Newman Real Estate Institute; a local law firm provided pro bono legal review of the task force's recommendations (City of New York 2007). The task force was asked to develop recommendations for revising the city's various building codes (construction, fire, water, sewer, and so on) in ways that would help the city meet their GHG reduction targets.

After 18 months of meetings, deliberation, and feedback, the task force produced a list of 111 recommendations for changes to the city's building codes. At the time of writing, 53 of these recommendations have been adopted and codified by City Council.[2] These include broad changes, such as introducing environmental protection as a fundamental principle of the construction codes, as well as specific changes, such as insulating exposed pipes during construction. The measures go beyond LEED certification standards for energy efficiency measures, and incorporate social equity goals (American Council for an Energy-Efficient Economy 2014). Taken together, the changes that have already been made to the building codes are estimated to generate a 5 percent reduction in the city's GHG emissions by 2030 (Urban Green Council 2010).

The collaboration underpinning the changes to the city's building code – what might be called "collaborative regulation" – is an important reason for the task force's success (Scheib et al. 2014). Members of the City Council and relevant stakeholders perceived their recommendations as being both *technically informed and supported by key political actors.* According to the American Council for an Energy-Efficient Economy (2014):

> Because the project was initiated by the Mayor and City Council Speaker, it obtained *legitimacy, recognition, and industry buy-in from the outset.* Urban Green Council played a critical role as an independent advisor and convener for the project. The organization has strong ties with both city government and industry, and is viewed as having a practical approach to achieving environmental goals. As a result, the report was able to identify many changes that city agencies or the real estate industry may not have been willing to consider on their own.

Acknowledgment of the need for legitimacy, recognition, and industry buy-in highlights that it is not only the presence of collaboration, or the opportunity for participation, that was important, but rather it was the particular way that the collaborative process tapped into the city's critical political leverage points. At the time, New York City had a powerful and popular mayor in Michael Bloomberg, and his support for the effort lent it credibility and buy-in that other mayors may have had more difficulty generating. Likewise, the task force was convened by an organization (Urban Green Council) that was seen to be relatively politically neutral and technically competent, with one foot in the realm of industry and one foot in the realm of policy. Incorporating technical and industry expertise along with environmental advocacy organizations helped to ensure that the recommendations were seen to be feasible and reasonable.

In many ways, the larger political challenge for these efforts has been that, while "greening" the city's building codes has the potential for large-scale transformation, it is a tedious and rather technical exercise. Indeed, urban transformation can be rather boring and can actually fail to capture the imaginations of commentators (Dolan et al. 2010; Solecki 2012).

The process of greening the city's building codes in this collaborative way has had longer-term implications for the politics of climate change policy in New York City. It generated significant buy-in from the real estate and development industries to the larger project of GHG emissions reductions, such that they are now considered an ally in these efforts rather than a source of political pushback. Mayor Bloomberg went on to use other task forces as he pursued his climate change agenda, such as the Climate Change Adaptation Task Force (2008) and the Building Resiliency Task Force (2013, which followed Hurricane Sandy and was also convened by the Urban Green Council).

Norms of collaboration are developing in New York City and have the potential to significantly enhance the city's ability to meet ambitious GHG reduction targets. In 2014, after being elected mayor, Bill DeBlasio expanded the city's climate change goals to include an 80 percent reduction target by 2050. As a step towards meeting this goal, the city appears to be building on the success of previous collaborative efforts to reduce energy use in the city's buildings, and has formed a Green Buildings Technical Working Group. Like the Green Codes Task Force before it, this technical working group is composed of representatives from real estate, architecture, labor unions, affordable housing, and environmental groups. However, the working group's ability to generate ideas and recommendations that are adopted by the city may depend on the mayor's own legitimacy in this area, the legitimacy assigned to the collaborative process itself, and the technical competency of the recommendations, which remain uncertain.

Returning to our earlier criteria for collaborative approaches that hold the potential for deeper urban sustainability transformations, this case illustrates significant efforts to equip participants with the technical and other skills required to deeply engage in the process (criterion two), but shows little evidence of tackling the root causes of unsustainability (criterion one). This New York City-based collaboration also focused mostly on action-driven types of work rather than deeper conceptual thinking (criterion three), but created relationships that have implications for other climate policy efforts in the city.

Case Study 2 Engaging Small- and Medium-Sized Enterprises in London

London already has an extensive history of climate change mitigation and adaptation action. The level of actions adopted and institutions created to facilitate London's efforts has positioned it as a key player in climate action at the city level (Gronewold 2010). Furthermore, Sadiq Khan, the Labour party mayor elected in 2016, is promising to produce a sea change regarding the environment; Khan himself pledges to become "the greenest mayor ever." He ran for office on an ambitious green platform, which included the promise to "ignite a clean energy revolution" and a vision for "100 percent green energy by 2050" for London (following the footsteps of other Labour-run, major UK cities). Promised measures include banning fracking in London, planting two million trees, providing more electric buses, divesting from fossil fuel industries, and expanding the Ultra Low Emission Zone[3]. Having already embarked on the latter within his first weeks in office[4], Khan's ambition is likely to make significant inroads. Based on interviews with municipal policy-makers, entrepreneurs, and other key stakeholders in London; policy documents; and prior scholarly work, we show how, on the back of strong mayoral leadership, the city is gradually developing its transformative potential through building a strategy of collaborations with the wider city, in particular with small and medium-sized enterprises, or SMEs.

One crucial enabling factor for London's climate actions is its administrative structure. Conceived as the Greater London Authority, or GLA, that administrative structure has a directly elected Assembly and Mayor and certain

---

[3] www.edie.net/news/11/Sadiq-Khan-wins-London-Mayor-election-2016-City-Hall-green-energy/
[4] www.theguardian.com/environment/2016/may/13/sadiq-khan-to-double-size-londons-clean-air-zone-pollution

autonomy in the areas of energy, planning, and transport policy, making it not only possible for London to govern climate change independently from the national government, but a statutory duty (Schroeder and Bulkeley 2009). Primarily under former mayor Ken Livingstone (2000–08), London set the foundations for its approach to climate governance, which is based on strategic partnerships with public and private sector actors (Bulkeley and Schroeder 2011). Livingstone set up the London Climate Change Partnership in 2001 to prepare the city for the impacts of climate change through raising awareness, developing adaptation guidance, and increasing the city's resilience more widely. In 2002, the London Hydrogen Partnership began providing research and development for new hydrogen technologies and, in 2004, the London Energy Partnership began assisting with the delivery of London's energy policy and creating new business opportunities for sustainable energy. Livingstone also issued an Energy Strategy for London in 2004, set up the London Climate Change Agency in 2005, and issued an Action Plan in 2007. This focus on partnerships emerged as a consequence of the mayor's and the GLA's rather limited ability to have significant impacts on the ways in which energy, a significant source of GHG emissions, is produced and used in London (Bulkeley and Schroeder 2008).

Mayor Boris Johnson (2008–2016) continued this trajectory to some extent by opening a cycle hire scheme in 2010 (nicknamed "Boris Bikes"), appointing a Cycling Commissioner for London in 2013, and, in the same year, announcing £1 billion of investment in infrastructure to make cycling safer in London. He also adopted a Climate Change Mitigation and Energy Strategy for London in 2011. It was based on the converging and intensifying challenges of energy security, waste management, and sustainable urban development, paired with the significant opportunities presented by investment in green energy. Crucially, SMEs are highlighted throughout the strategy, recognizing that 99 percent of total businesses in London are SMEs (employing under 250 people each). As SMEs are not covered under London's Green500, which focuses on larger organizations, the strategy outlines five programs specifically targeting energy efficiency in SMEs, some of which were already up and running in 2011, cofunded through the European Regional Development Fund. They included Ecovate – which gave businesses up to five days of support on energy efficiency and brokerage of service suppliers – and URBAN, which provided 81 SMEs with personalized climate change action plans (Bulkeley and Schroeder 2008).

In the past five to ten years, a variety of intermediary enterprises have been created to take advantage of funding (mainly through the European Regional Development Fund) to set up schemes and programmes to engage with SMEs, often in partnership with boroughs and business improvement districts, as well as the London Chamber of Commerce and the London Development Agency (for example, Funding London and Planet Positive). The main goal has been to help SMEs cut costs through reducing carbon emissions. In the words of an interviewee,

> the idea was to try to focus exclusively on the positive, the things that would have financial benefits to SMEs, recognizing that very, very few would have the time or the inclination to do anything for philanthropic or societally beneficial reasons. And so focusing on helping them understand how they could reduce energy use and therefore reduce costs, take advantage of government grants, et cetera. (Interviewee, May 2011)

Increasingly, initiatives can be found outside the mayor's purview. For example, after the GLA ended the Green500, the London Cleantech Cluster is not only continuing the concept but also extending it to all businesses, including SMEs. A key focus is on coordinating the many existing initiatives, networks, opportunities for finance, and business support services.[5]

Years of working with SMEs at small to medium scale throughout London highlights that what is needed as a next step is a more systematic approach, covering a wide range of concerns from overall policy, direction, and goals to an overhaul of procurement policies and procedures to "an organization-wide belief that this can be done" (GLA 2010). Overall, London's approach to engaging with SMEs has been more incremental than transformative, as actor-networks have expanded diagonally to including many actors outside the public sector. Will Mayor Khan reinvigorate engagement with SMEs, and perhaps push London onto a stronger sustainability paradigm? He certainly has pro-business credentials and, as of 2017, has begun to support small businesses more generally; London's SME sector is already engaging with him (for example, see Labour Business 2016).

Engaging a new set of actors – SMEs – in urban sustainability transitions presents an opportunity to deepen the capacity of an important sector to participate in the implementation of sustainability actions. The partnerships created here do not appear to address the root causes of unsustainability (criterion one), but do present an opportunity to equip SMEs to collaborate with government and civil society (criterion two). Some conceptual work (such as co-defining sustainability and identifying unsustainable business practices) and relationship building is clearly evident in this case, but ultimately, the focus here is on incremental action, and the long-term transformative potential is unclear.

---

[5] www.londoncleantechcluster.co.uk/london-cleantech-cluster-2/about-us/

Case Study 3 Innovation in Manizales, Colombia

In recent decades, Manizales, Colombia, has developed an innovative sustainability agenda that has incorporated disaster risk management into urban development policies (Institute for Sustainability 2012). Since the 1970s, Manizales had been expanding over river basins, steep slopes, and other risk-prone areas as a result of the immigration of populations displaced by armed conflict and rural poverty. The housing needs of these migrants, who could not buy into the official land market for housing, were readily filled by illegal land developers, eager to turn a quick profit (Hardoy and Barrero 2014). The occupation and land-use changes in these areas increased the number of landslides and resulted in significant economic and infrastructure losses (Hardoy and Barrero 2014). For example, the 1985 eruption of Nevado de Ruiz resulted in mudslides that buried several settlements and killed about 25,000 people; it still forms part of Manizales's collective memory. In 2011, heavy rains that hit Colombia killed 300 people nationally and resulted in slope failures and mudslides that washed away the pipes that transported water from the treatment plant to Manizales, leaving the population without piped water for ten days (Barrero 2013). Based on city documents and prior comparative work (Romero-Lankao and Gnatz 2013), we attempt to explore urban transitions in cities from Latin America.

Manizales has witnessed the development of social innovations to address sustainability challenges. Actions were taken locally to restrict land and resource use in areas the city shared with Villamaría, its neighboring municipality. The two municipalities partnered with private and civil society organizations, the National University of Colombia's Institute of Environmental Studies, and the Ministry of the Environment to implement joint environmental actions to manage water, tourism, transportation, and recreation (Hardoy and Barrero 2014). The federal government also played a supportive role by launching local environmental action plans seeking to implement UN Local Agenda 21 and to foster "better cities and towns." The National Institute for Natural Resources made a diagnosis of the country's environmental situation and established the Green Municipalities of Colombia program, which gave local authorities remit over these problems. This process created green councils and generated broad popular participation in environmental management.

These multilevel policies opened windows of opportunity for social innovations that, since the 1990s, have taken place in Manizales to integrate environmental and local disaster risk management concerns with an inclusive urban development agenda. Local authorities and universities coproduced an analysis of the risks related to urban development; that analysis supported the integration of disaster risk management with an Environmental Plan (Biomanizales), a Land Use Law (Ley de Ordenamiento Territorial), an Urban Development Plan (Manizales Calidad Siglo XXI), and a Local Agenda 21 Bioplan that fosters policy implementation (Barrero 2013). A strong tradition of participation by civil society and business organizations in implementation strategies, such as environmental observatories, the Slope Guardians program, and eco-parks, has contributed to Manizales progress in the area disaster risk management. In the 1990s, for instance, Manizales allocated 17 percent of its budget to environmental protections and disaster management. To expand the welfare and safety of poor communities situated in risk-prone areas, it constructed 2,320 houses, assimilated 168 hectares of protected green areas into the municipality, and, with university support, financed infrastructure works to lessen the risk of landslides (Hardoy et al. 2011).

Notwithstanding their innovative and pro-poor character, however, the actors involved in Manizales social experiments face a set of challenges. The city has not been able to institutionalize this socially inclusive and integrative approach, which is contingent on the support and political will of the administrations in place (Barrero 2013). Still, actors from civil society, universities, and the business sector have pressed to keep these issues within the urban development agenda of Manizales, even during the administrations of President Uribe (2002–2010), when such integrative approaches lost governmental support, and a managerial approach to disaster risk management focused on emergency responses and infrastructural works gained importance.

No matter how active and engaged civil society is, Manizales illustrates that these capacities are not enough to counter two powerful driving forces of urban development in Latin America and even in Asia: economic pressures to develop land located in risk-prone areas (Hardoy et al. 2011), and informal rules governing access to land, which continue to allow illegal developers to sell land to vulnerable groups (Romero-Lankao et al. 2015). Development in risk-prone areas is also common among developers of housing projects for middle- and high-income groups, who have the clout to obtain building permits (*curadurías*) outside of the regular permitting process. Thus, formal governmental controls and regulations are failing to protect populations even within the licensed developments of Manizales (Romero-Lankao and Gnatz 2013).

Manizales illustrates that innovative experiments can reduce risks in targeted communities and for some at risk populations. Furthermore, social experiments can empower the disenfranchised poor, who would otherwise be forced to live in illegal settlements at risk of floods and mudslides. Such social experiments also benefit sectors closer to the power structure in Manizales, such as the legal developers who build safe dwelling units for the poor. However, it has not been possible to scale up these innovations to counteract the forces of development and growth that are creating pressure for unsustainable and risky land use in Manizales and other cities worldwide. As such, these experiments remain isolated in their effect, and their transformative potential is dampened by the powerful inertia of status quo development.

In Manizales, it appears that collaboration is fraught with powerful economic pressures and informal rules, despite efforts to implement policies that benefit the most vulnerable. The partnerships described here offer evidence for the value of trust-building relational exercises (criterion three), and the value of an approach to poverty reduction that addresses the root causes of that poverty (criterion one). However, even with efforts to better equip stakeholders to engage meaningfully in participatory processes (criterion two), these small experiments are unlikely to have transformative effects without directly tackling the contested domain of pro-development forces.

15.5 Lessons for Research and Practice

As we find ourselves in the midst of the most dramatic migration in human history, from rural to urban areas, we are grappling with the social, environmental, and economic implications of rapid urbanization. The sustainability imperative demands that new strategies be explored to accelerate change, transforming urban systems, social practices, technologies, and governance models. This challenge is largely a social and political one, rather than a technical or economic one. While they are not uniquely urban, the politics we explored here illustrate that urban spaces present a compelling opportunity to draw together actors rooted in particular spaces with shared economic, ecological, and social experiences. The cases presented here demonstrate that the politics of collaboration are central to urban sustainability transformations.

Collaboration is vital as urban spaces transition towards sustainability, but the specific forms and functions of collaborations will vary by city and by objective. A lesson that can be applied in any case is that engagement and involvement serve as a transformation lubricant, allowing proposals that would previously have been politically untenable to move forward. In other words, not only collaboration, but the "right" kind of collaboration, is an important ingredient of sustainability transitions. In order to deliver the right kind of collaboration, cities must be prepared to play the collaboration long game. It takes time to build relationships and to see incremental changes become transformative. The necessity for gradual shifts predicated on strong relationships, however, may be at odds with the urgency of climate change and sustainability goals.

In New York City, we illustrated that collaboration has been central to a desirable outcome; however, this collaboration focused squarely on the development and implementation of regulation (rather than, for instance, market-based mechanisms or voluntary approaches). This case also illustrates that legitimacy, political influence, and reputation deeply influence the effectiveness of collaborative approaches to sustainability governance in cities. It further demonstrates that even when a goal is relatively incremental, the process followed to reach this goal may itself be transformative of governance models, multi-actor relationships, and social perception of the functioning of cities.

Ultimately, the reality of transformation may be mundane: actions that appear incremental may push an urban system towards a fundamentally different state in the future. For instance, as London works to reach ambitious climate change mitigation targets, it has chosen to engage directly with small- and medium-sized enterprises as a key set of actors, although predominantly in an incremental manner. It remains to be seen whether this approach will be scaled up and out in a way that might have a more fundamental impact on emissions, especially at the global level. Leadership on the part of the mayor has always been instrumental in London's case, as has been the availability of grants from the European Union, but many SMEs nonetheless suffer from capacity barriers that prevent equitable or pervasive uptake of opportunities offered by government

The case of Manizales, among others, demonstrates that a significant opportunity is missed by sustainability transitions scholarship that only addresses sociotechnical innovation in industrialized cities. In this case, the push to mitigate risk and manage vulnerability to climate change impacts presents the chance to build social equity, public participation, and alleviate poverty. In direct contrast to the New York case, government-directed regulation was less favorable than approaches led by civil society and private sector partners in Manizales. However, experiments in Manizales have not been able to effect the systemic change necessary to move the city to a more sustainable urban development trajectory. This illustrates the power of structural development dynamics, which can promote or prevent profound changes from within urban regimes.

As it may only be possible to recognize both local and global transformations with the benefit of hindsight, it is important to more rigorously explore and test early indicators of transformation. These indicators allow urban decision-makers, scholars, and practitioners to adaptively manage these complex socioecological systems, strengthen engagement with diverse actors, and reorient when necessary. It is clear that small changes (for instance, adjustments to building codes, job descriptions, and funding mechanisms) may gain momentum and influence over time, with powerful implications for an increasingly urbanized planet.

Ultimately, sustainability transformations may follow many paths, from the gradual reorientation of the system through accumulated incremental actions, to radical shifts or shocks that give rise to a nonlinear system shift. In a post–Paris Agreement world, it is the task of urban scholars to cast their conceptual and empirical nets widely, to explicitly acknowledge the complex politics of urban innovation, to explore models of governance that are inclusive and adaptable, and to delve into the power of a multitude of actors to effect change.

References

American Council for an Energy-Efficient Economy. (2014) New York City Green Codes Task Force. ACEEE; Location: Washington, DC. https://aceee.org/files/proceedings/2014/data/papers/6-921.pdf

Avelino, F., Grin, J., Pel, B., and Jhagroe, S. (2016) The Politics of Sustainability Transitions. *Journal of Environmental and Policy Planning* 18: 557–567.

Avelino, F., and Rotmans, J. (2011) A Dynamic Conceptualization of Power for Sustainability Research. *Journal of Cleaner Production* 19: 796–804.

Avelino, F., and Wittmayer, J.M. (2016) Shifting Power Relations in Sustainability Transitions: A Multi-Actor Perspective. *Journal of Environmental and Policy Planning* 18: 628–649.

Barrero, L.S.V. (2013) The Bioplan: Decreasing Poverty in Manizales, Colombia, through Shared Environmental, in Satterthwaite, D. Reid, H., and Bass, S. (eds.), *Reducing Poverty and Sustaining the Environment: The Politics of Local Engagement.* London: Routledge, pp. 44–72.

Biermann, F.H.B., Abbott, K., Andresen, S., Bäckstrand, K., Bernstein, S., Betsill, M.M., et al. (2012) Transforming Governance and Institutions for Global Sustainability: Key Insights from the Earth System Governance Project. *Current Opinion in Environmental Sustainability* 4: 51–60.

Bos, J.J., Brown, R.R., and Farrelly, M.A. (2013) A Design Framework for Creating Social Learning Situations. *Global Environmental Change* 23: 398–412.

Bos-Brouwers, H.E.J. (2010) Corporate Sustainability and Innovation in SMEs: Evidence of Themes and Activities in Practice. *Business Strategy and the Environment* 19: 417–435.

Bulkeley, H., Breitfuss, M., Coenen, L., Frantzeskaki, N., Fuenfschilling, L., Grillitsch, M., et al. (2015) *Theoretical Framework Working Paper on Urban Living Labs and Urban Sustainability Transitions.* Lund: Lund University.

Bulkeley, H., Castán Broto, V., and Maassen, A. (2014) Low-Carbon Transitions and the Reconfiguration of Urban Infrastructure. *Urban Studies* 51: 1471–1486.

Bulkeley, H., and Schroeder, H., (2008) Governing Climate Change Post-2012: The Role of Global Cities. Case Study: London, Tyndall Working Paper 123.

Bulkeley, H., and Schroeder, H. (2011) Beyond State and Non-State Divides: Global Cities and the Governance of Climate Change. *European Journal of International Relations* 18: 741–764.

Burch, S., Sheppard, S., Shaw, A., and Flanders, D. (2010) Addressing Municipal Barriers to Policy Action on Climate Change: Participatory Integrated Assessment of Climate Change Futures and the Use of 3D Visualizations as Decision Support Tools. *Journal of Flood Risk Management* 3: 126–139.

Burch, S., Shaw, A., Dale, A., and Robinson, J. (2014) Triggering Transformative Change: A Development Path Approach to Climate Change Response in Communities. *Climate Policy* 14: 467–487.

Burch, S., Graham A., and Mitchell, C. (2017). Permission to Fail: Enabling Governance Structures for Urban Climate Innovation, in S. Marvin, H. Bulkeley, Q.L. Mai, and K. Mccormick (eds.). *Urban Living Labs: Experimentation and Sociotechnical Transitions*. London: Routledge.

Burgess, J., Clark, J., and Chilvers, J. (2005) Going 'Upstream': Issues Arising with UK Experiments in Participatory Science and Technology Assessment. *Sociologia e Politiche Sociali* 8: 107–136.

Coenen, L., Benneworth, P., and Truffer, B. (2012) Toward a spatial perspective on sustainability transitions. *Research Policy* 41: 968–979.

Dolan, D.A., Soule, G.B., Greaney, J., and Morris, J. (2010) Warming Up to Climate Action A Survey of GHG Mitigation through Building Energy Efficiency in City Climate Action Plans. *Climate Law Review* 4: 161–172.

Farla, J., Markard, J., Raven, R., and Coenen, L. (2012) Sustainability Transitions in the Making: A Closer Look at Actors, Strategies and Resources. *Technological Forecasting and Social Change* 79 (6): 991–998.

Fischer, L.-B., and Newig, J. (2016) Importance of Actors and Agency in Sustainability Transitions: A Systematic Exploration of the Literature. *Sustainability* 8: 476–497.

Folke, C., Carpenter, S.R., Walker, B.H., Scheffer, M., Chapin, F.S.I., and Rockstrom, J. (2010) Resilience Thinking: Integrating Resilience, Adaptability and Transformability. *Ecology and Society* 15, Article 20: 20–29.

Geels, F.W. (2002) Towards Sociotechnical Scenarios and Reflexive Anticipation: Using Patterns and Regularities in Technology Dynamics, in Sorensen, K.H., and Williams, R. (eds.), *Shaping Technology, Guiding Policy: Concepts, Spaces and Tools*. Cheltenham: Edward Elgar, pp. 255–281.

Geels, F.W. (2005a) The Dynamics of Transitions in Socio-Technical Systems: A Multi-Level Analysis of the Transition Pathway from Horse-Drawn Carts to Automobiles (1860–1930). *Technology Analysis & Strategic Management* 17: 445–476.

Geels, F.W. (2005b) *Technological Transitions and System Innovations: A Co-Evolutionary and Socio-Technical Analysis*. Cheltenham: Edward Elgar.

Geels, F.W., and Schot, J. (2007) Typology of Sociotechnical Transition Pathways. *Research Policy* 36: 399–417.

Geels, F.W., and Schot, J. (2008) Strategic Niche Management and Sustainable Innovation Journeys: Theory, Findings, Research Agenda, and Policy. *Technology Analysis and Strategic Management* 20: 537–554.

GLA, (2010) *Delivering London's Energy Future: The Mayor's Draft Climate Change Mitigation and Energy Strategy*. London: Greater London Authority.

Gronewold, N., (2010) *NYC Begins Hard, Long Slog to Energy Efficiency*, New York Times, www .nytimes.com/gwire/2010/04/05/05greenwire-nyc-begins-hard-long-slog-to-energy-efficiency-78815.html?pagewanted=all.

Halila, F. (2007) Networks as a Means of Supporting the Adoption of Organizational Innovations in SMEs: The Case of Environmental Management Systems (EMSs) Based on ISO 14001. *Corporate Social Responsibility and Environmental Management* 14: 167–181.

Hansen, E.G., and Klewitz, J. (2012) Publicly Mediated Inter-Organizational Networks: A Solution for Sustainability-Oriented Innovation in SMEs, in Wagner, M. (ed.), *Entrepreneurship, Innovation and Sustainability*. Sheffield: Greenleaf, pp. 25–278.

Hardoy, J., and Barrero, L.S.V. (2014) Re-Thinking 'Biomanizales': Addressing Climate Change Adaptation in Manizales, Colombia. *Environment and Urbanization* 26: 53–68.

Hardoy, J., Pandiella, G., Stella, L., and Barrero, V. (2011) Local Disaster Risk Reduction in Latin American Urban Areas. *Environment and Urbanization* 23: 401–413.

Hekkert, M., Suurs, R., Negro, S., Kuhlmann, S., and Smits, R. (2007) Functions of Innovation Systems: A New Approach for Analysing Technological Change. *Technological Forecasting and Social Change* 74: 413–432.

Hughes, S., Pincetl, S., and Boone, C.G. (2013) Understanding Major Urban Transitions: Drivers and Dynamics in the City of Los Angeles. *Cities: The International Journal of Urban Policy and Planning* 32: 51–59.

Institute for Sustainability, (2012) *Best Practice Guidance for Successful SME Engagement*, London: Institute for Sustainability.

IPCC, (2012) *Managing the Risks of Extreme Events and Disasters to Advance Climate Change Adaptation, A Special Report Of Working Groups I and II of the Intergovernmental Panel on Climate Change*, in: Field, C.B., Barros, V., Stocker, T.F., D., Q., Dokken, D.J., Ebi, K.L., Mastrandrea, M.D., et al. (eds.). Cambridge University Press, Cambridge.

IPCC, (2014) *Climate Change 2014: Impacts, Adaptation, and Vulnerability*. Contribution of Working Group II to the Fifth Assessment Report of the Intergovernmental Panel on Climate Change, in Field, C.B., Barros, V.R., Dokken, D.J., Mach, K.J., Mastrandrea, M.D., Bilir, T.E., et al. (eds.). Cambridge: Cambridge University Press.

Johnson, C., Toly, N., and Schroeder, H. (2015) *The Urban Climate Challenge: Rethinking the Role of Cities in the Global Climate Regime*. London: Routledge.

Kates, R.W., Travis, W.R., and Wilbanks, T.J. (2012) Transformational Adaptation When Incremental Adaptations to Climate Change Are Insufficient. *Proceedings of the National Academy of Sciences* 109; 7156–7161.

Kemp, R., and Rip, A. (2001) Constructing Transition Paths through the Management of Niches, in Garud, R., Karnoe, P. (eds.), *Path Dependence and Creation*. Mahwah, NJ: Lawrence Erlbaum Associates, pp. 269–299.

Lawhon, M., and Murphy, J.T. (2012) Socio-Technical Regimes and Sustainability Transitions Insights from Political Ecology. *Progress in Human Geography* 36: 354–378.

Leftwich, A. (1983) *Redefining Politics: People, Resources, and Power*. New York: Routledge.

Lehmann, M. (2006) Government–Business Relationships through Partnerships for Sustainable Development: The Green Network in Denmark. *Journal of Environmental Policy and Planning* 8: 235–257.

Loorbach, D. (2010) Transition Management for Sustainable Development: A Prescriptive, Complexity-Based Governance Framework. *Governance* 23: 161–183.

Loorbach, D., and Wijsman, K. (2013) Business Transition Management: Exploring a New Role for Business in Sustainability Transitions. *Journal of Cleaner Production* 45: 20–28.

Markard, J., Raven, R., and Truffer, B. (2012) Sustainability Transitions: An Emerging Field of Research and Its Prospects. *Research Policy* 41: 955–967.

McCormick, K., Anderberg, S., Coenen, L., and Neij, L. (2013) Advancing Sustainable Urban Transformation. *Journal of Cleaner Production* 50: 1–11.

Meadowcroft, J. (2009) What about the Politics? Sustainable Development, Transition Management, and Long Term Energy Transitions. *Policy Sciences* 42: 323–340.

Meadowcroft, J. (2011) Engaging with the Politics of Sustainability Transitions. *Environmental Innovation and Societal Transitions* 1: 70–75.

Nelson, D.R., Adger, W.N., and Brown, K. (2007) Adaptation to Environmental Change: Contributions of a Resilience Framework. *Annual Review of Environment and Resources* 32: 395–419.

O'Brien, K. (2012) Global Environmental Change Ii: From Adaptation to Deliberate Transformation. *Progress in Human Geography* 36: 667–676.

Pahl-Wostl, C., Craps, M., Dewulf, A., Mostert, E., Tabara, D., and Taillieu, T. (2007) Social Learning and Water Resources Management. *Ecology and Society* 12: 5–34. www.ecologyandsociety.org/vol12/iss2/art5/main.html

Patterson, J., Schultz, K., Vervoort, J., van der Hel, S., Widerberg, O., Adler, C., et al. (2016) Exploring the Governance and Politics of Transformations towards Sustainability. *Environmental Innovation and Societal Transitions* 24: 1–16.

Pelling, M. (2011) *Adaptation to Climate Change: From Resilience to Transformation.* Abingdon: Routledge.

Pelling, M., O'Brien, K., and Matyas, D. (2015) Adaptation and Transformation. *Climatic Change* 133 (1): 113–127.

Pickett, S.T.A., Boone, C.G., McGrath, B.P., Cadenasso, M.L., Childers, D.L., Ogden, L.A., et al. (2013) Ecological Science and Transformation to the Sustainable City. *Cities* 32: S10–S20.

Revi, A., Satterthwaite, D., Aragon-Durand, F., Corfee-Morlot, J., Kiunsi, R.B.R., Pelling, M., et al. (2014) Towards Transformative Adaptation in Cities: The IPCC's Fifth Assessment Report. *Environment and Urbanization* 26: 11–28.

Rip, A., and Kemp, R. (1998) Technological Change, in: Rayner, S., and Malone, E. (eds.), *Human Choice and Climate Change.* Columbus, Ohio: Batelle Press, pp. 327–399.

Rockstrom, J., Steffen, W., Noone, K., Persson, A., Chapin III, F.S., Lambin, E., et al. (2009) Planetary Boundaries: Exploring the Safe Operating Space for Humanity. *Ecology and Society* 14: 32. www.ecologyandsociety.org/vol14/iss2/art32/

Romero-Lankao, P., and Gnatz, D.M. (2013) Exploring Urban Transformations in Latin America. *Current Opinion in Environmental Sustainability* 5: 358–367.

Romero-Lankao, P., Hardoy, J., Hughes, S., Rosas-Huerta, A., Borquez, R., Gnatz, D.M., and Governance, C.A.G. (2015) Multilevel Governance and Institutional Capacity for Climate Change Responses in Latin American Cities, in Johnson, C., Toly, N., and Schroeder, H. (Eds.), *The Urban Climate Challenge: Rethinking the Role of Cities in the Global Climate Regime*. London: Routledge, pp. 179–204.

Rotmans, J., Kemp, R., and van Asselt, M. (2001) More Evolution than Revolution: Transition Management in Public Policy. *Foresight* 3: 15–31.

Sarzynski, A. (2015) Public Participation, Civic Capacity, and Climate Change Adaptation in Cities. *Urban Climate* 14: 52–67.

Scheib, C., Unger, R., and Leigh, R. (2014) Greening a City's Building Codes: The NYC Green Codes Task Force.

Schroeder, H., and Bulkeley, H. (2009) Global Cities and the Governance of Climate Change: What Is the Role of Law in Cities? *Fordham Urban Law Journal* 36: 313–359.

Senge, P.M., Linchtenstein, B.B., Kaeufer, K., Bradbury, H., and Carroll, J. (2007) Collaborating for Systemic Change. *MIT Sloan Management Review* 48: 44–53.

Smith, A., Stirling, A., and Berkhout, F. (2005) The Governance of Sustainable Socio-Technical Transitions. *Research Policy* 34: 1491–1510.

Solecki, W. (2012) Urban Environmental Challenges and Climate Change Action in New York City. *Environment and Urbanization* 24: 557–573.

Steffen, W., Crutzen, P.J., and McNeill, J.R. (2007) The Anthropocene: Are Humans Now Overwhelming the Great Forces of Nature? *Ambio* 36: 614–621.

Stirling, A. (2014) From Sustainability to Transformation: Dynamics and Diversity in Reflexive Governance of Vulnerability. SPRU Working Paper Series 2014–06, Available at SSRN https://ssrn.com/abstract=2742113 or http://dx.doi.org/2742110.2742139/ssrn.2742113.

Svendsen, A.C., and Laberge, M. (2005) Convening Stakeholder Networks. *Journal of Corporate Citizenship* 2005: 91–104.

The City of New York, (2007) *plaNYC: A Greener, Greater New York*. City of New York, New York.

UN-HABITAT, (2011) *Cities and Climate Change: Global Report on Human Settlement 2011*. Nairobi: UN-HABITAT.

Urban Green Council, (2010) Executive Summary: NYC Green Codes Task Force.

van der Brugge, R., and van Raak, R. (2007) Facing the Adaptive Management Challenge: Insights from Transition Management. *Ecology and Society* 12 (2): 33. www.ecologyandsociety.org/vol12/iss2/art33/

Voytenko, Y., McCormick, K., Evans, J., and Schliwa, G. (2016) Urban Living Labs for Sustainability and Low Carbon Cities in Europe: Towards a Research Agenda. *Journal of Cleaner Production* 123: 45–54.

Westley, F., Olsson, P., Folke, C., Homer-Dixon, T., Vredenburg, H., Loorbach, D., et al. (2011) Tipping toward Sustainability: Emerging Pathways of Transformation. *Ambio* 40: 762–780.

Chapter 16: Seeds of the Future in the Present

Exploring Pathways for Navigating Towards "Good" Anthropocenes

Laura M. Pereira, Elena Bennett, Reinette (Oonsie) Biggs, Garry Peterson, Timon McPhearson, Albert Norström, Per Olsson, Rika Preiser, Ciara Raudsepp-Hearne, and Joost Vervoort

Chapter Highlights

1. The rapid urbanization associated with the Anthropocene provides an imperative for humans to think differently about the future.

2. The "seeds" approach describes how niche experiments can, over time, coalesce to shift the dominant regime onto a more sustainable trajectory.

3. To achieve positive urban futures, it is vital to ensure that more positive narratives inform our lived experience so that, as humans, we are able to act differently in the face of seemingly overwhelming challenges.

4. Novel scenarios can be developed by imagining futures in which seemingly disparate ideas must coexist; fostering this creativity is important if we are to create positive visions of futures that we would like to achieve.

5. Urban transformations are complex phenomena; the seeds approach is a tool that can help us understand how transformations occur and how to nudge them towards more sustainable trajectories.

16.1 Introduction: "Good Anthropocenes" in an Urbanized World

The past two centuries have seen dramatic gains in human well-being, largely achieved through conversion of land to agriculture and the appropriation of natural resources such as timber and fish. However, the extent and cumulative impact of human changes to the Earth have come to rival the great forces of nature, and have inadvertently shepherded us into a new planetary era – the Anthropocene (Steffen et al. 2015). Changes include profound alterations of the Earth's marine and terrestrial ecosystems and the services they provide to globally interconnected societies and economies (Carpenter et al. 2009). Humans have also radically altered the composition of the Earth's atmosphere (IPCC 2013), the elemental cycles (Steffen et al. 2004), and flows of water (Vörösmarty et al. 2010). By many measures, the changes humanity has caused in the last 50 years have now met or exceeded the variations seen through the entire Holocene, the geological era that started 10,000 years ago and that provided the relatively stable environment that enabled humanity's development of agriculture and complex societies (Rockström et al. 2009).

A central feature of the Anthropocene is the onset of rapid urbanization (United Nations 2009). The decisions made by the majority of the human population now living in cities affect the biophysical dynamics of the entire planet, and the urban demand for environmental goods and services is a major driver behind global environmental change (Seto et al. 2011; Bulkeley and Betsill 2005; Grimm et al. 2008). The choices urban citizens make are often disconnected from their environmental imprint in distant places; thus, urban lifestyles have altered the way people in cities perceive and interact with the biosphere (Andersson et al. 2014).

Despite the new threats, risks, and problems that arise from these changes and that dominate popular and scientific forecasts, the future does not have to be bleak. There are many examples of new thinking, new ways of living, and new ways of connecting people and nature that address aspects of global problems and that could create different trajectories of future change. For example, new, bottom-up processes are producing innovations that are reimagining the smart city concept and reshaping how urban citizens move around and reduce their energy consumption and carbon footprint (see Chapter 48).

Individuals, organizations, and governments have repeatedly stated their desire to create a just, prosperous, and ecologically sustainable world – or "Good Anthropocene." However, due to the complexity and scale of change required, the scientific community in general and the global change community, in particular, have undertaken very few analyses of positive futures or how to achieve them. A variety of different futures could constitute a Good Anthropocene, but all Good Anthropocene futures likely require dramatic social changes coupled to technological progress to create a future that meets widely held aspirations for equitable human development without undermining the capacity of ecosystems to support future human well-being (See Preiser et al. 2017). Such changes entail a transformation as radical as the shift from the Medieval period to the Industrial era in Europe – that is, a global scale renaissance that embodies fundamental shifts in underlying values, assumptions, cultures, and worldviews that govern the institutions and behavior of modern society (Bennett et al. 2016).

In this chapter, we present insights from an ongoing research initiative, "Seeds of Good Anthropocenes," that is at the forefront of approaches for exploring and articulating more positive futures in the Anthropocene. The project is based on a crowd-sourced database of "seeds": real initiatives that demonstrate one or more elements of a positive future that might contribute to creating a Good Anthropocene. We present a preliminary analysis of urban seeds and the types of projects that are emerging as important to sustainability transformations in this context. We then discuss how we have used seeds to generate creative, radically alternative, desirable visions of a better future. Such participatory exercises provide a platform for addressing and bridging different approaches to knowledge, views of how the world works, and values (Bennett et al. 2016; Wiek and Iwaniec 2014), and can be important in creating momentum for transformative change.

16.2 Theory of Change: How Seeds Can Create Transformative Change

The Seeds project is grounded in an emerging understanding of how change occurs in complex adaptive social-ecological systems, or SES. The framework that underlies this project is presented in Figure 16.1, and integrates two key existing frameworks: the sociotechnical transitions framework (Geels 2002), and the stages of social-ecological transformations (Olsson et al. 2006; Moore et al. 2014), which include the panarchy model (Gunderson and Holling 2002).

Macroscale change in SES comprises three interconnected phases: preparation, navigating the transition, and consolidation (Olsson et al. 2004). In the first phase (preparation), there is an emerging awareness of some systemic problem at a macro-level, such as the awareness growing since the 1960s, that society is on an unsustainable development trajectory (Meadows et al. 1972; Sawyer 1972). This inspires a diversity of experiments, typically at the micro-level. The examples contained in the Seeds project database constitute such micro-level experiments or initiatives that have emerged as responses to Anthropocene challenges.

The preparation phase can be subdivided into subphases of sense-making, envisioning, and gathering momentum (Moore et al. 2014). Sense-making is linked to a growing awareness of a systemic problem and involves an analysis of the structures that are most problematic in shaping the current trajectory. The major global environmental assessments of the past two decades, especially the Millennium Ecosystem Assessment (Millennium Ecosystems Assessment 2005) and the Intergovernmental Panel on Climate Change (IPCC 2013) assessments,

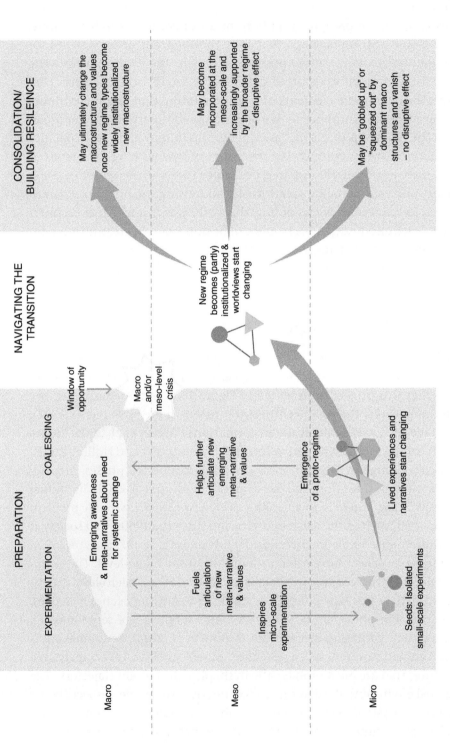

Figure 16.1 Macroscale systemic change typically emerges from a long period of preparation that entails experimentation, innovation, and the formation of new coalitions at the micro-level. Proto-regimes that emerge from this preparatory phase typically only become institutionalized at a meso-level once a window of opportunity emerges in the form of a crisis or anticipated crisis. Our understanding of how these meso-level regimes can then effect larger-scale systemic change is still limited. The symbols indicate new configurations, where the social and ecological components of the system are connected in new ways. Source: Authors' own.

can be seen as playing this role. The process of envisioning entails generating new innovations and visions for the future. Psychological and sociological research suggests that inspirational visions can be key components of transformations to sustainability (Wiek and Iwaniec 2014; van der Helm 2009): they can help shape the future by changing how people understand the world and what they expect from it. Together, visions and innovations can provide the basis for gathering momentum, involving self-organization around new ideas, the creation and mobilization of networks of support, and experimentation in protected niches. Social entrepreneurs or change agents are critical in this subphase, both for creating niches, and for helping to weaken the broader structures that prevent the scaling up or out of innovations (Westley et al. 2013).

The preparation and navigation phases are linked by a window of opportunity or the opening up of an opportuity context. As momentum builds in the preparation phase, small-scale experiments become connected or organized into "proto-regimes" (Geels 2002) that are amenable to institutionalization at meso-scales. For this to happen, however, there generally needs to be some crisis, or anticipated crisis, that destabilizes the existing regime and creates a window of opportunity for institutional change (for example, a change in government, a financial crisis, or an extreme climatic event). When these crises emerge, the proto-regimes then provide potential "solutions" that can be adopted by decision-makers in need of new strategies (see, for example, Gelcich et al. 2010). Institutionalization at the meso-scale is critical in the navigation phase in order to move into the consolidation phase and bring about larger systemic change.

Our understanding of how macroscale change emerges from meso- and micro-scale change is still somewhat limited, although there is a growing body of work looking at scaling up (growing bigger), out (replicating), and deep (changing underlying values) (Moore et al. 2015). In many cases, however, it appears that micro-scale innovations become captured by macroscale systemic structures and lose their innovative edge and potential for disruption. Adaptation and even more fundamental transformation of micro- and meso-scale structures may be required to engage with macroscale structures in a way that can bring about systemic change.

The Seeds project connects explicitly to the preparation phase and has three main objectives: 1) to survey and systematically compare seeds – based on their goals, activities, context, and impact – to identify the features of particularly transformative seeds, and to explore how different types of projects support and interact with one another to create protected niches; 2) to track and analyze particularly transformative seeds in more depth to further our understanding of how transformative processes occur; and 3) to experiment with new approaches for bringing diverse seeds together to stimulate further innovations and facilitate the development of proto-regimes. This experimentation step is being enacted through a process of envisioning, wherein the seeds are used as starting conditions for creating positive alternative visions of the Anthropocene.

16.2.1 The Seeds Database: Coding and Analysis

The starting point for the Seeds project is the development of a database of "seeds" (http://goodanthropocenes.net), which we define as initiatives (that is, a way of doing, an institution, a technology, a business, a project, or an organization) that exist in some form and that someone identifies as having the potential to contribute to a Good Anthropocene, but that are not currently dominant. We asked networks of sustainability scientists and practitioners from around the world to identify initiatives that could, given the correct conditions (for example, acceptability, cost-benefit analysis, ease of implementation), grow and transform to improve environmental conditions and human well-being. Contributors were invited through workshops, conferences, and via networks of sustainability researchers, and were asked to describe key attributes of the suggested seed by filling in an online questionnaire.

The initial seed collection represents a plurality of what types of initiatives could contribute to different concepts of what constitutes a "Good Anthropocene." This openness was essential to capturing a broad cross-section of initiatives. We wanted to maximize the diversity of seeds in order to expose the plurality of underlying values associated with them, and to explore how very different types of seeds could combine to create radically novel visions of the Anthropocene.

The seed attributes captured in the online questionnaire include the challenges the seed addresses, its innovative aspects, its size and duration, and the types of systems in which it is active. We also collected information about the key actors that are involved in initiating and sustaining the seed, and what types of activities it conducted. Attributes related to seed spread were included mechanisms for spread (growing, replicating, or inspiring); limiting and enhancing factors; globally relevant aspects of seeds (that is, seeds may be inherently local, but may have characteristics that could be relevant elsewhere); and state of implementation. These features are described in a mix of categorical and text statements, and are based on attributes that were iteratively identified as important during several workshops, focus group discussions, and pilot web surveys.

Members of the project team then consistently coded the seeds for analysis. This coding was based on responses to the online questionnaire as well as additional sources, such as websites of the seed initiatives, media articles, reports, and scientific articles. We also used the information from the questionnaire to write short blog posts (See Box 16.1) on some of the seeds for our website in order to engage with a broader audience and to encourage other people to contribute a seed to the database.

Box 16.1 A Seed Blog Post, from https://goodanthropocenes.net

Tyisa Nabanye

Tyisa Nabanye is a nonprofit urban agriculture organization growing organic food on the slopes of Signal Hill in Cape Town; it seeks to improve food security, promote sustainable livelihoods, and create employment for its members. Started in 2013 by a group of urban farmers from the townships around Cape Town, Tyisa Nabanye, which means "to feed each other" in isiXhosa (one of the official languages of South Africa), is an urban garden based on the principles of permaculture. The team consists of eight members: Mzu, Lumko, Unathi, Chuma, Lizza, Vuyo, Masi, and Catherine.

The land that Tyisa Nabanye occupies in Tamboerskloof was once used by the army and is now referred to as Erf 81. The land is owned by the South African National Defence Force, or SANDF, and is administered by the Department of Public Works, but the members of Tyisa Nabanye got permission from Andre Laubscher, the de facto caretaker of the property, to start growing some vegetables and moved into an uninhabited military storehouse on the property. At the moment, neither department has a clear plan for the property; as a result, they have not granted Tyisa Nabanye official tenure, although the department tacitly acknowledges their presence.

The urban farm at Tyisa Nabanye now hosts markets every second Sunday of the month, during which people can buy their fresh produce and homemade food from informal traders. Every Wednesday and Thursday, they hold yoga classes for volunteers on the farm and every so often they have a live music performance in the barn. Despite their uncertain status, they continue to innovate and learn, trying to create an environment where food can be grown, stories exchanged, and lives valued.

Urban initiatives such as Tyisa Nabanye have the potential not only to transform the relationships between people and the environment by reconnecting them to their food systems, but also to transform the relationships between people in a city that retains the apartheid legacy of fragmentation across race and class lines. By reappropriating space and integrating socially marginalized groups of people with others marked by affluence and access to resources, the problem of ghettoization and homeless city dwellers is being addressed in new ways.

16.2.2 Analysis of Urban Seeds

There are approximately 400 seeds currently in the database, 120 of which have been coded as urban seeds. To better understand the differences and commonalities among the seeds, we divided these urban seeds into a number of clusters based on their coded social-ecological attributes[1]. We clustered seeds based on how they were constructed socially, what "anthrome" (or anthropogenic biome, see Martin et al. 2014) they worked within, what Anthropocene challenge they addressed, and the extent to which they were social-ecologically integrated[2].

16.2.3 Preliminary Findings

The developing database reveals a rich diversity of seeds relevant to an urban context, ranging from new technologies and urban design that could reduce ecological footprints, to projects reconnecting people to their environment, especially through food systems. Figure 16.2 presents an analysis of the different attributes of the urban seeds.

A hierarchical cluster analysis of the urban seed traits identified eight clusters, which we have termed as follows: Future Sustainability, Climate Smart Cities, Green Design, Urban Agroecology, Conservation Ecology, Green Innovation, Social & Design, and Political Ecology (Figure 16.3).

The analysis illustrates that the largest number of seeds initiatives are aiming to innovate to achieve a good future; the analysis identifies culture – understood as everything from people's perceptions of nature to how they relate to each other – as the Anthropocene "challenge" being addressed by the greatest number of urban seeds (Figure 16.2). The various clusters give a glimpse as to what types of seeds (and their associated traits) people propose as being important for creating more positive urban futures. Notably, design and innovation are as important as more environmentally oriented traits, and social aspects – coded mainly in the political ecology group – are also emphasized.

The clusters we identified among the urban seeds largely correspond to the six main groups of projects identified by Bennett et al. (2016) in an analysis

---

[1] We coded the seeds using the statistical software R (R Core Team 2016) and the packages vegan (Oksanen et al. 2016), ape (Paradis et al. 2004), and ggplot (Wickham 2009).

[2] Because the seed traits were nonexclusive binary variables, we clustered them using Jaccard distances between seeds using Ward's hierarchical agglomerative clustering. We selected eight clusters to provide a balance between cluster size and the number of clusters. We named the categories based on the type of seeds found in each cluster.

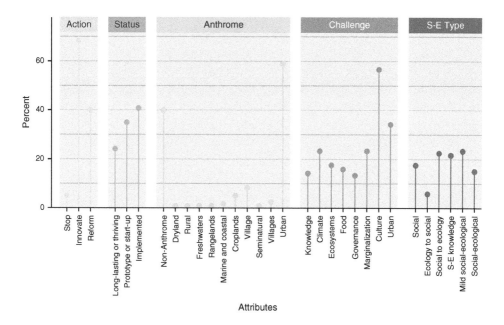

Figure 16.2 Attributes of 120 urban relevant seeds from the Seeds of the Good Anthropocene database. These seeds are classified across five categories based on a) what type of action a seed is encouraging (stopping, reforming, or innovating activities); b) the status of the seed (prototype, implemented, or a well-established project); c) which "anthrome" or social-ecological system the seed is oriented towards; d) what types of challenge of the Anthropocene the seed addresses; and e) the type of social-ecological integration the seed represents. The sum is greater than 100 percent because some categories are not mutually exclusive.

of the first 100 seeds in the database: (1) "Agroecology" – projects that adopt social-ecological approaches to enhance food-producing landscapes, (2) "Green Urbanism" – projects that improve the livability of urban areas, (3) "Future Knowledge" – projects which foster new knowledge and education that can be used to transform societies, (4) "Urban Transformation" – projects that create new types of social-ecological interactions around urban space, (5) "Fair Futures" – efforts to create opportunities for more equitable decision-making, and (6) "Sustainable Futures" – social movements to build more just and sustainable futures.

Further development of the seeds database will code for additional aspects of the seeds, and will likely identify other groupings. Nevertheless, our initial analysis identifies the substantial differences in approach, location, and activities that exist among the seeds, and suggests opportunities for considering how different types of seeds could interact with one another to enable or block transformations towards different types of futures.

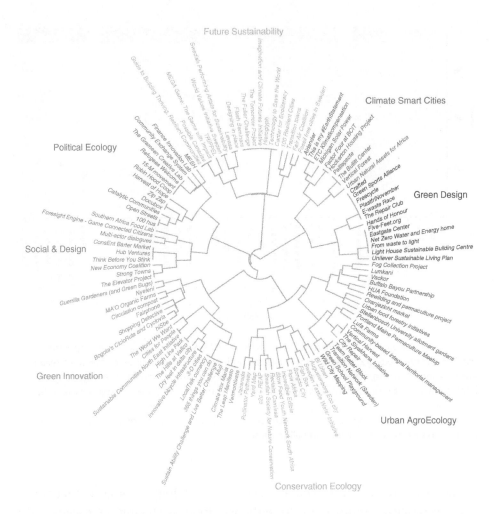

Figure 16.3 Urban seeds clustered into groups based on hierarchical clustering of the Anthropocene challenge(s) they address and their social-ecological type.

16.3 Using Seeds for Envisioning Alternative Futures

A central goal of the project is to use seeds as elements with which to envision radically alternative scenarios of Good Anthropocenes. The seeds-based scenario approach responds to the need to avoid creating purely dystopian, utopian, or business-as-usual futures, and the need to imagine futures that are at once truly novel and concrete enough to inspire practical action. It also aims to create a scenario approach that is effective at imagining emergent change. In the project, we are experimenting with a range of scenario creation methods for different purposes (analysis, learning, stimulating innovation, and action). These different approaches include:

1.   Testing a single seed against a range of Anthropocene challenges or fully formed scenarios, and coding its feasibility in these different futures, as well as how it would change different futures and if it would be successful enough to have a global impact – or, alternatively, what failure would look like. This creates a database of mini-scenarios or scenario elements that can, in turn, be clustered and combined into larger, more multidimensional scenario narratives.

2.   Combining, or "mashing up," different seeds selected by workshop participants, and using these combinations to imagine how different, contrasting seed initiatives could scale (up, out, or deep) and to create new composite ideas.

3.   Mashing up different seeds and, simultaneously, pitting them against different Anthropocene challenges or (partial) contextual scenarios, to create composite scenario narratives of combined seed growth or failure. This can be done by mixing up multiple seeds and Anthropocene challenges, either randomly or in a structured fashion, and discussing/describing the resulting narrative.

4.   Creating future scenarios via a game process in which players (initiative leaders, researchers, policy-makers) create coalitions of different seeds to take on different, contextual Anthropocene scenarios that are also represented by players in the role of researchers or policy-makers. The game includes a chance system to simulate uncertainty in seed development pathways. The combination of growing and failing coalitions of seeds changes and shapes the scenario context, resulting in a multidimensional scenario narrative.

Each of these options has been implemented in different versions at workshops, scientific conferences, with communities of innovative initiatives, and with students to test the consequences of different ways of designing seed-based scenarios development. In addition, rather than predesigning a given incarnation of a seed scenario development approach, we have also implemented a codesign process in which – in a workshop format – the participants conceptualize and experiment with how best to represent how seeds interact with their contexts and with each other (by designing game or other interaction rules). This codesign approach allows for conversations about the nature of transformative change in the face of the Anthropocene, as well as providing an open approach to incorporating inter- and transdisciplinary perspectives into scenario building methods.

In the following section, we provide a few summarized examples of how these different seed scenario-building methods have been applied to urban settings. The methods employed thus far in the project are experimental and need to be adapted for different situations. However, the results from some preliminary analyses indicate that this could be a useful framework for conceptualizing more positive futures.

16.3.1 Scenarios Created through Mashing Up Urban Seeds with Millennium Ecosystem Assessment Scenarios

We started to explore the possibility for combining different types of seeds in scenarios that explore radically alternative urban futures. Rather than testing single seeds (approach 1) or combining seeds with other seeds only (approach 2), we created more multidimensional futures by combining multiple seeds with each other, as well as with contextual scenarios (approach 3). The research team selected relevant urban seeds from different coded trait groups in the seeds database. In each iteration, we combined two seeds and imagined them within contextual scenarios. We used the Millennium Ecosystems Assessment scenarios (Millennium Ecosystems Assessment 2005) because they are relevant for the seed initiatives, and offer both desirable and challenging contexts. In this design, we present our scenarios in a more structured fashion to make the key questions transparent: What are the strengths and weaknesses of each combination in this context? How can the combination influence/change the scenario and its challenge? This process forces seemingly disparate connections between seeds to create more radical narratives. The time horizon for all scenarios is the year 2045, and the seed initiatives used in the mash-up are described in Box 16.2 as in the database by contributors and Table 16.1.

> **Box 16.2** Mash-up seeds as described by contributors in the database
>
> ### Vertical Forests
>
> Vertical Forests is a model for a sustainable residential building, a project for metropolitan reforestation that contributes to the regeneration of the environment and urban biodiversity without the implication of expanding the city upon the territory. It is a model of vertical densification of nature within the city that operates in relation to policies for reforestation and naturalization of large urban and metropolitan borders. The greener architecture will help absorb CO_2, oxygenate the air,

Box 16.2 (cont)

moderate extreme temperatures, and lower noise pollution. The bio-canopy is not only aesthetically pleasing to the eye, but it helps lower living costs.

Solar Airships

The airship has the potential to contribute to zero carbon development. This is important for developed and developing nations, since it would make growth without carbon pollution possible. Airships would carry payloads of 20,000 to 50,000 kg of cargo and would essentially replace the over-the-road trucks. They could travel to any point on the globe such that ships, trains, and trucks would be replaced by a method of transport capable of being powered by sunlight and a heat engine.

Espinaca

Spinach contains all six major classes of nutrients and it is one of the most highly affordable vegetables in the world. Espinaca Innovations wants to make this nutritious product more easily accessible to poor people. Espinaca Express Bakery is a company that aims to promote the consumption of spinach by producing innovative spinach products that are affordable for the poorest – creating access to nutritious and affordable food in informal settlements. It provides healthy food to people living in locations where healthy food has not always been available to them.

Urban Food Forestry

Urban food forestry, based in cities around the world, brings together elements of urban forestry, urban agriculture, edible landscaping, and agroforestry. It is an emerging form of urban food production visible in the form of community urban orchards, urban food forests, edible parks, and other edible landscape features. The main distinguishing features of urban food forestry from predominant forms of urban agriculture (such as allotment gardens) are a focus on utilizing public space and the planting of perennial crops. These characteristics result in more equitable access to fresh produce, particularly with the help of urban gleaning and fruit mapping projects.

Table 16.1 A brief comparison of each seed used in the mash-up

Name	Place	Challenges seed aims to address	Key actors	Approach	Innovative aspect	Scalability[3]
Vertical Forests	Milan, Italy	Urban disconnect from nature, Climate change, Energy use, Resource management	Architectural firm	Alternative design approaches	Sustainable management of ecosystem services in a high-rise building. It provides a model for future construction.	The model could be replicated elsewhere – scale out
Solar Airships	Saint Mary, Jamaica	Poverty eradication; Carbon pollution; Biodiversity loss; Global inequity in trade	International NGO	Adapting existing technologies to meet development needs	The idea makes use of tried and fairly simple technology to bring low-carbon solutions to remote and underdeveloped regions.	The technology can be used in many different locations – scale up

Espinaca Express Bakery	Khayelitsha, South Africa	Access to nutritious affordable food in an informal settlement	Social entrepreneur	Social enterprise model	Providing healthy, affordable food to poor people ensures the human right to food while maintaining a profitable business.	It is a business model that can be replicated elsewhere – scale out
Urban Food Forestry	Lund, Sweden	Food production shortages; Urban disconnect from nature	Local NGO	Mobilizing citizens to make use of green urban spaces for food production	The knowledge- and information- sharing between citizens and their model of cooperation is globally relevant.	It is replicable in cities around the world – scale out. It also changes citizens' relationship with green spaces – scale deep

[3] We refer to scalability as the seed's ability to scale up (increase its numbers, cover more space, and so on), scale out (replicate in different areas), and/or scale deep (change people's underlying values). See Moore et al. (2015) for more information.

16.3.2 Mash-Up 1: Vertical Forests and Solar Airships

Under Global Orchestration Scenario Facing Climate Change

The Global Orchestration scenario (Millennium Ecosystems Assessment 2005: 15) entails a "Globally connected society that focuses on global trade and economic liberalization and takes a reactive approach to ecosystem problems, but also takes strong steps to reduce poverty and inequality and to invest in public goods such as infrastructure and education." The main challenge with which we combine this scenario is extreme climate change.

In the resulting mash-up scenario, trees from the vertical forests provide food and other resources (with value addition in the cities in which they grow); these resources are transported to remote areas in the airships. This will be a lower carbon emissions value chain that is highly innovative and well funded. The problem with this outcome is that it is likely to reinforce our current, dominant model wherein the "periphery" relies on the "core"; that is, commodities being produced in the north or in cities in the south will be providing for the needs of poorer, remote communities, reinforcing their dependence.

This mash-up could be effective in addressing the Anthropocene challenge of climate change – for example, the shift from relying on production in rural areas that are vulnerable to climate variability and extreme events is shifted to more controlled urban contexts, which have access to irrigation and other high-technology inputs.

The overall scenario, while being more ecologically sustainable, does not shift significantly under the presence of this mash-up, which reinforces old models of dependencies.

Under Adapting Mosaic Scenario Facing Biodiversity Loss

The Adapting Mosaic scenario (Millennium Ecosystems Assessment 2005: 15) describes a world where "Regional watershed-scale ecosystems are the focus of political and economic activity. Local institutions are strengthened and local ecosystem management strategies are common; societies develop a strongly proactive approach to the management of ecosystems." The main challenge with which we combine this scenario is biodiversity loss.

In the mash-up scenario, the local production of vertical tree gardens has the ability to provide resources, such as food and medicine, to cities. However, airships are fundamentally about transport and connectivity, so local patchworks of urban trees' products will be connected by airships transporting their goods.

The development of tree gardens will improve local urban biodiversity greatly, but patches of biodiversity outside of urban areas (for example, in protected areas) will decrease as biodiversity loss from climate change goes unchecked and these areas remain unconnected.

The increased connectivity opportunities arising from the use of airships as goods transporters has the potential to shift the scenario away from relatively local self-reliance to a more strongly connected world.

16.3.3 Mash-Up 2: Espinaca and Urban Food Forestry

Under Order from Strength Scenario Facing Climate Change

The Order from Strength scenario (Millennium Ecosystems Assessment 2005: 15) describes a "Regionalized and fragmented world, concerned with security and protection, emphasizing primarily regional markets, paying little attention to public goods, and taking a reactive approach to ecosystem problems."

To combine Espinaca and Urban Food Forestry, the business model of Espinaca can be expanded to many commodities sourced from urban food forests, aiming for the most multidimensional and nutritious commodities.

In an Order from Strength world, the main benefits of a combination of these two seeds relate to self-reliance and resilience at the city level, which would be politically and socially attractive. The main weakness in this social and institutional context would be that the combined Espinaca and Urban Food Forestry practices need open and facilitative regulation, rather than the kinds of restrictive policies that would be more likely under Order from Strength.

However, these combined ideas could contribute to a shifting of activities in the food system to the local level, and provide more nutritional diets for poor people in cities, while potentially playing some role in changing dominant sources of power and organization and introducing elements of a more localized, networked world. This could also lead to greater degrees of urbanization and rewilding.

In the face of climate change, city-level self-reliance could be a benefit or a weakness, partly depending on what (perennial) crops are used. A lack of experience in managing climate extremes could be a key downfall.

Under Technogarden Scenario Facing Biodiversity Loss

The TechnoGarden scenario (Millennium Ecosystems Assessment 2005: 15) describes a "Globally connected world relying strongly on environmentally sound technology, using highly managed, often engineered, ecosystems to deliver ecosystem services, and taking a proactive approach in the management of ecosystems in an effort to avoid problems."

In this context, the key opportunity that emerges with the combination of Espinaca and Urban Food Forestry is transferring the Espinaca business model to Urban Food Forestry commodities; in this scenario, both the model of food production and the model of delivery would be more open and more replicable in peri-urban areas and outside of cities due to strong management of information, transport, energy sources, natural resources, and so on.

There would be an emphasis on smart, tech-based management of the combined projects, leading to a wealth of data. Learning networks between people who are involved in urban food forestry production and delivery to the poorest would foster innovations.

In the face of biodiversity loss, urban food forests could help supplement crop diversity as well as creating contexts for the enhancement of urban and peri-urban biodiversity more generally.

If the combined initiative were to follow the dominant mode of technology-heavy management too closely, this could create weaknesses through an overreliance on technology and an illusion of control, for instance, in the face of disease outbreaks. Yet, the city-focused and localized nature of the combined projects could also counterbalance this tech dependence to a degree, creating some resilience based on local diversity in a globalized world.

16.3.4 Mashing Up Seeds for a Vision for Urban Agriculture in Eindhoven, the Netherlands

An alternative approach that does not use the MA scenarios was employed in the city of Eindhoven, the Netherlands, where organizations are developing a shared vision for urban agriculture, led by Proeftuin040[4], a platform that aims to link diverse urban agriculture initiatives and to act in collaboration with the city council and diverse city-level actors, including many innovative urban agriculture projects and businesses.

To foster creative, novel, and concrete thinking about what elements could contribute to this vision beyond current practices and projects alone, we used the seeds approach, facilitated by the EU-funded FP7 TRANSMANGO[5] project on transitions to better food systems.

In the Proeftuin040 process, our main interest was in combining seeds to foster innovative ideas rather than in testing them against scenarios. To ensure our thinking went beyond present practices, participants identified a mix of Eindhoven-based seeds and urban agriculture seeds from elsewhere in the world. In this exercise, ten participants in the visioning process contributed and combined seeds. We paired participants with one Eindhoven-based seed and one seed from outside of the city, and we conducted multiple seed combination rounds.

Here are examples of resulting ideas:

---

[4] "Experimental garden 040" www.proeftuin040.nl/
[5] transmango.eu

- Polydome greenhouses on rooftops. In this idea, participants mashed up rooftop agriculture (Eindhoven-based seed) and polydome greenhouses (non-city-based seed). Polydome greenhouses on rooftops could increase rooftop production and serve recreational, community, and healthcare purposes if conducted with hospitals and schools, but they would also fit well on business properties and transport hubs. One political party in Eindhoven is currently interested in rooftop gardens.

- Combining the London Food Council's notion that a certain percentage of the city's food must be produced within a given radius – mixing local and non local supply sources – with the concept of giving large areas of underused public space to entrepreneurs guided towards producing public goods. First, a desired and feasible mix of local and non local food sourcing could be outlined, and then the identification and allocation of public spaces to entrepreneurs could be based on the need for local food production or activities organizing non local food sourcing in a sustainable fashion.

- Combining management of public green areas by neighborhood inhabitants with the maintenance, cultivation, and quantitative increase of local plant varieties. This was considered a viable commercial business model. In this scenario, people would organize green area maintenance policy to maximize benefits of this local varieties management scheme. Participants envisioned this combination as having value in enhancing local resilience through diversity, community building, education, and generating new livelihoods.

Reflections on the process by participants were positive – they saw the mash-up of local and non local seeds as providing a useful level of concreteness while stimulating creativity through the use of non local seeds, which also prevented conversations from getting too stuck in the present. This method can be applied across a range of topics that can allow free thinking to generate novel solutions in diverse groups of people – an important tool in addressing many of the complex and uncertain challenges facing urban settings in the future.

16.3.5 Reflections on Experimenting with Seed Scenarios

The above examples are only summaries of several ways in which new scenarios can be created using seeds. These examples are still somewhat limited – in the Millennium Assessment-guided examples, the existing scenarios provide a fairly dominant (and preexisting) top-down context for seed development; in the Eindhoven examples, the focus is only on mashing up seeds to create scenarios that are purely vision oriented – which can be perceived as good or bad, depending on the purpose of the exercise.

A number of ways to move beyond such limitations have been proposed, including:

- The use of more randomly combined Anthropocene elements, rather than fully developed scenario worlds to frame the seeds, could break the process out of limitations placed on it by existing scenarios.

- The combination of many such smaller scenario narratives in the context of a given preexisting scenario, and the exploration of how these narratives would change that scenario, could create a more emergent process.

- Iterations of seeds transforming their contexts and leading to new scenarios, setting the scene for new time periods would also allow greater influence of bottom-up scenario elements.

- If the goal is to test the seeds against extreme future conditions, we could introduce "wildcard" scenarios that stretch plausibility, but which would have major impacts (van Notten et al. 2005).

- Finally, researchers in the project organize codesign processes where many games and other methods for seed-based scenario building are created and explored, adding to an increasing understanding of the possibility space for seed-based scenario creation.

The similarity and lack of novelty among existing sets of scenarios is partly a result of their being developed by macro-level drivers or assumptions and being tied to notions of consensus about plausibility (van Vuuren et al. 2012; Ramírez and Selin 2014). The examples in this chapter provide an indication that the use of existing seeds as a starting point helps to develop concrete and tangible scenarios of future developments, while their combination, under diverse conditions, ensures novelty through recombination. A helpful next step could include the testing of the proposed scenario methods to combine seeds into novel futures, and comparison of the results with existing methods in terms of the novelty of their content.

16.4 Conclusions and a Future Research Agenda

Currently, negative – or even dystopian – visions dominate representations of the future in popular media as well as in scientific documents (see, for example, Chapter 43). We aim, through our seeds project, to bring a positive, realistic, social-ecological perspective to discussions of the Anthropocene, which are typically divided between visions of technological rapture and social collapse. We do this by collecting and analyzing seeds – examples of projects, ways of thinking, or initiatives that can lead towards a better future.

Scientists have long pointed to the urgent need for transformations towards sustainability (Clark 2001; Kates et al. 2001; Raskin et al. 2002; Schellnhuber et al. 2011). These shifts will likely require radical changes in values and beliefs, as well as in patterns of behavior, governance, and management (Olsson et al. 2014). Yet despite a growing number of promising conceptual frameworks for studying sustainability transformations, we have little practical, on-the-ground knowledge about how it actually happens. We believe that collections of seeds can be useful in at least four interesting ways:

1.   They can be used as part of transformation research projects to analyze how transformation occurs over a period of time. This aspect of our project links to testing and adding to the "Theory of Change" by tracking real-world examples of niche experiments that have the potential to disrupt the dominant regime. By tracking the progress of many seeds in different contexts as they interact, adapt, and scale, our project could bring enlightening new insights regarding how to create enabling environments for sustainability transformations.

2.   They can stimulate innovation and discussion, especially through combining and connecting seeds into new global scenarios. In particular, the seeds can be used to develop new, bottom-up scenarios that are concrete and holistic, yet challenging and novel. By creating these novel futures, seeds give decision-makers more creative tools for navigating towards more positive futures than the standard scenario archetypes (see Hunt et al. 2012).

3.   They can be used to analyze social-ecological diversity and interactions across scales. An analysis of seeds can help us understand where they arise and perhaps why or how they arise, as well as which types of seeds are common in which situations. Linking this understanding to bottom-up scenario processes can also aid in helping to achieve better cross-scale scenario linkages for understanding the relationship between ecosystem services and well-being from the local to the global levels, thereby inspiring new policy actions (see Kok et al. 2016).

4.   They can be used in action research. As seeds are linked to real people making real change on the ground, this provides the opportunity for action research that brings seed initiators together in an innovative, participatory engagement like a "Transformation-lab" or creative scenario process. This space can be designed to achieve a variety of objectives, such as to share insights and ideas on opening up transformative spaces, creating novel visions of the future, or strategic planning of a particular niche group of seeds. Because cities around the world may be more similar to one another than they are to the countryside nearby, this might be an invigorating way to spread positive urban transformation worldwide.

The recognition of a need for more engaged, interdisciplinary research that works with practitioners has been seen as an important shift within the sustainability community, but this requires "safe spaces" in which to experiment (Pereira et al. 2015). Our Seeds project is one such experimental space that is constantly adapting as new ideas or opportunities arise. The applicability of the seeds concept spans local to global levels, so the proposed research pathways are relevant to many different contexts. All four of the aspects outlined above have the potential to offer new insights for understanding and enabling sustainability transformations in urban environments in the Anthropocene. As the project continues to grow and learn, we hope that it will contribute significantly to our understanding of how it may be possible to create a "Good Anthropocene."

◆ References

Andersson, E., S. Barthel, S. Borgström, J. Colding, T. Elmqvist, C. Folke, and Å. Gren. 2014. Reconnecting Cities to the Biosphere: Stewardship of Green Infrastructure and Urban Ecosystem Services. *Ambio* 43 (4): 445–453.

Bennett, E.M., M. Solan, R. Biggs, T. McPhearson, A.V. Norström, P. Olsson, L. Pereira, G.D. Peterson, C. Raudsepp-Hearne, and F. Biermann. 2016. Bright Spots: Seeds of a Good Anthropocene. *Frontiers in Ecology and the Environment* 14 (8): 441–448.

Bulkeley, H., and M.M. Betsill. 2005. *Cities and Climate Change: Urban Sustainability and Global Environmental Governance*. Vol. 4. Oxford: Psychology Press.

Carpenter, S.R., H.A. Mooney, J. Agard, D. Capistrano, R.S. DeFries, S. D'ia, T. Diet, et al. 2009. Science for Managing Ecosystem Services: Beyond the Millennium Ecosystem Assessment. *Proceedings of the National Academy of Sciences* 106 (5): 1305–1312.

Clark, W.C. 2001. A Transition toward Sustainability. *Ecology Law Quarterly* 27(4): 1021–1075.

Geels, F.W. 2002. Technological Transitions as Evolutionary Reconfiguration Processes: A Multi-Level Perspective and a Case-Study. *Research Policy* 31: 1257–1274. doi:10.1016/S0048-7333(02)00062–8.

Gelcich, S., T.P. Hughes, P. Olsson, C. Folke, O. Defeo, and M. Fernández, et al. 2010. Navigating Transformations in Governance of Chilean Marine Coastal Resources. *Proceedings of the National Academy of Sciences of the United States of America* 107 (39): 16794–16799. doi:10.1073/pnas.1012021107.

Grimm, N.B., S.H. Faeth, N.E. Golubiewski, C.L. Redman, J. Wu, X. Bai, and J.M. Briggs. 2008. Global Change and the Ecology of Cities. *Science* 319 (5864): 756–60.

Gunderson, L.H., and C.S. Holling. 2002. *Panarchy: Understanding Transformations in Human and Natural Systems*. Washington, DC: Island Press.

Hunt, D.V.L., D.R. Lombardi, S. Atkinson, A.R.G. Barber, M. Barnes, C.T. Boyko, et al. 2012. Scenario Archetypes: Converging rather than Diverging Themes. *Sustainability* 4 (4): 740–772.

IPCC. 2013. Summary for Policymakers, in T.F. Stocker, D. Qin, G-K. Plattner, M. Tignor, S.K. Allen, J. Boschung, et al. (eds.) *Climate Change 2013: The Physical Science Basis Contribution of Working Group 1 to the Fifth Assessment Report of the Intergovernmental Panel on Climate Change* Cambridge: Cambridge University Press. doi:10.1017/CBO9781107415324.004.

Kates, R.W., W.C. Clark, R. Corell, J.M. Hall, C.C. Jaeger, I. Lowe, et al. 2001. Sustainability Science. *Science* 292 (5517): 641–42.

Kok, M.T.J., K. Kok, G.D. Peterson, R. Hill, J. Agard, and S.R. Carpenter. 2016. Biodiversity and Ecosystem Services Require IPBES to Take Novel Approach to Scenarios. *Sustainability Science* 129(1): 177–181. doi:10.1007/s11625-016-0354-8.

Martin, L.J., J.E. Quinn, E.C. Ellis, M.R. Shaw, M.A. Dorning, L.M. Hallett, N.E. Heller, R.J. Hobbs, C.E. Kraft, and E. Law. 2014. Conservation Opportunities across the World's Anthromes. *Diversity and Distributions* 20 (7): 745–755.

Meadows, D.H., D.H Meadows, J. Randers, and W.W. Behrens III. 1972. *The Limits to Growth: A Report to the Club of Rome (1972)*. New York: Universe Books.

Millennium Ecosystem Assessment. 2005. *Ecosystems and Human Well-Being: Synthesis*. Washington, DC: Island Press.

Moore, M.-L., D. Riddell, and D. Vocisano. 2015. Scaling Out, Scaling Up, Scaling Deep: Strategies of Non-Profits in Advancing Systemic Social Innovation. *Journal of Corporate Citizenship* 58 (June): 67–84.

Moore, M.-L., O. Tjornbo, E. Enfors, C. Knapp, J. Hodbod, J.A. Baggio, A. Norström, P. Olsson, and D. Biggs. 2014. Studying the Complexity of Change: Toward an Analytical Framework for Understanding Deliberate Social-Ecological Transformations. *Ecology and Society* 19 (4).

Oksanen, J., F. Guillaume Blanchet, M. Friendly, R. Kindt, P. Legendre, and D. McGlinn, et al. 2016. Vegan: Community Ecology Package. R Package Version 2.4.1.

Olsson, P., C. Folke, and T. Hahn. 2004. Social-Ecological Transformation for Ecosystem Management: The Development of Adaptive Co-Management of a Wetland Landscape in Southern Sweden. *Ecology and Society* 9 (4).

Olsson, P., V. Galaz, and W.J. Boonstra. 2014. Sustainability Transformations : A Resilience Perspective. *Ecology and Society* 19 (4).

Olsson, P., L.H. Gunderson, S.R. Carpenter, P. Ryan, L. Lebel, C. Folke, and C.S. Holling. 2006. Shooting the Rapids: Navigating Transitions to Adaptive Governance of Social-Ecological Systems. *Ecology and Society* 11 (1).

Paradis, E., J. Claude, and K. Strimmer. 2004. APE: Analyses of Phylogenetics and Evolution in R Language. *Bioinformatics* 20 (2): 289–290.

Pereira, L., T. Karpouzoglou, Doshi, S., and N. Frantzeskaki. 2015. Organising a Safe Space for Navigating Social-Ecological Transformations to Sustainability. *International Journal of Environmental Research and Public Health* 12 (6): 6027–6044. doi:10.3390/ijerph120606027.

Preiser, R., L.M. Pereira, and R. Biggs. 2017. Navigating alternative framings of human-environment interactions: variations on the theme of 'Finding Nemo'. Anthropocene 20: 83–87.

R Core Team. 2016. *R: A Language and Environment for Statistical Computing*. Vienna: R Foundation for Statistical Computing.

Ramírez, R., and C. Selin. 2014. Plausibility and Probability in Scenario Planning. *Foresight* 16 (1): 54–74.

Raskin, P., T. Banuri, G.C. Gallopin, P. Gutman, A. Hammond, R.W. Kates, and R. Swart. 2002. *Great Transition: The Promise and Lure of the Times Ahead*. Stockholm: Stockholm Environment Institute.

Rockström, J., W. Steffen, K. Noone, A. Persson, F. S. Chapin, E. F. Lambin, T. M. Lenton, M. Scheffer, C. Folke, H. J. Schellnhuber, B. Nykvist, C. A. de Wit, T. Hughes, S. van der Leeuw, H. Rodhe, S. Sörlin, P. K. Snyder, R. Costanza, U. Svedin, M. Falkenmark, L. Karlberg, R. W. Corell, V. J. Fabry, J. Hansen, B. Walker, D. Liverman, K. Richardson, P. Crutzen, and J. A. Foley. 2009. A safe operating space for humanity. *Nature* 461(7263): 472–475.

Sawyer, J.S. 1972. Man-Made Carbon Dioxide and the 'Greenhouse' Effect. *Nature* 239 (5366): 23–26.

Schellnhuber, H.J., D. Messner, C. Leggewie, R. Leinfelder, N. Nakicenovic, S. Rahmstorf, S. Schlacke, J. Schmid, and R. Schubert. 2011. *World in Transition: A Social Contract for Sustainability*. Berlin: German Advisory Council on Global Change (WBGU)(Flagship Report).

Seto, K.C., M. Fragkias, B. Güneralp, and M.K. Reilly. 2011. A Meta-Analysis of Global Urban Land Expansion. *PloS One* 6 (8): e23777. https://doi.org/10.1371/journal.pone.0023777

Steffen, W., M.O. Andreae, B. Bolin, P.M. Cox, P.J. Crutzen, U. Cubasch, H. Held, et al. 2004. Abrupt Changes: The Achilles Heel of the Earth System. *Environment* 46 (3): 8–20

Steffen, W., W. Broadgate, L. Deutsch, O. Gaffney, and C. Ludwig. 2015. The Trajectory of the Anthropocene: The Great Acceleration. *The Anthropocene Review*. 2(1): 1–18. doi:10.1177/2053019614564785.

United Nations. 2009. *World Urbanization Prospects: The 2009 Revision*. New York: United Nations.

van der Helm, R. 2009. The Vision Phenomenon: Towards a Theoretical Underpinning of Visions of the Future and the Process of Envisioning. *Futures* 41 (2): 96–104. doi:10.1016/j.futures.2008.07.036.

Van Notten, Ph. W.F, A.M. Sleegers, and M.B.A. van Asselt. 2005. The Future Shocks: On Discontinuity and Scenario Development. *Technological Forecasting and Social Change* 72 (2): 175–194.

Van Vuuren, D.P., M.T.J. Kok, B. Girod, P.L. Lucas, and B. de Vries. 2012. Scenarios in Global Environmental Assessments: Key Characteristics and Lessons for Future Use. *Global Environmental Change* 22 (4): 884–895.

Vörösmarty, C.J., P.B. McIntyre, M.O. Gessner, D. Dudgeon, A. Prusevich, P. Green, S. Glidden, et al. 2010. Global Threats to Human Water Security and River Biodiversity. *Nature* 467: 555–561. doi:10.1038/nature09549.

Westley, F.R., O. Tjornbo, L. Schultz, P. Olsson, C. Folke, B. Crona, and Ö. Bodin. 2013. A Theory of Transformative Agency in Linked Social-Ecological Systems. *Ecology and Society* 18(3): 27.

Wickham, H. 2009. *ggplot2: Elegant Graphics for Data Analysis*. New York: Springer-Verlag.

Wiek, A., and D. Iwaniec. 2014. Quality Criteria for Visions and Visioning in Sustainability Science. *Sustainability Science* 9 (4): 497–512. doi:10.1007/s11625-013-0208-6.

Supplementary Material

Website: https://goodanthropocenes.net/

Videos from workshops in South Africa: https://www.youtube.com/watch?v=3_pnVBdkhek
https://vimeo.com/215795841

Part IV

Provocations from Practice

Chapter 17: Sustainability, Karachi, and Other Irreconcilables

Mahim Maher

When I was an ugly little kid growing up in Karachi in the 1980s, my upwardly mobile mother used to hound me to get straight As so I could eventually go to a top university like Harvard. ("Look at Dolly Aunty's daughter Naila. She's going to Oxford!"). "Why can't she just let me be?" I inwardly fumed. All I wanted to do was read Anne Frank, listen to Wham!, and climb the Eucalyptus tree in the backyard. It ran up against our house's boundary wall, so I'd climb the tree, run along the top of the wall, and jump down into the alley below. I didn't want *total* freedom – just enough to have a bit of a romp in the neighborhood and loop around to let myself in at the front gate.

I wanted to be left alone but my mother's decade-long nagging persisted and eventually produced an intense revulsion in me for any exhortations to improve intellectually, morally, Islamically, physically, or domestically. At college my favorite book was Dostoevsky's *Notes from Underground* with its splenetic anti-hero. When I returned to Karachi after graduating (from McGill University, the "Harvard of the North"), I drove around listening to the "menacing leer" of P.J. Harvey.[1] When I started working as a journalist, all I wanted to do was drink chai in the "slums" with the boys, or ruffians. I was drawn to ugly. I was going in the opposite direction of progress.

It was, therefore, with great unease that I received the words "sustainability" and "resilience" when I began to cover Karachi as a journalist heading the metro section of a daily English newspaper. A fellowship on urban growth and conferences abroad brought me in touch with urban planners who kept talking about "smart" cities. (Just to spite them, a friend of mine and I created "The Dumb Cities Project." It never took off.) I didn't know enough urban planning theory to unpack "sustainability" or "resilience," and, of course, I agree that going forward these are crucial considerations for our global megacities. But somehow, I just wanted Karachi to be left alone. When the politicians running

---

[1] Taken from Ben Hewitt's article 'P.J. Harvey: 10 of the Best' in *The Guardian*, Jan 14, 2015. www.theguardian.com/music/musicblog/2015/jan/14/pj-harvey-10-of-the-best.

the city would talk about "improving" it and making it like Dubai, I would recoil inside. "Let us be," I'd say. I'd return from conferences with urban planners from New York and feel shame. It was with dread that we'd run news on how Karachi ranked 160th yet again on the green cities index. It didn't make sense for the city government to try to clean the city by removing the pushcart vendors it described as "encroachments."

And so it was from this position of ire, shot through with anxiety, that I approached this provocation. Before writing it, I began by looking up the meanings of "sustain" in the *Oxford English Dictionary*. Sustainable: able to be maintained at a certain rate or level. Sustain: bear the weight without breaking. Undergo or suffer. Cause to continue for an extended period or without interruption. These are semantics that fit Karachi. We keep going. We are. We will kind of be like this for a while.

No, we don't have enough water, housing, mass transit, sewage systems, or parks. We hitchhike.[2] We don't recycle unless Afghan rag-pickers are involved.[3] We regulate our bus schedule with paper tokens.[4] We suffer from "project-itis" instead of "long-term vision." We haven't had a census since 1998, so we don't even know how big we are.[5] But we continue to grow as one of the world's megacities. We don't have enough housing for the poor, but we have space for Burmese migrants and hungry villagers whose fields have dried up. We know. We know.

And so, perhaps the meaning of "sustainable" that fits is the one that lets people be. Karachi can't be prodded into progressing. Perhaps it will happen in time, organically. I'll never forget the comfort provided by Eugénie Birch after I was bummed out at a conference. She is the codirector of the Penn Institute for Urban Research and knows a thing or two about cities. She reminded me that cities like New York or London only very recently got their act together. I thought of the movie *Gangs of New York* and nodded. That's Karachi today.

We can learn from New York, of course. But perhaps Karachi can't apply "sustainability" or "resilience" in the same way. Our systems are different. We have grown to be a city run on informality, as has been brilliantly explored by

---

[2] Mahim Maher "What the Hitchhiking Women of Moach Goth can teach the Sindh Govt," April 3, 2015, *The Friday Times*, www.thefridaytimes.com/tft/what-the-hitchhiking-women-of-moach-goth-can-teach-the-sindh-government/

[3] Farhan Anwar "Solid Waste Management: Need for a Cohesive Approach to Make up for Failed Attempts," November 11, 2013, *The Express Tribune*, http://tribune.com.pk/story/630124/solid-waste-management-need-for-a-cohesive-approach-to-make-up-for-failed-attempts/

[4] Mahim Maher, "Timekeeping and Transport: The Minute Men of Karachi," May 22, 2014, *The Express Tribune*. http://tribune.com.pk/story/711471/timekeeping-and-transport-the-minute-men-of-karachi/

[5] "Census Not Put Off Indefinitely, Says Qaim," March 2, 2016, *The News*, www.thenews.com.pk/print/102248-Census-not-put-off-indefinitely-says-Qaim

Laurent Gayer in his book *Karachi: Ordered Disorder and the Struggle for the City.*[6] We need our own understanding of "smart city" based on our own knowledge. I keep going back to what postcolonial theorist Gayatri Chakravorty Spivak has argued: We have to speak for ourselves and not be spoken for. That can only come from our own people, the city government we elect – we just got a new one after a six-year void – and our home-grown urban planners. These professors need to be in elected office instead of in the classroom.

There are disconnects. Our people are just beginning to enjoy a relatively crime-free Karachi after decades of bombings, murders, gang wars, and terrorist attacks. We're making mistakes, of course, some of which perhaps can't be undone. We're building flyovers instead of transit lanes, and we prefer malls to open bazaars. But didn't Seoul rip out a highway and run a river through it?[7]

Perhaps cities like New York and London, Seoul and Singapore have become what they wanted when their people started knowing what their city should be (even if through debate and dissent and the push and pull of big business interests). Or perhaps it is the vision of one person who can implement it that counts. Karachi has neither right now. We have just elected a mayor, but even if he drives forward a vision acceptable to all in Karachi, he only controls one-third of the city – Karachi has 13 land-owning agencies, a majority of which are army-run cantonments. If sustainability is about resources, then we need to stop fighting over them before we can even think of renewing them. Knowing is key – knowing beyond just the basics of needing, perhaps starting with simple information and transparency in our transactions, especially the people-to-government kind.

I've often marveled at how building sites in London would have clearly displayed information about the entire construction project and permits. In Karachi, illegal buildings spring up overnight in parks, and even if journalists go digging, they can never really find out who permitted it and who is behind it. Sometimes it's simple information, such as the address of the town office where you can get a copy of your birth certificate. No map exists of the jurisdictions of Karachi's police stations (which is why we have cases of cops chucking

---

[6] "I decided to adopt a synoptic perspective, which would try to make sense of the wonder that is Karachi, as a whole. Journalists and scholars alike denigrated it as a 'chaotic city', an ungovernable, utterly unpredictable urban mass. If I wanted to counter these dominant narratives, I had to adopt the same wide frame of analysis and show that, as a whole, Karachi does work despite and sometimes through violent unrest," says Laurent Gayer in his interview with *Mid-Day*, July 3, 2014 (www.mid-day.com/articles/the-shiv-sena-and-mqm-share-similarities-laurent-gayer/15421151).

[7] Cheonggyecheon is an 11-km modern stream that runs through downtown Seoul as an urban renewal project. The stream was covered with an elevated highway after the Korean War (1950–1953). Then in 2003, the elevated highway was removed to restore the stream to its present form today (http://english.visitseoul.net/attractions/Cheonggyecheon-Stream_/35#).

bodies over the "line" to avoid the workload of investigating cases).[8] When I went hunting for a map of the city's electoral constituencies, I had to sneakily take photos of a handmade one from the election commission's office because none existed online and they weren't allowing me to take a copy.[9] Women find it hard to get around town because there is no publicly available and reliable information on the bus routes and schedules.

Don't get me wrong. The burden rests solely with us to make Karachi "liveable" and "sustainable." It's just that liveable and sustainable don't make sense to me right now. My instinct says that solutions lie in our informality, in our "ugliness." (To me Karachi's ugliness and informality is beautiful, but I am acutely aware that I speak of Karachi from an extremely privileged position.)

And so I search not for a way out and upwards, but by going around to return – just like climbing the wall of my house and letting myself in by the front gate.

---

[8] Faraz Khan, "Police Inspector Caught Leaving a Corpse in Another Station's Limits," *The Express Tribune*, January 12, 2012, http://tribune.com.pk/story/320395/police-inspector-caught-leaving-a-corpse-in-another-stations-limits/.

[9] Mahim Maher, "The Hunt for Karachi's Constituency Map," December 22, 2012, http://blogs.tribune.com.pk/story/15312/the-hunt-for-karachi%E2%80%99s-constituency-map/.

Chapter 18: What Knowledge Do Cities Themselves Need?

Robert McDonald

One of the stated big questions of this book is to ask what kind of knowledge is needed for smart urban environmental decision-making. This is an important question to ask, especially for long-term researchers looking to plan scientific activities over many years.

I work as science support for the Nature Conservancy's urban sustainability program. At any given time, we have projects in nearly 50 cities all over the world, with goals ranging from biodiversity protection to ecosystem service provision to youth empowerment. So while I still have (I hope) one foot in the world of academia, I also have another foot firmly in the world of the conservation practitioner. In the course of my job, I interact with municipal policy-makers, and work with Nature Conservancy staffers that live and work in these communities.

In all these conversations, I have never heard anyone working for a municipality ask to "coproduce" scientific knowledge with us. Many of these practitioners may not even know what this concept means. Similarly, the debate about whether good science should be interdisciplinary or transdisciplinary would seem sterile and boring to most policy-makers and planners. It isn't that these aren't good ideas – indeed, the best urban sustainability science projects involve deep involvement of those who would use the knowledge created. When setting project goals, having decision-makers involved ensures the sustainability science projects are asking the right questions. While designing the methodology, it is vital to make some practitioners understand and agree with the science methods used. And of course, while choosing how to communicate results, involving decision-makers ensures that they have a greater impact on decision-making.

The problem is that academics sometimes find it fascinating to study the process of collaboration itself. Academics can write whole papers on the process of the coproduction of knowledge, transdisciplinarity, and so on. We can then debate which theory about process is most effective, or sharpen the semantic differences between different theories. This is normal and healthy for an academic discipline, but every day spent studying the process is a day not spent creating practical knowledge that a city can use.

I am skeptical that there is a universal answer to what knowledge cities need, but I would much rather ask decision-makers themselves, "What knowledge do you need in *your* city?"

The quest for universal answers is, of course, part of science. But I doubt our ability as scientists to gaze into our crystal balls, our scenarios and models, and divine what the distant future will bring. The pace of technological and social change is so rapid that we have to have a lot of humility about our long-term predictions. I would much rather say we ask practitioners what decisions need to be made in the short term and what information is needed to inform those decisions. I am not saying that studies of the process of being relevant are not important. I just want to reserve a place in urban sustainability for works that answer the short-term, pragmatic questions that decision-makers have in a timely way. This work is sometimes not theoretically interesting, in the sense of creating brand new methods or models. Sometimes it just means taking existing information (for instance, forecasts from climate change models) and presenting it in a format that supports municipal decision-making. This is not the kind of science work that makes for novel, cutting-edge journal papers, perhaps. But it is often what urban managers and decision-makers actually need.

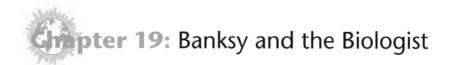

Chapter 19: Banksy and the Biologist

Redrawing the Twenty-First Century City

Debra Roberts

In my view, Banksy, the British street artist from Bristol, is one of the most insightful urban commentators of our time. His prankster performance art talks to us about the way cities breathe and sweat and create and destroy. His artistic vision has unsettled both the art world and city hall alike, and challenged us to see ourselves and our cities as they are, not as we think they should be. His images do not sit easily in rarefied art galleries (even though he has been known to smuggle his works into museums such as the MoMA), but rather reach out and challenge us where we live, surprising us on street corners, telephone boxes, and campervans. The element of risk is central to Banksy's art. In his words, "The greatest crimes in the world are not committed by people breaking the rules but by people following the rules" (Banksy 2005).

Perhaps intuitively following this guidance, I realized early on in my career as a biologist interested in cities that my science was best tested on the street rather than in a remote laboratory. As a result, over two decades ago, I traded in the ivory tower for city hall and now practice what I can only describe as "guerrilla street science." As a scientist-in-practice, I have become a hybrid personality, operating at and across the boundaries of science, policy, and practice with no fixed institutional allegiances. Much like Banksy's street art, this sort of street science is not politically correct or value neutral, and it is often viewed with suspicion and regarded as a political bad. It is seen as going where science should not go, challenging existing bases of power, and creating conflicting discourses. Its proponents are heavily criticized and interrogated: Can a good policy-maker really be a good scientist, or does science get in the way of good policy-making? By adopting this more fluid and uncertain identity, the scientist-in-practice becomes someone of whom all formal interest groups are wary; they can never be certain of which agenda those scientists-in-practice are advancing. Are we "bombing" – in graffiti terms "to bomb" is to paint many surfaces in an area – policy with science, or science with policy? Or ignoring both and simply getting the job done?

In this difficult environment, the risk-takers survive by finding others like themselves, building informal networks that are often more influential than formal reporting lines. Building trust and smart alliances within these subversive crews – a crew, krew, or cru is a group of associated writers or graffiti artists that often work together – helps create an ecology of revolutions that is more sustainable than just a single, winner-takes-all revolution. In this world, decision-making is more organic and processes more flexible, and the normative constraints of traditional science, policy, and practice do not normally apply. As a result, scientists-in-practice that can navigate the gray institutional spaces are generally better able to maneuver through complex institutional processes that might otherwise prove time-consuming and limit innovation. This suggests that the transgressive change required in the world's cities might be best catalyzed in these informal, noninstitutionalized shadows, rather than in the formal institutional limelight. Street art and street science have more in common than one might think.

Working in this unchartered territory also means reprioritizing conceptual reference points: Developing an understanding that political ecology is as important as ecology; that perception is as powerful (if not more powerful) than fact; and that it isn't what you know, but who you know. I have learned that good ideas have a limited political shelf life, even if they remain scientifically valid, creating an ongoing need to find new scientific motivations to justify the same actions. As a result, you will fight the same battles over and over again, often in different political cycles. Unfortunately, in the real world, science is not a silver bullet that removes the policy challenge with a single shot; it also does not tell you how to deal with the death threats linked to scientific decisions that frustrate unsustainable political or economic ambition!

The value of the informal networks of risk-takers and change-makers who work well beyond the reach of performance management plans and indicators cannot be overstated. They signal the diversity and complexity of skills required to drive real change and suggest the need to create a multiplicity of change agents, from research scientists to scientists-in-practice, rather than striving (rather unrealistically) for single individuals with a full range of transdisciplinary skills. How do we do this? My experiences suggest that the people with the capacity to harness the gray institutional spaces and to connect and challenge the formal systems benefit greatly from the creation of nexus points where the policy and scientific world engage on a regular basis. In the city I work in, we do this through research partnerships established with the local university that engages both the academic and local government officials. These interactions make the gaps and opportunities more legible to the institutional entrepreneurs in both environments. We also actively seek out people who are institutionally irreverent and encourage them to drive agendas of change by providing them with a community of support and ongoing opportunities to work on programs and projects capable of introducing new ideas and information into traditional systems. This creates a complex canvas for action on which we begin to sketch out multiple possible futures for our city.

As the challenges facing the world's cities grow, we must find ways of putting an increasingly diverse range of conceptual and tactical spray cans into the hands of our scientists and policy-makers – this will often blur the lines between science, policy, and maybe even art!

❀ Reference

Banksy, 2005. *Wall and Piece*. London: Century.

Chapter 20: Every Community Needs a Forest of Imagination

Andrew Grant

In the next 50 years, we need to transform every piece of urban landscape into a form that best supports the survival of the human race. This new urban landscape will increasingly provide our life support system, not just for air, water, and food – it must also become our refuge for creative inspiration and a catalyst for imagination.

I propose "Forests of Imagination" as a new type of urban landscape designed to evoke a sense of primal landscape and to encourage creative thoughts. They can be permanent or temporary, but their purpose will be to offer a particular place that reconnects us with the wonder, moods, and meaning of raw nature while offering inspirational experiences. I would like to see every community having easy access to a Forest of Imagination.

Wildness is synonymous with inspiration and contemplation. William Shakespeare, Percy Bysshe Shelley, Virginia Woolf, Albert Einstein, Rachel Carson, David Attenborough, Lucille Clifton all have used elemental nature as a source of inspired thought. I suggest we all need wildness in our daily lives to feed our imagination, just as we need vitamins to sustain our bodies. Charles Darwin recognized this need and made his own famous Sand Walk at Down House in Surrey, England. This provided him with a five-minute walk that passed through a formal garden, an open meadow, and the dark heart of a wood. This was his choice of place to think and be inspired by the natural world around him – his Forest of Imagination – which inspired him towards one of the greatest discoveries of all time.

In modern times, we have planned our cities around function and commerce, where nature is seen as a commodity to harvest, to set the scene, to provide air and water and food – but not as a fundamental part of our existence and certainly not as a source of natural wonder and inspiration. Instead, the modern city has tempered the wildness of nature to create an idyllic, gentle world far removed from the unpredictable "garden" of nature. Matt Ridley said, "Mountains may have more majesty, forests more fear ... formal gardens more symmetry – but it is the informal English parkland of Capability Brown that you would choose for a picnic, or for a visit with a potential lover. It feels natural" (Ridley 2016). Such ideas of nature have inspired countless urban parks across the world, but at what cost? The removal of encounters with more unexpected and challenging natural experiences within our cities has effectively anesthetized our engagement with the land and the very systems of life on which we rely.

Recent flooding in many UK cities has triggered a collective memory of our forgotten relationship with rivers and floods and weather. This echoes the astonishing growth of the Rewilding movement in the United Kingdom and across Europe, which is partly about ecological restoration of strategic habitats. But it's also about our emotional reconnection to nature. It promotes the reintroduction of key predators and keystone species into the wilder areas of our landscapes, but so far has not fully addressed the opportunities within cities. Anna Jorgenson of Sheffield University suggests that "we all need wildness" as both a projection of ourselves and also as a way of making sense of the world that is beyond our imagination (Jorgensen 2016). Her experiments into urban rewilding, based on the insertion of pockets of naturalized planting into more traditional parks, are proving there is an appetite for this urban wildness that, if introduced intelligently, can greatly enhance not just the working ecosystem of the city, but also the daily health and well-being of the local communities. It seems we are ready to be challenged and to welcome back the unknown and uncontrolled into our city environments. Still, just creating an additional urban habitat is not enough. These spaces must function at a higher level of engagement, since landscape can no longer be seen as the passive backdrop and stage set of Capability Brown and his followers. To survive the future, we need to foster curiosity, analysis, and understanding – but we also need spaces to encourage unimagined new worlds.

To achieve these goals, there has to be a major reinvention of our permanent public landscapes; large-scale changes can be complemented by a program of more experimental, temporary Forest installations. In my home city of Bath in the United Kingdom, we have introduced our own pop-up Forest of Imagination. This is a project about the creative ecology of the city and involves collaboration across generations and between industries. For the last three years, we have transformed a familiar but neglected piece of the city into an abstract Forest, brought to life by artists and scientists, carpenters, architects, landscape architects, school children, college students, parents, grandparents, young and old. It echoes Darwin's Sand Walk. It is a place to be inspired and where a number of different and dramatic experiences, light and dark, funny and sad, colorful and dull, are created around the theme of Forest. Here, the Forest is the home of Imagination.

I believe every community should have their Forest of Imagination, where people are invited to rediscover nature and which generate intuitive responses of delight and fear, senses of beauty and horror. Whether permanent or temporary, these Forests of Imagination can foster the creative genius present in each community and city. At a time when the future of humanity is on a perilous brink, they can and must inspire our future.

◆ References

Ridley, M. 2016. "How Capability Brown Recreated the African Savannah." MattRidley Online Blog. www.rationaloptimist.com/blog/capability-brown/.

Jorgensen, A. 2016. "Why We Need to Change Our Perceptions of Wildness." Sheffield Landscape Blog. https://sola-blog.com/2016/01/12/why-we-need-to-change-our-perceptions-of-wildness/.

Chapter 21: How Can We Shift from an Image-Based Society to a Life-Based Society?

Cecilia Herzog

How can twenty-first century cities sustain life if urban ecosystems, waters, and local residents are not prioritized in urban planning and design? High-tech solutions, disconnected from local natural processes, flows, and climate, are leading people to believe that sustainability is dissociated from nature. I would like to understand what sustainability means when a glass-covered building surrounded by a cosmetic garden, detached from the local culture and environment, receives a green certification.

In a society focused on financial capital, cities must be global in order to be part of the economic system and to attract international investment. So, how does a city become a "global city"? How can a city have a marketable brand recognized in this competitive world? The global city needs an "image" (Jhally 1990), generally represented by iconic architecture, and will thus become an *image-based* city. The image has become more important than substance at all scales, from the individual to the urban landscape. The image is created by outside drivers, market agents that focus on the most profitable and the fastest economic return. This exogenous force doesn't make any real compromises for long-term social and ecological sustainability; it is fluid, and flows with the winds of opportunity. The turns are fast and unpredictable. Frequently, politicians concentrate on the next election and their need for more money. It is easy to understand why decisions are made to invest public money in expensive works of engineering. Corruption is a key issue in this process.

The city I live in, Rio de Janeiro, is a good example. As host of the 2016 Olympic Games, the "Marvellous City" went through a structural transformation according to the values of an image-based society in search of a higher global position. Huge, disconnected, top-down public-financed projects were made to comply with short-term private economic interests. For example, the city has built iconic, image-based, green architecture – such as the Museum of Tomorrow – while its cultural and historic heritage is left to ruin. Likewise, Rio's ecological heritage has been damaged – urban sprawl took over wetlands vulnerable to flooding and sea-level rise through the construction of car-dependent, costly infrastructure and gated communities, perpetuating the mistakes of the past. The focus in this period was doing business as usual: building a marketable city while overlooking its natural, social, and cultural potential.

I strongly believe that cities should mimic nature and should systemically restore socioecological functions that sustain life and protect the environment. Life is our most precious capital to achieve real sustainability. We should enter a *life-based* society, where cities are planned and designed to provide hospitable and liveable environments for people and biodiversity. Economic forces should come from the communities; local potential should be the foundation for sustainable development. The buildings that shape the urban landscape should provide regenerative functions, such as green roofs, walls, and rain gardens that mitigate the urban heat island effect and prevent floods. Investments should incentivize comfortable, safe, and healthy housing for everyone. The economy and real estate development should be based on local and small and medium businesses, minimizing the turns of international economic flows.

Once we know that sustainability depends on ecological, social, and economic factors, what is missing? Ecological education and urban greening may be the bridge to a liveable future in sustainable cities. The challenges are many, but if urbanites don't have the opportunity to experience and learn about nature, they won't understand why they need nature or clean air and water to have healthy lives. They also won't collaborate to change the urban landscape. Educated and participative citizens are crucial in the process of legally control corruption, and monitor investments that will benefit the commons.

Life-based society is only possible if corruption is controlled; otherwise people's interest won't be prioritized, and participation will merely be a legal requirement to legitimate top-down decisions.

Being a green city is also a marketing strategy. Investing in soft-engineered green infrastructure (nature-based solutions – NBS), instead of traditionally built gray infrastructure, is essential. This is not new; however, in order to provide an effective long-term return, the greening of the city has to be genuine – supported by inherent social, cultural, and ecological capacities.

The paradigm shift to life-based society is already happening in many cities. For example, Paris is leading the way in promoting and recovering urban biodiversity (Legenne et al. 2015), and focuses on people and local businesses. Cars are gradually being removed from the urban landscape to prioritize people and green areas. The city has a comprehensive plan to mitigate carbon emissions and to adapt to climate change (PARIS 2012). Effective participation and ecological education have been essential to shift from the image-based city to a life-based city. No doubt, the city faces strong social challenges; justice is a complex issue that also depends on external forces. But Paris – the City of Light – is becoming the *City of Life*: greener, attractive, liveable, sustainable, and resilient.

References

Jhally, S. 1990. "Image-Based Culture: advertising and popular culture", in Dines, G., and Humez, J.M (eds.) *Race, Class, and Media: A Text Reader*. London: Sage Publications, Inc., pp. 249–257.

Legenne, C., Cornet, N., Acerbi, C., and Tedesco, C. 2015. *Redécouvrir la nature en ville. Les carnets pratiques du Sdrif*, n° 6. Paris: Institut d'Aménagement et d'Urbanisme [in French].

PARIS, 2012. "Plan Climat Énergie de Paris," Agence d'Écologie Urbaine, Direction des Espaces Verts et de l'Environment, Paris: Mairie de Paris. http://api-site-cdn.paris.fr/images/70921.

Chapter 22: A Chimera Called "Smart Cities"

Gurbir Singh

There is an obsession in India over the term "smart." People vie for smartphones, smart homes, and, lately, smart cities. After several rounds of competitive bidding, among Indian cities, the Narendra Modi government in the last week of January 2016 released a list of 20 cities that would be comprehensively developed. Another 13 cities were added to the "smart" list in May 2017, bringing the total to 33. The list included Bhubaneswar, the capital of Orissa, one of the most backward states of the country; and Lucknow, the capital of the most populous state of Uttar Pradesh. Two of the largest and most chaotic Indian cities with the largest slum populations – Mumbai and Kolkata – were not included.

The drive to build smart cities must be viewed in the context of the recently announced government policy to provide housing for all by 2022. India has a housing shortage of nearly 18 million units, and 25 percent of its urban population live in illegal shanty and slum hovels. Will the drive for smart cities ameliorate this ballooning problem of homelessness?

The idea of smart cities in India was first floated by Finance Minister Arun Jaitley in May 2014.[1] In his budget speech, he said the government was committed to developing 100 smart cities and allotted around $115 million to draw up plans and priorities. This initiative struck the right chord, as India is rapidly urbanizing. The McKinsey Institute has predicted that more than 590 million Indians, or around 40 percent of the country, will be living in cities and towns by 2030.[2] Conversely, most cities had become a planner's nightmare, with urban expansion mushrooming haphazardly.

No one in the government is quite sure what makes a smart city. It is a European term that identifies technology as the trigger to make life more ordered and comfortable. Sunil Mathur, Siemens India's managing director and CEO, said he had recently made a presentation to government on what

---

[1] www.thehindu.com/business/budget/rs-7060-crore-for-100-smart-cities/article6198022.ece.

[2] www.mckinsey.com/global-themes/urbanization/urban-awakening-in-india

the company thought should be the route to developing smart cities. "Ours was the fifty-sixth definition of smart cities," he acknowledged[3].

Initially, the central government thought it would be developing green field cities; the thinking then veered to retrofitting old cities as brownfield projects. Subsequently, the government realized it had neither the funds nor the planning capacity to complete the initiative for 100 cities together, so it reduced the scope of the project to a first round of 20 cities, wherein $7.7 billion would be invested over five years to develop infrastructure and technology. This is a drop in the funding ocean, considering that approximately $5 trillion is required over a decade to create 100 smart cities.

At best, this project represents tinkering around. For instance, among the 20 smart cities is the posh New Delhi Municipal Corporation area, where the rich live in their colonial-period bungalows. The dense, squalid Old Delhi has been passed over. "Investors' response to the Smart Cities programme is yet lukewarm, because they don't know yet what the fine print is, what they are getting into," Sunil Rohokale, CEO of the ASK Group, told me.[4]

Serious city planners have expressed concern that the concept of smart cities is more to do with erecting shiny glass edifices and icons of corporate well-being than about providing affordable housing or getting rid of slums.

Ranjit Sabhiki, an architect who drew up Delhi's master plan, has written that smart cities "are largely based on the areas developed for middle and high income housing"[5] and often take more than half of the urban land available in towns, whereas affordable housing takes 15 to 20 percent on average. "Because the units are small, and larger numbers can be fitted in small land pockets," he has written, "there has been a tendency to squeeze them into areas of leftover land. Such developments degenerate into squalid slums over short periods of time."[6]

An urban improvement program called the Jawaharlal Nehru National Urban Renewal Mission was launched under the previous Congress regime in 2005. With $20 billion to be spent over a decade, the scheme – with all its flaws – *did* address city-specific transport and housing issues, and strengthened local municipal bodies. The new, right wing BJP government has scrapped that program, replacing it with its own pet schemes. Prime Minister Modi's target of housing for all by 2022 hopes to garner and invest $65 billion over a decade to build 20 million homes. "India's poor can't be left to their fate. We are sitting

---

[3] Siemens India Managing Director and CEO Sunil Mathur made the comment speaking at a conclave on smart cities attended by the author.
[4] Interview with author.
[5] http://bwsmartcities.businessworld.in/article/Will-Smart-Cities-Be-Affordable-/19-02-2015-95841/.
[6] Ibid.

together to discuss how to improve life in cities. Had we recognised the importance of urbanization twenty-five to thirty years back, we would have been par with developed countries and cities," he says.[7] But on the ground, the smart city project has little to do with housing the poor, and much of the grandiose Homes for All project so far remains on paper.

Today, Indian cities are eyesores where a majority live in slums and commute in bestial conditions. People don't live in slums out of choice. They move into shanties when they can't afford anything better. Urban residential property is prohibitively expensive and out of reach for the teeming masses. There is little government supply of housing, and the residential market is largely in the grip of private builders. The last half-yearly survey by Knight Frank India, a consultancy, says that, in 2017, the country is facing the worst depression in the home-buying market in five years.[8] The all-India unsold inventory of homes is over 700,000 units; this would take more than three years to exhaust.

The government has to find swaths of urban land and construct millions of homes at affordable prices for buyers and renters. More importantly, slum communities and citizens' movements have to unleash struggles in the streets and in government planning forums to ensure that basic infrastructure, a hassle-free commute, and a decent home become part of the inalienable rights of new Urban India. The real battle is to not to make cities smart, but to make them livable.

---

[7] www.livemint.com/Politics/lzTVpTHgQ88ABan4KzmdwN/Narendra-Modi-launches-smart-city-housing-urban-renewal-sc.html.
[8] https://housing.com/news/residential-property-sales-fall-lowest-5-years-knight-frank-report/.

Chapter 23: Beyond Fill-in-the-Blank Cities

Cristina Rumbaitis del Rio

In the past few years, there has been a proliferation of city-network initiatives, most of which are donor-led. For donors and governments alike, there is a strong investment case for developing and participating in such networks. These networks have shown that cities are willing and able to learn from each other, and frequently take up innovations and good practice when it is pragmatic and makes sense for their contexts. City governments have resources of their own that can be used to implement solutions once they have been identified and tested. And when networked together, city leaders have amplified voices and greater influence on the global agendas that matter to them. In short, the potential impact of such networks can be tantalizingly outsized – leveraging large investment flows, shifting global agendas, and ideally improving the lives of millions through better urban governance.

The challenge is not that these programs exist or that they have multiplied in recent years. Nor is it necessarily a problem that these initiatives are largely donor-led. Most of these programs have very important goals that they aim to achieve, which would otherwise not get the attention they deserve if not for the external seed funding. The challenge is that most of these initiatives are structured and implemented in a generic, cookie-cutter manner that ignores the complexity of city governance systems, physical environments, and social dynamics. This simplified, reductive approach can unfortunately lead to wasted resources and unintended negative consequences.

Programs that seek to network a large number of cities, especially a highly diverse set of cities, often start their work with cities with a highly structured process. There are templates and worksheets to fill out, assessment tools to be completed, engagement meetings and working groups formed, 10-point plans drafted, and public commitment ceremonies and press events to be held. These can be applied rigidly and blindly at times. And although "templatizing" a process can help reduce the transaction costs of working across multiple cities and can facilitate comparison, it inadvertently gives an oversimplified and singular picture of what it means to be, and how to become, a more sustainable/

resilient/healthy city. It leaves the impression that the solutions that developed in and for London and New York are the only valid way forward. The standardized approach also reduces the opportunity of learning from a diversity of approaches (some of which may be quite replicable) that cities might develop if they were allowed more flexibility.

These rigid processes are often supported by external consultants, who fly in with global solutions but often have only a partial understanding of the challenges a city is facing, or the context in which they are operating. As a result, local-level engagement and goodwill are quickly lost, local capacity and creativity are crowded out, and solutions are misapplied and later abandoned once the funding ends.

The usual, cookie-cutter approach taken often masks the complexity of cities, and overlooks the forces that are really driving urban development patterns. Factors such as real estate and property development interests, or party politics, for example, are rarely examined. Worse, these programs, which are often a source of pride and media attention, can also be manipulated to draw attention away from issues that aren't getting worked on – inequity, social marginalization, and police violence, to name a few.

A better approach is perhaps to start with a localized understanding of the sustainability/resilience/health challenges facing a city by engaging citizens as well as the city leadership in defining the precise objectives of the initiative and the process to be followed. Providing some leeway in terms of defining objectives and process will help to contextualize the initiative's objectives within the priorities of the city, and may improve the relevance of the initiative to the reality of daily life of citizens.

Second, investing in high-quality facilitation is critical. Facilitators must be able to guide city leaders and stakeholders through a process, bringing soft skills as well as technical skills, blending global and local knowledge; yet, facilitators must not do it for the local constituents. It's important that the facilitation process be genuine and not a "facipulation" that seems participatory, but only superficially engages or even manipulates different stakeholders. The facilitation process needs to be open to a certain amount of messiness, including conflict; an open discussion of different interests, objectives, and values; and some inevitable meandering of the process.

Third, there needs to be room to experiment and innovate within the process. This can take various forms, from testing out ideas in pilot projects to developing new forms and processes for citizen engagement. Creating space for a culture of local innovation is critical to unlocking latent and, with luck, enduring capacity to innovate and change.

Working in this way will take longer and may stray at times from the funder's or the network's core objectives and plans. However, the deeper engagement, more flexible process, and an upfront investment in identifying and/or developing a cadre of skilled facilitators and local innovation capacity may well be worth it and lead to more durable and profound changes in urban systems. Ultimately, only evaluative evidence will tell us what approaches work best under which conditions, as well as what's most cost effective, efficient, and durable. However, in the meantime, it seems worthwhile to experiment with these different ways of working so that we can better understand how to catalyze the widespread changes in urban life and sustainability that are critical to improving the lives of billions and equally critical to maintaining and improving the health of our planet. Embracing the complexity of cities, rather than trying to simplify cities to make them fit into a standard template, will ultimately help city networks meet their objectives and create enduring change in cities.

Chapter 24: Persuading Policy-Makers to Implement Sustainable City Plans

Pengfei Xie

Persuading policy-makers and influencing governance is a complex art. The city is, indeed, a complex system. In achieving a healthy and smooth operation of the urban system, coordination and balance among various subsystems (natural-social-economic) are necessary. In recent years, the need to build sustainable, livable, climate-resilient, and inclusive cities has achieved global consensus. Those who hold these values for cities want to highlight balanced relationships and positive interactions among the subsystems of a city. To make this great idea happen, a city needs to have a roadmap (featuring balanced and coordinated development), and then to follow that roadmap. During this decision-making and enforcement process, the understandings, decisions, and actions of government officials are critical to the success of a government policy. This is especially true in strong, top-down administrations, such as China. As a worker at a nonprofit NGO who advocates for sustainable development in China, I have experience dealing with decision-makers at different levels. But sometimes, my and others' advocacy efforts do not yield expected results. What are the main obstacles in persuading policy-makers?

When city administrators, mayors, and city officials think about issues and make decisions, they bear full responsibility for safeguarding the interests of the whole city and its citizens. This is quite different from the standpoint and responsibility of scholars, professionals, and environmentalists. This simple truth differentiates what these different actors value and their ways of thinking, which, in turn, bring about different attitudes towards urban development strategies. Mayors and city officials have an affinity for operational and practical blueprints that can promote economic development, boost employment, and strengthen social stability. Conversely, experts and representatives of NGOs and civil society tend to recommend roadmaps that feature environmental protection, climate change adaptation and mitigation, and social equity. In my opinion, these are the main obstacles in practice.

Based on the Chinese context and my personal knowledge of working with NGOs, I have a few suggestions for navigating these complex scenarios.

The NGO community needs to show policy-makers the socioeconomic co-benefits that sustainable roadmaps bring through real-world case studies and empirical research findings. These benefits include but are not limited to (1) improved health and longer life expectancy due to better ecological environment (such as air, water, and soil quality); (2) higher quality of life and well-being due to a mix of land use, public transit-oriented development, and the allocation of more public space (which means better access to public services, reduced commuting distances, fewer traffic jams, and more open space for recreational activities); (3) increased employment opportunities in new (low-carbon) industries, such as renewable energy, electric vehicles, green building materials, waste disposal, and ecotourism; (4) the improvement of international recognition and, subsequently, the growth of investment in the city (by implementing a sustainable roadmap, the investment environment will be upgraded and thus likely to attract more capital); and (5) technical and business exchanges with other "like-minded" cities, extended relationships and networks (as a city actively implements the sustainable roadmap, it effectively joins a growing number of cities in the world who set the similar goal to move in the direction of low-carbon, sustainable development. These cities have a common language, and they can benefit through networking, knowledge sharing, and other interactions).

The NGO community should use various strategies to advocate for sustainable urban development, including (1) communicating frequently with city officials to understand their worries, cares, and needs through discussion meetings, workshops and seminars, and relevant conferences organized and hosted by various ministries and local governments; (2) uniting and speaking in one voice to mayors and city officials, as consistency and uniformity are more persuasive than discord and may offer a clearer route to a bigger impact on government policy; and (3) provide training for policy-makers on sustainable urbanization and low-carbon development. NGOs can collaborate with government-authorized training institutions (such as the National Academy for Mayors of China) to jointly compile teaching materials, organize training sessions, and arrange study tours. Sometimes, a respected person, a renowned expert, an admired senior official, and a real-world practice case exert great influence on local policy-makers. In such circumstances, the NGOs can invite the right persons to lecture in the training courses and select the right cases to be investigated in the study tour.

It is a complicated task for NGOs to persuade policy-makers and influence the decision-making process. The NGO community should work to understand the government officials' positions, use language within their lexicon, solve practical problems they care about, and strengthen the officials' capacity on urban sustainability.

Chapter 25: To Live or Not to Live

Urbanization and the Knowledge Worker

Takeshi Takama

Cities may not be viable places to live if people are threatened by lack of space and the accumulation of harmful or uncomfortable factors, such as traffic jams, pollution, and crime. This is a negative reality of urbanization, especially in developing countries such as Indonesia, because the fundamental infrastructure namely mass transportation and wastewater systems, for example, are still being constructed. Most jobs require people to be in the office, factory, or shop, requiring them to live in urban areas near their workplace. Improving the infrastructure that city residents use will be the mainstream approach to improving urbanization, as such improvements directly remove the obstacles to living comfortably.

If a job does not require one to be in these conventional workplaces, the worker no longer needs to live in the city. As such, their approach to work and a comfortable life can be different. These people are so-called knowledge workers, and I am one of them. My work involves telecommuting to a company based in an urban area; however, my company *could*, however be based in a rural area, too.

I live in a rural area of Bali called Canggu and run a think- & do-tank, su-re. co. Although urbanization is increasing here, the negative aspects mentioned above are largely absent. Our staff spends less than 10 minutes commuting to an island-style office without air conditioners; we can go to a beach after work for surfing at sunset. The only major downside is the difficulty of networking, and I still must travel on occasion, but most of my work, such as meetings, research, ordering goods, and outsourcing services, can be done online.

The term "knowledge worker" was first introduced by Peter Drucker in his 1959 book, *Landmarks of Tomorrow* (Drucker 1996). He described them, for example, as programmers, system analysts, technical writers, academic professionals, and researchers. The list can be expanded to some lawyers and schoolteachers, if their physical contact is not required. These knowledge workers develop or use knowledge that is transferred by information infrastructure, such as telephone lines and the Internet, from anywhere in the world.

Knowledge work was once only possible in advanced countries, but now there are opportunities to pursue such a lifestyle in developing countries, as well. In Bali, I have friends from across the globe and from multiple fields who have set up global businesses and start-up projects. In comparison with hard fundamental infrastructure, information infrastructure has improved and spread quickly. While I do not have access to public transportation in my area (save for Uber and Uber-like motorbike services) and there is not a sewage system, I have access to fiber optics and 4G mobile Internet.

There is macroeconomic evidence for an expansion in knowledge work in Indonesia. The Asian Development Bank's 2013 report, *Innovative Asia*, shows general low scores on knowledge economy in this country, but the situation is getting better. In the 1960s, the Indonesian economy was largely driven by agriculture. However, by the end of the last century, agriculture's contribution was less than 20 percent of the national GDP. Globalization and the Internet has accelerated knowledge work not only in Indonesia, but elsewhere as well. China is producing manufactured goods, but it is also selling added value in knowledge, namely through design and marketing. India works not only as the world's call center, but also as a Silicon Valley of sorts, with a bit more humidity and chaos. Why shouldn't Bali also have the same industries in a much nicer environment? In a 2007 World Bank Institute report, *Building Knowledge Economies*, Indonesia was already listed as one of the 18 most successful developing countries moving towards a knowledge economy.

Moreover, as David Kreps predicted in *Corporate Culture and Economic Theory* (1990), it does not matter where we work as long as a brand image and reputation are controlled by knowledge infrastructure. Before individual service providers were rated through sites such as on AirBnB or Uber, academic researchers were rated based on their knowledge, and their reputation was shared across the globe. The significance of research is determined largely by the number of times it is cited by others, and approval or criticism of its research result. These functions are the same as the "like" and "share" buttons or "comment" function on Facebook. Many other knowledge-based positions will rely on similar metrics in the future. There is already a social network service site for specialized computer graphic designers, behance.net. In the future, it will not matter if we sit in the middle of a traffic jam in Jakarta or on a surfboard in Bali before or after work. Instead, we will be judged by the quality of our knowledge products, not where those products came from.

Conventional, hard, fundamental infrastructure supports life in the city, while information infrastructure can help support lifestyles outside of urban areas. Both approaches will create more livable lifestyles – traffic-free commuting by good public transportation, or telecommuting. Hard fundamental infrastructure supports are necessary, as more than half of the global population has been living in urban areas since the end of 2008. However, it is becoming important to develop information infrastructure in developing and advanced countries, as hard infrastructure development may not catch up to the speed of urbanization. Let knowledge workers have the choice to stay in rural areas, which can mitigate urbanization by slowing its velocity.

🌐 *References*

Asian Development Bank. 2013. Innovative Asia: Advancing the Knowledge-Based Economy: Country Case Studies for the People's Republic of China, India, Indonesia, and Kazakhstan. Mandaluyong City: Asian Development Bank.

Drucker, P. 1996. *Landmarks of Tomorrow: A Report on the New "Post Modern" World*, 2nd Edition. Transaction Publishers.

Kreps, D.M. 1990. *Corporate Culture and Economic Theory: Perspectives on Positive Political Economy*. Cambridge: Cambridge University Press.

World Bank. 2007. *Building Knowledge Economies: Advanced Strategies for Development (WBI Development Studies)*. World Bank Publications. https://openknowledge.worldbank.org/handle/10986/6853.

Chapter 26: City Fragmentation and the Commons

Anna Dietzsch

For 500 years, the urban mass of São Paulo has voided out nature, spreading itself with speed and efficiency. Fragile institutions have given way to a private logic that disregards what is public. Cars have taken up the valleys and the river, while the land has been divided, and a fragmented territory exposed its culture. In the logic of the ruling state/city, there is no space for play or for meandering. There is no space for the collective good or collective memory.

The metropolitan area of São Paulo spreads over 8,000 square kilometers with a population of 20 million people, or 10 percent of Brazil's entire population. In the 1930s the city was remodeled to better accommodate cars and, since then, the urban logic of growth and development has followed that path.

Several consequences derived from that decision, including the disappearance of our rivers, which were buried and canalized, as our valleys became avenues. It also led to the decrease in use and importance of our public spaces, as our social lives migrated to the private realm, within walls and buildings. Today the best and the safest options for urban leisure happen in shopping malls, private condominiums, and private clubs. São Paulo became the anti-Jane Jacobs city, prisoner of a vicious cycle that walls up its buildings, abandons its streets and plazas, which then become even more dangerous and drive the walls to rise higher (Figure 26.1).

So when in 2002 the zoning rules changed to accommodate the real estate industry's need to sell more parking spaces and the public sector's need to deal with the ever growing car numbers, no one seemed to mind. The new ordinance stated that one could build aboveground garages without losing any of the allowed floor area ratio, giving developers "free" building area to accommodate cars. The results were disastrous (Figure 26.2).

New buildings were planned to have three to five garage stories above street level, resulting in walled-up fortresses and desolated streets. In some neighborhoods one can walk for up to three blocks without encountering a single opening, a single storefront, or any sign of street life. This new architectural

Figure 26.1 Downtown Sao Paulo in 2002. Photograph by Nelson Kon.

Figure 26.2 Walls isolate the street. Photograph by Anna Dietzsch.

element, along with a zoning ordinance that rules the city's development as an agglomeration of individual lots, created a city of walls.

Fortunately, the mindset has been changing in recent years, with citizens demanding better urban life, as several community groups and not-for-profit organizations have come together to occupy and care for public spaces. The best recognition of this change came with the city's new master plan in 2014, which tried to promote mixed uses, street life, and use of public transportation.

It is within this new understanding that we propose to act, liberating ourselves (and the city) from the pervasive and inefficient parceling of lots defined by walls. We are not against private property. We are not against anyone's right to own real estate. But we are against the fragmented vision of a city that imposes redundancy, isolation, and fear. We are against a city that prioritizes the car and becomes hostage within its own walls.

26.1 A Proposal

The experience of São Paulo exposes the weakness of the idea that a city should be the collection of individual lots in an ever-growing pattern of repetition and sprawl – each lot with its own garden, its own tree, its own swimming pool, its own playground, and its own walls, a fortified castle within many other castles.

To subvert this idea, Mind the Gap proposes to reclaim the common ground by acting in the microscale of the lot, unifying urban blocks through the collective management of interstitial spaces. In a city where public spaces are regarded as no one's land, our action provides private-owned spaces for public use (Figure 26.3).

We start by tearing down walls and other physical barriers within the block. Then we open up some of these spaces to the city and start connecting blocks, parks, plazas, and squares. We redirect the logic of flows and invite nature in. We call neighbors to cohabitate in common spaces and revert the isolation of anonymity, bringing back the basic virtues of common ground: spontaneous encounters, sedimentation of bonds, and recognition of the other (Figure 26.4).

The consumption rhythm of nature is reversed, as a new city structure is defined. One where the void is constant and the city develops and densifies around it, permeated by it. We advocate for the comeback of communal knowledge and the radical and simple idea of being able to practice that basic element of democracy's foundation: conviviality (Figure 26.5).

Figure 26.3 When walls come down, space can flow. Credit: Anna Dietzsch.

Figure 26.4 Open private spaces are joined and opened up for common use. Credit: Anna Dietzsch.

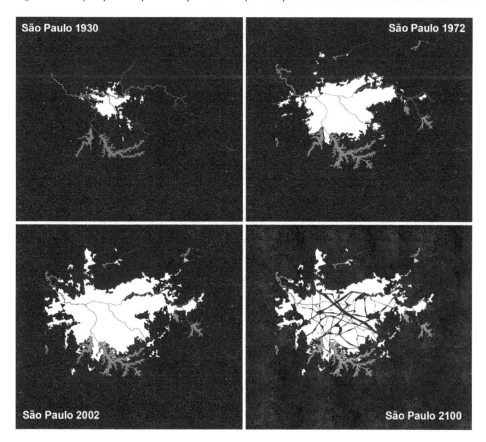

Figure 26.5 A timeline of expanding São Paulo, but in 2100 nature starts to come back in through green corridors and open spaces. Credit: Anna Dietzsch.

Chapter 27: Cities as Global Organisms

Oliver Hillel and Manuela Gervasi

Many have used the analogy that cities evolve much like living organisms in a planetary ecosystem, with mechanisms for competition but also for cooperation, mutualism, and symbiosis. If we consider that humanity's footprint on the planet is increasingly shaped by urban processes – and the perceptions and decisions made by urban citizens – and if we apply the analogy above, it makes sense that those "urban organisms," these consumption centers and laboratories of innovation, should play a commensurate, central role in informing and influencing decision-makers at the global level. The UN, for instance, is, and will continue to be, the planetary-level consensual instrument that we have to prioritize investments and actions towards sustainable human settlements and urbanization.

Yet, when we look at the influence of local authorities and other local policy- and decision-makers in the agenda and investment policies of the UN and international institutions charged with global governance, we are still largely confronted with a loosely organized and under-coordinated scenario, in spite of a few encouraging initiatives. Our global governance systems are still not successful enough in giving room to, and coordinating the specific contributions and common interests of, our urban centers, which increasingly compose the world's central nervous system – with our "sensory equipment" of the UN processes; our political, financial, and technical "muscles"; and our overall institutional "skeleton." There are also huge gaps in this nervous system's "central learning processes" – that is, in the production and distribution of knowledge on how best to promote and support, within the diversity of approaches across the globe, the coordination of governance efforts across different levels of government for sustainability.

Much progress has happened in the last ten years. At the Convention of Biological Diversity, when the coordination with subnational and local authorities first came up for deliberation in 2008, some delegates were concerned about the cost of additional demands of support from their numerous categories of subnational and local governments, and also by the political uncertainties linked to working with different levels of governance and their complex networks of influence. As the initiative matured, however, most realized that no additional resources were needed per se – in many countries, processes of articulation were already in place, and just needed to become more effective. For others, it was mostly a question of working with those subnational and local governments that were already leading, or interested, in the topic, and facilitating their encouragement to others. Today, on one hand, most parties report that they provide relatively low-cost guidance and technical support to subnational and local governments, and formally involve them in biodiversity strategies and actions plans, policies, and programmes; and on the other hand, many bottom-up approaches in which cities are leading in innovative global policies are developing around the world.

Local and subnational governments are supporting UN-Habitat within a Global Task Force in the Post-2015 Development Agenda and the New Urban Agenda. Many representative bodies and associations of cities are active in the UN, as well as in the international and regional arenas, and there are networks of cities and their mayors sharing lessons on collaborative processes to solve common problems.

Still, the current level of cooperation is limited when it comes to mechanisms that allow for global comanagement of programs, large-scale allocation of investments, and effective cooperation in knowledge generation and setting of targets. We need to expand these efforts towards another evolutionary leap. Let UN member countries explore innovative forms of cooperation with their subnational levels of government, each according to their circumstances – including at the global level. The International Labour Organization, for instance, is governed by a tripartite model where governments, representative bodies of businesses, and representative bodies of employees define joint agendas, each according to agreed mandates. The experience of municipal participatory budgeting can also be a source for inspiration for novel decision-making procedure at the global level.

We need organic, multilayered, and self-regulating governance systems for resource use, and we need sound scientific advice on how to set them up. For the UN's science-policy interface to produce the needed solutions, we need the engagement of scientists as well as policy-makers, to find ways for the UN to function as a global assembly of local governments.

The UN's New Urban Agenda and other outcomes of Habitat III, particularly the partnerships being prepared for action, are a great start. The full participation of knowledge producers as "neural systems" of our global urban planetary organism is required to translate needs and information across the science-policy interface. These academics, specialists, and knowledge-producers need to be aware of and be willing to influence the global politics of knowledge to help all levels of government to cooperate more closely, or they will miss the opportunity to make an enormous difference.

Chapter 28: From Concrete Structures to Green Diversity

Ecological Landscape Design for Restoring Urban Nature and Children's Play

Keitaro Ito and Tomomi Sudo

There has recently been a rapid decrease in the amount of open and natural space in Japan, and urban areas are particularly affected due to development. This has caused a decrease in the space available for children's physical play in natural environments (Ito et al. 2010). These are pressing issues; children's play is crucial for learning about the structure of nature and is an essential aspect of environmental education. Indeed, early studies by American environmental psychologists described the value of complex environments and wild lands for children, and how children perceive and experience wild lands as places of their own domain (for example, see Hart 1979 and Moore 1986).

Children build relationships with landscape areas by having direct, hands-on interaction with vegetation during play and participation. The greening of school grounds increases the diversity of children's school ground use, including more opportunities for pretend play. However, it could be even more beneficial and successful if children are included in the planning and long-term care of these spaces, from preliminary planning to assisting with ongoing maintenance. This would promote positive attitudes and caring behavior among children towards outdoor spaces as well as improve plant establishment.

If we convert even relatively small concrete structures in an urban area into functioning biotopes, they will also serve as stepping-stones for environmental and ecological education. Landscape diversity is related to different structures in topography and vegetation, which is important for children's spontaneous play and activities. School biotopes are created using many different methods. Some have been successful, while many have failed and been abandoned. In Japan, many school biotopes have been constructed. The main aim of school biotopes is to provide ecological education for the children in urban areas. Some of them have been successful and were created in collaboration with children, teachers, planners, and people in the region; all use the space freely, as they want. However, there are some biotopes that have not been maintained and are ultimately abandoned. There are several reasons why such biotopes fail. First, children are not allowed to utilize the biotope due to an emphasis on its protection rather than its use. Second, planners fail to consider the larger regional ecosystem, which can lead to more harm than help. Third, the biotope is too small to have an ecological function. Finally, children and teachers do not use the biotope because it was planned and constructed by the local council without their participation (Ito et al. 2016).

One successful project was created in Fukuoka, a city in the south of Japan. The aim of this project was to create an area for children's play and ecological education that could form part of an ecological network in their local urban area. The school actively sought to involve their students in the planning process in order to avoid the aforementioned problems. It aimed to create a place for children that could be easily approached, that safely utilized local flora, and that could help rehabilitate the regional ecosystem (Ito et al. 2016). As a result of this decision, children were able to freely use the space and felt more invested in its upkeep and use.

It is vital that planners and landscape designers consider landscape as an "Omniscape" (Numata 1996; Ito et al. 2016) in which it is much more important to think of landscape planning as a "learnscape," embracing not only the joy of seeing, but an exciting, more holistic way of using the body and senses for learning. Thus, it is very important to observe how children and teachers use their school's biotope, which can help landscape designers and planners to create a plan that caters to their needs. Giving children more experiences with nature during their formative years creates more diverse cultures and biodiversity, even in urban areas.

🌐 References

Hart, R. (1979) *Children's Experience of Place*. New York: Irvington Publishers.

Ito K., Sudo T., and Fjørtoft I. (2016) *Ecological Design: Collaborative Landscape Design with School Children: Children, Nature, Cities*. London: Routledge, pp. 195–209.

Ito, K., Fjørtoft, I., Manabe, T., Masuda, K., Kamada, M., and Fujiwara, K. (2010) Landscape Design and Children's Participation in a Japanese Primary School: Planning Process of School Biotope for 5 Years, in Muller, N., Werner, P., and Kelcey, G.J. (eds.), *Urban Biodiversity and Design*. Oxford: Blackwell Academic Publishing, pp. 441–453.

Moore, R.C. (1986) *Childhood's Domain: Play and Space in Child Development*. London: Croom Helm.

Numata, M. (1996) *Landscape Ecology*. Tokyo: Asakura shoten.

 Chapter 29: Building Cities

A View from India

Radhika Khosla

In discussions about cities of the future, or perhaps, the future of cities, it is worth noting that one of the largest shifts to urban centers in world history is projected to occur in India in the next few decades (United Nations 2011). It is estimated that the middle class in Indian cities will more than triple from 31 million in 2013 to 114 million in 2025 (*Economic Times* 2011). Demographically, India is expected to add at least 10 million people to the job market each year for the next two decades (FICCI-Ernst & Young 2013). And Indian cities are estimated to be responsible for 75 percent of the country's GDP in the next 15 years, with plans for a hundred new smart cities in the pipeline (Government of India 2014). Transitions of such scale place unprecedented pressures on energy resources: there is little doubt that the urban context promises to be a central determinant of the future of Indian energy, and by extension, of the future of India's development.

Unravelling this future, however, is not straightforward. India is starting from a low base of development and faces enormous unmet energy needs, poor energy access, and increasing pressure from interrelated environmental concerns. How then, can it urbanize in a manner where energy needs are met, the local and global environment is preserved, and the economy and energy security are not put at risk?

One urban component that can help answer this question is the city's built environment. There are three reasons for this. First, much of the energy consumption in cities takes place in buildings. Buildings consume more than a third of India's electricity, and this number is set for dramatic increase with development and access to improved lifestyles (Kapoor et al. 2011). Yet, buildings are largely untapped in energy planning and the scale of unexploited energy efficiency potential is estimated to be of the order of 3 gigawatts per year (Natural Resources Defense Council 2012). Second, timing is of essence. Two-thirds of the commercial and high-rise residential buildings to exist between 2010 and 2030 are yet to be built (Kumar et al. 2010). And given that buildings form long-lasting components of the economy and shape path dependencies for energy-use patterns, the next 15 years present a real occasion to lock in sustainable (or risky) consumption patterns. Third, unlike traditional pathways to meeting energy goals, the built environment offers benefits that go well beyond energy savings. These include carbon mitigation, improved energy security, job creation, and increased socio-environmental outcomes.

Given this context, how can the role of India's buildings be reimagined to enable better urban energy futures? Three interrelated aspects of the built environment can influence a transformative change in its energy use. The first of these is the technical, or the potential of available, accessible, and affordable energy saving technologies in the market. Most studies currently focus on this issue, in the form of macroeconomic and building-level analyses that determine the need and potential of technical efficiency. The next is the institutional or the formal and informal arrangements of regulations, finances, and capacities, which influence building energy policies and which are often in the form of voluntary or mandatory building energy codes or rating systems. And finally, it is the behavioral or the role of individual and organizational lifestyles in managing energy demand. Increasingly, a growing international literature points to the substantial potential that can be harnessed from tapping into behavioral solutions for energy savings, beyond technological fixes.

This framing deviates from India's current technical approach to the built environment, which no doubt is an essential basis for decision-making. But this needs to be complemented with a knowledge base of institutional functioning, such as the governance of building energy policies, and equally, with the social and behavioral practices that enable energy savings. Ultimately, energy use in buildings is determined not just by how they designed, but also how they are built, commissioned, and used.

Broadening current approaches to include these interrelated aspects of the built environment will help create the often envisioned cities of the future. Moreover, since India and other transitioning economies are at the verge of much new construction, there is opportunity to configure urban infrastructure in a manner that can shape energy-use preferences and practices. Such an alternative conceptualization will require emphasizing the relationships between consumption trajectories, development, and socioenvironmental priorities. India's built environment, where most of the energy demand infrastructure is yet to be built, provides a concrete space in which to stimulate such a shift.

⟨ *References*

Economic Times, 2011. "India's Middle Class Population to Touch 267 Million in 5 Yrs," Economic Times, February 6. https://economictimes.indiatimes.com/news/economy/indicators/indias-middle-class-population-to-touch-267-million-in-5-yrs/articleshow/7435793.cms.

FICCI-Ernst & Young, 2013. "Reaping India's Promised Demographic Dividend- Industry in Driving Seat." www.ey.com/Publication/vwLUAssets/EY-Government-and-Public-Sector-Reaping-Indias-demographic-dividend/$FILE/EY-Reaping-Indias-promised-demographic-dividend-industry-in-driving-seat.pdf.

Government of India, 2014. "Mission Statement and Guidelines" Ministry of Urban Development http://smartcities.gov.in/upload/uploadfiles/files/SmartCityGuidelines(1).pdf.

Kapoor, R., Deshmukh, A., and Lal, S. 2011. "Strategy Roadmap for Net Zero Energy Buildings in India," USAID India. www.nzeb.in/wp-content/uploads/2015/10/NZEB-Roadmap-2-Sept-2011.pdf.

Kumar, S., Kapoor, R., Rawal, R., Seth, S., and Walia, A. 2010. "Developing an Energy Conservation Building Code Implementation Strategy in India," USAID India. www.researchgate.net/publication/266382475_Developing_an_Energy_Conservation_Building_Code_Implementation_Strategy_in_India.

Natural Resources Defense Council, 2012. "Constructing Change: Accelerating Energy Efficiency in India's Buildings Market. www.nrdc.org/sites/default/files/india-constructing-change-report.pdf.

United Nations, 2011. "World Urbanization Prospects," Department of Economic and Social Affairs, Population Division. www.un.org/en/development/desa/population/publications/.../WUP2011_Report.pdf.

Chapter 30: The False Distinctions of Socially Engaged Art and Art

Todd Lester

In Gramscian terms, I believe in the role of the "organic intellectual" (Gottleib 1989). In Beuysian terms, I acknowledge an "extended concept of art" as was his idea of the Social Sculpture (Beuys 2004). However, these terms feel a little obscure or cultish for what I want to discuss here, even if they may be accurate, (art) historically speaking.

In considering the topic of urban sustainability – and specifically, *how can we produce or coproduce knowledge that will propel the better cities of the future?* – I think about a conspiracy between cultural production and dominant culture. I think of the instrumentalization of art and artists in the service of real estate agglomeration and the deadly perverse symbiosis of policy, such as "Quality of Life Enforcement" and the "Nuisance Abatement Action" (Goodman 2016) that can result[1] when a city succumbs to what Sarah Schulman terms "The Gentrification of the Mind" (Schulman 2013).

In *Representations of the Intellectual*, Edward Said enumerates a set of pressures – or "impingements of modern professionalization" – he believed can "challenge the intellectual's ingenuity and will." These include specialization, attainment of expert status, and the "drift towards power and authority" (Said 1996: 82). His critique is not intended to challenge the acquisition of knowledge, but an observation that sometimes pedigreed "knowing" is best deployed in tandem with lay wisdom among its other forms. Shils (1959: 179) asserts "In every society … there are some persons with an unusual sensitivity to the sacred, an uncommon reflectiveness about the nature of the universe, and the rules which govern their society." He is speaking of the intellectual in a way that can also describe the artist.

There is a double bind that serves to confuse the role of city building at the hands of nonexperts, the broader group to which artists are a subset when they

---

[1] The New York Police Department's role in the death of Eric Garner is an example. In this case the sale of single cigarettes was interpreted by police under the "nuisance" policy, leading to a string of events in which Garner was ultimately killed by the police.

go into residency at city agencies; are commissioned to make public art; and certainly when their interests and dedications become organically focused on social ills that societies encourage but fail to sustainably resource. This axis of obfuscation has traditionally rerouted the power of creativity (and perhaps what Said terms "ingenuity and will") under or into a subservience to capital throughout recent history. This has the effect of leaving the artist in the "sacred man" predicament. In his seminal work *Homo Sacer: Sovereign Power and Bare Life*, Agamben (1998) explains the original concept of *homo sacer* in Roman law, which is a person in the liminal state of being convicted of a crime not punishable by sacrifice (death), but who can be killed by a peer without the murder being considered homicide. He builds on the concept of *homo sacer* in order to show a contemporary society that maintains ambiguity through the use of positivist narratives, tropes, and wordplays may provide cover for maintaining the status quo.

Why do I put it in such harsh terms? It seems that the rhetoric of social practice art actually comes from the philanthropic fallout of the pan-Western subprime mortgage crisis that developed between 2007 and 2008. Raquel Rolnik, former UN Special Rapporteur on Adequate Housing and professor of architecture at the University of São Paulo, asserts that one important new development of social (specifically housing) movements is the expanding role of the cultural agent.[2] But the persistent loss of public money for art (as is typically the result of economic crises in a Western context) left a void. Into that void rushed a rhetoric of social art, social practice, creative place-making, artivism, and socially engaged art, as well as utilitarian and positivist sentiments. After the extreme and abrupt loss of culture funds, their replacement by "social art movements" was simply welcomed without being interrogated. Artists are faced with the double-bind of needing the social art money for their livelihoods, while also needing to critically engage the broader political economy in which they work: to understand and articulate the lived experience of precarity as a reality of neoliberal cultural production.

Cities need artists in the same way (or intensity) as Beuys suggests in a November 1969 interview in Artforum (Sharp 1969):

> Art alone makes life possible – this is how radically I should like to formulate it. I would say that without art man is inconceivable in physiological terms.

A couple years ago, I was in a room full of grant-makers and philanthropists in which this question was asked: "How can we make sure that artists are as

---

[2] Personal communication with the authors made during an interview in Rolnik's FAU-USP office in February 2015.

responsive to future natural disasters [as they were to Hurricane Sandy and the Calgary flooding]?" To which I reply: Art is as social as it has always been. Artists' ideas are as vibrant as they have always been. However, to only pay attention to their societal function when faced with crises misses the point of art.

Is there a distinction between socially engaged art and just plain art? There is none. Does art produce knowledge? Of course – except when art merely supports a status quo.

❖ References

Agamben, G. 1998. *Homo Sacer: Sovereign Power and Bare Life*. Palo Alto: Stanford University Press.

Beuys, J. 2004. *What is Art?: Conversation with Joseph Beuys*. West Hoathly, UK: Clareview Books.

Goodman, D. 2016. New York City Is Set to Adopt New Approach on Policing Minor Offenses. New York Times, January 20, 2016. www.nytimes.com/2016/01/21/nyregion/new-york-council-to-consider-bills-altering-how-police-handle-minor-offenses.html?_r=0.

Gottlieb, R.S. 1989. *An Anthology of Western Marxism: From Lukács and Gramsci to Socialist-Feminism*. New York: Oxford University Press.

Said, E. *Representation of the Intellectual*. New York: Penguin Random House.

Schulman, S. 2013. *The Gentrification of the Mind: Witness to a Lost Imagination*. Oakland: University of California Press.

Sharp, W. 1969. An Interview with Joseph Beuys. Artforum. November 1969.

Shils, E. 1982. *The Constitution of Society*. Chicago: University of Chicago Press.

Chapter 31: Overcoming Inertia and Reinventing "Retreat"

Andrew Revkin

Pursuing any vision of a thriving, agile city of the future requires grappling with a foe as ineluctable as gravity. That foe is inertia. It comes in two main varieties – infrastructural and societal. To convey what I mean, I'll start with two moments from New York City Mayor Michael Bloomberg's final term in office. In a 2013 report, his sustainability team featured this sobering finding: "Energy use in buildings accounts for 75 percent of New York City's greenhouse gas emissions, and 80 percent of the buildings that will exist in 2050 are already here today."[1] I hope you'll stop and read that twice, slowly absorbing each word's meaning in the context of what you've heard about grand visions for a rapid global transition to low-carbon societies in places for rich and poor. In older cities, a lot of what has to come is the kind of grinding door-to-door, boiler-by-boiler effort that isn't well conveyed in shiny architectural renderings. An analyst in Mayor Bill de Blasio's sustainability office told me in 2016 that, on closer look, 90 percent of 2050's buildings exist today.)

That's infrastructural inertia. It's arguably a tougher enemy to overcome than fossil fuel lobbyists.

Then there's societal inertia, much of which springs from basic reflexes embedded deep in human consciousness and is shaped by many of our social institutions, such as politics. People tend to overvalue the present, the familiar and proximal, while hyperbolically discounting future risks or hazards that are rare and unpredictable. This trait has served us well, so far. It's no wonder elected officials mostly lead from behind, too often offering voters pothole repairs more than new commuter trains.

I don't mean to pick on former Mayor Bloomberg, who in fact has been a tireless champion of action on climate change. But his final big speech on the subject as mayor, laying out plans for investing $20 billion by mid-century in

---

[1] New York City Mayor's Carbon Challenge Progress Report, April 2013. www.nyc.gov/html/gbee/downloads/pdf/mayors_carbon_challenge_progress_report.pdf.

making his city resilient, centered on a core theme that illustrates the potent pull of the status quo.

In the face of solid science pointing to centuries of sea-level rise ahead even with action to slow global warming, he said, "[A]s New Yorkers, we cannot and will not abandon our waterfront. It's one of our greatest assets. We must protect it, not retreat from it."[2]

It's easy to point a finger, but when talking to young people about climate change, I challenge them to pretend they're the press secretary to a mayor of a coastal city and tasked with writing an effective speech proclaiming, "We *will* retreat." I've tried many iterations myself and haven't come up with a formulation yet that any mayor would embrace.

I also challenge young people to invent a new relationship with climate change and its impacts – working for the long haul to blunt warming, but moving beyond a defensive posture and *embracing* the design opportunities faced in a world with, among other novel features, no new normal coastline for centuries to come.

This all might sound insurmountably daunting, but I've seen bright possibilities, often involving innovations in education and communication. When she was director of sustainability for the New York City Department of Education, Ozgem Ornektekin oversaw a retrofitting program for heating and cooling systems in hundreds of buildings. After discussions with the city's unions, she and others realized there weren't enough skilled building technicians in the city to manage the new technology. So she pursued the creation of the High School for Energy and Technology in the Bronx to teach the skills needed to fill those jobs. Students there now routinely tour the boiler room (which ran on hand-shoveled *coal* just 20 years ago!) as part of their curriculum, learning about the school as a system, not just a collection of classrooms.

Imagine the potential for spreading smarter energy choices if every school had a boiler room tour.

As for the challenge of re-envisioning coastal cities in a world with (essentially) endlessly rising seas, compromise will be essential. Geographer Peirce Lewis's description of New Orleans as both impossible and inevitable will increasingly apply to a host of metropolises around the world (Peirce 2013). In such instances, a managed (and politically tenable) retreat can be sold, as already has been the case in New York.

With federal funding and widespread support, New York City is taking the first steps by adopting the East Side Coastal Resiliency Project, which is seen

---

[2] Speech by New York City Mayor Michael Bloomberg, June 11, 2013, on the Brooklyn waterfront, outlining a long-term plan to prepare New York City for the impacts of climate change. www .mikebloomberg.com/news/nycs-plan-to-prepare-for-the-impacts-of-climate-change/.

as the first phase of a larger Dryline project – a buffer against storm surges that also serves as a public recreational and green corridor, designed by the Danish architectural firm Bjarke Ingels Group, with city involvement.

A day will come, perhaps not until well into the twenty-second century, when this defense will slide beneath the waves, given the inertia in the climate system and erosion of polar ice sheets.

But this is how the urban environment will evolve in the Anthropocene – Earth's Age of Us – step by imperfect step, learning and adjusting, testing and faltering, then testing again, impossibly and inevitably.

🌐 *Reference*

Peirce, L.F. 2003. *New Orleans: The Making of an Urban Landscape*. Charlottesville: University of Virginia Press.

Chapter 32: Money for Old Rope

The Risks of Finance Taking Over the New Urban Agenda

Richard Friend

The need for private sector finance is taking a commanding position in the emerging new urban agenda. Yet, there is an unavoidable tension between such calls and the ways in which current flows of private capital in land and property speculation are fueling urbanization across the world. For, at the heart of global urbanization is a challenge of rights – of access to and control over urban space, systems, and services, and of rights to decide urban futures.

This is, indeed, a super-wicked problem (Levin et al. 2012). On the one hand, it is argued that addressing climate change in urban areas requires market forces and private sector investment to fill the infrastructure deficit. On the other, the very problem of climate change and unbridled urbanization is a product of failures of the market and of state regulation. That which has caused the problem is now proposed as the solution.

That there is a need for investment in urban infrastructure and services is undeniable. Urban infrastructure in many parts of urban Asia is approaching the end of its lifespan and has been poorly maintained. In many cases, it has been designed for the demands of earlier decades, with little consideration of climate risks. Moreover, in many places, basic infrastructure is simply not there – whether it be water, sanitation, and drainage systems or public transport. It needs to be built and it needs to be paid for. The financial requirements are enormous, with estimates of global need from the World Economic Forum (n.d.) of one trillion dollars per year.

But the market is already hugely influential in how these systems take shape. Urban investment in much of Asia follows its own logic, often at odds with concerns for future climate change. That logic is often crudely profit-oriented – buy low, sell high. Such logic tends to target "low-value" land: vulnerable spaces such as wetlands and floodplain areas that are essential for water supply and drainage, or highly productive agricultural lands. Often, these lands are publicly owned or are utilized by marginalized people. National airports across

Asia are built on such lands. Thailand's international airport is built on the King Cobra Swamp.

Expansion of transport links also plays a role in fueling urban development, creating new values and additional opportunities for land speculation. As transport networks expand, established neighborhoods are pulled down and property prices in the newly created central areas are beyond the reach of many citizens.

Similarly, the industrial expansion that fuels much of the urbanization in Asia is itself dependent on dirty industries – coal provides much of the energy, and the petrochemical industry drives the new Special Economic Zones.

A common feature of all these investments is exploitation of weak legal frameworks for the environment and citizen rights (Friend et al. 2014). Rather than strengthening environmental legislation, requirements for Environmental Impact Assessments are being diluted by being presented as constraints on investment. Additionally, the basic monitoring information that could help manage specific investments and to reshape urban futures does not exist, or, if it does, it is not in the public domain. Most cities in Asia do not provide citizens access to basic information on air, water, and soil quality – let alone more contentious information on land-use plans.

Local government is often caught between playing the role of manager and entrepreneur, bearing the responsibility for attracting investment while also trying to play the role of regulator (Harvey 2006). Investment tends to win, with environmental legislation pushed aside in order to push through large-scale infrastructure development. Increasingly, public infrastructure, and even basic urban planning, lies in the domain of the private sector (Shatkin 2007). The whole urban experiment is increasingly a private sector affair. Urban infrastructure tends to attract dirty money and open space for corruption.

Without a strong and unequivocal commitment to environmental legislation and to the rights of urban citizens, we risk that infrastructure proposed and financed under poorly defined notions of climate resilience in the new urban agenda will merely exacerbate existing inequalities. They will create new climate vulnerabilities and lock us into to a path that leads to environmental catastrophe.

We need commitments to specific sets of rights. These have a long history. Principle 10 of the Rio Declaration of the 1992 World Summit on Sustainable Development, which most of the sovereign states signed, commits to strengthening access rights: access to information, access to participation in decision-making, and access to redress and remedy. Access rights have been enshrined in the Aarhus Convention, a Europe-wide commitment. A similar convention needs to be extended for cities across the world. Further, the Right to the City that took such a prominent role in earlier international negotiations about urban futures, talks of rights of access and control over key urban systems – water, food, energy, shelter, mobility – as well as a safe environment, and public space, should be expanded. At the heart of both sets of rights is the right of urban people – whether they are recognized as citizens or not – to determine and reshape their urban futures. Similarly, decision-making frameworks for infrastructure projects – such as that of the World Commission on Dams (2000) – that are grounded in concepts of "rights and risks" should shape urban investments.

However, these kinds of commitments remain sadly lacking in the discourse of the new urban agenda. This is not to say that some cities will not be able to make significant progress in addressing climate vulnerabilities and risks, and in transforming their urban futures. But with growing inequality across the globe – within and between cities, between cities and their rural hinterlands – the likelihood is that networks of privileged resilient cities, and neighborhoods within them, will prosper while the more numerous, nonresilient cities will flounder.

Bringing finance to the table is certainly necessary. But it is essential that environmental safeguards and rights be strengthened to ensure that infrastructural investments in the new urban agenda meet the needs and aspirations of urban citizens. This is a challenge that cannot be left to states or markets alone; it requires citizens to be organized and engaged, supported by a legal framework that is applied from the source of investment to where it lands. This itself requires financial and political investment.

🌐 References

Friend, R.M., J. Jarvie, S.O. Reed, R. Sutarto, P. Thinphanga, and V. Toan, (2014) "Mainstreaming Urban Climate Resilience into Policy and Planning: Reflections from Asia," *Urban Climate* 7: 6–19

Harvey, D. (2006) "From Managerialism to Entrepeneurialism: The Transformation in Urban Governance in Late Capitalism," *Geografiska Annaler Series B, Human Geo* 71: 3–17.

Levin, K., B. Cashore, S. Bernstein, and G. Auld. (2012), "Overcoming the Tragedy of Super Wicked Problems: Constraining Our Future Selves to Ameliorate Global Climate Change," *Policy Sci* 45(2): 123–152. DOI 10.1007/s11077-012-9151-0

Shatkin, G. (2007), "The City and the Bottom Line: Urban Megaprojects and the Privatization of Planning in Southeast Asia," *Environ Plann* 40: 383–401.

World Commission on Dams, (2000), *Dams and Development: A New Framework for Decision-Making: The Report of the World Commission on Dams*. London: Earthscan.

World Economic Forum (n.d.) "Infrastructure and Urban Development" https://www.weforum .org/communities/industry-partner-iu/

Chapter 33: Aesthetic Appreciation of Tagging

Emma Arnold

Imagine a baleen whale: immense, rendered in black and white, with a sliver of red – animated, yet evidently butchered – emerging from the meeting of brick and spackled walls. A spout of black liquid rises from its blowhole, its presence startling in an otherwise empty parking lot. Figure 33.1 is the work of Belgian artist ROA: aerosol paint applied meticulously in thin lines against exterior walls in the small coastal city of Stavanger, Norway. The piece is site-specific, sharply referencing to the Nordic welfare state as hunters of whales made rich by the discovery of oil. Is it possible to appreciate ROA's whale in the absence of this knowledge of media, artist, and context? What if you mistakenly believe whales to be fish? Must you know that it is a mammal to appreciate its grandeur, its *whaleness*? Would your aesthetic appreciation be augmented if you knew whales to be mammals, members of the Cetacean order, related to dolphins and porpoises?

Environmental philosopher Carlson (1984) argues that knowledge of taxonomy is fundamental to the appreciation of a whale, that scientific knowledge is vital to the aesthetic appreciation of nature (Brady 1998). Carlson's positive aesthetics likens the aesthetic appreciation of nature to the appreciation of art and suggests that, like art, all nature can be beautiful if only you possess the right knowledge. Applying this logic to the urban environment, the following discussion suggests that a positive aesthetics approach may lead to greater appreciation of tagging and graffiti and its cultural and political significance. An aesthetic appreciation for tagging may facilitate more informed and creative graffiti policy in cities and allow for more democratic use of public space.

The figurative nature of street art and new muralism, such as ROA's work, lends itself to aesthetic appreciation. It is easy to understand, admire, and respect. Tagging, on the contrary, is frequently maligned. It is a form of graffiti that involves writing a name in a consistent style in as many locations as possible. It has been linked to social disorder due to myths of moral panic and the "broken windows theory," which has inspired strict anti-graffiti policies

Figure 33.1 Mural created by ROA for the 2013 Nuart Festival in Stavanger, Norway. Photograph taken in 2014.

in many cities (Young 2014). Negative opinions of tagging have been shaped by a public conditioning carefully constructed by media and politicians, what Cresswell (1992: 332) describes as a "discourse of disorder." In such policy climates, there is no good *or* bad graffiti: there is only bad graffiti (Iveson 2009). Such approaches do not accommodate aesthetic appreciation.

Aesthetic appreciation may also be fueled by experience, perception, intuition, and imagination, as Brady (1998) suggests for the aesthetic appreciation of nature. This type of appreciation, however, comes more easily with the representational and figurative. Appreciation for tagging may require more, including a breaking free of conventional social, cultural, and political constructions of urban space. This requires something of the viewer: a shift of mind and a thoughtful reconsidering. A positive aesthetic approach may enhance appreciation of tags by encouraging the viewer to consider encountered pieces more carefully and thoughtfully.

Though they may seem indecipherable, tags are replete with meaning and made with skill and artistry. The tags of many graffiti writers are highly diverse in style and media, are spatially distributed throughout the city – indicative of profound knowledge of the geography of cities – and reflect calligraphic technique and a sense of design. Many tags are site-specific, sometimes mirroring aspects of the urban landscape (Figure 33.2). There is a beauty to

Figure 33.2 A tag by Vrom Seier mimics the adjacent wrought-iron fence in Oslo, Norway. Photograph taken in 2014

Figure 33.3 Various tags in Stavanger, Norway. Photograph taken in 2014

tags, proficiently executed, mindfully placed, betraying hidden respect for the landscape. There is also beauty in the collective expression that arises anonymously, in saturated and incremental collaborations that build up gradually (Figure 33.3). Challenging our views and fostering aesthetic appreciation may make policy-makers of us all, contribute to shifts in public opinion, acknowledge tagging and graffiti as forms of urban art, and open the city up for more democratic and creative expression and policy. As cities become increasingly commodified and citizens long for more free artistic and political expression, this type of appreciation and shift may be fundamental to creating more just and inclusive communities.

🌐 *References*

Brady, E. 1998. "Imagination and the Aesthetic Appreciation of Nature." *The Journal of Aesthetics and Art Criticism*. 56(2): 139–147.

Carlson, A. 1984. "Nature and Positive Aesthetics." *Environmental Ethics*. 6: 6–34

Cresswell, T. 1992. "The Crucial 'Where' of graFfiti: A Geographical Analysis of Reactions to Graffiti in New York." *Environment and Planning D: Society and Space*. 10: 329–344

Iveson, K. 2009. "War Is Over (If You Want It): Rethinking the Graffiti Problem." *Australian Planner*. 46(4): 24–34

Young, A. 2014. *Street Art, Public City: Law, Crime, and Urban Imagination*. New York: Routledge.

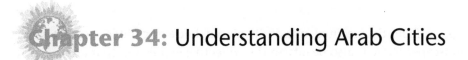

Chapter 34: Understanding Arab Cities

From National to Local

Huda Shaka

Cities have always been fundamental to the development and dynamic of the Arab world, which was only recently divided into nation states. However, when compared to cities in other regions, Arab cities are underresearched. The little data that is publically available on the Arab world is typically published by national government bodies and is thus focused on the national level. I was recently shocked when I could not find basic GDP data for a specific Arab capital city; all I could find were national statistics. The challenge of data availability is manifold, as it relates to the existence of comparable city-level data, to its public dissemination, and to the extraction of knowledge from this data. This chapter will focus on the first two aspects of the challenge: the creation and dissemination of data.

There are a number of emerging trends that will help nudge Arab cities towards action on this front. As cities compete regionally and globally for foreign investment, tourism, and talent, they will have to begin collecting and sharing data specific to their cities in order to better market themselves. Additionally, an increasing number of Arab cities are joining international networking and reporting initiatives, such as the C40 Climate Leadership Group (for example, Amman, Dubai) and the 100 Resilient Cities Challenge (for example, Byblos, Ramallah). These forums encourage cities to collect and share a wide range of data to inform city-level strategies and, ultimately, to contribute to global knowledge of cities. There is also a growing amount of spatial satellite data becoming publically available through research organizations (for example, the recent map of air pollution compiled by the Yale Environmental Performance Index). These data can act as incentives for cities to collect and share their own "bottom-up" data, or at least to better understand the existing data.

Where should cities begin on their journey of data collection? The recently released ISO 37120 (2014) standard sets out a series of indicators for city services and quality of life. These address strategic themes such as economy, health, environment, and governance, all of which are important aspects for cities regardless of scale or geography. Using this standard as a guide will allow cities to compare their performance against other cities, helping ensure that the data generated is meaningful and can catalyze action. The CDP (2016) question-naire is another helpful guide, particularly on emerging topics such as climate change adaptation.

Much of this information may already exist within one or more city depart-ment. Depending on the ease of access, format, and accuracy of this data, the city can decide whether to use the existing data collection processes or to set up new ones. Cities may also decide to set up independent bodies for the collec-tion and dissemination of this data or to delegate this responsibility to existing relevant authorities. When making this decision, it is important to keep in mind the strong tendency for individuals and organizations to be protective of their information. Setting up dedicated data collection entities may ultimately be the easier option.

The Abu Dhabi Spatial Data Infrastructure (n.d.) initiative, called AD-SDI, provides an example of a coordinated government effort to collect and share spatial data across entities. Currently, some of the data is also made available to the public. The AD-SDI is administered through the Abu Dhabi Systems and Information Centre and relies on the data contributions of over 60 gov-ernment and semi-government stakeholders. As described in the initiative's vision and illustrated in Figure 34.1, data are collected at a department level across all the involved stakeholders. It is then shared with and analyzed by an interdisciplinary strategic policy government body. Finally, the data are com-municated to the Executive Council and are used to track performance against the emirate's social, economic, and environmental vision. Each level is a two-way process, whereby the providers of data are simultaneously responding to and influencing a brief. It would be exciting to see this model applied at a wider scale, such that all the data collected can be influenced by and made available to the private sector, academia, and the wider public.

Herbert Girardet (2014) described most urbanists as living in a "pre-Galilean" time where the city is the center of the universe; as we dig deeper into under-standing the dynamics within a city, we must be cautious of falling into this trap. For example, even the most self-sufficient and sustainable cities rely on agricultural areas outside their borders, and often in other continents, to sup-ply their food. Only by acknowledging and understanding this dependence on other systems can cities address their areas of vulnerability and build resilience in their own systems. City databases should extend to relevant data beyond the

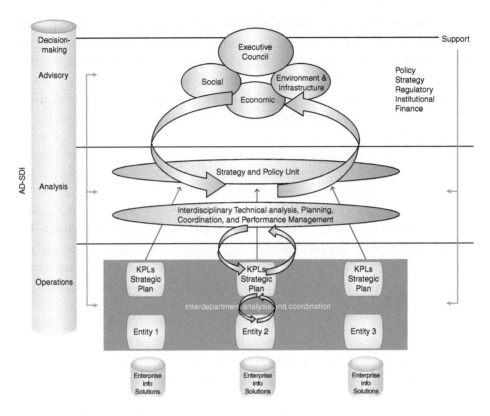

Figure 34.1 The Abu Dhabi Spatial Data Infrastructure Initiative's vision

boundary of the city in order to provide policy-makers and the public with a full picture.

With the availability of a new generation of data collection and dissemination technology, Arab cities have the opportunity to set up their databases to make the most of this technology now, rather than having to retrofit later. What we need in order to develop truly sustainable and resilient cities is data that is accurate, up to date, and available – not just at the national level, but at the city level. We are fortunate to live in an age where this is an achievable goal.

🌐 References

Abu Dhabi Spatial Data Infrastructure (n.d.) https://sdi.abudhabi.ae/Sites/SDI/Navigation/EN/About-AD-SDI/resources-geoportal.html

CDP. 2016. CDP Cities 2016 Information Request: www.cdp.net/CDP%20Questionaire%20Documents/CDP-Cities-Information-Request-2016.pdf

Girardet, H. 2014. "Creating Regenerative Cities". www.youtube.com/watch?v=lq_6batv2yE

International Standards Organisation (ISO). 2014. "ISO 37120 briefing note: the first ISO International Standard on city indicators". www.iso.org/iso/37120_briefing_note.pdf

Yale. 2015. Environmental Performance Index: Air Pollution Map. http://epi.yale.edu/ pollution-F/

Chapter 35: Who Can Implement the Sustainable Development Goals in Urban Areas?

David Satterthwaite

The Sustainable Development Goals (SDGs) are ambitious in what they set as goals and targets: eliminating poverty; universally providing risk-reducing infrastructure and services; ensuring access to safe, adequate housing and justice; and so forth – and all by 2030. But the SDGs say little about how, by whom, and with what support this transformation is to be accomplished. There is also little discussion of systemic change – implying that the national governments and international agencies that have failed to meet so many goals and targets in the past can now transform their approaches and effectiveness. We have over 40 years of promises going back to Habitat I, the first UN Conference on Human Settlements, where all government representatives endorsed recommendations such as the universal provision for water and sanitation. There are actually many nations that had a lower proportion of their urban population with water piped to premises in 2015 than in 1990. Most urban centers in Africa and Asia have no sewers or other means to safely collect and dispose of human excreta or, if they do, these serve a small percentage of the population.

Most SDGs and their targets for urban areas are entirely or in part the responsibility of local governments. Of course, the actual division of responsibilities between municipal/city/metropolitan governments and higher levels of government varies largely by nation. In most, however, urban governments have responsibilities relevant to housing quality, land use, infrastructure (local roads, drains, piped water, and excreta management), and services (schools, primary health care, solid waste collection, policing, and emergency services). However, urban governments were not invited to make commitments to the SDGs.

The SDGs emphasize the need for new data to support and monitor progress, but this is data for national governments. It is not for generating the data that every urban government needs to be more effective, such as which neighborhoods and streets lack needed infrastructure and services, which diseases and causes of injuries and premature deaths within their jurisdiction need attention, and which settlements have high infant, child, and maternal mortality rates.

The most important actors for meeting the SDGs in urban areas are urban governments working with their citizens and civil society organizations. The majority of cities that have performed best in relation to past goals are in Latin America. These were driven by well-functioning local democracies and a new generation of elected mayors committed to their city and its citizens. This success was bolstered by measures such as participatory budgeting that gave citizens the right to prioritize what public investments were made in their neighborhoods. Of course, there is still much to do in Latin America and places where there is little progress, but there are enough cities that have shown new possibilities. Most drew not at all on international agencies.

Then there is what is perhaps the most important change in much of Africa and Asia: in over 30 countries, there are now organizations and federations of slum/shack dwellers or homeless people. At their foundation are savings groups mostly formed and managed by women. These federations have chosen a different strategy of protest. They recognize that they have to change the way that local governments and international NGOs view them. So they come to local governments and offer them their knowledge and capacity. They show local governments how they can design, build, and manage community toilets more effectively and efficiently than local public works or private contractors. They have shown an amazing ability to document and map each informal settlement in a city – data that local governments usually lack and have difficulty collecting.

These slum/shack dweller groups have shown their capacity to build good quality housing and manage upgrading. Some have even shown how to manage unavoidable large-scale relocations in ways that did not impoverish those who were moved – as in the work of the Kenyan and Indian federations managing the relocation of those living close to the railway tracks. Both federations negotiated smaller setbacks on each side of the rail lines so fewer people had to move. Now there are over 100 local governments that work with them, which increase the scale of what they can achieve. There is also the example of the Asian Coalition for Community Action that has catalyzed over a thousand community initiatives in 165 cities in 19 countries all over Asia. The coalition also helps each initiative join with others in its city to press local government to work with it.

Where are the needed responses from the SDGs for supporting the work of these slum/shack dweller groups? The federations have their own funds that are carefully managed and through which external support could be channeled. The umbrella group to which they belong (Slum/Shack Dwellers

International) also manages an international fund to support member federations. Why do most international agencies ignore these? How can they claim to be participatory and accountable when they won't work with and support representative organizations of the urban poor and their partnerships with local governments? What transformations would be possible if community-driven responses to the SDGs got just 1 percent of development assistance each year (around a billion dollars)?

Chapter 36: Achieving Sustainable Cities by Focusing on the Urban Underserved

An Action Agenda for the Global South

Anjali Mahendra and Victoria Beard

We propose flipping the standard emphasis on economic growth as a means to reduce urban poverty by examining whether meeting the needs of the urban underserved can improve the economy and the environment of the city as a whole (Figure 36.4). This is our theory of change for how cities can become more sustainable.

Almost two decades into the "urban century," with about 3.3 billion people residing in cities and a further increase of 2.5 billion urban residents expected by 2050, cities are acquiring prominence in national and global agendas (Kourtit et al. 2015). Over 90 percent of the increase in urban population is expected in Asia and Africa (United Nations, Department of Economic and Social Affairs 2014), where urbanization can be a driver for poverty reduction and economic development (Figure 36.1). However, the unprecedented pace and scale of growth is placing heavy demands on urban services such as housing, transport, energy, water supply, and sanitation, and affecting people's quality of life while increasing their vulnerability to climate impacts. A major opportunity thus lies in informing, empowering, and equipping city leaders to focus on inclusive urban development, while advancing crucial environmental, economic, and social objectives towards a more sustainable city.

Achieving sustainable cities is particularly challenging in regions of the Global South, where the urban population is growing the fastest *and* where the majority of the world's urban population will reside in the coming decades (see Figure 36.1). For the first time in history, rapid urbanization is happening in countries where incomes have remained stagnant or economies are growing slowly, highlighting a weak relationship between urbanization and economic prosperity (United Nations, Department of Economic and Social Affairs 2014). In many of these countries, poverty is shifting from rural to urban areas, resulting

Projected Change in Urban
Population, 2015–2030

• <0%
0–15%
15–30%
>=30%

Figure 36.1 Highest Urban Growth Expected in Asia and Africa. Source: Beard et al. 2016.

in the "urbanization of poverty". While three-quarters of the world's poor reside in rural areas, the poor are urbanizing faster than the population as a whole, with poverty concentrating in cities (Ravallion et al. 2007; UN-Habitat 2003). In most countries, this phenomenon contributes to the decline of poverty at the national level, which may be viewed by many as a positive trend. However, from the perspective of cities, the urbanization of poverty presents one of the most significant challenges to economic prosperity, environmental sustainability, and meeting the needs of growing populations. Many of the poorest cities in the world have the lowest budgets per capita to deal with the challenges of providing basic urban services and a decent quality of life. While not a perfect measure of a city's capacity, budget per capita is a useful indicator of the resources available to a city. Budgets per capita of some of the fastest growing cities in the Global South are a fraction of that in cities of the Global North (Figure 36.2).

To solve challenges related to growing urban poverty, we must understand and operationalize the concept of urban poverty so that it can be linked to actions taken by urban practitioners and decision-makers. Conceptualizations of urban poverty range from those based on income or consumption deprivation, such as the standardized poverty lines that measure how many people live on less than two dollars a day, to broader, more multidimensional

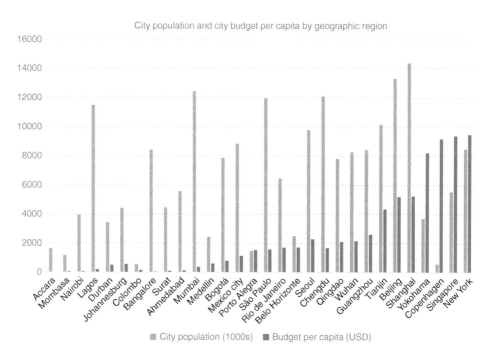

Figure 36.2 Comparison of city population and budget per capita in cities in Global South and North. Source: Beard et al. 2016.

indices of human well-being, and to those based on vulnerability, social exclusion, and the lack of political power. All of these have their utilities, as well as documented strengths and weaknesses.

As urban planners are concerned with the quality of life of all residents in a city and aware of the limited impact that national and subnational poverty reduction programs have had on stemming the rise of urban poverty, we propose a new way to operationalize urban poverty in the Global South in terms of the *urban underserved*. We define the *urban underserved* as low- and lower-middle income urban residents who lack access to one or more basic services such as housing, water, energy, and transportation. They lack access to these services across various dimensions of access – the quality and quantity of the service, proximity to the service (for example, distance to public transport stops and jobs), affordability of the service, and time during which access exists (for example, duration of power or water supply and wait time for public transport). In most cities of the Global South, the composition of the urban underserved correlates strongly with income level, although the concept is broader than simply an income-based poverty line (Figure 36.3).

Based on interviews in seven countries – India, Brazil, Mexico, China, Ghana, Kenya, and Nigeria – we find several common problems faced by urban residents in their level of access to reliable and affordable urban services. The urban services we include are secure and affordable housing; reliable and affordable potable water; clean, reliable, and affordable energy; and safe, convenient, and affordable transportation. These are all urgent needs that must be met in the short term; if not adequately addressed, the urban underserved are compelled

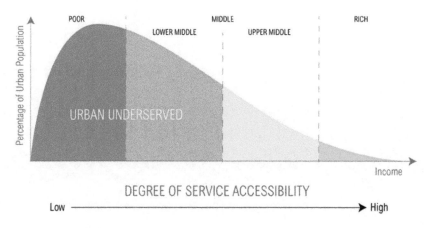

Figure 36.3 Income distribution in cities and the *urban underserved*. Source: Beard et al. 2016.

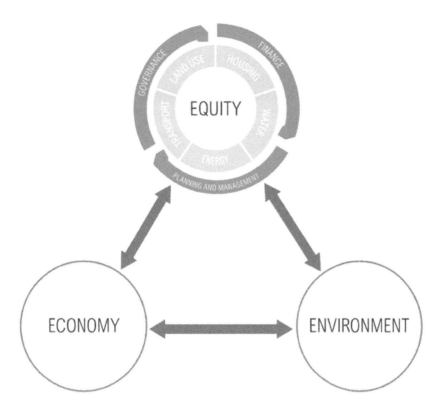

Figure 36.4 Equity as an entry point to a more sustainable city – a theory of change.
Source: Beard et al. 2016.

to self-provide them in informal, illegal, expensive, or unsafe ways. These are all also areas that involve the built environment and infrastructure choices, where making poor, myopic decisions can result in long-term consequences that are extremely difficult and costly to reverse. There is thus a serious lock-in effect.

Urban services that fall at the intersection of fulfilling urgent needs of a growing urban population and avoiding unsustainable lock-in are the highest priorities for cities to get right. If these issues are not resolved for the urban underserved, the costs to the city as a whole are enormous. Progress in these high-priority areas requires coalitions of urban change agents working towards a shared vision, working within important enabling conditions of governance, urban financing, and the capacity to plan, manage, and sustain change over time. When cities make progress in one of these high-priority areas that touch many people's lives, the momentum of these positive changes can affect transformations in other areas of urban development, with the potential to trigger broader, cross-sectoral, citywide transformation, as has been seen in cities such as Medellín and Surat.

References

Beard, V.A., Mahendra, A., and Westphal, M.I. (2016) *A More Equitable City: Framing the Challenges and Opportunities*. World Resources Institute.

Kourtit, K., Nijkamp, P., and Geyer, H.S. (2015) "Managing the Urban Century," *International Planning Studies*, 20(1–2): 1–3.

Ravallion, M., Chen, S., and Sangraula, P. (2007) "The Urbanization of Global Poverty," *World Bank Research Digest*, 1(4)

UN-Habitat, (2003) *The Challenge of Slums: Global Report on Human Settlements, 2003*. London: Earthscan.

United Nations, Department of Economic and Social Affairs, (2014) *World Urbanization Prospects: The 2014 Revision, Highlights*, New York: United Nations.

Chapter 37: The Rebellion of Memory

Lorena Zárate

Today is the day. Imagine that we wake up and, suddenly, everything has changed. The way we live, the places we live in. Social injustice, discrimination, poverty, hunger, homelessness, illiteracy; spatial segregation, lack of basic infrastructure and services; evictions and forced displacements; insecurity and violence; corruption, authoritarian and undemocratic regimes; environmental degradation and increasing vulnerability to disasters; unsustainable production, distribution, consumption, transportation; and settlement patterns, all are just a terrible memory from the past.

Today we wake up and, suddenly, our societies are guaranteeing that every human being on this planet and each member of the generations to come has the opportunity to live a fulfilling life "in dignity, good health, safety, happiness and hope."[1] Nobody suffers discrimination or violations of their human rights and fundamental freedoms; we all have access to adequate housing, food and nutrition, education, culture and recreation, health, sufficient income, justice, and peace.

Imagine that, today, every person and every community is playing a fundamental role in making all this possible. Imagine that every actor and sector participates in truly democratic and effective decision-making processes. Imagine that local, provincial, and national authorities and all other public institutions fulfil their mandate of *governing by obeying*, ensuring "responsiveness to the needs of people," respecting participation, transparency, and accountability. Imagine that multilateral agencies and the private sector are also working under the same principles.

---

[1] All quotations are taken from The Vancouver Declaration on Human Settlements and The Vancouver Action Plan approved at Habitat I in June 1976. http://unhabitat.org/wp-content/uploads/2014/07/The_Vancouver_Declaration_1976.pdf. Many of the same proposals and commitments were also include in the Istanbul Declaration and the Habitat Agenda, 20 years later. See http://unhabitat.org/wp-content/uploads/2014/07/The-Habitat-Agenda-Istanbul-Declaration-on-Human-Settlements-2006.pdf.

Imagine that, today, the economy (production, market, money) has changed its rules and mechanisms, which will now work on the basis of complementariness and solidarity, rather than of competition and competitiveness, to provide the goods and services for people's well-being. Imagine that our societies provide fair compensation to those in charge of socially relevant work, and that no one takes more than what is necessary for a good living.

Imagine that, today, we all operate with "respect for the carrying capacity of ecosystems, we all cooperate in a spirit of global partnership to conserve, protect and restore the health and integrity of the Earth's ecosystem." We all commit to "promote the conservation, rehabilitation and maintenance of buildings, monuments, open spaces, landscapes and settlement patterns of historical, cultural, architectural, natural, religious and spiritual value."

But how did we get here?

We decided to take seriously our commitments, understanding that to be able to meet them, we needed to get back and honor the different types of knowledge that our communities have been producing for generations, focusing on addressing social justice while respecting Mother Earth's rights.

We built social consensus around the worldviews that provided the ethical transformations we needed, making explicit the multiple links between the principles and values that promote and protect the commons, the responsibility to change urban life (right to the city) and the *buen vivir*[2] for all, respecting autonomy and self-determination through both individual and collective rights.

We finally understood that the urban life was neither inevitable nor the unique desirable way of living, and that a fulfilling life in dignity, multiculturalism, diversity, and peace was possible only if possible for everyone, everywhere.

We established a social, solidarity, sharing, and care economy that expanded access to products, services, and opportunities for human well-being, protecting and supporting nonprofit and cooperative institutions and activities.

We committed ourselves to the full implementation of the social function of land and property, guaranteeing democratic access to a place to live while promoting equitable and sustainable use of available land and the reuse of vacant or subutilized units in favor of social housing and community projects.

---

[2] The *buen vivir* condenses the ancient worldviews of indigenous people in the Andes region (whose principles undoubtedly resonate with those of many traditional groups in other regions of the world) and has taken on renewed conceptual, political, and programmatic relevance in several Latin American countries since the beginning of the new millennium.

We started prioritizing people suffering from homelessness and populations living in inadequate housing conditions.

Today might be the day to look behind, in order to see ahead.

The global community has just committed herself to a new, ambitious 2030 Development Agenda and an Urban Agenda for the next 20 years. But some fundamental questions are still floating in the air and should be tackled if we really want to move forward on implementation of these agendas. What kind of knowledge will we need in order to achieve them? What kind of knowledge, and for whom, will we produce in that process? What kind of capacity building do we need to provide for the different actors involved? What kind of professionals will we need to train? And how is all that going to transform us as individuals and societies?

It would certainly take more than a long, deep dream to make that day come true. Still, thousands of experiences all over the world are showing us that this utopia is possible.

Chapter 38: Cities Don't Need "Big" Data – They Need Innovations That Connect to the Local

Mary Rowe

Cities are an ancient form of human settlement. Successful ones continue to out-survive people, companies, cultural institutions, nonprofit organizations, and governments. The reason they do is because of their capacity to continuously adapt to the challenges particular to a place. Obviously, cities evolve differently based on their topography, natural resources, demographic composition, etc., *but the real success of any city is especially dependent on one thing: connectivity.* If a city's land use, design, and planning enable connections between people – easing the transfer of goods, services, knowledge, and resources – then public policy decision-making and private investment will reflect local conditions, and the city will thrive. But if a city's capacity to connect itself and operate holistically across sectors, communities, and jurisdictions is compromised, its viability is threatened.

Alas, over the last century, urban development in North America has been more informed by disconnection: land-use decisions were not properly connected to *local knowledge*; transit planning didn't benefit from *reliable data*, which was either not collected adequately or held proprietarily; housing designs and locations were set *without the insights of neighbors* who knew the unique needs and attributes of their communities and what would fit best, and any regional environmental impacts from new development weren't taken into consideration. The results from this disconnection can be seen in out-of-scale development that disrupts well-functioning streetscapes, expressways bifurcating vibrant commercial corridors, and public housing cited on flood plains. Sadly, the urban development mistakes committed over the last several decades in North America are being potentially repeated, as the Global South also rapidly urbanizes.

Were these development mistakes the result of a lack of knowledge? I doubt it. What continues to be lacking are reliable vehicles for locally generated knowledge to be incorporated into the decision-making processes that affect city livability. Will technology make it easier to ensure that decision-making affecting the built environment is informed by local knowledge? Proponents of big data and smart cities are suggesting yes. Perhaps, but only if they enable the sharing of tacit knowledge and hyper-local expertise, to produce place-specific innovations. These are tools, a means, not an end, for enabling agents within the city to communicate, collaborate, and codevelop. The proliferation of data and technology, advanced by private interests, also carries the risk that once again city leaders will be seduced by the promise of a "grand solution", this time to make your city "smart" or "data rich." Just as before when expressways, or large public housing developments were embraced as the latest universal big idea to solve an urban problem, we must be very wary of large-scale solutions that smother local knowledge and stifle innovation that is particular to place. Better data *are* valuable. But a smarter city is only that if it makes possible integrated decision-making that breaks silos, addresses policy fragmentation, and applies any new information in fundamentally innovative ways.

Communities know what makes their neighborhoods work well, as well as what inhibits them. The New Orleans Community Data Center (www.datacenterresearch.org/) demonstrated this after Katrina, identifying data gaps and local information sources, which proved critical to the city's advocacy for recovery investment. Boston's Office of Urban Mechanics http://newurbanmechanics .org/ and New York City's Civic Hall http://civichall.org/ are other examples of local entities that are providing a bridge between local urban challenges, knowledge and opportunities for innovation. Looser alliances in cities that connect people across sectors are also important to building knowledge, such as Future Capetown (http://futurecapetown.com/), the Bandung Creative City Forum (http://bandungcreativecityforum.wordpress.com), and Toronto's Civic Action (http://civicaction.ca/).

To be lasting and effective, we need multiple forms of bespoke urbanism. Outsiders have too often mistaken the complex weave of neighborhood exchange and improvization, that in fact make things work in a place, as examples of inefficiency and backwardness. But in fact, these patterns have evolved over time and work brilliantly within their local context. The determination of their effectiveness must be assessed locally, as should potential "fixes" to anticipate any unintended consequences. Contemporary city builders should observe the Hippocratic Oath, which reflects the Latin adage *Primum non nocere* ("First do no harm") when venturing into communities to "improve" them.

Various technologies have the potential to strengthen the city, but it is the particularities of a place, derived from local knowledge, practice, preferences, and culture – which will make it livable, sustainable, and real. Cities need innovations that connect to the local.

Chapter 39: Digital Urbanization and the End of Big Cities

Gora Mboup

We are moving to the era of digital towns and villages that are connected via the Internet for their commercial, financial, administrative, and social activities. Digital settlements will be the future of development; they are the trajectory of our urban planet.

With the urgent need for sustainable, inclusive, resilient and prosperous cities, as expressed in the Sustainable Development Goals and the Paris Agreement, and the New Urban Agenda cities must be reconsidered in terms of planning; housing; infrastructure development; economic development; environmental sustainability; social development; disaster exposure and resilience; and peace and security. The planning of twenty-first century cities must take into consideration the emergence of Information Communications Technology (ICT) infrastructure, social media, and the data revolution. This revolution is not only at the technical level but also reflects dynamic changes in modern life. More importantly, with the development of ICT infrastructure, workplaces are becoming more spatially mobile. The dichotomy between settlements, particularly between cities, towns, and villages, is becoming less relevant than it was traditionally perceived to be. Comparative advantages associated with urban settings, such as diffusion of ideas, innovation, economies of scale, and agglomeration, can also be achieved in connected sparse settlements. Today, settlements must be planned in consideration of these emerging parameters and conditions that point towards a new form of urbanization, one where digitally connected towns and villages offer social, economic, and political advantages traditionally only found in large, dense cities.

Over the past 15 years, national governments have created legal institutional frameworks to support regulatory mechanisms on the development and use of ICT. According to the World Bank (2016), between 2005 and 2015, the number of Internet users increased from 1 billion to 3.2 billion. Today, mobile phones are present in the majority of households (varying from 73 percent in sub-Saharan Africa to 98 percent in high-income countries), easing potential access to the Internet. By 2030, access to other ICT infrastructures will also be quasi-universal. Only 31 percent of the population in developing countries had access in 2014, compared with 80 percent in high-income countries (World Bank 2016). Making the Internet universally accessible and affordable should be a global priority.

The growth in ICT has given birth to e-commerce, e-banking, and so on – all of which have led to the creation of "digital villages" that will likely become the norm by the late twenty-first century, if not earlier. This will challenge all projections of urban population and size to 2050 and beyond. Although declines in the sizes of cities have been observed in past decades, the trend was mainly associated with suburbanization and the development of small- and medium-sized cities, it will be further pronounced with the emergence of new forms of digital human settlements, traditionally known as villages.

There are many examples of digitally served villages around the globe in which ICT advances have made spatial obstacles irrelevant and have opened up remote areas to the world with great local benefits. For example, the economy of the village Dongfeng in China's Jiangsu province drastically changed in 2006 when a migrant from the village returned to open an online shop (World Bank 2016). His successful experience was expanded to other sectors; four years later, the village had six board-processing factories, two metal parts factories, 15 logistics companies, and seven computer stores serving 400 households engaged in online sales throughout China and in neighboring countries. In Uganda, wider mobile phone coverage is contributing to increased sale of perishable crops, such as bananas, from farmers in remote areas (Muto and Yamano 2009). In India, e-Choupal is easing access to the Internet, making it possible for farmers to place orders for inputs and to directly negotiate the sale of their produce with buyers (World Bank 2016). E-Choupal services reach over four million farmers growing a range of crops in over 35,000 villages through 6,500 kiosks across 10 states (www.itcportal.com/businesses/agri-business/e-choupal.aspx).

ICT makes it easier for people to buy and sell products beyond geographical boundaries, reduces the cost of transactions by a large margin, and opens remote areas to new opportunities. Yet, it also renders cities and villages that lack versatility irrelevant through ICT's ability to shift to areas that can adapt and transform with its rapid evolution. Through ICT, villages have access to the latest innovations, can participate in democratic debates, and make their voices heard. Today, voices are not just originating from the cities but also from the villages. Finally, the emergence of these digitally served towns and villages will foster economic development without damaging the environment; there will be less consumption of land for private property and fewer cars, making streets friendly and healthy for walking and cycling. In the long term, this will reduce carbon emissions, promote the creation of low-carbon settlements, reduce land degradation, and promote biodiversity. These digitally connected settlements will provide economic advantages at a larger scale while safeguarding the environment. They will be sustainable, inclusive, and prosperous. This will mark the end of big cities and the rise of digital urbanization.

References

Muto, M. and Yamano, T. (2009). The Impact of Mobile Phone Coverage Expansion on Market Participation: Panel Data Evidence from Uganda. *World Development*, 12(37): 1887–1896.

World Bank. (2016). *World Development Report 2016: Digital Dividends*. Washington, DC: World Bank.

Chapter 40: The Art of Engagement / Activating Curiosity

Mary Miss

Artists are underutilized assets for cities and the environment: People often perceive climate change and other environmental risks as future events, happening to people in places far away, outside their own experience. Art has the power to involve people through visceral and place-based experiences, direct personal connection, and emotional engagement to evoke reaction and inspire action.

City as Living Laboratory (CALL) proposes that sustainability can be made tangible and accessible to communities through the arts. We have been developing our methodology since 2009 with the intention of articulating a replicable framework that can be used in other cities. CALL's framework consists of research, dialogues, and projects that intend to harness a sense of wonder and optimism to make people curious about their surroundings.

Results require long-term engagements and interdisciplinary teams: In Indianapolis in late September 2015, a community-wide project focusing on the tributaries of the White River was launched through with the support of a National Science Foundation grant. This grew out of FLOW, a project I completed in 2011 that drew attention to a six-mile stretch of the White River. That FLOW initiative was catalytic; it lead to the formation of a community organization, Reconnecting to Our Waterways, or ROW, that partnered on the grant, along with Butler University and the New Knowledge Organization. For this citywide project, I developed the conceptual framework and visual components of STREAM / LINES to highlight these five tributaries of the White River through contextual, immersive, and game-like experiences of the selected sites and their unique characteristics. It was a collaborative project involving a game designer, scientists, poets, musicians, and dancers.

Engagement benefits from multiple access points: In five modest neighbourhoods, a cluster of mirrors and red beams radiate out from a central point to nearby streams and waterways: these elements stake out a territory for observation. At the center, visitors can step up onto a pedestal to see their own image in a four-foot diameter mirror that places them in the middle of the reflected landscape while casting them in the role of the statue/activator/principal character. Single words and texts are reflected in the smaller mirrors that dot the site; some of the texts are poems, while others are prompts that encourage exploration. All are intended to provoke the visitor's curiosity and send them out to the nearby waterways.

Engaging all of the senses is key: Whether following a red beam out to observe habitat at a stream's edge, trying to walk at the same pace as the flow of the stream, or listening to music composed for each unique location, the goal is to engage citizens with a place-based experience of the waterways that supports every aspect of their lives. The installations are like anchors, the starting points for explorations, and will be activated over time by walks and dialogues with scientists and artists, by performances and readings. Engagement of the sites through programming is essential. The goal is to allow the people of Indianapolis to begin to imagine what they would like to see their streams, lakes, and rivers become in the future.

Diverse perspectives and community input are essential: The projects and contingent programming are part of a process of engagement that depends on the collaborative efforts of communities, various experts, and artists. Finding willing and enthusiastic participants is key. We look for people with very different ways of regarding the landscape, who can reveal their own observations to others: a climatologist points out the link between traffic patterns and ways to enjoy good weekend weather, while a poet reflects on the change over time of a particular place, or an ecologist reveals more about a day in the life of a turtle, or a community member describes the stream she knew before it was put in a pipe. Each of these "experts" can add a layer of insight into our surroundings. We are given a more complete picture of our landscape and our place in it.

Systemic challenges like global warming must be linked to the everyday: CALL proposes that rather than assuming only a top-down, governmental approach, we engage communities and citizens on the street with the pressing issues of our times. Rather than only focusing on a negative forecast of the future, the goal is to bring people together and to provide a platform to explore innovative, positive ways forward in creating socially and environmentally sustainable communities.

To promote/facilitate replication and scaling up, CALL focuses on specific principles and strategies: The City as Living Laboratory is building a methodology to engage artists with a process to be able to work with other experts, communities, and policy-makers to make lives of sustenance available to all.

The replicable framework we are developing focuses on:

- Encouraging inquiry and exploration

- Envisioning future possibilities

- Promoting interdisciplinary and dynamic thinking

- Encouraging and promoting innovation and practical solutions

- Bringing diverse cultural perspectives to the projects

- Harnessing interdisciplinary collaborations led by artists

- Producing distinctive artistic contributions

It is important that artists be recognized as essential members of the team addressing social and environmental issues in our cities and communities. We can have value beyond supplying artwork for the 1 percent of the population who are able to participate in the art market. Artists in the broadest sense – poets, musicians, dancers, and performers of all types – are an essential resource that must be recognized for the significance of the contribution they can make to help create an equitable and sustainable society.

Chapter 41: Nairobi's Illegal City-Makers

Lorraine Amollo Ambole

Like most cities, Nairobi has its good sides: a national park, fabulous nightspots, and a vibrant, youthful population. Unfortunately, this young population is growing faster than employment opportunities; hence, many Nairobians must resort to informal work, such as street vending.

Street vendors, better known locally as "hawkers," are the embodiment of what it is to survive in Nairobi. Out of sheer necessity, they break city bylaws with reckless abandon; they use any available street space to sell goods that range from insecticides to secondhand designer clothing. They also ingeniously display these goods on propped up carton boxes, which can be hurriedly folded up and sprung onto their backs as they dash off to escape the clutches of Nairobi City County, or NCC, officials. The NCC (colloquially referred to as *kanjo*) are themselves breakers of the law; they extort bribes and resort to violence in their frequent confrontations with the hawkers (Mungai 2016).

In its defense, the NCC, in its role as the local government of the city of Nairobi, is currently reviewing some of the city bylaws in a new attempt to bring order to downtown Nairobi. For instance, two large markets on the fringes of the city center have been designated for the hawkers (Odhiambo 2015). The hawkers, however, complain that they don't get enough customers in those markets, so they troop back into the heart of the city, where they set up shop in front of banks, offices, and hotels. Thus continues the Nairobi hawker menace – a menace that is the obvious result of poor planning and bad management by the city.

Considering that Nairobi is Kenya's capital, one would expect some foresight in its planning. Unfortunately, the city has expanded haphazardly and developed into fragmented neighbourhoods. There is an *Integrated Urban Development Master Plan* in the works (Niuplan 2016), but for now, Nairobians are left to their own devices. And this is not just the story of Nairobi; the development trajectory of most sub-Saharan African cities is haphazard, due in part to the inappropriateness of prevailing urban planning methods, which are, more often than not, borrowed from the Global North (Chen and Skinner 2014).

To remedy the urban planning debacle in downtown Nairobi, some negotiations have taken place between three interest groups: the hawkers (who formed their own Nairobi Street Hawkers Association), the NCC, and the Nairobi Central Business District Association, which is made up of business owners (Kamunyori 2007). For such talks to bear fruit, Nairobi needs urban negotiators who can creatively facilitate inclusive dialogue.

One possible way to enhance city dialogues in Nairobi is through design thinking, which provides methods for understanding and facilitating long-term societal change via a user-centered, problem-focused approach (Brown and Wyatt 2015).

A user-centered approach in planning Nairobi is urgently needed to ensure that the needs and knowledge of street hawkers and other vulnerable groups are brought to bear in developing the city. For example, the tacit design knowledge of street hawkers in navigating the city and dealing with daily challenges in downtown Nairobi could greatly enhance plans for better navigation and access in Nairobi's streets.

Ultimately, the quest for sanity and order in Nairobi is a long-term project. Design thinking experts, along with other professionals, can better contribute to such a project if they can negotiate the clash between formal, informal, and even outright-illegal processes that, together, assemble Nairobi.

❣ References

Brown, T., and J. Wyatt. (2015) "Design Thinking for Social Innovation." *Annual Review of Policy Design* 3(1): 1–10.

Chen, M., and C. Skinner. (2014) "The Urban Informal Economy, Enhanced Knowledge, Appropriate Policies and Effective Organization" in S. Parnell and S. Oldfield (eds.) *The Routledge Handbook on Cities in the Global South*. New York: Routledge, pp. 219–235.

Kamunyori, S. (2007) "A Growing Space for Dialogue: The Case of Street Vending in Nairobi's Central Business District." Unpublished Masters thesis, Massachusetts Institute of Technology.

Mungai, C. (2016) "African cities Are Crowded, But Not Necessarily Economically Dense. In Other Words, They Are Undergoing an Urbanisation of People, Not of Capital" *Mail & Guardian Africa*, April 18, http://mgafrica.com/article/2016–04-15-african-cities-street-hawkers-and-traders

Niuplan (2016) "Integrated Urban Development Master Plan for the City of Nairobi" http://citymasterplan.nairobi.go.ke/index.php/niuplan/background

Odhiambo, R. (2015) "Hawkers in Nairobi to Operate in Saccos as Plans to Revamp City Markets Underway." *The Star*, March, 4, www.the-star.co.ke/news/2015/03/04/hawkers-in-nairobi-to-operate-in-saccos-as-plans-to-revamp-city_c1095507

Chapter 42: Active Environmental Citizens with Receptive Government Officials Can Enact Change

Kate Scherer and Umamah Masum

Record-breaking weather patterns are becoming a defining feature of our world. Although to some people in the United States, this simply looks like odd weather, it is irrefutable that climate change is here. Unless we start taking care of Earth, it will soon fall to destruction. Every year, low-lying countries and communities face rising sea levels that are threatening their existence. For someone born and raised in the United States with roots in Bangladesh (Umamah), knowing that this country will be underwater by the end of the century[1] is sickening. Climate change affects us all, whether it be coastal cities in the United States or island nations all together, everyone will face the consequences of this global issue.

Despite the overwhelming evidence, many in the United States still doubt that climate change is real (or at least a threat). In New York City, though, there is little doubt. We have seen the effects of climate change firsthand in 2012's Superstorm Sandy. In author Kate's neighborhood in Queens, NY, many homes were damaged by fallen trees, and there was flooding all over the city. The damage was so severe that many of her good friends were forced to relocate permanently. The level of destruction was massive; entire neighbourhoods, such as Far Rockaway and parts of Lower Manhattan and Staten Island, were wiped out. It has been proven that storms have intensified due to climate change, producing storms such as such as Sandy, and future storms will only increase in severity[2]. In the aftermath of Superstorm Sandy, we realized how uninformed we were about climate change. We also learned that youth will be

---

[1] Harris, Gardiner, "Borrowed Time on Disappearing Land," *The New York Times*, March 28, 2014 http://nyti.ms/1eZlRjt

[2] Mathiesen, Karl, "Extreme weather already on increase due to climate change, study finds," *The Guardian*, April 27, 2015 http://bit.ly/1z65JsK

disproportionately affected by climate change because we are the ones inheriting a sick planet. Knowing this and realizing that apathy will not solve this problem, we decided to take action. Through our involvement with Global Kids, a nonprofit educational organization for youth leadership and global education, we became engaged citizens.

Although it may seem daunting, everyone, especially youth, can contribute to solving the climate change problem by encouraging, nudging, and even annoying government officials into taking action. Disinvestment campaigns promoted by hundreds of college students, which seek to drive academic institutions to disinvest from fossil fuel holdings, is an example of collective action's effectiveness.

Here in New York City, we have taken a stand locally with our climate change education campaign. It began in 2013 when, as high school students, we decided the best way for us to fight climate change was through education. Climate education has the power to enlighten people on the science of climate change and to prepare people to find solutions. We reached out to New York City Council Member Costa Constantinides to express our concerns for the lack of climate change education in all New York City public schools. Constantinides represents parts of Queens that were particularly affected by hurricane Sandy; therefore, he has a particular interest in climate change. In addition to his interest in safeguarding his district, Constantinides also had a history of advocating for youth and supporting similar resolutions. By working with him, we were able to make connections with other city officials to support the resolution. Thanks in part to our advocacy efforts, in August 2014, NYC Council Members Constantinides and Donovan Richards introduced Resolution 0375 calling for climate change education in all New York State schools, grades K–12.

Since the introduction of Resolution 0375, we have contacted more New York City Council Members, often on a daily basis, to gain their support. Prior to this campaign, many of us had no experience in lobbying. While this process requires dedication and commitment, it can be a surprisingly simple job. Every week we were either calling offices, writing letters, emailing, and/or visiting offices to lobby for the resolution. When we went on these visits, we would explain our cause and ask for support; if we already had the individual's support, we would ask for strategies to continue our momentum.

On April 19, 2016, along with ten other Global Kids high school students, we testified before the New York City Council's Committee on Education in support of Resolution 0375. After listening to the reasons why we demand climate education, the Education Committee unanimously voted in favor of the resolution. During the hearing, Council Member Constantinides noted that Global Kids youth activists "make government work." The next day, the resolution passed through the full City Council with overwhelming support.

It has been empowering to work on this campaign because it truly gives a voice to youth, those who have the most to lose from climate change. We learned that when we partnered with like-minded government officials, including our staunch ally, Council Member Constantinides, we could make a powerful difference. Youth will be the most affected by the damaging consequences of climate change, but youth also possess the energy, power, and enthusiasm to create real change to make better environments for all of us.

Chapter 43: The Sea Wall

Paul Downton

43.1 Preamble

Cities last for centuries – but when the climate is changing even faster than fashion, urban planning requires preparedness to experiment. Before entering the lexicon of the billions born *after* fateful decisions were made to cook the planet, city-making ideas that might repair past damage must be tested in practice, as fractals of the cities to which they aspire.

Then, the children can take the high ground.

Morally, it's already theirs.

43.1.1 4°C and Rising

Hot, humid, mid-winter in southern Australia. Space mirrors broken. Schools closed. Kids in the factories. Borgmol Industries bought the skies, stopped us frying. Borgmalazon drones deliver playthings and food. I have a license. I pay my fees. I know all my passwords.

Food's scarce, tastes awful; rationed, like the water. SiBorg's TerrorWatch stops crimes before they start. Petty criminals can't beat SmartCityData. The city is smarter than its citizens. Still, hackers run resistance. Water gets stolen. Wars are started over less.

43.1.2 2°C and Ecocities

I wake in turmoil, screaming. Matilda's cool hand on my brow. The wedding ring she laughed at glinting in the morning light. We lie quietly, sunlight playing across the sheets.

Out on the balcony, our vine adds dappled shade and grapes to the breakfast she brought from the café two floors down. We watch the morning flow down the street where people struggle to protect our world from Borgmol and drones and omniscient cities and oceans out of control.

Someone's got to do it.

The sea wall is being extended. Greenland's catastrophic ice melt is being matched by Antarctica and glaciers are shrinking fast. We've stabilised the climate but the sea will rise for centuries. So we're retreating in places where we have no choice, or building sea walls and platforms for our cities like Mesopotamians, shaping the land ocean-side to fit the flow of natural systems. Nay-sayers said don't interfere, let nature run its course – we said screw you, we are nature.

Old cities live on, fractals of the new are added. Adjustments between them take place. Ecological corridors fit the evolving urban form, embraced by new shorelines. If they're low enough, the sprawling suburbs of the infernal combustion engine are replaced by fish farms. Suburbanites and the rest of the dispossessed are relocated to ecocities.

Our Great Wall was the first. Brutally attacked when just an idea, it's evolving, its community fused together by our fight for survival.

Solar light rail connects our coastal town of 50,000 to others. Inland, sprawl is undone. Land is released for nature. We still have to fight for it. Wind farms float where coal carriers and tankers once spewed their filth. Our building datum is 15 metres; a pattern repeated: Shanghai, London, Cairo, Guyana, Florida, Mexico, Holland, Vietnam, Bangladesh, the Maldives ... we're achieving the "impossible!"

43.1.3 4°C and Rising

Sometimes, I see the yellow sky. But I've got drugs from the pharmadrones. Everybody takes them. It's what remains from the ruins of Welfare.

I'm a climate refugee. I came on a small boat, pregnant with hope and child. My son was born and died in a storm that spared everyone else aboard. God help me, haven't I paid my bills? Didn't I give you my password? Don't I have a license to live? Can't anybody HELP ME?

43.1.4 2°C and Ecocities

Greenery is everywhere. Matilda and I head up to our apartment building's roof garden. Circling the lightwell's cascading vegetation and handrail of flowing water, my 4° nightmare begins to fade.

"It's beauty-in-progress, eh?" says Matilda, "I remember when people thought all new buildings had to be ugly and nature was doomed!"

She's right. Shackled to a system run by the 1 percent, escaping from ugly reality meant images on screens tracking everything you did. In the prison of daily life you'd make choices as a conditioned consumer but never as a free citizen. There were troops in the streets. Now it's easy to walk and cycle; easy to meet without appointments, though not all the troops have gone.

In the face of climate change and fascist corporations, reshaping society was never going to be a picnic, but we are the apes that became a force of nature. Now we understand our power. For many, egalitarianism, compassion, and sharing are still dirty words but they're having to deal with increasing evidence that we can build cities that nurture our lives as citizens and restore the balance of nature.

And when they're sufficiently provoked to respond in kind, we are flattered by their mimicry.

43.2 PostAmble

We know enough to make the difference between an ecocity future and hell, but the decisions that make that choice must be made now, while the children are young enough to benefit – before they are old enough to express the anger and resentment their elders deserve.

Chapter 44: Academics and Nonacademics

Who's Who in Changing the Culture of Knowledge Creation?

Kareem Buyana

Now that urban sustainability is a global goal with the potential to undo the partitioning of disciplines within academic and nonacademic institutions, changes in the culture of knowledge creation are likely to differ in form and scale. Conventionally, urban development is a city-specific issue, limited to finding knowledge on urban forms that make it easier to live and work in the city. But because urban development has become a planetary and complex challenge, sustainability relies on knowledge beyond one's field of comfort. If we use the current economic model of extracting more from nature, it would mean production and consumption that is beyond what the planet can offer and an increase in international resource conflicts. So, how do we ensure less or recyclable use of resources for the same economic output by cities for the entire global population? This is a planetary and complex question, characterized by predictable and unpredictable scenarios; expected and unprecedented overlaps in stakeholder interests; and a multiplicity of solutions that are never completely right, but rarely completely wrong.

Because urban sustainability has posed multiple, interconnected layers of planetary and complex questions, collaborative knowledge creation – that is, knowledge cocreation – is necessary. Knowledge cocreation is a mechanism for solution-focused interfaces between academics and nonacademics (including industry figures, policy-makers, and members of society). The key principle that has defined knowledge cocreation globally is that nonacademics and academics should have an equal chance to contribute to the framing of research questions and to the design methodologies for finding and experimenting with options for urban sustainability. For academics and nonacademics to operate on equal footing requires putting a dent in the power structures that characterize many research processes – wherein academics, in consultation with a particular funding agency, frame the research agenda and use predetermined methodologies to broaden the understanding of urban sustainability *for*, rather than with, nonacademics. By viewing knowledge cocreation as a means of changing the rules and regulations of the game, scientists can be positioned to offer an open hand that invites nonacademics in as coproducers, rather than end-users, of knowledge.

Who is responsible for what in the process of changing the culture of knowledge creation? Is it the academics, nonacademics, or both? I explore this with three synchronized layers of empowerment: (1) individual; (2) institutional; and (3) the empowerment of collaborations. The analysis is both normative and applied, and points to the merits and pitfalls of changing the culture of knowledge creation.

44.1 Individuals

Empowerment of individuals means opening up the space to include all relevant actors (scientists, government officials, industry figures, civil society, and local residents) in the process of cocreating knowledge. For instance, if architects, engineers, and urban sociologists are to collaboratively work with the building industry to create commercially viable developments that enhance tenants' well-being while using scarce but precious metals sparingly, property owners in the city ought to have a front seat at the table. Their contribution would spring from ideas on how to manage properties in ways that reconcile the often-conflicting means of economic, environmental, and social viability. Policy-makers at municipal and central government levels also need to be involved from the start to realize a cohesive policy for the affected sectors. In such a scenario, individual actors would cocreate a sustainable urban design as the boundary object for learning beyond the limits of each person's expertise. Besides creating a personal learning network, individuals would broaden their understanding of a methodology that relies on fewer natural resources to generate buildings that offer equally good economic outputs and lifestyles for tenants. The academics would generate quality criteria for conducting transdisciplinary research on cities and buildings.

However, differences in corporate power and social context can position the elite as the voice for the nonelite and academics as the voice for the nonacademics, thereby minimizing the influence of certain actors on the outcome of the research agenda. This puts academics in a double-agent position; on the one hand, they would care about generating research questions and a methodology that is "scientifically credible," whereas, on the other, they would be expected to be ensure that the methodology produces a building design that is valuable to property owners, policy-makers, and tenant representatives. The question, then, is who among the academics or nonacademics is best suited to ensure that an outcome is scientifically valid and valuable to society, and what such an outcome would look like? Contestations among architects, engineers, and urban sociologists are very likely, and reconciliation of values and preferences among property owners, builders, policy-makers, and tenants is an uphill task.[1]

For these reasons, changing the culture of knowledge creation is nonlinear; this nonlinearity makes knowledge cocreation empowering for academics *and* nonacademics in two ways: (1) the nonacademics would learn how multiple disciplines operate alongside each other on a given policy and societal issue and (2) the academics would gain exposure to aggregating multiple policy and societal perspectives – a joint empowerment.

44.2 Institutions

As individual academics and nonacademics participate in coproducing knowledge, they are not acting in a vacuum. They are traversing institutional mandates and governance structures with different rules and regulations, as well as defined boundaries for collaboration. For example, it is possible for researchers in a university to sign a memorandum of understanding with municipal authorities to produce knowledge on governance structures that constrain capacity to plan and implement sustainability projects. However, this is likely to be a *collective* study as opposed to a *collaborative* one because knowledge would be extracted from urban policy-makers and residents using a predetermined framework for undertaking key informant interviews and citizen juries.

Pressing sustainability challenges – climate change, biodiversity loss, and interference in nutrient cycles, for example – are related to industry and societal struggles along gender and class lines, as well as to other patterns of inequality, which sustainability experts may not easily uncover unless policy-makers, industry figures, and the public all have the platform to validate and align their experiences to the issues of social change towards equity and justice. Therefore, depending on how institutional collaborations are designed, they can empower or disempower academics to exchange knowledge beyond the limits of their fields. Who should undo the institutional barriers to changing the culture of knowledge creation? And how should such institutional constraints be overcome? One option is for academics and nonacademics to imagine modalities of engagement that stretch across legal/illegal boundaries and formal/informal administrative routes to garner the support of their institutions. Such sidesteps can change power relationships among institutions and enable individual actors to negotiate a "gray space" between legality and illegality while creatively using the law.

---

[1] https://ugecviewpoints.wordpress.com/2016/08/23/transdisciplinary-research-in-urban-africa-a-coat-of-many-blended-colors/

44.3 Collaborations

Collaborations will require academics that have international research experience and the mentality to operate alongside differing disciplines and worldviews. Therefore, the definition of a global researcher has to change from a person who has conducted international studies with citations by other scholars and multilateral agencies to a person who provides space for voices that transcends the researcher's perspective and who participates in research collaborations that allow both academics and nonacademics in the Global North and South to flourish. While working from such a mindset, academics would work on projects that are valuable to industry and society in both hemispheres as opposed to partitioning international cases along developed/developing country lines. Such a collaboration would be manifest in a study on the feasibility of replacing disposable food containers with reusable containers, judged using criteria that focus on reduced operational cost and customer acceptance for industrial players; cutting down reliance on plastics and metal to attain efficiency in global supply chains; increased access to affordable food containers by school-going girls and boys in the Global South; and creation of jobs for youth that feel excluded by current employment policies. It would be critical for the academics in this research to work with nonacademics from both the Global North and South in framing key thematic issues that can constitute a science-policy-practice nexus in the context of sustainable food packaging.

In spite of the complexities associated with science-policy-industry-society interfaces, the culture of creating knowledge in cubicles is dying out, and not all academics are ready to lead or be part of the change. Academic and nonacademic institutions, such as Future Earth, have and will continue to invest in the technical aspects of coproducing knowledge; so, the value system of individuals and institutions within and outside the realm of transdisciplinarity ought to be studied in-depth, as culture and human factors are a precursor to the successful application of methods and tools across scales.

✿ References

Ambole, L.A. (2016). Understanding Coproduction through Sanitation Intervention Case Studies in South Africa (Doctoral dissertation, Stellenbosch University).

Campbell. L. K., Svendsen, E.S., Roman. L. (2016). Knowledge Co-production at the Research–Practice Interface: Embedded Case Studies from Urban Forestry. Environmental Management (2016) 57: 1262–1280.

Chapter 45: Private Fears in Public Spaces

Lesley Lokko

The title of this chapter is taken from a 2006 French film directed by Alain Resnais. Although it doesn't relate directly to the urban, per se, it speaks very clearly to a set of concerns that have been on my mind since I was a teen. I grew up yo-yo-ing between two very different cities, Accra and London, and therefore between two very different urban cultures.

Through a child's eyes, Accra was dense and close. Warm. Loud. Spontaneous. Anything could – and frequently did – happen. In the 1970s, it was fairly common to see a donkey trotting along, sandwiched between cars. Working traffic lights were few and far between. Kiosks selling bananas and oranges sat comfortably in the shade of suburban mansions. At lunchtime, municipal workers were as likely to sleep on the pavement as to walk on it. The city was gossipy, intimate, and indifferent. Peoples' lives unfolded in and around the city, almost in spite of it. A traffic jam was an opportunity to sell something – live puppies, toilet paper, sugarcane. A street could host a funeral or a carnival, depending on the mood. Church began at dusk and lasted all night. Passersby, anything goes.

London was different, and oppressively so. Quiet. Fast. Apart. Roads were for cars, not donkeys. People shopped in shops that stuck rigidly to opening hours. No woman ever settled herself down by the side of the road to sell bottles of warm Coke or powdered milk. Nothing ever seemed to happen. The difference was expressed not only physically – in the scale, form, and shape of buildings – but also (and perhaps more interestingly) in peoples' behavior, not just towards one another, but towards the city itself. Long before CCTVs sprang up on every corner, London's buildings maintained a watchful, beady eye, expressed clearly in signs and admonishments: No Smoking. Do Not Walk on the Grass. Residents Only. No Dogs. Citizen, know thy place.

Of course, these generalizations are a little predictable. But in my second year of architecture school, suddenly the childish observations began to deepen and crystallize: cities are shaped as much by how we behave in them as by their tangible fabric. Programs, which dictate – to a certain extent – what we do in buildings and how we structure and form them – don't hold quite as much sway in Accra, where adaptability, improvization, and an ability to just "go with the flow" are of more use to your average citizen than a well-mannered observance of the rules. Accra had attitude, in spades. London did too, but borne of arrogant confidence, not inventive contingency.

A decade ago, Richard Sennett wrote, "The cities everyone wants to live in should be clean and safe, possess efficient public services, be supported by a dynamic economy, provide cultural stimulation and also do their best to heal society's division of race, class and ethnicity. These are not the cities we live in."[1]

How true. I live in Johannesburg, possibly one of the least "healed" cities on the planet. The divisions of race, class, and ethnicity are alive and well in Jo'burg, shaping not just the physical city but our mental image of it as well. This is a city of nothing *but* difference, relentlessly and continuously expressed. Here, Africa – whatever that means – and Europe exist cheek by jowl, simultaneously codependent and determinedly apart. Opportunities for the myriad citizens of Johannesburg to spontaneously "come together" are few and far between. The FIFA World Cup; Mandela's passing; election day ... these are solitary moments where South Africans of all backgrounds self-consciously rub shoulders, thrilled on the one hand to have "discovered" a shared sense of their public selves, but on the other, equally worried that a single false comment or a sideways glance will "set it all off." The recent furor unleashed by the South African bigot Penny Sparrow illustrates this beautifully. Her Facebook comment,[2] which compared black South Africans to monkeys, hits the nail on the head, though it's safe to assume not in the way she intended: private fears in public spaces. Sparrow has been expelled from the Democratic Alliance political party and is said to have immigrated to Australia. Yet for all the hue and cry, there's an uncomfortable truth lying at the heart of the matter that few of us acknowledge: here in South Africa, there is – as yet – no common understanding around what it means to be urban. To be public. To share the city. To be *together*. Bourgeois values, lifted straight from nineteenth-century Europe and transplanted onto cultures that already had their own value system(s), make blanket, blind assumptions about all manner of behaviors, no pun intended. But urban cultures are formed, not imposed. They emerge out of shared experiences and shared histories, however contested. It takes a mature society to form not only the consensus around which public behavior – public "togetherness"– is molded but also the mechanisms by which it changes, develops, accommodates, renews itself. Sennett argues

---

[1] http://downloads.lsecities.net/0_downloads/Berlin_Richard_Sennett_2006-The_Open_City.pdf.
[2] www.news24.com/SouthAfrica/News/its-just-the-facts-penny-sparrow-breaks-her-silence-20160104.

Figure 45.1 Makola Market, Accra, midday. Man carrying bathing sponges for sale. © L. Lokko, 2014.

that cooperation is a skill.[3] It is learned, practiced, finessed. A healthy, tolerant, and resilient urban culture may also be viewed as a skill to which attention, effort, and energy must be paid. It's an aspect of sustainability we seldom discuss: to be sustainable is not only to refer to ecology and the environment, it includes ideas about equity and etiquette, too. Perhaps it's time we started practicing *how* to be together, learning how to fuse our often-contradictory attitudes about public and private together without friction and suspicion; understanding that these are not "universal" values, but are culturally determined and specific. It's time for us to learn the basic ropes of urban etiquette, trying – and, yes, failing – and trying again, instead of blindly assuming that we somehow already know.

---

[3] For a more thorough reading of Sennett's argument, see Sennett, R. (2013) *Together: The Rituals, Pleasure and Politics of Cooperation*, London: Penguin.

Chapter 46: Leadership

Science and Policy as Uncomfortable Bedfellows

Thomas Tang

In the eighteenth century, at the height of the Industrial Revolution, cities in the English Midlands were the pinnacles of technological advancement. The British Empire, served by vassal colonies, would have been the equivalent of major modern-day megalopolises such as New York and Tokyo. But failure to adapt – as, one by one, the empire lost its colonies and industries shifted elsewhere in the globe – led to the demise of once great English cities. Similar tales can be encountered in the United States (automobile manufacturers), Switzerland (watchmakers), and Germany (solar panels). How can other countries and their cities avoid a similar fate?

Climate change is one such major challenge facing several cities. Global warming is disrupting equilibrium; coastal cities, in particular, are at risk as sea level rises. People will have to reconfigure reclaimed land and design underground infrastructure, such as tunnels and submerged utilities, using climate protective measures. With many cities and towns approaching the limits of their carrying capacities and urban migration stretching resources, there is the added problem for cities of how to accommodate so many people let alone protect against the ravages of weather.

A partial solution can be offered by science and sound policies. The advanced production and distribution of food and other resources – so that a large number of the world's projected 8.5 billion people by 2030 (UN 2015) population are being fed through the efforts of a few – means that cities can yet thrive, and the construction of urban habitats and infrastructure that capitalize on economies of scale in heating, cooling, and mobility are a triumphant statement of modern urban development.

But the more science and technology come to the rescue, the more removed society becomes from appreciating nature. Plastic polymers are the epitome of the blessing and curse of science. Without plastics, from packaging to complex 3D laser printing, modern life would be almost inconceivable. Plastics are so commonplace today that they occur everywhere in our streets, countrysides, oceans, and in our food chains, where they will not break down for many decades. Society has become so imbued with consumer behavior that little thought is given to what happens after items are discarded. This is just one example of how behavior has been malformed as a result of science. Hence, science must be applied with good policies in mind to shape attitudes.

More enlightened cities these days are listening to scientists and drafting policies based on evidence instead of political populism. In tackling climate change, the C40 network of cities is an example of this type of thinking from cities worldwide. Conservation of resources makes sense, as does the protection of natural environments. The prudent use of energy and water means that current city dwellers will benefit from efficient use of resources but also that there will be enough of these resources for future generations. Investment now in renewable resources, linked with smart technologies, will result in meaningful long-term returns.

But if scientists are telling us how to get the policies right to conserve resources and execute the correct measures to address climate change, what is stopping us? A telling lack of statesmanship has dominated talks on climate change. Denial of climate change has long prevailed, spurred on by vested interests in certain sectors. The other major hurdle in solving climate change has been the lack of political will to make the hard calls, such as removal of subsidies on energy resources including oil and electricity, which garners popular sentiment, but does little good for the environment or the populace. The realization that externalities should be priced into resources such as water and energy is beyond the comprehension of most political dealers, which propels us onto our short-lived path of wanton consumption. This is not just irresponsible, but dangerous.

Science and politics should converge, even if they make uncomfortable bedfellows. Good political decisions coupled with science-based policies will "future proof" cities against climate change and other challenges.

Reference

United Nations (2015). Population 2030: Demographic challenges and opportunities for sustainable development planning. http://www.un.org/en/development/desa/population/publications/pdf/trends/Population2030.pdf

Chapter 47: Sketches of an Emotional Geography Towards a New Citizenship

Diana Wiesner (Translation into English by Juana Villegas)

A truly democratic city must empower its citizens and institutions as agents of change, through collective decision-making focused towards the common good. In order to achieve this, an urban pedagogy is necessary, aimed at encouraging collective decisions that include emotions and the advocacy of territorial governance; thus each citizen, along with institutions, in independent or organized fashion, exercise their capacity to self-govern.

This pedagogy would allow for citizens, schools, and universities, among others, to reactivate their social role, multiplying collective ways of solving local urban problems. Feelings and intuition can guide and be put to the service of a new democracy, for life is, in essence, both spatial and emotional (Nogue 2015). We interact emotionally with places by filling them with meaning that comes back to us through evoked feelings. Each geographical context transmits emotion, as does each landscape, because they are social and cultural constructions full of intangible meanings that can only be read or experimented through emotions.

The city's landscape acquires meaning through the significance and interpretation given to it by the particular vision of its inhabitants and visitors, making it nonexistent in the absence of an observer (Figure 47.1). Far from being a neutral space, landscape has the ability to transform itself through its two-way relationship with individuals: as they project their emotions onto it, it stimulates them, resulting in a sum of emotional geographies over the landscape (Luna and Valverde 2015). For this reason, a city's complexity isn't solely produced by the superposition of infrastructure systems, with their social and economic functions, but also by the sum of perspectives that increasingly demands for the existence of places that evoke emotions, positive feelings, and geographic roots.

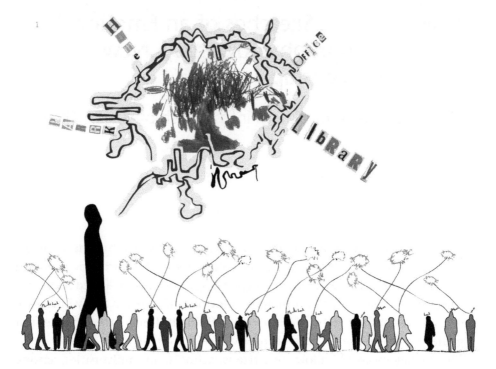

Figure 47.1 The city doesn't exist without an observer, by Diana Wiesner

The spaces each person travels through every day are key factors within the urban experience, and the enrichment of said experience materializes in places that allow for the city to be perceived through the feet, the body and the senses, places to walk, free the mind, and connect to the self (Figure 47.2). Along with the need for environments that promote urban living spaces focused on the growth of individuals, it's also crucial to propose urban projects that are framed within an urban ecology that is coherent with the ecosystem's regional corridors. Thus, nature's presence has a double functionality in the urban project. While contributing to the city's ecosystem service maintenance, it improves the quality of the urban experience, offering a range of safe meeting places that are rich in symbols and meaning.

The development of urban nature is not a "natural" process within city planning. The concept of nature in itself generates contradictions for planners who deem rivers, wetlands, mountains, and high vegetation areas to be wild places dominated by a fear of the unknown. This attitude results in a preference for high cost artificial comfort zones. Green infrastructure proposals, coherent with the aforementioned objectives, force that paradigm to be broken, for they seek to mitigate the effects of climate change and increase risk resilience strategies, procuring a balance between conservation and development.

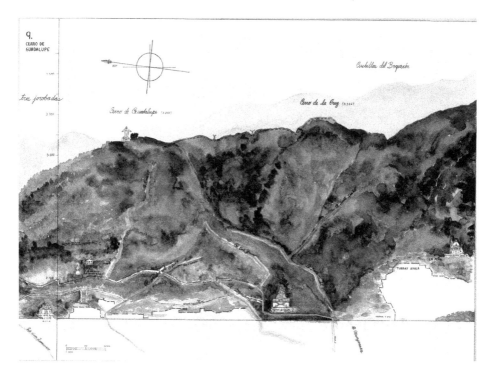

Figure 47.2 Section of a drawing by Colectivo Bogotá Pinta Cerros, 2017. Citizens who participated printed their feelings for the mountains of the region with a 12-hand watercolor in 16 plates of 11.2 meters, representing the 57 kilometers of mountains near the city

Another important challenge for these green spaces is to provide an identity to a diverse population. Heritage values and significant elements of a place must be rescued through methodologies that inquire into hidden stories and intangible memories, thus promoting a participative construction of public spaces where people can identify with an emotional geography. In addition, I suggest that indicators associated to the quality of life of human beings be established, for example what I call "soul resilience indicators," which measure people's intuitive ability to manage daily risks (Figure 47.3). This concept reclaims our ability to take mankind's adaptability and well-being into consideration.

Although humans are social beings that seek each other out, public spaces should also guarantee places for individuality, for the enjoyment of solitude, for silence, for encountering the self, and for mourning. The city is an extension of a person's home; it should offer multiple options, and it should use biodiversity as a tool to provide infinite possibilities for countless urban souls (Figure 47.4).

People look for distinctive elements they can identify with, which make the city feel like their own. This can only happen through the acknowledgment of

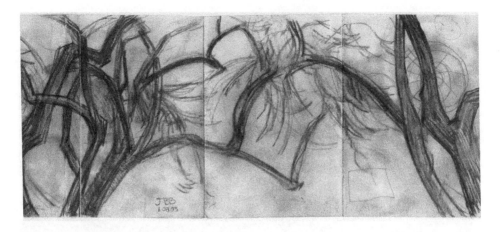

Figure 47.3 Soul Resilience, by María Ceciia Galindo

Figure 47.4 A Child Holding a Painting by Walter J. Gonzalez called "My Future Bogotá": from the south of the city he draws his image of the future

the culture and of the social groups that live in a given area. In this framework, local markets, artisanal production, and traditional practices gain recognition. In the face of imposed, foreign, globalized models, citizens yearn for those symbols that might be imperfect but are their own, that bring stories back to life and add value to their insufficient free time. The new citizen assumes his role like a musician in an orchestra, in which effective results are delivered through synchronization and group work, eliminating any type of protagonism. An urban concert could be achieved by a conductor-less orchestra, like the *Orpheus Chamber Orchestra*: a unique ensemble in which the musicians decided that instead of a conductor, they would all share in the responsibility of musical decisions (Figure 47.5). Could a city be conducted with the sum of citizen initiatives focused on the concepts of justice, equality, resilience, sustainability, and security, without the need for a sole governor? Is it possible that we're in a process of change, in which instead of focusing on the search for new city ideals, we're centering on the advocacy of a new citizenship, one that is capable of interpreting a symphony of democracy (Luna 2015) that yields more just, beautiful, emotional, and human cities?

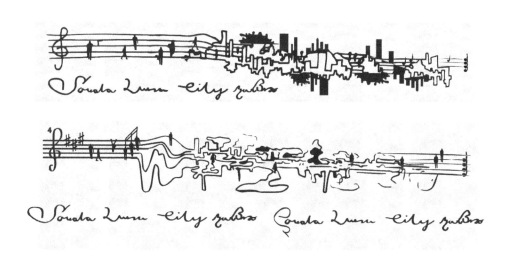

Figure 47.5 Symphony of Democracy, by Diana Wiesner in collaboration with Daniela González

● *References*

Luna, T., and Valverde, I. (eds.) (2015). *Paisaje y emoción. El resurgir de las geografías emocionales.* Barcelona: Observatorio del Paisaje de Cataluña; Universidad Pompeu Fabra. (Teoría y Paisaje; 2).

Nogué, J. (2015). "Emoción, lugar y paisaje" in Luna, T., and Valverde, I. (eds.) *Paisaje y emoción. El resurgir de las geografías emocionales.* Barcelona: Observatorio del Paisaje de Cataluña; Universidad Pompeu Fabra. (Teoría y Paisaje; 2), pp. 137–147.

Chapter 48: The Shift in Urban Technology Innovation from Top-Down to Bottom-Up Sources

Reyhaneh Vahidian

The role models of smart cities as technological utopias have changed over the last 28 years from tech titans such as IBM and Cisco, with their wonderful levels of innovation, to do-it-yourself entrepreneurs. A wide range of activists, entrepreneurs, and civic hackers are tinkering their way towards a different kind of technological utopia, and are reimaging the smart city concept through prominent enablers such as smartphones, low-cost broadband, open data, and open-source technologies (Shueh 2015). Local governments, with the assistance of large-scale and expensive technologies, have always shaped urban and suburban infrastructures. "Urban tech" describes the emerging technologies that are being used to solve problems at the intersection of urbanization and sustainability, from reducing energy use and greenhouse gas emissions to reducing crime and increasing government efficiency (Baptiste 2015). Accordingly, urban tech startups develop creative solutions to the urban challenges that all citizens face; their concepts have widely transferable applicability in the urban-centric areas of mobility, economic development, sustainability, and urban services (Stephens 2014).

One smart city trend identified by the International Data Corporation, or IDC, predicts a growing adoption and awareness of the smart city concept by an expanding set of government leaders. This demand for strategy development and implementation road maps includes a wide range of actors, from cities and counties to states and central or federal government agencies. IDC predicts that by 2017, at least 20 of the world's largest countries will create national smart city policies to prioritize funding and to document technical and business guidelines (Yesner Clarke 2015). Based on the benefits of Urban Tech for achieving sustainable development, it's strongly recommended that local governments promote friendly environments for meeting technology entrepreneurs' needs, such as setting rules, regulations, policies, and even easy access to technical requirements. Furthermore, by unlocking important public information and supporting policies of Open Government, urban managers will democratize access to services; enable innovation that improves the lives of citizens; and increase transparency and efficiency (NYC Digital 2011).

Most urban tech startups are less than a decade old, but they are already dramatically reshaping how citizens move around and reduce their energy consumption and carbon footprint (Abrahamson 2015). For instance, Uber is a mobile app that connects passengers with drivers for hire. One of Uber's stated visions is providing a simpler form of transportation while creating economic opportunities for all. In addition to these goals, they have set a target of promoting environmental sustainability ("Uber (company)" 2016). Rachio allows users to remotely control home watering systems for lawns or gardens. The Rachio app works through a connection to Rachio information through home Wi-Fi and automatically adjusts for the right amount of water needed for lawn and water savings. Waze is a free mobile navigation app for smartphones that allows drivers to use live maps, real-time traffic updates, and other road data. Traffic slows citizens down and pollutes cities. This app brings drivers together to find the best alternatives. (Urbantech Radar 2016). No one can predict what the future of cities will look like – but we can get a glimpse of what's possible by looking at some of the fastest growing startups currently reshaping the way people live and work in cities. The way cities work with emerging technologies is entering a new paradigm in which the city is not only the customer but, more often, the regulator and promoter of the best ideas as well (Baptiste 2015).

❂ References

Alexis Stephens, 2014, "Startup Funder Shoots for Maximum Urban Impact," last modified November 11, https://nextcity.org/daily/entry/urban-us-tech-startup-funding-city-apps.

Jason Shueh, 2015, "How Startups Are Transforming the Smart City Movement," last modified September 1, www.govtech.com/How-Startups-Are-Transforming-the-Smart-City-Movement .html.

NYC Digital, 2011, Road Map for the Digital City; Achieving New York City's Digital Future," Digital edition.

Ruthbea Yesner Clarke, 2015, "3 Smart City Trends to Expect in 2016," last modified November 23, www.govtech.com/dc/articles/3-Smart-City-Trends-to-Expect-in-2016.html.

Shaun Abrahamson, 2015, "Urban Tech Startups and the Cities of the Future," last modified March 31, http://knightfoundation.org/blogs/knightblog/2015/3/31/urban-tech-startups-and-cities-future.

Stonly Baptiste, 2015, "How Startups Solve Problems at the Intersection of Urbanization and Climate Change," last modified March 25, http://citiesspeak.org/tag/urbantech-startups.

"Uber (company)," 2016, last modified January 16, https://en.wikipedia.org/wiki/Uber_(company).

"Urbantech Radar," last modified January 18, 2016, http://radar.urban.us.

apter 49: Greening Cities

Our Pressing Moral Imperative

Troy Pickard

The movement for greening our cities is gathering momentum – but the time has come to move beyond tokenistic measures and to truly consider what type of cities we want to leave for future generations. It's time for those of us in leadership roles to "walk the talk" through our bold decisions and actions to ensure that the issue becomes a mainstream imperative rather than a side, niche movement that is viewed only as the domain of environmental activists.

There are numerous examples of approaches and projects related to "greening cities" throughout the world – all with good intentions; however, I fear that we often celebrate mediocrity and think that the job is done if we plant a few more trees.

This is not to diminish the fine efforts of all involved in this movement or tree planting. We must also acknowledge that many approaches to greening are already ambitious and bold and to be applauded, with the City of Melbourne (in my home country of Australia) setting a fine example.

Pockets of best practice, however, are no longer an option if cities throughout the world, no matter how large or small, are going to address the impacts of climate change and create urban places and spaces that are liveable and inviting; responsive to environmental factors such as pressure on water resources and increasing temperatures; and able to promote and protect biodiversity, as well as considering the health and well-being of urban communities – for both current and future generations.

We all need to be part of creating urban environments that present our children with opportunities to experience and appreciate nature in their urban environment by mainstreaming the urban forest paradigm as the standard, not the exception. This is much more than an environmental issue – it is the key moral and ethical issue of our generation. If we create green cities and provide opportunities for our children to connect with nature in our urban environment, we are more likely to produce future generations, through our example and their experience, who will respect the planet, preserve and conserve our valued natural environments, and continue to support and build urban environments that are healthy, ecologically diverse, and livable in the future.

Mainstreaming urban forests is, of course, not without its challenges – including inertia surrounding departure from traditional notions of the look and feel of cities, resource requirements, design conflicts, tree selection that encourages the use of native species, community engagement, and enthusiasm. These challenges need to be confronted globally and prioritized as an imperative, with greening cities promoted as an once-in-a-lifetime opportunity to transform existing urban environments and to breathe life and soul back into our cities. Of course, there will be significant economic advantages, including healthier and happier communities resulting in reduced health costs; healthy ecosystems resulting in reduced costs associated with redressing environmental issues; and vibrant and activated city spaces that attract and embolden people.

All leaders must prioritize, through bold action and example, the greening of our cities and to see it as an opportunity to create urban spaces that reconnect all of us and our children to nature – and to loudly and confidently promote green cities and urban forests as central to not only the health and well-being of our people and our communities but also to the economic prosperity and livability of our cities and, ultimately, the planet that we are all fortunate to share and to call home.

Chapter 50: Recognition Deficit and the Struggle for Unifying City Fragments

Pranab Kishore Das

Over the years, we have been deeply concerned about the abuse, misuse, and destruction of natural areas. We have been equally concerned about the systematic dismantling of the community and collective fabric. As a result, most cities across the world have been split into disparate and conflicting fragments.

Sadly, most governments and ruling elite continuously work towards dismantling the fabric of unity, sustainability, and justice. Such efforts are clearly reflected in the various policies and programs that, in most instances, are undermining larger public interest by stifling people's voices, their participation in decision-making, and active governance.

These governments and the ruling elite are driven by a host of selective and discriminatory recognition policies and programs. They are obsessed with recognition – or, more accurately, the lack thereof – for people and nature, insofar as they relate to building stronger market forces that dictate the terms of development and principles of governance. To challenge this dominant phenomenon is a tough battle for those people who are committed to the many struggles for achievement of social and environmental equity and justice.

In Indian cities, for example, a majority of the people comprising the poor and lower-middle classes are constantly denied recognition on multiple grounds, to an extent that their right to live itself is often questioned. They are denied access to land, housing, food, water, sanitation, healthcare, education, and transport – to name just a few restrictions. It follows that today we find high instances of social tension and violence between people and communities. Such social divides are seen and experienced on the basis of caste, creed, religion, gender, and other identities. Cities are increasingly divided on the basis of identity politics and their landscapes are reconfigured in the form of distinct colonies of ghettoized affluence and abject deprivation.

This practice of selective recognition – and the government's and ruling class's mindset, which enables the practice – is also evident in matters relating to natural areas and environmental conditions. The case of Mumbai is an extreme example of abuse, misuse, and destruction of the vast extent of natural areas and open spaces that constitute nearly 50 percent of the total area of the city. Successive governments have consciously avoided mapping and documenting these areas. By leaving them out, government has allowed these areas to experience aggressive land filling and real estate development, as well as rampant destruction of the mangroves, wetlands, rivers, creeks, hills, and forests, largely by unscrupulous builders and developers. Governments are active in proposing further construction in these areas.

Only after many citizens' movements in Mumbai demanding recognition of these natural areas and their environmental conditions has the city government begun documenting them for the first time in a development plan for the city. In fact, the first extensive mapping and comprehensive documentation of the natural areas of Mumbai, along with a clear action plan, was carried out by this author along with the Mumbai Waterfronts Center. A public exhibition which they held, titled "Open Mumbai," exposed the lack of recognition of such vital assets and the rampant destruction of these areas, and, importantly, suggested a way forward.

The growing level of intolerance arising from and incited by such selective and discriminatory recognition phenomena is beginning to threaten the stability of cities. Levels of intolerance are leading to a state of aggression and violence, expressed in relationships between people at individual and collective levels, as well as between people, nature, and the environment.

Further, recognition deficit is steadfastly eroding the idea of cities. A constant state of denial of public interest in various aspects of life and environment by city authorities is alarming.

50.1 Unifying City Fragments

As an urban planner and architect, the pursuit to connect the disparate parts of our cities – people as well as landscapes – is my greatest challenge, fueling my everyday work and engagements. I firmly believe that architecture and urban design are incredible democratic tools of socio-environmental change and, therefore, *must* not be reduced to being merely "professions."

Connecting people with urban planning and design exercises from the inception of preparing development programs is important. The implementation of city plans and programs with people's participation is a significant instrument for mobilizing larger political struggles for equality and justice. It is public action alone that can deeply influence decisions governments take.

In this sense, the key question before us addresses the lack of recognition of certain people, land, and resources. This inquiry must form the basis of our protracted struggles for evolving strategies and plans for the unification of our fragmented and divided cities. We will be surprised if we begin to prepare lists of the various denials that we accept and pursue, or of what we pretend not to see or recognize at individual and collective levels. Making these lists and critically reviewing them would help in liberating ourselves and our movements, thereby strengthening our influence on governments for the achievement of much needed socio-environmental justice. May we therefore consider the value of our work, engagements, and success be measuring the extent to which they contribute towards this goal: unifying disparate city fragments.

Chapter 51: Disrespecting the Knowledge of Place

Rebecca Salminen Witt

Innate, intuitive, and experiential knowledge is a significant resource that we cannot afford to ignore. I am writing from Detroit, Michigan, in the United States – a city of invention and industry with a long history of valuing the new and pushing the boundaries of knowledge through innovation. Detroiters are constantly generating knowledge and striving for progress measured by new ideas. We are so busy moving forward that we rarely look back, overlooking valuable knowledge that we have left behind. In the face of every exciting advance in science and engineering and with respect to the daily terrestrial, celestial, and aquatic discoveries that enrich our understanding of the world around us, I offer the wisdom of the elders – the knowledge of those who have been here all along, which we know intuitively, innately, from living in a place or experiencing it. This knowledge is not less serious, less important, or less legitimate than the hard won, peer-reviewed, technical, and academic knowledge that is being generated in our laboratories, design studios, and academic institutions. Moreover, I propose that the traditional, historical, innate, and intuitive knowledge of all of the parts of this living ecosystem be mined, preserved, and used with the same gravitas and effect as the papers, studies, journal articles, and reports that we cite in support of our proposals, arguments, and opinions.

Mrs. Smith is a gardener with more than 60 years' worth of hands-on experience growing flowers and vegetables in Detroit soil. She knows what plant varieties grow best here, when to plant each flower and vegetable that goes into her garden, and what soil amendments and practical pest-fighting remedies to apply to achieve the highest yields year after year. Mrs. Smith's annual sunflower patch is a thing of beauty. I know this. I have benefitted from Mrs. Smith's hyper-local and long-studied knowledge of her growing environment, and I have a desire to plant sunflowers as a part of a bio-remediation plan. Why should I rely upon a journal article generated by an academic in a far-off institution to tell me which sunflowers to grow, when I can look at the sunflowers that Mrs. Smith grows and ask her which varieties she's had the most luck with over time in the very city where I wish to grow sunflowers? Why should

Mrs. Smith's experience-based knowledge be taken less seriously by my funder than the results published in that journal? They were.

Detroit is beginning an ambitious attempt at landscape-scale redesign of its landmass. Scores of design and planning professionals are being hired to lead this effort. Phrases like "internationally renowned designer" and "nationally recognized talent" are being used as a promise that Detroit will move ahead with new ideas generated by the leading designers of our time. A promise that in this area, like so many others, Detroit will break new ground, innovate, invent.

Let us pause from our headlong pursuit of the new and innovative for a moment to consider the value of the resource that is already embedded in that landscape which is to be redesigned. What grows in a place can tell you what the soil will support, and even where rivers once ran. Paths created by today's travelers will tell you where sidewalks and streets would be most useful. People who are here now know what they need. Rather than assuming that the ideas and knowledge of talented outsiders are more relevant, useful, or reliable than the historical, innate, and intuitive knowledge of those who have been here all along, why not mine the knowledge and experience of Detroit's elders to inform the redesign? Why not look at the landforms and the flora and fauna that once graced this landscape for instruction on what is most appropriate for the future? Shouldn't the renowned designers that we are seeking, in fact, be expected to glean everything that they need to know from the plants, animals, and people who have experienced life in this place for so long?

Site-based, experiential knowledge is legitimate, valuable, and important. It can be found in the memories of our elders, in the patterns of nature, and in the traditions and history embedded within the culture of a place. There is much to be gained by a thoughtful and intentional attempt to capture, use, and respect this knowledge. We do ourselves, our research, and our future a disservice if we don't stop and pay attention to the knowledge that we have left behind or that we have ignored entirely.

Chapter 52: Broadening Our Vision to Find a New Eco-Spiritual Way of Living

Guillermina Ramirez (Translation into English by David Maddox)

The Mapuche nation has a philosophical and spiritual structure that draws on the relationship with Pu Newen forces of nature and various vital energies, which are telling us how the art of living can bring us closer to harmony. For thousands of years, our people developed their farms, their community, and their territorial organization, incorporating certain sacred spaces as the central driving force of life. At the core, this implies respect for the habitat of the watersheds, rivers, lakes, volcanoes, and land. We did not invade these spaces. We lived next to them, but not *on top* of them, so to speak. We understood that the territorial organization grew from the need to respect the other elements that lived there.

From this notion of "co-living," megacities would be unthinkable. However, the human crisis and global collapse facing the planet, along with the destabilizing impact of climate change, to which urbanization has significantly contributed, forces us to look for possible alternatives, both in the near and midterm, to set the stage for guaranteeing the continuation of human life on the planet.

To develop realistic strategies which might give concrete results, we have to think of a new urban design, which necessarily has to challenge and deconstruct the logic of capitalist development – which accumulates and concentrates resources for only a few. To do this, we must make progress in dismantling large estates, where huge tracts of land are owned by one person, family, or company, for speculation or exploitation, damaging mother earth, the Mapu – polluting and eroding her, killing her slowly to produce large business. While these companies destroy the countryside, many people are displaced and induced to settle in the cities in search of an opportunity to improve their lives. There they only find more misery and marginalization, which ultimately detracts from their humanity, stunting minds and spirits; in the end, they become *Homo economicus*, a kind of objectified human, an economic tool.

Poverty, misery, and violence generated by inequality are the constitutive elements of urban cannibalism. The megacities, such as we have conceived them, should disappear, transformed into small cities that are interconnected and coordinated with food production areas, natural medicine, and renewable alternative energy.

The spirituality of Indigenous peoples should not only be respected but also should serve as inspiration for these new urban structures. Population health is intrinsically linked to harmonious relationships with nature and, primarily, with the perceptible forces that interact in our territories. Sacred spaces are energetic centers in which forces and forms of life are harmonized. They must not be invaded by sports stadiums, buildings, or casinos, occurrences which have led to resistance and struggle of First Nations in various countries and cities, and which clearly violate the spiritual rights of the people.

The new ecological cities should redraw the maps of the persistent geopolitics of nations, doing away with the geographical boundaries of death, division, and racism introduced by nation states. It is irresponsible to think of the design of a new ecological urban model *without* proposing the construction of a new paradigm for civilizations, one that recovers the sense of reciprocity between people and nature. In a new humanity, a new design – and not only an urban, but a global peoples' movement – resistance and struggle will be the makers of this revolution of thought. It must emanate from the identity of ancestral lands and recovery of true spirituality that prioritizes the heart above reason, and which does not look for the base benefit of anthropocentric forces, but rather for the construction of a circular order, harmonized, horizontal, and reciprocal.

Humans are not an abstraction. We are part of nature. We say we are Mapuche: people of the land. The land is us; it is our identity-space. Each element of our culture is the expression of each element of nature. When an element of nature disappears, an element of our culture also disappears. If rivers are murdered with dams, the sacred song of the rivers is reduced to a sick silence, like standing water that pollutes our spirit. To keep us flowing as with the energy of flowing water, let us be guardians and respectful of it.

The economic crisis, the climate crisis, the humanitarian crisis are all symptoms of a single major disease: the matrix of Western civilization, the dominant culture based on anthropocentrism, materialism, individualism, patriarchy, and racism. So far, it has never been challenged by the great revolutionary movements of the world, which have only questioned social inequality, reducing the problem to a question of class struggle. We must broaden our vision, deepen our analysis, and develop new tools with innovative theoretical frameworks that allow us to approach multiple approaches to this great problem.

Synthesis

New Integrated Urban Knowledge for the Cities We Want

Xuemei Bai, Thomas Elmqvist, Niki Frantzeskaki, Timon McPhearson, David Simon, David Maddox, Mark Watkins, Patricia Romero-Lankao, Susan Parnell, Corrie Griffith, and Debra Roberts

S.1 What Do We Know about *Urban*?

We are already living on an urban planet (Chapter 1) and in the coming decades, about 2.6 billion more people will be added to world cities. Asia now has half of the world's urban population while Africa's urban population is larger than that of North America. Rapid urbanization in countries like China is considered to be one of the biggest human settlement challenges in human history, accompanied by profound social, economic, and environmental transformations (Bai et al 2014).

We also live in a time during which urban research and the development of urban theories are burgeoning, along with popular urban activism and practice. The past two decades, in particular, have witnessed an explosion of urban-focused literature with a rapidly increasing number of published research papers and practitioner reports (Wolfram et al. 2016).

Figure S.1 shows the trend in the number of publications with "urban" as keyword over the last five decades. In 1990, there were less than 5,000 papers published, whereas in 2015 nearly 70,000 papers were published.

What have these research efforts accomplished? At a macro level, we have established several key understandings. As highlighted in the Preface, Introduction, and many of the chapters, urbanization can be seen as a phenomenon that encompasses changes in demographic, land, and other resource use, environmental, social, cultural, and institutional aspects ranging across local, regional, and global scales (Box S.1) (Chapter 1). Urbanization is typically driven by traditional push and pull factors, but national policy is

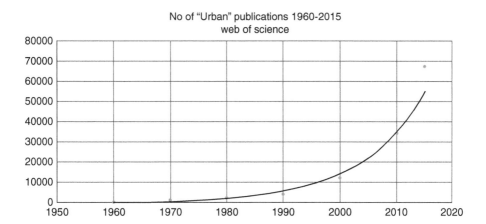

No of "Urban" publications 1960-2015
web of science

Figure S.1 No. of publications with "urban" as keyword 1950–2015 (Web of Science)

a critical driver shaping the process and outcomes (Bai et al 2014; Parnell and Simon 2014). Despite the multifaceted challenges, urbanization also brings about a unique window of opportunity for the cocreation and diffusion of innovative sustainable solutions. This parallels the growing recognition among policy-and decision-makers that cities have an important role to play in local and global sustainability.

Underpinning various aspects of these high-level understandings is knowledge and aspiration at a much finer scale. Each research-based chapter in our book takes a key element of urban knowledge and explores its state of the art, and probes the key knowledge gaps. Collectively these chapters showcase what we know about cities, where lie the frontiers and limits of urban research and practice, and the fault lines that point towards areas about which we need to know more.

But it is not only urban research that is flourishing. Cities around the world increasingly benefit from greater participation and activism by civil society, practitioners, and regular citizens. This activism has two key benefits. First, it facilitates the grounded practice of making better cities through not just knowledge but knowledge-based action and lived experience: the design of neighbourhoods, infrastructure, and open spaces – that is, places – that are better for both people and nature. Second, participation by urban citizens in decision-making and urban creation should be the driver in any connection between academic knowledge and policy. Indeed, what knowledge do cities themselves feel they need? Increased awareness of urban populations in the biophysical and urban design processes around them is key to building better cities by creating urban populations that demand better cities, and know what "better cities" can mean.

Box S.1

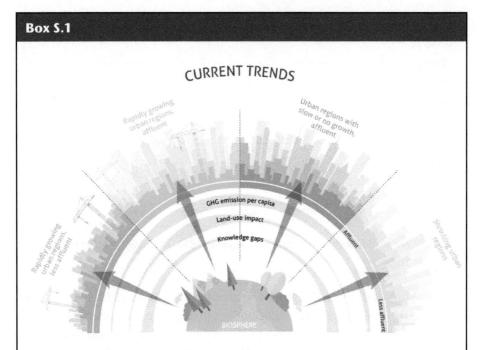

Figure S.2 Current trends

It is exceedingly difficult to generalize about urbanization and urban trends. Cities and city regions around the world are very different, and there is no such thing as one size fits all scenario (Jiang and O'Neill 2017. Cities are, for some, a specific form of human association that can be characterized based upon criteria of population size, built-environment form, and economic function (Wirth 1938; Minx et al. 2013; Seto et al. 2013; Chapter 9). Others understand urban areas as growth machines serving elite interests, inducing social inequality and damaging the environment (Harvey 2008; Heynen et al. 2006). Yet for others, cities are socioecological systems or sociotechnical systems, either of interacting biophysical and socioeconomic components, or social and technical components (McPhearson et al. 2016b).

While many cities in developing countries are growing rapidly, the pace of urbanization is slowing down in some countries, while some cities are shrinking. There is an absolute need for urban development policy to adapt to specific local and regional contexts. Here we illustrate current trends in urban development around the globe, based on two independent defining variables: (1) rate of growth, that is, whether a city may be rapidly growing, stable or shrinking and (2) economic state that is whether a city is less affluent or affluent. To describe some current trends, we have selected a few dependent variables: GHG emissions per capita, land-use impact, and

> **Box S.1** (cont)
>
> knowledge gaps, where there is at least some data available for analyses (Coulibaly et al. 2009, Bierbaum et al. 2010).
>
> In general, the conclusion is that affluence is the main factor behind GHG emissions per capita, with emissions still being large in affluent cities, irrespective of rapid growth, stable, or with no growth. As far as GHG emission is concerned, the impact associated with rapid urban expansion is significantly larger in affluent rapidly growing urban regions than in other types of regions. However, for many variables that we would like to analyze and that are highly relevant for policy, such as governance challenges, health impacts, adaptation capacity to climate change, it is currently extremely difficult to conduct analyses due to particularly large knowledge gaps for rapidly growing less affluent cities as well as for shrinking cities and city regions.

While playing a critical role in shaping our common urban futures, the perspectives of civil society, practitioners, and regular citizens are often missing from traditional academic treatments of urban ideas. Each of these practitioner-based contributions explores an element of city building from the "street level" points of view of designers, artists, and practitioners in civil society.

S.2 Highlights of the Four Parts of *Urban Planet*

S.2.1 *Part I: Dynamic Urban Planet*

The knowledge base around urbanization and its dynamics – drivers, impacts to the environment and environmental change, our conceptual frameworks, data, models, and methods have all advanced over the last decade and the chapters in Part I are a testament to this, offering a variety of perspectives.

Urbanization follows diverse patterns and pathways, each presenting unique policy challenges. Some urban regions are growing rapidly but others are shrinking (Box S.1). While megacities often receive more attention in global urbanization debates, many smaller urban centers are growing more rapidly (Chapter 1).

Cities do not exist in isolation: they are open systems, with various processes linking cities and their global resource/environmental hinterlands (Chapters 1, 2, and 3). Urban areas have a vast reach, both direct and indirect, (whether its resources or GHG emissions or food/energy/water) and there are global impacts/implications. On the other hand, urbanization is an opportunity to increase global sustainability. However, while we are making progresses, we still don't fully understand these systems interlinkages.

Scale is important in terms of how it impacts research and what we know, but also presents challenges or gaps (Chapters 2, 3, and 4). For example, a better understanding of the household or neighborhood scale is needed for reducing vulnerability (Chapter 4) or understanding variation in materials usage in cities/local or community levels that are rapidly growing.

There is a need for disciplinary integration, but particularly from the social sciences (integrative knowledge) – obvious in Chapters 4, 5, and 6. We've come a long way with more holistic approaches and frameworks, but knowledge gaps still remain when it comes to understanding politics and underlying power structures, political economy, urban macroeconomics, cultural traditions, preferences/behavior, and so on that influence urbanization.

Part I strongly suggests that there is a need for research to continue to develop and advance urban typologies and understanding of the different dimensions of urbanization at regional and global scales, both at medium- and long-term (beyond 2050) perspectives. However, at the same time there is also the need for knowledge underpinning very local, place-based solutions. How do we bridge the gap between the demand for these local and place-based solutions with the larger scale regional, global, and temporal insights on urbanization? We will return to this in Section S.3 of this synthesis.

S.2.2 Part II: Global Urban Sustainability

This part starts with Chapter 7 discussing and analyzing the word "sustainability." What does it mean to create sustainability on the ground? To do this we must connect to local issues, not only global patterns, since no blueprint or master plan will be locally appropriate and legitimate. One way to focus the idea of "sustainable cities" is to prioritize the areas of greatest need, namely the urban poor and the areas they inhabit. This addresses the most urgent and often severe aspects of unsustainability and has the potential to make a clear difference. Doing so effectively, moreover, requires complex tools and patience to work with the respective communities through inclusive and participatory or coproductive approaches such as those exemplified above.

In Chapter 8, the authors discuss the complexity of "the urban" and therefore the need to avoid oversimplification via measurement using simple indicators – hence the need for increasingly sophisticated indicators and efforts to ensure global relevance. Successive generations of indicators and multicriteria aggregation tools have improved our ability to capture urban complexity and dynamism, though there is often a trade-off between the increased sophistication of more holistic and composite indicators and the availability of the requisite data. Both the emergent fourth generation of indicators and SDG 11, the targets and indicators of which were formulated and piloted through an unprecedentedly long and penetrating process, illustrate this well. Implementation and the measurement of progress will be challenging for many urban administrations.

More inclusive intergovernmental agency approaches within and outside the UN system are discussed in Chapter 9. UN-Habitat, the specialist human settlements agency, has taken a leading role, initially through successive sessions of the World Urban Forum and most recently through the SDG and New Urban Agenda (NUA) processes. While still bound by UN rules attaching preferential rights to national governments ("parties" in UN language), this has done much to engage previously marginalized stakeholders and groups, also ensuring that the final versions of the SDGs and NUA have far greater buy-in and legitimacy than previous such initiatives.

In Chapters 10, 11, and 12, the role of urban living laboratories, big data and citizen science, coproduction and other innovative approaches are discussed. There has been a worldwide flourishing of such innovative approaches that decenter traditional, top-down, and expert-led knowledge production and implementation, providing alternative and often more meaningfully participatory engagement by key stakeholder groups and exploring new types of data. For instance, citizen science is an umbrella term for numerous ways in which ordinary urban dwellers and community groups worldwide can engage in knowledge creation as active data collectors and submitters using everyday devices like mobile phones, while undertaking their normal daily activities, or carrying out specific surveys and reconnaissance activities to complement conventional research.

Summary highlights from Part II: Avoid implicit overgeneralization in the search for apparently simple answers and replicable lessons in an era of unprecedented urban complexity and wider uncertainty. Comparative research – much necessarily applied and practice-oriented – undertaken particularly through transdisciplinary teams that combine academic and diverse nonacademic stakeholder groups, is one useful approach in this regard.

Overcome entrenched inertia and vested interests – especially sociotechnical agendas, for example, in smart cities discourses. Greater inclusivity and multi-stakeholder engagement do not, in and of themselves, overcome these barriers, although they might help to challenge them by engaging and perhaps empowering previously voiceless groups.

Consider the "deep" urban sustainability – via key features such as accessibility, greenness, and fairness – that is locally appropriate. It is important to pursue and integrate the main facets of sustainability so as to address the spatial and social diversity of prevailing conditions in different parts of individual urban areas. While some conflicts are inevitable and consensus may not be feasible, this is far from a zero-sum game in that carefully targeted interventions can achieve multiple objectives and cobenefits.

S.2.3 Part III: Urban Transformations to Sustainability

Part III explores the drivers and actors that play a role in urban transformations to sustainability. The introductory chapter sets the stage and identifies the main opportunities and challenges that city officials and private and civil society actors face in their efforts to develop governance solutions that support sustainable and resilient urban development (Chapter 13). The remaining chapters bring together four strands of urban research on urban transformations.

In Chapter 14, Frantzeskaki et al. illustrate how this changing role is evinced in contemporary case studies across Europe. In line with this, Pereira et al. (Chapter 16) extend our knowledge on where to search for and source innovative solutions for urban transformations by an extensive review and mapping of local initiatives that showcase positive transformations, being the seeds of the good Anthropocene. The evidence in these two chapters amounts to the understanding that living in an urban planet also means creating solutions that can be the stepping stones for positive trajectories to urban livability, inclusivity, resilience, and sustainability.

For counteractive nonsustainable and nonlivable urban futures, conflicts and contestations need to be examined and inform policy and planning – new urban realities between new sustainable solutions and conflicting or counteracting nonsustainable ones, create conflicts and contestations. In Chapter 15, Burch et al. provide an insight on the recent debates and knowledge on what governance for urban transformations to sustainability is all about, painting a rather different picture. Urban visions and pathways are always contested, given that they need to incorporate and accommodate interests and aspirations from multiple actors that are diverse. In this view, urban transformations become contested processes that will require new approaches and governance means to create collaborative outcomes to instigate, facilitate, and accelerate change. Next to this insight, Burch et al. introduce one more actor as paramount for urban transformations to sustainability: small-medium enterprises as the agile actor that can leverage innovations towards more systemic urban transformations.

In summary, Part III points to the need for a multi-actor governance and to new unusual "suspects" to play a role in transition processes, and proposes to deep research about relations between these urban change agents for new approaches and new collaborative and empowering means to facilitate urban transformations to sustainability. One common thread and perhaps at the core of these remaining challenges is the need for integration – integrating across disciplines, integrating other forms of knowledge, and integrating urban research into global policy processes.

S.2.4 Part IV: Provocations from Practice

While the provocations focus on a myriad of different topics and themes, they all tend to hover around a limited set of key ideas. Central to many of the chapters is the idea that the political reality of local sustainability is often ignored by academic treatments of the subject. For Mahim Maher of Karachi, this means that the concept of sustainability as it stands in New York and London is attractive but meaningless for her hometown, where there have been long periods without a mayor, there is little organized city planning, and water is sold by the mafia. To her, the meaning of "sustainable" that fits is the one that lets people be, and that allows for the city to progress in time. Ideas that remain in the academic realm – are not translated in common language, are not reported outside of academic journals, are not matched with workable solutions, and often do not address the needs of decision-makers in cities. Rebecca Salminen-Witt of Detroit and Mary Rowe of Toronto both agree that local knowledge has a place to address these gaps. Policy needs a human scale, and so does knowledge. The academic knowledge will mean nothing if the lives of people are not improved. For some of our provocateurs, the core Western economic model is fundamentally flawed, or even broken. For example, Guillerma Ramirex, an indigenous leader from the Mapuche region of South America, believes that sustainability solutions without social reform are bound to fail. For many writing from the street view, there is a great distance between academic knowledge and effective practice and city and neighborhood scales.

Other pieces point to the fact that cities around the world increasingly benefit from greater participation and activism by civil society, practitioners, and regular citizens. This activism has two key benefits. First, it facilitates the grounded practice of making better cities through not just knowledge, but action: the design of neighborhoods, infrastructure, and open spaces that better serve the needs of both people and nature. Second, participation by urban citizens in decision-making and urban creation should be the driver in any connection between academic knowledge and policy. Indeed, what knowledge do cities themselves feel they need? Increased awareness of urban populations in the biophysical and urban design processes around them is key to building better cities by creating urban populations that demand better cities, and know what "better cities" can mean. Diana Wiesner of Bogotá believes that a truly democratic city must empower its citizens and institutions as agents of change, through collective decision-making focused towards a common goal. This is a view of *democratic* knowledge-based cities that resonates among a number of these contributions.

Two things stand out when we take a step back and reexamine all the contributions in the book. First, there is lack of knowledge on and voices from from cities of the Global South compared to the Global North, which is an apparent and common knowledge gap demonstrated across all the academic chapters. Indeed, even in cases in which knowledge and experience from the Global South is well-developed, they often do not find its way into traditional academic forums, and even when they do, they tend to receive less attention and less prominent in traditional academic matrix. While cities in Global South are and will be the home for most of current and future urban populations, and they are confronted by very complex urban challenges, the reality is that more influential and dominant voices in academia are from the Global North. Books such as this one are an important advance, in which ideas and experience from the Global South are integrated into a book with global reach.

Second, there are drastically different perspectives between the provocations and the more academically oriented chapters. Here it is critical to note that there are many styles, sources, and uses of knowledge that typically exist in isolation from each other. In an attempt to pursuit more universal and scalable patterns and processes, academic knowledge can sometimes be agnostic on the idea of social values. It cannot remain so, as we are deeply fragmented, from Global North to South, and from rich to poor. As demonstrated by the diverse perspectives represented in the Provocations from Practice, various urban stakeholders other than researchers can hold deep insight into urban issues. Urban practitioners' knowledge of what works and what doesn't, based on long term experience of practice and context specific knowledge, can be equally important, and an invaluable complement to scientific knowledge. But, in traditional urban literature, these insights only receive peripheral acknowledgment at best. This is, in part due to the formalities of academic publishing, which discourage the "informality" of practice. But in general, there is a paucity of forums for sharing practice-based solutions among city and communities. This is starting to change, with books that summarize tools and practice, and international forums such as the Nature of Cities.

Some of the tensions revealed in this book, especially between the academic and practitioner worlds, present opportunities for synergies, while others represent fundamental frictions and clashes of world views and modes of knowing. The reason for such disparities vary across geography and communities of practice. It is not the intention of the book to present a thorough analysis of the underlying factors (although this would be a worth direction of research). Rather, by presenting them side by side, we wish to showcase the diverse perspectives, contrast the state of research insight with lived realities in communities of practice, and present different forms of knowledge and ways of knowing.

By doing so we point to the need to resolve the gaps and produce new types of knowledge that integrate traditional academic knowledge and insights in other forms and types. Indeed, there are many more bridges to cross in order to connect knowledge and lived reality (which is reflected more in the provocations). For example, does research-based knowledge truly reflect reality or does it cater to policy and practical needs? To what extent academic knowledge is translated into practice, or, more importantly, *correctly* translated with all appropriate constraints and caveats? These are just a few of the important questions suggested by discussing research and practice in a single volume.

Further, tensions also exist among individual chapters and pieces. We argue that bringing these into one volume is itself a pioneering attempt, and hope that the creative tensions presented can serve as a spring board to further discussions. We must strive to produce integrated urban knowledge.

S.3 Advancing New Integrated Urban Knowledge

So, where are the frontiers of urban knowledge production? What kind of urban knowledge is needed, how should we address these needs, and how would this knowledge be produced? New integrated urban knowledge will require new conceptual approaches, renewed understanding of the nature of urban knowledge, and new modes of knowledge production, all contributing to the ultimate goal of transforming towards more desirable urban futures. Such urban knowledge must first and foremost be based on a clear statement of the cities we want to create, and the values on which these creations are based, as discussed in detail in the following section. The new urban knowledge would need to extend our understanding of what contributes, instigates, and accelerates urban transformations. For example, understanding how systemic processes of change – urban transformations to sustainability and resilience – are triggered, amplified and/or facilitated by leverage points, emerging and often conflicting or counteracting change trajectories. What is the role of different actors (for example, civil society, small-medium enterprises, international organizations, global movements like Future Earth) in these urban sustainability transitions? What are conflicting and disruptive innovations or other developments within these trajectories?

Here we highlight three elements as crucial in future urban knowledge production, that is, (1) Systems approach, (2) Knowledge coproduction, (3) Solution-oriented research. We end this part with reflections on the inherent uncertainties about future trajectories we will have to address.

S.3.1 Systems Approaches

Cities are classic examples of complex systems (Batty 2007; Batty 2008; Bettencourt 2013; Pickett et al. 2001; Grimm et al. 2000; Bai et al. 2016a; this volume, Chapter 1.2) exhibiting emergent properties, some of which can be difficult to explain, such as nonlinear dynamics, feedbacks, and high inter-connectivity and unpredictability, while also having modular interlinked sub-systems that can create redundancy and exhibit resiliency. These and other complex behaviors make urban systems challenging to understand and, what is more, to govern, when seeking to improve resilience while transforming towards more sustainable development pathways and patterns (McPhearson et al. 2016c). In some cases, the complexity of urban system processes and patterns both within and across interconnected urban regions – where sustainable choices made in one place are not truly sustainable if they create social, economic, or environmental trade-offs elsewhere – clearly represent "wicked" problems faced by today's urban planners, policy-makers, and managers.

A systems approach can reveal the nonlinearity between drivers and effects of change that can be mapped and assessed and a broader understanding on where interventions can happen in tipping feedback loops and enabling structural shifts at system level. In this way, a systems approach can facilitate inputs across disciplines towards a deeper understanding of leverage points, driving forces and persisting feedback loops.

Many of the urban challenges, for example, natural resource, climate, energy, water, are not urban per se, but regional and global through urban metabolic processes (Chapter 3). Systems approaches are employed conjointly with other methods to investigate and dissect drivers of change in urban systems, identify patterns and metabolic flows as well as sourcing and evaluating of systemic solutions to achieve urban goals like sustainability, resilience, livability, and justice. For instance, Romero-Lankao et al. (Chapter 4) present a systems approach to urban risk and outline the necessary components of an interdisciplinary understanding of how environmental and societal processes such as global warming and urbanization contribute to sociospatial differences in exposure and in intra – and interurban vulnerability to heat waves, floods, droughts, and other hazards. Simon et al. (Chapter 7) support this in their chapter by highlighting that a systemic approach allows for analytical concepts like sustainability and resilience to integrate and better inform adaptation and mitigation solutions addressing climate challenges facing cities. Gomez-Alvarez et al. (Chapter 8) also point at the need for systemic approaches as the basis for developing new indicator schemes that adhere to sustainability. They address the need to formulate indicator schemes that take human well-being and ecological health at the core and promote a decoupling of urban well-being from economic growth. From the description of how indicator schemes evolved to their third generation, the Cities Prosperity Index showcases not only a systemic understanding of the dynamics of cities but also the positioning of cities as transformative entities in the world contributing to global prosperity.

In the context of this complexity and additional urban challenges, can we understand the dynamic socioecological, institutional, and infrastructural complexity of urban systems? Can we understand this complexity well enough to inform and improve decision-making for transitions towards more resilient and sustainable cities? Advancing urban sustainability and resilience agendas requires expanding the scope of inter- and transdisciplinarity approaches. It may require conceptually bridging two different disciplines, for example, urban ecology and industrial ecology through demonstrating how empirical evidence from one domain can contribute to revealing fundamental ecosystem characteristics of cities (Bai 2016), or moving beyond the often separate social-ecological and socio-technical approaches to jointly study socioecological technical infrastructure systems in cities (McPhearson et al. 2016c). A true systems approach in cities needs to embrace cities as complex, dynamic, and evolving system with multiple actors/constituents, structures, processes, linkages, and functions, all embedded within broader ecological, economic, technical, institutional, legal, and governance structures, and often causally interlinked, delivering in intended or unintended outcomes (Bai et al 2016a; Simon 2016) (Figure S.3). In light of achieving the New Urban Agenda and SDGs, where cities will be confronted by and measured against multiple targets and numerous indicators, pursuing synergies and avoiding trade-offs via systems approach is perhaps the only feasible way forward.

S.3.2 Knowledge Coproduction

New urban knowledge integrates across different scientific disciplines but also across multiple knowledge bases (for example, McPhearson et al 2016a). Connecting knowledge across societal spheres and positioning knowledge as a boundary object are considered findings and developments at the frontier of urban research. An active participation of different knowledge holders with the aim to coproduce knowledge that is actionable, reliable, and societally relevant is at the heart of the new urban science (for example, Palmer

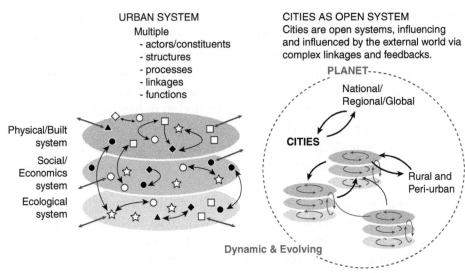

Current Opinion in Environmental Sustainability

Figure S.3 Urban system structure and interlinkages. The symbols represent various actors/constituents, structure, and processes across physical/built, social/economics, and ecological subsystems. The arrows represent complex processes and linkages within and between cities, and between cities and their hinterlands. The actors and constituents are typically self-organizing, and the structure, processes, and linkages and functions are dynamic and evolving, with nonlinear pathways. Source: Bai et al. 2016a.

and Walasek 2016). Diverse approaches have emerged over the last decade that respond to the need to connect urban knowledge from multiple actors to scientific processes that create knowledge legitimacy. These approaches help to integrate social, economic, and ecological needs/demands from cities and their citizenry to science and policy, supporting new agendas and development pathways. Urban knowledge in this way is a connective concept across multiple societal spheres and a boundary object for sociopolitical debate, contestation, and applicability.

Cities are ideal places to integrate different domains of knowledge, and indeed there has been a long history of codesigning and coproducing knowledge in urban settings. Participatory urban planning and design is one such example. Rather than oversimplifying complex and challenging situations, such an approach embraces complexity and uncertainty, and aims to find solutions together with the local actors and stakeholders.

The way knowledge is coproduced and the role it plays in addressing urban challenges and contributing to sustainable urban futures is a topic discussed by several contributions of our book. MacClune et al. (Chapter 12) point to a new model for urban citizen science, and the ways citizen science operates across scales, connecting local knowledge, contextual dynamics and contributes to an engaged citizenry that values knowledge coproduced. Burch et al. (Chapter

15) implicitly also address the ways we understand and create knowledge for governance for urban sustainability transformation, and point to the need to further integrate and therefore facilitate not only patterns of collaboration but also allow for contestation and conflicts in the urban sphere to surface. Thinking of urban transformations as multi-actor processes of innovation also points to settings of experimentation for coproducing actionable knowledge as well as trial systemic solutions for urban futures.

There are also settings where knowledge co-production for urban agenda setting and navigating solutions and perceptions have been tested. Examples include urban experimentation with living labs (see Chapter 10), with transition management arenas and with envisioning and scenario work in cities. Appreciation of multiple types of knowledge (tacit and explicit, global and indigenous) has been a foundation principle in designing such foresight arenas of urban agendas or development. The new urban science capitalizes, builds upon, and extends this line of coproduction processes as an indication of how processes that connect, integrate, and equalize multiple forms of knowledge come into play for understanding the urban planet and articulating ways to achieve the urban SDG and other local and global urban goals.

S.3.3 Solutions-Oriented Thinking and Approaches

Knowledge has no power unless it is shared and applied. When urban knowledge is examined in the light of application, a different and perhaps much more complex set of questions emerges. How do these topical or sectoral ways of knowledge interact with each other? When contradicting suggestions are presented from different research, each focusing on a particular task, how can they be incorporated into decision-making? For example, reducing urban energy use would suggest a higher density residential development, often translated in practice as much smaller lot single-standing house without backyard, or high-rising buildings. On the other hand, research shows that green backyards in old suburbs often have high biodiversity and provide important connectivity to wildlife habitats. In practice, decisions are often made focusing on one linkage and not on both. Solutions are required that take multiple interactions into account rather than partially addressing urban complexity and challenges. How to produce cutting edge, but also *integrated, actionable knowledge*, is an urgent task for urban researchers.

The notions of urban sustainability experiments and learning from practice are important in solution-oriented urban knowledge production (Bai et al. 2010; Palmer and Walasek 2016; Webb et al. 2017). Cities can be considered as living labs with many experimentations for cocreation of systemic urban solutions, which are created by civil society and its networks, contributing actively to more sustainable urban present and futures (Chapter 10). Civil society can be a transformative agent innovating, testing, and showcasing systemic solutions contributing actively in transformations in cities towards sustainability (Chapter 14). Analyzing the *seeds of good Anthropocene*, which are emerging solutions produced from civil society, businesses, public sector actors that illustrate the potentials for sustainable urban futures, provides a new way of understanding how systemic solutions emerge and how we can source inspiration and motivation from them (Chapter 16).

A solutions-oriented approach is also emerging in cities with a number of frameworks enabling this development. Signs of solutions-oriented approaches include the concepts of ecological design, water-sensitive cities, smart cities, and the recent work on nature-based solutions. While solutions-oriented approaches offer a way forward for cities as places where transformations can be accelerated towards sustainability, there are also critical views. For example, the development of smart cities as urban responses to resource challenges should also voice the different social aspects that often are inadequately addressed by the smart cities agenda, such as the digital divide across generations when smart technologies are adopted among many. However, a solutions-oriented approach may help in addressing questions on ways forward that invite multiple disciplines to contribute and advance our urban knowledge about and of those solutions.

Searching for sustainable solutions requires a broader view and exploration that looks across civil, public, and market actors. The evidence from recent years shows that civil society initiatives and the partnerships they create have the potential to reshape cities towards sustainability by changing practices, lifestyles, ways of organizing and forming new social relations (Frantzeskaki et al. 2016). Examining the way civil society interacts with other actors and the way it scales innovation can be a way forward to liveable urban futures.

S.3.4 Understanding Path Dependency and Transformation

As stated multiple times in the book, cities are already experiencing effects driven by climate change, and the extent to which cities will need to cope with these challenges will continue to increase dramatically 2050 and beyond. The need to develop urban strategies for flexibility to address the uncertainty and continuous state of change may, for example, lead to dramatically increased investments in innovative integration of gray, green, and blue infrastructure. In this context, urban strategies for flexibility based on a complex system view may be greatly inspired by advances in evolutionary theory to guide the future design of new urban infrastructure and the redesign of existing structures. Several decades ago, in a seminal paper in *Science,* the French evolutionary biologist and philosopher Francois Jacob pointed out how evolution is proceeding distinctly differently from a process that is de novo designed and engineered (Jacob 1977). He labeled this evolutionary process "tinkering" being primarily based on modifying and molding existing traits and occasionally resulting in totally shifting functions when conditions changed (for example, divergent evolution of base extremities to function as fins in water, legs on land, or wings in air). This contrasts greatly with a conventional designed and engineered process, which starts with tailor-made material and tools and always with a specific function in mind. Urban tinkering, as an approach, has the potential for moving beyond conventional urban engineering by replacing predictability, linearity, and design for one function, with anticipation of uncertainty and nonlinearity and design for a potential of shifting and multiple functions. There is a challenge with strong urban path dependencies where investments in infrastructure to fulfill one function often may prove to be a lock-in situation lasting decades or even centuries. An urban tinkering approach may help reduce such lock-ins, by designing infrastructure with an inherent potential to change function in the future if needed/desired. An urban tinkering approach may also help invent new functions of existing infrastructure and thus facilitate needed transformative processes (Elmqvist and McPhearson 2018).

S.4 Visions of the Cities We Want

Albeit long overdue, urban issues started to receive unprecedented attentions from policy arena in the last couple of years. The role of cities in preventing and abating climate change has gained official recognition, and cities are recognized as a legitimate key actor in achieving the Paris Agreement. A stand-alone urban goal is included in the 17 UN Sustainable Development Goals, and the New Urban Agenda was adopted in the UN Habitat III conference in 2016, both reflecting strong collective aspirations towards building the cities we want. Although the New Urban Agenda is aiming for 2030, it is important to note that principles for the cities we want does not stop at 2030, and we use the term the cities we want here with broader interpretation including NUA.

We argue that realizing these high-level policy goals and beyond would require *science* – a new integrated urban knowledge, *imagination* – formulating and utilizing collective visions of the future, and an *open mind* – understanding and embracing deep uncertainties and risks into the future. We also depict that *science needs to support* both *imagination* and an *open mind*.

A new integrated urban knowledge will play vital roles in achieving these policy goals. A stronger voice of researchers in the formulation of the global policy processes is called for in light of the development of the New Urban

Agenda (McPhearson et al 2016a). More importantly, the new integrated urban knowledge needs to contribute towards the design, monitoring, implementation, and evaluation of policy measures towards achieving these goals.

Pathways towards more desirable urban futures require concerted actions across jurisdictions (from global to local) and sectors (private, governmental, and social) (Figure S.4). The high-level international policy processes will inevitably trickle down, bringing more policy attention into urban issues at national and subnational levels, and eventually requiring each and every city to find out pathways towards the contextualized vision of the cities we want. Ideally, this should involve a process of identifying common societal goals, via exploring and identifying the plausible and desirable futures, and taking into account the diverse worldviews, values, cultures, and choices (Bai et al. 2016b). The lack of connection of policy and science to the attachment to *place* by people is repeatedly highlighted in the provocations in this volume. Visions need to be cocreated in inclusive experimental settings, varying from demonstrators, to civil society initiatives, to seed-projects and to urban living labs across cities in the globe. Uniform across all types of cities, is the need to create conditions for inclusive, just cities in which voices and aspirations across social

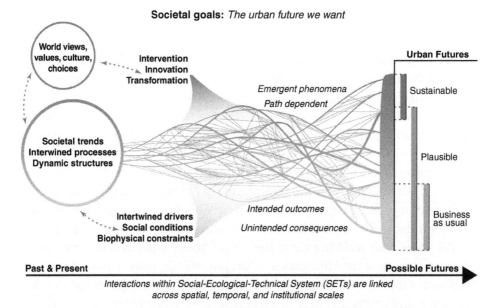

Figure S.4 Conceptualization of the interlinkages between factors and dynamic processes shaping urban futures. Visions are represented as societal goals influenced by worldviews, value systems, politics and power, culture and choices, and play an important role in intervention, innovations, and transformation that can lead to alternative and more desirable urban futures. Source: McPhearson et al. 2017, modified from Bai 2016b.

groups are heard and considered and citywide visions like smart cities are democratic and open for debate.

Visions, particularly shared positive visions, can play a critical role in shaping desirable futures (Figure S.4). We believe our book shows that visions alone are not enough, and that there is urgent need for action-oriented research and practice that links positive visions to on the ground transitions and transformations. While we acknowledge that the formal attribution of transformational change as a causal result of visioning is entangled with a myriad of social, political, cultural, ecological, and technological factors, examples of successful implementation of positive visions provide nodes of optimism and empirical basis for replication and scaling up of the cities we want.

Despite all efforts and massive knowledge generation, there are deep uncertainties about the Urban Planet in the long-term (2050 and beyond). As stated in the Introduction to the book, within this timeframe, the planet will face a complexity of drivers and interactions, with the potential of many of them interacting in unexpected ways, for example, migration, climate change, political instability, disruptions in financial systems, energy supplies, and pandemics to cite some. Although predictions about overall demographic growth and rates of densification of settlements may have a reasonably high certainty also in the long term, the way this will play out in spatial patterns by 2030, let alone much beyond 2030, is highly uncertain. The spatial pattern may be much more dispersed than we project today due to the number of factors that may disrupt and cause change, for example, constraints in scaling of renewable energy, global economic crises, and pandemics.

We need to fully embrace uncertainty and change from local to global scale in the long term, in particular addressing the multiple risks associated with hyper-cohesion. In an increasingly (and at increasing rates!) economically, digitally, socially, and ecologically globally connected network, there might be several risks associated with an ever more hyper-cohesive world (for example, increased vulnerability with over-connected power grids where outages cascade through energy systems to create widespread blackouts). At the same time, lack of connectivity can create risk by missing needed redundancy and availability of back-up systems characteristic of the resilience of the system. Intermediate modularity and connectivity in systems could provide an important new target for urban regional resilience building where energy, economic, and even social systems have protections in place for limiting impacts of failure in one part of the system while remaining connected. The Internet is a useful model for intermediate modularity and connectivity where protections such as firewalls are in place at multiple scales from individuals, to institutions, to nation states to protect subsystems in one part of the system from failing when subsystems fail in another part.

Achieving the critical, but extremely challenging task of transforming social, economic, ecological, and technical infrastructure systems towards global sustainability in the long term will require more than adding up combined efforts of cities to transform. No matter how transformative urban sustainability and resilience building efforts are, we cannot assume that *global sustainability* will be a granted end result. In fact, there are likely to be significant trade-offs, unforeseen side effects and consequences of urban sustainability initiatives at all scales. To address these challenges, globalization may have to take on a new face with a multipolar world developing, where thriving local and regional social, cultural and ecological diversity and governance is more central, and a new urban-rural regional integration is possible. Moving forward requires flexibility, understanding of what determines resilience, learning, visions and imagination, and open-mindedness to deal with the unexpected and deep uncertainties. This has all to evolve at the same time, on the foundation of a new intensity in generating innovative and integrated urban knowledge.

◆ References

Bai, X., Shi, P., and Liu, Y. (2014). Society: Realizing China's Urban Dream. *Nature*, 509(7499): 158–160.

Bai, X. 2016. Eight Energy and Material Flow Characteristics of Urban Ecosystems. *AMBIO: A Journal of the Human Environment*, 45(7): 819–830.

Bai, X., Roberts, B., and Chen, J., 2010. Urban Sustainability Experiments in Asia: Patterns and Pathways. *Environmental Science & Policy*, 13(4): 312–325.

Bai, X., Surveyer, A., Elmqvist, T., Gatzweiler, F.W., Güneralp, B., Parnell, S., et al. 2016a. Defining and Advancing a Systems Approach for Sustainable Cities. *Current Opinion in Environmental Sustainability*, 23: 69–78.

Bai, X., Van Der Leeuw, S., O'Brien, K., Berkhout, F., Biermann, F., Brondizio, E.S., et al., 2016b. Plausible and Desirable Futures in the Anthropocene: A New Research Agenda. *Global Environmental Change*, 39: 351–362.

Batty, M., 2007. *Cities and Complexity: Understanding Cities with Cellular Automata, Agent-Based Models, and Fractals*. MIT Press.

Batty, M., 2008. The Size, Scale, and Shape of Cities. *Science*, 319(5864): 769–771.

Bettencourt, L.M., 2013. The Origins of Scaling in Cities. *Science*, 340(6139): 1438–1441.

Bierbaum, R.M., Fay, M., and Ross-Larson, B. (eds.). 2009. *World Development Report 2010: Development and Climate Change*. World Development Report. Washington, DC: World Bank Group. http://documents.worldbank.org/curated/en/201001468159913657/World-development-report-2010-development-and-climate-change.

Buhaug, H., and Urdal, H. 2013. An Urbanization Bomb? Population Growth and Social Disorder in Cities. *Global Environmental Change*, 23(1): 1–10.

Coulibaly, S., Deichmann, U., Freire, M.E., Gill, I.S., Goh, C., Kopp, A.D., et al. (eds.). 2008. *World Development Report 2009: Reshaping Economic Geography*. World Development Report. Washington, DC: World Bank Group. http://documents.worldbank.org/curated/en/730971468139804495/World-development-report-2009-reshaping-economic-geography

Elmqvist, T and McPgearson, T 2018. Urban Earth. Re.think vol 2. Stockholm Resilience Centre

Frantzeskaki, N., Dumitru, A., Anguelovski, I., Avelino, F., Bach, M., Best, B., et al. (2016), Elucidating the Changing Roles of Civil Society in Urban Sustainability Transitions. *Current Opinion in Environmental Sustainability*, 22: 41–50.

Grimm, N.B., Grove, J.G., Pickett, S.T., and Redman, C.L. 2000. Integrated Approaches to Long-Term Studies of Urban Ecological Systems: Urban Ecological Systems Present Multiple Challenges to Ecologists—Pervasive Human Impact and Extreme Heterogeneity of Cities, and the Need to Integrate Social and Ecological Approaches, Concepts, and Theory. *AIBS Bulletin*, 50(7): 571–584.

Harvey, D. 2008. The Right to the City. *New Left Review*, II(53): 23–40.

Heynen, N.C., Kaika, M., and Swyngedouw, E. 2006. *In the Nature of Cities: Urban Political Ecology and the Politics of Urban Metabolism*. Vol. 3. Oxon and New York: Taylor & Francis.

Jacob, F. 1977. Evolution and Tinkering. *Science* 196(4295) 1161–1166. doi: 10.1126/science.860134

Jiang, L., and O'Neill, B.C. 2017. Global Urbanization Projections for the Shared Socioeconomic Pathways. *Global Environmental Change*, 42: 193–199.

McPhearson, T., Parnell, S., Simon, D., Gaffney, O., Elmqvist, T., Bai, X., et al. 2016a. Scientists Must Have a Say in the Future of Cities. *Nature*, 538:165–166.

McPhearson, T., Pickett, S.T.A., Grimm, N.B., Niemelä, J., Alberti, M., Elmqvist, T., et al. 2016b. Advancing Urban Ecology toward a Science of Cities. *BioScience*, 66(3):198–212, doi: 10.1093/biosci/biw002.

McPhearson, T., Haase, D., Kabisch, N., and Gren, Å. 2016c. Advancing Understanding of the Complex Nature of Urban Systems. *Ecological Indicators*, 70:566–573, http://dx.doi.org/10.1016/j.ecolind.2016.03.054

McPhearson, T., Iwaniec, D., and X. Bai. 2017. Positive Visions for Guiding Transformations toward Desirable Urban Futures. *Current Opinion in Environmental Sustainability* (Special Issue), 22: 33–40. DOI: 10.1016/j.cosust.2017.04.004

Minx, J., Baiocchi, G., Wiedmann, T., Barrett, J., Creutzig, F., Feng, K., et al. 2013. Carbon Footprints of Cities and Other Human Settlements in the UK. *Environmental Research Letters*, 8 (3): 035039.

Palmer, H., and Walasek, H. (eds.) 2016. *Co-production in Action: Towards realizing just cities*. Gothenburg: Mistra Urban Futures. Open Access from www.mistraurbanfutures.org.

Parnell, S., and Simon, D. 2014. National Urbanization and Urban Strategies: Necessary But Absent Policy Instruments in Africa, in Parnell, S., and Pieterse, E. (eds.) *Africa's Urban Revolution*. London: Zed Books, pp. 237–256.

Pickett, S.T., Cadenasso, M.L., Grove, J.M., Nilon, C.H., Pouyat, R.V., Zipperer, W.C., and Costanza, R., 2001. Urban Ecological Systems: Linking Terrestrial Ecological, Physical, and Socioeconomic Components of Metropolitan Areas. *Annual Review of Ecology and Systematics*, 32(1): 127–157.

Romero-Lankao, P., McPhearson, T., and Davidson, D.J. 2017. The food-Energy-Water Nexus and Urban Complexity. *Nature Climate Change*, 7(4): 233–235.

Seto, K.C., Parnell, S., and Elmqvist, T. 2013. A Global Outlook on Urbanization, in: Elmqvist, T., et al. (eds.) *Urbanization, Biodiversity and Ecosystem Services: Challenges and Opportunities*. The Netherlands: Springer Open, pp. 1–12. DOI 10.1007/978–94–007–7088–1.

Simon, D. (ed.) 2016. *Rethinking Sustainable Cities: Accessible, Green and Fair*. Bristol: Policy Press. https://oapen.org/search?identifier=613676;keyword=Rethinking%20sustainable%20cities.

Webb, R., Bai, X., Smith, M.S., Costanza, R., Griggs, D., Moglia, M., et al., 2017. Sustainable Urban Systems: Co-Design and Framing for Transformation. *Ambio*, pp. 1–21.

Wirth, L. 1938. Urbanism as a Way of Life. *American Journal of Sociology*, 44(1):1–24.

Wolfram, M., Frantzeskaki, N., and Maschmeyer, S., (2016), Cities, Systems and Sustainability: Status and Perspective of Research on Urban Transformations, *Current Opinion in Environmental Sustainability*, 22: 18–25.